A HANDBOOK OF INDUSTRIAL RELATIONS PRACTICE

Practice and the Law in the Employment Relationship

THIRD EDITION

EDITED BY

BRIAN TOWERS

KOGAN PAGE

First published in 1987
Revised edition, 1989
This third edition, 1992

Kogan Page Limited
120 Pentonville Road
London N1 9JN

© Brian Towers and contributors 1987, 1989, 1992

British Library Cataloguing in Publication Data
A CIP record for this book is available from the British Library.

ISBN 0 7494 0715 8

Typeset by J&L Composition Ltd, Filey, North Yorkshire
Printed in England by Clays Ltd., St Ives plc.

A HANDBOOK OF
INDUSTRIAL RELATIONS PRACTICE

Contents

Decentralisation of collective Bargaing.

Contributors

Brian Towers, editor of *A Handbook of Industrial Relations Practice*, is Professor of Industrial Relations in the Department of Human Resource Management at the Strathclyde Business School. He founded and has edited the *Industrial Relations Journal* since 1970 and has had a long practical experience in industrial relations as an arbitrator for ACAS. His lengthy research experience, interests and publications currently include trade unions in the UK and North America, the structure of collective bargaining and the European Community's social dimension.

Greg Bamber is Professor and Director of the National Key Centre of Strategic Management, Faculty of Business, Queensland University of Technology, Brisbane, Australia. His publications include *Militant Managers?* (Gower, 1986), and, jointly with Russell D Lansbury, *New Technology; international perspectives on human resources and industrial relations* (Unwin Hyman, 1989).

P B Beaumont is Professor in the Department of Social and Economic Research, University of Glasgow. He has published widely, including *Public Sector Industrial Relations* (Routledge, 1991) and most recently chapters in the *Handbook of Human Resource Management* (Blackwell, 1992).

Chris Brewster is Senior Lecturer in Industrial Relations and Personnel at Cranfield School of Management. He is currently leading a major European-wide research project in human resource management and it is in this area that he has recently had several publications.

Colin Duncan is Lecturer in Industrial Relations in the Department of Business Studies, University of Edinburgh. He was previously a personnel officer with the Lothian Health Board and a research officer for the Local Authorities' Conditions of Service Advisory Board. He is editor of *The Evolution of Public Management: Concepts and Techniques for the 1990s* (Macmillan, 1992).

Derek Fatchett is Labour Member of Parliament for Leeds Central and Shadow Industry Minister. Previously he was Lecturer in Industrial Relations at the University of Leeds. He has written a number of books and articles including *Trade Unions and Politics in the 80s*, a study of the Trade Union Act 1984, published by Croom Helm.

John Gennard is the Institute of Personnel Management Professor of Human Resource Management and Dean of the Strathclyde Business School. His many publications include the co-authored *The Closed Shop in British*

Industry (Macmillan, 1984) and more recently *The History of the NGA* (Unwin Hyman, 1990).

Colin Gill is University Lecturer in Industrial Relations in the Judge Institute of Management Studies at Cambridge University and a Fellow of Wolfson College. He is editor of *New Technology, Work and Employment* and author of *Work, Unemployment and the New Technology* (Polity Press, Oxford, 1985). He has recently written two reports for the European Foundation for the Improvement of Living and Working Conditions for an EC-wide survey on employee representative participation in technological change.

Paul Lewis is Head of the University of Leeds Business Services, a supplier of specialist courses to human resource managers throughout Great Britain. He is an experienced industrial relations practitioner and human resource management consultant, and has lectured in employment law for over 20 years. He has published extensively, particularly in the areas of unfair dismissal and redundancy, and is author of *Practical Employment Law*. He is currently working on a new book entitled *The Successful Management of Redundancy*.

Karl J Mackie is Chief Executive of the Centre for Dispute Resolution and Director of the Centre for Legal Studies at the University of Nottingham. He is a barrister and psychologist, and an arbitrator and mediator for ACAS. He is author of *Lawyers in Business* (1988); editor of *A Handbook of Dispute Resolution* (1991); and co-editor of *Learning Lawyers' Skills* (1989).

Mick Marchington is Senior Lecturer in the Organization and Employment Studies Group within the Manchester School of Management at UMIST. His principal research interests are in the area of employee involvement and the management of employee relations, and he has just completed a two-year project with the Department of Employment. He has published widely in the field, including *Changing Patterns of Employee Relations* (Wheatsheaf, 1990).

Ian Roberts is Lecturer in Sociology, University of Durham. He has had work experience in the shipbuilding industry and is currently researching small firms with special emphasis on industrial relations.

Derek Sawbridge is Honorary Lecturer at Durham Business School and Deputy Chairperson of the Central Arbitration Committee and an ACAS arbitrator.

Ramsumair Singh is Lecturer in Industrial Relations at the University of Lancaster. He is a chartered electrical engineer, and economist, with training and work experience with the General Electric Company and Texaco Trinidad Inc. He has published on third-party intervention and industrial disputes, and has contributed to the *Handbook of Human Resource Management* (Blackwell, 1992). He is an ACAS arbitrator.

Ed Snape is Lecturer in the Department of Human Resource Management at Strathclyde University. Prior to this, he worked at the University of Teesside in Middlesbrough. His research interests span the industrial relations and employee resourcing fields, and include the impact of total quality management on managers' jobs.

P J White is Senior Lecturer in Industrial Relations at the University of Edinburgh. He was formerly a civil servant and British Steel Corporation Research Fellow. He has published in a number of journals on a wide range of industrial relations themes and is co-author of books on worker–directors, and the role of information in government policy-making.

Foreword

Industrial relations, in all their manifestations, are changing rapidly. There continue to be significant shifts in the structure and patterns of employment, and radical changes in the ways business is organized and public services delivered. Trade union membership is still declining, in the main because of job loss in areas of traditional strength and the difficulties to be faced in securing recognition from employers for the first time, often from a limited membership base which then proves difficult to sustain. The process towards union amalgamations is being given impetus by the need to secure administrative economies, and to maintain and improve services to members, often now to be found in smaller units of employment.

Collective bargaining, and its style and content, are also changing, reflecting these and other developments, including the need to accommodate new and developing systems of remuneration, and more flexible job structures and working patterns. In recent years both industry-wide and company-wide bargaining have declined, although both remain important components of the industrial relations scene. The need to guard against complaints of discrimination, particularly sex discrimination, is of increasing influence.

Legal regulation of employment relationships and the conduct of industrial relations has continued to increase. Further domestic legislation is being proposed, to govern in particular proposed industrial action. Equally significant are developing proposals and the action being taken to progress social policies concerning employment within the European Community (EC). Increasingly, the law in the UK can be seen to be subject to EC law. In addition, domestic case law continues to develop with considerable impact on employment policies and practices.

For any practitioner or student of industrial relations, this revised edition of the *Handbook* should be invaluable. I welcome its focus on practice and on developments in the law. Only when these are mastered should there be scope for theory and advocacy.

Sir Douglas Smith KCB
Chairman
ACAS
London, June 1992

Introduction to the Third Edition

This third, fully revised 1992 edition of *A Handbook of Industrial Relations Practice* appears at an opportune and interesting time. Two major developments – of considerable significance for British industrial relations – have taken place since the second edition was published and both of them in 1992: the signing of the Maastricht Treaty in February, followed in May (as this book was going to press) by its rejection in the Danish referendum; and the British General Election in April. These events are, of course, closely linked. Should Maastricht be eventually implemented in some form in 1993, then the Government's present policy of remaining aloof from progress on the social dimension – in principle if not entirely in practice – will remain. Yet the social dimension itself, already clouded after Maastricht in political and legal ambiguity, has now been thrown into disarray along with the Treaty as a whole. But this is not the whole story. The obligations of the 12 under the original Treaty of Rome and the Single European Act remain. Under these the 'family' of health and safety directives continue to make progress by qualified majority, most recently in the form of the compromise agreement limiting the working week to 48 hours that the UK has reached with its partners. These complexities are discussed in Chapter 2, which provides the necessary framework for understanding further developments as they take place.

Domestically, the Government is currently preparing its eighth piece of employment and industrial relations legislation since 1980 which, among others, includes provisions intended to allow individual trade union members to choose the unions they wish to join without the involvement of the TUC's traditional regulation, and to have a three-yearly opportunity to cancel the automatic deduction of trade union dues from their pay. These provisions, as well as the approaching requirement for the ten-year renewal by ballot of political funds under the Trade Union Act 1984, pose further challenges to orderly collective bargaining, the membership and finances of trade unions and, possibly, their capacity to secure and maintain recognition, at a time when their strength continues to be weakened by unemployment and long-term changes in the economy and structure of employment. The outcome has been (and this is likely to continue) a strengthening of the non-unionized part of the private sector as Government industrial relations and privatization policies erode the collective bargaining culture and trade union strength in the public sector.

Yet it remains too early to say, if at all, that industrial relations in the UK is following the patterns of the US, which is dominated by the non-union option for employers with only 16 per cent of the labour force unionized and still falling. Collective bargaining as an institution in the UK is undoubtedly much weaker in 1992 than it was in 1979, or even 1989, but it retains a residual strength – especially in the workplace – which may not be easy to shift much further, especially as trade unions are showing signs of responding proactively to collective bargaining innovations by management. The Government is also showing signs that its next legislative 'step' will be its last – at least for a time.

This is the context in which this third edition has been prepared. Four new chapters are included. Three of these cover the impact of EC legislation on UK industrial relations, a discussion of the problems of trade union recognition and the always important implications of the decision within organizations as to the appropriate level at which to bargain with trade unions. The fourth new chapter is devoted to the growing importance of the legal background to health and safety, again, largely in response to EC legislation.

The health and safety at work chapter forms part of a revised and up-to-date Part Three covering the law in industrial relations which incorporates changes up to the spring of 1992, with some speculation on future developments. Major revisions – almost amounting to new chapters – are also evident in the background and overview chapters of Part One which cover the broad changes since 1989 in industrial relations, trade unions, the public sector, as well as including an industry case study style chapter on the impact of technical change on industrial relations.

Despite the essential revisions in content to keep the book up to date, this edition retains the style of the first and second editions which were so well received. Hence it remains a handbook of *industrial relations* practice, ie recognizing the still significant sway of traditional collective bargaining although reflecting the growing, and now familiar, approach of human resource management, as well as developments in collective agreements, participative mechanisms, payment systems and the like – all covered in detail in Part Two.

All the authors, again as in previous editions, write in an even-handed way, not least because they are mostly ACAS arbitrators. They are all therefore deeply experienced in the practices and compromises of industrial relations. The book is intended to appeal to practitioners, in all their variety, as well as its substantial and growing following in universities (old and new), business schools and colleges.

Finally, as before, may I once again thank the contributors to this handbook for the efficiency, good grace and good humour with which they have approached the task of revising existing chapters and writing new ones, as well as to Douglas Smith of ACAS for kindly contributing the Foreword at short notice. The publishers also deserve high praise for the extraordinary speed with which they have produced such a handsome volume. For this third edition I have again had the advantage of the managerial and editorial skills of Pam Arksey of the *Industrial Relations Journal*. For her essential contribution I was especially grateful at yet another difficult time.

Brian Towers
Department of Human Resource Management
Strathclyde Business School, 1992

Part One
The Background

Chapter One

British Industrial Relations and the Trade Unions: Background and Developments*

Brian Towers

In April 1992 the Conservative Party was re-elected with an overall, though much reduced, majority for the fourth consecutive time since 1979. The Government can now retain power at least until 1997 and, if returned for a fifth time, will have enjoyed a continous period in office of over 20 years, extending into the next century. This stable political dimension ensures that the new approach to industrial relations, and especially towards the trade unions, which was firmly established under the Thatcher administrations from 1979 to 1990, will remain and be confirmed through further legislation. Furthermore, even if the Conservatives are replaced at the next election by Labour (or possibly some other political realignment), it is clear that the substance of the legislative and policy changes progressively introduced since 1979 will not be reversed. The Labour Party, the trade unions and the Liberal Democrats had already adopted this position well before 1992 and the election defeat must at least confirm it. This political consensus – albeit one largely led by the Conservatives' continuing electoral victories – is now clearly an important factor in the consolidation of earlier reforms of the structure and processes of industrial relations, and provides a platform for further reforms.

But if the political context is of great significance it is not the only, or even the most decisive, influence upon industrial relations. For example, the dramatic and continuing decline in trade union membership since 1979 has been largely associated with a battery of powerful negative influences such as the decline in the size of the manufacturing sector, the persistence of high levels of unemployment and major changes in the composition of the labour force. While these developments have not been wholly independent of the effects of government policy since 1979, they clearly had origins going back much earlier than that and the legal instruments provided for employers by the government have not, in practice, been extensively used. Nor is the national political context as important as it used to be. Membership of the European Community (EC) has increasingly influenced British industrial relations. This influence must grow under the economic pressures of the single market and the social pressures towards greater

---

* The author is grateful to Jennifer Ross of the Law School, University of Strathclyde, for helpful comments in the redrafting of pp 22–30 of this chapter.

legislative protection for employees. The British 'opt-out' of the social dimension may be difficult to sustain in the longer term, while 'social dialogue' at EC level between employers and trade unions offers an alternative route.

It is also important to recognize that, while long-established institutions and patterns of behaviour *can* be quickly, even suddenly, transformed, it is more likely in relatively stable, complex societies that change will be both slow and piecemeal. It can also vary in both pace and extent between different levels of a system. Thus, the apparent significance of *nationally-measured* decline in trade union membership may be misleading. One can point to the relative stability of day-to-day industrial relations and trade union involvement and influence at workplace level. This observation has been a continuing feature of the Arbitration, Conciliation and Advisory Service (ACAS) annual reports throughout the 1980s, even though couched in increasingly less confident terms. Additionally, industrial relations in Britain – perhaps more than in most other comparable countries – has strong links with its past, which gives it some inbuilt resistance to reform and reformers. The influence of history, tradition, and custom and practice may have been weakened during the years since 1979, but this influence remains and it is important to take it into account if the present industrial relations system is to be adequately understood and evaluated, and the impact of reforms and reformers is not to be exaggerated.

This chapter has two purposes: first, to outline those changes in the economic, legislative and political background to industrial relations that have taken place since 1979; secondly, to describe the impact of these changes on industrial relations with special reference to the trade unions, including an assessment of their future development and prospects.

BACKGROUND

Changes in those factors which had had a direct influence upon British industrial relations since 1979 can be described and discussed under three headings: changes in the economy; changes in employment; and increasing government intervention. Such headings are, of course, devices of convenience, given the complexity of the relationships between them. Changes in employment are partly determined by economic change, and government intervention both influences, and is influenced by, developments in the economy and employment. Nor should 1979 necessarily be seen as marking a decisive break with the past, since current trends and present policies, even legislation, had their origins many years earlier. These important analytical and historical considerations cannot be discussed here but at least they should be borne in mind.[1]

The economy

The long post-war boom of the Western economies began to lose momentum in the late 1960s, a process accelerated by the 'oil shocks' of 1973 and 1979, and complemented by widespread deflationary and tight money policies – especially after 1979. In the UK the unemployment rate,[2] which had only exceptionally been above 2 per cent for more than 20 years, after 1967 began its long upwards drift reaching 5 per cent in 1976 and staying there until 1979. Then it doubled in three years and touched 12 per cent in 1985. However, early in 1986 unemployment began to fall as the economy boomed, reaching a low of 5.5 per cent in the middle of 1990. The promised boom was not sustained as inflationary pressures mounted. The government forced up interest rates at the same time as international recession was further slowing down the economy. These pressures reversed the fall in unemployment which by early 1992 had risen to 9.4 per cent.

In output terms gross domestic product (GDP) grew by an annual average of 2.8 per cent from 1980 to 1988 which, although less than Japan (4.0 per cent) and the North American economies (3.0 per cent), marginally exceeded the European average. This relative improvement in UK economic performance was especially evident from 1985 to 1988 when output and labour productivity accelerated to 3–4 per cent, outpacing the advanced industrial (OECD) countries as a whole, including the US, France, West Germany and Italy. Unfortunately, this promising performance was reversed in the late 1980s. Growth faltered and annual output in 1991 declined by 1.8 per cent, the lowest point of the deepest recession since 1945. The UK recession was more severe than that in North America, while for the OECD as a whole, growth continued, although at a much slower rate. However, by 1992 there were indications that the economy was beginning to revive, even though the recovery was slow and hesitant.

Inflation, as unemployment and output, reflected the economic cycle and government policy. From 12 per cent in 1982 a long decline took the annual rate to 3.3 per cent early in 1988. This, combined with falling unemployment, and rising output and productivity, offered some prospect of attaining the long-elusive goal of non-inflationary, self-sustaining growth. However, the government's monetary and fiscal stimuli to counter a potential fall in business and consumer confidence in the wake of the stock market crash of 1988 generated strong inflationary pressures aggravated by a credit and house purchase boom. The government pushed up interest rates to counter inflation which, by early 1991, was rising at an annual rate of 9 per cent. By the beginning of 1992 inflation had been cut to 4.1 per cent but at the price of unemployment at 9.4 per cent, or 2.7 million – a return almost to the crisis levels of the early 1980s.

Overall, the economy's performance throughout the 1980s and into the 1990s has been unimpressive. The marked improvement in the middle 1980s proved to be ephemeral and failed to compensate for the severe recessions at the beginning and end of the period 1979 to 1992.

This unimpressive performance must also be seen against certain structural weaknesses in the economy. The UK's traditional surplus on trade in manufactures has long been in decline under the influence of export competition, the shrinking of traditional markets and import penetration. These processes were accelerated by a major loss of manufacturing capacity in the recession of the early 1980s.

In 1982, for the first time in 200 years, the dwindling manufacturing surplus had turned into a deficit and by 1990 exports of manufactures, by value, had fallen to 86 per cent of imports. The strong oil-pound, at the same time, reduced the competitiveness of manufacturing exports. This erosion of the manufacturing sector has placed greater burdens on surpluses from oil and services to bridge the external payments gap. These surpluses, in the long run, cannot be sustained and are now raising the question as to the adequacy of the existing manufacturing base. It is of interest to note that the shrinkage of manufacturing in the UK is a phenomenon shared with the relatively unsuccessful US economy, but not with the still strongly performing economies of Japan and Germany. Whether the development of the EC's internal market from 1993 will provide a stimulus to UK manufacturing remains an open question. However, the government's declared approach to the Maastricht negotiations was to preserve the UK as a relatively low wage economy in order to attract inward investment. This strategy can clearly contribute to the revival of UK manufacturing – as for example in the car and electronics industries, with the growing contributions not least from Japanese multinationals – but at the expense of UK ownership and control. Serious questions are also still being raised about the UK's relative skill levels (compared especially to Germany, France and Japan) which may be inhibiting the economy's capacity to improve its competitiveness via the contribution of sustained improvements in productivity to unit labour costs.[3]

Whatever the prognosis, it remains clear that the contribution of the goods-producing industries to GDP will continue to decline – short of a very radical shift in government policy – and that private sector services will continue to grow in importance. In addition, the movement from manufacturing towards services continues to be strongly uneven in its regional impact. The lost manufacturing jobs are still mainly concentrated in the traditional manufacturing regions in the north, north-west and English midlands, as well as Scotland and Wales, although the preferences of inward investors may be beginning to change this picture. At the same time the growing service sector is essentially located, though not uniformly, and with some impact from relocation, in the already still relatively more prosperous south and east of England – despite the heavier impact of the 1990–2 recession on those regions. It is also clear that the general preference of high technology companies for location in the south and east remains intact.

The short and long-term problems of the UK economy are important in themselves: they also have wider implications. Successive government attempts to reform industrial relations and constrain the trade unions have, since 1968, been explained in terms of their contribution to improved economic performance. Furthermore, even without government reformers, structural economic change such as the shift from manufacturing into services continues to have a major effect upon industrial relations and collective bargaining through its weakening of trade union membership and finances. These matters will be considered in more detail later in the chapter.

Employment

Structural economic change is also influencing the occupational structure. The expanding service sector favours the growth of jobs traditionally performed by females. On present trends women will constitute 45 per cent of total employment by 2001, dominating support and personal service occupations. But even within contracting manufacturing industries certain occupations are being influenced by new technology applications, notably in the movement away from single-skilling to multi-skilling and the rise of the technician.[4] Furthermore, influencing both expanding and contracting economic sectors is the growth of the 'flexible workforce' (part-time, temporary and self-employed), which is about one-third of all employment. It is also dominated by women (two-thirds of all flexible workers) with the largest concentrations in hotels and catering, distribution, repairs, and professional and business services.[5]

Flexible work is of course not new, but it has been widely promoted among British management by agencies, consultants and some academic institutions through the familiar model of the 'flexible firm'* which distinguishes between core workers (multi-skilled, full-time, good pay, conditions and benefits); peripheral workers (short-term, temporary, part-time with less favourable pay, conditions and benefits); and external workers who are not employees of the firm (agency temporaries, workers in contracted-out services and the self-employed). The logic of the flexible firm is labour cost minimization by limiting core workers, relative to peripheral and external workers. It has potentially far-reaching implications for industrial relations and trade unions since the core is conventionally unionized in contrast to other workers.

In its comprehensive form the flexible firm is relatively rare,[6] although two specific kinds of flexibility have been very much in evidence. The first, multi-skilling, is common in collective agreements, even in industries such as ship-building and car manufacture where craft demarcations have been traditionally strong. The second, 'flexibility of time', has been long established in continuous process industries for technical reasons, but is now being extended by employers for market reasons to industries subject to seasonal or cyclical variations in demand. In its most radical form (known as 'annualization'), the employer con-cedes a cut in the average length of the working week without loss of pay. In return the union agrees for the employer to vary the actual length of the working week within upper and lower limits, and subject to an annual total of hours worked. Surveys in the 1980s showed that although all the forms of flexibility have normally been introduced through collective bargaining, the unions gene-rally do not welcome them and see them as a product of weakened trade union organization and influence.[7] Opposition has sometimes been more direct. In engineering, in the late 1980s, national negotiations broke down when the unions refused to link flexibility to their claim for a shorter working week. Perhaps even more significantly, early in 1988, rank-and-file workers in the car industry (notably Ford) included opposition to flexibility among their reasons for striking.

Another employer initiative in the use of labour, associated with the decline of the manufacturing sector, is a reduction in the number of manufacturing plants and the average number of employees in each plant – usually following mergers, takeovers and management buyouts. Part of this is in response to market pressures, but also the now apparently stronger relationship of smaller scale to higher efficiency via new technology applications.

Labour utilization innovations are usually thought to be associated with foreign firms, notably Japanese and American. This is undoubtedly an exaggera-tion. The introduction of radical changes in working practices ('Japanization')

---

* Interestingly, this model's antecedents come from the pioneering academic work in labour segmentation first developed in the United States which analysed, but implicitly deplored, the institutionalization of primary and secondary labour markets. The model of the flexible firm has, in contrast, been developed by some academics to encourage its adoption by firms.

in particular is not especially linked to Japanese companies.[8] American firms – which have total UK investments many times larger than Japanese in value terms – have had a much longer involvement in the UK economy without any marked tendency to innovation in labour utilization. For the Japanese the significance of their presence lies in their approach to collective bargaining. This will be returned to later in the chapter.

Government intervention, 1979–92

The strong commitment of the new 1979 administration to a monetarist, free market alternative to Keynesian intervention was compatible with the British, traditional 'voluntarist' or 'abstentionist'[9] approach to industrial relations. However, the perspective which saw trade unions in themselves as powerful, labour market monopolies which generated inflation and reduced efficiency, gradually came to supersede the simple reliance on monetary targets to control pay settlements. Monetary targets were in fact quietly dropped after 1983 and formally in 1986 at the same time as the free market, individualist perspective was being even more strongly promoted – complemented by the newer instruments of privatization and deregulation. The trade unions, with their traditional role in wage bargaining and collectivist pursuit of their goals, were seen as seriously impeding individualism and the working of free labour markets. The outcome was a strategy which sought to subordinate labour law and the trade unions to the government's economic and ideological goals, and which marked a sharp rejection of the old abstentionism. In implementing this strategy the government had its power to legislate as well as its direct role in the public sector both as major employer and ultimate paymaster.

The legislative programme has been put into effect 'step by step' in six Acts of Parliament: the two Employment Acts of 1980 and 1982; the Trade Union Act of 1984; and three further Employment Acts in 1988, 1989 and 1990. Most recently the legislation relating to trade unions, industrial action and individual trade union rights was brought together in the Trade Union and Labour Relations (Consolidation) Act of 1992. The following is an outline of the main changes introduced by the legislation. Detailed accounts of individual and collective employment law are contained in Part Three.

1. *Individual employment rights.* A range of statutory individual employment rights was introduced in the 1960s and 1970s by Labour (and to a lesser extent Conservative) governments. These statutory rights, under the jurisdiction of a system of tribunals established in 1964, made it possible to go to tribunal for compensation for redundancy, to claim equal pay, and to seek redress on race and sex discrimination, and on a limited number of health and safety matters. However, the work of the tribunals was, and is, dominated by unfair dismissal claims* which take about two-thirds of all cases, although since 1986 claims under the Wages Act have also become important.

   Since 1979 unfair dismissal claims have been subjected to a two-stage increase in the qualifying employment period before a claim can be brought,

---

* Unfair dismissal claims were introduced under Edward Heath's Conservative Government in 1971 and retained by the succeeding Labour Government after 1974.

ie from six months to one year and then two years. There was also a shift in the burden of proof: formerly the responsibility of the employer, it now rests equally with the dismissed employee. The number of unfair dismissal cases received by ACAS (which is required to conciliate at the initial stage) has remained fairly constant in the last ten years at about 40,000. However, cases actually proceeding to the tribunal itself (ie those not withdrawn or settled under ACAS conciliation) have declined from about one-third to one-sixth of cases received.[10] The employees' success rate is about one-third[11] although only about 1 per cent of successful applicants get their jobs back, the normal award being financial compensation.

Women's rights have had a mixed experience. Although maternity payments and access to maternity leave have been made more difficult, time off is now available for ante-natal care and recent EC directives have important implications for the protection of pregnant workers. In 1983, anti-discrimination provisions were introduced after the UK government had been found by the European Court to be in breach of the Equal Value Directive of 1975. Equal value claims have also been underpinned by a number of significant legal decisions.*

2. *Collective bargaining*. Recognition is a critical step in the extension of collective bargaining. Under the Labour Government's Employment Protection Act 1975 a unilateral *statutory* procedure to seek recognition was given to independent trade unions.** This statutory procedure was abolished by the Conservative Government in 1980, although the voluntary procedure† was retained. Hence since 1980 there has been a reversal to the pre-1975 position: British employers are not, in law, required to recognize or bargain with trade unions and can withdraw recognition previously granted. Since 1980 there has been a decline in the growth of recognition agreements although this decline has been in the context of more powerful pressures and even when the statutory procedure was in force it had a minimal effect (see Chapter 6). At the same time EC regulations have again worked in the opposite direction. Employment contracts, recognition and a collective agreements are protected following takeovers or the restructuring of existing companies.‡ There is also a general pressure for UK employers to follow

---

* See Chapter 18.
** An independent trade union ('independence' is assessed by the Certification Officer – a public official under the 1975 Act – using the criteria of history, membership base, organization and structure, finance, employer-provided facilities, and collective bargaining record) had the right to pursue a recognition claim against a recalcitrant employer via the services of ACAS. ACAS's enquiries did not necessarily require evidence of majority support in the bargaining unit to make a positive recommendation. Such a recommendation could be supported by a legally-enforceable award against the employer from the Central Arbitration Committee (CAC).
† At the request of either a union or an employer, ACAS can be asked to conciliate in a dispute over recognition. The outcome can be the employer voluntarily agreeing to recognition, either full or partial (ie grievance representation only).
‡ This right became law in Britain under the Transfer of Undertakings (Protection of Employment) Regulations 1981. The right may, however, be difficult to enforce. An

the more developed procedures for consultation and employee involvement which exist in other European countries.*

A further change influencing collective bargaining was the 1988 removal of the remaining statutory immunities protecting closed shop agreements, ie affecting those in employment or *post-entry* closed shops. Dismissal (or action short of dismissal) of an employee for not being a member of a trade union, or of a particular trade union, was 'unfair' in all circumstances and industrial action to enforce union membership was unlawful. Under the Employment Act 1990 the law reached out to include *pre-entry* closed shops, ie the refusal of employment on grounds of non-membership of a trade union.

3. *Statutory pay regulation.* The UK (unlike the US and other countries) has never provided for a statutory minimum wage covering all employees. However, it has long had a mix of statutory institutions and procedures providing defences against low pay, and supporting claims based on comparisons between different groups of workers. The most notable institutions are the wages councils with a history going back to their trade board predecessors of 1909. The 'tripartite' (trade union, employer and 'independent' representatives) wages councils over time had their original statutory powers to set minimum wage rates extended to include piecework and overtime rates, holiday pay and holiday entitlements. In 1986 the government reversed this trend restricting the councils to the setting of a single minimum hourly and overtime rate and removed young people under 21 from their jurisdiction. The councils currently number 26, covering some 2.5 million workers. Government proposals for total abolition have been opposed by both employers and trade unions.** The use of pay comparisons with other workers was given statutory support under the Employment Protection Act 1975 (Schedule 11). Unions could apply for legally enforceable awards to the Central Arbitration Committee (CAC), based upon arguments that their members were being paid less than the generally prevailing rates in their particular trade or industry. Schedule 11 was abolished in 1980. A similar prop to pay comparability applied to workers employed by companies having contracts with government, both central and local. Successive fair wages resolutions of the House of Commons (ie a simple majority of members, the last in 1946) guaranteed, though without the force of law, that workers on public sector contracts would be paid no less than their counterparts in their trade or industry as a whole. These resolutions were overturned by the House of Commons in 1982.

---

industrial tribunal, in a case involving the formation of a new company from three existing ones, has ruled against the transfer of employment rights and recognition. The decision was upheld on appeal. *Banking, Insurance and Finance Union* v *Barclays Bank plc* 32146 (1986); *BIFU* v *Barclays Bank and others*, EAT 479 (1987).
* See Chapter 2.
** The Government has, however, now indicated its intention to abolish the councils.

4. *Industrial action*. The Trade Union Act 1984 (s 11) defined industrial action as 'any strike or other industrial action by persons employed under contracts of employment'. Its main expressions, apart from the strike, are the overtime ban, go-slow, and work-to-rule. Furthermore, since under British *common law* virtually all industrial action is illegal (ie in breach of contract) the 'right' to take industrial action needs to be guaranteed. The practice in Britain, which developed in the 19th century, has been to confer *statutory* immunities (against court actions by employers) upon workers involved in industrial disputes.* More precisely, immunity has been available 'in contemplation or furtherance of a trade dispute' since the Trade Disputes Act of 1906. However, in 1982 the statutory definition of a trade dispute was significantly restricted 'wholly or mainly' to terms and conditions of employment. This correspondingly widened the scope of prohibited 'political' as opposed to industrial action.**

In 1984 the immunities were further restricted to those unions securing majority support in a secret ballot held no more than four weeks before the planned action. Failure to comply with the law on balloting leaves a union and its officials open to civil actions by employers and, since 1988, by union members. Injunctions can be sought prohibiting the action and, if it still takes place, fines and sequestration of union assets. Further sanctions available are receivership and even imprisonment. The financial penalties can be onerous. In the case of the 1984–5 strike of the National Union of Mineworkers (NUM) the total of fines and costs was some £1 million or 5 per cent of the union's total available funds. The much smaller National Union of Seamen (NUS) was, in 1988, subjected to fines and costs totalling £1–3 million. The Acts of 1988 and 1990 made balloting procedures even more complex. Employers also have the option of seeking damages from the union or unions involved and the immunities are at risk during the industrial action itself.

Picketing (now limited in practice by the police, supported by the courts and the Department of Employment's Statutory Code of Practice on Picketing† to six persons) was previously also allowed at the premises of the employer's direct suppliers or customer. This limited form of secondary action under the 1988 Act was disallowed by the Employment Act of 1990. Now virtually all forms of secondary action have lost immunity. Industrial action must be peaceful and wholly restricted to the employee's place of work. Furthermore, under the Employment Act 1988 individual trade union members are now protected against disciplinary actions by their unions should they refuse to take part in a strike or other industrial action even if the action has majority support and is in accordance with all the statutory

---

* Thus, for example, there is no positive right to strike under British law, in contrast to other comparable countries. How this arose is a matter of historical debate.[12]
** For example, industrial action by a union against privatization because of its potential impact upon its members' jobs was prohibited: *Mercury Communications Ltd* v *Scott Garner and POEU* (1984) ICR 74.
† A new revised and more restrictive Code became effective in May 1992.

requirements.* Trade union (as opposed to individual) liability was introduced in the 1982 Act and up to 1990 was confined to official industrial action, that is the acts, in accordance with the rule book, of the union's full-time employed officials and/or its committees. The 1990 Act extended a trade union's liability to the unofficial actions of all union officials even if not union employees, ie shop stewards and committees, and even if not in accord with, or contrary to, the union's rules. Unions can avoid this liability by repudiating the unofficial action. The process is not, however, an easy one requiring the early sending of individual repudiation notices to the employer and all shop stewards and members involved. Nor, under the Act, can the union hold a retrospective ballot rendering the action official without first repudiating the action.

Finally, the circumstances under which workers involved in industrial action can be fairly dismissed were changed in 1982 and unofficial action dismissals were covered by the 1990 Act. Under the Employment Protection Act of 1975 workers taking industrial action (including action across a number of plants) could not be dismissed selectively or, following the action, re-engaged on a selective basis. Now selective dismissal in official industrial actions is only unfair at the actual place of work ('establishment') of the workers claiming victimization. Hence employers can dismiss workers taking industrial action on a plant-by-plant basis. Selective re-engagement is also within the law if it takes place three months after dismissal. For unofficial action, since 1990 employees can be dismissed selectively and lose their right to claim unfair dismissal.

5. *Trade union organization and ballots.* The government's enthusiasm for balloting extends beyond its application to industrial action. Thus all members of a union's national executive body, including its senior officers of president and general secretary, must now be elected by the membership at least every five years by an independently scrutinized secret postal ballot. Furthermore, unions which wish to pursue 'political objects' have, since 1913, been required to ballot their members to seek majority support to set up a political fund separate from their general funds. The fund is financed by special contributions, the 'political levy', from which individuals can 'contract out' without penalty. Since 1984 affirmative ballots must be achieved at ten-year intervals to retain a union's political fund.** Since 1988, as with ballots for national executives and senior officials, they are to be by post and independently scrutinized.

Since 1980 unions have been able to claim part of their balloting costs from the government via the certification officer.† This subsidy is only available for secret postal ballots and for the following purposes: industrial action, union elections, rule changes, amalgamation, political funds and employers'

---

* Individual members taking their unions to law may also have the advice and assistance of a Commissioner for the Rights of Trade Union Members established under the 1988 Act. This assistance was extended to common law actions under the 1990 Act.
** Through affiliation fees and substantial special payments for general elections the political funds are the principal source of the Labour Party's finances.
† In 1990, 85 unions received a total of £2.6 million for 680 ballots: in 1986, 40 unions received £0.74 million for 399 ballots.

offers on pay or its equivalent. For industrial action workplace ballots are still lawful, but these do not qualify for financial support.

The potential impact of this surge of legislation is far-reaching but the new legal remedies available against strikes require *employers* to initiate action. Such initiatives seem to be growing in incidence, but, according to one study, still apply 'mainly at the margins'.[13] In major disputes the anti-strike laws have been limited to their use by newspaper publishers against the printing unions and by sea-going ferry operators against the NUS. Actions against the NUM and its leaders in 1984–5 were taken by members and under common (not statutory) law for breach of union rules.

The balloting requirements of the Trade Union Act 1984 were designed as an important and direct constraint on industrial action. The number of ballots totalled 152 for 1985–6 rising to 280 in 1987. However, the 1987 figure was little more than a quarter of the Department of Employment's recorded stoppages of work in that year (which includes unofficial strikes for which ballots are not required) and of the 280 ballots 90 per cent resulted in majorities for industrial action. However, votes in favour did not often result in actual industrial action and were sometimes presented, and used, as a means of strengthening unions' negotiating positions.[14] Thus, while it is probable that ballots are becoming an established feature of the negotiating process it is thought to be too early to assess their longer-term impact on behaviour. Even more uncertainty must be attached to the effect of the provision in the Employment Act 1988 which allows individual members to ignore a strike call, following a lawful ballot, without fear of disciplinary action. It also remains to be seen how the new Code of Practice on Industrial Action Balloting, approved by Parliament in 1990, influences trade union behaviour.

A much clearer outcome of the new balloting procedures was the complete endorsement of trade unions' political funds. It was feared by many in unions that the balloting requirement would cut them off from 'political' campaigns (such as supporting the National Health Service) and undermine the financial base of the Labour Party to which most of the major unions are affiliated. In the event, following vigorous campaigns among their memberships, all trade unions with political funds (totalling 38) retained them mostly by very large majorities and 14 unions have so far set them up for the first time.[15] Yet the need to ballot every ten years remains and it is far from certain, given changing political circumstances, that such a positive reaction can always be guaranteed. However, the core issue is the role of the political funds in financing the Labour Party. Without the funds, or an alternative such as state subsidies and/or mass membership subscriptions, the Labour Party is quite unable to compete financially with the Conservative Party's business backing.

In addition to lawmaking, the government has intervened directly, and vigorously, in public sector industrial relations through its role as employer. In 1984 it banned trade unions at the Government Communications Headquarters (GCHQ) as incompatible with the national interest, replacing them with internal staff associations The ban led to condemnation of the government by the ILO and drew it into bitter political controversy and a major confrontation with three civil service unions, which included the small but influential First Division Association (FDA), the union of senior civil service advisers to government. The unions eventually exhausted their legal action against the government with the rejection of their case in 1986 by the European Commission on Human Rights. This inevitably soured relationships still further and two of the three unions (but not the FDA) later initiated a strike over pay during the 1987 General Election campaign. The most recent episode of this long and bitter dispute has been the dismissal at GCHQ of those who have retained their union membership.

But undoubtedly the most vivid case study in intervention was in the miners' strike of 1984–5. The government in the summer of 1984 abandoned its initial non-interventionist stance in favour of the large-scale national mobilization of its physical, financial and propagandist resources[16] in direct support of a public sector employer, which in 1985 resulted in the defeat of, and division within, the NUM. British Coal was then free to run down loss-making capacity and to prepare the industry for privatization.* The privatization of coal was promised by the government as an early outcome of the General Election 1992. This confrontationist style emerged again in the long-running struggle with the teachers' unions over bargaining machinery and educational reform. The teachers lost their negotiating rights and were eventually given a pay review body, reforms imposed largely in the face of strong, professional opposition and further condemnation from the ILO in 1988.

Finally, the government's overriding belief in the efficacy of market forces has led to strong intervention in the rationales and processes of pay bargaining. It has virtually eliminated the comparability principle in public sector pay negotiations promoting the case for ability-to-pay, performance-related pay and regional flexibility considerations. It has also strongly attacked national pay bargaining, seeking to dismantle it for decentralized forms in the civil service and has influenced local government to move towards a framework approach while some authorities have broken away from national bargaining. Privatized industries such as water, electricity supply, telecommunications and steel have also been at least partly influenced in their decentralization policies by the government and the new hospital trusts are beginning to adopt local bargaining arrangements. The private sector has long been replacing the old national agreements with company and plant bargaining. This trend accelerated in the 1980s, partly again under Government advocacy. Perhaps the most significant examples of the trend are the large, but declining, engineering industry (the 'model' of framework bargaining), which has now ended national negotiations as well as banking, in which the multi-employer arrangements collapsed in 1987.**

Assessing the future

The overall strength and direction of those economic and political factors which influence industrial relations, and the role and power of trade unions have been significantly enhanced by the General Election of 1992. On present economic policies (ie the primacy of anti-inflation policy within the ERM) and in the

---

* The NUM offered minimal resistance. Between 1985 and 1990 the effect of pit closures, manpower cuts and the founding of the Union of Democratic Miners (UDM) was to reduce NUM membership from 248,000 to 53,000.
** See Chapter 9 for a detailed consideration of the pros and cons of decentralized bargaining.

context of continuing balance of payments deficits, the resumption of economic growth at a level which will significantly reduce unemployment seems unlikely. At the same time the goods-producing industries' contribution to GDP will continue to decline in favour of private sector services, a process encouraged by the Government.

The Government has also renewed its interest in further employment and trade union legislation. The Employment Act 1990 was widely believed to have satisfied the Government's reforming ambitions, but further legislative plans were announced early in 1992, in preparation for the General Election.[17] The proposal to make collective agreements legally binding was dropped, faced with the objections of employers as well as trade unions and reminders of the experience of 1971–4.[18] A further proposal, to make the deduction of trade union subscriptions from pay to employers subject to annual confirmation, was revised to three years after employer as well as trade union objections. The main proposals which are likely to be incorporated into the Bill announced in the Queen's Speech in May 1992 are as follows.

1. *Individual employment rights.* All employees working in excess of eight hours a week, within two months of starting work, would be entitled to a statement on pay, hours, holidays and other terms and conditions. For discrimination against workers on the grounds of age the government proposed the encouragement of improved employer practice, although eschewing legislation on the sex and race discrimination models.
2. *Collective bargaining.* All individual employees would be given the right to join any union of their choice, irrespective of existing arrangements under the TUC's Bridlington Rules.[19] On the deduction of subscriptions (the 'check-off') trade union members would be required to indicate their agreement within 12 months of the legislation and then to confirm it every 3 years. Additionally, employers would have the duty of informing union members of increases in subscriptions at the same time as their right to review membership.
3. *Industrial action.* The government's predilection for postal ballots was again demonstrated with its intention to apply them to industrial action in cases where more than fifty are to be balloted. Furthermore, all ballots in favour of action would be subject to seven days' notice and members of the public would have the new right to seek legal redress to prevent unlawful industrial actions by workers in the public services, such as hospitals, transport and refuse collection.
4. *Trade union organization and ballots.* The 1988 requirement that ballots for union office should be by post and independently scrutinized are planned to be extended to give additional powers to the scrutineer to oversee membership registers and voting papers, as well as a requirement for elections to be conducted by an outside agency.[20] The rules on election ballots would also be extended to ballots on mergers. On the financial affairs of trade unions the certification officer would have new powers of investigation and unions would be required to provide all members with an annual report.

These proposals are, in substance, milder towards trade unions than the legislation of the 1980s and are placed in the wider context of the Government's continuing attempts to improve skills and job opportunities. Furthermore, EC pressure towards the extension of individual employment rights is evident in the proposals for employees working more than eight hours and with regard to older workers. Nor do the trade unions now have any serious objections to the extension of industrial action balloting, which has frequently enhanced their bargaining leverage, although some employers follow the unions in the case for workplace, rather than postal, ballots as a means of encouraging involvement. However, two of the proposals have caused serious concern in trade union circles: the proposed elimination of the Bridlington Rules and the proposal for three yearly renewal of the check-off.

The right of employees to join any union of their choice could undermine existing bargaining arrangements, including single union agreements, as well as provoke inter-union rivalry. These possibilities have even alarmed some employers who see them as a threat to orderly collective bargaining.[21] The check-off is now a widespread practice and a regular renewal procedure could seriously adversely affect already declining trade union membership. Yet some trade union opinion draws comfort from the highly successful campaigns to retain trade union political funds which are subject to similar renewal rules to those proposed for the check-off, albeit the latter would be subject to individual rather than collective endorsement.

Aside from the government's influence on industrial relations through its powers as legislator and over the direction of economic policy, it retains substantial influence as an employer. It shows little sign of relaxing its robust attitude towards public sector trade unions and its continuing intention to decentralize collective bargaining in the civil service is also being extended, as major paymaster, to local government. But countervailing influences remain. A government with a smaller majority has arguably less authority than its predecessors. There is also the generally positive effect of EC legislation. Employees' rights which, even after the 1992 Maastricht agreement, can still be advanced under the social dimension provisions continue to bind all 12 member states and should the special arrangements binding the 11 come into effect they would pose difficulties which could threaten the UK position.[22] Furthermore, collective bargaining remains a widespread, established activity with trade unions retaining much of their strength, influence and legitimacy at local level.

Yet for the trade unions their capacity to resist trade union demands is much weaker than it was in 1979 or even a few years ago and this capacity has suffered a severe setback in the result of the General Election of 1992.

THE TRADE UNION CRISIS

From 1968 to 1979 membership of British trade unions grew by almost a third, standing at 13.3 million in 1979. The rate of increase of total membership outdistanced that of potential trade union membership (which itself grew steadily from 1972 to 1979) so that trade union density* rose from 44 per cent in

---

* This important and much used and abused statistic is *actual* trade union membership (as reported by unions themselves) as a percentage of *potential* trade union membership. For these figures the denominator is civilian employees in employment (which includes managers with contracts of employment) plus the unemployed. The problems of measuring density are discussed on pp 35–6.

Table 1.1   *Trade union membership and density in the UK, 1979–91[a]*
(000s and %)

	Trade union membership[b]	Potential membership		Trade union density %	
		c	d	e	f
1979	13,289	24,505	23,244	54.2	57.2
1980	12,947	24,509	22,409	52.8	57.8
1981	12,106	24,366	21,602	49.7	56.0
1982	11,593	24,223	21,126	47.9	54.9
1983	11,236	24,249	21,170	46.3	53.1
1984	10,994	24,683	21,464	44.5	51.2
1985	10,821	24,906	21,633	43.4	50.0
1986	10,539	24,947	21,718	42.2	48.5
1987	10,475	24,731	22,035	42.4	47.5
1988	10,376	24,543	22,496	42.3	46.1
1989	10,158	24,471	22,832	41.5	44.5
1990	9,947	24,502	22,652	40.6	43.9
1991	(9,479)[g]	24,436	21,884	(38.8)[g]	(43.3)[g]

Source: Employment Gazette (various issues), Department of Employment.
[a] At the year end.
[b] This series is derived from two main sources (for Great Britain and Northern Ireland) to give the UK as a whole. For Great Britain they are those unions holding a statutory Certificate of Independence issued by the Certification Officer (see footnote on p 23). For Northern Ireland the figures are those of the Department of Economic Development.
[c] Civilian employees in employment plus the unemployed subject to changes in methods of enumeration and coverage of the unemployed over the period.
[d] Civilian employees in employment.
[e] Trade union membership as % of c.
[f] Trade union membership as % of d.
[g] Author's estimates based on reported TUC membership decline Dec 1990 to Dec 1991, *Financial Times*, 27 February 1992.

1968 to over 54 per cent in 1979. Even this high water mark, as an average, concealed wide variations. Although in agriculture, construction and private services densities were substantially below the average, they were greatly exceeded in manufacturing at 70 per cent and were above 80 per cent in the public sector.

Since 1979 the engine of growth has gone into reverse. The total gains in membership from 1969 to 1979 have all been lost and density, which had declined to 43 per cent in 1985, is estimated at less than 39 per cent at the beginning of 1992 (Table 1.1). Losses of membership of this magnitude, *should they continue*, would take density to below 30 per cent by the year 2000, that is as low as it was in the period between the wars. A possible reaction to these dire predictions is that it has all been seen before. Density stood at 45 per cent in 1920, halved over the next 13 years and by 1952 was back to the 1920 level.[23] It should also be noted that commentators were then predicting permanent stagnation under the twin influences of rising prosperity and consensus politics. These predictions were then, of course, followed by the 11 years of sustained growth described earlier.

However, although it is possible to exaggerate the scale of the crisis facing British trade unions – and this will be returned to later – it would nevertheless be wrong, not least in trade union circles, to deny that a crisis exists. We must now turn to describe in more detail, and assess, the scale of that crisis since 1979.

Table 1.2   *Trade union membership in the UK: all trade unions and TUC unions, 1979–91*

(000s and %)

	All trade unions		TUC trade unions		TUC membership % all membership
	Number	Membership	Number	Membership	
1979	453	13,289	109	12,172	91.6
1980	438	12,947	108	11,601	89.6
1981	414	12,106	105	11,006	90.9
1982	408	11,593	102	10,511	90.7
1983	394	11,236	98	10,082	89.7
1984	375	10,994	91	9,855	89.6
1985	370	10,821	88	9,586	88.6
1986	335	10,539	87	9,243	87.7
1987	330	10,475	83	9,127	87.1
1988	315	10,376	83	8,652	83.4
1989	309	10,158	78	8,405	82.7
1990	287	9,947	74	8,193	82.4
1991	na	(9,479)[a]	72	(7,800)[a]	(82.3)[a]

[a] Author's estimates based on reported TUC membership decline Dec 1990 to Dec 1991, *Financial Times*, 27 February 1992.
Source: Employment Gazette (various issues) Department of Employment; Trades Union Congress.

Membership and density since 1979

The steep decline in membership is shown in Table 1.1. Total losses between 1979 and 1991 were almost four million or 28.7 per cent. The fall in membership exceeded the fall in employment over the whole period largely because of the continuing contraction of the unions' traditional manufacturing and industrial areas of recruitment. Rising employment between 1983 and 1990 was mainly concentrated in the service sector where unions have greater organizational problems so that total membership and density continued to fall at much the same rate. Since 1990 the effects of prolonged and deep recession have seriously hampered the trade unions' attempts to recover membership with employment falling and unemployment resuming an upward path. Table 1.1 also illustrates two approaches to the measurement of density. This is discussed later (pp 35–6). Table 1.2 compares the decline in membership of trade unions as a whole (ie those with the certification officer's certificate of independence) with unions affiliated to the TUC. TUC unions, since 1979, have lost more members proportionately than trade unions as a whole (36 per cent and 29 per cent respectively) with the consequence that TUC membership, though remaining substantial, is significantly less important than it was in the 1970s. This partly explains the recent weakening in TUC authority and influence, an aspect discussed later.

The fortunes, or misfortunes, of the 20 largest unions affiliated to the TUC are illustrated in Table 1.3. The Electrical, Electronic, Telecommunication and Plumbing Union (EETPU), although expelled in 1988, is included as an important former affiliate and because of its possible readmission following the 1991 merger with the Amalgamated Engineering Union (AEU). Some of the big affiliates (notably the Transport and General Workers Union (TGWU) and

Table 1.3   Change in membership[a] of the 20 largest trade unions affiliated to the Trade Union Congress, 1979–90

			Number of members			Increase or decrease 1979–90	% increase or decrease	
			1990	1989	1979		1979–90	1989–90
1	Transport & General Workers' Union	TGWU	1,223,891	1,270,776	2,086,281	−862,390	−41.3	−3.7
2	General, Municipal, Boilermakers & Allied Trade Union	GMB[b]	933,425	823,176	967,153	−33,728	−3.5	+13.4
3	National & Local Government Officers' Association	NALGO	744,453	750,502	753,226	−8,773	−1.2	−0.8
4	Amalgamated Engineering Union	AEU[c]	702,228	741,647	1,298,580	−596,352	−45.9	−5.3
5	Manufacturing, Science, Finance	MSF	653,000	653,000	691,954	−38,954	−5.6	—
6	National Union of Public Employees	NUPE	578,992	604,912	691,770	−112,778	−16.3	−4.3
	Electrical, Electronic, Telecommunication & Plumbing Union	EETPU[c,d]	366,650	367,411	420,000	−53,350	−12.7	−0.2
7	Union of Shop, Distributive & Allied Workers	USDAW	361,789	375,891	470,017	−108,228	−23.0	−3.8
8	Union of Construction, Allied Trades & Technicians	UCATT	207,232	258,342	347,777	−140,545	−40.4	−19.8
9	Confederation of Health Service Employees	COHSE	203,311	209,461	212,930	−9,619	−4.5	−2.9
10	Union of Communication Workers	UCW	201,200	202,500	203,452	−2,252	−1.1	−0.6
11	Banking Insurance & Finance Union	BIFU	171,101	170,481	131,774	+39,327	+29.8	+3.6
12	National Union of Teachers	NUT	169,007	171,990	248,896	−79,889	−32.1	−1.7
13	Society of Graphical & Allied Trades '82	SOGAT'82[e]	165,635	176,144	205,784	−40,149	−19.5	−6.0
14	National Communications Union	NCU	154,783	157,060	125,723	+29,060	+23.1	−1.4
15	National Graphical Association (1982)	NGA[e]	122,834	125,003	111,541	+11,293	+10.1	−1.7
16	Civil & Public Services Association	CPSA	122,677	127,976	233,884	−101,207	−45.2	−4.1
17	National Association of Schoolmasters/Union of Women Teachers	NAS/UWT	119,816	118,230	122,058	−2,242	−1.8	+1.3
18	National Union of Rail, Maritime & Transport Workers	NURMTW[f]	118,000	103,000	180,000	−62,000	−26.4	+14.6
19	National Union of Civil & Public Servants	NCPS	113,488	115,606	154,161	−40,673	−34.4	−1.8
20	Institution of Professionals, Managers & Specialists	IPMS	91,713	89,730	102,142	−10,429	−10.2	+2.2
	Total TUC membership		8,192,664	8,405,359	12,172,508	3,979,844	−32.7	−2.5
	Number of TUC affiliates		74	78	109			

Source: TUC; EETPU.

a At year end.
b Formed from GMBATU, APEX merger 1989.
c Merged to form the Amalgamated Engineering & Electrical Union (AEEU) 1991.
d Expelled from TUC 1988.
e Merged to form GPMU 1991.
f Formed from merger of NUR and NUS 1990.

AEU) lost members at a rate well above the average for the period 1979 to 1990. Merger and absorptions slowed down individual membership losses and improved viability. There were a number of significant ones over the period including the GMB's absorption of the Amalgamated Society of Boilermakers in the early 1980s, the formation of the MSF and the series of mergers in printing, culminating in the GPMU in 1991.

Natural growth was, however, the experience of a few unions, notably BIFU which gained almost 30 per cent more members. NALGO also lost relatively few over the whole period and GMB improved its position in 1989 to 1990, although a large part of the explanation was its merger with APEX. The 20th union in size (IPMS) reversed its long-term decline in 1990, a performance now exceptional without the benefit of a merger or absorption. Two unions with substantial National Health Service memberships (NUPE and COHSE) continued to lose members in 1990 above the average for all affiliates.

Unions important in British trade union history continued to contract. Both the steelworkers (ISTC) and the mineworkers (NUM) now have memberships of little more than 60,000 and 50,000 respectively, and are well out of the top 20 and the critical figure of 100,000* – a fate which looks likely to overtake the railway workers in the next few years with the merger with the also declining seamen (NUS) only affording a temporary respite. More recent TUC estimates for 1991 only give limited comfort. The impact of recession has been less serious than expected with an overall TUC loss of 5 per cent with both NALGO and the CPSA increasing their membership. However, the AEU lost 10 per cent in 1991, double its loss for 1990.[24]

Inevitably there are now fewer large unions, although the recent spate of mergers and merger proposals will counter this trend. Excluding the then ASB in 1979 and the EETPU in 1990 26 unions passed the 100,000 mark in 1979 compared with 19 at the beginning of the 1990s. The TGWU was the only union to exceed 1 million in 1990 (two did so in 1979) but had fallen from more than 2 million 11 years earlier.

Trade union finances

The main source of British trade union income derives from its membership. In 1979 84 per cent of all income came from subscriptions and it was still 82 per cent in 1989.[25] Substantial falls in membership can therefore pose serious financial problems for British trade unions. However, contrary to what might be expected, serious financial problems are still not widespread and even in recession unions experiencing special difficulties can find solutions to their problems.[26] Solvency has been preserved by a substantial increase in subscription income, which from 1979 to 1985 more than doubled to almost 64 pence per week and by 1989 it was 85 pence.[27] Furthermore, as membership falls

---

* To secure an automatic seat on the TUC's governing body (General Council) an affiliate must report a membership of 100,000. The wish to maintain influence in the trade union movement through a place on the General Council *can* lead to affiliation at inflated membership figures. This practice needs to be borne in mind when using the figures of membership in the tables.

income from other sources, such as investment, can be shared out among fewer members.[28] Even the TGWU, which has lost more than 860,000 members since 1979, still had assets and funds of £75 million and £72 million, respectively, at the end of 1989, compared to £40 million and £38 million ten years earlier.[29]

There is also scope for unions to increase their income from members even beyond the already substantial increases since 1979, even though increases are always subject to the obvious constraints of competition between unions and resistance from members. Again the TGWU, faced with an accumulating deficit of £1 million per month, is proposing to balance its budget with an 18 per cent increase (ie 21p per week) taking its weekly dues to £1.35, below the average for all unions but slightly above its competitor, the GMB.[30] However, £1.35 is only 0.48 per cent of average weekly earnings which is low in international terms*.

The continuing financial viability of most trade unions acts as a counterweight to membership decline but not in the long run. Continuing membership losses on the scale experienced since 1979 must seriously weaken the bargaining power and financial health of British unions. Even the richest unions with room for financial manoeuvre remain poor relative to the company sector. For example, the combined *funds and assets* of the (still richest) TGWU in 1989 at £147 million are equivalent to the *annual profits* of a successful, medium-sized company and represent only £116 per member.

The unions' financial problems also have serious implications for the TUC. The TUC's income from its affiliates decreases with affiliated membership. Yet the affiliates faced with their own problems are resistant to increases in affiliation fees to bridge the TUC's accumulating deficits and current fees of £1.23 per member have increased from £1 in 1990. The TUC is seeking to link affiliation fees to increases in union subscriptions from members and has achieved cuts in TUC staff, committees and services. However, its reduced role and increasing cost to the unions already pressed for cash leads to the questioning of its role and functions – and even existence in its present form – by the affiliates.

Explaining trade union decline

Although there is clear evidence for declining membership and density from the high point of 1979, the evidence does pose some measurement problems. For example, the key statistic of trade union density can be measured using three different statistical series for trade union membership and a further three for potential membership. Density, using these statistics, can therefore be measured in nine different ways. For example, in research using the 1985 figures the nine measures gave a range *from* 51.4 per cent to 35.8 per cent.[34] The problem is further compounded by the unreliability of the membership figures reported by the

---

* In the US a 1977 study[31] reported that a large majority of unions required an initiation fee for new members and this was generally less than $40. Current United Automobile Worker (UAW) dues (which *may* be typical) are on the basis of two hours' pay per month, representing 1.15 per cent of regular monthly income.[32] In the UK 'admission' fees, once common among the craft unions, have been phased out over the past three decades. UK dues (as a proportion of earnings) are about half of the West German level and two-thirds of the French and Italian.[33]

unions, and the uncertainty and controversy surrounding the official unemployment figures in those measures which include the unemployed in the denominator.

The inclusion or exclusion of the unemployed also raises an analytical issue. Bain and Price include the unemployed on the grounds that their links with unionized, employed workers are not immediately severed – if at all – when they fall out of work.[35] But for measuring the strength of trade union organization at the workplace, or *bargaining power*, excluding the unemployed and using employees in employment as potential membership, gives a more appropriate indicator.* The Bain and Price method can then be reserved for measuring trade union *influence* in the wider society.[36] There is also a possibility that the distinction is more than 'academic'. A 1986 workplace survey concluded that despite the negative effects of high unemployment and job losses: '. . . union density remained high and the formal structures of workplace organization appeared generally to be intact'.[37] This still appeared to be the case in 1991.[38]

Yet despite this reservation and the frequent search in trade union and academic circles for some sign of a 'bottoming-out' in overall membership decline the trade unions' present plight is both undeniable and serious.

General explanations of decline and growth have attracted a good deal of attention in both Britain and the US. One group stresses the effects of war and social unrest as primary influences either directly, or through intervention by government to maintain industrial peace by passing laws favourable to trade unions. Another sees underlying longer-term influences at work.[39] An influential British review in the context of earlier comparative studies combines the determinants of growth under six headings which seek to explain both variations in rates of unionization *over time* as well as differences *at any one time* between groups, occupations and industries.[40] The six are:

1. *composition of potential union membership*, which includes the impact of the growing numbers of women and white-collar workers in the labour force and the associated shift in the economy towards services;
2. *the business cycle*, in particular the influence of inflation, and changes in wages and unemployment upon trade union membership;
3. *employer policies and government action*, ie the role of government, through its legislation and policies, in encouraging or discouraging employers to recognize trade unions;
4. *personal and job-related characteristics*, such as age, gender, incidence of part-time employment, labour turnover, as well as occupational status and its influence on unionization;
5. *industrial structure*, by which is meant the extent to which industry is organized in large groups of employees;
6. *union leadership* or their influence upon growth via their success in organizing new members.

The Bain and Price approach does have the merit of being comprehensive although the relative importance of each of their determinants in explaining British trade union decline since 1979 is not easy to assess. It is, however, clear, on the Bain

---

* This has been done in Table 1.1, column f.

and Price analysis, that membership loss from 1979 to 1987 is very largely attributable to unemployment (within the 'business cycle' determinant) and that this was most in evidence when its level was both high and increasing at a strong rate.*[41] This was especially the case between 1979 and 1981 when the economy was moving into recession and again after 1989. However, the negative effect of unemployment upon unionization both assisted, and was assisted by, the sharp reversal in government policy after 1979 including the abolition of the statutory recognition procedure and the negative influence of government on attitudes to recognition. Bain and Price, in discussing the influence of government upon employers' approach to recognition after 1979, suggest a 'vicious circle' relationship as employers took advantage of declining density to limit, or push back, recognition pressures.[42] In the early 1980s the effect was perhaps more to inhibit recognition rather than towards actual derecognition. However, in the late 1980s and into the 1990s growing trade union weakness and continuing anti-union legislation could encourage a more active derecognition process.[43]

Government is obviously a powerful influence upon unionization, especially when employers are susceptible to official example-setting. But this influence is short term (and can eventually even be reversed) relative to the compositional and structural changes which have been exerting an inexorable and accelerating influence over a longer period. The shift in the balance of the economy towards services; the increasing numbers of women and white-collar workers; the growing incidence of temporary, part-time and peripheral employment; and the decline in the number of workplaces employing large groups of people** have come together to dimininish those environments and circumstances favouring trade union growth, and enlarge those in which recruitment and recognition are an uphill trudge.

Trade union responses

Up to 1983 it was realistic for British trade unions to work towards the return of a Labour government with the prospect of expansionist economic policies favouring the goods-producing industries (which would have at least partially restored their membership strongholds), as well as a return to the industrial relations policies and legislation of the 1970s. The Labour Party's heavy electoral defeat in 1983 was followed by slowly accumulating evidence that changes in the economy and labour force were eroding the unions' traditional membership base. By 1985 a number of unions, and the TUC, were beginning to devise, fund and implement revival – or in some cases survival – strategies. They were encouraged by the success of their post-1985 campaigns to retain their political funds but once again lost their main political lifeline with the further defeat of the Labour Party in 1987. Out of the post-1987 debates and reappraisals six strategies – some traditional, some new, from which unions were choosing –

---

* But note that unemployment need not necessarily weaken trade union bargaining *power* following the distinction between influence and power discussed earlier (p 36).
** According to the findings of the 1980–4 Workplace Industrial Relations Survey 'the greater loss of employment by large, highly unionized workplaces is a major factor behind the contraction of trade union membership since the end of the 1970s'.[44]

could be identified: work for a Labour government and supportive legislation; merge with other unions; recruit new members in the fastest growing industries and among previously neglected groups; improve services to members; revise trade union purposes; and look to the institutions, legislation and trade unions of the EC for support.

The strategy of working for the election of a Labour government – as old as the Labour Party which was itself the creature of the TUC* – served the unions well until 1979. The Labour Party was in power for 17 out of the 34 years from 1945 to 1979, enacting a whole raft of legislation favourable to the unions, especially after the defeat of the Heath Government in 1974. This policy has, however, never implied not trying to work with Conservative governments, except following the Industrial Relations Act of 1971. For their part, Conservative governments have normally sought constructive relationships with the trade unions, mainly for *realpolitik* reasons. After 1979 this began to change. The Government progressively diminished the TUC's role in consultation and representation on tripartite bodies with employers and itself; stiffened its attitudes towards its own employees and unions in the public sector; and enacted its industrial relations and trade union legislation over TUC and union protests. These rebuffs left the trade union movement's only route to political influence through the Labour Party. The most notable initiatives were the founding of the campaigning, fund-raising body 'Trade Unions for a Labour Victory' and its successor 'Trade Unions for Labour'. The former organized the successful political funds campaign. The latter provided a major organizational contribution in the constituencies in preparation for the 1987 general election and contributed £3.8 million of the Labour Party's election fund of £4.6 million.

After the 1987 defeat efforts shifted towards the formation of a nationally-focused, low subscription, mass membership party of trade union and constituency members – on the European social democratic model. The largest unions themselves undertook to support the concept with an increase in their per capita affiliation fees to the party. The eventual outcome was a failure with membership remaining at less than 300,000. However, the unions continued to play a major part in funding and offering substantial organizational manpower resources to the Labour Party's election campaigns, especially when political and economic developments after 1989 seemed to offer the party a real prospect of success.

The Labour Party's fourth successive defeat in 1992 has clearly severely weakened the trade unions' hopes of an early and favourable political context. It has also encouraged a lively debate on the degree to which, if at all, the close relationship between the Labour Party and the trade unions serves their respective interests. Yet in the medium term it remains highly unlikely that the TUC and its affiliates – although some have reservations – will seek to abandon a strategy which was established even before the formation of the Labour Party as the other 'wing' of the labour movement. Undoubtedly the Labour Party's ability to form a government would be seriously weakened, in both financial and organizational terms, by the rupture or weakening of the trade union

---

* The Labour Representation Committee, the precursor of the Labour Party, was created by the TUC in 1900. The Labour Party was founded in 1906.

connection. For their part, the trade unions' prospects of at least slowing the decline in membership would be greatly assisted by favourable government policies, especially those which would encourage recognition and advance collective bargaining. As long as there remains the prospect of a Labour Party in government then the trade unions must seek to sustain its chances of election, although maintaining the same level of financial support will become increasingly difficult as pressure upon trade union income becomes more acute.

Mergers, amalgamations and absorptions have a long tradition as a means of survival and growth. Between 1949 and 1979 about 300 trade unions were absorbed in this process[45] and since 1979 the number of TUC unions has fallen from 109 to 72 – almost entirely from mergers. The mergers in the early 1980s involved GMB's absorption of the boilermakers (ASB) and the emergence of two enlarged printing unions – SOGAT '82 and NGA (1982) – from mergers among the original four. In 1989 GMB merged with the much smaller clerical union, APEX, followed by the NUR's absorption of the seamen in 1990.

This traditional process of merger and absorption led to the formation of bigger, more viable unions, often simply involving smaller unions seeking the resources and protection of the larger. However, in 1987 the merger process was stepped up to involve the bringing together of already large unions to form 'superunions'. The first of these was the somewhat unstable creation of MSF from ASTMS and TASS which is the fifth largest TUC union with 653,000 members. In 1991 the final rationalization of the print unions took place with the emergence of the GPMU from NGA (1982) and SOGAT '82 – a combined membership of almost 300,000. In 1992, by an overwhelming majority of those voting, the AEU and EETPU combined forces to form the AEEU with a combined membership exceeding 1 million on their 1990 figures and the second largest TUC union.

The formation of the AEEU has quickened the pace of tentative discussions in other quarters. The smaller, higher education unions AUT and NATFE may yet see the logic of coming together now that the old distinction between universities and polytechnics has gone. In the big league, NALGO, NUPE and COHSE – should their negotiations and consultations bear fruit – would form a union of some 1.5 million, ahead of the TGWU and confirming the gradual shift in power within the TUC affiliates towards the white collar and public sector unions. A consequence of the formation of the AEEU could be to rationalize the unions in manufacturing and combining manual and white collar strengths with a further merger with MSF. This would result in a combined membership, again on 1990 figures, of 1.7 million. Most recently, and perhaps the ultimate merger, is the intention to bring together the combined strengths of the much-troubled TGWU, and the still confident and growing GMB, to form a union approaching 2.2 million although this would not be much above the TGWU's membership at its peak in 1979.

Merger or absorption are often sought as means of survival where finances are shaky. Sometimes, as in the formation of the MSF, the process is seen as a prelude to further 'natural growth'. Natural growth, with or without merger, through the recruitment of new members has been strongly promoted by the two big general workers' unions (TGWU and GMB), which have together lost nearly 900,000 members since 1979. Their organizing efforts have been especially concentrated in the service sector industries, which combine growing employment with low union density, high levels of female employment, a large proportion of temporaries and part-timers, high employee turnover and low member retention. Thus the industries with the greatest opportunities for membership growth present the most difficult problems.

Both the TGWU and GMB have begun to use 'workplace audits' among part-timers to assess the levels of unionization and the TGWU is having some success through agreements with employers to extend permanent workers' wages and conditions to temporaries. It has also polled the attitudes of young workers towards unions as a prelude to special organizing drives geared directly to young people.

Women workers (who already represent one-third of all trade union members) are an important target group for both unions. The TGWU now has a national women's officer with special responsibilities to organize more women members, and raise their profile and influence within a union traditionally led and dominated by men. The GMB has reserved 10 out of 40 places on its National Executive Committee for women, and in workplaces and branches is introducing women's discussion groups and equality officers.* It has also turned its attention to the self-employed (another expanding group) offering administrative help and services without the need for membership.

Other unions, notably the printing union (SOGAT '82), which is now part of the new GPMU, and the shopworkers (USDAW) have responded to membership loss with similar policies. SOGAT, following its defeat in its dispute with Rupert Murdoch's News International and with a membership vulnerable to new technology and the breakdowns of occupational demarcation in printing, is running organizing campaigns to appeal to young people and women in its traditional strongholds of papermaking, books and magazines.

The development of membership services has long been a feature of professional, managerial and white-collar unions. More recently, blue-collar unions have set the pace with advisory and financial services in insurance, savings, investment and bond/equity purchase. The EETPU has, for a number of years, even succeeded in including private health insurance in some collective agreements and now provides new technology training for its members, an example which has been followed by the engineering union (AEU) using government training grants and equipment. The NGA, now part of the GPMU, has also been active in new technology training. The development of these services has been greatly assisted by the development of accurate, computerized, membership records. Paradoxically the government has assisted this process by its strong preference for secret postal ballots in the conduct of union business which clearly requires accurate membership registers. These registers were made a legal requirement in the Trade Union Act 1984.

The TUC, under General Secretary Norman Willis, has played an active role in support of these strategies. Willis himself even advocated (contrary to TUC

---

* An interesting recent finding on women in British trade unions is that '. . . full-time women employees are as likely to be trade union members as full-time men employees, but that part-time women employees are half as likely to be members as full timers . . . part-time employment . . . rather than gender might well lie at the root of the difference'.[46]

traditional non-intervention in such matters) a merger of the two big teachers' unions (NUT and NAS/UWT) in the context of the failure of their industrial action in 1987. The two unions' deep rivalry, rather than Willis's intervention, prevented any progress. He has also firmly supported the unions' new emphasis on organizing new members, developing services* and attracting women workers – especially temporaries and part-timers. The TUC is also considering its own computerized balloting service for affiliates. Another TUC enthusiasm is the video film – influenced by the experience of US trade unions and the successful use of videos in the trade unions' political funds campaign. The TUC's credit card was also influenced by the US experience and the cards are now becoming commonplace in UK unions.

The inter-union conflict over single union agreements was partly about an issue of *principle*, ie the alleged willingness of the EETPU in particular to exchange its freedom to strike in return for recognition. In response the EETPU claimed that the 'right' to strike has remained since the agreements are not legally binding and that its rivals (especially the GMB and TGWU) have negotiated identical agreements. Principle has, however, been confused with *tactics*, ie competition for members, which is traditionally regulated by the Bridlington Rules. The case against the EETPU on these grounds was, first, that it had reached single union agreements with employers before work had begun (and before it even had workers in membership) on new ('greenfield') sites, using the strike free clauses as inducements, and secondly, that it had signed single union agreements with employers on existing ('brownfield') sites where other unions already had members. The first part of the case clearly allowed no scope for workers to choose their union by ballot. The second, when it occurred, constituted a clear breach of the Bridlington Principles. Protracted discussions within the TUC to draw up a Code of Practice on single union agreements acceptable to all parties failed to resolve the dispute and the EETPU was suspended and expelled following its refusal to withdraw from two agreements ruled to be in breach of Bridlington.**

Yet the dispute over single union deals was not simply about competition for members but also ideology, even though one should not exaggerate the differences between the two positions or hope to find homogeneity within them. The AEU, for example, is somewhat disenchanted with its famous agreement with Nissan, manufacturing cars in the north-east of England. AEU membership in the plant remains, on some reports, at only 20 per cent and the opinion within the AEU and EETPU with reservations over single union deals will not disappear in the merger process. Indeed, the EETPU's expulsion from the TUC in 1988 was later followed by the affiliation of the small, breakaway Electrical and Plumbing Industries Union (EPIU).

---

* The TUC has now introduced its own package through its own bank (Unity Trust) including personal pensions, financial advice and services, legal advice, banking and travel, and a credit card.

** It should be noted here that the action against the EETPU was not because of its preference for single union/strike free agreements, but its refusal to accept the rulings of the TUC.

The debate over trade union purposes has emerged in response to the decline in membership and influence since 1979, and the continuing defeats of the Labour Party, although this debate is an old one echoing the controversies of the late 19th and early 20th centuries. Two broad streams of opinion have emerged as responses to membership decline since 1979: the *new realist* and the *new traditionalist*.

The new realists are closely associated with the expelled electricians (EETPU) and, with a more ambivalent commitment, the engineers (AEU) now in the new, merged union. They argue that the primary, even exclusive, purpose of trade unions is to improve the pay and conditions of individual members. This is seen as 'realistic' in that it is what most members want, and that wider social, community and political goals are at best an irrelevance and at worst a threat to the primary purpose of trade unions – and even their existence – should the political climate become hostile. However, principle is assisted by practice. The craft skills of, for example, electricians tend to give them 'core' worker status (therefore bargaining strength) and the ability to upgrade their skills through new technology.

The new traditionalists are led by the big general worker unions, the TGWU and, to a lesser extent, the GMB. They largely represent the interests of the 'non-core' groups most threatened by changes in the economy and labour markets, and are seeking to extend their membership into what the GMB calls the 'new servant class' in the growing service sector. This involves developing a wider, community-based approach to potential trade union members, notably women, the young and the disadvantaged. Such an approach strengthens these unions' identification with the Labour Party at local and constituency levels.

The conflict between the two approaches manifested itself in the competition for members and the bitter disputes over single union/strike free agreements which culminated in the expulsion of the EETPU. The first single union agreement was between the EETPU and the Japanese company Toshiba in 1981. The EETPU's then national engineering officer (Roy Sanderson) maintained that this agreement arose from a *joint* identification, with management, of the causes of industrial conflict in Britain and the best method of reducing these causes.[47] Such agreements have been primarily sought by Japanese companies and typically, although not universally, have six principal ingredients: recognition of a single union; labour flexibility; single status (ie extension of white-collar conditions to blue-collar employees); a commitment to worker participation (ie company councils for all employees, unionized or not); binding pendulum arbitration (ie the arbitrator has to choose either the employer's offer or the union's claim without a compromise); and a no strike provision (ie arbitration as a mandatory, final stage).[48]

But accepting the inconsistencies there remains a difference between the two camps (which is confirmed by the differences within them) that goes back to the old controversy over trade unions' industrial and political purposes. The EETPU, its leadership and the other unions which support it, is firmly identified with 'business union' objectives and, under its now retired general secretary, Eric Hammond, openly derided the political goals and ambitions of its rivals, especially in the use of strikes and in its opposition to the 1984–5 miners' strike and its leadership, a position which generated acute and bitter conflicts within the unions and the Labour Party, but largely isolated the EETPU. Traditionally leading the 'political union' camp, the TGWU has had a long line of politically active leaders with a strong influence within the Labour Party. It still draws support from the GMB just as the AEU maintained its close relationship with the EETPU. It opposed the EETPU's expulsion, and eventually both pursued their joint interests towards the merger. Yet some of the bitterness of the 1980s remains. The question of the reaffiliation of the EETPU to the TUC, despite being part of the AEEU, is attracting strong opposition from unions insisting that the EETPU first returns members 'poached' from other unions before and after expulsion, and withdraws from the single union agreements which led to the TUC's ruling, the union's refusal to comply and the subsequent expulsion.[49]

The EC option came to life when the Labour Party, the TUC and most of the affiliates converted their principled opposition to the EC to one of firm support. This was strongly signalled at the 1988 TUC when the president of the European Commission, Jacques Delors, addressed the Congress and was received with remarkable enthusiasm. The support within the Community and the member countries for the principles of the Social Charter, in the form of the Social Action Programme and the associated proposed directives of the Commission, held out the prospect of a series of legislative initiatives which could extend UK employment protection in areas such as health and safety, working time and offering parallel rights to part-time and temporary employees. The obvious attraction to the trade unions of the social dimension – not least in the context of the prospect of real progress via the extension of qualified majority voting* – was complemented by progress on the 'social dialogue', ie through the duty of the Commission, under the Treaty of Rome and Single European Act, to encourage European-wide and sectoral, voluntary collective bargaining as an alternative to the compulsory, legislative route of the directives under the social dimension. The 'social partners' in the social dialogue are the European employers' association UNICE (to which the CBI belongs) and the European Trades Union Congress (ETUC) which includes the TUC.[50] Associated with these collective bargaining developments, but through the legislative route of a Commission directive, is the proposal to make consultative, information-receiving European Works Councils mandatory for European multinationals operating in at least two countries of the EC.**

Individual unions themselves, encouraged by these positive developments and their industrial and political problems at home, have pursued European initiatives with growing enthusiasm. They have offered strong support to the proposed directive on European Works Councils but, more importantly, have

---

* A qualified majority in the Council of Ministers, following a proposal of the Commission, requires 54 out of 76 states voting in favour. The distribution of votes is: France, Italy, UK, Germany (10 each); Spain (8); Belgium, Greece, Portugal, Netherlands (5 each); Denmark, Ireland (3 each); Luxembourg (2). For a detailed consideration of qualified majority voting and the implications of the Maastricht agreement in 1992 see Chapter 2.
** See Chapter 2 for a more detailed treatment of European Works Councils.

sought to extend their direct links with European trade unions, even towards the prospect of eventual merger.[51] The AEU's development of a closer relationship with IG Metall has been paralleled by other unions, notably MSF, with French trade unions and the GPMU with its counterparts in the European printing industry. Of even greater significance was the founding in 1990 of the Euro Cockpit Association from the airline pilots' unions in the EC with the intention of moving to eventual merger.[52] Nor has the TUC been idle within the ETUC, reversing its earlier aloof stance of the 1960s and 1970s. The STUC is also playing an increasingly active role as representative of its affiliates in Scotland, not least on the Economic and Social Committee of the European Community.

CONCLUSION: THE PROSPECTS FOR THE TRADE UNIONS

The Labour Party's defeat in the 1992 General Election was a major setback for the trade unions, especially in the context of being the fourth in a row with a further opportunity unlikely to be available until 1997. If the direction of union growth is dependent upon a triangular and '. . . crucial inter-relationship between economic forces, employer policies and government action'[53] then under a Labour government a programme would have been implemented within at least the second and third sides of this triangle (ie employer policies and government action), followed by the eventual movement of the economy out of recession, all of which would have stimulated some recovery in the trade unions' fortunes. The Labour Party has moved a long way from its early promises in the 1980s to return to the labour laws existing before 1979, accepting with most unions' acquiescence the bulk of the Conservatives' reforms. Yet on certain critical issues – a return to some form of statutory support for trade union recognition, the promotion of collective bargaining and some limited return to the freedom to impose secondary action – a 1992 Labour government would have been a welcome lifeboat for its brothers and sisters in the unions. Now there is even a prospect that the Labour Party will seek to distance itself from the supposed political liability of the trade unions and that a realignment of the anti-Conservative parties for the 1997 election will further loosen the Labour Party's links and commitment to the unions. Nor, from some trade union perspectives is this necessarily a bad thing; NALGO, one of the stronger of the TUC unions, is not affiliated to the Labour Party despite its record of political campaigns against government policy on privatization. The 'business union' lobby also remains strong, not least within the EETPU section of the AEEU which is not without followers in the unions as a whole, large numbers of whose members voted Conservative in the 1992 General Election. However, it is by no means certain that full-blown, apolitical business unionism will revive the trade unions' fortunes. The example of the US is certainly not helpful where membership continues to decline to marginal levels and the non-union option is already the norm in most states and most industries.[54]

But if the political route to revival is presently blocked, and may even remain so, what can the trade unions do for themselves? One option is recruitment of new members.

Structural economic change is clearly handicapping the recruitment campaigns which have been a continuing feature of trade union activity since the middle 1980s including two co-ordinated by the TUC itself. So far the positive impact has been minimal, although the decline in membership may have been steeper without the campaigns. The TUC's view that recruitment campaigns are materially assisted by the availability of sophisticated packages of services such as personal insurance, financial advice, loans and discounts is widely shared among the unions. This view is close to accepting the concept of 'associate membership' prominent in the US in the AFL/CIO and its affiliates, that is that the decision to join a trade union is essentially determined by services offered. In contrast, recent British research suggests that recruitment may be more influenced by pay, ideological commitment and the expectation of protection, rather than an attractive range of services.[55] Other research questions the organizational commitment of trade unions to the high priority given to recruitment efforts finding '. . . a gap between theoretical commitment and existing practice'.[56]

Possible weaknesses in the approach, and low priority given, to recruitment are serious when set against the scarce resources available and the scale of the recruitment problems facing the unions. Some British commentators, as is commonplace in the US and referred to earlier, are beginning to discuss the non-union option available to British employers as union membership dwindles and derecognition, once virtually unknown, is showing some signs of spreading. Even single union agreements which could secure trade union recognition and a strong presence may be seen, by employers, as a prelude to full or partial derecognition should trade union membership fall below what is considered an acceptable level. Indeed, an expert observer of the Japanese approach to industrial relations has suggested that Japanese companies in Britain would prefer, if possible, to organize their industrial relations without trade unions.[57] Retention of members can be as crucial as recruitment. Some industries, such as hotels and catering, have natural problems in this respect. A further dimension was added in the 1980s, as public sector industries were privatized, undermining traditionally strong trade union cultures and hastening membership decline and derecognition.[58]

The strategy most within the control of the trade unions themselves is the traditional one of merger. As we have seen, major developments towards 'superunions' seem to lie ahead, some of them in the possible wider context of the EC. This may not be a moment too soon should the Government revive the earlier view of trade union 'monopolies' as the labour market equivalent of those in the product market. Indeed, its present legislative proposals provide for the application of rules on election ballots to be equally applied to those for mergers. This may yet suggest things to come. Mergers also have their 'downside'. As defensive strategies against declining membership and financial non-viability they have much merit but inevitably distance the members from the leadership and may not provide a basis for natural growth in membership unless associated with vigorous recruitment campaigns attractive to potentially new members – as we discussed earlier.

As for the TUC, unlike its German counterpart the DGB, it traditionally plays no broker role in these marriages of convenience. Indeed, it would be difficult for it to do so as has been recently observed: '. . . suffering from dwindling resources and credibility problems with some of its major affiliates [it] is unlikely to be either able or inclined to impose a coherent pattern on the current round of amalgamations'.[59] The TUC also has the additional problem that superunions may have sufficient resources to pursue wider purposes more effectively and for themselves.

These wider purposes are increasingly associated with the EC. Whatever happens to the Commission's pressure to convert the Social Charter into a battery of approved directives – and the prospects are not auspicious as the EC stumbles in the Maastricht ratification process – UK trade unions must seek to respond to the growth of the single market and the associated development of Europe-wide multinationals, including their increasing penetration of the Eastern European economies. A number of possibilities remain open. The social dialogue reflects the 'social partners' traditions of continental EC members with the automatic legitimacy conferred on trade unions. The dialogue is taking place at EC and sectoral levels with the encouragement of the Commission providing opportunities for the active involvement of the TUC (within the ETUC) and its affiliates, although the institutional involvement of the Commission may be under threat if the Maastricht Treaty is not ultimately ratified. There also still remains a now very limited possibility of a directive establishing European Works Councils with the UK finding itself unable to resist* Finally, as we have seen, some UK unions have begun to work more closely with their counterparts in Germany, France and elsewhere. They may be beginning to value the experience and its potential outcome. Indeed, given the quite unexpected developments in the EC in the wake of Maastricht this may become the main route to follow.

References

1. For an account of the historical forces shaping current industriial relations see Fox, A (1985) *History and Heritaage: the Social Origins of the British Industrial Relations System*, Allen and Unwin, London.
2. Comprehensive employment, unemployment and consumer price data are published monthly in the Labour Market Data section of the Department of Employment's *Employment Gazette*. These, and subsequent figures are drawn from that source.
3. The comparative economic statistics cited here are taken from two sources: the summaries in the statistical appendices of the quarterly *National Institute Economic Review* of the NIESR; and the OECD's annual *Employment Outlook*, most recently the July 1991 edition.
4. A study of occupational change in the UK is Rajan, A and Pearson, R (1986) *UK Occupation and Employment Trends to 1990*, Butterworths, London.
5. Hakim, C (1987) 'Trends in the flexible workforce', *Employment Gazette*, 95, No 11, November, pp 549–60.
6. Pollert, A (1991) *Farewell to Flexibility*, Blackwell, Oxford; *Employment Gazette*, 100, No 5, 1992.
7. 'Flexibility examined', Labour Research Department, Bargaining Report, No 56, November 1986, pp 5–12.
8. See, for example, Oliver, N and Wilkinson, B (1992) *The Japanisation of British Industry*, Blackwell, Oxford.
9. For a perceptive, socio-political analysis of the Thatcher Government's policies

* See Chapter 2 for a further discussion.

towards the trade unions, as well as a comprehensive exposition of the principles of British labour law see Wedderburn, Lord (1986) *The Worker and the Law*, Penguin, Harmondsworth.
10. 'Tribunals and the recession', *IDS Focus*, Incomes Data Services, March 1992, pp 14–16.
11. 'Industrial Tribunals and the Employment Appeal Tribunal', *Employment Gazette*, 95, No 10, October 1987, pp 498–502.
12. For a thorough discussion see Wedderburn, op cit.
13. Evans, S (1987) 'The use of injunctions in industrial disputes', May 1984–April 1987', *British Journal of Industrial Relations*, XXV No 3, November pp 419–35.
14. Annual Report 1986, ACAS, March 1987, p 11.
15. Leopold, J (1988) 'Moving the status quo: the growth in trade union political funds', *Industrial Relations Journal*, 19: 4, Winter, pp 286–95.
16. For analysis of the wider issues see Towers, B (1985) 'Posing larger questions: the British miners' strike of 1984–85', *Industrial Relations Journal*, 16: 2, Summer, pp 8–25; Adeney, M and Lloyd, J (1986) *The Miners' Strike 1984–85, Loss without Limit*, RKP, London; Beynon, H (ed) (1985) *Digging Deeper: Issues in the Miners' Strike*, Verso, London.
17. *People, Jobs and Opportunity* (1992) Cm 1810, HMSO, London.
18. Under the Industrial Relations Act 1971 collective agreeements were presumed to be legally binding unless the parties wished otherwise. The outcome was that agreements were concluded with 'Tina Lea Clauses' (ie 'This is not a legally enforceable agreement').
19. The Bridlington Rules or Principles which date from 1939 (although similar arrangements existed before then) regulate, among other things, inter-union competition for members. Disagreements are resolved by binding decisions of the TUC Disputes Committee.
20. This is, in any case, a common practice among unions. The Electoral Reform Society is the usual agency employed.
21. A view recently confirmed by Sir Douglas Smith, chairman of ACAS.
22. These possibilities are discussed in Chapter 2. See also Towers, B (1992) 'Two speed ahead: social Europe and the UK after Maastricht', *Industrial Relations Journal*, 23: 2, Summer, pp 83–9.
23. Bain, G S and Price, R (1983) 'Union growth, dimensions, determinants and destiny' in Bain, G S (ed) *Industrial Relations in Britain*, Blackwell, Oxford.
24. Smith, M (1992) 'TUC estimates membership is down by only 5 per cent', *Financial Times*, 27 February.
25. Annual Reports, 1980 and 1990 Certification Office for Trade Unions and Employers' Associations, Appendix 4.
26. Kelly, J (1987) 'Trade unions through recession, 1980–1984', *British Journal of Industrial Relations*, XXV, No 2, July, pp 275–82.
27. Annual Report, 1990 Certification Office for Trade Unions and Employers' Associations, op cit.
28. Willman, P and Morris, T (1988) *The Finances of British Trade Unions*, Research Paper No 62, Department of Employment.
29. Annual Report, 1990 Certification Office, op cit.
30. Goodhart, D (1992) 'TGWU plans higher fees to combat debt', *Financial Times*, 10 February.
31. Hickman, C W (1977) 'Labor organizations' fees and dues', *Monthly Labor Review*, 100, No 5, May, pp 19–24.
32. 'The UAW makes us strong', United Automobile Workers' Education Department.
33. 'Europe's unions – what do members pay?' *Labour Research*, 77, No 6, June 1988, pp 8–11.
34. Kelly, J and Bailey, R (1988) *British Trade Union Membership and Density in the 1980s*, LSE, Department of Industrial Relations (mimeo), pp 9–13.
35. Bain, G S and Price, R (1980) *Profiles of Union Growth: a Comparative Statistical Portrait of Eight Countries*, Blackwell, Oxford, p. 7.

36. Kelly, J and Bailey, R, op cit, pp 15–21.
37. Batstone, E and Gourlay, S (1986) *Unions, Unemployment and Innovation*, Blackwell, Oxford, p 264.
38. According to interview statements, reported in the media, made by Sir Douglas Smith (chairman of ACAS) at the time of the publication of the 1991 Annual Report.
39. For a US review of these explanations, see Stepina, L P and Fiorito, J (1986) 'Towards a comprehensive theory of trade union growth and decline', *Industrial Relations*, 25, No 3, Fall pp 248–64.
40. Bain, G S and Price, R (1983) op cit, pp 12–31.
41. Ibid, p 18.
42. Ibid pp 18–19.
43. *Annual Report 1991*, ACAS, March 1992, pp 20–1.
44. Millward, N and Stevens, M (1986) *British Workplace Industrial Relations, 1980–84*, Gower, Aldershot, p 303.
45. Buchanan, R T (1985) 'Mergers in British trade unions: 1949–79', in McCarthy, W E J (ed) *Trade Unions*, Harmondsworth, Penguin. For a more recent contribution to the merger literature see Buchanan, R T (1992) 'Measuring mergers and concentration in UK trade unions, 1910–1988', *Industrial Relations Journal*, 23: 4, (forthcoming).
46. Witherspoon, S, reported in Millward and Stevens, op cit, pp 61–2.
47. Bassett, P (1986) *Strike Free: New Industrial Relations in Britain*, Macmillan, London, p 122.
48. Ibid.
49. Smith, M (1992), 'More at stake than mere machismo', *Financial Times*, 4 February.
50. For a recent discussion of these developments see Towers, B 'Two speed ahead: social Europe and the UK after Maastricht', *Industrial Relations Journal*, op cit.
51. See, for example, the statement of Bill Jordan, the AEU's president, prior to a meeting in Dusseldorf with IG Metall; the union's German counterpart. 'European-wide union mergers forecast', *Financial Times*, 7 February 1992.
52. Gapper, J (1990) 'Pilots to form pan-European body', *Financial Times*, 7 November.
53. Bain, G S and Price, R (1983) op cit, p 33.
54. The most recent research on US trade union membership is in Curme, M A et al (1990) 'Union membership and contract coverage in the United States 1983–88', *Industrial and Labor Relations Review*, Vol 44, No 1, October, pp 5–33.
55. Sapper, S (1991) 'Do members' services packages influence trade union recruitment?', *Industrial Relations Journal*, 22, No 4, Winter, pp 309–16.
56. Mason, R and Bain, P (1991) 'Trade union recruitment strategies: facing the 1990s', *Industrial Relations Journal*, 22, No 1, Spring, pp 36–45.
57. Thurley, K (1988) 'Changing the agenda: learning from Japanese industrial relations', *The Anglo-Japanese Economic Journal*, 2, No 2, July–September, pp 15–17.
58. Dibden, J and Millward, N (1992) 'Trade union membership: developments and prospects', *Policy Studies*, Vol 12, No 4.
59. Industrial Relations Review and Report, No 508, 'Union mergers: for growth or survival?', *IRS*, 1992, pp 12–15.

Chapter Two

British Industrial Relations and the European Community

Colin Gill

INTRODUCTION

The EC will occupy a prominent place on the political agenda during the 1990s. As we move towards the completion of the internal market from 1 January 1993 a new wave of Europeanization has been generated throughout the Community. Business organizations, politicians and trade unions in all the 12 member states are preoccupied with matters stemming from greater economic and political union among the member states. The Maastricht summit of heads of government in December 1991 represented a landmark in Community affairs. One of the most controversial issues at Maastricht was the social dimension of the internal market programme; in other words issues about to what degree the Community should adopt positive policies and legislation on such matters as employment and working conditions – health and safety issues, information and consultation rights, working time arrangements, training, job placement schemes etc, so that the citizens and employees of the Community would have some sort of 'safety net' to protect them from the substantial economic changes which were expected to accompany the establishment of open markets in Europe.

The purpose of this chapter is to assess the implications for British industrial relations of the social dimension of the internal market within the context of the EC generally. Given the refusal of the UK government to agree to qualified majority voting for social and employment affairs at the Maastricht summit, it is important not only to clarify the post-Maastricht legal situation with regard to how EC legislation affects British employees, but also to speculate on how such legislation might evolve during the rest of the 1990s. In order to assess current and future developments, it is first necessary to outline the evolution of Community social policies up to the present time and how such developments have affected British workers.

THE DEVELOPMENT OF EC SOCIAL POLICY

The period of economic neo-liberalism: 1957–72

Prior to Britain joining the Community in 1973, there was little in the way of social policy action at Community level. The period 1957–72 was a period of economic boom, and most member states introduced legal and welfare rights for employees. At Community level, the principle of the freedom of movement of persons from one member state to another was regarded as an adequate check on any distortion of competition within the labour market. There were, however, a small number of social policy measures introduced, the consequences of which have not been adequately clarified even today.

The first such measure was the authorization of nationals of one of the member states to take up employment in another member state if there were no available workers in the national labour market. Even today it is still not clear whether Community preference should be given to nationals of one of the member states, or whether states such as Germany or France could continue to utilize migrant labour from non-Community states to maintain an economic advantage; the application of this measure is still largely outside Community competence.[1]

The Community also passed Regulations to set up an Administrative Committee to settle questions of administration and interpretation of social security matters relating to the free movement of labour. Even today there are still vast differences in levels and coverage of social security benefits between the member states; in some countries tax and social security systems are integrated and in others they are not. Each member state designs its social security system for different purposes and Community influence is concerned with co-ordination rather than harmonization.

Little else characterized Community social policy during this period. The European Social Fund became operational in 1962 and was used largely as a means of cross-subsidization of contributions from the larger states (France and West Germany) to Italy. The Commission also established an Industrial Health and Safety Division in 1962, but only one directive was adopted by the Council of Ministers – relating to harmonization of classifying and labelling certain dangerous substances.

Adopting a Community 'human face' in social policy: 1972–80

Just before Britain (along with Denmark and Ireland) joined the Community, a Declaration was issued after the Paris Summit of October 1972 stating that the member states were equally committed to establishing a social union as to establishing economic and monetary union. The final communiqué stated that the member states:

> . . . attached as much importance to vigorous action in the social field as to the achievement of economic union . . . it is essential to ensure the increased involvement of labour and management in the economic and social decisions of the Community.[2]

During this period a number of measures were introduced which affected Britain at a time when a large number of company mergers were taking place, both in Britain and in the EC generally. In the four years from 1976 to 1980, three directives were adopted by the Council of Ministers which established Community-wide legislation on workers' rights in situations of mass dismissals, transfer of undertakings and insolvencies.[3] Under the Community legal system, member states are able to implement Community directives so as to fit in with their existing legal traditions and customs. This means that it is frequently the case that some countries use this provision to 'soften' the impact of directives in the employment area. This was certainly the case in Britain because the

British government subsequently failed to give full effect to these three directives.

First, the Employment Protection Act gives a narrower definition of 'redundancy' than is provided by Article 1 of the Collective Redundancies Directive which means that fewer redundant workers are covered by the provisions of Article 1. Secondly, Article 2 of the Collective Redundancies Directive requires the employer to consult workers' representatives 'with a view to reaching agreement'. However, the provisions of the Employment Protection Act do not require the employer to consult with the aim of reaching agreement. It is sufficient that he should consider representations made to him on behalf of workers and state why he chooses to reject any of these representations. Thirdly, Article 2 indicates that consultations are to cover 'ways and means of avoiding collective redundancies or reducing the numbers of workers affected'. There is no such provision in the Employment Protection Act in Britain. Finally, the Employment Protection Act obliges the employer to consult only the representatives of 'recognized' unions. Where he does not recognize any union, in apparent contrast to the directive, he does not have to consult anyone. This means that the growing numbers of British workers being made redundant as the current recession continues are not being given the rights due to them under EC law (for a more detailed outline of redundancy law see Chapters 17 and 18).[4] The European Commission issued a draft directive that proposed revisions to the Collective Redundancies Directive in early 1992 which sought to strengthen its impact; however, since the proposals are based on Article 100 of the Treaty of Rome they are subject to unanimous voting in the Council of Ministers, and given the present stance of the British government, are likely to be vetoed.[5]

The Transfer of Undertakings Directive found its way into British labour law in the Transfer of Undertakings (Protection of Employment) Regulations 1981. The intention of this directive was to ensure that when a business changed ownership, employees' terms and conditions of employment would be protected under the new owner. In fact, the Regulations only apply in Britain where there is a takeover of a business other than by share purchase, and since share purchase is the most common form of takeover, British workers have limited protection.

Despite the fact that EC initiatives in employment affairs had a limited impact in Britain, the period 1972–80 did see increasing intervention on the part of the Commission into the employment area, even though such initiatives were piecemeal and limited in scope. However, by the end of the 1970s, this impetus for a social dimension to the Community was faltering, largely because of rising unemployment throughout the Community member states, and economic pressures arising from the need of companies to adapt to new technology and competition from the US and Japan. In particular, as restructuring of industry gathered pace in the early years of the 1980s, it became clear that 'labour market flexibility' was the key to increasing the competitiveness of European enterprises. These changes were reflected in Community policies in the first half of the 1980s.

Stagnation in EC social policy: 1980–6

Several initiatives were taken in EC employment policy between 1980 and 1986, nearly all of which could be described as measures to enhance flexibility in

European labour markets and to give protection to workers in the new forms of 'atypical' work (particularly part-time and temporary employment) that were emerging. The measures were designed to make forms of 'atypical' work more attractive to workers by giving them legal protection. This period coincided with the election of a Conservative Government in Britain from 1979 onwards. As a result, most of these measures were blocked by the UK government in the Council of Ministers.

These measures included a non-binding Recommendation on the Reorganization of Working Time, which was vetoed by the UK government in the Council of Ministers, even though major modifications had been made to the proposal to incorporate UK objections to an earlier version.[6] It also included draft directives which were issued by the Commission which would have given *pro rata* rights for part-time and temporary workers – both of which were opposed by the British delegation.

Britain is almost alone in the Community in not providing for parental leave (as opposed to maternity leave).[7] Despite this deficiency in providing for parental leave for British workers, the Thatcher Government opposed an attempt by the Commission to introduce Community-wide legislation to provide for family and parental leave. Finally, Britain resisted the Commission's attempts to establish Community legislation giving workers information and consultation rights in complex organizations – the popularly known Vredeling Directive (see section on information, consultation and participation for workers later in this chapter). As a result of the British government's opposition, virtually no social legislation was ratified by the Council of Ministers during the early 1980s, apart from a small number of health and safety proposals. The period 1980–6 was therefore one of stagnation as far as EC employment initiatives were concerned.

The 1986 British Presidency of the EC: labour market flexibility

When the UK assumed the Presidency of the Council of Ministers in 1986, it was anxious to neutralize the Delors plan and, as an alternative, produced its own plan for the future of Community employment policy, called the 'Action Programme for Employment Growth'. Essentially, the plan reflected the flexibility and deregulation policies already being pursued in Britain, and it largely consisted of measures which would encourage the promotion of flexible patterns of work, measures to assist in the training of the long-term unemployed, the promotion of managerial and entrepreneurial skills, and realigning the priorities of the Social Fund to promote small and medium-sized businesses. The Action Plan was adopted at the December 1986 meeting of the Council of Ministers after Britain had obtained the co-sponsorship of two other member states – Italy and Ireland.

As Teague has noted:[8] 'On paper, the Thatcher government had pulled off a remarkable victory, for it is seldom that a proposal that is not supported by the Commission is adopted by the Council of Ministers.' However, the Commission has since largely ignored these proposals for devising and implementing flexibility and deregulation policies, instead choosing those items which it prefers and overlooking those items which contradict its interventionist philosophy.

The beginnings of the single market

When Belgium took over the Presidency of the Council of Ministers in 1987, the foundations for the present social dimension of the internal market were laid. The new measures contained in the Single European Act of 1986 were seen as a means of extending the use of qualified majority voting and co-operation procedures to all areas dealing with the social dimension of the internal market.[9]

The Belgian government was worried that the British Action Programme would undermine established statutory guarantees for workers throughout the Community, and proposed a range of social and employment rights that later became enshrined in the 'Social Charter' (or more accurately termed the Community Charter of Fundamental Social Rights for Workers), which was subsequently adopted at the Council of Ministers in December 1989 with Britain voting against. The European Commission was charged with the responsibility for drawing up an 'Action Programme' of measures to put the Social Charter into effect.

Before we consider the Social Charter it is important to see this initiative in the context of the Single European Act which was agreed between the 12 member states in 1986 and was ratified by a sparsely attended House of Commons in that year. The Single European Act was adopted to give the 1992 internal market a legal base. It had the effect of amending the Treaty of Rome and new clauses were inserted into the Treaty – some of which, as we will see later, concerned social policy.[10]

Jacques Delors and the internal market

Jacques Delors, who became President of the EC Commission in 1985, was determined to surmount the legislative problems of the use of the veto in the Council of Ministers by linking social policy law to the objectives of realizing the internal market by 1992. Delors believed that it was important to have equivalence of social laws throughout the Community in order to prevent 'social dumping' whereby member states with low levels of social protection could gain a competitive edge and thus disrupt the workings of the internal market. His proposals, entitled *l'espace sociale Européenne*, represented 'a clever piece of thinking'[11] and provided for the establishment of a social dialogue at the European level.[12] The Social Dialogue, known as the 'Val Duchesse' process (named after the château just south of Brussels where the initial talks took place), involved the trade unions and the employers' organizations (ETUC and UNICE/CEEP) taking over the initiating role in labour market policy and employment matters from the Commission. More particularly, it envisaged that the so-called social partners could do this by concluding joint opinions – not agreements – which would then be used as the basis of proposals for Community labour legislation. Unfortunately for Delors, the employers' organization UNICE made it very plain from the outset that it would only take part in such talks if the Commission gave an undertaking not to produce proposals for legislation from any joint opinion that might emerge.[13] The objective of Delors was to circumvent some of the criticism frequently made by employers that the Commission failed to take into account the business needs of European companies by incorporating them into the decision-making approach. However, as Teague pointed out,[14] 'the success of this project required the social partners not only to fully co-operate, but also to adopt a more visionary approach to Community affairs than had hitherto been the case. It was on this crucial issue that the project foundered.'

The social dialogue

The first conference on the Social Dialogue was held in Val Duchesse in November 1985 on the initiative of the Commission, and new avenues for discussion between the social partners were opened. Eventually, in March 1987, these discussions led to the expression of a Joint Opinion on information and consultation as to the introduction of new information technologies in firms. In this document the social partners

> 'recognized the need to make use of the economic and social potential offered by technological innovation in order to enhance the competitiveness of European firms and strengthen economic growth thus creating one of the necessary conditions for better employment and, taking particular account of progress in the field of ergonomics, for improved working conditions'.[15]

The Joint Opinion of Val Duchesse emphasized the importance of information and consultation practices in European enterprises, and leaves room for manoeuvre for both sides. However, it has led to very limited results, and there is a need to make the Joint Opinions which emanate from the Val Duchesse process binding on the parties. Others would argue that it can be regarded as a first, open concept for social change within European enterprises and it should be seen as one of the main achievements within the social field.

The Social Dialogue has led to several Joint Opinions. Among them, the double agreement of 6 March 1987 on the new technologies (training and motivation, information and consultation) provides guide-lines of major importance for the two sides of industry throughout the Community, even though there are more developed systems of worker information and consultation in some member states (for example, Denmark, Germany and The Netherlands) than others.

In 1990–1, further Joint Opinions were concluded on the 'Creation of a European Occupational and Geographical Mobility Area and Improving the Operation of the Labour Market in Europe', 'New Technologies, Work Organization and Adaptability of the Labour Market', 'Education and Training' and 'The Transition from School to Adult Working Life'. The first of these assigns primary importance to training throughout the working life of employees in order to promote a workforce which is better trained, more motivated, more mobile and able to adapt to change, and the new qualification requirements. The second and third of these Joint Opinions re-emphasized the importance of effective information and consultation procedures in training, and also stated that 'all workers in the firm, whatever the size of the firm for which they work, should be entitled to the same health and safety protection at the workplace'. Recently, the Social Dialogue has been extended to sectoral level, notably in construction, the public sector and transport.

Recently, the Social Dialogue has been seen as the main means of implementing many of the measures in the Social Action programme to put into effect the

Community Charter of Fundamental Social Rights for Workers. Directives will only be issued in circumstances where the Social Dialogue process is seen as inappropriate for introducing such measures (see the section on the Social Charter below).

How does the Social Dialogue affect Britain? Given that it is now seen as the main procedure whereby Community employment initiatives linked to the Social Chapter which John Major refused to sign at the Maastricht summit in December 1991, does this mean that Britain is unaffected by its deliberations? The answer to this question is not as clear as it might appear to be at first sight. Even though the present Conservative government continues to refuse to be bound by the social measures accepted by the other 11 member states, Britain will continue to play a role in the social dialogue by virtue of the respective affiliations of the TUC to the ETUC and the CBI to UNICE. In any case, the Social Dialogue will continue to discuss employment matters concerned with the Single European Act which provides for qualified majority voting on health and safety matters which Britain is obliged to follow (see later in this chapter). Indeed, the Secretary General of UNICE, Mr Tyszkiewicz, recently emphasized that Britain would still continue to play an active role in the Social Dialogue deliberations.[16]

The Single European Act

The Single European Act of 1986 had the effect of amending the Treaty of Rome by introducing new provisions in the Social Policy area; these were Articles 100A, 118A and 118B.

Prior to the passing of the Single European Act, the legal base for all employment law directives was Article 100 of the Treaty, which required unanimity on voting in the Council of Ministers. This meant that on important issues, any one member state could prevent directives being adopted by refusing to make the Council of Ministers' decision unanimous. As we saw earlier, the Conservative government in Britain was able to veto a number of measures which were proposed from 1980 to 1986 – on *pro rata* rights for part-time and temporary workers, parental leave, reorganization of working time and the Vredeling Directive on worker consultation and information rights. The Single European Act extended the range of matters on which a Council decision could be taken by a 'majority' or more precisely, a *qualified* majority.

In order for a measure to be adopted in the Council of Ministers by *qualified majority voting*, it needs 54 of the 76 votes in the Council. The allocation of votes to member states is that the four major countries, France, Germany, Italy and the UK, each have ten votes; Spain has eight; Belgium, Greece, Portugal and The Netherlands five; Denmark and Ireland three; and Luxembourg two. This means that any three of the four major states can, if united, prevent an effective majority; and if the proposal does not come from the Commission, eight states must be in favour.[17] This voting procedure also means that if the UK is to exercise a veto on a particular measure effectively, it probably needs to secure the support of at least one other of the big four member states.

The new Article 100A(1) at first sight appears to surmount the problem of member states vetoing social policy initiatives by providing for majority voting on measures on the 'establishment and functioning of the internal market'.

However, Article 100A(2) limits its applicability by deliberately excluding from majority voting those provisions 'relating to the rights and interests of employed persons'. On the other hand, the new Article 118A provides for qualified majority voting on measures that 'pay particular attention to encouraging improvements, especially in the working environment, as regards the health and safety of workers'. The conflict between these two new articles is all too evident to see.

For example, is the length of the working week a 'health and safety' issue or is it concerned with the 'rights and interests of employed persons'? Are protections for pregnant women in the workplace concerned with health and safety? What is meant by the 'working environment'? The term 'working environment' has a much wider meaning in member states in northern Europe than it does in the UK; in Britain it tends to be associated with lighting, heating, ventilation, noise, work layout etc, whereas elsewhere it can cover job design, the quality of working life, manning, pace of work and other matters which might arguably be covered by the 'rights and interests of employed persons'. It could also be broadly interpreted to regulate aspects of the working environment which particularly affect women, such as the protection against foetal hazards and sexual harassment at work!

There are also interpretation problems attached to Article 100A(2). One eminent European labour lawyer[18] maintains that the concept of 'rights and interests of employed persons' could have three different meanings:

(i) Any proposal which bears *directly, indirectly or partially* on the rights and interests of employed persons is excluded from the majority voting procedure.
(ii) Only proposals which *predominantly* affect the rights and interests of employed persons are excluded from the majority voting procedure.
(iii) Only proposals that are *solely* concerned with the protection of the rights and interests of workers require unanimity.

The ambiguity between the two new Articles 100A and 118A in the Single European Act has enabled the Commission to put forward draft directives under the Social Charter Action Programme which not only interpret Article 100A very broadly but also widen the coverage of Article 118A. The reason for doing this is to attempt to accelerate the Social Action Programme by cleverly putting forward some of its draft directives under a legal basis, so as to ensure that qualified majority voting can take place rather than having draft directives blocked by member states such as the UK. Of course, the legal basis for such draft directives could always be challenged by the UK or any other member state in the European Court of Justice; what the European judges would say to any such challenge is hard to predict, although the Court would possibly be more likely to rule against such a challenge.

A member of the Social Affairs Cabinet of the European Commission recently claimed that 27 out of 47 proposals of a legislative nature contained in the Social Action Programme had already been dealt with by the Commission.[19] Even so, each draft directive has to undergo the cumbersome decision-making procedure of the Community (preparation by COREPER (the Committee of Permanent Representatives; the opinion of the Economic and Social Committee; the opinion of the European Parliament; discussion by the Commission; discussion by the Council of Ministers), for at every stage there exists for each proposal the possibility that it will be amended or blocked.[20]

THE SOCIAL CHARTER

Why was the Social Charter necessary?

The Social Charter was proposed in order to offset 'social dumping' within a completely liberalized single market. 'Social dumping' has never been properly defined, but it refers to a scenario whereby a liberalized internal market without a floor of employment rights would lead to peripheral member states taking advantage of their relatively low wage status and their 'softer' employment laws at the expense of Germany and other more prosperous northern countries in the Community.

Under such a scenario the peripheral countries would seek to take advantage of their lower employment standards to encourage their own industries at the expense of those countries with better employment standards. As a result, a price-cutting war would develop, whereby managers throughout the Community would concentrate on rationalization and cost reductions in order to retain their competitiveness, all at the expense of social welfare provisions and employment standards. Thus, the drive to upgrade the quality of existing products, to increase investment in new technology and to enhance product innovation would be put in jeopardy in the Community as a whole. In short, advocates of the 'social dumping' argument are saying that the 'Social Charter' is necessary in order to ensure 'a level playing field', so that member states following low employment standards are not at an economic advantage compared to the more prosperous countries in northern Europe which have superior employment standards.

Those who subscribe to the 'social dumping' argument point out, first, that with the accession to the Community of Spain, Portugal and Greece, the divergence between labour standards has widened considerably; secondly, the pressures of global competition would, in the absence of a floor of employment rights, make it more likely that European firms would seek to employ an increasing number of 'marginal' workers – part-timers, temporary workers, young people on 'training schemes', subcontractors etc – all of whom would be paid lower wages. All this does not mean that the Social Charter necessarily entails a monolithic harmonization of employment policies and practices across the Community; instead, in the words of Vasso Papanderou, the Social Affairs Commissioner:[21]

> The point is not to impose a strait-jacket of all-embracing detailed measures, but rather to establish a common set of principles and general measures. Without Community regulation, national deregulation could very quickly depress social conditions if business responded to the need to improve their relative competitiveness by cutting costs on all fronts, labour costs included.

Thus, such employment standards could be introduced to take account of the particular customs and traditions of industrial relations systems in each member state – a process known as 'subsidiarity'.

Subsidiary

The process of subsidiarity is explained by the Commission in its Action Programme as the principle: 'whereby the Community acts when the set of objectives can be reached more effectively at its level than at that of the member states'.[22] The Action Programme's 'subsidiarity' approach limits its proposals for regulations and directives 'to those areas where Community legislation seems necessary to achieve the social dimension of the internal market and more generally to contribute to the social and economic cohesion of the Community'.[23] Hence, proposals involving fundamental collective workers' rights (eg union recognition and the right to strike) and also participation requirements in the 'European Company Statute' (see later sections) come under the 'subsidiarity' principle.

This shift on policy on the part of the Commission from seeking to harmonize across the board by Community instruments to one of leaving, where it is appropriate to do so, more matters to be left to the legislation of national governments or the 'social partners' (employers and unions), is particularly significant and is pertinent to the political debate in Britain about the Social Charter. The reason for this is that the European Employers' Federation, UNICE (to which the CBI is affiliated) and the European public sector employers, CEEP, made an agreement with the European Trade Union Confederation at their meeting on 31 October 1991 as part of the Social Dialogue (see above), which called on the Maastricht Summit meeting in December to agree on the following.

1. On the joint request of the social partners, a member state may entrust them with the implementation of directives in areas covered by Article 118 (health and safety and the Social Dialogue) – though retaining ultimate responsibility for ensuring compliance.
2. Prior to making proposals in the social policy area, the Commission would be bound to consult the social partners.
3. When proposals in this area have been made, the social partners would be consulted on their content.
4. The social partners may, if they wish, reach Community-level collective agreements. These would be implemented either according to the procedures and practices of the social partners and the member states or, in the case of agreements on matters referred to in Article 118, the social partners could make a joint request for the Commission to propose a Decision, based on the agreement, to the Council. The Council could then implement the agreement through the Decision.
5. During the consultation procedure following the making of a proposal by the Commission, the social partners could jointly express their wish to put into operation the collective agreement procedure summarized above.

The Maastricht Summit subsequently agreed to amend Article 118B of the Treaty to provide for a consultation period of nine months for both sides at Community level to consider a social policy proposal. If the social partners could not come to an agreement on this proposal, then the Commission would produce its own directive. Of course, this amendment only affects the 11 member states in the separate Social Chapter which was incorporated as an Annex to the Treaty to which Britain was specifically excluded. In this way 'subsidiarity' worked against the arguments that the UK government was putting forward against the Social Charter. The provisions of the Charter will be tailored to the traditions of those whom it affects, and the Social Dialogue between employers and unions at European level can reach framework agreements which can then be implemented according to the traditions and practices in each member state rather than employment matters being harmonized across the board. This has the support of both UNICE and the ETUC. As the shadow employment secretary, Tony Blair, puts it when arguing for the adoption of the Social Charter: 'It provides binding principles and flexible means'.

Does this process of 'subsidiarity' via the Social Dialogue affect Britain even though the Conservative Government has refused to sign the Social Chapter? British employers and unions will still be involved via their representatives in being able to scrutinize and propose employment legislation through the Social Dialogue, but the UK will be unable to influence the form and direction of the Social Charter in the Council of Ministers except in those areas covered by the pre-Maastricht Single European Act (ie where qualified majority voting on health and safety matters still applies) and matters covered by unanimity as a result of the Single European Act. However, the UK government will be unable to influence the form and direction of proposals covered by the post-Maastricht Social Chapter. This means that if and when the UK agrees to ratify the Social Chapter some time in the future, it will have had no influence in the Council of Ministers where the key decisions are made.

In any case, UK companies which have operations elsewhere in the EC will be affected by the Charter. Moreover, the CBI[24] itself has expressed doubts about the value of 'opting out'; a paper issued by its governing council in January 1992 stated: 'There is unlikely to be any lasting advantage to UK businesses if the rest of the EC is handicapped by a social affairs regime characterized by a centralized approach to determining employment decisions.' In any case, the present situation is untenable and is unlikely to last for long. The absurdity of the 'empty chair' policy at the Council of Ministers when employment matters are being discussed is all too evident.

What are the provisions of the Social Charter?

The Social Charter was adopted at the Strasbourg Summit on 8 December 1989 with only one dissenting voice – that of Mrs Thatcher, who once described the Social Charter as 'Marxism by the back door'. Before it reached the Summit, it had been amended at the October 1989 Council of Ministers for Labour and Social Affairs in an unsuccessful bid to gain British backing. It covers a range of social and employment rights, including freedom of movement, employment and remuneration, and equal treatment, information and consultation of workers, and health and safety in the workplace. The accompanying Action Programme, which contains a 'shopping list' of 47 proposals, of which 17 are draft directives (10 of which deal with health and safety), 5 recommendations (which are not legally binding on member states), 5 unspecified instruments, 3 decisions and 3 regulations, is arguably of much more significance than the Charter itself.

The Action Programme consisted of 12 parts, each of which were related to particular sections of the Charter; these 12 parts are summarized below.[25] For the purposes of brevity, only the basic outline of each proposal is given and readers will be able to consult the notes at the end of this chapter if they required more detail.

Freedom of movement   The aim of this part of the Charter was to enable people in the Community to move freely within its borders and to be able to 'engage in any occupation or profession in the Community in accordance with the principles of equal treatment as regards access to employment, working conditions and social protection in the host country'.[26] Specifically it aimed to tackle a long-standing problem of the refusal of some member states to recognize qualifications from other countries and the difficulties experienced by non-working family members. It also called for an improvement in the conditions of workers living on one side of a frontier and working on the other.

Progress on this relatively non-contentious matter has been very slow. Only one of the two detailed technical regulations – on worker's rights after their employment ceases and the application of social security schemes to the self-employed – has so far been agreed. We are still a long way from the day when British employees can have their occupational or professional qualifications recognized in other countries of the Community. However, a draft directive on the working conditions for subcontract workers in other member states was published by the Commission in June 1991. This would require foreign subcontractors to be given the same employment rights (holidays, hours, minimum pay) as domestic workers. This would clearly have implications for British workers who are engaged in subcontract work in the Community (eg Germany). This directive has not yet been discussed in the Council of Ministers but is subject to majority voting.

Employment and remuneration   This section is one of the most important parts of the Charter. The Charter here seeks to ensure that all employment is 'fairly remunerated' so that workers receive 'an equitable wage' regardless of whether they are part-time, temporary or permanent. However, the Charter does not propose a binding minimum wage across the Community; it merely committed the Commission to publish a non-binding Opinion, which was published in December 1991, calling on all member states to ensure that workers have 'a decent standard of living'. The manifesto pledges of the Labour party to introduce a minimum wage of not less than £3.40 an hour go much further than this.

The Commission has already submitted draft directives on part-time and temporary workers, or 'atypical' workers as they are described by the Community. This was done by publishing three linked draft directives on Atypical Work in June 1990.[27]

All these draft directives apply to temporary and part-time workers – a growing proportion of the British labour force. The three draft directives are particularly significant for Britain because it has more part-time workers (6 million) than nay other EC member state; not only that, but those who argue the need for directives of this kind claim that the UK currently avoids paying social security benefits to 2.5 million part-time workers.

The first of these three draft directives covers access of 'atypical' workers to vocational training and services, and the various social security benefits associated with training. It also lays down that such workers should be included in the head-count of employees for workers' representative bodies, eg Works Councils and, in Britain, Health and Safety Committees (this would also apply to European Works Councils – see under 'Information, consultation and participation for workers', below). However, this draft directive is issued under Article 100, which requires unanimity in the Council of Ministers. The other 11 member states who signed the Maastricht Social Protocol will make further progress on this draft directive later in 1992.

The second of the 'atypical work' draft directives is issued under Article 100A, which can be adopted in the council by qualified majority voting (QMV). It provides for *pro rata* rights for part-time and temporary workers on social security benefits, dismissal payments, holidays, seniority allowances and occupational pension schemes. It covers all 'atypical' workers who work for at least eight hours per week. This draft directive has already been discussed in the Council of Ministers and is vehemently opposed by Britain. Michael Howard, the secretary of state for employment, has challenged the legal basis of the draft directive. In a speech on 29 June 1990, he stated that the Commission's proposed extension of social security coverage to those working over eight hours but earning under £46 per week would mean that:

> these people would see a reduction in their earnings; and their employers, who would also have to make contributions on their behalf, might well decide that the costs were too great and simply wind up those jobs. In other words this proposal would hit the income and the jobs of some of the lowest paid people in Britain. The Commission's proposals are therefore wholly unrealistic. They ignore the fact that in the UK some 5.5 million people work part-time – more than 20 per cent of the workforce.

The third linked directive under 'atypical work' is more innocuous and is issued under Article 118A (Health and Safety); it provides for equivalent access to health and safety as full-time workers. This directive was finally agreed in the Council in June 1991.

Improvement of living and working conditions   The aim of this part of the Social Charter begins with a clear statement: 'The completion of the internal market must lead to an improvement in the living and working conditions of workers in the European Community'. This article in the Charter then went on to call for every worker to have a weekly rest period and annual paid leave, improvement in redundancy procedures and for the conditions of employment of every EC worker 'to be stipulated in laws, in a collective agreement or in a contract of employment'.

Already a directive has been approved which requires employers to provide their employees with a document setting out the main details of their employment contract. When the appropriate legislation has been enacted, British employers will have to provide all workers (apart from casual workers) who are employed for over one month and for more than eight hours a week with information on the place of work, a brief job description, the date of commencement of employment, the expected length of employment, the amount of paid leave, notice requirements for both parties, the length of the working week and details of remuneration. This directive is only of marginal significance to existing legislation.[28]

A Draft Directive on Working Time is also about to be decided upon during 1992; this has been vehemently opposed by Britain (see below). Finally, a revised Directive on Collective Redundancies (see section earlier in this chapter 'Adopting a Community "human face" in social policy: 1972–80'). This would extend consultation rights in firms whose ownership is in another EC state.

Social protection   Here, the aim of the Charter is for every EC worker to 'have a right to adequate social protection' and assistance if they lose their jobs or have never been able to work. The Commission has only published two non-binding recommendations on this part of the Charter, and measures under this section are still a matter of unanimity, even for the group of 11 countries other than Britain who signed the Social Protocol at Maastricht.

Freedom of association and collective bargaining   Although the aim of this part of the Charter is that every employer and every worker 'shall have the freedom to join or not to join' professional organizations or trade unions, and that they should be able to negotiate their terms and conditions, the Commission never had any intention of going any further than simply producing a communication on the role of the social partners. In any case, the Social Dialogue (see earlier section) is now the main avenue for such discussions. Even among the other 11 countries, unanimity is required.

Vocational training   It is well known that Britain compares very unfavourably with its EC partners in the area of training. This part of the Charter presented the prospect of every worker in the Community having 'access to vocational training' and to receive it 'throughout . . . working life'. Such a prospect would entail setting up permanent training and retraining systems, and so far the results have been patchy. There has been some progress in ensuring comparability between occupational and professional qualifications gained in different member states; there is currently a proposal to provide for recognition in all member states of qualifications which are awarded by competent bodies for which training of less than three years' duration is required.[29] However, it will take a very long time indeed to arrive at a satisfactory situation. A proposal on the key area of workers' access to training is expected at the time of writing.

Equal treatment for men and women   This area had already had a substantial impact on British industrial relations, particularly in terms of equal pay for women and in sex discrimination in employment. The Equal Pay Act 1970 and the Sex Discrimination Act (1975) can both be traced to European developments. Article 119 of the Treaty of Rome contains a broad legal obligation to implement the principle of equal pay for equal work and there was an Equal Pay Directive adopted in 1975 which brought in the concept of 'equal pay for work of equal value'. The Employment Protection Act 1975 also provided for maternity leave and pay.

In 1981, the European Commission took the UK government to the European Court for failing to implement the Treaty of Rome, specifically Article 1 of the 1975 EC Directive on Equal Pay, by not providing in its national legislation for individuals to pursue claims for equal pay where they were engaged in work of equal value compared with other workers. Thus the Government was compelled to introduce measures to conform with EC standards. The response of the Conservative Government came in the form of the Equal Pay (Amendment) Regulations 1983, which were written in such tortuous language that the labour lawyers themselves were unable to decipher them, and even Lord Denning criticized them for their 'tortuosity and complexity . . . beyond compare'.

The first case under the new regulations to hit the headlines was that of Julie Hayward,[30] a cook at Cammell Laird in Birkenhead, who successfully argued that her job was of equal value to that of men working in the shipyard as painters, engineers and joiners. Since then there have been a number of cases under the new Regulations, although the whole process is cumbersome and very slow.

Despite the impact of these developments from the EC, British women's employment rights generally lag behind those standards enjoyed by their counterparts in other member states,[31] in areas such as pay, maternity provisions, child-care and job security.

The aim of this article of the Charter is to 'ensure the implementation of the principle of equality' and develop measures to 'reconcile job and family responsibilities'. Recent progress under the Charter in this area includes the Directive on the Protection of Pregnant Women at Work, which was ingeniously drafted under Article 118A (Health and Safety) of the Treaty so as to ensure adoption by qualified majority voting. It was agreed in principle in October 1991 in the Council of Ministers (Britain abstained), and is likely to be formally adopted in June 1992. It provides for 12 weeks' paid maternity leave at 80 per cent of usual pay (no continuity of employment is necessary). It also lays down that there is no obligation on the part of pregnant women to do night work. The EC has also agreed an Action Programme on Equal Opportunities for Men and Women, which primarily provides for a range of training projects, as well as monitoring the progress of existing equality legislation. However, given the very inferior provisions for child-care in Britain compared to the rest of the EC, it is unfortunate that EC action in this area has been restricted to a non-binding recommendation. Further movement in this area of the Charter is only likely in the 11 member states who signed the Maastricht Social Protocol.

If equal pay, maternity rights and sex discrimination are covered by equal treatment between men and women in European legislation, what about pensions? Here, there has been an important case[32] in the UK whose implications are immense. Douglas Barber, who was employed by Guardian Royal Exchange Assurance Group, was made redundant in 1980 and complained that the pension package he received was less favourable than would have been the case had he been a woman. The case dragged on through the industrial tribunal system for ten years and eventually reached the Court of Appeal. The Court of Appeal requested a preliminary ruling from the European Court of Justice on the interpretation of Article 119 of the EEC Treaty, which, as we saw above, established the principle of equal pay for work of equal value, and the 1975 Directive on Equal Pay and the 1976 Directive on Equal Treatment. Even though Barber died in May 1989, his widow continued with legal proceedings.

The European Court of Justice ruled that occupational social security benefits were to be treated as pay for the purposes of Article 119 – thus implying that occupational pensions schemes would have to set common pension ages and benefits for men and women. The court stated that the ruling could not be used to support claims for pension entitlement with effect from a date prior to the ruling (17 May 1990), except for cases already before the courts. This ruling had to be taken into account by the 11 member states who signed the Maastricht Social Protocol and they placed a narrow interpretation on the *Barber* ruling stating:

> For the purposes of Article 119 of the Treaty establishing the European Community, benefits under occupational social security schemes shall not be considered as remuneration if and insofar as they are attributable to periods of employment prior to 17 May 1990, except in the case of workers or those claiming under them who have before that date initiated legal proceedings or introduced an equivalent claim under the applicable national law.

Finally, the Council of Ministers has agreed a non-binding recommendation on child-care which calls on the member states to make it more widely available, as well as introducing other measures to make it easier for parents to combine child-care and work. Another recommendation, on a code on sexual harassment, has also appeared.

Information, consultation and participation for workers   Lord Bullock, who chaired the Committee of Inquiry on Industrial Democracy which was set up by the Labour Government in 1975 and which issued its Report[33] in January 1977 with its famous '2X+Y' formula for worker participation in British industry, once said that 'the issue of industrial democracy will never disappear from the political agenda'. Despite the fact that this issue remained largely dormant in Britain until very recently, it now occupies a high priority in Britain once again as a result of developments in the EC.

The European Commission's recent draft directive on the establishment of European Works Councils, issued in December 1990 under Article 100 (which requires unanimity in the Council), in European-scale companies is the most recent of numerous attempts – mostly unsuccessful – to legislate on employee participation at the EC level.[34] These include the Draft Fifth Directive on company structure and administration in 1972; the revised Draft Fifth Directive on company structure and administration in 1983;[35] the Draft 'Vredeling' Directive on procedures for informing and consulting employees in large national and multinational firms (1980); the revised Draft 'Vredeling' Directive in 1983; the Collective Redundancies Directive embodied in the Employment Protection Act 1975 (referred to earlier in this chapter); and the Transfer of Undertakings Directive (again mentioned earlier), which found its way into British labour law in the Transfer of Undertakings (Protection of Employment)

Regulations 1981; and finally, the European Company Statute (1989), which was a redraft of previous initiatives in 1970, 1975 and 1979.

The European Works Council's draft directive proposes that all companies with at least 1000 employees in the EC, and with at least two establishments in different member states with at least 100 employees each, or at least two group undertakings in different member states, each employing at least 100 workers, should provide the option for either management or the workforce to set up European works councils made up of members elected/appointed from the workforce for information and consultation on company policy. The minimum requirements provide for an annual meeting with management to be informed of the progress of the undertaking or group's business and its prospects; probable development of business, production and sales; employment situation and probable trends; and investment prospects; consultation on any management proposal likely to have 'serious consequences' for employees' interests. A growing number of companies already operate on this basis in the EC, including Volkswagen, Renault, Gillette, Ford of Germany, Bull etc.

So far, there has been no progress on this draft directive in the Council of Ministers, largely because of British opposition. However, progress is likely to be made by the other 11 member states who signed the Maastricht Social Protocol, with or without Britain. In fact, Britain cannot fully escape the effects of this proposal whether it eventually signs the Social Protocol or not; this is because many of the European-wide companies which operate across Europe and which are therefore covered by the provisions of the draft directive are *British* companies. Are British workers to be excluded from participating on works councils of Dutch, French and German companies, for example, which have undertakings in the UK? Clearly, the present situation is untenable.

Finally, under the information, consultation and participation of workers part of the Charter, non-binding recommendations on profit-sharing and financial participation are likely to be adopted.

Health and safety at the workplace   A great deal of progress has been made on this part of the Charter because it is covered by the Single European Act and qualified majority voting. The Commission has issued a Health and Safety Framework Directive[36] which embraces numerous initiatives in the health and safety field, including manual handling, protective clothing, safety on construction sites, safety signs at work, vibration risks etc. The minimum health and safety requirements for work with visual display units (VDUs) require employers to take measures (including regular ophthalmological examinations at no extra cost to the employee), as well as satisfactory ergonomic design of workstations and periodic breaks from working with VDUs.

Protection of children and adolescents   The aim of this part of the charter is to prohibit employment – other than certain light work – for those below school-leaving age or in any case under 15, and requires young people who are in work to be protected in terms of their pay, hours of work and access to training. To date there has been no progress in this area, although at the time of writing a draft directive was expected at any time.

Elderly persons   This part of the Charter seeks to ensure that everyone retiring should have a decent standard of living. Since the main means of implementing these aims are through pension and social security systems which are in the hands of national governments, progress has so far been limited to an Action Programme on the Elderly which was agreed in November 1990. The year 1993 will be the European Year of the Elderly.

Disabled persons   Progress in this area has been limited to a Draft Directive on Mobility of Handicapped Workers which was issued under Article 118A (qualified majority voting) in February 1991;[37] it has yet to be discussed in the Council of Ministers. This part of the Charter seeks to improve the integration of those with disabilities into work and society through training, ergonomics, better accessibility and mobility, and changes in housing. It will be years before these aims are achieved.

CONCLUSIONS

The refusal of the UK government to agree to majority voting on social and employment matters at the Maastricht Inter-governmental Conference in December 1991 was a severe disappointment to those who believed that a stronger social dimension was essential for the success of the 1992 internal market. The anathema of the UK Conservative Government towards influence on British employment law and practices which resulted in the 11 other EC member states signing a separate Protocol to permit qualified majority voting (QMV) on social and employment affairs does not mean, however, that British industrial relations will be immune from EC influence. In any event, Britain will still be influenced by EC directives emanating from the Single European Act 1986, which provides for QMV on health and safety matters. In addition, there is still a great deal of legal confusion surrounding the outcome of the Maastricht Summit and it is by no means certain that Britain can be entirely exempt from decisions made by the other 11 countries within the terms of the Protocol. In any case, the Maastricht Treaty still has to be ratified for the national parliaments of all the member states before the end of 1992.

There are signs that the newly-elected Conservative Government is willing to compromise on its opposition to many of the draft directives issued under the health and safety areas (eg the maximum length of the working week and maternity leave), although it is too early to suggest any softening of British opposition to EC initiatives on social and employment policy.

The compromise reached at Maastricht arguably raised more questions than it answers. Will British workers be able to participate on European Works Councils? What is the Social Protocol's status in Community law? How is it possible to use the institutions and mechanisms of the EC to develop social and employment policy for only 11 member states? Will the absence of Britain from the Protocol mean that Britain will become a 'paradise for investment' and become the 'Hong Kong' of Europe?[38] Will UK representatives in the European Parliament and other bodies be able to participate in formulating legislation under the agreement? Where does the compromise leave the Social Charter proposals and other contested items of draft legislation proposed under existing social policy Articles of the European Community Treaty?

Whatever the answers to these and other questions, one thing is certain. British industrial relations will continue to be influenced by developments in the EC for the rest of the 1990s and well beyond.

POSTSCRIPT: THE IMPLICATIONS OF THE DANISH MAASTRICHT REFERENDUM RESULT

The rejection of the Maastricht Treaty by the Danish electorate in a referendum in May 1992 casts doubts on the whole basis of the Maastricht Treaty throughout the EC. At the time of writing it was unclear whether the Treaty would ultimately be ratified by each member state before the end of 1992.

What effect would this have on EC social and employment matters if the Treaty were not ratified? In the short term it would mean that the separate Social Protocol which was annexed to the Treaty would not come into effect. Therefore, the other 11 member states who signed the Social Protocol would not be able to use its provisions for qualified majority voting on social and employment policy matters, other than those covered by the single European Act. Nor would the Social Dialogue between the ETUC and UNICE/CEEP be used as a means of putting into effect EC employment legislation. In other words, the position reverts to what it was before the Maastricht Treaty was negotiated, until such time as other Treaty modifications are made and are ratified by all 12 member states. Social and employment draft directives, other than those on health and safety, will still require unanimity in the Council of Ministers.

As far as the UK is concerned, little has changed. Qualified majority voting still applies on health and safety issues as a result of the Single European Act. As we mentioned earlier, there are a number of draft directives introduced under Article 118A (Health and Safety) which are still under discussion in the European Council of Ministers for Social Affairs. These include the Draft Directive on the Protection of Pregnant Women at Work with its enhanced provisions for maternity rights and the three linked Draft Directives on Atypical Work (*pro rata* rights for part-time and temporary workers, and the maximum length of the working week). It is ironic that Britain assumes the Presidency of the Council of Ministers just as these draft directives are drawing to a conclusion and when the Community has to solve the crisis following the Danish rejection of the Maastricht Treaty.

References

1. Szyszczak, E (1992) 'Race discrimination: the limits of market equality?', in Hepple, B and Szyszczak, E (eds) *Discrimination: the limits of law*, Mansell, London.
2. Quoted in Nielsen, R and Szyszczak, E (1991) *The Social Dimension of the European Community*, Handelshøjskolens Forlag, Copenhagen, p 28.
3. Robbins, B (1985) 'The EEC's new Social Dimension', *Personnel Management*, March.
4. For a discussion of the effects of these three directives, see Lewis, R (ed) (1986) *Labour Law in Britain*, Blackwell, Oxford, pp 588–90.
5. See the *European Industrial Relations Review* (1992), No. 216, January.

6. Welsh, M (1987) *Labour Market Policy in the European Community: The British Presidency of 1986*, Royal Institute of International affairs, London, Discussion paper No 4.

7. For a comparison of parental leave provisions in other Member States of the Community, see *European Industrial Relations Review*, 142, November 1985; for an overall appreciation of labour market trends and statistics in the EC see *Employment in Europe* (1989), Commission of the European Communities, Office for Official Publications of the European Communities, Luxembourg.

8. Teague, P (1989) 'Constitution or régime? The Social Dimension to the 1992 Project', *British Journal of Industrial Relations*, November, p 319.

9. Bercusson, B (1990) 'The European Community's Charter of Fundamental Rights for Workers', 53 *Modern Law Review*, 624.

10. There are many EC documents which explain the social dimension of the EC. See in particular *Social Europe*, the special edition on the social dimension of the internal market published in 1988 and the issue in March 1990; see also Venturini, P (1990) *1992: the European Social Dimension* Office for Official Publications of the European Communities, Luxembourg.

11. Teague, P op cit, p 318.

12. See in particular Venturini, P (1989) *1992: The European Social Dimension*, Commission of the European Communities, Office for Official Publications of the European Communities, Luxembourg, pp 61–6.

13. Tyszkiewicz, Z (1986) 'The achievement of the Internal Market by 1992 and the European Social Space: the employers' view', speech given to the Management Centre of Europe.

14. Teague, P op cit.

15. Commission of the European Communities (1991) *Joint Opinions*, European Social Dialogue Documentary Series.

16. *Financial Times*, 21 December 1991.

17. Article 148 of the Treaty of Rome.

18. Vogel-Polsky, E (1990) 'What future is there for a social Europe following the Strasbourg Summit?', *Industrial Law Journal*, Vol 19, No 2, pp 70–3, June.

19. Seminar on 'EC Social Policy, Maastricht and the UK' held at St John's College, Cambridge on 20 February 1992.

20. Vogel-Polsky, E op cit.

21. Papandreou, V (1991) Postface, in Spyropoulos, G and Fragnière, G (ed) *Work and Social Policies in the New Europe*, European Centre for Work and Society, European Interuniversity Press, Brussels-Maastricht, p 175.

22. *Action Programme*, 1/3.

23. *Action Programme*, 1/5.

24. *Financial Times*, 24 February 1992.

25. The following section is based on an article which appeared in the January 1992 issue of *Labour Research*.

26. *Social Charter*, Title I.

27. Full details of these directives can be found in the *European Industrial Relations Review* (1990), September.

28. For fuller details of this Directive, see European Industrial Relations Review (1991), No 214, November.

29. For further details, see the *European Industrial Relations Review*, February 1992, p 15.

30. *Hayward* v *Cammell Laird Shipbuilders Ltd* (1984) IRLR 463(IT): 502 (152).

31. See, for example, Deakin, S (1990) 'The floor of rights in European labour law', *New Zealand Journal of Industrial Relations*, 15, pp 219–40; Deakin, S and Garnsey, E (1990) 'Part-time work and sex discrimination: the relationship between British labour law and European Community standards', in *Part-time Work*, *Report of the Select Committee on Employment of the House of Commons*, HMSO; Zalabza, A and Tzannatos, T (1985) *Women and Equal Pay: the effects of legislation on female employment in Britain*, Cambridge University Press, Cambridge; McCrudden, C

(1983) 'Equal pay for work of equal value', *Industrial Law Journal*; Treu, T (1988) 'Equal pay and comparative worth: a view from Europe, *Comparative Labour Law Journal*, 8, pp 1–33; Fitzpatrick, B (1989) 'The significance of EEC Directives in UK sex discrimination law', *Oxford Journal of Legal Studies*.
32. The full details of the *Barber* case can be found in the *European Industrial Relations Review*, 198 (July 1990) and 216 (January 1992).
33. *Report of the Committee of Inquiry on Industrial Democracy*, (1977) HMSO, Cmnd. 6706, January.
34. The full text of this draft directive can be found in the *European Industrial Relations Review*, 206 (March 1991).
35. *European Industrial Relations Review* (1983) 117.
36. For full details on the Community's health and safety laws, see the Labour Research Department's booklet *1992 and Health and Safety*, January 1992; see also *Social Europe*, 2/90.
37. See the *European Industrial Relations Review* (March 1991).
38. For a discussion of this question see *Financial Times*, 25 February 1992.

Chapter Three
Industrial Relations and Technological Change

John Gennard

FRAMEWORK OF APPROACH

Industrial relations is the study of the reconciliation of the different economic interests of the suppliers of (employees) and the buyers of (employers) labour services. The latter, like all buyers of services and products, seek the 'lowest acceptable price', while the former seek the opposite. However, both employees and employers have a common interest in ensuring that their differing economic interests in determining 'the price of labour' are reconciled, since to engage in constant conflict over this price is not in the interests of both parties.

The reconciliation of the different economic interests of employees and employers is expressed in two broad types of agreements – substantive and procedural. These agreements have varying degrees of formality (written/ custom and practice), different kinds of authorship (unilateral and/or joint) and are concluded at different levels (industry, company, plant). They are arrived at by the use of various industrial relations processes, for example, joint consultation, employee participation and involvement, collective bargaining, unilateral enforcement by management or the union, third party intervention (conciliation, mediation and arbitration), industrial sanctions and legal enforcement. However, the extent to which these agreements are concluded closer to the interests of the buyers or the sellers of labour services, and the processes whereby they are reached depends upon the balance of bargaining power between the two interested groups.

The relative bargaining power between the two goups is determined by three factors external to the workplace. These are the level of economic activity at the macro and micro level, the legal framework and the implementation of new technology. If the level of economic activity is increasing, then relative balance of bargaining power tips in favour of the sellers of labour services and vice versa. Technological change influences relative bargaining power by its impact on the demand for labour in general and on the demand for particular types of labour. It can create skill shortages as well as eliminating the need for existing jobs. Although this chapter is concerned with examining the impact of the implementation of new technology on industrial relations institutions, arrangements and processes, with reference to the coal mining, banking and printing industries, it has to be borne in mind that technological change could, and should not, be seen in isolation from other factors, such as economic, that influence the balance of bargaining power in the industrial relations system.

TECHNOLOGICAL CHANGE

General and specific developments in technology are always taking place, but the speed and general applicability at which these happen varies. When the speed of change accelerates very rapidly, it becomes more difficult for employers and employees to adjust to its impact. When rapid technological change affects all industries and services, it is common to refer to such events as 'an industrial revolution'. In the last 20 years the UK has experienced such a revolution which it is anticipated will continue throughout the 1990s.[1]

This 'industrial revolution' has been based on broad technological developments based on computers (which have been smaller, cheaper, but more powerful), lasers and telecommunications. The implementation of new production techniques based on these developments in the workplace has received the general support of employers, employees and their organizations. Opposition has been greater where the organizational change that usually accompanies the introduction of new technology threatens the employment prospects of certain groups. The employers see new technology as providing the opportunity to maintain, increase or improve their product market competitiveness, to obtain greater output or service, to enhance labour productivity, to employ less labour and undermine the bargaining power of trade unions. For some employers (for example those in national and provincial newspapers) it is and was also viewed as an opportunity to end long-standing relationships with trade unions which, under the existing production technology, held the upper hand in the balance of bargaining power.

The general attitude of UK trade unions to new technology, over the last 20 years, has been to favour and co-operate with its introduction, so long as it is done jointly with management, rather than by unilateral decision-making by management (change by agreement). The continued commitment to 'joint regulation' of the industry or service has also been fundamental to the attitude of trade unions co-operating with the implementation of new technology. Other issues important to trade unions in this regard are access to information, redeployment, no compulsory redundancy, retraining, and stringent standards of health and safety for new equipment.

Trade unions have also favoured new technology since it enables them to be seen as progressive and 'at the cutting edge'. Unions have also viewed new technology as providing them with the opportunity to gain, for their members, improved employment conditions, which include improved wages, shorter hours, longer holidays, and better sick pay and pension provisions. It is fundamental to UK trade unions' philosophy in co-operating with the implementation of new technology that all parties – employers, employees and trade unions – participating in industry and commerce should be able to see a future 'stake' for their interests in the 'new world'.[2]

Contrary to conventional wisdom, survey results have shown that there is often little worker resistance to the introduction of new technology into the workplace.[3] Resistance comes from groups of employees who see no future in 'the new world' because the changes in work organization that will accompany the change in technology threaten the continued need for their skills. Workers see, in new technology, the possibilities of a more conducive working environment (safer, less noise, less dirt etc), enchanced wages and other conditions of employment and greater employment security. Computer-aided methods of coal-mining have, for example, brought relatively safer and more pleasant working conditions for coal-miners. The introduction of cold composition techniques in the printing industry had the same effect by replacing hot metal.

If the impact of the implementation of new technology on industrial relations institutions, arrangements and processes is to be understood, then it is necessary to examine its effect on product and labour markets and on the method by which employers introduce new technology. This broad framework will also include an examination of the effects of new technology on trade union organization and the scope of collective bargaining. Additionally, the introduction of new technology has important implications for training. These will be discussed in the final section of this chapter.

PRODUCT AND LABOUR MARKET EFFECTS

Industry changes

By changing customer tastes, new technology can reduce the bargaining power of the sellers of labour services. Computers have enabled production systems to emerge that can be applied to a wide range of industries and services. This has led to a decline in the demand for equipment manufacture for use in some industries and, with it, an increase in unemployment in some equipment manufacturing industries. There has been employment contraction, for example, in the machine textile manufacture industry, while the introduction of computer-based origination systems in the printing industry has resulted in a dramatic decline in the demand for hot-metal composing machines, such as linotype and monotype machines. The growth of plastics, at the expense of paper, as the basis of packaging materials has reduced the demand for paper for packaging purposes and thereby reduced employment in the papermaking industry. This can be illustrated by the growth of frozen foods in supermarkets. These products require packaging materials which can withstand very low temperatures and which will not damage the food. Paper-based package materials cannot achieve this, but plastic-based ones can.

Although technological change has reduced the bargaining power of employees and the employment opportunities in industries such as textiles, printing, paper and coal-mining machinery manufacture, it has potentially enhanced that of other workers by giving rise to new industries, such as computer manufacture and the electronic media. Prior to the 1970s, the communications industry was based on paper and ink processes. However, the 1970s and 1980s have witnessed the rise of a 'new communications world' based on electronic devices – for example, teletext, viewdata, Prestel, Ceefax, videos and cable television. This 'new' communications industry is expanding at an expotential rate, while the old communications industry based on paper and ink is shrinking.

Over the past 20 years, the application of computer technology to industry and commerce has removed boundaries between previously clearly separated industries. In the 1970s and the 1980s the dramatic changes in production techniques whereby printing work is originated have blurred the boundaries between the printing industry and other industries. Prior to the 1970s, if employers wanted to produce origination work for print on a viable basis, they had to employ craft compositors. Without a five- or six-year apprenticeship, an individual did not possess the skills to operate hot-metal composition systems, to set type and to assemble advertisements or pages. Computerized origination systems, especially desk-top publishing, however, mean that origination work could be done outside the printing industry, for example in instant print shops, in art and advertising studios, and in-house by, for example, local authorities, nationalized industries, banks and finance houses, the civil service and engineering companies. The completed origination work can then be sent to a printing firm for printing. The employees in these organizations outside the printing industry tend to be non-union, or members of unions other than print ones, and to have inferior terms and conditions of employment to the printing industry. One effect of this blurring of the previously clear distinction between the printing industry and other industries, with respect to origination work, has been to reduce the bargaining power and employment levers of origination workers in the printing industry but enhance those of printing machine craft employees.

The implementation of computer technology over the last two decades has blurred the division between the banking industry and retail food distribution. Previously these industries were clearly separated. Customers paid for their food at the cash point by cheque etc. The supermarket food chain would then process the cheque through the bank by the paying-in procedure and the bank then operated its clearing procedures to transfer the money from the customer's account to the supermarket's account. However, today it is possible for the employee at the 'checkout' to transfer, instantaneously, money from a customer's bank account to the supermarket's bank account. In this way the retail food industry and the banking industry boundaries almost disappear, and there is a potential decline in the employment of bank clerical staff.

Merging of tasks

The application of new technology has also removed boundaries between previously separated tasks in the production process or the provision of service process. Before the widespread application of computer-based origination systems, newspaper production involved five separate processes – editorial, advertising, composing, printing and distribution. Computer-based systems have integrated the editorial, advertising and composing processes, enabling access straight to the printing process. Typesetting which was always 100 per cent trade union organized has been transferred to areas which are unorganized or the preserve of other unions, and where employees receive lower pay and conditions of employment. Traditionally, magazine and periodicals production had four stages – 'creative' origination from authors or journalists, typesetting, printing and distribution. Typesetting and printing were 100 per cent organized. 'Creative' origination was either unorganized or some other union's preserve, but employees received inferior employment conditions to employees engaged on typesetting and printing. Computer technology has enabled the 'creative' and typesetting stages to merge into a single process and 'typesetting' to be removed from highly organized and well-paid labour to, at best, lowly organized and low-paid labour. The result is that the balance of bargaining power has tilted significanctly towards the employer.

The application of information technology to the banking industry has also changed the relative importance of certain tasks in the provision of service to the customer. In the past the major tasks in a retail bank were carried out in the 'back-office', where staff worked with, essentially, ledgers and pens. The 'front' office, where the cashier related face to face with the customer was relatively small and cramped. The implementation of new technology means that large 'back rooms' are no longer necessary, since the tasks previously carried out there are now mechanized. The 'front office' has thus become much bigger and the general environment in which the customer interfaces with the counter staff has improved markedly in quality terms. This move has been assisted by the 'high street' banks becoming retail outlets which design personal financial packages to sell to customers. With continuing developments in banking technology it is likely that the existence of the 'back office' in the branches of banks will disappear.

There are many other examples which can be given where the implementation of new technology has affected job tasks to the detriment of some workers and to the potential advantage of others. In the tobacco industry, for example, the production of cigarettes has traditionally involved fast machine technology in contrast to the slower-paced machine-assisted processes of cigar making. Machine innovations have transformed cigar making which in speed and processes is now technically much closer to cigarette manufacture. This has displaced older skills (including the blurring of old demarcation lines of mechanics and electricians) and reduced manning levels, but at the same time has created some new jobs and new skills.

In coal-mining in the 1960s, the introduction of power loading joined together what were previously separate tasks, cutting and conveying, while eliminating the intermediate task of handfilling. In the late 1970s and the early 1980s the National Coal Board began to introduce a standardized computer system, known as MINOS (mine operating system), for control at collieries. This system merged previously separated tasks via the computer making key decisions automatically. The worker acts as a machine minder. MINOS threatened the bargaining power of the coal-miner by diminishing his job control, limiting human decision-making and reducing the number of miners required.[4] Yet it also created some new surface jobs for workers monitoring and controlling the computer systems.

Employment effects

Overall   An examination of the impact of technological change on the labour market can be assessed against a number of different criteria. These include questions like what is its impact on the general level of employment? On the content of jobs? On the number of jobs (contraction versus expansion)? On job control? On the employment structure in a company or industry etc? There is no general consensus as to what is the impact of new technology on the general level of employment in an economy. Some argue that the effect is to reduce the general level of employment, but there are those that argue the opposite, pointing to the fact that the impact of new technology is never one way. On the one hand it destroys/modifies existing jobs, but on the other creates new jobs/new industries and expands existing jobs, such that the net effect is probably an overall increase in employment. There is no doubt that in some industries, such as coal-mining, shipbuilding, railways, steel manufacture, docks and textiles, technology has been a factor in accounting for the long-run decline in their employment levels. However, it has also been a factor in the growth of employment in such industries as air transport, chemicals, financial services and public utilities such as gas, water and electricity.[5]

Occupational structures   There is more evidence available, at the industry level, as to the impact of the application of new technology on employment. In the banking industry, it has led to an increase in the overall level of employment, but a change in occupational structures, in that there has been a decline in the employment of clerical workers, but an increase in the employment of computer operators, technicians and technologists. The overall increase in employment in the banking industry has also brought new types of workers into the industry. In some parts of the country, they were not individuals with anti-trade union, anti-industrial action attitudes. This is in contrast to the traditional bank employee attitude which was broadly to accept a master–servant relationship. Many of these new bank employees had been, or come from, families that had been employed in factories and some have experienced difficulty in becoming retail bank workers (ie shop workers).

In the 1970s, the banks began automating existing processes and this led to some redundancies that were achieved by natural wastage. The introduction of 'hole-in-the-wall' cashpoints resulted in a reduction in the employment of tellers. However, the contraction of employment in these traditional areas of employment was taking place against an increase in demand for technicians, technologists and managers whose skills were enhanced via increased responsibility, since the cost of error was now greater, given the investment cost of the new equipment. In general, in banking, the impact of technology has been to increase the number of employees employed servicing the provision of banking services and to a reduction in the number employed in the direct provision of the service.

In addition to changes in the occupational structure, the implementation of new technology in the banking industry, over the last two decades, has also brought changes in the content of jobs. This has taken the form of employees becoming multi-skilled and flexible between jobs and functions on a scale greater than in the past.

The recession of the late 1980s and early 1990s, along with technical change, brought other labour problems for the banks. Increased competition from building societies etc led banks to come under pressure to introduce more sophisticated technology to substitute capital for labour. This led to pressures to offset the costs of the implementation of more sophisticated new technology by reducing staff costs. This was done by negotiating redundancy and redeployment packages with the representatives of the workforce. In response to the increased product market competition, banks have sought to maximize their revenue by becoming the designers and sellers of personal financial packages. However, new technology had reduced the number of staff employed in the branches and therefore it was difficult to sell these products there. In an attempt to tackle this problem, some banks have started to reduce the numbers employed in head office and redeploy some of their headquarters staff into the branches or to conclude employment severance packages with such employees.

The technological revolution that has occurred in the printing, paper, publishing and packaging industry, over the last 15 years, has also changed the occupational structure and thereby increased the bargaining power of some groups of employees while reducing that of others. Like the banking industry there has been a relative increase in the proportion of employees engaged on servicing production, rather than directly employed on producing the product. In 1971, the proportion of non-manual employees (supervisors, administrators, scientists and technicians) employed in the industry was about 18 per cent, but by 1990 the figure was in excess of 25 per cent. Technology has moved employment into areas where unionization is weak or non-existent from the direct production areas where manual worker unionization is high and among whom the closed shop is still prevalent. It was, in the late 1980s, estimated that some 200,000 non-manual employees in the printing industry were not in trade unions. It was the presence of such workers in the industry that caused the former NGA and former SOGAT to attempt to extend their membership and influence into these areas. However, resistance from employers on the grounds that membership of the print unions is appropriate for such workers, combined with the general industrial climate of the 1980s led to a general apathy towards membership among non-manual workers in the communications industry; the outcome was little success in recruitment for the two unions.

In 1990, the dominant printing process was lithography, while 30 years previously it had been letterpress. The growth of litho was linked to photocomposition, replacing hot metal systems in the late 1960s and early 1970s as the dominant mode of producing print origination work. Hot-metal composition and litho printing techniques were incompatible, but photocomposition and litho were not. Lithography is predicted to continue to expand further in the 1990s, and its machines to have robotics and electronic attachments, which are expected to eliminate many ancillary and unskilled jobs in the press room.

These changes in printing processes are reflected in the industry's current occupational structure relative to the past. Today there are few hand and mechanical compositors. In the mid-1950s, mechanical composition was replaced by photocomposition which was subsequently replaced in the mid-1970s by computerized composition. Photocomposition involved setting on film or paper rather than the manipulation of metal type. It changed the nature of the work rather than the number of compositors required; although output was considerably increased, compositors were able to maintain control of the supply of labour and their bargaining power. The tasks of the hand compositors, for example, changed from the assembly of metal type and blocks, to paste-up or assembling film on a transparent backing. Mechanical compositors found that photocomposition created new jobs for them as 'Qwerty' keyboard operators or as photocomposer operators.

By 1990 computerized composition techniques were the dominant form and, as was shown above, merged previously separated tasks in newspaper, magazine and periodical publishing, and enabled print origination work to be done by employees employed in other industries. The effect of computerized composition systems has been the virtual elimination of the occupational groups, 'compositor' or 'typesetter' from the industry. This weakened their bargaining power and their dominance within the former NGA. The days when 'high levels of specialist skills' were essential in operating pre-press equipment have gone for ever. However, the decline in pre-press printing areas has been countered by recent developments in press room and litho plate-making technology which have brought dramatic increases in bargaining power and therefore employment benefits (more money, greater job security, enhanced job opportunities and permanent retraining provisions) to the employees who operate such equipment. These employees are now responsible for operating expensive and sophisticated equipment, particularly web offset multi-colour printing machines that operate at very high speeds. In the hi-tech machine rooms of every sector of the printing industry, the litho machine manager is dominant. They are highly skilled, highly paid and have considerable bargaining power. They are members of the former NGA (now the Graphical Paper and Media Union) and are the basis of the GPMU's continued dominance and influence in today's modern printing industry. Newspapers where little use is made of high-quality colour printing are an exception to this situation. However, a common misconception about the former NGA was that it was a newspaper based union. At the peak of its membership, only 10 per cent were employed on provincial newspapers and 5 per cent in national newspapers. The remaining 85 per cent were employed in the general printing trade, the periodical trade, the packaging and tin industry, and book manufacture etc.

However, for unskilled and semi-skilled workers in press rooms, where the former SOGAT was the appropriate union, the impact of technological change, such as automated reel-handling systems, has seen a dramatic fall in their employment. Some, nevertheless, have been retrained to reach skilled status and the enhanced employment conditions of the litho machine minder. In the finishing and distribution stage of the printing production process, the implementation of change has also reduced the bargaining power of these employees. It has brought them few benefits and little or no increase in job opportunities. The employees in this stage of the production process are mainly semi-skilled and female workers, and they have suffered huge reductions in their numbers employed. Technological change in this area has also brought moves towards casual, seasonal and part-time employment. All these existing trends in employment in the finishing and distribution areas of printing are predicted to continue in the 1990s.

Former SOGAT members in the machine room and finishing departments sought to offset these employment losses by amalgamating with the NGA. The alternative, given the favourable trends in technological change towards craft employees in print machine rooms, would have been ultimately complete elimination of employment opportunities for former SOGAT members in the high-tech modern printing plant. These trends in new technology were important factors in the NGA and SOGAT merging in September 1991 to form the Graphical, Paper and Media Union (GPMU). Technological change is thus an important factor in causing trade union mergers, although these do not always follow the lines of industrial logic and many small single industry based unions often seek protection in one of the large general unions such as Manufacturing, Science and Finance (MSF). As is shown below, if the unions in an industry or firm cannot agree a combined approach to the acceptance of technological change, the employer's relative bargaining power is enhanced and they are likely to be able to introduce new equipment on terms more favourable to their economic interests.

THE IMPLEMENTATION OF TECHNOLOGICAL CHANGE

Different employer strategies

Although employers will nearly always say that they favour new technology, very few are prepared to be the '*leaders*' in implementing the latest production and service delivering techniques. Most employers prefer to see others introduce the latest developments and bear the costs of correcting technical faults in the system, and of solving any industrial relations difficulties (eg employee opposition, changed pay structures, health and safety problems) that can arise from being the first to introduce new machinery. The vast majority of employers prefer to be '*followers*' in implementing technical change. They prefer to let the leader 'iron out the faults'.

In monopoly producer industries, like coal-mining, this leaders/followers situation does not exist, but the coal industry has to be a leader in introducing technological change if it is to maintain a competitive market position relative to other forms of energy. In industries like banking, where there are few producers, and there is much knowledge about competitors, the leaders in the introduction of new technology have been the big English clearing banks. In the provincial newspapers the 'leaders' in the introduction of computerized origination systems were the large firms such as Sunderland and Portsmouth Newspapers, the Midlands News Association and Thompson regional newspapers, all of which are part of large multinational company groupings.

In implementing new technology in recent years, employers, in general, have adopted two broad approaches. Some have realized that as soon as they introduce new techniques of production into the workplace, a familiar situation changes for employees. This can produce insecurity and, in a few cases, may be the cause of rejection of the change by some or all the employees. Trade unions can make a strong issue of this insecurity among employees and exploit it to their advantage. To cope with this situation, managements have negotiated a new social order that establishes acceptance and commitment of the employees and their representatives. In adopting this approach, managment seeks the co-operation of its employees with the implementation of new technology, on the basis of joint agreement rather than confrontation, as well as a commitment to continued joint regulation of the industry. Although the approach of negotiating in new technology has been the most common among employers, the economic circumstances of the 1980s meant that the bargaining power favoured the employer and they have been able to implement new technology peacefully on terms more favourable to themselves. The negotiation of the introduction of new technology through the use of the TUC model comprehensive New Technology Agreement, as issued to affiliated unions in 1979,[6] has been little in evidence, as trade unions have negotiated from a position of weakness, but have recognized their common interest with the employer that the enterprise must survive in the longer term.

On the other hand, there are employers who adopted a completely opposite approach in that they introduced new technology into the workplace on a unilateral basis and without the co-operation of the workforce and their representative organizations. Such employers were prepared, if necessary, to take industrial sanctions from their employees and, in some cases, to ignore existing procedures for the introduction of change or resolving disputes between employers and employees.

These differing employer new technology implementation strategies are well illustrated in the mid-1980s in the provincial newspaper industry. The former NGA found itself dealing with some employers who peacefully negotiated jointly the implementation of new technology and, where appropriate, jointly with other unions. On the other hand, it faced some employers who introduced computerized composition systems unilaterally, took industrial action from the union and ultimately excluded it from their plants. Also, it encountered some provincial newspaper employers who were prepared to make an accommodation with some other unions, for example, SOGAT, as a means of isolating the NGA and resisting successfully any industrial action it might take.

The bulk of provincial newspapers peacefully negotiated new technology into the pre-press area with the former NGA, individually or jointly with another union. Although the number of provincial newspapers introducing new technology without an agreement with the union was extremely small, they were significant in shaping the manner in which new technology was introduced into the industry. Indeed, it was only after a number of key disputes (for example[7] with the *Wolverhampton Express and Star* newspaper and the *Kent Messenger*) over the introduction of computerized origination systems, where, with inter-union problems between the NGA on the one hand and SOGAT and the NUJ on the other, that the employers were able to overcome NGA resistance and set the basis on which single-keystroking, including a reduction in the employment of compositors, would be introduced into the provincial newspaper industry. Other provincial newspaper employers then negotiated the same terms for the peaceful introduction of computerized composition systems.

Multi-union situations

In unionized situations, employers have been able to introduce new technology on more favourable terms to themselves where there is inter-union competition and especially where new technology enhances the job interests of one union, but threatens those of another. In the UK banking industry, the Banking, Insurance and Finance Union (BIFU) focused its new technology policy in a demand for new technology agreements. It sought comprehensive new technology agreements containing provisions which would govern the implementation of new technology. Such an agreement was seen as the key to regulating jointly the introduction and impact of new technology on BIFU members. The agreement was to safeguard its members' interests by providing for employment security, for guaranteed earnings, for enhanced health and safety provision and for job content changes to be met by retraining. A new technology agreement was also demanded by the English Clearing Banks' Staff Union. However, they insisted solely on consultation and information rights. This was in direct contrast to BIFU policy which placed strong emphasis on negotiating rights.

With their differing demands, the UK banking unions found themselves dealing with an aggressive response from the clearing banks who dismissed the demands as being unacceptable because they challenged managerial prerogative. As a result, with a few exceptional cases (for example, the Co-op Bank), BIFU requests for new technology agreements were firmly rejected. The implementation of new technology in the UK banking industry was usually a non-negotiable issue. However, the banks were prepared to give limited employee institutions representation via participation programmes aimed at 'greater co-operation and identification with the organization, but within the context of managerial prerogative and control'. BIFU representation was marginalized. The banks had been able to play off the BIFU against the staff associations.

The clash of job interests between unions that can arise on the implementation of new technology and enable the employer to determine the terms on which change will be introduced was seen, as hinted at above, even more vividly in the newspaper industry. The introduction of computerized origination systems brought a radical change to the production process by introducing into the advertising areas VDUs, which are directly linked with a typesetting computer. The function of the tele-ad individual is combined with the typesetting and correcting functions which had traditionally been that of the NGA compositor. It transferred keystroking from a former NGA area to an area which is the province of the former SOGAT or non-unionists. Exactly the same relocation and merging of processes took place with the origination area (fully organized by former NGA) and the editorial area, which is the province of the NUJ or non-unionists. The introduction of computerized composing systems meant the traditionally separated editorial, advertising and production functions were merged and the former NGA control of the production process undermined. If the NGA could not make an accommodation with the NUJ and/or SOGAT, its bargaining power in newspapers would change dramatically and, given the relatively low degree of unionization in the editorial and advertising areas, the fear was that the newspaper industry would become a deunionized and low-paid area of employment.

In provincial newspaper employment, over the period 1984–7, the issue of computerized origination from advertising departments caused difficulties between the NGA and SOGAT. The latter rejected the NGA's proposal that where new technology was introduced into the entire new 'merged' origination area, typesetting should remain unionized and that only members of the three unions (NUJ, SOGAT and NGA) should be allowed to operate typesetting equipment. Relationships became severely restrained when SOGAT refused to respect NGA picket lines in crucial disputes with provincial newspapers over the introduction of new technology and then actively co-operated with the managements involved to undermine the NGA position in those disputes.

Why did SOGAT adopt an anti-NGA stance over the introduction of new technology into provincial newspapers? It saw computerized origination systems as potentially increasing its bargaining power and decreasing that of the NGA. It viewed the NGA as a declining influence in the industry. By collaborating with provincial newspaper employers, SOGAT felt it could quicken the NGA's decline and the advent of its own perceived enhanced bargaining power. It believed its best interests were served by standing on the side-lines watching the NGA being defeated by employers, assisting in the process if necessary and then picking up the pieces, and using a new found bargaining power to improve the terms and conditions of its members.

The NGA sought, to no avail, to dissuade SOGAT of these views by arguing that technology by itself would not bring enhanced bargaining power if it were not accompanied by 100 per cent organization. In the advertising departments of newspapers, unionization was low. It also told SOGAT that it was naïve to think newspaper employers would neuter the bargaining power of the former NGA, in order to give the NGA's former bargaining power to another group of workers or unions. The failure of the NGA and SOGAT to have a common approach to the implementation of new technology resulted in the fact that, by the late 1980s, the NUJ and SOGAT were weaker in their areas than in 1980, while the NGA had seen reductions in the employment of composing room staff by a half to two-thirds of that which existed in the early 1980s. The provincial newspaper employers had introduced new technology on favourable terms to themselves and in doing so had transferred traditional highly paid and highly unionized work to poorly paid areas that were usually non-union or trade union in name only. Wages and conditions of employment had been cut, profitability increased and the origination side of the industry effectively deunionized.

In the general printing industry the clash of job interests between SOGAT and the NGA enabled employers opening 'greenfield sites' and installing the latest hi-tech printing machines to have union arrangements only with the NGA rather than multi-union arrangements with the NGA and SOGAT. By collaborating with these employers over the introduction of new technology, the NGA was able to eliminate SOGAT from the machine rooms of modern, large-scale printing plants. By 1990, both the NGA and SOGAT had recognized that to continue to engage in mutually destructive interunion conflict would simply enhance the bargaining power of the employers and that an accommodation between them was essential. To this end, in September 1991, the two unions came together to create the GPMU which, with 300,000 members, is the largest printing union in the world.

A clash of job interests between the print unions and the EETPU enabled News International to use the implementation of technological change to divest itself from its relationship with the traditional print unions. This happened when it opened, in 1986, a new 'greenfield site' at Wapping in East London and transferred the production of four newspaper titles to this new plant from Fleet Street. The dispute, however, was not essentially over new technology since the origination system and the presses to be used in the machine room were relatively old in relation to the provincial press. The litho machines to be used in the machine room were some 25 years old. However, it was new technology for national newspapers, in that the printing machines in use in the past had been letterpress.

The print unions in the Wapping dispute were not resisting the company decision to implement technological change and, in October, 1985, in negotiations with News International, had accepted the proposed changes in production techniques. The dispute was over the company's insistence on four non-negotiable conditions that were to accompany the changed production techniques at Wapping. These were that the agreement would be legally binding, would contain a no strike clause, would not permit the closed shop and would give the company the unfettered right to manage, by which was meant that if the company felt it appropriate to consult with the unions it would do so, but if not, it would not. These conditions were unacceptable to the NGA, SOGAT, and the AEU, but were acceptable to the EETPU. This acceptance by the

EETPU members was crucial because it meant, as they had collaborated with the company in secretly training people to operate printing machines, that the company could staff the Wapping machine rooms if the NGA and SOGAT members opted to strike. The employees secretly recruited by the EETPU union were used to produce the paper when the print unions went on strike in January 1986. The printing machines, being over 25 years old, could be operated by relatively 'green labour'. This would not have been the case if News International had equipped Wapping with the latest hi-tech printing machines. The ability of News International to obtain an alternative workforce, together with its ability to obtain an alternative distribution system for the national newspaper and willingness to use the 1980 employment laws were crucial factors in its ability to undermine the print union's industrial action and divest from a long-standing relationship with the traditional print union and operate in a non-union environment.

The reorganization of work that usually takes place with the implementation of new technology is easier to cope with, for the union and the employees, where there is only one union in the industry. New technology can destroy or modify existing skills, and at the same time increase the demand for some existing skills and create new ones. This can result in one union's members suffering large-scale unemployment, while another union's members experience severe skill shortages. The solution for such a problem is the redeployment, with appropriate training if necessary, of the unemployed workers to the areas of labour shortages. Such redeployment is easier to facilitate where the employees are all in the same union, rather than separate unions who compete with each other to defend their members when employers introduce new technology which has very different effects on the separate unions.

In non-union situations, technological change can be implemented more quickly than in a unionized situation. However, the co-operation of the workforce still needs to be gained and they must be able to see a future for themselves in the 'new world'. In industries like electronics, where the technology of production changes very rapidly, the ability to implement new technology very quickly is crucial to maintaining competitiveness. Rapid technological change and the need to implement it quickly is a major reason why many household-name electronics firms prefer to operate without a union. Where they do accept unions, it is only one union and to avoid costly industrial action being imposed against them, some, by far the minority, of electronics firms have compulsory arbitration (usually in the form of pendulum arbitration) as the final stage of the disputes procedure.

TRAINING ARRANGEMENTS

An important aspect of the implementation of new technology is its implications for existing training arrangements. New technology eliminates, or dramatically reduces, the demand for existing jobs, changes the content of existing jobs, and creates new ones. If employees are to take a co-operative attitude to the acceptance of the implementation of new technology, then it is important that their fear of employment insecurity is minimized by the provision of retraining provisions to upgrade existing skills or to acquire the new skills. Such provisions are therefore common in agreements and arrangements for the implementation of new technology, whether the workplace situation is a unionized one or not.

In some firms and industries radical and new production techniques may make existing training schemes inappropriate, such that a fundamental change is necessary. This happened in the general printing industry with respect to skilled operatives. The 1983 Recruitment, Training and Retraining Agreement between the NGA and the British Printing Industries Federation is the most progressive, far-seeing and comprehensive package on training in British industry. No other industry in Britain has a set of training arrangements that are as positive and as flexible as provided for under the 1983 agreement. The agreement ended the apprentice system, based on a restricted intake of trainees on time-serving, rather than training to standards, and on young boys. The 1983 agreement covers young and adult workers entering the industry for the first time, skilled workers undergoing retraining and other skilled employees who need to undertake skills training. Their training is modular, to set standards, and based on human resource planning. Trainees acquire skills to agreed standards at their own pace. Young trainees receive 60 per cent of the basic rate of qualified skilled employees, while adult trainees receive 80 per cent. A training agreement for each trainee is drawn up by management and the union chapel, which includes the training modules and further education to be completed. In the case of young people, the employer is obliged to pay for the trainee's further education. The training system is overseen by a Joint Training Council which comprises equal representation from both the employers and the unions.

In 1988 the NGA took an initiative in the form of a proposed National Printing Skills Centre to provide a solution to the acute skill shortage in high-tech areas, such as scanning, page planning and multi-colour sheet and web presses, that hit the industry in the late 1980s. The NGA considered that the industry should ensure that the right skills become available at the right time, or else both employees and employers would not benefit from the implementation of new technology in these areas, since an advantage would be given to foreign producers in the home and overseas markets.

The National Training Centre was to be a consortium of five organizational partners: the NGA, the largest printing employers (both these partners would invest £1 million each in the venture), the printing machine equipment manufacturers, the EC and a local authority. The Centre, which was to be located in Salford, was to be equipped with a range of 'state of the art' sheet-fed and web-offset machines and high-tech repro equipment. It was to undertake the retraining of NGA members from one high-tech skill to another, and to provide skills development training. In addition, it would undertake retraining and training of employees of the participating companies and sell its services to non-participating companies. In all these ways, the National Skills Centre would become available to the whole industry, thus helping to overcome the shortage of skilled labour in repro and machine rooms of the general printing industry. The Centre was to have state-of-the-art trainers seconded from industry. The employers were initially willing to attempt to solve the acute shortage of high tech skills, jointly with the NGA. However, by 1991, the deep recession in the economy meant that the employers were less able, or willing, to support the project. In 1991, the NGA's desire to provide the printing industry, in collaboration with the employers and printing machine manufacturers, with a high-tech National Skills Centre at Salford, which would have enabled its members to train and retrain for operating new technology, was thwarted by the failure of a sufficient number of large employers to agree, at the end of the day, to support the project.

Other unions have also adopted policies towards retraining of members to enhance their employment security in a rapidly changing technological environment. The EETPU offers training and retraining services to its members, as well as offering training services to other organizations on a commercial basis.[8]

References

1. For a fuller discussion of these issues see Gill, C (1989) 'New technology and industrial relations', in Towers, B (ed) *A Handbook of Industrial Relations Practice* (revised edn), Kogan Page, London, pp 55–77.
2. See, for example, *Employment and Technology* (1979) Trades Union Congress.
3. See, for example, Daniel, W W (ed) (1987) *Workplace Industrial Relations and Technical Change*, DE/ESRC/Policy Studies Institute/ACAS, Heinemann, London, and Daniel, W W and Hogarth, T (1990) 'Worker support for technical change', *New Technology, Work and Employment*, Vol 5, No 2, Autumn, pp 85–93.
4. See Burns, A, Feickert, D, Newby, M and Winterton, J (1983) 'The miners and new technology', *Industrial Relations Journal*, Vol 14, No 4, Winter.
5. For a full account of the implication of new technology in the printing industry over the period 1950 to 1989 see Gennard, J *A History of the National Graphical Association* (1990) Unwin and Hyman, London.
6. See *Employment and Technology* (1979) Trades Union Congress.
7. For a fuller account see Gennard, J (1987) 'The NGA and the impact of new technology', *New Technology, Work and Employment*, Vol 2, No 2, Autumn.
8. See Rainbird, H (1991) *Trade Unions and Training*, Blackwell, Oxford.

Chapter Four

Industrial Relations in the Public Sector*

P B Beaumont

The analysis and recommendations of the Donovan Commission (1965–8) viewed the problems of British industrial relations as being very much problems of the private sector. This was because in the mid-to-late 1960s the public sector was an area of employment where authoritative national-level collective bargaining was subject to little challenge or threat from fractional bargaining or unofficial industrial action at the level of the individual workplace. And at the same time, formal, comprehensive incomes policies were in their relative infancy in Britain so that the wage outcomes of the public sector had not, as yet, been subject to any sustained and substantial 'attack from above'. The result was that the public sector hardly figured at all in discussons of the desired direction(s) of reform in British industrial relations in the 1960s.

More than 20 years after the Report of the Donovan Commission, the position has changed to such an extent that many commentators now view any industrial relations problems in Britain as being overwhelmingly centred in the public sector. This view has been particularly stimulated and enhanced by the various instances of national-level industrial action which occurred in the public sector throughout the 1980s.

However, most commentators have taken a somewhat longer time perspective and viewed the whole of the 1970s as constituting a significant turning point or watershed in public sector industrial relations in Britain. Indeed, in the 1970s one saw the traditional model of public sector industrial relations challenged, undermined and at least partially replaced by a new model, the latter involving, among other things: the decline of the principle of comparability with the private sector; the pressure for decentralization of rule making; and the development of circumscribed collective bargaining.[1] The details of these various components which are elements of this new (still emerging) model of public sector industrial relations will, we hope, become clear as a result of our subsequent discussion.

Throughout the 1970s, academics began increasingly to compare and contrast public and private sector industrial relations arrangements in Britain, with the implicit assumption in such work being that the extent and nature of industrial relations differences between the two sectors far outweighed any differences that

* The author wishes to thank David Evans of Incomes Data Services and Paul Thompson of Industrial Relations Services for the provision of a good deal of the information contained in this chapter.

existed within each of the two sectors. It is certainly possible, and indeed desirable, to identify a number of *structural* features that differentiate public sector from private sector industrial relations arrangements in Britain. A list of the historical distinguishing features of public sector industrial relations arrangements would typically include the following:

- the key role of the government as a direct (or indirect) employer of labour;
- the relative remoteness of market (as opposed to political) forces;
- the relatively high level of unionization;
- the relative strength of national-level bargaining arrangements;
- the 'mixed' management side (ie immediate, local employers and relevant central government department) representation on a number of negotiating bodies in the public sector.

In pointing to these (and other possible) differences between the public and private sectors, it is important, however, not to lose sight of certain important industrial relations differences within the public sector itself. For example, in the case of the public corporations, there is not the mixed management side representation on negotiating bodies that exists in the case of the health service.

Table 4.1   *UK public sector employment 1979–91 by major categories (1000s)*

Headcount	Central government	Local authorities	Public corporations	Total public sector
1979	2387	2997	2065	7449
1980	2393	2956	2038	7387
1981	2419	2899	1867	7185
1982	2400	2865	1756	7021
1983	2384	2906	1662	6952
1984	2359	2942	1610	6911
1985	2360	2958	1261	6579
1986	2337	3010	1199	6546
1987	2312	3062	996	6370
1988	2322	3081	924	6327
1989	2315	2940	844	6099
1990	2313	2969	797	6079
1991	2177	2948	747	5872
Full-time equivalent				
1979	2188	2368	2034	6590
1980	2196	2343	2007	6546
1981	2225	2306	1862	6393
1982	2198	2274	1736	6208
1983	2181	2301	1641	6123
1984	2149	2320	1589	6058
1985	2144	2325	1247	5716
1986	2116	2352	1182	5650
1987	2091	2377	980	5448
1988	2084	2379	905	5368
1989	2084	2265	824	5173
1990	2077	2280	778	5135
1991	1965	2267	707	4939

Source: 'Employment in the public and private sectors', *Economic Trends*, No 458, December 1991, p 101

Accordingly, in the discussion that follows, any relevant differences within in the public sector itself will be highlighted. This discussion is presented under four basic headings, namely; joint procedures; pay determination; the changing context of public sector industrial relations; strikes and the union response. However, before turning to the first of these headings, it is useful to consider the size (in employee numbers terms) of the overall public sector, and its individual components, and the extent to which this has changed in recent times. The contents of Table 4.1 help provide some perspective in this regard.

The contents of Table 4.1 indicate (on the headcount basis) that public sector employment as a whole declined by some 21 per cent in the years 1979–91. The extent of the reduction in public sector employment has, however, varied a great deal between the different parts of the public sector. The local authority sector declined by some 1.6 per cent in these years, and central government declined by 8.8 per cent, whereas the level of employment in public corporations fell by fully 63.8 per cent; the reasons for the disproportionate concentration of employment reductions in the latter area will be discussed in a later section. In mid-1991 approximately 22.4 per cet of the total workforce was in the public sector (compared to nearly 30 per cent in the late 1970s), with the public sector employment total (5.9 million) consisting of 3 million (11.3 per cent) in local authorities, 2.2 million in central government (8.3 per cent) and 0.7 million (2.9 per cent) in public corporations.

JOINT PROCEDURES

The public sector has long been the most highly unionized part of the economy, a position that still pertains today. This relatively high level of unionization, which is not confined to essentially manual employees, has been variously attributed to the traditional government (management) encouragement of union membership and the concentration of employment in relatively sizeable

Table 4.2 *Union density rates in the public and private sectors, various European countries, mid-1980s*

	% Public	% Private
Austria	71	52
Denmark	82	81
France	42	13
Germany	58	28
Great Britain	82	31
Italy	49	39
Netherlands	46	17
Norway	95	50
Sweden	87	77
Switzerland	67	25

Source: Anthony Ferner, 'Changing public sector industrial relations in Europe', *Warwick Papers in Industrial Relations No 37*, October 1991, Table 4

individual employment units. Moreover, this relatively high level of union density in the public sector is not unique to Britain, as the contents of Table 4.2 illustrate.

Unions in the public sector, however, have not been immune from the general membership fall that has occurred in the 1980s and into the 1990s. Most of the leading unions in the public sector have experienced declining membership in these years, with the most notable exception to this trend being the Royal College of Nursing (RCN), whose membership increased by some 76 per cent in the years 1979–89, for instance. Closely related to the relatively high level of union density indicated in Table 4.2 is the relatively high level of collective bargaining coverage, with the public sector also traditionally being dominated by national or industry-level collective bargaining. This particular level of bargaining has historically had a number of important industrial relations effects and implications in the public sector. These include an above-average suscepti- bility to attempted control via incomes policies, the relative underdevelopment of shop steward systems and the personnel management function at the individual establishment level, and the fact that strikes in the public sector have made a disproportionate contribution to the total number of working days lost through strike activity in given periods of time.

The 1980s and 1990s have seen the traditional dominant role of national-level collective bargaining challenged and undermined, with much more diversity characterizing the present-day arrangements. A recent report, for example, highlighted the following sets of arrangements:[2]

1. pay review bodies – with the addition of teachers in England and Wales, there are now some 1.5 million employees working under such arrangements;
2. pay formulae – both the police and fire service have their pay linked to average earnings movements by means of a pay formula;
3. personal contracts – such as for unit general managers in the NHS;
4. traditional national bargaining, such as at British Rail;*
5. national pay negotiations with increasing local flexibility – such as in local government and the NHS;
6. pay comparability – such as in parts of the civil service where pay is negotiated within a predetermined settlement range;
7. decentralized bargaining – as in the Post Ofice, where pay decisions are made at the business unit level.

The Conservative Government throughout the 1980s and into the 1990s has attached a relatively high priority to stimulating and facilitating moves away from national level bargaining in the public sector. A view or belief to the effect that there should be more decentralized collective bargaining in the public sector did not, however, originate with the Conservatives. The McCarthy review of industrial relations in the NHS in 1976, for example, contained a recommenda- tion in favour of more bargaining being conducted at the regional level, while a report by the Prices and Incomes Board in 1967 recommended that payment

---

* These arrangements have also been questioned by management as a result of a movement towards individual profit centres with BR.

by results or bonus schemes be extensively adopted in the local government sector in order to improve productivity and ameliorate the low-pay problem there.

In considering joint procedures it is also relevant to note that another traditional distinction between the public and private sectors has been the greater presence of unilateral arbitration arrangements in the former area of employment. However, a Department of Employment report prepared in the early 1980s examined 17 arbitration agreements in the public sector and recommended that, in 11 of them, the employers withdraw from and renegotiate the existing arrangements. The essence of the recommended change was a move away from the right of unilateral reference to arbitration on the grounds that such existing arrangements encouraged irresponsibility among the parties (in that they had no responsibility for the final agreement and thus tended to hold to their original bargaining positions); favoured the union side; and were potentially inflationary in that they tended to undermine the effective operation of incomes policy and cash limits. In 1981, for instance, the government removed the right of unilateral access to arbitration in the education sector. The Conservative government's more general disquiet with the operation of arbitration arrangements was well evidenced by its rejection of its usage in the civil service and NHS disputes of the early 1980s, and in the more recent ambulance dispute. The government's general (critical) view of arbitration in public sector disputes is that it is not appropriate on the grounds that arbitrators are not accountable to the public at large, and tend to try and fashion compromise solutions by splitting the difference between the positions of the parties in dispute.

One of the government's most well-known, not to say widely criticized, actions in the public sector was the decision to ban or derecognize trade unions at GCHQ at Cheltenham from March 1984. Following the House of Lords' ruling in November 1984 in favour of the government, an employee ballot resulted in the establishment of a staff association at GCHQ. The union offer of a no strike agreement as a substitute for derecognition was not accepted, the TUC temporarily withdrew from the NEDC, local protest stoppages occurred when the remaining union members were transferred or dismissed and the Council of Civil Service Unions unsuccessfully took the case to the European Court of Justice. This particular derecognition experience seems to have been largely a one-off case in the public sector, which has not stimulated other moves in this direction. Admittedly, however, British Rail senior management staff no longer have a union recognized for collective bargaining purposes, while more recently the Ministry of Defence has raised the issue of derecognizing unions (affiliated to the Labour Party) for their security guards.

There has nevertheless been considerable speculation over the question of whether public sector management has broken sharply from traditional practice and taken an increasingly 'hard line' with the unions over the course of the 1980s and into the 1990s. For example, during the course of a dispute in the Post Office in 1985 (over the introduction of new technology, the extension of part-time work and the further development of local productivity schemes), management threatened, in the face of union opposition, to introduce the desired changes by unilateral action, but senior management were insistent at the time that this tactical threat did not indicate that they were becoming determinedly anti-union. The threat to unilaterally impose (or the actual imposition of) terms and conditions of employment has undoubtedly become much more a feature of public sector management practice in recent times. For example, pay settlements have been unilaterally imposed on members of the NUM on a number of occasions since the 1984–5 dispute, while more recently the BBC management threatened to impose a settlement involving a simplified grading structure on its 22,000 non-managerial staff.

Throughout the 1980s it was also abundantly clear that the government as an employer actively sought to set an example for the private sector to follow in relation to closed shop arrangements. In the hope of encouraging a generally tough, anti-closed shop line from management, the public sector was very much to the forefront in the removal of closed shop arrangements: British Gas, British Telecom, the water authorities (all now privatized), British Rail and the Post Office all withdrew from agreements providing for such arrangements.

PAY DETERMINATION

To many commentators, public sector industrial relations is essentially about pay determination arrangements. This sort of view reflects the 1970s experience in which governments of both political persuasions came into open conflict with public sector unions as they struggled to reconcile their responsibility for macro-economic management with that for the well-being of their own employees. Throughout that decade, public sector unions frequently claimed that the government of the day had dishonoured their traditional commitment to act as a good employer of labour by seeking to enforce the restrictions of incomes policy most vigorously on their own employees. The *intent* of governments to act in this way is open to little doubt, but in practice it would *not* appear to be the case that the public sector *as a whole* bore a disproportionate burden of *actual* wage restraint achieved during *all* periods of incomes policy in the 1970s.

The lack of a clear-cut, consistent pattern in this regard should occasion relatively little surprise when it is noted that the content and administration of these various episodes of incomes policy was far from homogeneous in nature, and that the extent and nature of union bargaining power is highly variable between the different parts of the public sector.

The Conservative Government has frequently stated its opposition to the introduction of any sort of formal, comprehensive incomes policy. Such statements need, however, to be viewed in the light of frequent critical calls by ministers for the exercise of 'responsible' wage behaviour, and the government's use of the cash limits approach in the public sector. The essence of the latter has been: first, the government's *prior* announcement of a pay provision figure for central government services (ie 1981–2 to 1984–5), followed by the usage of the mechanisms of departmental running costs and 'public service pay'; second, strict limits in the rate support grant and rate-capping for any over-spending authorities in local government; and third, the use of external financing limits to constrain the spending of public corporations and the setting of performance targets for these corporations.

It is against this background that the figures in Table 4.3 should be viewed.

Table 4.3 *Public and private sector pay since 1970/71: annual percentage increases*

Year (April–March)	Private sector earnings	Public services pay*	Public services pay relative to private sector earnings
1972/73	14.6	9.7	–4.9
1973/74	13.3	9.2	–4.1
1974/75	23.3	22.4	–0.9
1975/76	22.8	27.7	4.9
1976/77	13.7	12.3	–1.4
1977/78	9.8	5.8	–4.0
1978/79	14.9	9.9	–5.0
1979/80	16.8	17.3	0.5
1980/81	18.4	23.5	5.1
1981/82	12.4	9.4	–3.0
1982/83	9.4	6.5	–2.9
1983/84	8.3	5.5	–2.8
1984/85	6.8	5.5	–1.3
1985/86	9.2	6.4	–2.8
1986/87	8.0	7.6	–0.4
1987/88	7.3	10.0	2.7
1988/89	9.1	8.0	–1.1
1989/90	9.5	6.9	–2.6

Source: Chris Trinder, *Trends and Cycles in Public Sector Pay*, Public Finance Foundation, 1990
* public sector figures represent the weighted average of the annual increase in public sector pay of the nine largest groups of public sector workers

In essence Table 4.3 reveals a pattern of relatively sharp, short-run changes and movements in the public–private sector (average) wage relationship. For the 1980s, however, relative pay movements in general were against the public sector, with the years 1980–1 and 1987–8 being exceptions in this regard (these exceptional years were ones of major comparability awards). It has recently been reported that public sector pay on average rose by 37 per cent in the years 1988–92, compared to 40 per cent in the private sector, although there was some notable variation within the public sector;[3] local government and the civil service saw increases of 34 per cent in these years, compared to 40 per cent for the police, 42 per cent for the armed forces, and 38 per cent for health and education.

In the 1990–91 wage round public sector employees did rather better than their private sector counterparts. According to the pay settlement bank maintained by Industrial Relations Services, the weighted (unweighted) median settlement figure for the year to July 1991 was 9.5 (8.5) per cent in the public sector, compared to economy-wide figures of 8.7 (8.2) per cent.* These relative gains

---

* An update for the 12 months to April 1992 gives a weighted median settlement figure for the public sector of 6.3 per cent, which is exactly the same figure for the economy as a whole.

in the public sector were particularly true for groups that settled relatively early on in the round, and generally resulted from the retrospective orientation of pay review body arrangements and substantial restructuring exercises. The 1991 New Earnings Survey figures also revealed that the (April to April) increase in average gross weekly earnings in the public sector exceeded that in the private sector. The public sector figures were 9.1 per cent for male manuals (compared to 5 per cent in the private sector), 11.5 per cent for male non-manuals (7.5 per cent), 9.4 per cent for female manuals (6.7 per cent) and 12.2 per cent for female non-manuals (8.9 per cent). Furthermore, a more recent report suggested that public sector pay in the financial year to March 1993 was likely to increase by some 7 per cent, which was estimated to be one percentage point higher than the private sector and 3.5 percentage points above inflation.[4] Table 4.4 lists some of the leading individual public sector settlements in the 1991 wage round.

Table 4.4   *Public sector pay settlements in 1991*

Group	Settlement date	Method of determination	Increase (%)	Comments
British Rail	8.4.91	national negotiations	7.75	following arbitration
Civil service: executive grades	1.4.91	pay comparability	7.8 (basic increase)	government rejected arbitration
Further education: lecturers	1.9.91	national negotiations	6.1	
Local authority: manuals	1.9.91	national negotiations	6.4	slightly higher for lower grades
NHS: administrative and clerical	1.4.91	national negotiations	7.9 (or £11.50 per week)	higher increases for ancillary staff
Police	1.9.91	pay formula	8.5	
University academics	1.4.91	national negotiations	5.0	interim increase

Source: Industrial Relations Review and Report, No 499, 1 November 1991

As suggested by the contents of Table 4.4, in keeping with recent years, the largest public sector increases (although staged) tended to go to the groups covered by review body arrangements, thus raising issues and concerns about intra-public sector equity. This is of particular interest in view of the rather surprising decision of the government to withdraw the Teachers' Pay and Conditions Bill (which would have restored negotiating rights) and replace the Interim Advisory Committee (established following the abolition of the Burnham Committee bargaining machinery) with a pay review body for teachers in England and Wales. The government has, however, resisted demands and pressure to establish review body arrangements for both ambulance drivers and university academics.

As noted earlier, a number of the recent public wage settlements have involved restructuring exercises in which various quid pro quos have been attached to the wage increases. For example, the substantial pay rise for NHS ancillary workers was seen as having cleared the way for a radical overhaul of their pay structure which would include:

- local flexibility to allow recruitment and retention concerns to be tackled;
- locally agreed performance packages;
- a single pay structure, combining the present supervisory and non-supervisory spines; and
- a reduction in the number of basic pay increments.[5]

In 1991 there was also an agreement to reduce the hours of local authority manual workers from 39 to 37; this reduction, which is to be achieved through local negotiations by January 1994, follows the establishment of a joint working party on harmonization in 1990 (sick pay arrangements were harmonized early in 1991).

Prior to the mid-1980s, major and even minor salary structure adjustments were relatively few and far between in the public sector. However, the government's general desire to see pay related more closely to performance and market forces, together with the practical pressures and problems of recruiting and retaining an adequate supply of labour in various parts of the public sector (at least prior to the present recession), have brought about a substantial amount of change in this regard. The various individual wage rounds from the mid-1980s have witnessed, for instance, the introduction of various merit or performance-related pay measures, changes to existing salary scale arrangements and special pay additions in hard to fill vacancy areas. Many of these early initiatives, taken in response to immediate local labour market pressures, were essentially *ad hoc* in nature, and confined essentially to managerial and white-collar grades of staff, particularly in local government. More recently, however, these initiatives have become more formalized in nature, and begun to spread beyond white-collar grades of employees. The restructuring of ancillary staff grades in the NHS in April 1991, for instance, introduced local pay supplements of up to 30 per cent of salary for staff in the Thames region, with the added facility for local managers to pay recruitment and retention packages where appropriate.

There are also at least 30 local authorities which have formally broken away from national-level bargaining in local government; Kent County Council (with some 11,000 Administrative, Professional, Technical & Clerical (APT&C) employees) is one of the largest authorities to have moved in this direction. A recent survey by Incomes Data Services also indicates a number of less formal departures from national level terms and conditions in both local government and the NHS.[6] The Local Government Management Board in early 1992 also put forward a proposal for more flexibility in existing bargaining arrangements,[7] a proposal which is the subject of ongoing discussions.

Above it was noted that the Conservative Government has been strongly in favour of public sector pay being more closely related to the movement of market forces and measures of individual and organizational performance. In fact, by the 1989 pay round approximately 400,000 civil servants (out of a total of 585,000) had some part of their pay determined by performance appraisal. The Inland Revenue Service in particular has seen a great deal of controversy about the practical operation of performance-related pay, with a recent employee survey suggesting relatively little positive impact on employee motivation and performance.[8] The other side of the same coin is the government's desire to reduce significantly the role of comparability in the wage determination processes of the public sector. Comparability has, in fact, been a major principle of pay determination in much of the public sector over a number of decades, although various bodies such as the National Board for Prices and Incomes (1965–70) were highly critical of this fact. The commitment to comparability has been most explicitly institutionalized in the case of the non-industrial civil service where arrangements have frequently come into conflict with the operation of incomes policies and subsequently cash limits. The report of the Megaw Committee of Enquiry, following the 1981 civil service dispute, downgraded, rather than eliminated, comparability as a factor in civil service pay determination. And in October 1991 the Treasury gave notice of their intention to withdraw from six long-term pay agreements covering 550,000 civil servants in order to pave the way for more performance-related pay developments and decentralized bargaining arrangements. In mid-1992 these proposals were the source of some obvious difficulties in ongoing wage negotiations.

Two other tangible indicators of *any* government's desire to 'deprioritize' the comparability factor in public sector wage determination would be, first, the ending of any formal, intra-public sector wage relationships and, second, reducing the coverage of review body arrangements, or else limiting any further groups of public sector employees being covered by such bodies. In fact the Conservative Government has enhanced the coverage of review bodies (ie nurses and midwives, and teachers in England and Wales), although it has resisted similar demands from other groups (eg ambulance drivers and university academics), and certainly the comparability arrangement between manual workers in local government and the NHS was ended in 1980.

THE CHANGING CONTEXT OF PUBLIC SECTOR INDUSTRIAL RELATIONS

As we saw earlier, in Table 4.1, a leading feature or facet of change here has been the decline in public sector employment since 1979. This decline should be seen in the light of, first, the Conservative Government's stated intention to control and bring down the level of public expenditure. In Britain public expenditure as a proportion of GDP was 38.2 per cent in 1988, the lowest figure since 1966.[9] However, in November 1991 the government's public expenditure plans (announced in the context of recession and a General Election looming closer) indicated that the ratio will rise to 42 per cent in 1992–3 (from 40 per cent in 1990–1) and 41.75 per cent in 1993–4.[10] Needless to say, a great deal of controversy has surrounded the alleged success of the Conservative government in bringing public expenditure under control. The second relevant consideration to bear in mind when considering the fall in public sector employment is the government's privatization programme.

This programme has essentially involved:

■ denationalization of public corporations and the sale of public assets;

- liberalization, or the removal of restrictions on private competition for public services; and
- contracting out or compulsory competitive tendering.

Interestingly, the privatization of public enterprises was hardly prominent on the Conservative Party's agenda at the time of its initial election in 1979. However, as the contents of Table 4.5 indicate, a substantial number of organizations were privatized during the course of the 1980s.

Table 4.5 *Some leading examples of privatization in Britain in the 1980s*

British Aerospace	[February 1981]
Cable and Wireless	[October 1981]
National Freight Corporation	[February 1982]
Amersham International	[February, 1982]
Britoil	[October, 1982]
Associated British Ports	[February 1983]
Enterprise Oil	[June 1984]
British Telecom	[November 1984]
Trust Ports (GB)	[April 1985]
British Shipbuilders (warship yards)	[various from July 1984]
British Gas	[December 1986]
British Airways	[February 1987]
Royal Ordnance	[1987]
British Airports Authority	[1987]
National Bus Company	[1984–9]

To this list can be added the British Steel Corporation, the water authorities and electricity supply, with coal-mining and railways scheduled for privatization during the Conservatives' fourth consecutive term of office. The disproportionate concentration of employment reductions in the public corporations (as indicated in Table 4.1) is very much associated with privatization, as the following examples indicate. The privatization of British Aerospace in 1981 reduced employment in public corporations by some 23,000, the transfer of Britoil (1982) and the Associated British Ports (1983) to the private sector reduced employment in public corporations by some 14,000, British Gas (1986) involved an employment reduction of some 89,000, British Airways (1987) reduced employment by 36,000 and the privatization of National Bus Company subsidiaries (1987–8) reduced public corporation employment by some 30,000.* The significance of such moves can be gauged from the fact that total public sector employment fell by 12.5 per cent (headcount) or by 15.6 per cent (in full-time equivalent terms) in 1983–9, but if the employment effects of privatization are excluded, then the scale of reduction was only 5 per cent (headcount) or 8 per cent (full-time equivalents) in these years.[11]

What have been the industrial relations consequences of privatization? Have

---

* In total some 29 major organizations, with approximately 800,000 employees, were privatized during the 1980s.

there been any significant changes in the structures, processes and outcomes of collective bargaining since these public corporations were transferred to the private sector? Not surprisingly, such questions have generated considerable debate and disagreement, although the volume of systematic, empirical research to inform the debate has been rather limited. The unions have pointed to increased decentralization of decision-making tendencies within management, the derecognition of management unions and the associated growth of individual contracts of employment for managers, and increased initiatives to communicate directly with individual employees in the privatized corporations. However, such tendencies are not unique to such organizations; they are very much features of the remaining public corporations.

There is no denying that significant industrial relations changes have occurred in a number of these organizations post-privatization. For example, since the water authorities have ended national-level collective bargaining, Welsh Water has embarked on an extensive, step-by-step programme of harmonization; in Northumbrian Water the trade unions have only one advisory seat on a new (employee–management) company council which discusses pay; while single table bargaining arrangements (three sets of negotiations replaced by one) have been introduced in Yorkshire Water. However, as to the question of whether the post-privatization changes have disadvantaged the unions, it would appear to be difficult to generalize both between and within individual corporations.[12] Nevertheless, one recent review has suggested a potentially interesting line of development for the future in at least some privatized corporations:[13]

> The shape of things to come may be represented by the failure of BT's unions to win recognition and bargaining rights in the corporation's new cable television and equipment manufacturing subsidiaries. With water and electricity companies likewise planning to diversify into other activities, one can foresee a dual pattern of industrial relations in which many of the aspects of the traditional public sector industrial relations – high unionization, pervasive bargaining and consultation – are preserved in the core sectors, but the expanding new activities are a test bed for a range of new initiatives in industrial relations based around an 'individualistic' rather than collective approach to the workforce.

This is clearly a line of possible development in industrial relations of the privatized corporations that should and will be watched closely by both practitioners and researchers.

In the NHS there has been compulsory competitive tendering for cleaning, laundry and catering services from the mid-1980s, whereas in local government contracting-out was initially a voluntary process associated with a relatively small number of Conservative-controlled local councils; mandatory competitive tendering only applied in relation to construction, direct labour organizations (1980) and municipal buses (1985). However, the Local Government Act 1988 contained compulsory competitive tendering provisions for a range of services, including refuse collection, cleaning buildings and other cleaning, school meals and welfare catering, other catering, repair and maintenance of vehicles, and ground maintenance; a new Bill before Parliament (at the time of writing) proposes to extend compulsory competitive tendering to a wide range of white-collar services in local government. Mandatory competitive tendering has also existed for certain services (eg cleaning) in the civil service, although in this particular case the in-house workforce has had little opportunity to compete with external contractors.

For the individual employees concerned, competitive tendering is seen as likely to involve job losses, pay reductions and a general decline in conditions of service; such adverse effects have been documented in various studies.[14] Furthermore, the process poses a threat to the unions (as organizational entities) in the NHS and local government because of its capacity to reduce membership levels. In fact, however, typically 75–80 per cent of contracts put out to tender at any point in time in the NHS have been retained in-house, while some 70 per cent of the 2558 contracts put out to tender in the first four rounds of compulsory competitive tendering by English and Welsh local authorities were won by the in-house bid[15] (this represented 84.3 per cent of the total value of contracts on offer). These in-house win rates have been attributed to major reorganizations of council services into quasi-companies (direct service organizations) in many councils, and to a significant renegotiation of terms and conditions of employment at the local level.[16] However, important questions remain as to whether these in-house win rates can be maintained over time,* and at what cost to the individual employees and unions involved. More generally, the process of compulsory competitive tendering has contributed to an undermining of nationally negotiated terms and conditions of employment, and increased the involvement of elected representatives in industrial relations matters (ie a more overtly 'politicized' process has resulted) in local authorities.

A number of the individual hospitals which moved to trust status in 1991 announced some sizeable staff reductions which generated considerable media and political attention. A review of the initial 57 trusts by Industrial Relations Services suggested that the majority would initially maintain national bargaining arrangements, but favoured a move to local bargaining in the longer term;[17] in fact, two ambulance trusts (covering Lincolnshire and Northumbria) have already moved away from nationally negotiated terms and conditions of employment.[18] The ACAS Annual Report for 1991 noted that the lack of local bargaining expertise and experience on both the union and management sides had resulted in a number of trusts approaching them for advice and assistance. Decentralized bargaining and industrial relations arrangements also characterize those parts of the civil service (eg HMSO) which have been moved to executive agency status,[19] a process which will undoubtedly increase in the course of the present government's term of office.

STRIKES AND THE UNION RESPONSE

Although individuals may disagree about the strength of the particular causes involved (eg reaction to incomes policy, changes in workforce composition,

---

* A survey of 513 local authorities in Britain as a whole reported that 42 per cent had contracted out none of their main services to the private sector, 28 per cent had contracted out one, 13 per cent had contracted out two, and 18 per cent had contracted out three (*Financial Times*, 26 May 1992).

changes in the political complexion of union leadership), it was generally held that the changing nature of public sector industrial relations in the 1970 derived from, or was at least most clearly manifested in, important changes in the *character* of the unions concerned. In essence it was argued that employee representation bodies, particularly in the civil service, the NHS and education sector, became increasingly less staff-association-like, and, conversely, more union-like in their attitudes and behaviour during the course of the decade. This was indicated by a variety of actions that departed from traditional practice, such as increased strike action and affiliation to the TUC.

The level of strike activity in the public sector in the 1970s should certainly not be exaggerated, but there is no denying that it came increasingly to the forefront in discussions of the problems of British industrial relations. There are arguably three major reasons for the disproportionate amount of attention given to public sector strikes in the 1970s (and subsequently). First, a number of national disputes involved groups of public sector employees that had never previously been on strike (eg civil servants, firemen). Secondly, a considerable number of them were viewed as having constitutional overtones in that they were directed essentially against government policy of the day; certainly, virtually all episodes of incomes policy in Britain have been broken, at least formally, by public sector strikes, with groups of public sector employees spearheading the resulting 'pay explosions'. And, finally, these strikes have been alleged to be particularly high-cost ones, being especially harmful to the public at large and in some cases raising the possibility of threats to public health and safety.

Since the Conservative party came to power in 1979, the level of strike activity in the public sector has increased considerably. For example, the public sector accounted for between 44 and 88 per cent of total working days lost in the years 1980–5.[20] (In the period 1974–9 the range was from 10 to 48 per cent). National-level strike action in the public sector occurred in virtually every year of the 1980s, with most of these centring around wage issues. However, the miners' dispute of 1984–5 and the teachers' disputes in the period 1985–7 involved much larger direct challenges to the government's overall public sector expenditure and employment strategy. Over and above the well-known instances of national level industrial action in the public sector in the 1980s (eg the so-called 'summer of discontent' in 1989 on the railways and London Underground), there have also been many instances of local-level industrial action. For instance 42 per cent of the (provisionally estimated) total working days lost through industrial disputes in January 1991 occurred in public administration and education, with the relevant figures for February, March and April being 58, 72 and 87 per cent respectively. Much of this industrial action in the public administration and education sector involved disputes over staffing levels, redundancies and job cuts; at Liverpool City Council, for instance, some 750 white-collar workers engaged in some five months of industrial action over redundancies. The prison service was a particular centre of 'problems' in 1991, with some 82 disputes, largely centring around manning levels, being reported in 45 English and Welsh prisons in the latter part of that year.

Major public sector disputes in Britain have frequently been followed by calls from various organizations for the introduction of 'no strike clauses' in essential services. The Conservative Government was known to be initially keen to proceed in this direction, although little tangible progress was evident due to disagreements over the definition or scope of essential services in the public sector and over the desirability of institutionalizing compulsory arbitration arrangements in return for removing the right to strike. As a consequence a 'second-best' approach of encouraging the increased representation and status of 'non-militant' employee organizations in the public sector was pursued. For example, the Union of Democratic Mineworkers (UDM) in Nottinghamshire and South Derbyshire, the Professional Association of Teachers (PAT) (with its no strike clause) and the Federated Union of Professional and Managerial Officers in local government (which favours the break-up of national bargaining arrangements there) were all accorded national-level recognition status. More recently, the Green Paper on proposed industrial relations law reforms contains measures to try and limit certain strike actions in essential public services.

The increased levels of strike activity in the public sector in recent times, together with the number of public sector unions that have established political funds for the first time, seem to point to a continuation, and even enhancement, of the union character changes observed in the public sector during the course of the 1970s. This being said, it is important to recognize that membership growth in the 1980s and into the 1990s has been very much associated with 'less militant' unions like the Royal College of Nursing. The declining membership of a number of public sector unions has promoted a number of important merger discussions, with the potentially most significant of these being the ongoing discussions between COHSE, NUPE and NALGO; the more long-standing merger discussions between CPSA and NUCPS in the civil service, however, appear to have come to an end, with no change in the status quo. The Public Services Committee of the TUC (established in 1979) has also sought to enhance the level of public sector union co-ordination in recent years, with such co-ordination, at least at the national union level, also being stimulated by the threat posed by compulsory competitive tendering. In general the unions have sought to oppose compulsory competitive tendering by a variety of means: various local level strikes against such proposals; attempts to forge links with political pressure groups at the local level who favour the maintenance of in-house public services; the seeking of various legal rulings in the courts on aspects of the process; and extensive media publicity of the 'poor performance' of private sector contractors. Some success has been reported to have resulted from this package of opposition measures, although a lack of inter-union co-operation at the local level has allegedly hindered the extent of gains in this regard.[21]

CONCLUSIONS

Public sector employees and unions have, for more than a decade, faced a government highly committed to public expenditure restraint, privatization, the adoption of decentralized decision-making arrangements and to reducing the power of unions in the public sector. Although such tendencies have been observed in other European countries in the 1980s and into the 1990s, it appears that the British case has been the 'most extreme' in this regard.[22] Has the result been a major substantive change in public sector industrial relations structures, processes and outcomes? This is certainly the view of some commentators, as indicated by the following:[23]

> Size, however, is virtually the only thing static in today's public sector. For the rest, change is more rapid and far-reaching than at any time since the 1940s. These old-style public services, each a national monolith with a single organizational structure, ethos and rigid set of pay and conditions, are withering fast. Choice, standards and quality are the catchwords; flexibility, performance, and local management the tools; the private sector the model. The Citizens' Charter unveiled by the government earlier this week reverberates to them all

In fact, the available, albeit inadequate, research evidence does not support such a 'rosy' view of widespread, deep-seated change in public sector industrial relations. This is because it is difficult to find evidence of a sizeable set of internally consistent structural changes underpinned by the processes of attitudinal and behavioural change which all point in the same direction.[24] The relative absence of change along these lines should perhaps occasion relatively little surprise when it is recognized that the process of translating government strategy into operational managerial decisions and actions in the public sector is far from being a straightforward, mechanical process. This is because of the relatively 'blunt' nature of many of the government control mechanisms, together with the fact that public sector management is not an undifferentiated mass solely committed to the achievement of the government of the day's strategic objectives.

Finally, there is the question of whether some of the changes initiated to date will gradually accumulate and add up over time to a coherent change programme, or whether some of them will not survive the test of time. In seeking to answer this question it is interesting to note that there is some public opinion poll data which raises some important questions about the extent to which the public at large favours further public expenditure restraint, privatization and curbs on unions.[25] It will be interesting, to say the least, to see how the government responds (or not) during its fourth consecutive term of office to these public opinion signals, as the nature of this response will clearly have some important implications for the future shape of public sector industrial relations in Britain.

References

1. Hepple, B (1982) 'Labour law and public employees in Britain', in Wedderburn, Lord and Murphy, W T (eds) *Labour Law and the Community*, Institute of Advanced Legal Studies, University of London, London, pp 75–9.
2. *Industrial Relations Review and Report*, No 499, 1 November 1991.
3. *Financial Times*, 20 December 1991.
4. *Financial Times*, 31 January 1992.
5. *Financial Times*, 22 March 1991.
6. IDS Report No 602, October 1991.
7. *Financial Times*, 17 January 1992.
8. *Financial Times*, 27 September 1991.
9. *Social Trends 20* (1990) HMSO, London, p 105.
10. *Financial Times*, 7 November 1991.
11. Fleming, A (1989) 'Employment in the public and private sectors', *Economic Trends*, No 434, December, p 72.
12. Thomas, D (1984) 'Privatisation and the unions', *New Society*, 21 June.

13. *Industrial Relations Research Unit Newsletter*, No 8, Winter 1990, p 3.
14. Institute of Personnel Management and Incomes Data Services (1986) *Competitive Tendering in the Public Sector*, London, p 66.
15. *Financial Times*, 13 May 1991.
16. Beaumont, P B (1991) 'Privatization, contracting-out and public sector industrial relations: the Thatcher years in Britain', *Journal of Collective Negotiations in the Public Sector*, Vol 20, No 2, pp 89–100.
17. *Financial Times*, 9 July 1991.
18. *Industrial Relations Review and Report*, No 497, 4 October 1991.
19. *Financial Times*, 21 November 1991.
20. 'Public sector trade unions', *IDS Public Sector Digest*, 187, p 8.
21. Asher, K (1987) *The Politics of Privatisation*, Macmillan, London, pp 125–32.
22. Ferner, A (1991) 'Changing public sector industrial relations in Europe', *Warwick Papers in Industrial Relations*, No 37, October.
23. *Financial Times*, 26 July 1991.
24. Beaumont, P B (1991) *Public Sector Industrial Relations*, Routledge, London, Chapter 8.
25. Beaumont, P B, ibid.

Part Two
The Practice of Industrial Relations

Chapter Five
Managing Industrial Relations

Chris Brewster

It is now accepted as axiomatic that management plays a key role in industrial relations. It was hardly challenged before the 1980s that industrial relations was 'about' trade unions; in industry, managers saw their job as coping with the situation in which the unions put them. To caricature the position, most managers saw industrial relations as like the weather; something they could bemoan, but do little to influence. In the academic world the subject of management was simply disregarded as an area of study for industrial relations specialists.

Things have changed. Developments in industry and commerce have led to a manifest weakening in the influence of the unions in the UK. This has been paralleled by an upsurge of academic discussion of the role of management in industrial relations. The combination of these factors has led to a clarification of the fundamental importance of the process and policies of management, and an emphasis on the capacity which managements have to plan and influence industrial relations.

Managers, of course, are an extremely varied and heterogeneous group. The term covers individuals who may be very different in terms of function, status, age, income, philosophy – and capability. In industrial relations, too, managers perform very different roles. There are a few managers whose primary concern is with industrial relations, but many have industrial relations as a small part of a complex of responsibilities. On the narrowest definitions of industrial relations, those involving managerial relationships with trade unions, only a very limited amount of managerial time and resources is committed to the subject. Even on wider definitions, which involve managerial relationships with employees, whether formal or informal, group or individual, there are few managers who devote more than a minority of their time to the issue.

It is arguable, of course, that on the widest definition almost anything that a manager does has some effect on the other, non-managerial, employees. Such an argument is valid in its own terms, but the danger of so comprehensive a definition is that it conglomerates industrial relations with many other subjects and makes it of little analytical value. The occasions on which managers deal consciously with issues concerning their employees are fewer than the pundits sometimes like to admit.

The importance of industrial relations in the managerial consciousness is both less and greater than is usually understood. Again, the issue is definitional. The obvious occasions – annual wage negotiations, disciplinary or grievance hearings, bargaining over rosters, meetings with shop stewards – are distinct and comparatively isolated incidents within a complicated managerial workload. In this respect the importance of the subject can be exaggerated.

Yet if it can be exaggerated, it is also easy to underestimate the importance of industrial relations to an organization's management. For most organizations, even those in high-technology areas, the major operating costs are those associated with their human resources. Financial success or failure, even survival or non-survival, can be determined by such issues as $\frac{1}{2}$ per cent on wage costs, a lack of commitment on the part of employees, the need to spend extra money on recruitment, or the difference between a cost-effective shift roster and an expensive one. In times of economic crisis it is not surprising that the first area that management examine with the objective of cutting costs is the workforce – hence the wave of redundancies in Britain in the early 1980s and early 1990s. This is a message that has not been lost on managements. Employees are the largest operating cost, the most important resource, and above all the one that requires greater attention and increasingly cost-effective management.

This chapter reflects the current interest in management's role in industrial relations. It does so by addressing three closely related areas of debate, and arguing that a theoretic dichotomy can be identified in each area. First, the developing literature on human resource management, as compared to personnel management, is reviewed. Second, a contrast is drawn between social awareness and cost-effectiveness based approaches. Third, the newly resurgent ideas of performance-related pay and total quality management are examined.

None of these elements is entirely new and it is probably true that nearly all organizations are making changes in at least some of these areas. Because these dichotomies are all based upon the relationship of managerial behaviour towards non-managerial employees, this analysis inevitably overlaps with many of the issues covered in later chapters of this book, and with other subjects often defined as being outside industrial relations – manpower planning, recruitment, development and training, even marketing, production technology or finance. Practising managers will not need this book to know that problems come to them as issues, with all these ramifications; not in neat academic packages where solutions have no implications in other areas. Those managements who are developing a strategic view of industrial relations are building on these overlaps, rather than ignoring them. A brief summary attempts to set these dichotomies in perspective.

HRM AND PERSONNEL MANAGEMENT[1]

The concept of human resource management (HRM), and the associated concept of strategic human resource management, is being debated increasingly in the literature and used increasingly within employing organizations. The history of the concept of HRM has been summarized elsewhere.[2] It developed initially from work in the US in the 1960s and 1970s, and since the mid-1980s has been an ever more visible feature of the academic literature, of consultancy services and of organizational terminology. The concept of HRM was taken up most enthusiastically in the related cultures of, first, Great Britain and then Australasia. The terminology has begun to spread into Scandinavia, and to a lesser extent, into continental Europe. In France, for example, the first book to address the topic of strategic HRM specifically was not published until 1988.

Critics of HRM stress that the concept of HRM is hardly distinguishable from the term personnel management.

> . . . It might well be asked why the language of HRM has gained the currency it appears to have – not least among management groups themselves. After all . . . there is little real difference between normative HRM and personnel management models and, in practice, it is probable that managing employee relations in the vast majority of companies remains a pragmatic activity, whether labelled personnel management or HRM. Furthermore, many of the techniques of HRM can be found in any personnel management textbook of a decade ago.[3]

HRM is, strictly speaking, more a bundle of overlapping notions than a concept in its own right. In particular two distinct approaches ('hard' and 'soft') have been identified regularly in the literature.[4] These 'hard' and 'soft' views were emphasized most clearly in the mid-1980s by two competing texts, the first edited by Fombrun et al;[5] the second by Beer et al[6] standing, in essence, as a manifesto for the then newly developed HRM element of Harvard's MBA. It is only necessary in the context of this chapter to point out the key distinctive features of each approach.

The 'hard' approach focuses on the 'resource' side of the phrase 'human resource management'. It argues that people are organizational resources and should be managed like any other resource: obtained as cheaply and used as sparingly as is consistent with other requirements such as those for quality and efficiency; and that they should be developed and exploited as fully and profitably as possible. The words 'human' or 'people' are used rather than 'employees' because techniques such as outsourcing, subcontracting and franchising would, in certain circumstances, be seen as entirely appropriate to a hard view of HRM. The approach tends to have a much closer relationship to corporate strategy – with HRM often seen to follow such strategies. It is most typically linked to contingent analyses of corporate strategy, or product life-cycle theories or organizational growth theories. Fombrun et al express this view as follows: 'Just as firms will be faced with inefficiencies when they try to implement new strategies with outmoded structures, so they will also face problems of implementation when they attempt to effect new strategies with inappropriate HR systems.'

British consultants Cook and Armstrong sum this up very clearly[7] using data from a British electrical firm: 'In Thorn EMI, as elsewhere, corporate strategy sets the agenda for HR strategy . . . it should not in itself be over-influenced by HR factors (HR strategies are about making business strategies work).'

By contrast the 'soft' approach to HRM concentrates upon the 'human' side of 'human resource management'. It argues by contrast that people are a resource *unlike* any other – for most organizations far more costly than other resources, but for all organizations the one factor which can create value from the other resources. This is the resource whose creativity, commitment and skill can generate real competitive advantage. This most precious resource therefore requires careful selection, extensive nurturing and development, proper rewards and integration into the organization. As such this approach will tend to concentrate on 'employees' and stands clearly in the long tradition of human relations and developmental studies. In this approach human resource management is more symbiotically related to corporate strategy; the presence or absence of certain skills may push the organization into or out of certain markets or products, for example.

The 'soft' view of HRM typically refers to a (unitary) view of the organization in terms of a team, competing against other organizations, and with the development and growth of the team players inevitably contributing to the success of the whole. This viewpoint was captured in an American text on human resource planning and development (HRPD)[8]:

> In an ideal HRPD system, one would seek to match the organization's needs for human resources with the individual's needs for personal career growth and development. One can then depict the basic system as involving both individual and organizational planning, and a series of matching activities designed to satisfy mutual needs . . . growth and development must be organized to meet both the needs of the organization and the needs of the individuals within it.

Thus, although Schein admits that there will sometimes be a need to have components 'that reflect the need for either a new growth direction or a process of disengagement of the person from his or her job', key objectives will include such things as the need to reduce costly turnover.

These US views of HRM have come under increasing criticism in Europe. The concept has been criticized for being: imprecise; prescriptive; and lacking evidence as to its acceptance by employers; it has been attacked for being just 'personnel management' in another guise; and for being inappropriate to, for example, British industrial relations practice.

How these theories of HRM translate into day-to-day factory, shop or office level practice is very much a moot point. In simple terms the fact is that although there have been attempts to relate the concept to practice (mainly through case-study examples), there has been a lack of real evidence of the development of trends in either policy or behaviour. It is at this point relevant to begin to address two closely related issues: whether managerial styles in managing industrial relations are moving from social awareness (soft HRM) to cost-effectiveness (hard HRM) and what is happening in respect of two of the ideas most closely associated with the concept of HRM: performance and quality management.

CHANGING STYLES

British managements are in a situation markedly different from that of a decade or so ago. From their point of view there are several factors which put pressure on their approach to industrial relations: increased competition (particularly internationally and with the advent of the single European market); a free-market oriented government and increased pressure on employment costs. At the same time, other changes have increased opportunities for managements to organize industrial relations as they desire: a high level of unemployment; an increasing segmentation of the labour market; reduced trade union power and influence; and reduced legal constraints. Inevitably these pressures and opportunities will operate differently in different sectors of the economy: increased international competition will be more central for sectors of manufacturing; government action will have a greater impact on teachers, and so on. Overall, however, most managers in Britain in most sectors of employment are faced with greater pressure for the cost-effective use of human resources and greater opportunities to achieve it.

The different objectives that personnel and industrial relations specialists among managements can pursue in such circumstances can be considered under the two headings of social awareness and cost-effectiveness. Both aspects have been and will continue to be important for most organizations, but there is a clear trend from the former to the latter.

Prior to the 1980s these specialists were concerned with *social awareness:* responsibility for the workforce and even responsibility to society at large. Forward-looking specialists in industrial relations judged themselves, and were judged by others, on their ability to maintain good relationships with their trade unions. They sought and achieved the increases in formality recommended by the Donovan Commission in 1968: written-down recognition arrangements; established procedures; and formally-minuted substantive agreements. They aimed for an image in the community at large as a caring and concerned employer. Above all, they tried to avoid industrial disputes.

With such criteria, the personnel and industrial relations specialists adopted a role within the management team akin to that of a 'loyal opposition'; ever ready to criticize, ever keen to put the point of view of trade unions or employees before those groups heard of anything threatening or worrying.

From the watershed of the early 1980s more and more managements were first of all forced, and then chose, to define different objectives for themselves in their relationship to employees and of the most productive use of the workforce. The touchstone became *cost-effectiveness*: the cost-effective use of the human resource.[9]

Many specialists found this a difficult change to make. The Institute of Personnel Management still attempts to develop a 'professional' approach, based on the old criteria, whereby a professional specialist can, like the older legal, accountancy or medical professions, argue that they have different standards, above those of the organization for which they are currently working.

Other specialists, however, have embraced the cost-effective approach enthusiastically. These are the ones who are most likely to have adopted the 'HRM' terminology. They argue that their department must aim to contribute to the efficient and successful running of the organization in the same way as any other department. Indeed, because the workforce is in most cases the major operating cost, because it is where the major benefits of productivity, innovation and service are found, and because poor industrial relations can ruin all other policies while organizations with good industrial relations can often overcome deficiencies elsewhere – for all these reasons it is argued that cost-effective industrial relations can be the key to organizational survival and success.

The specialists who argue this way are not crudely discarding previous policies. The different objectives may lead to similar policies. Socially aware policies would include opposition to racial and sexual discrimination, since these are unlawful and socially repugnant; the provision of company training and development would give employees the chance to make a contribution and better themselves; providing good facilities for senior shop stewards would improve the relationship with the union.

Cost-effectiveness might involve the same policies, but with a different rationale. Thus, discrimination would be opposed because it limits managerial ability to obtain the maximum output from all employees equally; company training and development makes employees more efficient and in Britain at least makes their skills less transferable to other organizations; and good facilities for senior stewards make it easier to keep the full-time officials out of the workplace.

In some areas the rationale will run against old policies. Here managements pursuing cost-effective policies are prepared to risk the relationship with the unions, operate increasingly through informal agreements, subordinate the organization's image in the community and even face up to industrial action (and take steps to win it) in order to achieve the goals of control, flexibility and productivity.

One area of focus in this approach is on labour flexibility. There is clear evidence from a number of surveys and case studies that there were extensive and widespread changes in working practices in Britain in the 1980s. Much of this evidence is from the beleaguered manufacturing sector. The sort of changes most frequently made have been concerned with such issues as the introduction of new technology or increased efficiency with existing equipment, more flexible working practices and flexibility in working times. The overwhelming majority of these working practice changes have been introduced without the conclusion of new technology agreements or indeed any other agreement. Managements have, quite simply, just reorganized the work.[10]

From a managerial viewpoint, the most common reason for introducing increased flexibility of working practices is greater cost-effectiveness. In particular, this increased flexibility gives a more effective use of existing equipment and constantly updated technology. In most cases the unions have accepted readily the need for increased task flexibility.

While the organization and performance of many areas of work has been subject to substantial changes, the concept of *work time* has remained remarkably stable until quite recently. However, there is now an enormous variety of working time arrangements being developed. The following examples could be multiplied.

Part-time work in Great Britain expanded considerably in the 1980s. By the end of the decade over one-fifth of all people in work, more than five million people, were in part-time employment. Britain has a higher proportion of part-time workers in its workforce than most other European countries. Of this part-time labour force the vast majority are women, who often combine work with domestic and family responsibilities. From the management point of view, the use of part-time workers enables specific peak demands to be met without incurring the costs of full-time staff whose services may not be required for a full week. Furthermore, part-time workers are less often absent and tend to have higher productivity per working hour. It also has the added advantage for managers of committing them to rather limited legal rights for the employee.

Shift working has been a common feature for many manual employees over many years. It is now spreading to non-manual employees and to service industries. Furthermore, companies are moving towards matching their hours of work to suit their productive needs. This is resulting in an ever-increasing variety of shift arrangements; there is hardly any longer a normal or standard pattern.

Variable working patterns other than shift arrangements are also widespread. Flexitime arrangements, where employees can vary their daily hours of work, largely at their own discretion, provided that the required hours are completed over a longer time-scale, is now common in many offices. Annual hours arrangements, where hours are varied by management to suit business needs subject to an overall yearly total, are not so far widespread but they are becoming more common.

'Standard' working hours are still the norm for many employees but fewer than half of those in employment in the UK now work a straightforward nine-to-five day. Increasingly, managements are devising working patterns which reflect the needs of the business, such as those of production or sales cycles, the longer opening hours of shops or pubs, the need to contact organizations in other countries and other time zones. Flexible working time arrangements are continuing to increase.

The third key area of flexibility concerns contractual arrangements. Many companies are now moving away from an automatic assumption that all work will be done by full-time employees on indefinite contracts. Three types of labour force have been identified: a core group; a secondary labour market; and a peripheral labour market. Those employed in the core group perform essential tasks which are specific to that firm and they are likely to be assured of a full-time permanent career. Those in the secondary labour market include part-timers, job-sharers and those on short-term contracts employed subject to the fluctuations in the market demand experienced by the firm. They cannot rely upon the security of permanent jobs, have no career structure, and limited training and development. At the periphery is a labour market consisting of self-employed workers, agency temporaries and others who can be called on to perform specific tasks for a specific time period and who have no commitment for any great length of time to that one firm.

It is argued that the central employment distinction is not now between manual and staff status, but rather between core and non-core workers. By the mid-1980s almost half of all establishments employed non-core workers. By 1991 flexible working practices were well established across Europe. For example in a survey of ten countries, only three (France, Spain and Italy) reported less than 20 per cent of organizations using part-time workers.[11] Furthermore such practices had grown rapidly (Figure 5.1).

Such moves have not been uncontroversial[12], though the controversy has tended to centre on whether employers have developed the use of atypical working as a conscious strategy, whether that is a strategy that should be approved in some moral sense and whether growth is related to developments in industrial structure. Despite the controversy it seems clear that such atypical forms of working are now more widespread than they have been in the recent past.

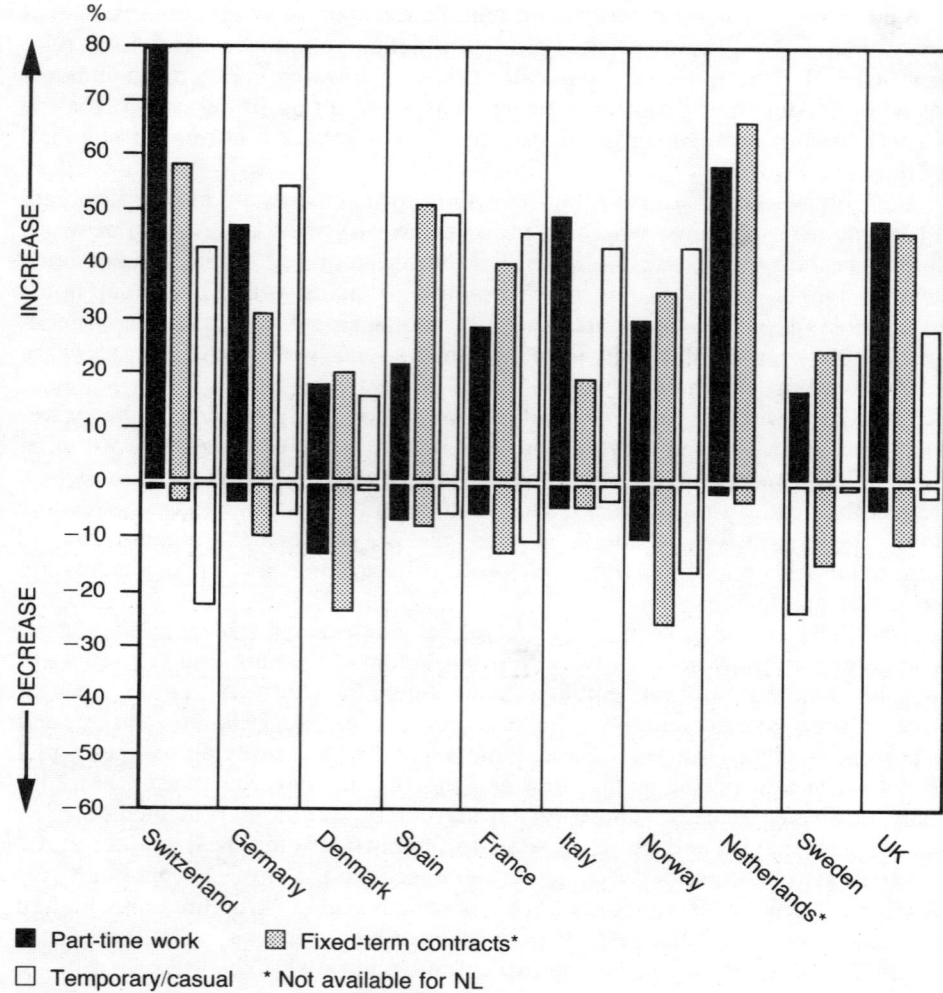

Source: Price Waterhouse Cranfield Report 1991, Cranfield, UK

Figure 5.1   *Changes in part-time, temporary and fixed term contracts in Europe*

Nor are these examples the only ones. Managements make use of temporary workers, job-sharers, youth trainees and semi-retired people. Other options are homeworking, networking, minimum–maximum contracts and first-call contracts. Many organizations are subcontracting whole areas of work to other organizations or to self-employed workers. Some companies are making use of the many individuals operating in the black economy.

The many variations in these forms of 'casualized' employment have all grown rapidly in recent years. It remains to be seen how far the use of these contractual forms will be developed or maintained. From the managerial viewpoint peripheral employment contracts provide opportunities to develop a dynamic, flexible workforce structured in ways that management deems appropriate, and responsive to short-term restructuring. It is difficult to see much decline in their use in the next few years. And this, of course, raises important issues in industrial relations.

PERFORMANCE AND QUALITY

Two of the most popular 'new ideas' associated with human resource management are performance-related pay (PRP) with its extension into the wider concept of performance management and total quality management (TQM). Analysis of the two approaches is complicated by the fact that each term spans a variety of arrangements. This section nevertheless attempts to summarize these two aspects of the received wisdom about how organizations should be managed; to assess their advantages for management and to evaluate these against the disadvantages to draw some conclusions about the nature and extent of their use.

Performance-related pay (PRP)

In the UK, at least, performance-related pay is one of the most fashionable topics in HRM. PRP has been defined as 'the part of the financial, or financially measurable, reward to an individual which is linked directly to individual, team or company performance'.[13] As such it includes a wide range of merit pay, bonuses linked to results, shares or gifts related to performance and payment-by-results (PBR) schemes. Usually, however, these latter schemes which link pay directly to output measures, rather than performance measures, are excluded. PBR schemes are reducing in number. The focus of PRP is assumed to be merit or contribution rather than number of units produced; indeed in many cases, particularly for managerial staff, PRP is termed 'merit pay'.

The performance management and performance-related pay concepts are now the received wisdom among commentators. The UK's Institute of Personnel Management has embraced the concept with enthusiasm. Many consultants now make considerable amounts of money out of helping organizations in the private and public sectors to introduce PRP. The CBI has claimed that PRP is directly related to the national growth in productivity of the 1980s. PRP has also found favour in more exalted circles. The British government of the 1980s and early 1990s, for example, has pushed it hard: forcing it into the areas of employment the government controls and exhorting the private sector to do likewise.

The benefits that these various authorities expect to flow from PRP are manifold – though there is limited evidence that they exist in practice. The claimed advantages include the following.

1. Increased motivation. If pay can be seen to be related to performance, and the assumption is made that employees perform in order to receive pay, then the linkage of the two will lead to an increased motivation to perform at a high level. There is an obvious 'fairness' in paying more to those who contribute more; and less to those who perform badly. There will be an increased understanding of goals and targets among employees; it will be easier to reward the best employees and easier to identify, and handle, the worst. From a wider perspective, the Conservative Government's backing of

the concept is presumably based on this vision of the motivation of employees and the resultant positive impact on the economy as a whole.

2. Fairness. Not only can PRP achieve a greater sense of 'felt fairness' on the part of employees, but many managers are attracted by the idea that they are paying for what they get rather than for availability. Whether or not such programmes motivate employees, managers like the idea that those who contribute most get more of the organization's cash: and vice versa.

3. PRP enables managers to reward individuals who are performing well but who, perhaps because of tough economic circumstances, cannot be promoted.

4. Managerial accountability. The notion of relating pay to performance is, almost by definition, one that can only apply if local managers, who know their employees' performance levels, are responsible for its implementation. Furthermore, it makes local managers clearly accountable for the financial impact of their assessments of performance. As such, it fits well with other fashionable ideas of devolvement and decentralization.

5. Individual accountability. PRP can be related to groups, but in practice in the UK it is almost always targeted at individuals. The result is that PRP is an addition to the armoury of those who wish to move from a collective (union oriented) to an individual (non-union) culture. As employees' pay rates are increasingly varied by performance rating, rather than grade or function, so the solidarity of the grade or function becomes weakened.

6. A challenge to collective bargaining. Related to these moves towards individualization is the obvious concomitant of a decrease, or total absence, of union influence. This happened, for example, at Cable and Wireless, which moved from a highly unionized and cohesive workforce, through PRP and the breaking down of group loyalties to an individualized approach to pay. When the company finally withdrew union recognition, MSF, the union concerned, was unable to generate any counter-action. There are, however, other cases – including British Telecom and the Society of Telecom Executives, Associated Newspapers and the National Union of Journalists, the Inland Revenue and the Inland Revenue Staff Federation – where the introduction of PRP schemes, perhaps badly managed, has been met by the provision of more individual union services or has strengthened the union.

That these supposed benefits have been widely accepted in the UK is clear from the growth of PRP.[14] Evidence from a study of organizations in ten European companies shows that, while the practice is marginal in the Scandinavian countries, PRP is widespread in France, Italy and Switzerland as well as the UK.[15]

Quality management

The other widely bruited approach to HRM has been 'quality management'. It is less widely practised in the UK than PRP, but it is perhaps even more widely discussed, and even proselitized. Its proponents tend to have an almost religious adherence to the concept and to invest it with great power: 'Commitment to Total Quality is a way of life. It is the fundamental ingredient which makes all other Business Goals attainable at a competitive cost. Where the question is survival, the answer is quality.'[16]

Like the concept of performance, that of quality is bedevilled by numerous definitions and discussions which fail to define the term clearly. They range from what most American textbooks refer to as 'conformance to requirement or specification' through to the detailed 14–point prescription by Deming, the leading 'guru' in the field (see Box, below).

Many of the benefits claimed for quality management, or in its more grandiose guise, total quality management (TQM), fall outside the human resources area – customer satisfaction, reduced defects, lower inventories. In HRM claimed benefits include the following.

1. *Reduced costs*. If employees are concentrated on improving quality there will not only be fewer physical costs, in terms of lower inventory, reduced recalls and fewer corrections or replacements, but manpower costs will also be reduced. Employees may find ways of increasing production or improving service which require fewer employees, inspection teams will be unnecessary, complaints departments reduced.

2. *Shared objectives*. The literature continually stresses the need for the full commitment of everyone in the organization, from top to bottom, to quality. As such it provides a unifying theme for transactions between different levels in the hierarchy.

3. *Increased motivation*. Full commitment to TQM provides employees with substantially increased control over their own work, with greater opportunities to train and to experiment and with reduced managerial control. As such great motivational benefits are claimed for it.

THE WORLD ACCORDING TO DEMING: HIS 14 ESSENTIAL POINTS FOR MANAGERS

1. Create constancy of purpose toward improvement of product and service, with the aim to become competitive and to stay in business, and to provide jobs.
2. Adopt the new philosophy. We are in a new economic age. Western management must awaken to the challenge, must learn their responsibilities, and take on leadership for change.
3. Cease dependence on inspection to achieve quality. Eliminate the need for inspection on a mass basis by building quality into the product in the first place.
4. End the practice of awarding business on the basis of price tag. Instead, minimize total cost. Move toward a single supplier for any one item, on a long-term relationship of loyalty and trust.
5. Improve constantly and for ever the system of production and service, to improve quality and productivity, and thus constantly decrease costs.
6. Institute training on the job.
7. Institute leadership. The aim of supervision should be to help people, and machines and gadgets to do a better job. Supervision of management is in need of overhaul, as well as supervision of production workers.
8. Drive out fear, so that everyone may work effectively for the company.
9. Break down barriers between departments. People in research, design, sales and production must work as a team to foresee problems of

production and in use that may be encountered with the product or service.

10. Eliminate slogans, exhortations and targets for the workforce asking for zero defects and new levels of productivity. Such exhortations only create adversarial relationships, as the bulk of the causes of low quality and low productivity belong to the system, and thus lies beyond the power of the workforce.

11a. Eliminate work standards (quotas) on the factory floor. Substitute leadership.

11b. Eliminate management by objective. Eliminate management by the numbers, numerical goals. Substitute leadership.

12a. Remove barriers that rob the hourly worker of his right to pride of workmanship. The responsibility of supervisors must be changed from sheer numbers to quality.

12b. Remove barriers that rob people in management and in engineering of their right to pride of workmanship. This means, *inter alia*, abolishment of the annual or merit rating and of management by objective.

13. Institute a vigorous programme of education and self-improvement.

14. Top management will accomplish the transformation.

Source: Serlen, B 'W Edwards Deming: The Man who made Japan Famous for Quality', *NYU Business*, Fall 1987/Winter 1988, pp 16–20

Performance and quality: what impact?

The concepts of performance and quality management are the received wisdom of the age. It is difficult to argue that the management of any organization should not be concerned with, and focused on, improving performance and quality. In their manifestation in PRP and TQM, however, two notes of caution must be sounded: they concern the impact of these approaches, and their compatibility.

The impact of PRP is, at best, unclear. It is worth noting, for example, that the 1991 New Earnings Survey showed eight out of ten of all workers received no form of incentive payments. And where there were incentives they amounted to no more than 4.1 per cent of earnings. Furthermore, it has been argued that PRP may not be entirely positive. Commentators such as Douglas Smith, the chairman of ACAS, and researchers, have argued that PRP is costly and inflationary. The economist Richard Layard has challenged any link to productivity. Nor is there any straightforward evidence of its impact on industrial relations: 'PRP has not in itself resulted in any weakening in trade union power or representation and . . . where it is poorly applied or where the industrial relations climate is not based on high trust, it may provide unions with a powerful issue over which to negotiate'.[17]

The impact of TQM is also uncertain. Many of the individual elements or tools are widespread, but a full-blown TQM programme is rare: the same few companies – Corning Glass, IBM, Rank Xerox, Nissan, Hewlett Packard – are quoted repeatedly. Perhaps the challenge to existing managerial cultures is too great.

Part of the reason for the low levels of evidence that the concepts of performance and quality have had much impact may lie in the incompatability between them. It is clearly expressed by Deming who argues that quality is incompatible with 'annual or merit rating and . . . management by objective'. In order for a full TQM programme to operate employees have to be free to experiment, free to take risks and make mistakes, and not be driven by pre-established targets. For PRP to work there must be effective, tight, pre-established targets against which performance can be kept to the mark and evaluated.

A fully operating performance system allows a much reduced role for industrial relations. In particular it differentiates between similar workers and breaks up collectivities; and it takes important elements of pay and rewards out of the collective bargaining arena. A full quality system allows almost no role for industrial relations. It is predicated on the basis that the whole employee workforce, from top to bottom, work together with no partial or divisive objectives.

In summary, although there can be little doubt that PRP and total quality management have made a big difference to industrial relations in some companies, there is equally little doubt that in many cases the words themselves are not followed through into any significant or effective change in practices.[18]

MANAGERIAL PRACTICE IN INDUSTRIAL RELATIONS

In order to pull together these disparate, if related, strands of thinking about managerial practice it is necessary to return to the central question in industrial relations: that of the relationship between managements and trade unions.

Prior to the 1980s it would have seemed idiosyncratic to write so much about managerial policies in industrial relations with so little mention of trade unions. That it is relevant to do so now reflects another key element of 'human resource management' strategies; managerial attempts to individualize and localize industrial relations. The rationale for such policies is to avoid the errors of the past. It is generally accepted, not least by union officials, that within a workplace it is managerial action that has the major impact in creating collective thinking, trade unionism and effective opposition to management. Many managers also believe that significant problems have arisen from the involvement in industrial relations of those outside the workplace or the organization. It is as a direct reaction to these two views that managements are seeking to individualize and localize industrial relations.

New technology aids this approach in two ways: by improving and reducing the size of workplaces, and by its potential for aiding communication. Apart from the new technology, managements are exercising deliberate choice to develop relationships with individuals rather than groups. It is particularly the direct, face-to-face mechanisms that are becoming increasingly fashionable. One popular new approach has been dubbed MBWA (to distinguish it from the widely accepted, cold, scientific MBO, management by objectives). MBWA stands for 'management by wandering about' (ie 'visible' management). This is, of course, what managers in small organizations have always done but it has now been rediscovered as a 'new' management fad. Alongside such simple prescriptions there has been a growth in other forms of direct communication (see Chapter 11).

A second strand in this process of individualization is that of variable pay. The whole thrust of the move towards PRP involves both a greater role for immediate managerial superiors in determining each individual's pay; and an increasing differentiation of pay even among groups who are performing identical roles. The earlier discussion of this issue (and that in Chapter 14) shows how, from a managerial viewpoint, one advantage of such pay systems is their ability to discriminate, at a detailed level, between individuals – to split the interests of members of a workgroup.

The new working arrangements, varied working hours and more casualized forms of employment contract also act to fragment the workforce. Together with individually tailored training and development programmes, career planning and promotion policies, they act to differentiate between employees. Increasingly, each individual has less in common with the other people employed at the same workplace. Each of these policies has an intrinsic logic of its own, but for managements the increased segmentation of the workforce that each provides is more than just a bonus: it is a calculated strategic benefit.

Individualization goes hand in hand with management strategies for localization (see Chapter 9). But there is a limit to the processes of individualization and localization. For the foreseeable future most managers will have to deal with trade unions. Analysing the management of trade union relationships is a difficult task. At the very least there are a number of potential strategies available, and no evidence that any one is more closely correlated with the overall efficiency and success of the enterprise than any other.

Managerial support for trade unions remains widespread in the UK. There is evidence, though, that in the 1980s managers choose to deal with a non-union workforce if they can. Most new businesses set up in new towns are non-union. On greenfield sites managements have preferred not to recognize a union or only to recognize a single union for all employees (Chapter 9).

Commentators have identified two distinct managerial strategies in the non-union companies. The first of these has been dubbed traditionalist: all-out forceful opposition to the unions. The second has been given the title of *sophisticated paternalists*: non-union companies (mostly) who devote considerable resources to ensuring that their treatment of employees gives little ground for trade union complaint and spend considerable sums on promoting the company to its own employees. Marks and Spencer is the most famous British example, and the group includes US companies like IBM and Kodak, and some of the Japanese companies operating in the UK.

For most managers a non-union or single union workplace is not feasible. They have little choice but to deal with a number of unions. Two distinct strategies have been identified here, too. The *sophisticated moderns* recognize trade unions but encourage extensive consultation procedures and practices. They, too, tend to have centralized arrangements and to encourage a commitment to the overall company. The *standard moderns* are decentralized and pragmatic, with different approaches adopted at different locations or at different times.

This analysis of strategy[19] is helpful in distinguishing between such approaches. It was developed at a time when the trade unions were felt to be very strong. The distinctions may be becoming blurred. There are two key decisions to be made by managements in industrial relations: do we accept the trade unions and, if we do, how do we manage them? The two approaches to keeping the unions out are clear and are used by many successful organizations. Most managements, however, prefer to, or feel they have to, deal with unions, and with a multiplicity of them. In general, larger companies in the public and private sector are developing strategies which amount to an amalgam of the sophisticated and standard modern approaches. These involve an extensive and heavily resourced internal communications exercise, built around the concept of individualization, the encouragement of localization or decentralization on a pragmatic basis and the development of a planned, strategic approach to industrial relations.

Managements are not, in general, 'taking the union on'. Rather, a more subtle process is taking place. Managements are changing the nature of their relationship with their unions. They are organizing complementary forms of communications channels alongside traditional collective bargaining arrangements. Many of these amount to a form of 'internal PR'; public relations for the employees rather than the customers. Thus, many companies now regularly tell employees about new orders or contracts, new technological breakthroughs or current advertising campaigns. Fifty-eight per cent of organizations in the UK with over 200 employees have developed coherent 'mission statements' that they spend much time propounding to employees.[20] In modern industry or commerce and in most areas of the public sector, it is employee commitment and enthusiasm that marks out the successful organization. Communications channels are being used as part of the attempt to generate such commitment.

At the same time managements are looking for genuine upward communication, as long as it is related to work and quality of production or service. Upward communication on policy issues is not encouraged. There is substantial evidence that employees can make a positive and valuable contribution in terms of ideas about efficiency and quality if they are encouraged to do so. Managers are increasingly looking at the variety of quality circles, work improvement schemes and other techniques to harness these ideas.

The effect of these developments is to downgrade the union functions. Straightforward, head-on attacks on the unions generate employee commitment to their representative group and are often counter-productive. A more subtle process of providing far more channels and more opportunities for employees to make a contribution means that the union ceases to be the main channel and becomes one of many. The collective bargaining system is increasingly limited to straight 'pay and conditions' issues. Employees are encouraged to look elsewhere for means of dealing with management on all other issues.

Developments in the collective bargaining arena are covered in detail in Chapters 6, 8 and 9. Here it suffices to note that as union strength, real or perceived, has decreased, and as managerial pressure for flexibility and adaptability has increased, so managers are developing policies built around the concept of single bargaining units. Managers are insisting that they will only meet with the unions as a single body; they are refusing to deal with each union in turn, and asking the unions to resolve any differences among themselves before any subject is brought to management. Such a strategy risks uniting the unions against management, but diminished union power has reduced any threat here. The corresponding benefits for management are substantial.

Managers must balance two facts: the pressure to manage human resources as efficiently as any other resources; and the fact that this particular resource is unique, it thinks and reacts. Hence the evidence, continually galling to a succession of Conservative Government speakers in the 1980s, that managers, strong as they are in relation to the unions, are still in general prepared to work with them and to negotiate wage increases above inflation.

For the purpose of this chapter the different elements of a managerial approach to industrial relations have been described in broad outline and with few caveats. It must be recognized, however, that clearly-thought-through managerial policies on industrial relations are rare. While many managements have developed or adapted particular aspects of the approaches outlined here, few have created a coherent, consistent and comprehensive set of policies. And, of course, there are many managements who pay very little attention to their employees.

Nevertheless, the elements identified here are significant. It is more likely that such approaches will be extended than that they will be reversed. The pressures that led to these developments and the opportunities that made them possible were identified at the beginning of this chapter and are, in the main, unlikely to change. There is much debate about whether Britain is developing a 'new industrial relations'; less antagonistic, more consultative and co-operative. If there is a new industrial relations is it simply a temporary reaction to recession, or is it a major change? On one side the argument runs that nothing has changed the inherently conflictive nature of industrial relations, that union quiescence is determined by weakness, that major disputes among miners, teachers and telecommunications workers show that a change in the economy will re-establish old patterns. On the other side it is argued that there are fewer strikes, declining union and employers' association memberships, increased consultation and co-operation: a new climate.

The analysis proffered here suggests a third interpretation; that managements have learnt from the past and are developing new policies in industrial relations. These policies are being built carefully upon new working practices, new working patterns and new contractual arrangements. They recognize the antagonistic possibilities and the conflicts of interest which go alongside the conjunction of interest of management and employees. Rather than fight that battle head-on, however, they are utilizing a more subtle and complex strategy, using consultation and collective bargaining together with other channels, and working carefully to reduce the importance of the trade union relationship.

The elements of this new approach, taken separately or together, raise many issues far beyond the scope of this book. However, it would be disingenuous not to note that this approach raises at least three wider questions. The first concerns the extent to which society at large can, through the medium of social security payments, employment support schemes and training schemes, support the costs of maintaining flexible workforces in employing organizations. The second question is about the overall effect on society and the economy of large numbers of people pressured to be, rather than choosing to be, in marginalized employment. The third area of debate is whether the analysis is accurate. Is it cost-competitiveness that is the fundamental problem? How does this relate to the argument that it may be more important to develop the ability to switch product or service quickly in response to markets, ie 'flexible specialization'?

Whatever the answers to such questions, the fact remains that there are increasing numbers of managements devoting substantial attention to their human resources, and developing planned strategies for dealing with their employees and the trade unions. Such policies and strategies have proven to be largely successful in helping managements to achieve predictability and control in industrial relations. Changes in employment law will affect the speed of these developments but will not reverse them. Managements will remain the dominant players on the industrial relations stage over at least the next decade.

References

1. Aspects of this analysis of HRM are drawn from Brewster, C and Bournois, F (1991) 'Human Resource Management: a European perspective', *Personnel Review*, 20, 6 pp 4–14; and Brewster, C and Holt Larsen, H (1992, forthcoming) 'Human Resource Management in Europe: evidence from ten countries', *International Journal of Human Resource Management*, Vol 3, 3.
2. See, for example, Storey, J (ed. 1989) *New Perspectives on Human Resource Management*, Routledge, London; Freedman, A (1991) *The Changing Human Resources Function*, The Conference Board, New York; Hendry, C and Pettigrew, A (1990) 'HRM: an agenda for the 1990s', *International Journal of Human Resource Management*, Vol 1,1, pp 17–25; Beaumont, P (1991) 'The US Human Resource Management literature: a review', in Salaman, G (ed) *Human Resource Strategies*.
3. Legge, K (1989) 'Human Resource Management: a critical analysis', in Storey, op cit, p 40. See also Guest, D (1989) 'Personnel and HRM: can you tell the difference?', *Personnel Management*, January, pp 48–51.
4. Hendry and Pettigrew, op cit; Beaumont, op cit; Legge, op cit.
5. Fombrun, C, Tichy, N and Devanna, M (eds) (1984) *Strategic Human Resource Management*, John Wiley, New York.
6. Beer, M, Lawrence, P R, Mills, Q N and Walton, R E (1985) *Human Resource Management*, Free Press, New York.
7. Cook, R and Armstrong, M (1990) 'The search for strategic HRM', *Personnel Management*, December, pp 30–3
8. Schein, E (1987) 'Increasing organizational effectiveness through better HR planning and development', in Schein, E (ed), *The Art of Managing Human Resources*, Oxford University Press, New York, pp 25–45.
9. Brewster, C and Connock, S (1985) *Industrial Relations: Cost-Effective Strategies*, Hutchinson, London.
10. Daniel, W W (1987) *Workplace Industrial Relations and Technical Change*, Frances Pinter, London.
11. Price Waterhouse Cranfield Project Annual Report 1991, Cranfield School of Management, UK.
12. See Pollert, A (ed) (1991) *Farewell to Flexibility*, Basil Blackwell, Oxford; and Syrett, M and Leighton, P (1989) *New Work Patterns: Putting Policy into Practice*, Pitman, London.
13. Wright, V (1991) 'Performance-related pay', in Neale, F (ed) *The Handbook of Performance Management*, IPM, London. See also Chapter 14 of this *Handbook*.
14. ACAS Annual Report, 1989; Ingram, P (1991) 'Ten years of manufacturing wage settlements: 1979–89', *Oxford Review of Economic Policy*, pp 93–106; Bevan, S and Thompson, M (1991) 'Performance Management at the Crossroads', *Personnel Management*, November, pp 36–39.
15. Hegewisch, A (1991) 'The decentralisation of pay bargaining: European comparisons', *Personnel Review*, 20, 6, pp 29–37.
16. Ward, J M (1988) Foreword, in Chase, R L (ed) *Total Quality Management*, IFS Publications/Springer Verlag, Berlin.
17. Guest, D (forthcoming) 'Current perspectives on Human Resource Management in the United Kingdom', in Brewster et al *Human Resource Management in Europe*, Routledge, London.

18. For more on the debate about quality management, see Hill, S (1991) 'Why quality circles failed but Total Quality Management might succeed' *British Journal of Industrial Relations*, April, pp 541–68; and Wilkinson, A and Witcher, B (1991) 'Fitness for use? Barriers to full TQM in the UK', *Management Decision*, August, pp 46–51.

19. Purcell, J and Sisson, K (1983) 'Strategies and practice in the management of industrial relations', in Bain (ed) *Industrial Relations in Britain*, Blackwell, Oxford; following Fox, A (1974) *Beyond Contract. Work, Power and Trust Relations*, Faber and Faber, London.

20. Price Waterhouse Cranfield Project Annual Report 1991, Cranfield School of Management, UK.

Chapter Six
Approaches to Trade Union Recognition

P B Beaumont and B Towers

INTRODUCTION

The period 1979–92 represents the longest ever period of sustained decline in union membership in Britain since records began in 1892. Although there is some disagreement as to the leading individual factors responsible for this fall in membership, there is now general agreement that union membership is disproportionately concentrated in older industries, older companies and older plants, with the union movement very much needing to make membership inroads into newer, more recently established organizations.

This perspective has resulted in the subject area of recognition assuming a much higher profile in union discussions, deliberations and activities in recent years. At the same time, however, the ACAS Annual Report for 1991 (p 21) suggested that a slowly growing number of employers were increasingly beginning to question the benefits (and costs) of union recognition and to consider the possibility of derecognizing unions.[1] Accordingly in this chapter we look in turn at the experience with statutory recognition provisions in Britain, consider various voluntary routes or mechanisms for achieving recognition, examine the recent thinking of the TUC on recognition arrangements, briefly refer to the workings of statutory recognition arrangements in the US and Canada, and then look at the issues of single recognition deals and union derecognition. As a preliminary comment to these discussions it is important to note the traditional distinction in Britain between full recognition (ie the establishment of collective bargaining arrangements) and partial or limited recognition, the latter typically giving unions representational rights on behalf of individual employees within disciplinary and grievance procedures.

STATUTORY RECOGNITION PROVISIONS IN BRITAIN

In Britain, at least since the Report of the Royal Commission on Labour of 1891–4, numerous public pronouncements have been made in favour of encouraging union organization and collective bargaining arrangements. However, such pronouncements were rarely backed up by tangible measures, with no general legal support for union recognition existing before the 1970s. Such legal support was not historically sought by the unions because when they were growing they could use their bargaining strength to achieve recognition and, in any case, were afraid of unacceptable quid pro quos being attached to the legal support. In 1969 the Commission on Industrial Relations (CIR) was established (without any detailed working rules laid down in statute) and reported on 13 recognition references before the Industrial Relations Act came into force in 1971. This Act's provisions for statutory recognition procedures (s 46) were broadly in line with the Donovan Commission's recommendations (except that they could be initiated by both trade unions and employers, as well as by the Secretary of State) and did not lead to any significant changes in the methods which had been developed by the Commission for handling recognition references in the first two years of operation. Between 1971 and 1974 the Commission reported on some 30 recognition cases.

In total, approximately two-thirds of the cases handled by the CIR between 1969 and 1974, which involved the principle of trade union recognition, resulted in recommendations in favour of the union(s). However, one study found that only about half of these recommendations had been implemented in practice, with the result that collective bargaining coverage had been extended to approximately 14,000 extra employees.[2] The same study also raised some important questions about the length of time taken to hear recognition claims (as in the US where the longer it takes to hear a recognition claim, the less likely the union is to win it), as well as the strength of sanctions for employer non-compliance with recommendations for recognition.

The second experience with statutory recognition procedures (ie ss 11–16 of the Employment Protection Act 1975) occurred in the years 1976–80. These procedures allowed an independent trade union to refer a recognition issue to ACAS, which then had a duty to examine the issue, to seek to resolve it by conciliation if appropriate and, failing that, to make further inquiries and prepare a written report. The available procedures appeared to give ACAS wide discretion and flexibility in pursuing its recognition inquiries and reaching its conclusions (similar to the position of the CIR), although it was required to:

- have regard at all times to the desirability of encouraging the settlement of the issue by agreement and where appropriate to seek to assist a settlement by conciliation;
- consult all parties whom it considered would be affected by the outcome of the reference;
- ascertain, in the course of its inquiries, the opinion of workers to whom the issue related;
- prepare, if the issue was not settled and the reference not withdrawn, a written report setting out its findings, any advice in connection with those findings, and any recommendations for recognition, with reasons, or the reasons for not making a recommendation;
- specify in any recommendation the employer, trade union and description of workers to whom it related, whether it was for recognition generally or in respect of specified matters, and the level at which recognition was recommended;
- send a copy of such a report to every trade union and employer concerned in the issue, and to such other persons as ACAS thought fit.

The Act provided that a trade union which had received a recommendation for recognition could complain to ACAS of any non-compliance by the employer. In certain circumstances such a complaint of non-compliance could lead to an award of terms and conditions by the Central Arbitration Committee (the CAC).

Some research has revealed that essentially similar problems (from the unions' point of view) to those during the CIR years (ie employer delays at the ballot stage and non-compliance with recommendations) were also associated with this particular set of arrangements.[3] These procedures were repealed by the Employment Act 1980, following the expression of difficulties and concerns by ACAS in operating them. At the time, the unions were not strenuously opposed to the repeal of these procedures on the grounds that, first, they had derived only limited *direct* gains (ie a 35 per cent union win rate, resulting in some 65,000 additional workers being covered by collective bargaining) due to a combination of i) employer delays (particularly centring around the definition of the appropriate bargaining unit) at the ballot stage; ii) a failure to negotiate first agreements; and iii) an increasing entanglement in complex, unfavourable court proceedings and legal judgments (such as in the highly publicized Grunwick case). Second, their belief that a more satisfactory, alternative public policy based route to recognition (ie voluntary conciliation facilities), which had yielded a higher union win rate (ie 43 per cent) in the years 1976–80 was still to remain in force. In the next section, however, we indicate that this initial union satisfaction with the voluntary conciliation route to recognition has essentially evaporated in recent times. As a footnote to the 1976–80 experience, it is worth noting that statutory recognition provisions have remained in place much longer in Northern Ireland, were operated in a rather different manner* and certainly yielded a higher union win rate (ie 51 per cent) at least in the years 1977–8/1982–3.[4]

VOLUNTARY ROUTES TO RECOGNITION

In the years prior to the decade of the 1980s, one can reasonably characterize the role and process of membership recruitment and organizing within union circles in Britain as being non-specialist, reactive, decentralized and low profile in nature. This characterization follows from the following facts: relatively few unions employed specialist recruitment officers; the full-time officers of most unions spent only a limited amount of time on recruitment activities; union training courses were overwhelmingly concerned with developing negotiating, as opposed to recruitment skills; the alleged existence of a centralized recruitment strategy in an individual union rarely involved anything more than a tendency to concentrate on larger-sized organizations; and the norm in recruitment tactics was for unions to react or respond to potential or actual members who first approached them about organizing possibilities at their particular place of employment. (To some researchers,[5] this characterization remains a reasonably accurate picture of the present-day position, despite union rhetoric to the contrary.)

This view of the organizing/recruitment process by unions should be seen in the light of the following facts and considerations. First, as mentioned in the

---

* For example, the Northern Ireland Labour Relations Agency, in contrast to ACAS, had more discretion to commence and complete inquiries, and had an express right to refer disputes to the relevant inter-union machinery.

previous section, statutory union recognition procedures have only ever operated in Britain in the years 1971–4 and 1976–80. Traditionally, British unions
have attempted to recruit members and obtain recognition for collective
bargaining purposes by essentially voluntary means, including some limited use
having been made of third party conciliation facilities. (This fact should not
obscure the all-important, historical role of the government in successfully
'pressuring' employers' associations to recognize unions in the two war-time
periods.) Secondly, even the high union growth years of the 1970s (when overall
union density increased from some 45 to 55 per cent of the workforce) were not
particularly associated with new, innovatory union recruitment strategies and
tactics in the relatively underorganized areas of the labour market. These years
essentially involved the growth of closed shop and membership dues check-off
arrangements, and the consolidation of membership in the already relatively
highly organized public sector and manufacturing industries sector. The result
was that in the 1970s the proportion of the workforce covered by collective
bargaining arrangements showed nothing like the growth that occurred in union
membership. Finally, the conventional academic wisdom prior to the 1980s[6] was
that an overall growth in union membership was highly contingent upon a
favourable economic and political environment, with the particular recruitment
strategies and tactics of individual unions (such as they were) often not being
particularly successful, and certainly contributing little to overall membership
growth.

Historically, the leading voluntary routes to union recognition in Britain have
been:

- negotiation;
- recognition by extension (ie the recognition arrangements of existing plants
  in a multi-plant firm being automatically extended and applied to any new
  plants acquired or built); and
- voluntary conciliation.

In the remainder of this section we will present in turn various facts, findings
and developments centring around these three particular routes or mechanisms.
As an initial starting point, the 1980 workplace industrial relations survey
contained information on the means by which a sub-set of written recognition
arrangements for both manual and non-manual workers had come about in the
period 1976–80. The basic results obtained from an analysis of this data set were
as follows:[7]

	Manuals	*Non-manuals*
By negotiation/discussion	71.6%	73.9%
By extension	18.7%	14.5%
By ballot (ACAS)	5.2%	11.6%
By industrial action	4.5%	—

The obvious point to make here is that the vast majority of these cases of
recognition had come about through (the potentially heterogeneous) means of
discussion and negotiation. Furthermore, the 1984 workplace industrial relations
survey asked the sub-set of non-union establishments whether any union had

attempted to recruit members and/or obtain recognition there in the five years 1979–84. The basic information from the survey revealed the following picture:[8]
1) for the 501 establishments that did not have manual unions present in 1984 there were 73 attempts to recruit members and 19 requests for recognition, and 2) for the 788 establishments that did not have non-manual unions present in 1984 there were 87 attempts to recruit members and 21 requests for recognition. In short, it appears that recruitment/recognition attempts (albeit all unsuccessful) were made for manual employees in some 18 per cent of non-union workplaces in 1979–84, while for non-manual employees the figure was some 13 per cent.

At first glance these figures would not seem to suggest a particularly 'impressive' organizing performance by the unions; the vast majority of non-union workplaces saw no organizing attempt made in these years, and the proportion where an attempt was made was greater for manual than for non-manual workers, which does not seem an obviously desirable tendency in view of the current trends in the overall occupational distribution of the workforce. However, any judgement along such lines needs to recognize the fact that, firstly, we have no information on the extent and characteristics of successful organizing attempts among the population of non-union establishments in these years; and secondly, it needs to be acknowledged that the supply of union organizing services is not without limit. That is, unions need to balance their institutional needs for new members against the needs to adequately service their existing members, particularly in the adverse labour market circumstances of the time.

In recent years a number of unions have sought to build on the traditional, negotiating route to recruitment and recognition by initiating a number of more non-conventional organizing campaigns. Prominent among these has been the TGWU's 'Link-Up' campaign which was launched in 1987 to consolidate existing areas of strength, and extend organization into new and neglected areas of the labour market (eg women, young workers, ethnic minorities). The TUC also orchestrated concentrated recruitment and recognition campaigns at Trafford Park and London Dockland, although by all reports these were not obviously notable successes. Such commentators have raised some questions concerning the unions' ability to adequately sustain these campaigns over the course of time in view of the existing workloads, priorities, training etc of the full-time officers of the unions concerns.[9] Furthermore, other academics have questioned the extent of tangible commitment to these union campaigns. For example, the questionnaire responses obtained from 56 unions revealed that:[10] 79 per cent had initiated recruitment campaigns in the years 1985–9 (compared to only 39 per cent in the period 1980–4); only 15 unions could assess the success of these campaigns; only 10 had designated a union officer with the responsibility for national recruitment; and only 9 had a specific recruitment budget.

The second voluntary route to recognition has been that of 'extension', whereby a multi-establishment organization which recognizes unions in its existing establishments automatically extends recognition to any newly opened or acquired facilities, as, for example, the well-known arrangements or agreements along these lines which exist between Asda stores and GMB. As we saw from the earlier figures from the 1980 workplace industrial relations survey, this has been a not insignificant route to recognition in the past. Unfortunately, there has been relatively little systematic research on the characteristics of organizations which operate such arrangements, and any resulting impact on the level of union membership etc. However, some individuals have voiced certain criticisms of the nature of such arrangements, such as the following:[11]

> The move into the country has not necessarily meant the establishment of non-union plants. While it would be reasonable to expect lower levels of unionization in these areas, in-going plants, especially those of larger companies with established recognition agreements and elaborate industrial relations systems, will often have stitched up recognition deals for outlying plants before they have even opened their gates. A captive membership may gladden the heart of union finance officers . . . but it will do little for those long-sighted enough to appreciate the value of spontaneity.

In short, the contention above is that recognition by extension arrangements may not result in a membership reasonably highly committed to the union concerned. However, this may be the least of the unions' worries if employers in Britain become increasingly reluctant to recognize and not least to automatically extend recognition to any newly opened facilities. For example, Unigate Dairies in 1991 originally excluded the TGWU from recognition in its new greenfield site plant (where it was determined to introduce team working, single status arrangements etc), although it recognized unions in its ten other plants. If more and more employers seek to make moves along these lines then one will increasingly observe (what has been termed in the US) 'double-breasted' operations, whereby multi-establishment organizations operate both union and non-union establishments, with the latter being very much the newer, more recently established ones. Indeed, the current extent of non-uniform recognition arrangements, particularly among white-collar employees, in large, multi-establishment organizations, is not inconsiderable in Britain.[12]

The final, traditional voluntary route to recognition in Britain has involved the use of third-party conciliation facilities. The use of conciliation to resolve recognition disputes has not always been popular with individual conciliation officers (who feel they may be viewed by the employer as an agent working on behalf of the union), and certainly the unions have generally viewed it as a weapon of 'last resort' – ie to be utilized only when all other avenues of approach have been used and exhausted. This being said, we noted in the previous section that the union win rates via voluntary conciliation exceeded that under the statutory procedures in the years 1976–80. However, what has happened since then? The first point to note is that the number of union recognition claims going to conciliation has fallen quite substantially (ie 697 in 1976 to 174 in 1991). Secondly, the union win rate has also fallen; in the Scottish region of ACAS the union win rate (ie full recognition achieved) fell from 41 per cent in 1976 to 29 per cent in 1985.[13] The contents of Table 6.1 below, which covers three ACAS regions, clearly indicates the small number of claims and the limited extent of union success in obtaining recognition in recent years.

In short, what is observed here is that, since the repeal of the statutory recognition procedures (with their all-important *indirect* effects on the operation of the voluntary conciliation process) and the changed labour market

Table 6.1 *Union recognition claims and outcomes, three ACAS regions, 1990–1*

	Region 1		Region 2		Region 3	
	1990	1991	1990	1991	1990	1991
Claims	12	8	16	5	12	13
Full recognition	3	0	4	2	3	3
Partial recognition	1	1	1	0	0	3
No recognition	8	7	11	3	9	7

circumstances of the 1980s and 1990s, the voluntary conciliation route to recognition has essentially 'dried up' from the union point of view: the 1991 ACAS Annual Report indicated that the union win rate was 33 per cent, approximately half of which involved full collective bargaining rights and the remainder, representational rights. This is undoubtedly an important part of the background to the recently revived interest of the TUC in the possible role and value of statutory recognition procedures. It is to this subject which we now turn.

RECENT TUC THINKING CONCERNING STATUTORY RECOGNITION PROCEDURES

At the 1989 Trades Union Congress one of the motions passed called for the future establishment of a legally enforceable threshold of trade union membership at individual workplaces, which would lead to automatic trade union recognition. In 1991 this process was moved a stage further forward with the publication of a TUC discussion document which suggested the following four-stage procedure.

1. *Representation* – any worker would have the right to be represented by a union in, for example, health and safety, maternity rights, equal pay and discrimination issues, even in the absence of any other union members in the workplace.
2. *Union facilities* – where the union had 10 per cent membership there would be a right for representatives to time off work for union duties and training.
3. *Consultation* – a 20 per cent membership figure in a given bargaining unit would give the union the right to be consulted on issues such as the procedures for declaring redundancies.
4. *Negotiations* – this would result from the union's demonstrating via a petition the existence of a membership level of 40 or 50 per cent.

These proposals have undergone considerable discussion and some revision within union circles (eg the 40–50 per cent threshold for recognition being dropped in favour of reference to 'substantial membership support'), and are likely to remain the focus of considerable further debate and examination. The urgency of this will, however, have receded considerably, with the Conservatives winning a fourth consecutive term of office. Questions and reservations on the substance of the proposals do, however, remain. For instance, is the staged approach feasible, what membership levels are appropriate for each stage and what enforcement mechanisms (eg binding arbitration?) are necessary? More generally, it is not difficult to detect some considerable unease and uncertainty among unions about the future possible role of statutory recognition provisions in the British system. Indeed, conversations with individual trade union officers suggest that there are three primary areas of concern in this regard. The first is the view that statutory procedures have not worked well in the past and hence are unlikely to work well in the future. The worry here is that certain past problems (eg defining an appropriate bargaining unit, employer delays at the ballot stage, the difficulty of ensuring employer compliance with any recommendations in favour of recognition) are *inherent* in the nature of such provisions. The second concern is about *quid pro quos*. The fear here is that a logical accompaniment to statutory recognition provisions is statutory derecognition provisions, with the operation of the latter likely to undermine or offset any membership gains made through the former arrangements. The third is a more general concern that statutory recognition provisions will be given undue importance by individual unions and absorb too much in the way of their organizing resources, to the detriment of their larger, voluntary based organizing initiatives.

In considering the possible future of statutory recognition provisions in Britain, the TUC have expended some considerable time and effort in looking at experience with such arrangements in other countries, with a view to identifying any possible useful lessons. The next section follows a similar approach by looking at the positions in the US and Canada. The reason for choosing these two particular countries is that they appear to convey very different messages about the potential value of statutory recognition procedures. That is, one (the US) appears to offer an essentially negative lesson for unions in Britain, whereas the other (Canada) appears to offer a much more positive one. This divergence in experience is all-important, as it seems to call into question any view that problems (from the unions' point of view) with statutory recognition procedures are inherent in the nature of such procedures.

STATUTORY RECOGNITION PROVISIONS: THE US AND CANADA

In the US, s 7a of the Wagner Act, enacted at the time of the New Deal, enshrines in law the right of employees 'to form, join or assist labor organizations'. The agency established to administer this, the National Labor Relations Board (NLRB), is authorized to conduct elections among employees in a designated bargaining unit to determine whether there is a majority support for a union. Where this is found to be the case, the union is certificated as the bargaining agent for the unit for the purposes of collective bargaining. In recent years it is apparent that the unions are losing the majority of union representation elections, a result generally attributed to the strength of employer opposition which may take either legal forms (eg delays, use of consultants) or illegal (eg unfair labour practices, such as the dismissal of union activists).[14] Moreover, even in the minority of cases where the unions win at the ballot stage, recognition or representation has not come about in a substantial number of cases due to management opposition hindering the negotiation of first contracts.

In the unions' view they are no longer operating on a 'level playing field' in the matter of securing representation or recognition, with the loopholes in the

The difficulty is that such a supportive approach is not on the present political agenda, given Labour's defeat in the General Election. The remaining, and longer term question is should it be? This question can be approached in two dimensions – at the place of work and in the wider, political context.

Collective bargaining is still widely supported by employers who see value in continuing relationships of trust with elected representatives who can speak for a substantial number of employees. This practical aspect does, however, lie alongside a *moral* issue. If a substantial proportion of employees in a bargaining unit (arguably in excess of 50 per cent) are members of a trade union or trade unions and wish that fact to be reflected through collective bargaining and representation arrangements, should this be a *right*? In the US, for example, this has been the case for over 50 years in the private sector and more than 20 in the federal services. Furthermore, in the case of unions already enjoying full recognition, should employers have the unfettered legal freedom to reduce it to representation only or even remove it entirely?

In the wider, political context individual employers refusing recognition or withdrawing it have a collective impact upon trade unions in society which has implications much beyond the effective management of their individual enterprises. Trade unions, for all their faults, remain an integral and important part of the system of checks and balances which make up capitalist, liberal democracies. The trade unions' ability to oppose, to bargain, to organize – even to exist – is already under some challenge and this would be strengthened should a derecognition movement prosper. Government and employers should at least give some thought to the wider implications of their policies and actions.

References

1. See also Towers, B (1988) 'Trends and developments in industrial relations: derecognising trade unions: implications and consequences', *Industrial Relations Journal*, Vol 19, No 3, pp 181–5.
2. James, B (1977) 'Third party intervention in recognition disputes: the role of the Commission on Industrial Relations', *Industrial Relations Journal*, Vol 8.
3. Beaumont, P B (1981) *Trade Union Recognition: The British Experience 1976–80*, Employee Relations Monograph, Vol 3, No 6.
4. Beaumont, P B (1987) *The Decline of Trade Union Organisation*, Croom Helm, London, pp 76–84.
5. Mason, R and Bain, P (1991) 'Trade union recruitment strategies: facing the 1990s' *Industrial Relations Journal*, Vol 22, pp 36–46.
6. Bain, G S (1970) *The Growth of White Collar Unionism*, Oxford University Press, Oxford.
7. Beaumont, P B and Harris, R I D (1992) 'Double breasted recognition arrangements in Britain', *International Journal of Human Resource Management*, Vol 3, No 3, September.
8. Beaumont, P B and Harris, R I D (1990) 'Union recruitment and organising attempts in Britain in the 1980s', *Industrial Relations Journal*, Vol 21, No 4, Winter.
9. Kelly, J and Heery, E (1989) 'Full time officers and trade union recruitment', *British Journal of Industrial Relations*, Vol 27, No 2, July, pp 196–213.
10. Mason and Bain, op cit.
11. Lane, T (1982) 'The unions caught on an ebb tide', *Marxism Today*, Vol 26, No 9, September, p 9.
12. Beaumont and Harris (1992) op cit.

13. Beaumont, P B (1987) 'Individual union success in obtaining recognition: some British evidence', *British Journal of Industrial Relations*, Vol 25, No 3, November, pp 323–34.
14. Freeman, R B and Medoff, J L (1984) *What Do Unions Do?*, Basic Books, New York, Chapter 15.
15. Weiler, P (1980) *Reconcilable Differences*, Carswell, Toronto, pp 37–56.
16. Chaison, G N and Rose, J B (1990) 'New directions and divergent paths: the North American labor movements in troubled times', *Proceedings of the Industrial Relations Research Association*, Spring, pp 591–6.
17. *IRS Employment Trends No 482*, 22 February 1991, p 5.
18. Beaumont, P B and Harris, R I D (1992) 'Scotland: where have all the trade union members gone?', *Quarterly Economic Commentary, Fraser of Allander Institute*, Vol 17, March, pp 47–64.
19. Freeman, R B (1989) 'The changing status of unionism around the world', in Huang, W-C (ed) *Organized Labor at the Cross Roads*, Kalamazoo, Michigan, Upjohn Institute, pp 111–38.
20. Blanchflower, D G and Freeman, R B (1991) 'Going different ways: unionism in the US and other advanced OECD countries', *National Bureau of Economic Research*, Working Paper No 3342.
21. Claydon, T (1989) 'Union derecognition in Britain in the 1980s', *British Journal of Industrial Relations*, Vol 27, pp 214–24.
22. Cited in *Industrial Relations Review and Report*, No 388 May 1991.

Chapter Seven
Negotiations

Ramsumair Singh

Negotiating plays a central role over a wide range of human activity. Dunlop has rightly observed that, 'Negotiations is (sic) the process of changing positions and making concessions from initial positions in the course of moving towards an agreement.'[1] Negotiating is, of course, used to resolve disputes in fields other than industrial relations. These include disputes between husband and wife, between children, and between nation states. But negotiating is more than a possible method of settling differences; it is also a means of preventing them from arising.

There are two primary purposes to negotiating in the industrial relations context. The first is to reconcile differences between managements and unions and the second is to devise ways of advancing the common interest of the parties. The first of these purposes attracts the greater attention in practice, but the second is of no less importance. Indeed, most of the issues that come within the ambit of negotiations are usually a mixture of conflicting as well as common interests. Successful negotiations are therefore *not* conducted only to advance the sectional interest of one party.

This is not to deny that negotiating is conducted by persons who have distinctive purposes of their own. Union representatives are often aspirants for higher office, with supporters and opponents within their own union and sometimes rivals in other unions. Likewise, representatives of management may see negotiations as a way of fostering their own aspirations, and the interests of various parts of the company. Thus the two sides are not *monolithic*, and negotiations must therefore reconcile differences *within* groups as well as *between* groups.

Among managements and trade unions that deal with each other on an ongoing basis, negotiating may at the outset take the character of mutual problem-solving. The process involves the recognition of the common interests of the parties, the areas of agreement and disagreement and possible solutions, to the mutual advantage of both sides. The negotiator's task is not only to gain advantage for his own constituents, but also to develop long-term constructive relationships between the organizations involved in negotiations.

These introductory remarks have been intended to draw attention to the importance of negotiations in resolving disputes. Many disputes could be more efficiently resolved if the negotiators were more skilful and the negotiation process more widely understood. We will therefore explore the practical side of negotiating with some theoretical analysis, with the aim of helping managements and unions to negotiate with each other with greater understanding and insight. The main focus is on negotiations in industrial relations in real-world situations.

PERSPECTIVES ON NEGOTIATIONS

Many influential writers have argued that negotiating is an art. Dunlop states that, 'I am inclined to believe that the art of negotiation can only be learned by experience – often hard experience.'[2] Yet Dunlop concedes that a framework for analysis, and a statement of principles, of negotiations may reduce the learning time or, perhaps, the pain of experience.

Raiffa has argued that there is both an art and science of negotiations.[3] The science is concerned with a systematic analysis of problems, while the art includes interpersonal skills, the ability to convince and be convinced, the ability to use bargaining ploys, and the wisdom to know when and how to use them. Raiffa has, moreover, observed that the art of negotiating has not been well documented; the science is not only in its rudimentary stages but also not very accessible to the practitioner. He concludes that both the art and science have a role to play in negotiating as they can act synergistically.* To a large extent, negotiating in industrial relations is unique and can be differentiated from other types by the following characteristics.

1. Employers and unions expect to have a long-term relationship. Agreement over terms and conditions of employment, and their administration in practice, are essential for the efficient functioning of the organization to which they both belong.
2. The negotiators from managements and unions represent organizations within which there are important differences, and thus the parties to negotiations are not monolithic. Aspirations of a wide range of groups and individuals have to be satisfied. Negotiating is the art of putting together a package that both sides could 'sell' to their constituents. It is therefore essential not to have a 'winner' and a 'loser' in negotiations as this not only makes the agreement hard to sell, but does not make for good industrial relations. It could also reflect on the credibility of the negotiators on the losing side, and affect their attitudes to future negotiations.
3. In general, negotiating is concerned with more than a single issue, or with one issue that can be broken down into a number of component parts for analysis and solution.

Practitioners, of course, often act intuitively in negotiating situations, in ways that are far more sophisticated than they can conceptualize and articulate. Even experienced negotiators can, however, benefit by examining negotiations within a theoretical framework. In this way they gain a deeper understanding of what they are actually doing and can better communicate their insights to others.

MODELS FOR ANALYSING NEGOTIATIONS

A wide variety of models has been used to explain the negotiating process. These models, although mathematically elegant, tend to make a variety of assumptions that are far removed from real-world situations and therefore of

---

* ie work together to the better understanding and greater effectiveness of negotiating.[4]

little use to practitioners. A basic assumption in most theoretical models is that trade unions and managements are made up of monolithic and homogeneous entities. In fact, as already noted, there are often wide differences of opinion within organizations or between members of negotiating teams. These differences are not static but vary over time. A consensus within each party to negotiations is often necessary before a negotiated settlement can be arrived at. Thus, when two organizations are party to negotiations, it takes, in effect, *three* agreements to achieve a negotiated settlement between the parties: an agreement *within* each party and *between* them.

One of the most influential models used in analysing negotiating was proposed by Walton and McKersie. They distinguished four systems of activity or subprocesses in labour negotiations, each having its own functions for the interacting parties. The following subprocesses were distinguished:

- *distributive bargaining*, the function of which is to resolve conflicts between the parties;
- *integrative bargaining*, the function of which is to find common or complementary interests;
- *attitudinal structuring*, the function of which is to influence the attitudes of the participants toward each other;
- *intra-organizational bargaining*, the function of which is to achieve consensus within each of the interacting groups.

While the subprocesses are related and can occur simultaneously, particularly the integrative and distributive subprocesses, conceptually they are quite different.[5]

In discussing the subprocesses in labour negotiations, Walton and McKersie identified distributive bargaining as the dominant activity and noted that:

> Distributive bargaining is central to labor negotiations and is usually regarded as the dominant activity in the union-management relationship. Unions represent employees in the determination of wages, hours, and working conditions. Since these matters involve the allocation of scarce resources, there is assumed to be some conflict of interest between management and unions. The joint-decision process for resolving conflicts of interest is distributive bargaining. The term itself refers to the activity of dividing limited resources. It occurs in situations in which one party wins what the other party loses.[6]

We shall concentrate mainly on distributive bargaining, as it is central to negotiations.

THE DYNAMICS OF NEGOTIATIONS

The purpose of negotiations is to achieve a settlement, often moving from positions that are initially far apart. One may conceptualize this process in the case of two parties bargaining over a wage increase, as shown in Figure 7.1.

In negotiations, managements and unions tend to select the positions most favourable to their own interest. In the case of the union this would be its initial demand (UID) and of management its initial offer (MIO). In reality, one party is unlikely to persuade the other to accept its initial demand or offer, and thus

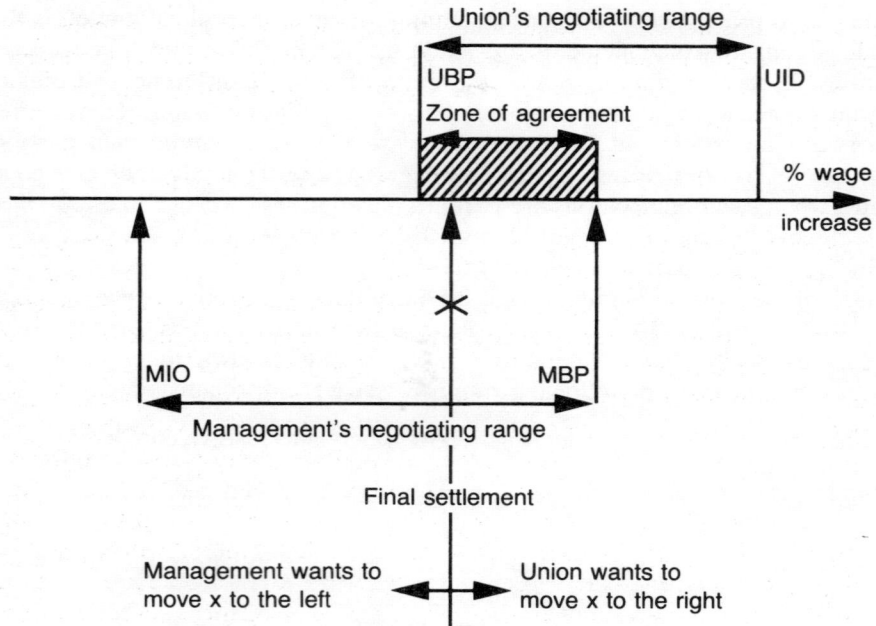

Figure 7.1   *Dynamics of bargaining*
Note if MBP is less than UBP there is no zone of agreement

would have to move towards the other party's position. There is, however, a limit to this process, sometimes referred to as the break-point or fall-back position. This is the critical point beyond which the parties would not go. In Figure 7.1 the union's break-point (UBP) overlaps with the management's break-point (MBP), thereby indicating a zone of agreement. The final settlement x is located within the zone of agreement, and the position of x depends on a number of factors including the relative bargaining power and negotiating skills of the parties.

If the management's break-point is less than the union's break-point, there is no zone of agreement and negotiations may become deadlocked. In this situation one or both parties may resort to sanctions to persuade the other party to adjust its limit and thus achieve a zone of agreement. Alternatively, the parties may resort to third party assistance, such as conciliation, mediation or arbitration, to break the impasse. These methods of intervention are discussed later in the chapter.

In wage negotiations it is usually possible to find a zone of agreement, and to achieve a final settlement within this zone. There are, however, a number of disputes where the parties may feel that fundamental principles are at stake, or for other reasons, such that they are unable to move from their initial positions. The grading of jobs and disciplinary issues often come within the ambit of this category. In this situation the parties may have little alternative but to seek third party assistance to the resolution of the dispute if overt conflict is to be avoided.

Frequently in practice, the parties have an imprecise perception of their own break-points, and make little or no attempt to locate the other party's break-point. Moreover, negotiations are a dynamic process and the break-points may change as negotiations progress. The astute negotiator not only influences the movement of his opponent's break-point in his favour, but also closely monitors this movement.

PREPARATION FOR NEGOTIATIONS

Negotiations cannot be conducted fruitfully unless there is adequate preparation. For successful results the most intensive and detailed preparation is required. The extent of preparation will become readily evident at the negotiating table. A badly-prepared negotiator soon demonstrates that he has little knowledge of the issues under discussion and is not only a liability to his own team but loses the respect of his opponents. In sharp contrast, the well-prepared negotiator stands out and can lead events rather than reacting to them.

Preparing for negotiations is a year-round activity; every piece of information relative to one's negotiating position should be collected and collated, and its future use considered. Management and union, moreover, need to be making continuous studies of changes in wage rates, markets, the introduction of new technology and of industrial trends generally in order to obtain an informed view as to what changes are needed in the union-management agreement. From time to time, specialized studies are made of problems of particular interest to employers or unions and the results of such material could help the parties in negotiations. Moreover, with the use of computers it is now possible to analyse claims in terms of costs and benefits using different parameters.

There are many factors involved in the preparation for negotiations and it is not possible to consider them all. It is, however, helpful to examine a few strategic factors, especially bargaining objectives, bargaining power, and the role of the respective negotiating teams.

Objectives

Only the parties can decide what their objectives are for a particular negotiation. In different negotiations the objectives of the same party may be different. They may, however, be summed up as meeting one or more needs of the participants involved. This view of negotiations is often referred to as the 'need theory of negotiations'.[7] It is useful not only in preparing one's objectives, but also in analysing the strengths and weaknesses of the case of the other side. By defining their objectives the parties will be in a position to set up criteria for evaluation of their negotiating performance.

The formulation of objectives is a multi-disciplinary task, and should not be left entirely to personnel specialists. Persons with expertise in finance, production, sales and other functions have a vital role to play and their views should be sought before agreeing on a set of objectives.

All objectives do not carry the same weight, and exploration of priorities among issues is therefore an important pre-negotiation task. Objectives can conveniently be ranked under three subheadings: essential (E), desirable (D), and optimistic (O). The essential objectives are those which are fundamental to one's negotiating position; the desirable objectives are important but less so than those that are fundamental; the optimistic objectives would be a bonus if achieved, and may be a prelude to some subsequent negotiations. The objectives can be viewed along a *continuum* as shown in Figure 7.2, with essential at the lower end, optimistic at the higher, and desirable in between. Objectives are not static and expectations can change with the circumstances of the negotiations.

Having ranked one's objectives it would be necessary to determine the bargaining range for each issue in accordance with Figure 7.1. Likewise, it would be necessary to establish the linkages between issues and the effect that changes in the parameters of one issue would have on others.

Ranking involves judgement and is to some extent subjective. Objectives when ranked, however, provide a framework for negotiations.[8]

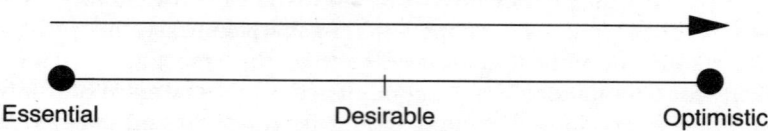

Essential   Desirable   Optimistic

Figure 7.2   *Ranking of objectives*

Bargaining power

Bargaining power has been defined as 'the ability to induce the other side to make concessions that *it would not otherwise make*'.[9] Clearly, it means more than the mere fact of obtaining concessions. Hawkins has suggested that a crucial test of bargaining power is 'whether the cost to one side in accepting a proposal from the other side is higher than the cost of not accepting it'.[10] Bargaining power is, moreover, not static but varies over time. To be of value, assessments of bargaining power would have to be related to a particular time in the negotiating process.[11]

Bargaining power is inherent in any situation where differences have to be reconciled. It is, however, not an end in itself, and negotiations must not rely solely on bargaining power. One side may have enormous bargaining power, but to use it to the point where the other side feels that it is impossible to deal with such a party is to defeat the purpose of negotiations.

The negotiating team

The number of people and specialisms that may compose a negotiating team will depend on many factors, including the importance of the negotiations, the difficulty involved and the time available. In most instances, negotiating will be a team effort because a single negotiator may not have the scope and depth of expertise required. An evaluation of the skills and functions of team members is therefore of crucial importance.

There are three fundamental roles in negotiations: that of team leader or chief negotiator; that of the secretary or recorder; and that of the analyst. The chief negotiator will normally be the most senior member of the team, and his role is to undertake most of the negotiating and to steer the negotiation towards a successful conclusion. The secretary, of course, is responsible for keeping minutes of the meetings but, in addition, should be alert to recognize verbal and non-verbal signals from the opposition. The analyst's role is to scrutinize what is being said; to ask for clarification of ambiguous points; and to summarize the issues, if and when this is appropriate.

Other technical specialists may also be members of the negotiating team, but it is important to define their roles. It may simply be to observe and listen carefully and report on what the opposition is saying. Before going into the negotiations it is essential that team members should understand their roles. The objective is to improve negotiating performance and to facilitate agreement on more favourable terms, or more rapidly, or both.

Role of a deadline

It is now common practice to have an expiry date in substantive agreements, and this allows both sides to plan for negotiations before the agreement expires. Thus, much of the planning can take place in a more relaxed atmosphere than would be the case if the agreement had already expired.

If the parties can agree on a deadline for the negotiating process this serves a useful function: it compels each side to establish priorities and make decisions within a time limit. With a deadline, the temptation to procrastinate is reduced. Conversely, without a deadline both parties can drag their feet and avoid confronting the issues under consideration. If union negotiators perceive management as behaving in this way they may well resort to industrial action to preserve their credibility in the eyes of their members and to focus management's attention on the importance of their claim. This is particularly true where the issue is a major one, such as a pay claim. There can be little doubt that a deadline encourages the parties to make decisions and to keep in focus the consequences of non-agreement.

Agenda

The primary purpose of the agenda is to bring order and structure to the negotiating process. To some extent the agenda reveals the positions of the parties in advance and thus permits each side to prepare a reaction of the issues that are to be discussed.

The issues might be listed so that the major ones are discussed first. Alternatively, minor issues regarded as relatively non-controversial might be listed just so that one side can begin the negotiations by making concessions, hoping that as the issues become more important they will receive concessions in return. Of course, the fact that one side makes concessions may be regarded by the other side as setting a precedent and a feeling may be established that concessions from the conceding side should continue. However, minor issues are sometimes easier to resolve, and their resolution creates an atmosphere of goodwill which can be of great value to both sides when the major and more contentious issues are being discussed.

It may not be possible to negotiate on an item-by-item basis. Items may be strongly linked as, for example, a union's claim for a wage increase which may be linked with management's proposals for increases in productivity. In such a situation it may be useful to combine the items in a package and to conduct negotiations on the package as a whole. If it is perceived by both parties that there are mutual benefits in negotiating on a package basis, the agenda can be planned accordingly and room for manoeuvre may be found which would otherwise be lacking. On the other hand, if a rigid issue-by-issue approach is adopted, both sides may lose room for manoeuvre and a failure to agree on one item may prevent progress from being made on the others. Thus, a valuable means of making progress in negotiations is through the linking of issues which have previously been treated separately.

STAGES OF NEGOTIATIONS

Meetings of any negotiating team may well be said to pass through at least four stages. Initially, there are meetings to review formally the proposals submitted by each side, then comes the development of the cases, followed by the phase of seeking agreement. The final meetings will deal with the closure of negotiations.

Stage 1: the opening moves

There are no strict rules about conducting negotiations but there are some widely accepted negotiating conventions: negotiating should be fair and equitable; existing agreements should be honoured; each side should be prepared to move from its initial positions; sanctions should only be used as a last resort, and then only to assist negotiations and not in place of them. Most importantly, each side should act so as to encourage the development of respect for those on the opposite side of the negotiating table. Mutual respect facilitates understanding and is conducive to successful negotiations.

The introductory stage should set forth the importance of the negotiations and give an indication of the reasonableness of the proposer's case and the premiss on which it rests. The benefits to be gained by the other side if it accepts the proposals should be clearly demonstrated. The need for both parties to gain something from the negotiations cannot be over emphasized.

The position of 'take it or leave it' at the beginning of negotiations is a dangerous ploy for all but the strongest and most prescient. Movement from initial positions is the usual course of negotiations; this is the central aspect of distributive bargaining.

At the beginning of negotiations there is often ambiguity as to the status of various proposals and it is therefore important to clarify ambiguities at the earliest opportunity. Very often there are small issues that can be cleared up immediately, but there may be others that are out of the ordinary which should likewise be clarified. Otherwise, at a given stage in the negotiations it may be unclear as to what exactly is in dispute. In negotiating it is important to remember that there is no agreement until all items in dispute are resolved one way or the other, unless explicitly specified.

Stage II: developing the case

After the first review has been completed a break is necessary to allow each party to examine the proposals advanced by the other party. It is at this point that the negotiator has an opportunity to assess all the proposals together thoroughly.

Some conclusions can now be drawn as to whether a proposal can be accepted in principle, its negotiation range and possible settlement value. It is, moreover, important to note carefully the size of the gap between the two parties in a consideration of one's responses. The chief negotiator should now be in a position to brief team members on how individual items can be dealt with at the bargaining table. This will allow the negotiating team to direct their efforts to possible areas of settlement.

If a compromise is offered it should be drafted, since in drafting it additional features may come to mind and these can be discussed at the time that the proposal is put forward. Nothing is worse than to agree in principle to a proposal, only to find that one side wants to make so many exceptions or refinements to the proposal that the other party feels the need to utter charges of bad faith.

Stage III: seeking agreement

In entering the third stage of negotiation both parties should be in a position to advance specific proposals for settlement. It is, moreover, at this point that management can take the initiative and make the first offer. After all, it is usually the union that has probably made most of the demands, and it is difficult for union negotiators to begin with a reduction in the magnitude of their proposals before there is a definite offer from management.

Such an offer must, moreover, be sufficiently realistic to command the attention of the union side but, more importantly, if an impasse is reached and the offer is rejected by union negotiators or by the union membership, it must not prove an embarrassment to the union negotiators.

In the search for an agreement it is not unusual for requests for concessions from initial positions or previous offers to be accompanied by such phrases as 'this is our final offer' before some deadline or projected break-off in negotiations. There is a wide variety of gambits that negotiators use to encourage the other side to change their positions in distributive bargaining. Two important ones are summarized below.

The pattern of making concessions The number of concessions made would depend on the context, but concessions should be made at the same pace and linked to those of your opponent. In the quest for movement from fixed positions the approach of the hypothetical linked concession is often used. The essence of this approach is that a proposal is made in a hypothetical form, as this allows each side the opportunity of moving from fixed positions without commitment. The hypothetical proposal may call for the abandonment or reduction of some items in response to movement by the other party: 'If your side would reduce your claim from A to B, we would be prepared to reconsider our position on C.' The concession is hypothetical but it is likewise conditional, and it is an attempt to get real movement towards a compromise. Once the opposing side has accepted the hypothetical proposal in principle, this should form the basis of a negotiated settlement. Clearly, the linking of proposals should not be left to chance; they should have been considered during the preparations for negotiations.

Helping the opponent to change positions It may be to one's advantage to let the other side change positions without loss of face. One could, for example, imply that the situation has changed, that new information has come to light or that there has been a genuine misunderstanding. In these circumstances it is not unreasonable for the other party to change its position. Conversely, if a negotiator wishes to move from a position, one approach is to invite the other side to help. It is important to let either side retreat gracefully and with dignity, so that the credibility of negotiators is not undermined in the eyes of their constituents.

Stage IV: closing the negotiations

By the closing stage of negotiations the main features of an agreement should be readily apparent. The task now is to get a successful closure, the end product of which is a formal agreement ready for implementation.

It is not uncommon to find negotiators unable to terminate their negotiations. This is understandable, as they may not know when they have squeezed out every concession from their opponents. Unable to close, they keep negotiating and conceding what appear to be minor concessions but which, taken together, could be costly in financial terms and in setting precedents for future negotiations. The decision as to when to close negotiations is a matter of judgement, but there are some techniques used to get closure, and to a discussion of these we now turn.

1. The *concession closure*. This terminates the negotiations by offering a concession to secure agreement. If the opponent is near to making a final commitment he may be assisted by the offer of a minor inducement conditional on immediate acceptance. The concession should be made in such a way as not to be construed as an indication on the part of the conceding side that further concessions are to be had for the asking.
2. The *summary closure*. This terminates the bargaining procedure by summarizing everything that has been agreed up to that point, emphasizing the concessions made and the benefits to the other side if they accept what is on the table. The party using the summary closure should stress that this is their final offer and that there will be no further movement. If the opposing side accepts, then agreement is possible; if not another strategy may have to be resorted to.
3. The *all or nothing closure*. If the outstanding item is part of a total package, the rest of the package having been agreed to, then an indication is given that unless full agreement can be reached, the entire package is at risk. While this may be an extreme position to take, it can be justified if the negotiations have been on the basis of a package deal or one in which the issues were expressly linked from the outset.

Recording the agreement   When agreement is finally reached, perhaps after long and protracted negotiations, there is often a high degree of euphoria on both sides as the tensions of the negotiations dissipate themselves in the natural relief of achieving an agreement. The euphoria can be soporific, and the negotiators may be tempted to call it a day. This temptation must be firmly resisted until both sides are absolutely clear about the terms of the agreement. A detailed summary must be written and agreed between the parties. The golden rule is: 'Summarize what has been agreed and get agreement that what has been summarized was agreed.'[12] The more complex the subject matter of the negotiations, the more room there is for misunderstanding and memory lapses. The negotiator's task is incomplete until all the items that have been agreed have been put in writing.

Implementing the agreement When the negotiating process has ended in agreement the terms will have to be interpreted and administered. Yet no agreement can provide for all contingencies and there may be minor gaps left in the agreement because full understanding cannot be achieved. It could be that certain administrative problems may have been overlooked during the negotiations. There should therefore be agreed procedures for resolving questions concerning the implementation of the agreement and in filling in such lacunae.

In the process of interpretation and administration of any agreement the parties should develop a set of questions and answers concerning the interpretation of particular clauses, and a complex body of common understandings. This is an ongoing process involving persons at various levels in the firm and in the union, reflecting the symbiotic ties between negotiation, interpretation and administration of an agreement. It is this process which puts flesh on the bare bones of the written agreement.

Adjournments

An essential feature of all negotiations is the timing of adjournments. The number, length and frequency of adjournments will depend on the negotiations and, in general, adjournments are readily conceded if either party requests them.

The primary purpose of an adjournment is to review and assess progress against the objectives you have set. An adjournment also facilitates the consideration of each party's response to the other side's proposals; it also allows each party time to reconsider both its own offer and also the alternatives of not reaching agreement. At this stage the negotiating situation is delicate: each side would prefer the other side to move to avoid a further concession itself, but such a move may create the impression of weakness and may be interpreted as a willingness to move all the way to the position of the other side. It is therefore important to bear in mind that whatever expectations an adjournment may create in the minds of the other side, one's own responses should be consistent with one's essential objectives.

We have been looking at adjournments to consider specific proposals from the opposition, but there are, of course, adjournments for natural breaks – meals, sleep, weekends and so on. Such adjournments provide opportunities for informal discussions with the other side. They can relieve the tension of negotiating and can assist in reaching a settlement, especially when the issues are reasonably few, limited in scope and well defined. The distances between the parties should furthermore be relatively small. Thus, the final steps to agreement may be taken away from the negotiating table – although they must be ratified there.

Ronald Reagan, commenting on his experience on this aspect of negotiations as President of the Screen Actors' Guild, said:

I was surprised to discover the important part a urinal played in this high-altitude bargaining. When some point has been kicked around, until it swells up bigger than the whole contract, someone from one side or the other goes to the men's room. There is a kind of sensory perception that gives you the urge to follow . . . Then, standing side by side in that room that levels king and commoner, comes an honest question, 'What do you guys really want?' . . . Back in the meeting, one or the other makes an offer based on this newly acquired knowledge . . . Then the other returnee from the men's room says, 'Can our group have a caucus?' That is the magic word, like the huddle in football – it's where the signal is passed.[13]

The use of sanctions

The primary purpose of sanctions in the context of negotiations is to alter the position of one side or the other. In the pursuit of their objective, workers resort to a wide variety of sanctions: go-slow, work to rule, overtime ban, strike, to name a few. Management can likewise resort to a lockout but this sanction is now rarely used.* Thus, negotiations may take place against a background of a strike, lockout, litigation, or with campaigns to win public support for a case. Such overt conflict is, moreover, the most dramatic form of pressure directed to the bargaining table. Negotiations may be profoundly affected by it as the results of the conflict may alter the position of one side or the other, thus inducing agreement.

Good negotiations are, however, conducted by experienced individuals on both sides. Neither side is therefore likely to resort to sanctions without making a final offer or concession that represents a position on which the party is prepared to face the possibility of industrial action. Generally, the parties realistically appraise each other's position, and frequently a negotiated settlement is achieved before industrial action is resorted to. This does not mean that the parties might not reach an impasse at times, with a strike or other form of sanction being used. It does mean, however, that the parties are less likely to stumble into taking action without considering the consequences.

All this is not to deny that at times sanctions are used by workgroups without the approval of their union officials, as a spontaneous protest against something management has done, or to indicate support for their union leadership in negotiations. Such unofficial action has continued to occur in spite of legal prohibitions and lack of official union support. Nor do workers take industrial action lightly. There are no easy solutions to unofficial spontaneous outbursts, but the answer probably lies in the particular tenor of management–union relationships, the types of procedure available to resolve disputes and how well these procedures fit the problems to be resolved.

The role of third parties

When the negotiating process has reached an impasse or deadlock, the parties may seek the assistance of a third party as a catalyst in the search for a solution. In Britain, such assistance in the form of conciliation, mediation and arbitration

---

* Of course, it is common, however, for the sides in a dispute to describe a stoppage of work as both 'strike' and 'lockout'.

is provided free to the parties by the Advisory, Conciliation and Arbitration Service (ACAS).

The timing of third party intervention is, however, important. Where disputes have not been taken through all the stages of procedure, or where in the absence of formal procedure negotiations have been incomplete, the introduction of a third party may undermine the bargaining machinery by encouraging half-heartedness in the negotiations in the hope that a third party will save the situation. Not surprisingly, before considering requests for third party assistance, ACAS takes into account any dispute procedure agreed between the parties and whether it has been fully used for the dispute in question.

Conciliation, mediation and arbitration have in common the introduction of a third party into the negotiating process to assist the parties in the resolution of the dispute. The need for such involvement arises from a recognition by the parties that voluntary agreement is not likely to be reached without some outside assistance. Conciliation and mediation are a continuation of the negotiating process, whereas a recourse to arbitration is a recognition that further negotiation will be fruitless and that a settlement will have to be imposed from the outside. In essence, the role of the conciliator is to clarify the areas of agreement and disagreement between the parties; that of the mediator to make recommendations for a settlement or to reach a basis for a settlement; the arbitrator to hear the cases presented by both parties and made an award – that is, make a settlement of his own which the parties normally agree to accept beforehand.

THE TRUST FACTOR

Negotiations cannot be fruitfully conducted if there is distrust between the parties. In negotiations, management and unions may be forced to recognize that their survival is dependent on reaching an accommodation with each other. As Purcell succinctly puts it: 'We must find some way of reconciling our differences. We must learn to live together.'[14] Negotiations may not be possible unless there is a certain degree of trust between the parties.

The climate for negotiations is also profoundly important, as Walton and McKersie noted:

> A supportive and trusting climate facilitates joint problem-solving. Defensive and low-trust atmospheres inhibit the process. A supportive climate is marked by encouragement and freedom to behave spontaneously without fear of sanctions. A defensive atmosphere is one in which the parties perceive threat and risks associated with provisional behaviour . . . when support is lacking and a person anticipates threat, he behaves defensively, diverting energy from the problem-solving task.[15]

The need for trust stems from the complex nature of negotiations, and trust provides the basis on which negotiators deal with each other as they seek to reach agreement. The quest for trust between the parties is a learning process, and opportunities should be given to each other for a high-trust relationship to develop and flourish between them.

The personal ingredient

Agreements are made not merely between organizations but also between individuals. It is, however, difficult to generalize about personality factors in negotiations, yet these factors are not inconsequential and some comments of practical importance may be made.

Some negotiators get on well with other members of their team, and with the opposing side; some do not. In many situations this does not make much difference, but in others it could be crucial. It is, for example, not unusual for the chief negotiators, sometimes with a colleague, to talk 'off the record' about a proposal for settlement. Clearly, in this situation personal relationships are important.

The astute negotiator will appraise the personal ingredient in negotiations, and take it into account in preparing and presenting his case. It may not be an analytically neat exercise but its practical importance cannot be overemphasized.

TRAINING FOR NEGOTIATIONS

We have been concerned in this chapter to examine the general rules and guidelines that can be of use to negotiators involved in distribution bargaining. Knowledge about negotiating is, however, intimately associated with negotiating skills. Competence in both knowledge and skills can enhance the performance of the negotiator.[16] While opinions may differ as to what are the essential attributes for an effective negotiator, it is generally agreed that the art of negotiating can be developed by practice, and by a keen interest in the developments within the field of negotiating. There is an increasing number of specialized texts on negotiating, some of which have been discussed in this chapter, and courses designed to improve the skills of negotiators are now widely available. Negotiators should take full advantage of the opportunities available to improve both their knowledge and skills.

THE FUTURE OF NEGOTIATING

As means of resolving differences between employers and trade unions, negotiating towards the concluding of collective agreements has a number of advantages over other methods of regulating their relationships. For the significant feature of an agreement is that both parties are committed to live by it, and the likelihood of the parties enforcing their own agreement is far greater than that of accepting a decision adverse to one party from the outside. Furthermore, the two sides are in a better position to resolve their own differences, since they presumably know more about their problems than outsiders do.

The leadership qualities of the parties involved in negotiations are profoundly important in a rapidly changing economic and political environment. Improving their relationship and the process of negotiation should be a conscious goal of the parties. For negotiations not only play a vital role in conflict resolution today, but all the indications are that they are likely to be even more significant in the future.

References

1. Dunlop, J T (1984) *Dispute Resolution*, Auburn House, Dover, Mass, p 21.
2. Dunlop, J T, ibid. p 10.
3. Raiffa, H (1982) *The Art and Science of Negotiations*, Harvard University Press, Cambridge, Mass, pp 7–8.
4. Raiffa, H, ibid, p 8.
5. Walton, R E and McKersie, R B (1965) *A Behavioural Theory of Labor Negotiations,* McGraw Hill, New York, pp 1–7.
6. Walton, R E and McKersie, R B, ibid, p 11.
7. Nierenberg, G I (1968) *Fundamental of Negotiating*, Hawthorn Books, New York, Chapter 7.
8. Kennedy, G, Benson, J and McMillan, J (1980) *Managing Negotiations*, Business Books, London, Chapter 3.
9. Slichter, S H, Healy, J J and Livernash, R E (1960) *The Impact of Collective Bargaining on Management*, The Brookings Institution, Washington DC, p 918.
10. Hawkins, K (1979) *A Handbook of Industrial Relations Practice*, Kogan Page, London, p 192.
11. Atkinson, G (1983) *The Effective Negotiator*, Negotiating Systems Publications, London, Chapter 2.
12. Kennedy, G, Benson, J and McMillan, J, op cit, p 13.
13. Reagan, R and Hubler, R G (1965) *Where's the Rest of Me?*, Dell Publishing Company, New York, p 225. Quoted by Dunlop, J T, op cit, p 17.
14. Purcell, J (1981) *Good Industrial Relations, Theory and Practice*, Macmillan, London, p 237.
15. Walton, R E and McKersie, R B, op cit, p 141.
16. Kniveton, B and Towers, B (1978) *Training for Negotiating: A Guide for Management and Employee Negotiators*, Hutchinson, London.

Chapter Eight
Collective Agreements: Old and New Styles

Chris Brewster

Collective agreements set the basic terms and conditions of employment for most people in the UK. That, however, is one of the few generalizations that can be made with any certainty. As in other areas of industrial relations the formal outcomes of the system – the agreements – are complex, diverse and differentiated. The fact that substantial elements of pay and benefits are set by collective agreements for well over two-thirds of all people in employment means that at the national level the overall economic impact of these agreements is considerable, if still much debated. The impact of the agreements at the organizational level is also clear: pay is the major operating costs item for most public and private sector organizations. In the private sector particular collective agreements can mean the difference between profit and loss, even survival and non-survival. In the public sector the ever-increasing pressure of labour costs puts a real strain on tightly controlled public expenditure. Even at the individual level, in the employees' pay packets, or in the way they work, the importance of collective agreements is hard to overestimate.

This chapter examines the role of collective agreements in the UK. It considers in turn their nature and content, their importance, current trends (and in particular the trend towards new-style single-union deals) and makes some suggestions about what may happen to collective agreements in the near future. This chapter should be read in conjunction with Chapter 6 on developments in the trade unions and Chapter 7 on levels of bargaining.

THE NATURE OF COLLECTIVE AGREEMENTS

The UK is remarkable for having a great diversity of forms of collective agreement, some of them informal, some perhaps even unlawful, some hidden from senior management and union officials. Some of the agreements will have been reached with much satisfaction on both sides; others will have been made with much unhappiness under real pressure and difficulty. The majority, however, share a number of features in common and it is useful to note these first.

Trade union recognition

In broad terms all collective agreements are dependent upon union recognition. It takes two parties (at least) to reach an agreement. There can be no collective agreement until management has decided to deal with its employees, at least partly, through a trade union or trade union-like body. There does not, in the British tradition, need to be a formal recognition agreement before there can be a collective agreement. But if management does not accept that the unions represent one channel through which it can deal with its workforce, then agreements cannot exist. In practice, most collective agreements are made with independent unions formally recognized by the employing organization for collective bargaining purposes.

It is now understood that managerial attitudes are a key influence on the growth or decline of trade union membership. It should not be assumed that managers are opposed to trade unions in any automatic sense. Many managements are very positive towards the unions and actively encourage their recognition and participation in specific areas of organizational policy. They find that the unions provide a useful channel for communications with employees and that collective agreements are a simple and comprehensive way of altering employment contracts for many employees simultaneously. More importantly for these managements, the trade unions and collective agreements provide a means of generating commitment. Collective agreements have a strong moral force: the parties to them will not breach their terms except in case of real pressure. The unions want collective agreements because they formalize improvements to terms and conditions that the unions have negotiated, and because they restrict managerial prerogative. The managements want collective agreements because they commit unions and the employees they represent to the terms of the agreement. Agreements are two-way processes: managers and unions both gain from them. Hence the readiness of managements to recognize the unions for negotiating purposes.

Once the union (or unions) is recognized the possibility is opened up for all forms of collective agreements. There are the formal, deliberate, planned negotiations leading to an annual wage increase. There are also local deals, developed more or less informally and with greater or less visibility. Many of these deals will not be conceived of as collective agreements, even by the parties concerned. The night duty manager agrees with the shop stewards that to prevent the problems caused by a new bus timetable the late shift will finish, and the night shift will start, 20 minutes earlier than indicated on the shift rosters. To create as little fuss as possible, the individuals concerned continue to log, and be paid, the same hours as on the roster. The legal position may be uncertain, there is nothing in writing, senior management does not want to know, but another collective agreement has been struck. Such deals would be difficult, perhaps even impossible, if the night duty manager had to convince each employee individually that this was an acceptable arrangement. Where a union is recognized, however, the manager is well placed to make such agreements.

Most collective agreements will be more open and more formal than this. They will still depend upon management being prepared to deal with or 'to recognize for negotiating purposes' (as the jargon put it) a trade union representing the employees.

. . . not legally binding

Collective agreements have a unique status in the UK. They are, with a few exceptions, deemed not to be legally binding between the parties. If either management or union break the agreement the other party is debarred from going to court to enforce it. The presumption has always been that collective agreements cannot be enforced by the courts. During 1971–4 the Conservative Government changed the law so that the agreements were held to be legally enforceable unless the parties specifically stated otherwise. Almost every agreement during that period included a 'Tina Lea' clause: 'this is not a legally enforceable agreement'. Before the 1992 General Election the Conservative Party, in its proposals for the sixth major piece of union legislation to be introduced since 1979, suggested again that agreements should be presumed to be legally enforceable. In any event, the parties to a collective agreement can make them legally enforceable if they so choose and if they write them in a way that the courts find acceptable. Hardly anyone does.

The arguments for and against legally binding agreements have been well rehearsed.[1] Essentially, the culture of British industrial relations is such that both parties prefer to make their own deals without lawyers, and to retain flexibility. The case in favour of legally binding collective agreements is made most strongly, in general, by those not directly involved in industrial relations.

It is, however, oversimplistic to state baldly that collective agreements are not legally enforceable. By the legal process of incorporation, clear terms made by parties with the authority to act as agents become part of individual employees' contracts of employment. Thus a wage increase, say, will become part of the individual legal contracts of the employees covered by that particular collective agreement. If the increase is not paid action can be taken by or on behalf of the individual; but not by or on behalf of the unions which were party to the agreement.

Format of collective agreements

The lack of intention to negotiate legal documents explains the format of most collective agreements. The non-practitioner, on first seeing a documented agreement, finds it hard to credit that events of such significance can be covered by such thin paperwork. The agreement that may determine living standards for dozens or hundreds of families, and have a critical effect on an organization's operating costs and competitiveness, will cover one or two sheets of foolscap, hastily typed and idiosyncratic. That these collective agreements are so thin and insubstantial reflects the negotiators' concept of their nature. They are not legally binding; rather they are reflections of an understanding, binding in honour upon those who drew them up. They are incremental; each agreement builds upon previous deals and arrangements. They reflect a present consensus, which is open to renegotiation, and are not intended to establish definitive or final positions.

Typically, in the UK, wage agreements last for one year. This is shorter than the norm in many other countries, which will have two-or three-year deals as typical and it is a comparatively recent development in the UK, too. Agreements for different lengths of time are far from rare, even in the UK. This is dependent to some extent on subject matter: agreements on working practices may last only a few weeks; agreements on pay typically will last a year; agreements on hours may last several years; and in some areas – such as pensions, expenses and dirt money – agreements may well last for decades. There are now indications that from the mid-1980s onwards even wage agreements are tending to last longer. Deals lasting for two years or more are becoming more common in the car and components industries, and in petroleum and the docks. Employees in areas as diverse as the Greene King brewery, British Aerospace, Ford and the teaching professions have recently agreed long-term settlements.

It is important not to overgeneralize. Some companies have long-term, substantial, carefully worded agreements running to many pages and covering all sorts of subjects comprehensively. They are, though, very much in the minority. For most, the rather elemental few-page agreement is typical. This typical format and the incremental and complex understandings that it represents are central to any analysis of collective agreements in the UK. The negotiating of agreements in myriad forms and myriad different places is a continuing and never-ending feature of the industrial relations scene.

THE CONTENT OF COLLECTIVE AGREEMENTS

The subject matter of these flimsy, temporary, incremental and legally uncertain agreements is perhaps more open to generalization. There is a simple distinction between procedural agreements, which are concerned with methods of conducting the relationship between the parties involved (covered in Chapter 9) and substantive agreements, which are concerned with the terms and conditions of employment.

The subject matter of collective agreements varies widely. Given the complexity of agreements, the different forms that they take and the varying levels at which they are made, it is not surprising that this is the one statement that can be made with confidence. The substantive agreements may be about one or more of a wide range of topics. What is or is not agreed will be determined by history and tradition, by the forms and levels at which the agreements are reached, by the strength and confidence of the parties to the agreement, and by the particular resources and issues of the moment. They are usually about pay, ie salary, remuneration, wages, incentive schemes, premium payments. They are often about working conditions or working arrangements. They are sometimes about other terms and conditions of employment; hours or pensions, training or holidays. Very occasionally they cover other topics. But agreements on such issues as recruitment, investment and product or service quality are rarities.

There are issues which are not covered. A recent, very comprehensive US agreement included sections on the company slimming plan, self-defence training and the allocation of tickets to the local football team. Few British agreements have a similar content. Agreements in Britain are more likely to include some or all of the following subjects.

1. *Pay levels and structures.* The basic collective agreement is about pay. Typically, this has been restricted to details of a general uplift of, perhaps, a certain percentage. Increasingly these agreements involve a more extensive re-examination of pay structures. These agreements, or separate ones, also cover many other elements of the cash equation, such as bonuses, shift and overtime premium, dirt money, uniform allowances, salary scale incremental points.

In the past, particularly when governments have been operating incomes policies to control the growth of wages, there has been much discussion of 'wage drift'. This term was used to refer to the way in which less structured, local agreements act to push actual earnings above those established in more formal agreements. From the Donovan Commission onwards millions of words were written about this phenomenon, nearly all addressing it as a problem for which a solution was needed. This concern has abated, largely because economic circumstances have forced managers to control labour costs more rigorously, but also because there is a greater understanding of the complexity of collective agreements, a wider acceptance of local responsibility for wage costs and the virtual abandonment of interest in formal incomes policies in government circles.

2. *Other terms and conditions.* Subjects such as hours of work, holiday entitlement, sick schemes, pensions, and health and safety are, less frequently than pay (but still frequently), included in collective agreements.

3. *Job evaluation.* The majority of systematic job evaluation schemes rely on the involvement of employees. They are usually introduced and often administered by joint agreements between management and unions. All organizations of any size over a dozen or so employees will have schemes for comparing one job against another. In many cases this will be entirely informal and *ad hoc*, undertaken solely by the manager or owner of the business. Where formal and systematic means of assessing jobs against each other are adopted – in about one-fifth of all workplaces employing more than 25 people[2] – the schemes are normally the subject of collective agreements.

4. *Working arrangements.* The phrase covers a multitude of different activities around the immediate work area. Depending upon the workplace, issues such as manning levels, allocation of work, the structure of workgroups and the manner in which the work is conducted, may be determined unilaterally by management, in some few cases by the employees or their union representatives, or frequently by joint agreement.

5. *New technology agreements.* During the early 1980s several unions, and the TUC, devoted considerable attention to agreements on the introduction of new technology. These agreements have retained some interest in the private manufacturing sector but have not become widespread: among establishments which recognize trade unions, negotiation over the introduction of technical change occurred in only 10 to 15 per cent of cases.[3] There are three reasons for this: it is often difficult to disentangle agreements on new technology from agreements on changing working practices or pay; new technology is a blanket term and in practice each situation is different, making general recommendations inappropriate or difficult to follow; and it quickly became clear that the economic circumstances and the managerial confidence which characterized the 1980s meant that managers were able to introduce new technology without having to reach agreements with unions.

6. *Flexibility and productivity.* The concept of productivity bargaining enjoyed a great vogue in the 1960s. A form of it is now back in favour, but is in a distinctly different form. The earlier productivity agreements involved payments over and above cost of living or incomes policy basic rises, and were frequently concerned with limited changes to working arrangements such as

reductions in overtime, shorter meal breaks and abolition of tea breaks. It was not uncommon for such agreements to be undermined, gradually, by a series of less formal agreements (or turning of blind eyes), so that the same practice might be bought out by management several times. In the 1990s agreements are more far-reaching, focused on flexibility among the workforce and linked explicitly to workforce reduction rather than to substantial extra payments.

7. *Redundancy*. There were large numbers of redundancies in the first half of the 1980s (more than 40 per cent of workplaces reported reductions in their workforce in the early 1980s[4]) and another surge in redundancies at the beginning of the 1990s. Although many workplaces effect these redundancies by agreement, and not just management *diktat*, many of these 'agreements' will be grudging, unhappy and often forced on unwilling unions. In broad terms, the unions have concentrated on raising the compensation paid to redundant workers rather than attempting to retain the workforce at its original size.

8. *Training*. Traditionally the unions have limited their interest in training to apprenticeships. In some few industries, such as electrical contracting, the unions have developed a more comprehensive approach, but this has been rare. The virtual collapse of the apprenticeship system, and the requirement for workers to train and retrain during a working lifetime, have changed union attitudes. Unions are now much more prepared to bargain over training opportunities. Agreements on training are now common in many workplaces.

THE IMPORTANCE OF COLLECTIVE AGREEMENTS

The discussion so far has emphasized the continuing importance of collective agreements in the British economy. Indeed, during the economic turbulence and widespread changes of the 1980s and early 1990s, collective agreements exhibited a remarkable tenacity. However, things are changing.

There is considerable debate as to whether the decline and change in collective bargaining is a temporary feature or represents a real watershed. Those who argue that it is temporary point out that many of the reasons underlying union weakness can be reversed: Conservative governments may fall, manufacturing industry can be revived, unemployment could be cut. In sharp contrast, it will be argued here that industrial relations in Britain have reached a watershed, that collective bargaining will continue to decline, and that collective agreements, while they will remain influential across a wide range of employment, will continue to fall in importance. There are long-term reasons why we should expect collective agreements to diminish in importance. These, among others, are as follows.

1. The structural changes in employment are unlikely to be reversed. Technological change is blurring boundaries in employment, leading to retrenchment and retraining, even in successful organizations, and requiring greater employee flexibility. This creates difficulties for union recruitment and retention, and for the collective bargaining process.

2. Workplaces are becoming smaller. There is a proven relationship between small workplaces and low levels of unionization.[5]
3. More workers have 'peripheral' contracts of employment. Part-timers, temporary workers, youth scheme workers and so on are very much less likely to join trade unions.
4. Groups that the unions have in the past found more difficult to organize are becoming a bigger percentage of the workforce: the percentage of non-manual workers is increasing (even as the distinction between manual and non-manual becomes increasingly blurred), and there are more women and non-whites among the labour force.
5. The climate of opinion has changed. This is difficult to prove and capable of differing interpretations. There is at least some evidence that the basic legitimacy of the union role is now more frequently challenged, that union officials' confidence is less and that employees are not prepared to support their unions as totally as they did in previous decades.
6. The unions have problems. These are not insurmountable; the unions will remain and will recover some of their influence. But they are in general in financial difficulties, uncertain of their future and not well organized to meet the changing circumstances in which they find themselves. They are struggling to adapt. By the mid-1980s the EETPU and the AEU were offering members and potential members very significant financial benefits in areas outside those which could be obtained through collective agreements – cheap car purchase, cut-price holidays, medical cover, discounts and insurance, and so on. By the late 1980s the TGWU had launched a recruiting campaign for part-time workers and the GMB was aiming to recruit the self-employed. The potential development of half a dozen 'superunions' (see Chapter 1) is another response to the unions' problems. In the way of the British trade union movement, a wide range of different approaches to their problems was being developed.
7. In contrast, managements now have a new confidence in their ability to deal with industrial relations. Managers do learn. Much of the debate about the future of collective bargaining and collective agreements seems to assume that managements have gained nothing from recent history. Managers have increasingly seen the advantages of different forms of employment structure, different ways of relating to staff and a more planned approach to industrial relations. It is not necessary to be too cynical or too jaundiced about management to argue that they are likely to want to continue those developments that left them with greater autonomy.

It is against this background, of new opportunities for managements to develop and manipulate the employment situation and an increasing willingness by management to do so in a subtle, planned and coherent manner, that a discussion of trends should take place. Collective agreements were the bedrock of industrial relations during most of the post-war period. They will not disappear, but they are decreasing in importance in two respects. First, the number of employees whose main terms and conditions are set by collective agreements is decreasing. Second, the influence of those agreements in the employing establishment is also being reduced.

Fewer people are covered because of the following reasons.

- Growth in employment is in new industries, new towns, new locations, small units, service industries. All are difficult for unions to organize, and are much less unionized than the traditional industries and large sites where employment is declining.
- In the private sector, companies are increasingly prepared to refuse union recognition, or withdraw it once granted, especially for higher-level employees.
- In the public sector, areas of employment are being 'privatized' or subcontracted, often to non-union employers.
- Overall, the considerable increase in the number and proportion of peripheral workers will not be reversed. By the nature of their employment many of these will have their terms and conditions determined individually.

The impact of these changes is likely to be long lasting. The effect has been to reduce the extent of collective negotiation between managements and unions, and hence to reduce the coverage of collective agreements. The early evidence of this trend was already apparent in the first half of the 1980s; and has continued since then. It is worth noting that although only a minority of larger British organizations have over 50 per cent of their employees in membership of a trade union (see Table 8.1) 72 per cent of them recognized trade unions for collective bargaining purposes.* These figures vary markedly around Europe: in Norway,

Table 8.1 *Percentage of Organizations (over 200 employees) having Proportions of Employees in Union Membership.*

Country	UK	Denmark	Norway	Sweden	France	Spain
0%	16	0	3	0	9	4
1–25%	20	5	3	0	73	59
26–50%	18	7	7	3	9	17
51–75%	24	17	18	10	3	7
76–100%	18	60	68	85	1	2
Don't Know	3	11	0	1	4	11

Country	Italy	Germany	Netherlands	Switzerland
0%	2	3	1	19
1–25%	27	34	52	39
26–50%	35	23	26	15
51–75%	28	17	6	10
76–100%	8	10	3	6
Don't Know	1	12	12	10

* Figures from Price Waterhouse Cranfield Project on international strategic HRM, 1991 data. For more detail on the project see Brewster, C, Hegewisch, A and Lockhart, T L 'Researching Human Resource Management' *Personnel Review*, Vol 20, 6 (1991), pp 36–40

Table 8.2   *Percentage of organizations with over 200 employees recognizing trade unions*

SWITZERLAND	GERMANY	DENMARK	SPAIN	FRANCE	ITALY	NORWAY	NETHERLANDS	SWEDEN	UK
*	*	91	73	*	91	96	43	*	72

* Question not asked: position determined by legislation, not managerial decision.
Source: Brewster, C and Bournois, F (1991) 'Human Resource Management: A European perspective', *Personal Review* 20, 6 pp 4–14.

for example, 96% of all organizations with over 200 employees recognize trade unions, while in The Netherlands only 43 per cent do so (see Table 8.2).

Even where agreements exist their influence is being reduced. This is because of the following.

1. Changes in the nature of the workforce, particularly the growth in peripheral employment, mean that the proportion of workers in the establishment covered by each agreement is reduced.
2. Companies in the private sector are tending to refuse to accept or to withdraw recognition from groups within the workplace, especially managerial staff (see Chapter 6).
3. Some issues are being dealt with more frequently by different forms of representation, such as briefing groups or consultative committees, which do not lead to collective agreements.
4. Other issues are simply not being put into the arena of collective bargaining by management. Managers continue to refuse to bargain over strategic issues like investment and the location of particular sites. The authors of the most authoritative workplace surveys struggled to come to terms with the fact that managers reported widespread joint regulation of many non-pay issues, but very little joint regulation in other areas.[6] It may be quite straightforward: some things, such as pay and physical working conditions, are subject to collective agreement and some, such as the introduction of new technology, are not.

Overall Figure 8.1 shows that according to senior human resource specialists the influence of trade unions in the UK has declined in many organizations – as it has also in France and in Italy. However, it is also important to note that this is not a common development throughout Europe.

Again, these trends are likely to develop discontinuously and with variations, and they will be subject to a range of external factors. Here too, however, it seems that the overall trend will be towards the reduction of influence of collective agreements.

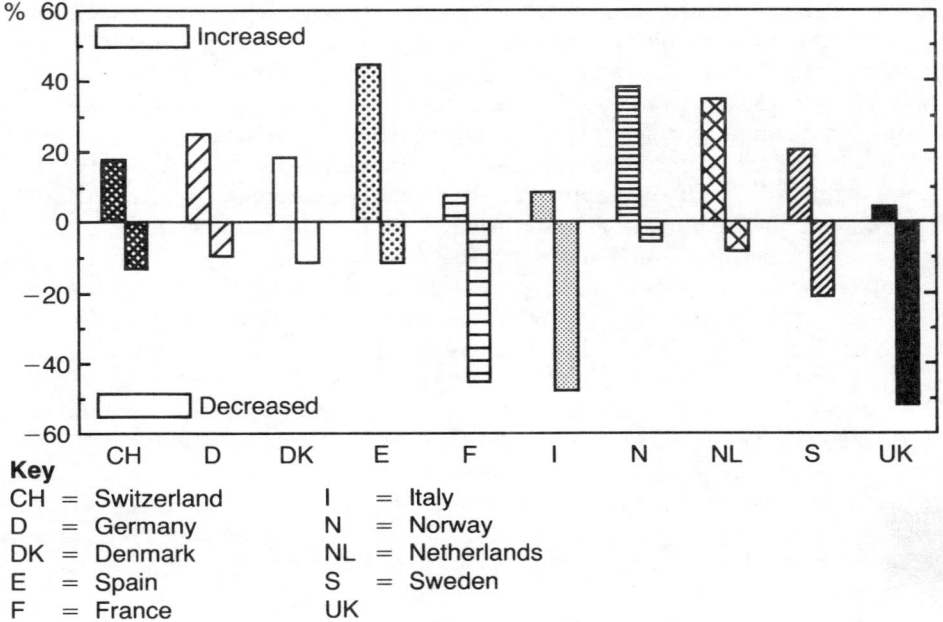

Key

CH	=	Switzerland	I =	Italy
D	=	Germany	N =	Norway
DK	=	Denmark	NL =	Netherlands
E	=	Spain	S =	Sweden
F	=	France	UK	

Figure 8.1 *Percentage of organizations reporting change in union influence*
Source: Brewster, C and Bournois, F (1991) 'Human Resource Management: A European perspective', *Personnel Review*, 20, 6, pp 4–13.

CURRENT TRENDS IN COLLECTIVE AGREEMENTS

This section of the chapter focuses on some continuing trends in the nature of collective agreements in the UK and then considers what have been termed the 'new style' or 'single union, strike free' deals which have been the subject of so much attention. In terms of the 'old-style' agreements (to coin a phrase) attention is directed towards a reduction in formalization, changes in content, a reduction in the willingness of managements to 'package' their negotiations and, perhaps pointing in a somewhat different direction, a move towards more comprehensive agreements.

The 1980s and 1990s have seen a *move away from the increased formalization* developed in the 1960s and 1970s. In general terms, formalization benefits the weaker party to an agreement. The stronger party is in a position to make changes anyway; breaching a written agreement remains a constraint. In many areas, especially those outside the standard pay and conditions areas, managers are now preferring to work through informal and unwritten 'understandings'. Much new technology is introduced this way. Even in the pay areas managers are seeking enabling agreements that leave them an unwritten degree of flexibility (see Chapter 14).

The *variation of subjects* within collective agreements is to a large extent a part of this process. A substantial number of non-wage items are the subject of collective agreements, but the number of companies and establishments in which such issues formed the subject of collective agreements has dropped markedly.

Issues such as recruitment, manning levels and work practices are increasingly being excluded from that minority of agreements where they were included and held as part of the management prerogative. Other issues, which have traditionally been the subject of collective agreements, are becoming less widespread. Thus, for example, the spread of formal job evaluation schemes which occurred in the 1970s has been halted: managements are finding that such schemes are often subject to joint regulation. If job evaluation schemes are reduced, joint agreements about them will be reduced. Equally, payment schemes, such as payments-by-results, which normally have a high degree of shop steward involvement, are also losing popularity. The fact that such pay schemes are built around joint agreements is probably a contributory factor in management's decision to replace them. The effect is again to remove an issue from the collective bargaining arena.

The addition of new items into collective agreements is a paradoxical approach. From a managerial viewpoint the rationale for such action lies in the greater commitment that can be achieved through an agreement. So some managements are beginning to include in their collective agreements a series of items that they want accepted by the employees. Agreements may include clauses on flexibility (of task or working time), on product or service quality, on confidentiality or security, and on training and retraining.

Changes in the scope of negotiations arise from the more planned approach to industrial relations that some managements are developing. Where strategic decisions are being taken against the criterion of the cost-effective use of manpower, management's options in negotiation are reduced. Traditionally, management negotiators have been given overall cost targets and been charged with reaching a deal as far below them as possible. To do this negotiators have become skilled at packaging and repackaging the elements of their offer in order to make it more acceptable.

Management negotiators can now find themselves in a much stronger position, given their greater strength – compared with the 1960s and 1970s – to face down threatened industrial action or to win if it takes place. Management negotiators thus feel themselves to be in a better position to make realistic first offers, and to move only a little way from them in the course of the negotiations.

A strategic managerial approach to industrial relations both builds on this situation and feeds off it. As an example, consider a company that has decided to subcontract some services, reduce overtime, encourage a faster turnover of staff, particularly among older employees who may find it difficult to adapt to new training requirements, extend flexible working practices and increase the flexibility of working hours. Such policies will have clear implications for collective agreements in the workplace. They will mean that management negotiators are restricted in what they can 'package' into an offer. So, if the management has decided to subcontract services, the negotiators may be unable to offer employment security guarantees. The objective of reducing overtime means that the negotiators have limited scope in overtime rates: any increase would tend to increase the attractiveness of overtime and employee resistance to its reduction. Equally, if the management wanted to encourage turnover, especially of older staff, it would be unlikely to offer pension improvements. Conversely, it may well want to make early retirement packages available.

Policies of extending flexibility will lead managers towards reducing any element of the package which adds to distinctions between parts of the workforce. So there would, at a minimum, be no improvement of individual or group payments-by-results schemes; differential conditions or rosters would be reduced; and management would attempt to limit payments for shift or unsocial working hours. These give employees a stake in limiting the flexibility of working hours.

These are, of course, just examples, but they are far from uncommon. The implication of such policies is that managerial bargainers increasingly find that their room for manoeuvre in the negotiations is restricted and they cannot move very far before they come across another issue of principle which they must not jeopardize. It is still undoubtedly the case that managements are sticking close to first offers mainly because they feel themselves to be in the ascendancy. However, as the strategic approach to industrial relations becomes more widespread, so that in turn will also constrain managerial flexibility in what they can allow in collective agreements.

Paradoxically, perhaps, given these changes noted above, recently there have been signs of the development of more comprehensive agreements of longer duration. The contrast between this movement and that towards less formalization should not surprise us: on both management and union sides there are those who wish to move towards simpler and less restrictive agreements, and those who want to see more substantial, perhaps even legally binding arrangements. The results of these differing tensions vary from organization to organization. In some cases agreements are becoming more comprehensive in so far as managements are consolidating numerous small agreements into one. Those managements who are consciously reviewing all aspects of industrial relations will not want to leave various elements of the employment package lost in the mists of an agreement reached many years ago. They will at least want to reaffirm it, and often want to amend it. This can be done alongside all the other agreements that come up for regular renewal. In this respect at least, agreements, though usually not those on basic pay, will be of shorter duration. Agreements on the basic pay package, however, are being extended in duration because managers, in particular, see the benefit of having some predictability about wage and salary costs over as long a period as feasible. The reduction of the rate of inflation in the 1990s made this process more acceptable to the unions. Longer-term agreements were typical in Britain prior to the 1960s and are still the norm in most competitor nations. British agreements in the 1990s may follow suit.

'NEW-STYLE' AGREEMENTS

The widely-publicized 'new-style' agreements are perhaps the furthest extension of this comprehensive approach to collective agreements. These 'single union, strike free' deals, as they are sometimes called, consist of a number of related elements:

- single-union recognition;
- a reliance on arbitration procedures (sometimes including what's been called 'final offer' or 'pendulum' arbitration) to exclude industrial action;

- a high degree of disclosure of information by management, and participative structures such as company advisory boards;
- considerable flexibility in working practices;
- extensive training and retraining;
- single status conditions for all employees (holidays, sickness, restaurant facilities etc).

Not one of these elements is new. Single union agreements are widespread in Britain, particularly outside manufacturing in areas such as printing, retail distribution and the public sector. The 1984 workplace industrial relations survey showed that 65 per cent of all establishments recognizing unions for manual workers recognized only one manual union and that 82 per cent had only one manual bargaining unit. Of establishments which recognized unions for non-manual workers, 39 per cent recognized a single non-manual union and 61 per cent had only one non-manual bargaining unit. Arbitration is a traditional part of the UK industrial scene: industrial action has always been a minority activity in Britain and is now rare. 'No strike' clauses are not unknown elsewhere in the UK.[7] In any case, the 'pendulum arbitration' or insistence that the arbitrator can only decide on either the union or the management's final position, which was imported from the US by the then EETPU, is a restriction on industrial action − but cannot eradicate the possibility of it occurring altogether. Information disclosure and participation in management are far from uncommon (see Chapter 11). Flexibility is now widespread; and whilst the UK's record on training and retraining is still open to criticism, it is not for want of many examples of good practice. Single status is now almost the received wisdom. However, as ACAS recognized as long ago as 1984, in a confidential briefing document, while the elements are familiar, their combination 'to create a whole package . . . can be seen as unique'.[8]

These new-style agreements have been the subject of much controversy in the trade union movement and elsewhere. They have been identified with what was the EETPU and a number of Japanese companies which have come to the UK in recent years. In practice, though, such agreements are rare in the EETPU and far from the norm among Japanese companies. Moreover, they are not restricted to the one union or the one nationality of company. By the early 1990s they were to be found not only in a number of other foreign-owned subsidiaries (eg companies from US, Sweden and Norway), but also in an increasing range of indigenous organizations which have set up new plants and offices. They also involve a growing number of unions (eg the AEU as it was, TGWU, GMB, ISTC and the MATSA section of the GMB). Although the number of these 'new-style' agreements is growing, they are as yet few in relation to the overall number of employers with conventional agreements with unions: a few dozen agreements covering less than 100,000 employees.

These new-style agreements have been controversial because it is argued that they have, in some cases, been made without due consideration for the interests of other unions; and because it is argued that the restriction of the right to take industrial action prevents the union carrying out its role effectively in the future. The unions involved, particularly the AEEU's electrical section, make the point that they wish to sign more of these deals − but that the opposition to them comes in general from employers. The employers like the idea of restrictions on industrial action – but are very cautious about signing agreements which require them to 'open the books' on financial performance, to work with trade unions in joint committees and to accept final-offer arbitration. Their concern about the latter is expressed as a fear of taking the final decision on key issues like the wage bill out of the hands of the management who are responsible for organizational results.

The controversy led to the establishment of a Special Review Body by the TUC at its 1987 Congress – and, more dramatically, the expulsion of the EETPU at the 1988 Congress. The controversy was fuelled by the link to single unionism: some unions were either excluded from negotiating rights in some workplaces where they had long held them, or found themselves, on greenfield sites, participating in 'beauty contests' where several unions each tried to persuade an employer to grant them sole negotiating rights.

THE FUTURE FOR COLLECTIVE AGREEMENTS

Overall, despite the interest in new-style agreements, it is likely that they will remain a minority concern for the immediate future: if only because of the challenge they present to the established industrial relations culture of the UK. By contrast, the development of more traditional 'old-style' agreements is likely to continue. In particular it is increasingly likely, fuelled by the development of the 'superunions', that single-table bargaining – where several unions meet prior to negotiations with management and agree to act together (more or less as one plant-level union) – will continue to be extended. The TUC Special Review Body's second report 'Organizing For the 1990s' gave an enthusiastic endorsement to single-table bargaining.

The role of government in the development of collective agreements may be less than is sometimes claimed. However, government action does have an impact. The Conservative administration of the 1980s and early 1990s took pains to reduce the role of government in industrial relations. Its policies were, and are, concerned with establishing a scenario in which managerial power in industrial relations was strengthened and union power reduced – and then leaving the parties as free as possible to make their own collective agreements. This outcome was reinforced by the government's pressure on the public service sector to contract out, or 'privatize', as much work as possible and by the objective of denationalizing as many State industries as possible. These approaches had the effect of removing many strongly unionized sectors from direct government responsibility, and again of allowing management and unions to come to collective agreements unfettered by any political or social factors.

In the area directly or indirectly under its control, the Conservative Government has tried as far as possible to reproduce the conditions under which collective agreements are negotiated in the private sector. Attempts have been made to reproduce 'market place' analogies (except in the notably exceptional cases of the groups covered by the Top Salaries Review Board, judges, senior civil servants and the police). The aim was to move away from the comparability arguments of the 1970s and move closer to the 'ability to pay' criterion.

The re-election of a Conservative Government in 1992 makes it likely that the trends outlined above will continue; and not just for the public sector. The cautious development of performance or merit linked pay in that sector, and in the private sector the increase in collective agreements below national level, and the extension of collective agreements to such issues as flexibility, quality and training are likely to be supported by all political parties. Collective agreements in Britain are in a process of change and development, and of some decline. But they will remain the most important means of establishing employees' terms and conditions.

References

1. A particularly clear recent analysis is provided by Lewis, R (1986) 'The role of law in employment relations', in Lewis, R (ed) *Labour Law in Britain*, Blackwell, Oxford.
2. Millward, N and Stevens, M (1986) *British Workplace Industrial Relations 1980–1984: the DE/ESRC/PSI/ACAS Surveys*, Gower Aldershot, p 255.
3. Daniel, W W (1987) *Workplace Industrial Relations and Technical Change*, Frances Pinter, London, pp 130, 149.
4. See *Employment Gazette*, various issues; Millward, N and Stevens, M, op cit.
5. Bain, G S and Elias, P (1985) 'Trade union membership in Great Britain: an individual level analysis', *British Journal of Industrial Relations*, xxiii, 1, pp 71–92; Millward and Stevens, op cit, p 58.
6. Millward and Stevens, op cit, p 250.
7. Bassett, P (1986) *Strike Free: New Industrial Relations in Britain*, Macmillan, London, p.118.
8. ACAS Staff Briefing Paper 3/1984, quoted in Bassett, P op cit, p 87.

Chapter Nine
Collective Bargaining Levels*

Brian Towers

In spite of the diminishing role of collective bargaining in the UK in the 1980s and into the 1990s it remains a widespread and still important activity influencing, directly or indirectly, the terms and conditions of about 70 per cent of all employees. Even trade unions – the other party to collective bargaining – though they have serious and continuing problems, remain significant. As a proportion of the labour force trade union membership, currently at 38 per cent, is still much higher than in many industrialized countries and is close to twice that figure in the public sector. It has even been estimated by one authority that in the long term UK trade union density will not fall below 35 per cent.[1]

If collective bargaining has the capacity to remain a significant activity then an important aspect of collective bargaining, influencing both the bargaining process and the context of agreements, is bargaining structure. This has several dimensions: the number and characteristics of employees covered by the bargaining arrangements, ie the bargaining unit or units; the identification, and recognition, of the organization or organizations representing the employees in the bargaining unit, ie the bargaining agent; the scope or content of the matters covered by the collective agreement; and the level or levels at which bargaining takes place.

These dimensions are, in practice, closely related. For example, a corporate decision to decentralize the level at which pay is negotiated to the plant, profit or cost centre increases the number of bargaining units. It will also normally enhance the role of shop stewards representing their unions, ie the representatives of the union as bargaining agent. Additionally, it can significantly widen the scope or content of local bargaining and local agreements through the addition of pay and related matters which may formerly have been negotiated centrally.

Decisions on the level, or levels, at which collective bargaining takes place are therefore very important and are normally seen by trade unions as lying within management's discretion, even though changes in bargaining levels have important implications for trade unions. However, despite the vogue for decentralization it does not follow that the balance of benefits over costs in making such a decision is always favourable to the organization. Indeed, the centralization of bargaining, or in a form combining it with decentralization, may be more appropriate to some organizations in certain circumstances.

* This chapter draws upon research for a study of bargaining levels commissioned by the Institute of Personnel Management in 1991 and completed in 1992. The financial support of the Institute is gratefully acknowledged.

This chapter is concerned with these issues, among others. It will, first, outline the recent trends in bargaining levels in the UK and indicate the influences lying behind these trends. Secondly, it will list and discuss the basic industrial, organizational and industrial relations criteria which should influence management's choice of the bargaining level, or levels, most appropriate to an organization's or industry's circumstances. Thirdly, it will use these general criteria to evaluate the experience of UK organizations over the past decade who opted for a change in their bargaining levels. Fourthly, it will briefly consider the wider implications for economic policy and UK membership of the EC and internal market of different bargaining levels,especially the decentralized form. Fifthly, and finally, the chapter will close with a summary and some conclusions.

TRENDS IN BARGAINING LEVELS

Collective bargaining can take place in multi-employer or single employer contexts. Multi-employer bargaining has traditionally combined two levels, ie the setting of framework terms and conditions at industry level with bargaining on other matters left to individual companies – as in the long established but now dissolved arrangements in the engineering industry. The actual distribution of responsibility between the multi-employer and company levels varies between industries, and also changes over time.[2]

Single employer bargaining can also take place at two levels, centralized or decentralized – or some combination of the two. Complete functional decentralization to the plant, business unit, cost or profit centre is rare. Within the organization it is likely to be considered appropriate to keep some functions at the centre with others decentralized – as at GEC where financial accounting remains centralized in contrast to the personnel function.[3]

Within this framework two major trends can be identified. First, since the 1950s, there has been a long-term and fairly consistent decline in multi-employer bargaining and this trend has accelerated in the 1980s. A CBI survey[4] found a significant decline between 1979 and 1986 as does recent academic research.[5] The Workplace Industrial Relations Survey in the early 1980s reported that multi-employer bargaining was the principal means of settling pay levels for only 20 per cent of private sector employees[6] and it is probable that the next WIRS Survey to be published later in 1992 will report a further fall in this proportion.

Secondly, there has been an equally clear (though not always consistent) long-term trend which has also accelerated in the 1980s towards decentralized bargaining within organizations. The CBI 1986 survey reported that nearly 90 per cent of all employees in plants with collective bargaining had their basic pay negotiated at company or establishment level. The less complete case study evidence post-1986 still strongly suggests that decentralization has continued to grow in incidence and that even where multi-employer bargaining exists its content progressively excludes pay.

However, these trends, though apparent, need to be read with some reservations. The CBI survey found that 13 per cent of companies had moved towards more centralized arrangements. Furthermore, although multi-employer bargaining is clearly in serious decline, logic rather than inertia explains its persistence in some industries, while in a small minority industry-wide bargaining has been recently established.[7] Again, in earlier periods there have been trends *towards* centralization rather than decentralization or, at the least, the seeking of an optimum balance between centralized and decentralized bargaining.[8] The continuing experience of British Steel in the 1980s indicates a careful search for such a balance within its separate business organizational structure.[9]

Nor should a declared policy of decentralization of functions necessarily be taken at face value. Some organizations with multi-divisional organizational structures seem not to have recognized the appropriate strategic/operating distinction in decision-making.[10]

Others seem to have done so, but for pay disregard it in practice, retaining centrally determined parameters within which local bargainers must operate.[11] This may be understandable but it can pose problems of credibility.* There are also the potential problems arising from widening differentials between separate bargaining units inspiring leapfrogging claims. The absence of local bargaining skills may also rekindle enthusiasm for the expertise and disciplines of national bargaining.

In the public sector the capacity to implement decentralized bargaining poses more difficulties, not least the deep, long-established national bargaining culture in a context of still strong trade unions. However, the government's enthusiasm and pressure for decentralization of its social and economic policies has begun to fragment the older structures. In the civil service it has promoted a policy of decentralization to make employing units more sensitive to variations in local labour market conditions. It has abolished school teachers' long-established bargaining machinery and may yet opt for the wholesale privatization of individual schools with the obvious corollary of local implementation of pay and conditions even without trade unions – in line with the parallel developments in the NHS trusts. For universities, continuing impasses over pay settlements and their funding are increasing opt-out pressures on individual universities, although as yet there has not been a permanent breaking of ranks. In the former public sector the water industry's national bargaining structures were abolished by statute in 1983 before privatization; and the 20 privatized electricity supply companies are now beginning to withdraw from the 44-year-old national bargaining machinery with the apparent intention of using company bargaining to implement labour flexibility and single table arrangements. Furthermore, the EETPU is now accepting local bargaining and apparently even sees advantages in it.[13]

In local government decentralization pressures have made themselves felt, although their impact has not been uniform and they have been largely con-fined to Conservative-controlled local authorities in the south-east of England.

---

* For example Lucas, which centralized its bargaining in 1989, has been accused by the AEU in the 1992 pay negotiations of attempting to achieve a company-wide settlement of 3 per cent, regardless of local conditions in its 40 plants. Lucas, defending its decentralization decision, conceded that there remained a 'going rate' across many plants. Most Lucas plants in 1992 seem to be settling around this figure with a few above it via local productivity deals.[12]

The most publicized defectors were Brentwood District Council in 1989 and Kent County Council in the same year, both withdrawing from the national Administrative, Professional, Technical & Clerical (APT&C) agreement. Kent's rationale for this step was acute problems in attracting and retaining staff in the south-east labour market.[14] While these problems are now much less acute the grip of national level bargaining in local government is less strong. However, a balance between central and local bargaining has always been a necessary practice in the context of local authority autonomy. What now seems to be emerging is a shift in that balance towards decentralization but within a framework of 'core' and 'non-core' items, in particular for APT&C and manual employees. This would leave national pay structures, hours, related conditions and premia within 'national joint negotiations based on Whitley principles . . .'.[15] An indication of the balance in 1990 between central and local bargaining is shown in Table 9.1.

Table 9.1   *Current status of national agreements by bargaining group [district councils 1990 %]*

	Local conditions	Local conditions with some reference to national	National conditions modified by local variations	National conditions unmodified
Chief executive	6.1	13.6	55.4	24.4
Chief officers	5.6	13.6	54.9	25.8
APT&C	4.2	11.7	57.3	26.8
Manual	4.7	12.7	46.0	33.8
Craft	3.3	11.3	43.7	38.0

Source: Association of District Councils' 1990 survey of 213 local authorities; cited in Beaumont, P B (1992), *Public Sector Industrial Relations*, Routledge, p 113

Product market pressures have largely lain behind organizational change in the private sector; however, the public sector has been more under the influence of labour market changes. For example, the housing prices and cost-of-living pressures which posed acute problems of staff recruitment and retention in local government, and which led to strain on traditional national bargaining and the withdrawal of some authorities from national agreements, have now largely gone into reverse and the threat to national bargaining in local government is less evident. In another part of the public sector labour market pressures are also influencing the decentralization option. It has been predicted by senior management that hospital trusts will, in due course, dominate the NHS, and that these will determine their own pay and conditions not necessarily through recognized trade unions.[16]

Overall, although the trend towards decentralized bargaining is clear it should not necessarily be seen as a one-way process, indeed some organizations have returned to centralized bargaining following their experience of decentralization and in earlier periods a trend towards corporate bargaining reflected a wish to maintain central control. It may also be, according to the chairman of ACAS, that the trend towards decentralization has run its course as employers struggling with rising labour costs from unduly expensive performance-related pay schemes return to the controls of centralized pay bargaining.[17] However, it seems unlikely to be a pendular process[18] since there is much long-term logic in decentralization decisions related to regional and local labour market considerations – as in the public sector. Yet, although it is unlikely to be reversed, the decentralization trend of the 1980s may be slowing down, not least because of its extent. However, much of its impact will remain, leaving the overall pattern of bargaining levels far more decentralized than in earlier periods. In industrial relations terms it has not, however, been a costless exercise. British collective bargaining is now more fragmented than it was ten years ago. The benefits of a more flexible system have to be set against the problems it poses for employers and/or governments searching for co-ordinated strategies. There is also the added, and very important, dimension of the degree to which British collective bargaining needs to adapt itself to the generally much less fragmented patterns which prevail in other EC countries – as well as the preferences of the EC's institutions for European-wide and sectoral collective bargaining.

Yet, whatever the potential problems, a clear preference by employers for decentralized forms of collective bargaining in both the private and public sectors is a now well-established feature of UK industrial relations. There are a number of reasons explaining this important development. First, a necessary condition has been present, ie trade union weakness. While trade unions do not, as a rule, contest management's traditional practice, even 'right', to choose bargaining levels, their normal preference for national bargaining is evident and this can influence managerial decisions. This influence has been minimal throughout the 1980s except in the well-publicized and exceptional cases of the Fire Brigades Union's defence of its national agreement and the former NUR's successful retention of national bargaining in BR, even only perhaps in the short term. Secondly, it is clear that organizational devolution has normally preceded the decentralization of collective bargaining, ie organizational considerations rather than an industrial relations rationale has predominated. Thirdly, bargaining at lower levels in the organization has allowed management negotiators to make connections between indicators of business success and failure, productivity and appropriate pay increases. More particularly, there has been a growth in performance-related pay schemes, although it is difficult to establish whether this has been mainly a motive for, rather than a consequence of, decentralization of bargaining.

CHOOSING BARGAINING LEVELS

Basic criteria

The choice of bargaining levels – where industrial relations considerations are of prime importance – can be guided by well-established criteria. These criteria may change in relative importance over time but are sufficiently durable to provide a first basis for sound policy decisions. For example, although multi-employer level bargaining is increasingly a minority activity with a bargaining content of diminishing importance research and organizational experience shows it to be an attractive option in industries where all, or most, of certain criteria are present. These are:

- a large number of companies of relatively small size;
- geographical concentration;
- strong competitive pressures;
- high trade union membership;
- high labour costs.

Small employers with limited time, resources and expertise are attracted by bargaining arrangements which secure negotiating skills, limit the influence of unions in the workplace, reduce vulnerability to competitive pay pressures in circumstances of labour intensity and set industry-wide standards.

This 'convoy' bargaining ensuring collective protection is seen in industries like ceramics in Staffordshire (56 companies and 2500 employees), and cotton weaving in Blackburn and North-east Lancashire which set up its own machinery for the remaining small firms following the breakdown of national bargaining in textiles. There are also several cases where even large-scale employers find a balance of advantage in staying within multi-employer bargaining such as RTZ, Albright and Wilson, and ICI as members of the Chemical Industry Association's two-tier bargaining system, the CIA viewing the industry's bargaining structure as '. . . a highly flexible and efficient concept'.[19]

Yet, in general, it is large scale employers who are most likely to feel the need to withdraw from multi-employer bargaining. This normally involves a second choice, ie whether or not to bargain at corporate level or to decentralize bargaining to the plant, business unit, cost or profit centre – or some combination of the two with each bargaining item linked to its appropriate bargaining level. Thus, performance-related pay schemes are clearly best associated with decentralized bargaining while pension schemes are more sensibly negotiated across the organization at national level. More generally, corporate level bargaining is suggested where all or most of the following criteria are present:

- single product company;
- stable product market;
- centralized organizational structure;
- preference for centralized functions;
- standardized terms and conditions across operations;
- preference for negotiating with national trade union officials.

In contrast, decentralized bargaining is indicated using the tests of the following criteria:

- multi-product company;
- unstable product markets;
- multi-divisional organizational structure;
- preference for decentralized functions;
- decentralized terms and conditions across operations;
- preference for negotiating with shop stewards.

The flexibility associated with the decentralization route can be seen to advantage in a commercial crisis. For example, following the withdrawal of Philips from the EEF after the 1979 national strike the company opted for corporate level bargaining. The company's growing problems in the 1980s led in 1989 to a decision to decentralize its bargaining below group level, except for its manufacturing components division. After heavy losses in 1991 the company then split the division into two and ended national bargaining altogether. The five unions involved reluctantly accepted the situation and, indeed, the perceived bargaining power of the unions in 1979 may have largely explained Philips's initial preference to stay at the corporate level when decentralized bargaining seemed to offer a better organizational fit.[20]

The decentralized organizational form allows organizations to respond with sensitivity to different market changes across its product range. A decision to adopt this form inevitably pre-empts the decision to decentralize collective bargaining. The decentralization decision also offers management the possibility of moving to single table bargaining or single union agreements at decentralized, autonomous plants or even the reconsideration of recognition rights. These possibilities emphasize the significance of trade union weakness in explaining collective bargaining developments since 1979.

ORGANIZATIONAL EXPERIENCE

Management's choice of the level or levels at which to conduct collective bargaining does not need to be an act of faith given the useful broad industrial and organizational criteria that exist to inform decision-making which have been outlined. Furthermore, these criteria have been deepened by the experience of organizations over the past decade. This experience has continued to be researched and reported by academics who have long had an interest in the field, although there has been a significant survey/case study contribution from Industrial Relations Services (IRS) and Income Data Services (IDS) which has been referred to throughout this chapter. Some practitioners have also usefully reported their own organizational experience.[21]

Organizational experience can be reported in several dimensions. First, what are the circumstances in which it is appropriate for an organization to break away from multi-employer bargaining? Secondly, within the organization, what motives and factors should inform a decision to decentralize collective bargaining and what are the available options on the form of decentralization? Thirdly, what do we know of the experience of organizations which have followed a decentralization path? Fourthly, how important are the 'knock-on' effects and wider organizational implications of the decentralization decision?

Withdrawing from multi-employer bargaining

A 1989 survey of 30 multi-employer bargaining groups found that in recent years 16 had broken up and 9 had reduced their bargaining coverage.[22] However, five new multi-employer agreements had been established in two cases by small employers following the withdrawal of large companies, as with the Retail Food Joint Committee and cotton weaving in Lancashire. In the other three, new bargaining arrangements or amendments to existing ones were influenced by the restrictions imposed by the Wages Act 1986 on wages councils. Where multi-employer bargaining has survived or been renewed, companies were influenced by national bargaining as a defence against 'leapfrogging' pay claims, the time-saving aspects of central negotiations and the benefits of a national disputes procedure, ie a clear indication of the attraction of the 'convoy principle' to small companies. However, multi-employer bargaining is still clearly in general decline and this survey confirmed the presence of two of the principal influences: the search for greater flexibility through organizational decentralization; and the wish to introduce performance-related pay schemes. Conversely, some large organizations have retained their confidence in the benefits of multi-employer bargaining, such as in the CIA, which has three national agreements involving three large companies among a total of some 200. The CIA stresses the local pay flexibility which the arrangements offer within an advantageous national framework agreement.* Two-tier bargaining does in fact remain the most common pattern in multi-employer agreements which its adherents see as combining stability at industry level with maximum flexibility for individual members. Nor is the view widely held among employers that national bargaining is inflationary or contributes to unemployment. The system is claimed to stabilize wage costs at industry level while remaining sensitive to variations in regional and local labour market circumstances.

What seems clear from actual experience is that individual decisions to withdraw from multi-employer bargaining or collective decisions to dissolve existing arrangements need very careful consideration. Such decisions are not self-evident. Some organizations do, however, stress the need for frequent review and a pragmatic response to changing circumstances. This was well put by the British Printing Industries Federation: 'An industry agreement remains valid provided it maintains its relevance to the parties involved, and this requires recognition and acceptance of change according to the needs of the particular industry.'[23]

The decision to decentralize

A 1987 survey of nine companies found that organizations which operated in a variety of markets found it appropriate to decentralize their production and marketing decisions, and budgetary processes.[24] These organizations also tended to seek greater labour flexibility, set pay locally and relate it to performance. If, therefore, there is a natural relationship between decentralized organizational forms and decentralized bargaining, it follows that a decision to shift the locus of decision-making downwards should be matched by the bargaining arrangements. In summary, organizational experience offers a number of clear advantages in following the decentralization route:[25]

- an enhanced responsibility for line managers;
- more flexible and performance-related payment systems;
- the opportunity to recruit and retain new types of staff;
- the introduction of changes in working practices;
- greater flexibility in responding to product and labour market changes;
- the introduction of technical and organizational change;
- closer contacts with employees, especially shop stewards;
- the distancing of trade unions from influence over decisions such as corporate stategy and investment.

---

* See p 172.

However, the same 1989 survey reported that the decentralization decision involves a number of disadvantages:

- wasteful duplication of effort in pay negotiations;
- problems associated with limited negotiating experience of local management;
- the potential problem of leapfrogging pay claims as central control is weakened;
- the fragmentation of staff development and deployment.

Furthermore, in some cases it is clear that in relation to pay, decentralization can be more apparent that real. A survey in the late 1980s revealed that of 30 organizations with decentralized pay bargaining for manual workers, 'Only 17 per cent of establishments reported that there was no higher-level policy or guidelines or prior consultation'.[26] Plant autonomy in relation to the key issue of pay may therefore be an 'illusion' or a 'myth'.[27] This is not to imply that pay arrangements need to be either wholly centralized or decentralized: there is a clear case for a combination of both levels. This 'best of both worlds' approach is also suggested in Purcell's 'Decentralization Planning Checklist'.[28]

The research of Marginson, Kinnie, Purcell et al clearly indicates that even when decentralization offers a clear balance of advantage to an organization its form also needs to be considered. Kinnie argues against 'polarization' so that head office managers of industrial relations in large enterprises 'achieve central control over the key issues fundamental to the running of the business without undermining the autonomy of managers in the plant'.[29] But how is the appropriate balance between centralization and decentralization to be discovered and achieved?

Purcell's checklist is of clear value in the initial decision whether or not to follow the road to some form of decentralization. Indeed he reports that experience suggests that decentralization is not a 'universal panacea' and two organizations, after using his checklist, decided against their *a priori* view that decentralization was an obvious development. But where the decentralization decision is taken central co-ordination can still be retained through 'the budgetary control mechanism, where labour cost targets are often specified in line with broader targets or rates of return on sales and capital employed.'[30]

Financial guidelines or parameters can allow for meaningful local discretion within the clearly-defined constraints, without being seen in Kinnie's term as an 'illusion of local autonomy'. The Marginson 1988 survey did in fact find that 37 per cent of organizations circulated guidelines before local negotiations began. However, 'illusion' was in evidence in the majority of the surveyed organizations with 10 per cent of head offices issuing instructions, 17 per cent requiring approval of proposed settlements and 20 per cent holding meetings with establishment managers to discuss policy on pay settlements. Generally, it is difficult to see these concealed authoritarian approaches as options in finding a position at a point along the central-local continuum which best fits the characteristics and circumstances of individual organizations.*

Experience suggests a number of other options in relation to the form which

---

* Such approaches can also attract trade union hostility, as in the case of Lucas (see p 169).

decentralization can take, for example, an IRS ten company* survey of decentralization reported, in 1989 and 1990,[31] a number of significant variations. Some companies decentralized pay determination to divisional level while others chose the business unit or site. Pay bargaining could also be conducted across a number of locations. There was also a choice between decentralizing to relate to a company's product or labour markets.

The experience of decentralization

Organizations which have decentralized their bargaining have had a mixed experience. IRS's surveys of 1989 and 1990 reported the familiar advantages of an enhancement of the authority and responsibility of local management, and an easier ability to introduce changes in payment systems and working practices. Yet the familiar problems were also evident, ie the duplication of negotiating effort, the need to train negotiators and the vulnerability to 'leapfrogging'. The outcome was that only four of the ten companies anticipated further decentralization with four maintaining the status quo and two even contemplating some return to centralized decision-making.

Furthermore, the trend towards decentralization has undoubtedly been stimulated by the opportunities it provided to link pay to performance. Research is now suggesting that performance-related pay is proving a disappointment in itself, nor is there evidence that it has yet done anything for corporate performance.[32] This may encourage disillusion with decentralization and adds credibility to the prediction of a return to centralized bargaining in order for companies to regain control of their labour costs.[33]

Some prominent private sector organizations do, however, remain encouraged by their experience of decentralization. The most notable example is British Steel[34] which, following its privatization in 1988, organized itself into five businesses: strip products; general steels (the two largest); stainless steels; diversified products; and distribution. Each business had the option of decentralizing its bargaining arrangements to meet its own needs. However, there were some common elements:

- each business guaranteed there would be no change in current recognition and bargaining rights – some 95 per cent of British Steel employees are unionized;
- bargaining over pay and conditions was decentralized to business units under 'single table' arrangements covering the industry's industrial and craft unions;
- bargaining over pension arrangements was retained at the centre, ie business level;
- grievance and disciplinary procedures were retained but within the limits of the business unit;
- arbitration was subject to joint, not unilateral, reference.

British Steel believes its decentralization path has generally been a success in giving identity and responsibility to the individual businesses, as well as

---

* The companies were Associated British Ports, British Airports Authority, Cadbury, CMB Speciality Packaging, Coats Viyella, Legal and General, Lucas, Pilkington, Royal Insurance, STC (communications and information systems).

shortening the lines of problem resolution. The changes also provided the opportunity to introduce single table bargaining which has minimized inter-union differences. Local bargaining has also been assisted by the long experience, in the 1980s, of local management–union negotiations over the lump-sum bonus scheme which survived into privatization. There was also a well-established training programme in negotiating skills for managers.

More recent research in British Steel suggests that further decentralization is likely in some businesses, with each plant controlling its own sales and marketing functions.[35] However, British Steel maintains that its interest in further decentralization would be judged by its potential for increasing management's ability to bargain more flexibily and effectively with local bargaining groups.

The organizational effects

The decentralization of bargaining, especially since it is associated with organizational restructuring, can have far-reaching implications which need to be taken into account in the decision to decentralize and the process of implementation.

Purcell,[36] working with companies who used his decentralization planning checklist, found that the 'knock-on effects' which caused most difficulty were the restructuring of company-wide job evaluation schemes; the removal of the corporate layer from disputes procedure appeals; and the reduction in the numbers employed in, and influence, of personnel departments – sometimes involving transfers to local offices.

The IRS ten-company survey in 1989 and 1990 confirmed the existence of the 'knock-on effects', although with an uneven incidence. Three companies needed to reform their job evaluation schemes; two reported implications for their disputes procedures; and six found it necessary to revise the role of corporate personnel. Those indicating personnel's new role pointed to 'support services', 'advice' and 'guidance' in place of direction as well as the need to train local line managers in negotiating skills.

Implications for corporate personnel were reported in two detailed 1991 case studies of Prudential Assurance and the Automobile Association (AA).[37] Prudential transferred the personnel function from the corporate level to the business divisions where senior personnel are now controlled by the managing director in each business. Corporate personnel remains but has devolved all its operational activities retaining a strategic, co-ordinating role.

At the AA (a traditionally highly centralized organization) personnel professionals and certain key responsibilities were transferred from group to the four new divisions. All pay and conditions were to be negotiated at divisional level under the control of senior line management. Group personnel retains control of matters still negotiated centrally, ie pensions, health and safety, job security, and equal opportunities. At both the Prudential and the AA senior personnel and industrial relations specialists took a proactive role in the decentralization decision and its implementation. However, it proved difficult in both organizations to achieve acceptance by personnel of its new, decentralized role, although this problem was more acute in the AA given its tradition of centralized decision-making.

The potential resistance of personnel staff can be heightened by a reduction in staff and/or redeployment. At the Prudential, for example, the old corporate personnel department used to employ 180: this has now fallen to 30. However, IDS's 1991 survey found that decentralization can sometimes involve an increase rather than a reduction in personnel staff as organizations may need more people to ease the process of organizational change.[38]

Obvious casualties of decentralization (cited in the IRS ten-company survey), especially when personnel is itself decentralized, are corporate job evaluation schemes. Such schemes, in large, multi-plant organizations are the product of many years of negotiation and consensus-building between employers and trade unions. If there is also a parallel shift towards performance-related pay, as well as the restriction of industrial relations procedure appeals to divisions, potential adverse reactions from trade union officials as well as personnel staff will require careful handling. Yet, aside from the 1989 rail strike and the dispute over the abolition of the National Dock Labour Board, the trade unions have followed a generally pragmatic line. This is current TUC policy which is mindful of growing competition in the EC's internal market: 'Unions attempting to oppose all moves to decentralization and flexibility – some of which have clear immediate financial benefits to members – would be in danger of finding themselves bypassed.'[39] This approach was also evident in the EETPU's reluctant acceptance of separate pay talks with the electricity supply industry's private companies, beginning in some cases in 1993.

The trade union response, within organizations, can be determined by the degree to which individual unions are themselves decentralized organizations. In some cases unions have found it necessary to match management's decision to decentralize. This has been the case with the UCW in its response to the decentralized structures in the Post Office and British Telecom where bargaining responsibility has been partially devolved from the General Secretaries.[40] In other cases companies have considered it necessary to assure their trade unions that they had no intention of changing recognition and bargaining rights, notably in British Steel[41] and at Coats Viyella.[42]

The British Steel and Coats Viyella experience also show that, like local management, some unions have found it difficult to respond to the duplication of negotiations and lack of negotiating experience. Nor have these problems for trade unions been eased by management frequently taking the opportunity arising from decentralization to insist on single table bargaining from their trade unions – as at British Steel where the production and craft unions have experienced difficulty in finding common approaches.

SOME WIDER CONSIDERATIONS

The structure of collective bargaining has not been a matter which modern governments have wished to leave to the parties to industrial relations. Especially since the 1960s bargaining structure has been seen as a central influence upon key macro-economic variables, ie pay movements and pay levels, the state of inflation and labour productivity. The present government, in particular, as public sector employer, has actively sought to break up the traditions, processes and institutions of national level collective bargaining as a counter-inflationary instrument. It has used its power as ultimate paymaster to promote a similar movement in local government; and it has encouraged the private sector – as it follows a decentralization path – to believe that it is acting in the national interest, as well as its own, in marginalizing the role of trade unions and forging links between pay and performance.

The trend towards decentralization and the government's direct and indirect involvement in the acceleration of this process has given rise to a lively national debate among government, employers, trade unions and academics on the decline of national bargaining and the implications of decentralization for national economic policy objectives, especially in relation to non-inflationary pay movements. This debate has also been conducted in the wider, comparative context of other members of the EC in that their apparently more centralized collective bargaining arrangements may, or may not, be associated with greater control over movements in unit labour costs and a generally more successful economic performance than the UK. This gives rise to the possibility that as the internal market of the EC develops the UK may find that the labour cost implications of its decentralized collective bargaining place it at a permanent, competitive disadvantage. This argument has recently become more acute, given the limited freedom of the UK within the Exchange Rate Mechanism (ERM) to devalue its currency in order to restore competitiveness while minimizing the unemployment consequences.

On economic policy those who regret the break-up of centralized pay arrangements argue that centralized forms assist the synchronization of pay settlements, especially in the context of tripartite national economic assessment machinery existing in several European countries – notably Germany. Those who support this approach, however, maintain that the fragmentation of bargaining associated with decentralization can be exaggerated given that 'pay bargaining points' are much smaller in numbers than bargaining units and diminish substantially with organization size.[43]

Opponents of synchronized pay and the national economic assessment emphasize the virtues of decentralization which can link pay more closely to productivity and performance, and allow market forces to control local settlements without the inflationary mechanisms of national agreements. The benefits of market forces and the break-up of national bargaining are also stressed in relation to the public sector.

Aside from the arguments over devising effective means for co-ordinating settlements in the pay round and the prospects for tripartite agreement under a national economic assessment, it is difficult to accept the view that national agreements are inflation transmission mechanisms via comparability and leapfrogging. The experience of decentralization reported in this chapter does in fact strongly suggest that the possibilities of repercussive claims and settlements pose a major problem for decentralized bargaining which often needs to be approached with guidelines and parameters for bargainers set at the centre. Another approach is the two-tier structure within some private sector organizations which in some form could develop in local government. This two-tier model echoes the old national agreements which imposed disciplines on all the components of labour costs, as well as pay, at national level, while allowing for local variations in earnings reflecting differences in productivity and ability-to-pay.

Within the EC it is apparent that the prevailing level of bargaining is sectoral with some limited tripartite national arrangements and a recent, though still minor, accretion of company bargaining. This bargaining context is very different to the UK's largely decentralized arrangements. The much more centralized bargaining of most EC countries is associated with their generally superior performance over the long term in unit labour costs, inflation, productivity and unemployment. If it is accepted that decentralization in the UK allows unit labour costs to get out of control, then the bargaining differences between the UK and its more successful EC partners assume a significance beyond mere accidental association. One explanation for those bargaining differences could lie in the tradition of employer combination in the EC to defend their interests in contrast to the more individualistic propensity of British employers.

SUMMARY AND CONCLUSIONS

It is evident that the level or levels at which collective bargaining takes place is an important dimension of collective bargaining structure. It relates to and closely influences the other dimensions; it has implications for the process of collective bargaining and the distribution of power between and within the parties; it affects the content of collective agreements and has important 'knock-on' effects for the role and status of the personnel function and trade unions. It is also of major significance in the control of labour costs by organizations as well as in the wider, associated, context of national economic policy objectives of containing inflation without adverse effects on employment and economic growth. At the level of the EC, prevailing bargaining levels need to be evaluated in terms of the degree to which they assist or retard the performance of organizations and the economy as a whole as the internal market develops. However, in choosing bargaining levels UK employers have, in large numbers, opted for decentralization to the plant, business unit or profit centre.

The growing decentralization of collective bargaining in the UK has involved the progressive break-up (or a reduction in scope and influence) of multi-employer collective agreements with a consequent growth in corporate bargaining. Within corporations there has been a clear trend towards, and strong preference for, decentralization to business units, profit centres or plants. These trends have not been confined to the private sector: the public sector has been influenced by the private sector's example, as well as the direct policies and indirect influence of government, especially in the 1980s. These policies and influences are most clearly seen in the civil service and privatized agencies; the former state industries of electricity supply, telecommunications, steel and water; and British Rail within the public sector. In local government the old hegemony of national bargaining has been eroded by opting out and the search for new forms combining weaker central controls with strengthened local autonomy.*

---

* For example, the most recent proposals of the Local Government Management Board (formerly LACSAB) offer three options: maintain the present system of national bargaining on pay scales and rates with increasing local discretion; a two-tier system with only part of the annual increase enhancing national scales and rates, the remainder

In the NHS the eventual demise of national pay bargaining and decentralization to hospital trusts with (or even without) trade unions looks probable.

Within this picture of change and transformation there remains a limited continuing preference, on strictly instrumental grounds, for multi-employer bargaining, notably in industries such as chemicals, printing and ceramics, as well as those regrouping following the withdrawal of a large employer or employers. It is also possible that the trend towards decentralization has run its course, given the difficulties of implementation, such as the need for local level bargaining skills, the duplication of effort and the vulnerability to leapfrogging pay claims and settlements. There is also evidence that some organizations have diluted local autonomy by retaining central controls and parameters on pay settlements, while others may have backtracked to centralization to regain control over labour costs. However, it seems unlikely that there will be a wholesale retreat from decentralization of collective bargaining given its origins in, and close relationship to, organizational devolution in response to growing competition in markets. The search by organizations for new, devolved organizational forms has been the major explanation of the trend towards decentralization. Collective bargaining clearly needs to follow a parallel devolution. Trade unions, for their part, largely arising out of their continuing weakness in the 1980s and 1990s have reluctantly acquiesced in the process, but in some instances have already given greater emphasis to devolving their own organizational structures in response to those of management, an approach which has been endorsed by the TUC.

Decentralization has also been closely associated with the introduction of performance-related pay, although recent research suggests that the outcome in enhanced performance has been generally disappointing. Management has also, in some cases, used decentralization as an opportunity to insist on single table bargaining. This has been notable in the water industry, in British Steel and could, as we have noted, develop in NHS trusts.

However, the decision to decentralize is far from a panacea and needs very careful consideration in relation to the characteristics and contexts of organizations. Even if the decision is appropriate, the form of decentralization requires equal consideration. These decisions can be informed by readily available general criteria drawn from the actual experience of organizations. These criteria have been developed in recent years in the form of 'checklists' tested in practice which, in some cases, have led organizations to reverse an initial preference for decentralization.

The form of decentralization can be usefully considered along a centralization–decentralization continuum. This continuum can be related to bargaining content. For example, some items may be appropriate to bargaining at the corporate level with pay determined locally. Organizational experience suggests a list of appropriate items, ie premia, hours, holidays, pensions, sick pay, redundancy arrangements, cost of living indexation, and health and safety

---

applied locally; and 'kitty bargaining', ie a national agreement on a percentage increase on the pay bill with each authority having total discretion in the distribution of the increase which would allow for performance-related pay.[44]

matters. Local pay negotiations in themselves can be contained within appropriate guidelines or parameters set centrally or through co-ordinating meetings with local management. However, this approach may be seen by trade union negotiators as an attempt to avoid the implications of the decentralization decision. Trade unions may also need to be reassured that decentralization poses no threat to existing recognition and negotiation arrangements.

Even a well-planned and successful decentralization strategy requires careful evaluation at each stage of implementation. This may suggest a slowing-down or even a partial return to centralization. However, decentralization can offer clear advantages in terms of the organization's capacity to respond to a commercial crisis – as in the recent experience of Philips. There are also advantages, such as enhancing the responsibility and authority of local management, and the opportunity of linking pay to performance, as well as introducing single table bargaining. These advantages do, however, remain potential, and require detailed planning and implementation. Actual disadvantages, from organizational experience, include the duplication of effort, inadequate negotiating skills, and the danger of leapfrogging claims and settlements.

Organizational experience indicates the need to consider a number of the implications or 'knock-on' effects of decentralization. For example, corporate-wide job evaluation schemes are an obvious potential casualty of decentralization itself, especially given the preference for performance-related payment systems. The disruption and fragmentation of job evaluation schemes can attract the hostility of corporate personnel departments which may be aggravated by the devolution of personnel responsibilities to operating units and, in some cases, the reduction in numbers employed in personnel. However, the organizational changes involved in decentralization may require an increase in personnel staff rather than a decrease, given the problems of implementing change.

The fragmentation of job evaluation schemes is also likely to attract trade union resistance. In this respect trade union representatives may find common cause with personnel staff with whom they have been involved in the negotiation, construction and implementation of long-standing schemes. Trade union opposition may also arise from the abolition of grievance and disciplinary procedure appeals at the corporate level. In practice, however, trade unions have rarely taken their opposition to decentralization and its knock-on effects beyond protest and regret. This must be largely explained by their relative weakness in the 1980s and 1990s, although some trade unions have sought to maximize the benefits for their members from decentralized arrangements, and to achieve this have decentralized their own organizational structures.

References

1. Goodhart, D (1991) (reporting an LSE seminar given by D B Mitchell, a prominent US academic) 'Stabilisation expected for union membership', *Financial Times*, 4 December.
2. Industrial Relations Review and Report (IRRR) (1989) No 440, *Developments in Multi-employer Bargaining*, 1 IRS, pp 6–11.
3. Incomes Data Services (IDS) (1991) IDS Focus 59, *Decentralization*, June.
4. Confederation of British Industry (1988), *The Structure and Processes of Pay Determination in the Private Sector, 1979–1986*.

5. Brown, W and Walsh, J (1991) 'Pay determination in Britain in the 1980s: the anatomy of decentralization', *Oxford Review of Economic Policy*, Vol 7, No 1, pp 44–59.
6. Millward, N and Stevens, M (1986) *British Workplace Industrial Relations 1980–84*, Gower, Aldershot.
7. IRRR No 440, op cit.
8. Kinnie, N J (1985) 'Single employer bargaining: structures and strategies', *Industrial Relations Journal*, Vol 16, No 4, pp 76–81; (1985) 'Local managers' control over industrial relations: myth or reality?', *Personnel Review*, Vol 14, No 2, pp 2–10; (1987) 'Bargaining within the enterprise: centralised or decentralised', *Journal of Management Studies*, Vol 21, No 5, pp 463–77.
9. Leopold, J and Jackson, M P (1992), 'Decentralisation of collective bargaining within British Steel', unpublished research, University of Stirling.
10. Marginson, P et al (1988) *Beyond the Workplace: the Management of Industrial Relations in Large Enterprises*, Blackwell, Oxford.
11. Marginson, P (1986) 'How centralised is the management of industrial relations?', *Personnel Management*, October, pp 52–7; Leopold, J and Jackson, M P (1990) 'Decentralisation of collective bargaining: a case study', *Industrial Relations Journal*, Vol 21, No 3, pp 185–93.
12. Goodhart, D (1992), 'Lucas accused over centralised pay', *Financial Times*, 20 January.
13. Smith, M (1991) 'EETPU gives way on national deals', *Financial Times*, 9 December.
14. Beaumont, P B (1992) *Public Sector Industrial Relations*, Routledge, London.
15. Local Authorities Conditions of Service Advisory Board, 1990.
16. Smith, M (1991), 'NHS manager foresees trusts ending national pay bargaining', *Financial Times*, 25 October.
17. Smith, D (1991), 'Return to centralised bargaining predicted', *PM Plus*, Vol 2, No 4, 1991.
18. IDS Focus 59, op cit.
19. IRRR (1989) No 443 *Developments in multi-employer bargaining 2*, IRS, pp 6–12.
20. Summers, D (1991) 'Philips stops centralised pay bargaining', *Financial Times*, 3 July.
21. For example Avis, B (1990) 'British Steel: a case of the decentralization of collective bargaining', *Human Resource Management Journal*, Vol 1, No 1, pp 90–9.
22. IRRR No 440, No 443, op. cit.
23. IRRR No 443, op cit.
24. IRRR (1987) No 397 'Pay bargaining: to centralise or decentralise?', IRS pp 13–14.
25. IRRR (1989) No 451 'Decentralised bargaining in perspective', IRS, pp 11–14.
26. Marginson, P et al, reported in IRRR No 451, ibid, p 14.
27. Kinnie, N J (1987), op cit.
28. Purcell, J (1989), 'How to manage decentralised bargaining', *Personnel Management*, May, pp 53–5.
29. Kinnie, N J (1987), op cit, p 464.
30. Purcell, J (1989), op cit, p 55.
31. IRRR (1989) No 454, *Decentralised bargaining in practice 1*, IRS, pp 5–10; (1990) No 457, *Decentralised bargaining in practice 2*, IRS, pp 13–14.
32. Bevan, S and Thompson, M (1991) 'Performance management at the crossroads', *Personnel Management*, November, pp 36–9; IDS (1991) Focus 61, *Performance Pay*, December.
33. Smith, D, op cit.
34. IRRR (1990) No 474, *Decentralised bargaining at British Steel*, IRS, pp 11–14; Avis, B (1990), op cit.
35. Leopold, J and Jackson, M P, op cit.
36. Purcell, J (1989) op cit.
37. IRRR (1991) No 479, *Devolving Personnel Management at the AA and Prudential Corporation*, IRS, pp 4–9.
38. IDS Focus 59, op cit.

39. Trades Union Congress (1991) *Collective Bargaining Strategy for the 1990s*, p 4.
40. IRRR (1991) No 483, 'Changing industrial relations in the Post Office', IRS pp 10–14.
41. IRRR, No 474, op cit.
42. Leopold, J and Jackson, M P (1990), op cit.
43. Brown, W (1983) 'Central co-ordination', in Robinson, D and Mayhew, K (eds) *Pay Policies for the Future*, Oxford University Press, Oxford; Brown, W and Walsh, J (1991) op cit.
44. Smith, M (1992) 'Council bargaining change proposed', *Financial Times*, 17 January.

Chapter Ten

Industrial Relations Procedures*

P J White

This chapter explains the term 'industrial relations procedures', and considers why such procedures have become widespread in British industry; some key procedural arrangements are then introduced and explained; problematic issues are highlighted; and some concluding reflections are made.

THE MEANING AND EXTENT OF PROCEDURES

Procedures which are entered into jointly by management and employee representatives are designed to ensure that certain standards of industrial behaviour and conduct are adhered to. Such procedures also encourage fair, consistent and prompt methods of dealing with alleged misbehaviour or misconduct on the part of employers or employees.

There are many types of procedures to be found in contemporary British industry. The principal ones (on which we shall concentrate) deal with negotiating (including disputes), grievance, disciplinary and dismissal, redundancy, and health and safety issues. (Examples of other procedures include disclosure of financial information to employees, grading and job evaluation, and participation or employee involvement.)

According to the investigation by Millward and Stevens,[1] the proportion of surveyed establishments possessing some sort of industrial relations procedure increased from 85 per cent to 94 per cent between 1980 and 1984.

As a generalization, such procedures were more in evidence: in the public sector; in larger enterprises; and where trade unions were recognized. Even in smaller firms, there was a tendency for procedures to be expressed in written form, and there seemed to have been increased provision for 'outside' assistance (eg senior managers, or a body such as the Advisory, Conciliation and Arbitration Service (ACAS)) when a dispute or issue could not be solved lower down.

One reason for the prevalence of procedures was the encouragement given to them by the Donovan Royal Commission Report of 1968,[2] which treated

* The author wishes to thank many individuals and organizations for their assistance in the use of examples in this chapter, including the Automobile Association (AA), ACAS, Bovis Construction Ltd, Tony Cormack, Kevin Hawkins, Alan McCreath, the Scottish Print Employers Federation, Seaforth Maritime Ltd, United Distillers Plc, and George Waterston and Sons Ltd. Thanks are also extended to Colin Duncan for helpful comments on an earlier draft.

inadequate procedures 'as a major cause of industrial disputes'. The Commission therefore recommended the introduction of written, joint procedures.[3] Since the Commission's Report, other factors have also played a role, including various industrial relations statutes, codes of industrial relations practice and government pronouncements. But the fundamental reason for the spread of procedures lies in the advantages which employers and trade unions have found in such an approach.

THE MERITS AND LIMITATIONS OF PROCEDURES

Procedures can do the following:

- lay down accepted standards of conduct and behaviour in the workplace;
- help management and employees to avoid conflict;
- provide early warning of potential problems;
- place emphasis upon fairness and rationality, and reduce the possibility of inconsistent or uncontrolled action; and
- influence the morale of the enterprise and the people who work within it.

Nevertheless, procedures are by no means a panacea, for they also have their drawbacks, and they highlight problematic issues. Procedures reduce the autonomy of both parties: each is bound to acknowledge the rights and interests of the other in any action that they take. However, it is extremely fanciful to suppose that procedures reduce each party's autonomy in equal measure. In some instances, the stronger party might successfully resort to procedures, but a weaker party might also be able to gain concessions by resorting to procedures as a delaying or frustrating tactic. Intra-party considerations might also be relevant, for a procedure might be seen by the employer as a means of curbing the power of workplace representatives and/or their constituents. Senior managers can exert control over individual managers in a similar fashion.

There is considerable debate in industry over whether procedural arrangements should take a predominantly written or oral form. There are several advantages in having written procedures:

- the mere act of writing joint procedures encourages discussion as to their purpose and scope;
- an agreed text reduces the possibility of misunderstandings and ambiguities of meaning;
- written documents can be readily transmitted to, and retained by, those to whom the procedures relate;
- managers and trade union representatives leave and go elsewhere, taking with them their recollections of oral arrangements.

On the other hand:

- oral arrangements, or 'custom and practice', allow the opportunity for experiment, or for trying out novel arrangements without commitment on either side;
- written procedures can be restrictive – those managers who do not have written redundancy procedures, for example, might be able to cut their

workforce more speedily, and some trade unionists would prefer not to sign a redundancy agreement for fear that they are seen to be admitting to the inevitability of redundancy;

■ written procedures can introduce a 'legalistic' element into industrial relations, and can prejudice a relationship between management and unions which relies upon mutual trust, flexibility and a preparedness to compromise.

The written/oral distinction finds echoes in the formal/informal distinction in industrial relations. Formality can tend towards an over-rigid observance, while some degree of informality – or departure from the strict letter of a procedure – might be desirable when an extremely speedy decision is called for. Similarly, a dogged adherence to all stages in a procedure might prolong conflict, preventing concessions being made by those most directly involved in the issue.

Where it is decided to have written procedures, a further general problem might arise: they are expensive to produce and can create a daunting impression to the reader. In these circumstances, an enterprise might wish to produce a company handbook which summarizes the key features of each procedure, and which is handed to each new employee as part of the induction process. However:

■ the handbook must contain a comprehensive summary – a drastic summary can be meaningless and counter-productive;
■ employees must be made aware of the locations of the full copies;
■ the full copies must be readily available for inspection at short notice;
■ full copies should be given to all 'key' personnel, eg trade union representatives, first-line supervisors.

Another general problem area concerns the question of whether various procedures (eg grievance, disputes) should be separate or combined. It seems usually to be preferable to have separate procedures for distinct eventualities:

■ some procedures are 'triggered' by management (eg disciplinary), whereas others (eg grievance) are invoked by employees;
■ some issues (eg grievance) might be felt to require less elaborate appeal mechanisms than might others (eg disciplinary).

Nevertheless, it is useful to conceive of procedures as possessing parallel paths, for example, where the same senior management are involved in hearing appeals. Similarly, some interrelationship should also be allowed for, such as where an individual grievance escalates into a matter of collective contention.

It must already be clear that procedural issues are complex. Accordingly, managers and trade unionists who are contemplating the introduction or modification of procedures might wish to seek advice from sources external to the establishment. In the case of managers, higher level management (eg at head office) might be consulted, and management consultants might have a role to play; federated enterprises can call upon their employers' association. Workplace trade union representatives might seek guidance from full-time officials, local trade councils, shop steward combine committees and trade union research units. Where a joint management/union approach is felt to be called for, then the advisory function of ACAS clearly has a role to play. Indeed, recent reports of the service demonstrate that ACAS is especially heavily involved in advising industry on its industrial relations procedures.[4]

NEGOTIATING PROCEDURES

A negotiating procedure lays down a framework in which the parties determine terms and conditions of employment.* Given the potential for conflict over such matters, some provision must also be made for the resolution of collective disputes. In some instances, 'disputes procedures' might be separate from, though connected to, those providing for negotiations, but our focus is upon negotiating procedures which incorporate measures to resolve disputes. It must also be borne in mind that some individual grievances, for example, grading claims, or a woman's claim for equal pay for work of equal value, can have collective attributes. There can be knock-on effects for an entire group or enterprise. Accordingly, the individual grievance/collective dispute distinction is often blurred in practice.

Elements in negotiating procedures

There are usually four elements in such procedures.

1. The definition of the area (in terms of geography, occupational group or otherwise) in which the union's representative role is acknowledged, including the laying down of 'spheres of influence' where more than one union is involved.
   Example: This agreement regulates the industrial relationship between XYZ Company plc and those trade unions signatory to this Agreement and regulates the Conditions of Employment of hourly paid operatives (or, those holding positions up to Grade X) employed by the Company in Scotland.
2. Issues which are to be the subject of negotiation, ranging from wages and salaries to normal hours of work, from trade union membership to promotion.
3. The steps by which agreement is to be sought, including the determination of authority and seniority for both management and employees.
   Example: Stage 1. In the first place the meeting will be between the divisional personnel director and the divisional officer of the trade union. Either person may be accompanied by colleagues who have a specific interest in the negotiations.
      The union side will consist of the divisional officer and no more than four accredited representatives with a maximum of two from each factory. If any matter cannot be agreed at this level the matter will be referred to Stage 2.
      Stage 2. At this stage the committee will consist of the regional personnel director, the divisional chief executive, the divisional personnel director and one or more colleagues, together with the national officer of the union, the divisional officer and one or more representatives. If agreement still cannot be reached at this stage the matter will be referred to Stage 3.

---

* The distinction between 'framework' and 'terms and conditions of employment' is often referred to as a distinction between 'procedural' and 'substantive' matters.

Stage 3. At this stage the matter will be discussed by the company's regional chief executive and the appropriate union official.
4. The steps to be taken when there is a failure to agree.
Example: Should there be a failure to agree (at Stage 3) the matter may by mutual agreement be referred for conciliation and, if necessary, arbitration, either independently or through ACAS.

Some problems and issues

While negotiating procedures are designed to resolve disputes, they also acknowledge that disputes can and do arise. One of the functions of this sort of procedure, then, is to channel disputes and their resolution in a controlled manner. Otherwise, either party might be tempted to bypass procedure. For that reason, it is common to find a 'peace clause' built into procedures:

Example: The parties agree that at each stage of the procedure every attempt will be made to resolve issues raised, and that until all such stages have been carried through there shall be no disruption to normal working or other unconstitutional action by either party.

At the same time, agreements also acknowledge an important feature of such collective agreements in Britain: unless the parties specify to the contrary, such agreements are *not* legally enforceable contracts.

Example: It is the spirit and intention of the signatories that the terms of this Agreement shall be respected and implemented by both parties. It is not the intention of the signatories that the terms of this Agreement should in any way be binding in law.

As our earlier example made clear, provision can be made for conciliation or arbitration by a person or agency external to the establishment. Our example also made a distinction between the two principal methods of collective dispute resolution.

Conciliation (undertaken by ACAS conciliation officers) takes the form of attempts to persuade the parties to reach, by negotiation, a settlement of their dispute. Arbitration is provided either by arbitrator(s)* nominated by ACAS or by someone who is directly approached by the parties. Arbitration takes the form of an award after the arbitrator has heard the respective cases of the parties to dispute. In general, arbitration is more appropriate to *disputes of rights* (ie disputes over the interpretation or application of an existing agreement), than it is to *disputes of interest* (disputes over new terms and conditions of employment). In the former case, an arbitrator would usually be expected merely to clarify existing rules, but in the case of disputes of interest, the parties might be reluctant to entrust the proposal of innovations, perhaps of a fundamental nature, to an outsider.

There are several reasons why procedures have increasingly allowed for third-party involvement in negotiating and other procedures, reasons which are underlined by the fact that the parties in Britain are not usually compelled

---

* In some instances, a panel of up to three people might undertake arbitration.

by law to seek outside involvement or to abide by the outcome of such involvement.

A body such as ACAS can provide *bargaining assistance* to the parties where: there may be an impasse in negotiations, indicated by a breakdown in the disputes procedure; one or both parties might be lacking in experience of negotiations; or conciliation or arbitration can be viewed as constructive alternatives to industrial disputes which are costly in economic and psychological terms.

ACAS can also serve as an *outside authority* over a dispute, for conciliators and arbitrators are not connected with or involved in the dispute. This has several advantages: some disputes can be extremely protracted, so that eventually the parties might not be able to 'see the wood for the trees', or the factors which truly divide them; negotiating positions can become so entrenched that suggestions or proposals by outsiders might enable one or the other party to soften its negotiating position without loss of face; emotions, or clashes of personalities, can sometimes cloud reason, whereas an outsider can encourage the parties to look at their situation more dispassionately.

Potential disadvantages with third-party involvement include the possibility that management and unions come to treat resort to conciliation and arbitration as a 'soft option' along the lines of 'let ACAS sort it out'. In consequence, procedures might be undermined and rendered meaningless. However, before agreeing to intervene, ACAS satisfies itself that serious attempts have been made to follow a procedure through all of its stages. Third-party involvement might also prolong the resolution of conflict by postponing rather than averting a trial of strength between the parties. In consequence, the conflict might be more embittered and deep-seated.

A criticism which is levelled at arbitration is that arbitrators 'split the difference' between the parties – they, too, take the 'soft option'. It is partly for such a reason that 'flip-flop', 'pendulum' or 'last offer' arbitration has recently received some attention in British disputes procedures, often in conjunction with a 'no strike' clause.[5] Last offer arbitration requires an arbitrator to choose only between the latest claim of the union and the latest offer of the employer. Supporters of this practice maintain that:

- the incidence of stoppages would be cut – arbitration must be attempted first;
- negotiators would be more cautious in their expectations, for when an arbitrator is forced to choose between positions, negotiators are more likely to compromise beforehand;
- because the negotiators are being encouraged to narrow the distance between their respective positions, there is a greater likelihood of mutually agreed settlements being reached without recourse to arbitration;
- arbitrators would no longer be able to avoid tricky issues by 'splitting the difference' or compromising between the two positions.

However, the claims in favour of a no strike clause, combined with last offer arbitration, are somewhat exaggerated.

1. Arbitrators do not always 'split the difference' – indeed, many disputes of right (for example, over dismissal or grading) can involve a straight choice between one position and another.

2. Last offer arbitration might not readily lend itself to complex cases, where parts of both claim and offer might have considerable merit in the eyes of the arbitrator.
3. The arbitration decision might itself be the source of some dispute between employer and union.
4. Where arbitration is built in as an automatic stage, then the parties might be tempted not to negotiate in earnest, on the grounds that the arbitrator 'will solve our problem', but most managers and unions would feel that this was an abdication of their responsibilities. It is partly for this reason that requests to ACAS for conciliation, leading to jointly negotiated agreements, far exceed request for arbitration, where the parties could be said to forfeit some autonomy. (We give further consideration to the role of arbitration in Britain in our concluding remarks.)

GRIEVANCE PROCEDURES

Grievance procedures enable an individual employee to express a grievance or problem to immediate or, if need be, to higher management. There is much to be said for establishing a grievance procedure which is separate from negotiating procedures, for the former cover individual issues, in contrast to the collective focus of the latter. The distinction is not clear-cut, however, as we have already observed. In consequence, there should be some provision for grievances eventually to be routed through the negotiating procedures, although it is generally advisable for all concerned that grievances are settled by the people who are directly involved.

Example: Both parties accept the principle that it is important to settle grievances as near to the point of origin as possible.

Elements in grievance procedures

These procedures should specify *how and to whom* employees can raise a grievance.

Example: Stage 1. Any employee who wishes to discuss the matter with management will, in the first instance, discuss the matter with his/her immediate superior.

It is customary for such procedures to spell out the *stages* through which the grievance should go. It is usually considered to be important to specify the *time limits* at each stage in order to ensure speedy resolution of the grievance. The *rights of representation* on behalf of the employee should also be spelt out; in non-union establishments, or among non-members, individuals should have the right to select as representative an employee of their choice.

If, therefore, at Stage 1 the supervisor has been unable to resolve the matter within 24 hours of its being raised, Stage 2 can be attempted.

Example: Stage 2. The employee may consult with his/her shop steward during the next break in working time. The shop steward, accompanied by the employee, should if necessary then discuss the matter with the employee's immediate superior.

Stage 3. Failing satisfaction, the shop steward should discuss the matter with the departmental manager who should endeavour to resolve the matter within 48 hours of its being brought to his attention.

Stage 4. If there is no settlement at departmental management level, the senior shop steward should request a meeting with his general manager and may, if necessary, involve the local trade union official at the earliest opportunity. No time limit is put on this stage of procedure, but it is accepted that serious matters will be dealt with in a prompt manner.

Stage 5. If there is no settlement, a meeting will take place between senior management and the regional trade union official.

In common with other arrangements, grievance procedures tend to allow for external reference (eg to ACAS) where internal procedures have been exhausted.

Some problems and issues

The first stage of grievance procedures (the employee to the supervisor) could be said to be of especial importance.

1. A supervisor who through inaction regularly fails to resolve grievances may lose the respect of his employees, and suffer diminished authority.
2. Senior management must permit supervisors some delegated authority, at least on certain of the more routine problems, otherwise employees with grievances will be tempted automatically to bypass their supervisor.
3. On the other hand, senior managers tend to treat such procedures as controlling mechanisms, ensuring some consistency of behaviour among all supervisory staff, as well as reducing the supervisor's autonomy.
4. Some procedures at Stage 1 allow for the grievance to be presented either by the individual or by the individual in company with his representative. There are merits in permitting an immediate role for a shop steward where, for example, the individual lacks self-confidence and is reluctant to raise the issue in person. On the other hand, most workplace union representatives would prefer to withhold their intervention until they are truly needed: the notion of automatically involving the shop steward would not usually be helpful to that official, and it might also have the effect of alienating the supervisor and undermining his ability, or willingness, to resolve the difference directly with the individual.

The above-mentioned example of a grievance procedure included time limits at the various stages. However, there is an argument against including explicit time scales, on the grounds that an issue might sometimes prematurely force its way up the procedure, whereas a grievance stands a better chance of being effectively resolved by the parties who are directly involved. There might also be problems where trade union officials are difficult to contact within the prescribed time. For these reasons, the time limits might either be waived, along the lines of the final section of Stage 4 above or:

Example: The foregoing time limits may exceptionally be waived by mutual consent if both parties agree that the circumstances of the case may prove hard to ascertain, or where relevant personnel are not readily available.

Whether or not time limits are explicitly included, there seems to be great merit in preparing, for completion, special grievance handling forms. The employee can note the date of the initiation of his grievance, the issue which was raised, the manager who was approached and the action which was taken. From the manager's standpoint, the recording of grievances ensures that complaints are tackled speedily and are not allowed to fester. The personnel department, or manager who is entrusted with such functions, might be given the task of monitoring the firm's grievance handling arrangements, for the incidence of grievances might indicate areas where industrial relations are under some strain, and where there is scope for training both supervisors and shop stewards in the use of procedures.[6]

DISCIPLINARY PROCEDURES

Disciplinary procedures are to some extent the other side of the procedural coin: grievances are raised by employees, whereas disciplinary procedures specify the steps which managers are expected to take against employees.

The significance of these procedures cannot be understated. When determining unfair dismissal claims, industrial tribunals pay close attention to the manner in which individuals are disciplined and dismissed. Where unfair dismissal is established, then tribunals can order employers to pay compensation, or give re-employment, to affected individuals. The need for written disciplinary procedures has also been underlined by the ACAS Code of Practice on Disciplinary Practice and Procedures 1977.* While failure to observe the Code does not in itself render an employer liable to proceedings, tribunals might nevertheless take the Code into account when determining complaints of unfair dismissal against an employer.

Elements in disciplinary procedures

According to the Code of Practice, disciplinary procedures should embody several elements. It is recommended that they:

- should be in writing, preferably including an explanation as to why it is felt to be important to encourage certain standards of conduct and performance from all employees, as well as to strive for uniform and equitable treatment of all employees;
- specify to whom they apply (according to Millward and Stevens,[8] the vast majority of procedures applied to all employees within the establishment – ie manual and non-manual);
- provide for matters to be dealt with speedily;

---

* ACAS has subsequently produced a booklet designed to complement the Code of Practice with more practical guidance: *Discipline at Work*, HMSO (1987). According to one commentator,[7] such was the demand from industry that the handbook quickly achieved a third printing, and 120,000 copies. The importance of disciplinary procedures in unfair dismissal cases was underlined in 1987 by the House of Lords decision in *Polkey* v *AE Dayton Services Ltd*, which went against the employer. See also Chapter 18 on dismissal procedures in small firms.

- indicate the levels of management which have the authority to take the various forms of disciplinary action, and ensure that immediate supervisors do not normally have the power to dismiss without reference to senior management;
- provide for individuals to be informed of specific complaints against them, and to be given an opportunity to state their case directly to those who are considering disciplinary action before such decisions are taken;
- give individuals the right to be accompanied, either by a trade union official where a union is recognized, or by a fellow employee of their choice;
- ensure that any investigatory period of suspension is with pay (unless the contract of employment clearly specifies otherwise) and specify how pay is to be calculated during such a period;
- ensure that disciplinary action is not taken until the case has been carefully investigated;
- ensure that individuals are given a written explanation for any penalty imposed;
- provide a right of appeal and a description of the procedure to be followed and the action which may be taken by those hearing the appeal.

Some problems and issues

The Code sets great store by giving the individual an opportunity to state his case, in the company of his representative. The purpose of this facility is to allow the person to explain his side of the story, or version of events, before it is decided whether to take action against him.

It is also to be noted that the Code draws a distinction between 'gross' and less serious misconduct, to which different reactions are advised. Clearly, it is impossible to make a sharp distinction between types of offence, nor is it practicable to compile an exhaustive list. Accordingly, the following form of words might be considered suitable.

Example: Management reserves the right to dismiss without prior warning and without notice if an act of gross misconduct is committed. The following list, which is not exhaustive, gives some examples of offences which are treated as gross misconduct:
fighting, assault of another person on company premises;
being severely under the influence of drugs or drink while at work and thereby likely to endanger self or others;
theft from company premises of property belonging to the company, employees, suppliers or customers;
deliberate disregard of safety rules;
deliberate release of confidential company information to unauthorized persons.

Offences which might be felt to be less serious, calling for a series of verbal and written warnings before dismissal is contemplated, might also be spelt out.

Example: Other offences which have been repeated despite warnings will also lead to dismissal. Such offences include, but are not limited to, the following:
poor attendance and bad timekeeping;
poor workmanship and/or work performance;

unauthorized absence from the designated place of work;
repeated and/or sustained unauthorized absence from work.

A prime purpose of warnings is to rectify the behaviour or conduct of an employee. Clearly, then, it is important for management to monitor the individual's behaviour after warnings have been issued. But it is also advisable for the individual's shop steward to ensure that his member is given full opportunity to show improvement.

Generally, warnings are allowed to lapse after a specified period.

Example: Provided that there are no further breaches of discipline for a period of one year following the issue of the first formal warning, then it will be considered null and void and will be removed from the employee's record.

Where a serious offence has been committed, the warning might remain 'on the record' for more than one year, depending upon circumstances.

Even where an individual is felt to have committed gross misconduct, justifying summary dismissal rather than a warning, employers are nevertheless expected to allow an appeal against the decision, perhaps on a form specially devised for the purpose:

Example: Where an employee is dismissed summarily (eg for reasons connected with gross misconduct) the dismissal shall stand but it will be open to the employee or his trade union representative to contest the dismissal. An intention to appeal must be lodged in writing with the employer within 72 hours of the receipt of the disciplinary action. Unless the appeal is lodged within 72 hours, it will be assumed that the employee accepts the decision.

It is to be noted in the examples quoted that drunkenness can be treated as a serious offence, whereas absence is usually treated less seriously. But the question arises as to suggested company policy in the case of employees who are afflicted by alcoholism as distinct from excessive drinking on random occasions. One company (Seaforth Maritime Ltd) has attempted to tackle the issue in its procedures in an especially imaginative fashion.

First, the *background* is sketched in for all employees by quoting statistics to indicate that approximately 3 per cent of a company's workforce will suffer from alcoholism to some degree. The Health and Safety at Work etc Act 1974 is also cited as a reminder that employers have a duty to ensure the health, safety and welfare of all employees, while each employee has a duty 'to take reasonable care for the health and safety of himself and of other persons who may be affected by his acts or omissions at work'. (Health and safety procedures are discussed later in this chapter.)

Second, the company's procedure acknowledges that, although alcoholism as an illness is very difficult to recognize, nevertheless it might be *indicated* by any of the following: absenteeism, or uncertified sickness; decreased work performance – poor productivity, poor timekeeping; behaviour – moodiness, irritability, lethargy, uncooperativeness; drinking habits – suspicion of drinking at work, before work or at lunchtime; hand tremor; facial flushing and bleary eyes; accident record – proneness to accidents.

Third, where management forms a suspicion that an employee suffers from alcoholism, managers are encouraged to *interview* him, with a representative if need be. Where the suspicion is confirmed, management will suggest that the employee consider making an approach to an independent alcoholism counselling agency. Should the employee be off work for this reason, then he would be covered by the company's sick pay scheme and would not suffer loss of pay.

Fourth, the company liaises closely with outside agencies (possibly including medical specialists) to draw up a *rehabilitation programme* for the individual.

Finally, 'following a return to work after or during treatment, should work performance again suffer as a result of alcoholism, each case will be considered on its merits and, if appropriate, a further opportunity to accept and co-operate with treatment will be provided'.*

In the various examples cited, opportunities for appeal have been mentioned. It is fairly commonplace for such appeals to be heard by a special committee or panel, and, in some instances, trade union representatives seem to feel that they can provide better protection for their members where they argue the case to a body consisting solely of managerial personnel.

Where there is a failure to agree on a question of discipline, then an external stage (similar to that in other procedures) might be included, in the form of ACAS conciliation or arbitration. In any case, when an individual makes a formal complaint of unfair dismissal against his former employer, a copy of that complaint is automatically sent to ACAS for possible conciliation.

A conciliation officer from the service will then attempt to approach the employer and the individual, with a view to resolving the difference between them. Certain features of the role of ACAS can be stressed:

- conciliation is completely separate from the industrial tribunal system (conciliation officers are not members of tribunals);
- neither the employer nor the individual is compelled by law to discuss the matter with the officer;
- nevertheless, the officer provides an opportunity for a troublesome issue to be settled calmly and speedily;
- the conciliation officer has no power to compel either party to settle their difference;
- he will explore whether a disciplinary procedure has been fully used, and if it has not, he will encourage its full use;
- he will explore with the *employer* whether he is prepared to consider the re-employment of the individual, failing which he will consider the scope for the voluntary payment of compensation to the individual;
- he will explore with the *individual* whether he is determined to proceed with his complaint to an industrial tribunal or whether he would prefer an agreed settlement without a tribunal hearing – he will also explore the individual's preferred solution, eg re-employment or compensation;
- where an individual withdraws his complaint, or where an agreed settlement

---

* For further discussion of a policy on alcoholism, including the suggestion that consultation with trade unions is a prerequisite for success, see Mortimer, B (1988) 'Alcohol and work – an explosive cocktail', *Employment Gazette*, 96, February.

is reached under the auspices of ACAS, then the complaint to the tribunal automatically lapses, and the individual forfeits any entitlement to take his case to a tribunal, while the employer cannot renege on his decision (to re-employ or pay compensation) by then 'appealing' to a tribunal.

It is clear that a tribunal hearing is an alternative to settlement at ACAS, but it must be borne in mind that such hearings are held in public, with the attendant consequence of unwelcome press publicity. Compensation awards against employers tend to be higher than are those agreed at the ACAS stage, and tribunals have increasingly been attended by legal representatives, with the consequence that complex legal arguments tend now to be used in tribunal proceedings. Conciliation and tribunals do have certain features in common, however, for it is equally rare for a dismissed person to be re-employed by the former employer at either stage.

REDUNDANCY PROCEDURES

It might be argued that the negotiation of redundancy procedures is an admission of an inefficient business, and that the acknowledgement of the possibility of redundancy demotivates employees. However, redundancy procedures have a positive dimension, and (as recent British experience affirms) there are few enterprises which have avoided the need for redundancies.

Elements of redundancy procedures

A procedure might include a preamble along the following lines:

Example: Under normal operating circumstances, it is our intention to provide regular employment to all employees. However, reductions in manning may sometimes be felt to be inevitable, eg the demand for our product/service is unpredictable and might fluctuate.

The procedure might then itemize the steps which management would endeavour to take to reduce manning by means other than compulsory redundancies. Depending upon circumstances, such steps might include: early retirement; natural wastage and/or the non-filling of vacancies; reducing or eliminating overtime working; slight reductions in basic weekly hours through negotiations; the redeployment or transfer of employees within the enterprise, with training where appropriate; terminating the employment of temporary employees; the reduction or elimination of subcontracted work; voluntary redundancies.

Nevertheless, these steps might be insufficient to meet an employer's requirements. For instance, the measures as outlined might not bring about the desired reduction in numbers: that element of overtime working which is required to carry out essential repair or maintenance work places a lower limit on the extent to which overtime can be cut; early retirement can be extremely costly to an enterprise; and certain workers who are vital for continuing operations might leave first. In these circumstances, the issue arises of the selection of employees.

One frequently used method is last in first out (LIFO). This arrangement has advantages to employers, for it avoids their having to make invidious choices between individuals. It also appeals to trade unions, for it reduces the possibility that management might make selections on the basis of 'favouritism'.

But the application of LIFO is not without its problems. Should it, for example, apply by department or across the whole organization? Also, it might be inappropriate where operational requirements call for the retention of certain key occupational groups, such as computer personnel. Accordingly, employers might feel justified in considering other criteria, perhaps in the following sequence: operational and job requirements of the enterprise; skills and training levels; suitability for retraining; length of service; standard of performance, including past *verified* attendance record.

> *Example*: Misconduct (as defined in the disciplinary procedure) would not normally be treated as the sole reason for selection for redundancy but any current warnings issued (in accordance with the section on discipline) will be taken into account; personal circumstances.

As far as is possible, the selection criteria must be objective, in the sense that they are capable of some sort of independent assessment.

Some problems and issues

There are certain trade unionists in Britain who refuse, as a matter of principle, to negotiate redundancy procedures with employers, on the grounds that a joint procedure might render redundancies less easy to resist. Other trade unionists view the matter differently, on the grounds that a joint agreement enables them to influence the employer's manpower strategy, including the taking of measures short of redundancy (see above). There is also the risk that a union's outright refusal to negotiate over redundancies will leave inadequate scope for the negotiation of the most favourable terms of compensation on behalf of those who are made redundant.

It is not uncommon in British industry for redundant workers to receive payments in excess of the minimum laid down by redundancy payments legislation. When trade unionists perceive that some redundancies are inevitable, and when all alternatives to compulsory redundancies have been found wanting, then the best possible terms for affected members can be negotiated. In this connection, it is to be noted that the statutory scheme is linked to length of service, and that no one with less than two years' service with an employer would be legally entitled to any payment from him.

In some circumstances, the need for redundancies occurs with little warning, by virtue of a major, unforeseen, external cause. In general, however, any changes in manpower can be anticipated and therefore planned. It seems to be a growing practice for employers to consult with trade unions, and, in larger-scale cases, this is required by law.*

Extracts from an agreement between the AA and APEX exemplify attempts at greater consultation over the issue.

---

* For the current legal requirements on consultation over redundancies see Chapter 17.

Example: The AA agrees to disclose to APEX annual corporate and business plans. Twelve months' notice of proposals with job security implications will be given. Consultation takes place every six months on manpower forecasts and overall manning levels. This entails disclosure of all information concerning the proposals and allows reasonable time and opportunity for the trade union to examine and seek clarification on each proposal. Revised proposals will be given full consideration.

The criteria for the selection of redundant workers can be fraught with difficulty. Moreover, a worker who has been 'unfairly' selected for redundancy might be able to claim unfair dismissal where an employer has unreasonably departed from a procedure or customary arrangement. It is therefore advisable for management to consider the establishment of an appeals procedure, to which aggrieved employees can submit their case.

HEALTH AND SAFETY PROCEDURES

It would appear that formal health and safety procedures received encouragement in the post-Donovan climate through the publication of the Robens Report in 1972,[9] and the introduction of two statutory instruments: the Health and Safety at Work etc Act 1974, amplified by the Safety Representatives and Safety Committees Regulations 1977.

Elements in health and safety procedures

The basic philosophy of the legislation is that it is the responsibility of all people within an organization to seek to achieve safe and healthy working conditions. Alongside this universal obligation, the ultimate responsibility for health and safety policy in an enterprise rests with managers, in the following basic respects:

- the provision and maintenance of plant, systems and places of work that are safe;
- the safe handling, storage and transport of articles and substances;
- the provision of information, instruction, training and supervision to ensure the health and safety of employees;
- the provision of a working environment that is safe and without risks to health;
- the provision of adequate welfare facilities.

It is, then, the duty of every employer, usually at board level, to prepare a written statement of his policy concerning health and safety, and to bring this policy to the notice of employees. It is also incumbent on the employer to ensure that the system of recruitment, supervision and training within the enterprise reinforces the policy laid down.*

---

* For a dramatic instance of corporate neglect, see the Department of Energy, *The Public Inquiry into the Piper Alpha Disaster* (1990), Vol 1, Cm 1310. According to the report, there were 'significant flaws in the quality of Occidental's management of safety . . . (managers) adopted a superficial response when issues of safety were raised by others . . . platform personnel and managers were not prepared for a major emergency' (para 14.52).

In the case of hazardous substances or operations, for example, it is clearly necessary to ensure that people who are *recruited* to work with these possess the requisite specialized knowledge. Or, to take another example, when the atmosphere is polluted, it is not enough for management to issue protective clothing to employees: *supervision* must also ensure that such clothing is worn. Nor does it suffice for policy and associated standards merely to be introduced; they must also be *monitored*, by such means as collating statistics, conducting investigations, and preparing reports on health and safety incidents.

The 1977 Regulations envisaged a prominent role for employees, notably through the employees' appointment of safety representatives and joint safety committees (JSCs). Several functions were conferred upon a safety representative, the most notable being:

- to investigate potential hazards and dangerous occurrences at the workplace, and to examine the causes of workplace accidents;
- to investigate complaints made by any employee whom he represents, relating to that employee's health, safety or welfare at work;
- to make representations to the employer on the foregoing matters;
- to make representations to the employer on general health, safety or welfare matters within the workplace;
- to carry out inspections of the workplace, or of documents in the employer's possession, or to obtain relevant information from the employer;
- to attend meetings of JSCs in his capacity as safety representative.

It must be stressed that the powers that are outlined above apply to representatives, not to JSCs. It is also to be noted that the representatives must be members of a 'recognized trade union'; in other words, the statutory system of safety representation is trade union based.[10]

For the purpose of clarity, it is important for the employer to identify the relevant manager to whom the safety representative should report. The manager concerned should also have detailed knowledge of the matter and operations under discussion. It seems advisable, therefore, for the line manager or supervisor to be the first point of contact rather than, say, the personnel or safety officer. Nevertheless, a representative's written report to his supervisor, perhaps on a specially prepared form, might be copied to other relevant people. The supervisor's reply to the representative could take a similar course. In other instances, the supervisor might initiate the completion of a special form, when, for example, an accident occurs.

Under the Regulations, an employer is obliged to establish a JSC with employees where at least two safety representatives request him in writing to do so. A JSC must then be established within three months of the employer's receipt of the request. Some JSCs operate under a constitution, containing the following elements:

- composition of the committee (the presence of a senior manager would affirm to employees the seriousness with which management regards the JSC);
- duration of office of the committee members;
- training provision for management and worker representatives;
- dates of meetings;

- determination of the agenda;
- functions and powers of the JSC;
- minutes of meetings – their writing and distribution;
- the role and status of invitees (including safety officers) and subcommittees.

Attention has to be given to a hierarchy of safety committees, where more than one workplace is involved. The health and safety procedure at Lehrer/McGovern Bovis's Canary Wharf development had the following provision.

Example: An overall Project Safety Committee chaired by LMB will receive reports from individual Site Safety Committees and monitor overall safety and health on site.

Regard has also to be paid to the relationship between JSCs and conventional Joint Consultative Committees (JCCs).* Given the technical nature of health and safety considerations, there is much to be said for having separate committees, specifically for such matters.

The legislation is enforced by the Health and Safety Executive (HSE), through its inspectors. It is within an inspector's power to issue an employer with an 'improvement' or 'prohibition' notice in connection with an employer's infraction, but, in reality, the inspector is more likely to attempt conciliation with the employer. It is extremely rare for the HSE to take enforcement action.[11] ACAS might also have an advisory or conciliatory role to play, but only after the relevant disputes/grievance procedure had been exhausted.

Some problems and issues

The extent to which health and safety issues are truly a subject for dispute between employers and employees is debatable. The Robens Report best exemplified a 'unitary' perspective, contending that there is a high degree of common interest, given best effect through consultation between the two sides. The Regulations, in contrast, assigned an extremely prominent role to union representatives; a pluralistic perspective was stressed, and negotiations were seen as the best means of resolving conflicting interests.

Two interrelated matters for consideration can thus be seen to arise. First, are health and safety issues more rightfully appropriate for consultation than negotiation? Second, to what extent should safety representatives come from shop stewards' ranks, thereby emphasizing their links with the unions?

The process of consultation between employers and employees in Britain is often said to be characterized by shared interests: the parties jointly seek out all relevant information, they share it fully, they jointly work out solutions, they indulge in a positive-sum game (where both sides gain), and adversarial behaviour is eschewed. In general, managers tend to be more enthusiastic about consultation, for it allows them to retain their decision-making powers.

In the case of negotiations, on the other hand, the degree of information sharing is restricted, the parties engage in a zero-sum game (a win to one side entails an equivalent loss to the other) and the tactics of bluffs, threats and

---

* See Chapter 11 for a detailed discussion of JCCs.

sanctions are used. Trade unionists tend to favour this approach, because it affords an opportunity for them to make decisions jointly with the employer. Trade unionists also tend to have a suspicion that an employer's fostering of consultation might serve to undermine the strength of workplace bargaining.*

In common with many such generalizations, the distinction between consultation and negotiation is, in reality, blurred: some consultative processes have elements of joint decision-making, whereas some negotiations occur in an environment of shared assumptions and constructive efforts.

In the case of health and safety, there is some doubt whether assumptions and interests are so fully shared that consultation is the solely appropriate mode. Thus, the creation of a safe environment carries a cost which the employer must bear and which he might seek to temper.

Evidence suggests that, when health and safety issues involve significant financial expenditure, safety representatives tend to process these through collective bargaining procedures rather than through consultation.[12] Trade unionists are unlikely to see JSCs as the principal vehicle for improvement, for several reasons: JSCs meet only occasionally, and are more suitable for long-run policy issues, whereas some problems call for immediate action; fully 'consultative' JSCs would have little or no power to authorize decisions; and representatives might receive more solidaristic support from their constituents through collective bargaining.

The links of solidarity between representatives and their constituents help to explain why some trade unions prefer their shop stewards to serve as safety representatives, too. The need to have people with considerable 'representing' experience is another reason. But other trade unions prefer a separation of roles. The danger of an overload of work is a prime factor (health and safety can involve many 'technical' issues, calling for specialist workplace knowledge), and it might often be more satisfactory for the workers' side to have one of their number catering for 'quasi-consultative' issues, leaving the shop steward to develop the more controversial ones in a negotiating framework.

There are several features of the safety representative structure which call for agreed procedural arrangements between management and workers.

1. The law places no restriction on the number of representatives that a union may appoint, but the significance of this issue would be reduced somewhat were the representatives to be drawn from the ranks of shop stewards.
2. The constituencies of the representatives require to be identified, bearing in mind that representatives have the right of inspection; different shifts, or distinct occupational groups, might have to be catered for.
3. In multi-union situations, each trade union would have the right to appoint a safety representative, but it might be decided that some representatives should cater for more than one union where the constituencies are small.
4. Attention has been given to the position of non-union employees, who have no representative rights under the legislation.

---

* See Chapter 7 for a detailed analysis of negotiations.

preferable for trade union representatives to react to managment decisions rather than attempt to share them.*

There seems to be little doubt that statutory forces have encouraged the development of certain procedures in Britain, notably in the spheres of discipline, and health and safety.[16] The implementing of these procedures has also been overlaid by a legislative apparatus. In consequence, workers have a right of 'appeal' against management decisions to independent external bodies. Whether, in consequence, workers' interests are better protected is more debatable, however. Of course, the mere existence of the law might act as some constraint upon management, so that workers are disciplined, not dismissed, or working environments are rendered safer than they otherwise might have been. Nevertheless, the experience with unfair dismissal legislation does not seem to suggest substantial relief for workers,[17] and there is evidence that not even the minima as provided for in the health and safety legislation are always laid down.[18] Moreover, it is by no means certain that trade unions in Britain can hope for considerable advance in procedural safeguards from EC sources. In the light of these realities, trade unions demonstrate scepticism towards attempts at the statutory reinforcement of procedural arrangements. Statutory proposals might become heavily diluted, in response to business concerns about 'costs' or 'competitiveness'. The law itself can have double-edged effects, serving to confirm management decisions, and adding a layer of extreme complexity and uncertainty to workplace industrial relations.

In marked contrast, the widespread incidence of negotiating and grievance procedure owes little to statutory encouragement, although such measures have been contemplated, and attempted, in connection with collective agreements as a whole. According to the Conservative Government's 1981 Green Paper[19] two main advantages were likely to stem from the legal enforceability of collective agreements, which, as we noted earlier, British industry has shunned. First, enforceability would bring peace and stability to industrial relations; and secondly, it would encourage the development and use of disputes procedures. However, the Green Paper mentioned several drawbacks to such an approach, the most noteworthy for our purpose being that legal enforceability required clear agreements that were capable of interpretation in the courts, whereas the 'vast majority' of collective agreements in Britain were underpinned by *informal* understanding and arrangements.[20]

That employers were at best apathetic to the attempt of the Industrial Relations Act 1971 to declare agreements legally enforceable suggests that managers also seem to regard the law as sitting uncomfortably with procedural matters. Indeed, employers' emphasis seems to be on autonomous developments, as exemplified by the recent extension of last offer arbitration in Britain.

---

* For example, an ACAS survey[15] found widespread incidence of redundancy policies or practices, as distinct from agreements. The survey concentrated on those employers who either had standing redundancy arrangements or had recently declared redundancies. Those employers who had no policies or practices, let alone agreements, were therefore excluded from the survey. On the lesser likelihood that disciplinary or dismissal procedures are jointly agreed, compared to negotiating procedures, see Millward and Stevens, op cit, p 189.

It appears that such arrangements are especially to be found in the private sector, among multinationals, and in conjunction with single union and no strike agreements.[21] It also seems that the arrangements might have the effect of achieving the objectives of legally enforceable agreements – stability in industrial relations, a declining incidence of industrial disputes, more 'responsible' bargaining – with a flexibility which asociation with the law might impair.

In certain cases, as Lewis makes clear,[22] a pendulum award can be accompanied by the formulation of an acceptable compromise by the arbitrator. However, the procedure must admit this approach, and the circumstances (eg management–union relations) must be favourable. But that, in turn, raises questions as to whether last offer arbitration is truly innovatory. There appear to be close similarities between the 'strike free' clauses of last offer processes and the 'peace' clauses which have long been a feature of British procedures. Nor could last offer arbitration be said to be innovatory in other respects, for disputes of right generally require the arbitrator to make a straight choice between one party and the other.

It is clear that mass unemployment and economic recession have fostered a mentality of 'survival of the fittest' among the unions, and have encouraged the more entrepreneurial (eg the EETPU) to perceive recent recognition/dispute/ arbitration arrangements as a lifeline to membership consolidation. But the recent experience with industrial relations procedures suggests that employers continue to play the dominant role in their introduction and operation. The trade unions are unlikely to obtain much relief from any statutory framework that can be presently envisaged. The potentially most favourable set of circumstances for unions would envisage a Labour government, but it is unclear how the law in itself could bring about a marked transformation in trade union recognition procedures. Such procedures are inextricably linked to those for negotiations, while the law concerning health and safety, and redundancy assigns a prominent place to the unions, yet there is little evidence that the unions have been able to use the law as leverage to enhance their influence. Similarly, the most recent versions of the Social Charter/Chapter exclude any involvement in rights of association for employees in member nations. Nor will the state of the economy hold much promise for the foreseeable future. Forces of competition, technological change and increasingly footloose enterprises will continue to compel (and enable) employers to control staffing levels and labour costs, exercise strong discipline, and enjoy considerable autonomy over health and safety measures. Such control will probably be exercised more through the consultative mode than through the negotiating one. It would seem, therefore, that the unions will have to rely and draw heavily upon their own resources to utilise the large elements of informality which procedural arrangements continue to offer.

References

1. Millward, N and Stevens, M (1986) *British Workplace Industrial Relations 1980–1984, The DE/ESRC/PSI/ACAS Surveys*, Gower, Aldershot, p 169.
2. Royal Commission on Trade Unions and Employers' Associations (1968) *Report*, Cmnd 3623.
3. Ibid, paras 68, 162–6.
4. ACAS (1992) *Annual Report 1991*, ACAS, p 79.

5. See Leese, J (1988) 'The Nissan agreement – a work philosophy', *Employment Gazette 93*, August, p 327; Lewis, R (1990) 'Strike-free deals and pendulum arbitration', *British Journal of Industrial Relations*, 28, 1, March.

6. For a discussion of a grievance procedure under strain, see Pendleton, A (1991) 'Workplace industrial relations in British Rail: change and continuity in the 1980s', *Industrial Relations Journal*, 22, 3, Autumn.

7. Hunter, I (1988) 'Discipline at work', *Employment Gazette*, 96, May. According to the ACAS *Annual Report 1991* (p 63), nearly half a million copies of *Discipline at Work* have now been published.

8. Op cit, p. 176.

9. Committee of Inquiry on Safety and Health at Work 1970–72 (1972) *Report*, Cmnd 5034.

10. For details of representation in non-union situations, see Beaumont, P B (1983) *Safety at Work and the Unions*, Croom Helm, Beckenham, p 186.

11. Walters, D (1987) 'Health and safety and trade union workplace organisation – a case study in the printing industry', *Industrial Relations Journal*, 18, 1, Spring.

12. Walters, op cit.

13. On AIDS, see 'AIDS and the workplace', *Employment Gazette*, 98, May 1990; on workplace sources of ill-health amongst office workers, see *Employment Gazette*, 95, April 1987, p 217. Certain collective agreements are already providing for female employees to have time off for breast and cervical cancer screening. The British Printing Industries Federation has such an agreement with the GPMU. Although there is no precise equivalent in the Scottish industry, the Scottish Print Employers Federation recommends that all of its members should provide on-site facilities where these are justified by the number of employees.

14. Purcell, J and Sisson, K (1983) 'Strategies and practice in the management of industrial relations', in Bain, G S (ed) *Industrial Relations in Britain*, Blackwell, Oxford, p 114.

15. *Redundancy Arrangements: The 1986 Survey* (1987) Occasional Paper 37 ACAS, London, p 12.

16. Millward and Stevens, op cit, p 170.

17. See the author's 'Unfair dismissal legislation and property rights – some reflections', *Industrial Relations Journal*, 16, 4, Winter 1985.

18. Walters, op cit, p 48. It must also be observed that the author's study was in the printing industry, where trade union activity and vigilance would normally be expected to be relatively keen.

19. *Trade Union Immunities* (1981) Cmnd 8128 p 55.

20. The Conservative Government subsequently resurrected discussion on legal enforceability, on the grounds that circumstances had changed since the early 1980s. One such change had been the increase in 'no strike' clauses; another had been a 'much greater acceptance of the role which the law can play in helping to bring about better industrial relations behaviour and practices' (para 8.7). Accordingly, it was then proposed that collective agreements would be presumed to be legally enforceable, unless the parties specified to the contrary. See *Industrial Relations in the 1990s* (1991) Cm 1602.

21. Lewis, op cit.

22. Ibid.

Chapter Eleven
Employee Participation

Mick Marchington

The idea of employees participating in some way in the administration of their working lives has long been a source of interest for practitioners and academics alike. Some would argue that such ideas are an unnecessary diversion from the primary job of management – that is, to supply a profitable and cost-effective service to customers – and that employers should have the right to make decisions without being forced to consider employee interests. Others would suggest that an unbridled managerial prerogative is quite contrary to the democratic ideals upon which developed societies are based, and that employees ought to have a say in decisions which affect their working lives.

Indeed, the terminology itself serves to illustrate the quite different interpretations of employee participation; while employers talk of employee involvement (EI), trade unionists talk of industrial democracy. That is, one starts from the assumption that managements might be willing to *allow* some degree of involvement by employees in the process of decision-making, while the other has its source in notions of democracy and the *right* of the governed to control those in positions of authority. The last 20 years have seen practical illustrations of this conflict of interpretations, with initiatives ranging from worker directors through to team briefing and profit-sharing, along with a resurgence of interest in joint consultation. In other words, while it might have become commonplace among progressive managers and trade unionists to argue that employee participation is a 'good' thing – for whatever reason – the operationalization of this concept has also led to significantly different forms of participation in practice.

Notwithstanding the debate over terminology, a whole range of participation initiatives have been adopted by employing organizations within the UK. What matters to practitioners is whether these schemes actually provide advantages to those involved, either in terms of substantive benefits or improved working relationships. Of course, the consequences of such schemes might not be those which their designers intended and it is important to assess success (however measured) against practical examples rather than exhortations or rhetoric.[1] In this chapter, the concern is to describe and analyze practice in a number of different forms of participation, chosen for their relevance to contemporary industrial relations activity.*

---

* The decision to focus upon team briefing, quality circles and TQM, joint consultation, worker directors, employee share ownership and profit sharing was made on this basis. Inevitably, other practices could have been examined, the most important of these being autonomous work groups, information disclosure, pension fund trustees and safety representatives, but there was insufficient space to do justice to all of these techniques.

FORMS OF EMPLOYEE INVOLVEMENT AND PARTICIPATION

A distinction can be made between these different forms of employee participation in the following way.

1. Direct participation is concerned with face-to-face contact between managers and their subordinates, and may primarily involve the passage of information from the former to the latter, communication between the two parties or the exercise by subordinates of some kind of decision-making activity. The type of techniques which can be included in this category would be team briefing and quality circles. The basic point about this form of participation, however, is that employees are involved on an individual level rather than through their representatives.
2. Indirect participation is concerned with the situation in which employees are involved in the process of management decision-making via their representatives, who have generally been elected from among their number to undertake such duties. Schemes may vary from worker representatives on the board of the company through to joint consultative committees which could operate at any level within the organization, and indeed may link together managers and shop stewards from a number of establishments in a large enterprise. Since individual employees delegate powers (explicitly or implicitly) to their representatives on such committees, these people have to achieve a balance between the potentially competing requirements of both parties to the employment contract. Understandably, this has led to some concern about the appropriate role for employee representatives on such bodies.
3. Financial participation is concerned with economic involvement by employees in the success (or failure) of the organization, and the link between a proportion of their pay and company or departmental performance. Typically, this would include profit-sharing schemes, employee share ownership and value-added payment systems. These may or may not be associated with mechanisms for involving employees in decision-making processes, and this in itself has led to criticism of such schemes.

The 1980s and early 1990s have seen developments within each of these different categories, although primarily in the first and the third. Direct employee involvement has become something of a growth industry, as managements have increasingly sought to inform their employees of the organization's position in the market place, in an attempt to win their co-operation (or at least acquiescence) in achieving the process of change. Indirect participation tends to be through joint consultative committees, and despite a move towards more direct EI during the latter part of the 1980s, a substantial number of organizations still retain this form of participation. Worker directors have become a rarity, even in the public sector, following the decade after the publication of the Bullock Committee of Inquiry, although we may see a renewed interest in this if the UK moves closer to the practice of some other European countries. Financial participation was stimulated by the Finance Acts of 1978, 1980 and 1984, and grew rapidly during the early part of the 1980s.[2] Why should these trends towards greater employee participation, particularly of a 'soft' nature –

that is, those initiated by managements, which do not challenge existing forms of decision-making – have taken place? Several general reasons can be put forward:

- employers have been seeking ways in which to elicit employee commitment to corporate rather than trade union goals (in particular, quality, productivity and competitiveness) and it is felt that this is more likely to be forthcoming if employee involvement is developed;
- managements may take the view that employees are more likely to co-operate in the process of change if they are aware of the circumstances confronting their company, the reasons behind the need for change and their knowledge of the alternatives;
- a desire on the part of employers to avoid the consequences of industrial action by trade unions resentful of a failure to involve them in decision-making processes, and a preference to spend time and money in channelling conflict into peaceful and manageable procedures;
- increasing expectations on the part of working people who have learnt from a more democratic socialization that they ought to have some influence over their conditions of employment and the quality of their working lives;
- the eventual likelihood that developments in EC legislation will require employers to develop one or more forms of employee participation and involvement.

Since the Employment Act 1982, there has, of course, been a requirement for companies covered by the provisions of the Companies Act, and which employ more than 250 people, to report on action taken during the previous financial year to introduce, maintain or develop employee involvement. The focus on action, rather than policy as in the case of employing the disabled, is meant to ensure that companies describe what is *actually* happening, rather than what ought to happen. Four areas are specified: the provision of *information* on matters of concern to employees, which could be through a variety of mechanisms such as employee reports, house magazines and briefing groups; *consulting* with employees or their representatives so that their views can be taken into account on decisions likely to affect them; *financial* involvement of employees through schemes like share ownership or group-wide productivity incentive systems; helping to achieve a *common economic and financial awareness* on the part of employees, which could be achieved via any of the other categories or mixtures of all three. The information is included in the annual report.

Welcome though legislative pressures are to analysts who consider that employers do little or nothing to realistically involve their employees in the affairs of the company, the requirement of this particular provision has not actually *forced* employers to do anything more. If they feel inclined, there is no sanction against employers who choose to file a 'nil' return, because there is no obligation to actually involve employees, only to report on what is being done on the participation front. Some employers did nothing and, unfortunately, many used the same form of words to describe EI over the course of several years. In addition, there is a feeling that the reporting requirement merely creates unnecessary work, encourages pious expressions of intent and focuses attention on structures rather than the processes of employee participation. As we shall see in subsequent sections, the mere existence of a particular form of participation can tell us little or nothing about the *nature* of involvement, and the commitment of the parties towards it.

Having introduced the subject, the remainder of this chapter focuses on a series of employee involvement and participation activities that are, or might be, practised by employers and employees within the UK. With the exception of worker directors, the rest are management initiatives. This reflects not only prevailing structures of power and authority within employing organizations, but also the current economic, social, legal and political context within which industrial relations take place. In the concluding section there will be a brief discussion of future possibilities in the area of employee participation.

TEAM BRIEFING

Team briefing is a system of communication operated by line management, based upon the principle of cascading information down the line. Its objective is to make sure that all employees know and understand what they and others in the company are doing, and why. It hinges around the principle of leaders getting together with their teams on a regular basis in a small group, in order to put across information relevant to their work. Although there is provision for information from the top, the major priority is local or departmental matters, and it is the leader's job to ensure that this occupies most of the meeting.

As a technique, team briefing and its variants have increased in popularity within British industry since the early 1980s. There is nothing especially new about the idea of informing employees about company or departmental affairs, but the major proponent of team briefing – the Industrial Society – insists that the current schemes are different in that the emphasis is on local matters and supervisory explanations (and therefore to some extent interpretations) of a central brief. Experience with team briefing has now extended well beyond manufacturing industry, and there are examples of the scheme in practice within public corporations and the National Health Service.

According to the Industrial Society booklet on *Team Briefing*,[3] the system has a number of crucial benefits. In addition to the general objectives – of improving efficiency and satisfaction – there are *meant* to be a variety of highly practical advantages to be gained from this form of structured communication, such as the following.

1. It reinforces the role of line managers and supervisors as leaders of their teams, by virtue of their being seen as different from their subordinates. In addition, it also enhances their reputation as the providers of information to team members, and reminds supervisors that they are accountable for the performance of their unit.
2. It increases workforce and supervisory commitment to the primary task, and also to the organization as a whole. While team briefing will not succeed in making a boring job interesting, it will provide employees with a greater sense of purpose and direction in their activity. Also, while individuals may not agree with a particular course of action, they can accept it if they understand the reason for it.

3. It reduces misunderstandings if information is communicated to employees, and prevents a considerable amount of wasted time and rumours over potential decisions. There is often an assumption that people know what is happening, but it might be better to rely on the old saying that 'It is better to reinform the informed than to leave the uninformed uninformed!'
4. It helps people to accept changes at work because the early provision of information can assist understanding about the changes and the reasons for them.
5. It helps to control the grapevine, not by preventing it, but by ensuring that employees receive the 'official' version of any decision from their manager. Because individual supervisors have to provide the information themselves, there is also pressure upon them to understand any communications, and on the company to ensure that they are regularly briefed about activities.
6. It improves upward communication, since people will begin to feel after their initial exposure to team briefing that they now know some of the facts, and can therefore contribute to the organization in a more meaningful way.

In practical terms, team briefing has several key principles which have emerged over years of experience. These are:

- the central message should be based upon ideas following a senior management or board meeting;
- at each level, the central message should contribute no more than 30 per cent of the total message;
- teams should be based around a common production or service area, rather than an occupation;
- the team should comprise between 4 and 15 people;
- meetings should be held at least monthly and on a regular, prearranged basis;
- the aim should be to brief all employees within 48 hours;
- the meeting should not last for more than 30 minutes;
- there should be no more than four levels in the cascade system from senior management to the office or shop floor;
- general discussion should be discouraged;
- time should be left for questions about the brief at the end of the input from the leader;
- the leader should be the manager or supervisor of the section concerned;
- leaders must be trained in the principles and skills of how to brief.

The above list of benefits and principles illustrate how team briefing *should* work if all operates smoothly. However, it is not unusual for problems to arise.[4] On a practical level, experience has shown that companies can run into problems when trying to tailor the principles of team briefing to their own organizational requirements. This is particularly the case for organizations with a pattern of work organization which makes it difficult to operate the system effectively; for example, in establishments with extensive shift-working arrangements and large numbers of part-time employees, more sessions have to be arranged than would otherwise be the case, and there may be difficulties in getting information across to people who are not at work for several days; in organizations like the NHS, where substantial numbers of people are employed in the community, it is rare for all individuals to be at the main office for more than a few minutes each day; on continuous production or process operations, it may be impossible to brief all staff, since a skeleton service has to be provided at all times. Of course, given commitment on the part of the management, it is always possible to minimize the problems, and perhaps allow for rotation or, in exceptional circumstances, longer periods of time in which to push out the information.

Team briefing is also heavily reliant upon the skills of the leader as the imparter of information, the controller of the meeting, the fielder of questions and the achiever of objectives. Not surprisingly, such a range of skills is not found in all that many managers – especially first line supervisors – and it is crucial that training is provided for briefers. But, the training itself may not be of the right nature, nor may the practical benefits be sustained by individual briefers beyond the first few sessions. Training requires not just the development of an appropriate set of skills, but also the continuous monitoring of those skills and regular reviews of progress against objectives. In addition, if briefing is to be more than a flash in the pan and actually bring about a change in attitudes and style of management, the system has to be sustained by the provision of relevant and comprehensible pieces of information. This may be somewhat easier in certain organizations than others, especially those in which financial, production and order statistics are compiled on a monthly basis. A lack of meaningful information, or repetition of historical material, can easily lead to disillusionment on the part of briefers and their teams, and to the degeneration of meetings into moaning sessions.

There are also more fundamental objections to any briefing system. The whole language of team briefing is managerial in tone and is concerned with reinforcement of managerial prerogatives. Notions of teams – as groups or organizations as a whole – flow from a unitarist perspective,* as does the view that the interpretation of management decisions should not be undertaken by shop stewards. Not surprisingly, for this reason, workplace trade union representatives may be suspicious of management motives when introducing such a scheme, and see it as little more than an attempt to weaken union organization by the back door. Indeed, this was the line taken by the TGWU when the West Yorkshire Passenger Transport Executive attempted to introduce team briefing into their organization a number of years ago. The union was strongly opposed to any proposal that management should communicate directly and systematically with the workforce, feeling it to be a part of a deliberate attempt to undermine the trade union, and bypass normal consultative and negotiating procedures. Union opposition continued and actually became more entrenched once team briefing had been implemented, with the result that there were low attendances at meetings among certain groups of employees.

It would appear that team briefing has the greatest likelihood of implementation in two quite different sets of circumstances: on the one hand, where there is little or no union organization, and management's interpretations of events

---

* Unitarists are keen to view organizations as football teams, in which all participants are aiming for the same goal, have similar objectives and are not in conflict with one another.

are those which are more likely to secure acceptance from the workforce: on the other, where unions are well organized, have good channels of communication with their members, and are supported by a progressive management philosophy, they may have little to fear from this new communications initiative. Conversely, where there is a history of distrust and overt conflict between management and the unions, there is more likely to be suspicion of any new initiative directed at individual members and workers. Paradoxically, it could be argued that a system such as team briefing probably has the greatest chance of success when it is least needed, and the least chance of success when it is most needed.

In addition, some of the potential benefits of team briefing also appear to rest upon highly questionable and unestablished assumptions. For example, the notion that people may accept decisions they do not agree with – just because they understand the reasoning behind such decisions – can only really be sustained in the context of a massive power imbalance in the employment contract. There must also be doubts that the management chain can be reinforced via briefing, when one considers the essentially problematic role of first line supervisors, especially so with people who have been promoted from the shop floor, and neither share the same value systems as managers, nor possess some of their interpersonal and presentational skills.

Nevertheless, team briefing has been introduced into a great many organizations over the last decade, and it must therefore be providing participants with something they value. If team briefing is used in conjunction with other forms of participation – notably those in which workers and/or their representatives have the opportunity to interact with senior management – the information provided by the system may prove to be of benefit to different interest groups within the employing organization. Similarly, if managements are seen not to use team briefing to subvert other regulatory processes, unions are less likely to challenge its existence. Finally, it should be anticipated that, as employees become more knowledgeable about the organization and more confident in their views, briefing is likely to evolve into a two-way communication process.

QUALITY CIRCLES AND TOTAL QUALITY MANAGEMENT

Quality circles typically consist of small groups of employees who meet voluntarily on a regular basis to identify, analyze and solve quality and work-related problems. The membership of the circle would normally comprise between four and a dozen volunteers from the same work area, or those doing similar work, who meet under the guidance of the group leader. Usually, supervisors act as leaders of quality circles, and it is their task to encourage volunteers to set up the group, and then help to develop it into a cohesive team. Training of circle members is done by facilitators, who are available as a source of information and encouragement, and who act as a liaison between individual circles and the rest of the organization. Usually, in addition, the whole concept will have been initiated and continues to be monitored by a steering committee, which comprises representatives from various departments within the organization.

A leading writer on the subject[5] has identified three distinctive features of quality circles: the principle of *voluntary* membership; the encouragement to *solve* job-related problems, rather than merely spot them; and the provision of *training* to enable people to solve problems in an organized and effective manner.

Quality circles were first introduced in Japan, although the original ideas behind such systems stemmed from the US. There are now estimated to be over 1 million quality circles in Japan and over 10 million workers are involved in them. They have also taken off more recently in the US, Germany, France, Italy and the UK. Some of the best-known experiments in the UK have been in companies such as British Telecom, May and Baker, Blackwell's, Wedgwood, Mullard and Jaguar cars. In other companies, similar principles and practices are undertaken, but under a different name – for example, the implementation of EI at Ford. However, despite the amount of media attention which quality circles have attracted over the years, they are not practised on any significant scale across the UK as a whole. Indeed, by the end of the 1980s, the CBI estimated that a quarter of all organizations used quality circles, only one-third of which had been in operation for more than three years.[6] Apparently, many companies have either tried to implement quality circles or been forced to suspend them for one reason or another.

Some of the benefits claimed for these quality programmes are similar to those seen for team briefing, namely the likelihood of a greater commitment to work and interest in the job, but quality circles go further in that they actively encourage employee involvement in decision-making, albeit at task level and within specified boundaries. The aim is to improve decision-making and to iron out problems at the earliest possible opportunity. It is also felt that quality circles can have a positive effect on the atmosphere within an organization, and can assist in the development of individual abilities gained through training and participation in meetings, as well as improving the viability of the company in terms of cost and quality.

Key components of quality circles are that: meetings should be held weekly or fortnightly, in working time; the place and time for meetings should be arranged in advance; meetings should last for about one hour; members should be trained in a variety of techniques and interpersonal skills; leaders keep groups to the central task of dealing with work-related problems; the group endeavours to enlist support from top management.

Based upon extensive research over a long period of time, the following factors have been identified by Collard and Dale[7] as being necessary for success:

- secure the commitment of the board and senior management to the principle of quality circles, and ensure they understand that this means providing time and resources if they are to work properly;
- involve middle managers and supervisors, since this group will be central to any initiatives emanating from circle discussions, and can provide invaluable specialist assistance on particular issues;
- seek the support of the trade unions in a unionized environment in order to involve representatives in the process, and allay any fears that this will undermine the role of the union;
- delegate decision-making so that once circles have reached a satisfactory conclusion on a particular aspect of the job, they will either have the authority

to implement the decision, or the right (in the case of a more strategic-level matter) to present proposals to senior management;

- provide adequate structured training both to circle leaders and members in order to assist them in fulfilling their roles;
- use a pilot study approach which will allow for a thorough evaluation of the benefits and drawbacks without a high-profile company-wide introduction.
- monitor events on an ongoing basis, assist in reinforcing the work of circle members and assist them in propagating their ideas to fellow employees.

As mentioned above, however, many quality circles fail at the introduction stage, or after a short period of operation; the first three years appear to be critical for establishing long-term viability. While lack of top management support is often given as a reason for failure, trade unions can also have significant objections to the quality circle concept. As with briefing groups, there is a legitimate concern that quality circles – or for that matter any direct employee involvement technique – will be used as a mechanism to bypass or compete with the trade unions. This is more likely to be the case in circumstances when managements fail to convince union representatives of the value of quality circles, or when they are imposed unilaterally in a climate of hostility or tension. More specifically, trade unions will be particularly concerned that modifications may be made to working practices without proper consultation and negotiation, and without any improvement in associated terms and conditions. Furthermore, quality circles may be seen as an altogether more dubious form of participation, in that the feeling of involvement is greater, although the actual control and influence over strategic decisions is likely to be minimal. As with any other aspect of industrial relations, quality circles have significant implications – in this case, implicit and unwritten – for the balance of power in the workplace, and for conflict and co-operation.

In a number of organizations, quality circles have either been replaced by, or incorporated into, total quality management (TQM) programmes. It is not altogether surprising that this should happen given that TQM offers a more integrated approach than some other forms of EI, which have often been 'grafted on' as a quick-fix solution to organizational problems. Again, contrary to quality circles, TQM is *compulsory* for employees as opposed to voluntary, and its aim is to improve service to customers (both internal and external), produce error-free work and build quality into the product/service – rather than check quality standards by inspection. In short, the TQM approach aims to combine both 'hard', production-oriented, statistical principles with softer, more qualitative notions of employees as the organization's most important resource. Some of the early leaders in this field were IBM, Rank Xerox and Ciba-Corning, although other big-name companies have recently followed suit.

Some studies suggest that there have been tensions between the hard and the soft components of TQM, especially if the champions behind different aspects of the programme come from different functions or levels in the organization. Since the operations management drive for TQM is predicated upon conformance to clearly-defined instructions, it is bound to conflict with the view that employees should continually search for ways of improving their own performance and use their discretion to ensure that their actions 'add value' to the organization. Nevertheless, since participation is viewed as one of the key aspects of TQM, at least some of managements' efforts need to be tailored to the creation of a culture and structure which aims to maximize the effective involvement of all employees in the pursuit of quality.[8]

JOINT CONSULTATION

Traditionally, joint consultation has had a somewhat tarnished image. It has been described variously as a waste of time, the three Ts (tea, toilets and trivia), irrelevant to the main needs of the business or conversely as a challenge to trade union organization and collective bargaining. Even though some form of joint consultative committees (JCCs) have existed in a number of organizations throughout the whole of the 20th century, interest has definitely waxed and waned within industry overall. There have been periods of growth in the 1940s and 1970s, interspersed with a general decline in the 1960s. Since 1980 the proportion of workplaces with JCCs has declined again, particularly in the manufacturing sector.

For some analysts, JCCs are viewed as unstable and problematic, both in principle and in character. Two assumptions lie behind this view. First, that shop stewards view consultation as in direct competition with negotiation, and a choice has to be made between one or the other. In fact, stewards in well-organized workplaces may value *both* processes, and find that they can cope with the different problems imposed by them. Second, that managements actually wish to use consultation as a mechanism for undermining union organization within workplaces. Although some may well use JCCs for this purpose, the evidence would suggest that many employers are also keen to maintain both consultation and negotiation, and provide facilities for workplace representatives on both sorts of committee.

Joint consultation is a process by which management seeks the views of employees, usually via their elected representatives, before final decisions are taken. To work effectively, it involves the provision of considerable amounts of information and time, and a willingness on the part of management to actually listen to alternative views, discuss implications, and if appropriate explain and justify why a certain line of action is proposed. It requires a degree of openness and trust on the part of both managers and shop stewards, which will allow for meaningful-discussion of problems and solutions. It is usually the case that joint consultative committees do not have decision-making powers formally allocated to them, but it is always difficult to firmly establish where, how and when decisions are made in practice, and JCCs may actually influence the eventual outcome of any discussion.

The precise structure and design of a consultative system depends crucially upon the shape and character of the organization in which it is operating, but there are a number of key questions which need to be posed if JCCs are to be seen as successful both by managers and workplace representatives. Success can be measured in terms of the quality of decision-making, working commitment, management awareness and sensitivity, as well as job satisfaction and company efficiency. Drawing upon examples of organizations which have had a long history of joint consultation, and where both stewards and managements express satisfaction with the outcomes, the following factors seem to be important.

First, there needs to be a clearly defined statement that the JCC will not be allowed to discuss issues which are subject to negotiation, and this clarification will probably be equally desired by both managers and stewards, either of whom may act as the custodians of any collective agreements in a unionized concern. In a sense, consultation serves to fill in the gaps left by collective bargaining, and as such, can be relatively fluid in its exact area of coverage; indeed, it is this fluidity which causes greatest anxiety among analysts who argue that a clear distinction cannot be maintained between the two bodies, and consequently this must prove advantageous to management. Once again, though, this rests upon the dual assumptions that managers *wish* to gain such an advantage through JCCs, and that stewards possess neither the resources nor the ability to prevent this from happening or the awareness of management tactics.

Second, management needs to demonstrate its commitment to meaningful consultation, by producing evidence that JCCs are to be taken seriously. This means that attendance at committees needs to be obligatory for managers who are of sufficient status to be the appropriate decision-makers at whatever level the committees operate. Consequently, at a departmental committee, it could be the plant manager; at establishment committee, the works director; at divisional level, the divisional chairman; and, at group level, the company chairman. Employee representatives are soon going to question the value to management of a committee which purports to allow for influence over decision-making within the company, when attendance is by managers who are seen to lack status themselves, who fail to progress issues, or who regularly fail to turn up at meetings.

Third, in order to be effective, worker representatives need to command the support of their constituents, and in a unionized company, shop stewards are usually likely to be the people who attend JCCs. While the task of drawing up the constituencies and preparing the groundwork for effective representation may be relatively easy in a single union establishment, it can be rather more complex in a multi-site, multi-union organization. In addition, any attempt by management to ask for representation which may be based upon a non-union or non-steward presence is also likely to be viewed with some consternation by the appropriate unions, and reduce the commitment of the latter not only to the JCC, but also to other industrial relations institutions.

If management are committed to joint consultation, other details of the JCC which need proper consideration would be:

- timing of meetings and their regularity;
- role of the chair, and its possible rotation between managers and employee representatives;
- location and length of meetings;
- adequate representation of employees;
- agreed process of agenda-formation;
- opportunity for pre-meetings for employee representatives;
- use of subcommittees for detailed or more problematic items;
- nature of the subject matter appropriate for the JCC;

- completion and circulation/publication of minutes;
- list of action points and named individuals;
- induction of new members/broadening of membership;
- distribution of papers in advance of the JCC;
- training in presentation and interpersonal skills;
- training in the interpretation of financial/strategic information;
- planned turnover of committee members;
- process for regular monitoring and review of JCC effectiveness, including the use of independent analysts.

It is probably indicative of the reputation of JCCs that considerably more has been written about failure than success, of JCCs which are marginal and deal with all types of accumulated trivia. In this case, consultation is likely to stagnate and may ultimately collapse.[9]

Equally, some employers have used consultation as a mechanism to resist collective bargaining and union recognition, especially in sectors in which there is little tradition of unionism or independent representation. Since consultation requires time and commitment on the part of management, this approach is rather more likely in establishments where a sophisticated paternalist policy is used. In such cases, the process of consultation will primarily be one-way and educative in its objectives; that is, a process designed to make employees aware of the economic circumstances of the company, and the effort which senior managers are expending for the good of the corporate whole.

The notion of consultation being used as a direct competitor with an already-established system of collective bargaining has been briefly discussed already. This works on the principle that, by providing employee representatives with a considerable amount of information and involving them in the process of decision-making within companies, managements are able to 'incorporate' stewards and convince them of the logic and inescapability of company policies and proposals. Thus, according to this approach, trade unionism may be weakened – if the policy is successful – by the back door rather than head on.[10]

WORKER DIRECTORS AND WORKS COUNCILS

For some analysts, none of the schemes which have been discussed so far offer an acceptable form of employee participation, because they fail to challenge existing systems of control and authority within employing organizations. The idea of workers securing a place on the board or having guaranteed access to senior management, while not actually producing workers' control, is seen as somewhat more promising in that at least employee representatives get closer to the point at which strategic decisions are made. Not surprisingly, given this scenario, the concept of worker directors and works councils has attracted a considerable degree of hostility from employers. Given the political circumstances which characterized Britain in the late 1980s and early 1990s, there are very few examples of this aspect of employee participation, despite developments elsewhere within the EC (see below).

The British debate on worker directors was at its most extensive in the 1970s. The Labour Government of the time and the TUC (especially via the general secretary of the TGWU, Jack Jones) initiated the Bullock Committee of Inquiry.* Its terms of reference related to how, rather than whether, representation on the board of directors of private sector companies could be achieved, while taking into account the essential role of trade unions, and having regard to the interests of the national economy, employees, investors, consumers and company efficiency. There were problems from the outset, not only in securing an appropriate membership for the committee, but also with the eventual reports. In addition to the majority report, to which there was a note of dissent, a minority report was also published, containing the views of the industrialists. Even so, the latter report probably went much further than many employers would have wanted, especially those antagonistic to the principle itself. The reaction to Bullock was vitriolic and, despite a much-diluted attempt in a subsequent White Paper (May 1978), the proposals on worker directors were never enacted.

Experience with the concept of worker directors is extremely rare in the private sector, and research based upon seven of the companies which operated such a scheme has demonstrated the substantial influence of managements over its implementation and operation.[11] It has been argued that each of the schemes was used in order to strengthen or reassert management control, rather than to redistribute that control. The worker directors themselves experienced great difficulty in handling the information received at the board, partly because they were not party to the informal discussions which took place among senior management, but also because they lacked the resources to interpret or make effective use of the information. Consequently, the schemes tended to be regarded in a relatively poor light by the workforce, and the unions were either indifferent to them or ensured that they did not interfere with independent representation.

There is greater experience of board membership in the public sector, and two schemes – at British Steel and at the Post Office – have been the subject of detailed analyses.[12] Worker directors were appointed to the group boards of the newly-established British Steel Corporation in 1965, and for the initial period these nominees were required to give up their formal union positions. Although there was some hostility among the other directors to the principle of board membership at the outset, their stance softened over the course of the next year, and they – like shop stewards and ordinary employees – eventually supported the idea of worker directors. A majority of middle managers, however, remained opposed to the scheme. The 12 worker directors themselves were enthusiastic and strongly committed to their new role, seeing themselves as central to communication, co-operation and the exchange of ideas, and the other board members defined them as experts on the shop floor view. None the less, there were also problems for the worker directors in moving into the new world of the boardroom, and in understanding the rules, language, customs and symbolism which operated therein. Also, the worker directors came to realize

---

* The Committee of Inquiry on Industrial Democracy was chaired by Lord Bullock, and its members were drawn from both sides of industry and a group of independents. It was set up in December 1975, and it reported in January 1977.

that there were a variety of forums for discussion and decision-making outside the board.

The Post Office experiment with worker directors commenced in 1978, but was discontinued two years later due to managerial and governmental opposition to the concept. Many of the outcomes were similar to those mentioned above in the Steel case; for example, union nominees contributed most to discussions on personnel and industrial relations – often with a critical perspective – and rarely to those on other matters. Similarly, the board changed its character and adopted a blander nature with managerial disagreements being acted out elsewhere. Moreover, the worker directors themselves experienced some conflicts between their traditional union role and that of board member.

Overall, though, independent assessments of both schemes argued that the representatives operated as directors first and workers second, finding it hard to resist the logic of efficiency, markets and institutions. In the Post Office case, although industrial democracy brought few gains to the unions or management, it brought few losses either. It certainly could not be seen as a severe threat to management authority or as a mechanism for achieving workers' control.

In summary, previous UK experience both in the public and private sectors, suggests the following conclusions about worker directors.

- managements are generally opposed to the principle of worker representation, especially through trade unions, on the board;
- the trade union movement is ambivalent about worker directors, although certain unions are hostile to the concept due to fears of incorporation, role conflict and a reduced ability to resist management actions;
- workers themselves express no great desire for board representation on their behalf;
- worker directors experience difficulty in coming to terms with boardroom norms and customs;
- there will be little change to the outcome of board discussions.

Given these findings, it is sometimes difficult to appreciate why employers have been so hostile to the concept of worker directors, beyond seeing them as an extra burden rather than an aid to efficiency. However, throughout the 1980s, a campaign has been waged by some UK industrialists and the government, against EC legislation and European Works Councils, as well as against the details of the Social Charter. The former legislation has been on the cards since the early 1970s, having been diluted somewhat from its original form. Now, if enacted, the Fifth Directive would allow member states to choose from one of a number of options* for the installation of formal systems to involve employee representatives in company decision-making structures. It would also allow for

---

* These options allow for unitary or supervisory boards, and for a process of election or co-option on to one or other of these bodies. In addition, there is provision for an alternative to workers on the board, in the form of a joint arrangement concluded by collective agreement so long as this applies the same principles of participation as would be achieved by board membership. This is the one which would cause least disruption to current UK arrangements.

the possibility of participation through collective agreements, rather than board membership, provided that employees acquired the same rights and information as they would through representation on the board. The Vredeling Directive would apply to multinationals with a head office outside of the EC, which have large undertakings within Europe. This requirement, if enacted, would be for information disclosure and consultation with employee representatives about decisions liable to have serious implications for employees' interests. Many of the issues covered by Vredeling are already the subject of information and consultation within more progressive UK companies, although these are provided on a voluntary not a statutory basis.

The proposals for European works councils (EWCs) are a much more recent initiative (1990) designed as part of the move towards greater harmonization in EC Social Policy issues across the member states. In brief, this proposal states that in organizations with at least 1000 employees, and at least two establishments in at least two member states – each of which has at least 100 employees – representatives would be free to request the formation of a European works council. Ultimately, assuming that employee representatives still desire this, the EWC would allow for participation on a wide range of issues – although managements would retain the right to withhold information of a confidential nature. Since it has been estimated that approximately one-third of the EC firms which would be affected by this proposal are UK-owned, and of course many other foreign-owned organizations would have sufficiently large establishments in the UK, the implications of this directive could be significant for Britain. At the time of writing, only one company (Elf Aquitaine) had set up an EWC.

In the short term, the actual impact of these developments on British employment relations is likely to be limited. The Conservatives have made clear their opposition to compulsory models of participation, preferring the voluntary approach which has operated throughout the last decade. The government managed to block adoption of the Social Charter (including the provisions discussed above) at the Maastricht Summit of December 1991, in what the *Financial Times* referred to as 'an astonishing compromise'. This amounted to the creation of a two-tier Europe whereby the other 11 member states can progress with new initiatives (either by qualified majority voting or unanimity, depending upon the issue), which can then be incorporated into national legislation. Britain, on the other hand, is free to remain outside of this new framework of employment relations. Given a Conservative government during the 1990s, it is unlikely that the UK establishments of British-owned companies would voluntarily opt for an EWC structure.

Beyond this, of course, foreign-owned companies with employment units in the UK (and which qualify under the criteria outlined above) would be free to set up EWCs, and membership would be open to employee representatives here. This could create an interesting problem for a future Conservative government, especially if workers in these companies were seen to be getting a better deal – in terms of information and consultation – than their colleagues employed in UK-owned organizations. Similarly, there might be pressure on British-owned firms with employment units elsewhere in the EC (say France or Germany) to set up EWCs, either from employees or other national parliaments. Whether this would have the net effect of encouraging or discouraging employers to locate or remain in Britain is as yet a more open question. So too, assuming the continued isolation of Britain, is the argument that a future government would be obliged to adopt laws over which it had exerted no influence.

PROFIT-SHARING AND EMPLOYEE SHARE OWNERSHIP

While profit-sharing and employee share ownership schemes are by no means a recent development, with examples of the former going back into the 19th century, it is only during the 1980s that there has been a resurgence of interest in them, largely due to legislative encouragement via the Finance Acts of 1978, 1980 and 1984. Since such schemes are also part of the total pay and benefits package, they will be dealt with in rather more detail in Chapter 14, but by its very nature, economic and financial involvement is also a form of employee participation. Some would argue that to provide the opportunity for employees to share in the financial success (or otherwise) of their employer is an essential part of any employee involvement package.

Profit-sharing by itself represents a very dilute form of employee involvement, and it is only when financial participation is associated with mechanisms for creating industrial democracy, that it can represent anything more than an additional form of payment to employees. Government initiatives, via profit-related pay, come into the former category (again see Chapter 14), while value-added systems which allow for employee representation via works councils do at least formalize the relationship between participation, organizational productivity and individual reward. By so doing, calculative orientations held by employees can be recognized and placed within a participative context.[13]

In broad terms, the arguments in favour of profit-sharing and employee share ownership are that they:

- help to increase individual identification with and commitment to corporate success;
- increase co-operation within the company;
- make employees more conscious of business needs and the value of profit to the organization;
- ensure employees benefit from company profitability;
- help to attract and retain key staff due to extra financial inducements.

The critics of such schemes, however, produce a number of equally convincing counter-arguments. First of all, it is suggested that profit-sharing fails to conform to one of the most basic rules of payment systems, namely that there should be a clear and identifiable link between effort and reward. Individual employees find that no matter how hard they have worked during the previous financial year, this is not reflected in the amount of profits which come their way, nor in the value of shares quoted on the stock exchange. Equally, share prices may rise in order to produce high bonuses in a year when individual employees have worked less hard. Not surprisingly, therefore, profit-sharing may consequently be seen as nothing more than a windfall bonus, and shares may be sold as employees get the opportunity or need the money.

Secondly, it is felt that profit-sharing and share ownership merely doubles the insecurity of individual employees. Not only do they risk losing their job if the company runs into financial difficulties, but they also face the prospect of losing any capital which may have accrued through such schemes. Employees might not always be fully aware of this possibility when they enter into such schemes, because they only conceive of a successful outcome.

There is also an objection to stand-alone profit-sharing schemes – that is, those without any associated mechanism for participation – in that employees have no means by which to contribute to, or challenge, management decisions. Strategic decisions may be made by senior management which have significant implications for profits – for example, a decision to invest in new technology, or market a new product line overseas – whereas employee representatives, given the interests which their members have, might take an altogether different line. While senior managers may see value in implementing profit-sharing schemes on current terms, this would soon turn to hostility if it were linked to realistic employee participation in and control over strategic decisions. None the less, it was probably indicative of the political climate during the 1980s that share ownership increased, fuelled to a large extent by the government's privatization programme.

CONCLUSIONS

There is little doubt that the range of participation and involvement systems which are used by organizations in the UK depends to some extent on political circumstances. Despite pressure for greater harmonization of employment relations throughout the EC, there are likely to be only limited moves towards representative participation and a continuing commitment to voluntary measures. In effect, this will mean an even greater emphasis on forms of direct EI.

Irrespective of developments at Westminster and Brussels, it is highly unlikely that managements will discard the initiatives in direct EI which have been developed over the last ten years. Equally, given that their members are now more accustomed to receiving information from management, it is unlikely that trade unions would want these to be removed. Accordingly, direct communication techniques such as team briefing can be expected to retain their popularity, as too can quality packages which tie together EI and customer service concerns. There may also be an increase in the number of organizations which operate some form of JCC structure, particularly if the spectre of EWCs assumes greater prominence; after all, it may be possible to extend some of these enterprise-wide bodies from the level of single-nation to multi-nation.

Whatever systems emerge on a political level in pure structural terms, however, there will always be examples of organizations which are more successful than others in making employee involvement and participation work in practice. Much depends upon the commercial environment in which companies find themselves, and upon the kinds of issues which confront them, so facilitating or hindering the achievement of organizational objectives. Joint publications by the Involvement and Participation Association and the Institute of Personnel Management provide a range of examples, as well as statements of principles and practice, and a guide to effective action. Rather than prescribe how participation should operate, the action guide poses a series of questions which need to be considered by organizations which are reviewing their position.[14]

Beyond this, the major point at issue concerns attitudes to participation, and the total process of conducting industrial relations in the workplace, office, plant or company as a whole. Participation packages can be bought off the shelf, but whether or not they work depends upon the quality of management–employee relations within the undertaking, upon the history of previous dealings, the level of trust and, above all, on the commitment of management to making the system effective. Participation is not easy, but is a difficult and time-consuming process, which needs to develop over time and cannot be discarded once its initial objectives have been met. Since it ought to involve employees taking part in management decisions in one way or another, it is also beset with tensions and potential contradictions. But, the fact that organizations continue to experiment with employee participation surely demonstrates that it offers some hope for the development of more constructive and permanent relationships at work.

References

1. Each of the participation and EI techniques dealt with in this chapter are discussed in much greater detail in another publication of mine. See (1992) *Managing the Team: A Guide to Employee Involvement*, Blackwell, Oxford. For a further view, see also Ramsay, H (1991) 'Reinventing the wheel? A review of the development and performance of employee involvement', *Human Resource Management Journal*, 1(4).
2. Baddon, L, Hunter, L, Hyman, J, Leopold, J and Ramsay, H (1989) *People's Capitalism: A Critical Analysis of Profit Sharing and Employee Share Ownership*, Routledge, London.
3. Grummit, J (1983) *Team Briefing*, Industrial Society, London.
4. For the results of a critical analysis of team briefing, readers should refer to Marchington, M, Parker, P and Prestwich, A (1989) 'Problems with team briefing in practice', *Employee Relations*, 11(4).
5. Robson, M (1984) *Quality Circles in Action*, Gower, Aldershot.
6. Confederation of British Industry (1989) *Employee Involvement – Shaping the Future for Business*, London.
7. Collard, R and Dale, B (1985) 'Quality circles – why they break down and why they hold up' *Personnel Management*, February.
8. See, for example, Wilkinson, A, Allen, P and Snape, E (1991) 'TQM and the management of labour', *Employee Relations*, 13(1); and Hill, S (1991) 'Why quality circles had to fail, but TQM might succeed', *British Journal of Industrial Relations*, 29(4).
9. Nicholson, N (1978) 'Can consultation work?', *Personnel Management*, November.
10. For a short review of each of these approaches, see Marchington, M (1988) 'The four faces of employee consultation', *Personnel Management*, May.
11. Towers, B, Chell, E and Cox, D (1981) 'Do worker directors work?', *Employment Gazette*, September; and (1981) *Worker Directors in Private Manufacturing Industry in Britain*, Department of Employment Research Paper No 29.
12. For a useful summary of both these experiments, see Brannen, P (1983) *Authority and Participation in Industry*, Batsford, London.
13. Marchington, M (1977) 'Worker participation and plant-wide incentive systems', *Personnel Review*, Summer.
14. Involvement and Participation Association/Institute of Personnel Management (1990) *Employment Involvement and Participation in the United Kingdom; the IPA/ IPM Code*, London.

Chapter Twelve

Managing Professional and Managerial Staff

Ed Snape and Greg Bamber

Professional and managerial staff are often treated rather differently from other employees, particularly manual workers. In this chapter, after defining the professional and managerial category, we consider such issues as recruitment, selection, mobility, education, human resource management, economic rewards and the unionization of managers.

WHO ARE PROFESSIONAL AND MANAGERIAL EMPLOYEES?

In defining managerial employees, we include all those employees in the hierarchy above first-line supervisor but below the level of executives who report directly to the board. In addition, we include professional and technical staff of comparable status. For convenience, we use 'manager' to cover the whole group, thus including people such as personnel and marketing specialists, professional engineers and administrators, as well as line managers.

There is some ambiguity about whether managers are *employers* or *employees*. Even if they do not have direct line authority, such staff often have a relatively high level of discretion in their jobs. Subordinate grades generally see managers as bosses, while the directors may see managers as agents of the employer, and expect them to act accordingly.

There was a dramatic increase in the absolute and relative numbers of managers in the decades after the Second World War. The increase has prompted employers to pay increasing attention to the management of this category of employee.

RECRUITMENT, SELECTION AND MOBILITY

Appointing managers by internal promotion is an explicit policy of many large employers. Many large organizations aim to recruit externally only if they lack suitable internal candidates, when they require specialist skills, or when wishing to bring in 'new blood'.

Thus, many managers have been promoted from within, especially in the longer-established industries. In recent years, however, most employers have recruited young people as management trainees, or have recruited people externally to particular managerial positions. It has become less usual for people to be promoted from a shop floor job into management unless their shop floor role was part of a management traineeship.

We can distinguish between four typical recruitment patterns for managers. In the first pattern, external recruitment is restricted to junior levels of the organizational hierarchy, and managerial jobs are filled by promotion from within. This is typical of the finance sector, particularly the larger banks, who have traditionally recruited most of their staff at junior clerical level and thereafter promoted from within.

This may, however, lead to an organization becoming too inward looking, and fail to yield sufficient staff with the necessary potential for promotion to the senior positions. Hence, in many organizations, there is an increasing use of 'tiered' recruitment patterns. This second pattern involves external recruitment at junior managerial levels (often new or recent graduates), along with some promotion from among manual or clerical workers, usually via technical or first-line supervisory positions. Higher level managerial positions are then filled mainly by internal promotion.

A third pattern involves external recruitment into junior managerial posts, with subsequent internal promotion to fill higher level jobs. In this case, however, there is no significant promotion into managerial jobs from among manual or clerical workers, who rarely progress beyond the first-line supervisory level. This situation often arises where managerial jobs are more technical, requiring specific qualifications, for example retail chemists, where managers must be professionally qualified.

The fourth, an 'open' recruitment pattern includes the possibilities of external recruitment and internal promotion at all levels. This pattern often develops where labour markets are tight and highly competitive, or where organizations are growing rapidly, so that they may be faced with shortages of managers and use any available means to recruit. Some retail chains pursue such a policy, as do some companies in the expanding, high technology industries.[1]

Recruitment patterns have implications for employee attitudes and personnel management. Our research in a bank revealed systematic differences between those managers promoted from within ('natives'), and those recruited from other banks ('migrants'). The migrants were more career-oriented, in that they were better qualified, were more willingly mobile, had greater expectations of mobility, and were less likely to be content with the bank's provision for training and career development. Most of the migrants had moved to this bank in search of better career opportunities, they often brought new ideas, and they tended to become a career 'élite' within the organization.

Apart from press advertisements, how are managers recruited? The now privatized Professional and Executive Recruitment agency mails advertisements to eligible job-seekers. This service is generally seen as most appropriate for junior management positions. Several private consultants and professional institutions run recruitment registers, but these are used mainly for specialist jobs such as finance, scientific or technical posts.

Rather than relying on their own expertise, an increasing number of employers use recruitment agencies to design and implement an appropriate advertising programme. Particularly for recruitment at senior levels, there is also an increasing number of employers using executive search consultants ('headhunters').

Selection

When selecting managers, many employers are concerned not only with technical qualifications but also with how well they would 'fit in', with their leadership qualities, and with other personality factors.

How do organizations select managers from among the available candidates? While some large organizations are using increasingly sophisticated procedures for selecting managers, many still rely almost exclusively on formal and/or informal interviewing. Many larger companies use panel selection boards. Relatively few use tests, and then mainly for graduate recruitment.[2]

Many employers recruit graduates by interviewing extensively at universities and colleges, before inviting some of the more promising candidates to intensive second interviews. This process, the 'milk round', is a useful way of dealing with mass applications from what intially appears as a fairly undifferentiated group. Such employers usually have a management induction scheme. The exact form of scheme varies considerably, but 'management trainees' may complete off-the-job training courses and projects before taking up a junior managerial position. Such schemes often involve a series of short placements in various departments. These schemes may extend from six weeks to over two years. More and more employers have introduced such schemes, as a growing number of organizations aim to recruit graduates.

Many graduates are, however, soon disillusioned with their first job. Many induction schemes are inadequate, and there is a mismatch between what graduates and employers expect of each other. Hence, graduate turnover from first jobs approaches 50 per cent after five years.[3] Ambitious individuals in their 20s often move between employers, in an attempt to win more experience and more rapid promotion than they would get with one employer.

It is likely that the recruitment and retention of graduates will become increasingly difficult in the next few years as demographic trends point to a marked contraction of the 18–24 age group. Inter-firm competition in the graduate labour market is likely to intensify, and employers may need to look to other groups, such as married women and older workers, to make up any shortfall in graduate recruitment.[4] One implication of this is that the number of women managers will probably increase, particularly if, as seems likely, employers attempt to accommodate women by extending career-break schemes.

Mobility

As more employers recruit managers externally, there has been an increasing tendency for managers to change jobs.[5] For the individuals concerned, a change of job can bring new stimulation and/or problems of adjustment. The main problems for managers in locational moves are: the disruption of their children's education, the disruption to friendships and social life, and the quality of health, educational and social facilities within the new area.[6] Managers seem less concerned about the problems of house-moving, leaving members of the family, the effect on their spouse's job, and uncertainty about the new job itself. Relocation has become an expensive issue. Many employers pay substantial sums as disturbance allowances. Some employers pay an incentive to encourage managers to move. To advise on such matters, in 1986 the Confederation of British Industry (CBI) established an Employee Relocation Council.

In spite of some cross-functional mobility, British managers are less likely than Americans to move beyond their own specialism. Many British organizations have a rigid 'functional' structure. Nevertheless, an increasing number of organizations are trying to introduce more flexible structures which foster more cross-fertilization between functions, especially in their promotion policies for potential high-flyers.

MANAGEMENT EDUCATION

A traditional view has been that 'leaders are born and not made'. This was reflected in the relative lack of management education in Britain, at least until the 1960s. British managers still tend to be less well qualified than those in many other countries.

In spite of some rhetoric from managerial interest groups, management is not a 'profession'; particular qualifications are usually required only where the job involves specialist, technical work. Many firms do not systematically train their managers for the jobs they hold.

A few universities have been teaching management since before the Second World War and several colleges have run short courses for managers for much of the post-war period. However, universities did not initiate specific graduate business schools until 1963, following the Robbins and the Franks Reports.[7]

By 1983, more than half of Britain's universities had management departments or business schools, offering postgraduate Master of Business Administration (MBA) degrees. In that year, however, less than 1350 MBAs were awarded in Britain, and while the intake on to MBA programmes had grown to around 8000 by 1990, Britain still falls well short of the numbers needed to match the US proportionately.[8] Several institutions have recently developed novel forms of MBA programme. These include part-time study, distance learning and in-house schemes for particular employers or groups of employers. Nevertheless, MBAs are still accepted much less readily by most British employers than by their North American counterparts.

Besides MBA courses, many institutions offer shorter executive courses; these may either be broad or concentrate on particular fields such as finance, marketing or human resource management. Partly arising from an apparent dissatisfaction with open courses, which are allegedly 'too general', many large employing organizations commission specially designed courses for their own managers. As management education is increasingly competitive, more business schools are willing to 'tailor-make' courses to suit particular employers.

Many of the new universities (ex-polytechnics) and some of the established universities also offer full degree courses in business studies at undergraduate level. Some also offer part-time diploma courses, mainly to those already working in management. Study for professional qualifications is mainly by day-release, evening, or correspondence course, while doing a relevant full-time job. Relatively few employers seem willing to allow managers to have a substantial period of paid study leave, although many will provide financial assistance for evening-class fees.

The British Institute of Management (BIM) was set up in 1947 to help promote managerial effectiveness. The BIM publishes journals, along with various books and reports on management topics. It maintains a library, publishes research and organizes conferences. While the BIM does not seek to represent managers *vis-á-vis* their employers, it does represent its members' views to the government on such issues as pensions, fiscal policy and employee participation. BIM membership is open to individuals educated at least up to a diploma or degree level, who have several years' management experience.

Although there has been an expansion of management education and training, the provision is still varied and somewhat *ad hoc*. Too many British employers seem to regard such provision as being *costs* to be cut, rather than as carefully-planned *investments* in their human resources. Most British employers seem to give too low a priority to education and training, compared to their foreign competitors.

The growing concern about Britain's relatively poor management education, training and development was highlighted in two major reports published in 1987.[9] They recommended increased provision of management education and training, with greater flexibility to improve access, and more co-operation between employers and educational institutions. In addition, they called on employers to give greater emphasis to careful recruitment, training and development, and on large corporations to set a good example in these areas. In response to these debates, the BIM and the CBI, with government backing, established the Management Charter Initiative in July 1988, to develop recognized standards of competence in management and to promote good practice in management training and development.

HUMAN RESOURCE MANAGEMENT

Before training managers, it is important for employers to evaluate their training needs, not least by appraising their current strengths and weaknesses, and their career development potential. Appraisal should also form the basis of a firm's promotion practices. Most employers have an appraisal system for their non-manual workers, particularly managerial staff. Appraisal may have several other objectives including:

- facilitating the planning of an individual's career development and setting future goals;
- providing a basis for annual salary reviews where pay is related to individual merit;
- motivating individuals, even in the absence of merit pay, by providing feedback on job performance;
- improving communications by encouraging managers to gather information on the views and concerns of their subordinates;
- assisting the process of personnel planning by helping to identify those staff with promotion potential.

Properly conducted, appraisal is a useful technique in relation to managerial staff, whose motivation and performance is crucial to most organizations, yet who have much more discretion in the performance of their jobs than most other employees. Appraisal became even more widely used during the 1980s, partly because of the increased use of performance-related pay (see below).

A problem with some appraisal systems is that they lack a clear set of objectives. Furthermore, linking pay to appraisal may encourage the individual being appraised to conceal job difficulties in order to safeguard a pay increase. This may conflict with the use of appraisal for career development and training purposes. Where merit pay is to be used it is worth trying to separate merit awards and appraisal interviews in the minds of employees, perhaps by keeping them several months apart and by emphasizing non-pay issues in the appraisal interview.

An appraisal may raise expectations, as it questions staff about their career ambitions and training needs. Where these expectations are not then realized, there may be a loss of morale. Hence, appraisal schemes should match the organizational realities, as well as the needs of the staff concerned. Schemes aimed at 'career' staff should emphasize their professional development, while those for non-career employees should focus more on immediate job issues.

Another problem often arises with appraisal schemes which are designed and initiated by a central personnel department, but left to line managers to implement. If the latter have not been involved in designing the scheme, nor fully trained in its operation, it rarely works as well as originally hoped, since most line managers have many other more immediate priorities than operating what they may see as personnel's 'airy-fairy schemes'. For appraisal schemes to operate effectively, it is important for the implementers to feel some degree of ownership of the scheme. This can be achieved if they are involved in designing and reviewing the scheme.

Most large organizations have specialists responsible for appraisal and management development; often they are also responsible for managerial succession planning. In practice, only a small minority of companies seem to have a systematic approach to such aspects of personnel management. Ideally, however, all of these aspects should be part of an integrated strategy for developing human resources.

Career blockages

Many organizations have found it difficult to meet the career aspirations of their younger managerial staff, who are confronted by a 'career blockage' of older managers. Such problems are exacerbated in organizations which have retrenched or grown more slowly than hitherto. Low morale and poor performance may result, as staff become frustrated, especially if their career aspirations remain high, given the more favourable experience of their predecessors.

The lack of career opportunities is a problem for many organizations in the public sector, in manufacturing, and for larger banks and financial institutions. There are some exceptions to this, however, in expanding sectors such as finance, retailing and electronics, and in certain occupations, such as computing and marketing.

There are many remedies to the career blockage problem. These include changing organizational structures and introducing 'intrapreneurial'* ventures, which may provide new opportunities for managerial staff. Redesigning career paths, with lateral transfers and even downward moves towards the end of a career, can make better use of managerial resources. Other remedies include job rotation, job sharing, part-time working and outward secondments. Some large employing organizations have seconded managers to work for periods of up to two years in educational institutions, government agencies and community projects. Such secondments may be a way of enriching the experience of younger managers or of easing out managers near the end of their careers.

Many organizations have encouraged staff to opt for early retirement to ease career blockages for their younger colleagues. But this may fail to provide a long-term solution to the career blockage problem, as it allows for only a once and for all displacement, unless their successors can also be retired early. Such early retirement is generally preferable for individuals than the harsher alternative: redundancy.

Redundancy

Managerial employment used to be seen as secure, but the view that managers have a 'job for life' has changed. In recent years, many organizations have reduced the size of their workforce, including their cadre of managers, and many companies have specifically aimed to 'flatten' their managerial hierarchies.

The broad occupational category of managers suffered a greater proportionate increase in unemployment in the early 1980s than most other categories. The expertise of managers is more likely to be organizationally specific than is the case for other categories of worker. Hence, redundant managers may find it more difficult to find another job in comparison, say, with craft or professsional workers whose skills are more easily transferable to other employers. Also, as some managers put it, 'the higher you rise, the harder you fall'.

Management vacancies generally remain unfilled for longer than other categories. Good managers are relatively scarce and employers also take longer to fill such vacancies, because managers have to give longer periods of notice than other staff and the selection methods are more elaborate than those used for subordinate grades.

A Durham University survey of 91 large manufacturing companies found that 63 per cent of them had reduced their number of managers between 1979 and 1984. Of these, 20 per cent had an in-house resettlement unit to help those managers being made redundant. In some cases this involved helping them to start their own business. Several independent agencies provide outplacement counselling for redundant managers, although only a few companies hire such external help for their managers.[10]

Managers may receive a full pension and a substantial cash payment on being made redundant, particularly in the case of those over 55 years old, and those working in the public sector and for the larger firms. The cost of such redundancy payments can reach £75,000 per head. Compensation for unfair

* An intrapreneur is an employee who runs a quasi-autonomous business within a larger organization.

dismissal can be much higher. One recent out-of-tribunal settlement (via ACAS) was almost £1 million.

Equal opportunities

By the early 1990s, women accounted for almost half the labour force, but were only 27 per cent of managers and only 1 per cent of top managers.[11] There is a significantly lower percentage of women employees in managerial jobs in Britain than in Germany, France, the US, Canada and Australia. Women managers tend to be concentrated at the lower levels; in particular functions, such as personnel, purchasing/contracting and sales/marketing; and in industries such as paper, printing and publishing, retailing and other services.

Why are there relatively few women managers? One explanation for the lack of women's career progression is that they may be less mobile than men. Many employers in banking, finance and retailing have mobility clauses in their contracts of employment for managers, which may deter women from seeking promotion. More generally, management may be seen as requiring certain 'male' characteristics, such as aggression and drive. The stereotypical female is assumed to lack those qualities and so is presumed unsuitable for a managerial career. Women are socialized into 'female' attitudes and behaviour, which discourage them and others from seeing them as ideal managers. This is compounded by personnel policies which have thoughtlessly discriminated against women, by assuming an uninterrupted and typically 'male' career pattern. Also, women have not usually been sufficiently encouraged to study for professional qualifications.

The proportion of women managers will continue to rise, and there is increasing pressure to change personnel practices, by introducing provision for child-care and extended periods of paternity, as well as maternity leave. Social stereotypes are changing, albeit slowly; there is a growing proportion of women in higher education, and an increasing tendency for women graduates to enter industrial and commercial employment. Further, men's opposition to women managers seems to be declining.[12]

Women are not the only people who are under-represented in management. There are disproportionately few managers from a working-class background and from the ethnic minorities. There has been increasing concern by some politicians and practitioners that 'something should be done' about the lack of managerial recruitment from women and ethnic minorities. Part of the concern is that managerial talent is scarce, and that discriminatory recruitment practices increase the scarcity. The contraction in the number of 18–24 year olds is likely to increase the pressure for equal opportunities (see above).

Several public policies have attempted to prevent such discrimination. Both the Equal Oppportunities Commission (EOC) and the Commission for Racial Equality (CRE) have launched 'codes of practice', encouraging employers to promote equal opportunities and to develop their own 'monitoring systems'. Some large employers have responded; in some cases by appointing an equal opportunities officer to monitor recruitment and promotion. Unlike some of their US counterparts, however, few British employers have yet begun to pursue positive action in favour of women and ethnic minorities. Some unions have also appointed equal opportunities officers, to promote the interest of women and ethnic minorities.

ECONOMIC REWARDS

In the 1970s, there was a compression of pay differentials between managers and their subordinates, but this trend was reversed in the 1980s. This reverse reflects the end of formal incomes policies, the increased tax efficiency of pay relative to other benefits and employers increasingly aiming to reward individual performance, particularly among the more senior staff.

Those who design salary structures have to meet several objectives, which may conflict with each other. The patterns of rewards in an organization are shaped internally, by considerations of motivation, incentives, status, differentials and relativities;* and externally, by such considerations as the capacity to recruit and retain the appropriate people.

The pay of a particular manager may be related to two factors internal to the organization: first, the job level; and secondly, the manager's performance within the job. Organizations place differing degrees of emphasis on these two factors, according to labour-market conditions and their own corporate culture. Compare the individualistic ethos and merit pay systems of an electronics company, for instance, with the rigid salary scales and service-based pay increments of the civil service (although the latter is changing; see later).

Job evaluation** and salary structures

Most large organizations evaluate managerial jobs, in particular, into an approximate hierarchy and relate salaries to the level of the job within the hierarchy. There are various techniques of job evaluation, but most of them fall into one of two categories:

1. *Non-analytical approaches* involve either ranking jobs, or allocating them to predetermined grades on the basis of simple subjective comparisons.
2. *Analytical approaches* analyse jobs in terms of several factors, such as 'responsibility' and 'knowledge'. Each job is allocated a number of points per factor, the sum of points then determines the evaluation of the job.

A job may be allocated to a grade which carries a specified salary range. Alternatively, the points score from the analytical approach may be converted directly into a salary level, using a conversion formula.

How is an individual's salary determined within a given job? Most jobs have a salary scale or a range based on specified percentages of the evaluated job value (say 90 to 110 per cent). Progression through the scale may be on the basis of annual increments, perhaps denied only to poor performers; or on the basis

---

* *Relativities* refer to the differences in the levels of pay (and/or other benefits) between comparable jobs in different employing organizations or negotiating units, whereas *differentials* refer to the pay difference between different jobs within one employing organization or a single negotiating unit.
** Job evaluation techniques in general are described in more detail in Chapter 11.

of a regular assessment of the individual's performance. Some salary systems involve a mix of automatic increments and merit payments; for example, progression up to a certain point in the scale may be automatic, with movement beyond this depending on merit, perhaps with several ceilings for different standards of performance. In addition, some organizations also pay cost-of-living increases independently of any incremental or merit award. This practice was particularly widespread during the inflationary period of the 1970s.

In designing salary structures for managers, there are several pitfalls to avoid. If salary scales overlap by too much, this may create problems in getting staff to accept job mobility and even promotion, since this may involve only a limited financial gain for an individual. Those who try to implement one salary system to cater for all of an organization's managers often experience problems in accommodating specialist groups. For example, some employers attempt to pay their professional computer staff on the same scales as middle managers. While this satisfies the desire for equity, it may compromise the organization's ability to recruit and retain computer staff, who command a premium in a competitive labour market. Separate salary grades or pay supplements for such staff may be necessary in order to recruit and retain them, but this may upset other staff and so reduce morale. Other solutions include having computer staff as self-employed contractors, or subcontracting all the computer operations to an agency.

An additional problem may arise when individuals reach the maximum salary level for their particular job, and when promotion is not possible, perhaps because of a general lack of promotion opportunities. Individuals may then become demoralized, in the absence of further salary increases. One way to avoid this is to offer occasional incentive payments or good performance bonuses to such staff. Again, the emphasis is on flexibility to cope with particular circumstances.

In recent years, some organizations have introduced performance-related pay for the first time, while others have reintroduced it, having abandoned it during the 1970s. Many of those organizations which already had such schemes have extended them to account for a higher proportion of an individual's salary, sometimes abandoning general cost-of-living increases and automatic salary increments altogether.

The use of performance-related pay has increased for at least three reasons. First, it provides a mechanism for increasing pay differentials. Secondly, the reduction in the level of inflation has reduced the need for general cost-of-living increases. Thirdly, it reflects a perceived need by corporate policy-makers to link rewards more closely with performance, as competition has intensified. This is often associated with attempts to change the corporate culture. Furthermore, some organizations try to link earnings to company or divisional performance, for example, by paying incentive bonuses. This became more common in the 1980s, particularly at senior levels, where an individual's performance can have a significant impact on that of the company as a whole.

Many large corporations are organized into profit centres or subsidiary businesses. There is a trend towards greater autonomy for such units. In some organizations this extends to differentiating between the types and levels of reward in these units, depending on their profitability, local labour markets, product markets or business policies. Increasingly, those responsible for profit centres and subsidiary businesses find that they can choose to implement their own policies and practices, without being fully tied to a monolithic corporate arrangement. One disadvantage of introducing such differentiation is that it can then become more difficult to give managers a wide experience by moving them around. Therefore, unlike many other innovations in personnel management, such differentiation of terms and conditions for managers happens less readily than for subordinate categories, who are less likely to be mobile.

The remuneration package

Although most perks are now taxable, pay has long been more liable to tax than non-pay rewards, particularly for the more highly paid staff. This has contributed towards a proliferation of fringe benefits for managers.

In 1991, almost 80 per cent of senior managers and 20 per cent of junior managers received a company car, with a continuing trend towards providing status cars further down the managerial and professional hierarchy.[13] Other typical fringe benefits include health insurance, a telephone, assistance with children's education costs, housing loans or subsidies, allowances for clothing or consumer durables and expense accounts. Since 1978, tax concessions have been granted to encourage profit-sharing and employee share ownership generally, but the majority of share option schemes have been registered under the post-1979 Conservative Government's legislation, which allows schemes restricted to directors and managers.

After 1979, the reduction in marginal rates of income tax, and the heavier taxation of fringe benefits, has increased the relative tax efficiency of cash payments. This is reflected in the increasing use of performance-related pay and cash bonuses. However, fringe benefits remain popular. For example, the number of company cars increased fourfold during the 1980s, although it remains to be seen whether the increasingly heavy taxation of company car benefits will check this trend in the 1990s.

Organizations are beginning to introduce greater flexibility and choice into their remuneration packages for managers and professionals. While the adoption of fully-developed 'cafeteria-style' benefits programmes is less common than in the US, some experts are expecting them to spread. Such programmes allow individual managers to choose from a range of alternative benefits, up to a maximum annual cost to the employer. Depending on individuals' personal circumstances, they may select particular perks, or choose to maximize their level of salary.

The rationale of these programmes is that if an employer provides the individual's preferred remuneration package, this should maximize value for money in terms of recruitment, motivation and retention.[14] Some employers are considering such flexibility for a broader category of employees. However, in view of the larger numbers of people involved, the salary administration becomes more complicated.

The public sector and privatization

The public sector has traditionally had salary scales through which managers progress on the basis of automatic annual increments. The emphasis has been on standard rates of pay, with individual performance being recognized through seniority and promotion. After privatization, former public sector corporations have aimed to move away from such standard rates, towards greater flexibility. There have been similar moves, even in those parts of the public sector not subject to privatization. There has been much subcontracting of services such as cleaning, catering, transport and maintenance, as well as computing.

The public sector has also been seeking to relate pay to individual performance. These schemes reflect, first, the decline in promotion opportunities, which threatens to demoralize staff, secondly, the government's desire to introduce private sector type management styles, and thirdly, a need to raise pay in key areas to deal with recruitment and retention difficulties. In 1985, the government introduced a performance bonus system for senior civil servants. The scheme met with considerable union opposition, mainly because of the differences in implementation between departments, which the unions saw as arbitrary and divisive. However, performance-related pay seems set to become increasingly important in the public sector, not least in the hived-off executive agencies.

Personal contracts

By the end of the 1980s 'personal contracts' were being introduced for senior management in the National Health Service and in the newly-privatized corporations such as British Telecom and the electricity supply industry, while a few organizations, notably in newspaper publishing, had begun to offer them to their middle managers and even to more junior staff.[15] Such contracts involve the settling of terms and conditions on an individual basis with the senior manager concerned, and in many cases take the individual outside the scope of an existing collective agreement.

Such personal contracts can be seen as the logical extension of many of the developments described above. The move to a more flexible and individualized remuneration package, the offer of a stake in the success of the organization and the acceptance by the employee of the risks that go with it, are all taken further with personal contracts, and their introduction was often accompanied by performance-related pay and bonuses.

UNIONIZATION OF MANAGERS

Traditionally, compared to junior staff, managers and professionals tend to be treated on a more individual basis by the employer. Nevertheless, the 1989 Labour Force Survey shows that 42 per cent of managerial and professional employees were unionized, ranging from 96 per cent in rail transport and 83 per cent in electricity and gas, to 8 per cent in business services and 7 per cent in wholesale distribution.[16] The unionization of managers and professionals is higher in the private sector and in the recently-privatized utilities, largely because of historical differences in employer policies on collective bargaining.

The 1970s saw a growth in the unionization of managers and professionals, as the economic and political climate was generally conducive to union growth (see Chapter 1), although its impact remained negligible outside the public and co-operative sectors and certain large companies.[17] Since 1980, unions have been on the retreat, and union derecognition, while so far limited in general, appears to have had a disproportionate effect on managers and professionals.[18] While managerial and professional unions have tended to be moderate, and have often accepted the introduction of performance-related rewards, some employers have taken senior staff outside the scope of collective bargaining in an attempt to increase their ability to treat them on an individualized and flexible basis (see above).

CONCLUSION

Managers and professionals play a vital role in implementing the objectives of most organizations, so that the management of such employees is crucial. Moreover, employers' innovations in managing managers are particularly significant as they are often subsequently applied to other categories of employee. Examples of such wider applications include more sophisticated methods of selection, induction and development; pay systems based on job evaluation, which include performance-related elements; and other schemes ranging from appraisal to early retirement.

In recent years, there has been some discussion about whether or not managers and professionals, particularly those in the middle levels of the organizational hierarcy, have become less committed to their jobs.[20] One view is that such employees increasingly feel that they are excluded from 'management' as they are more closely monitored and controlled, and as career prospects have become more uncertain and managerial prerogatives have been questioned. While some have questioned such pessimistic views,[21] it is likely that organizations will have to adapt their employment policies to account for the non-work interests of their staff, and that the loyalty and commitment even of managers and professionals cannot be taken for granted. The development of more flexible policies aimed at encouraging the full participation of women is a step in this direction, as is the movement towards 'family-friendly' employment policies. The recruitment, retention and motivation of a high-quality managerial and professional workforce is among the key challenges facing organizations in the future.

References

1. For further details of these four types see Snape, E J and Bamber, G J (1987) *Managerial and Professional Employees in Britain, Employee Relations Monograph*, **9**: 3, MCB University Press, Bradford, p 16.
2. Institute of Personnel Management/British Institute of Management (1980) *Selecting Managers: How British Industry Recruits* London.
3. Mabey, C (1984) 'Managing graduate entry', *Journal of General Management*, **10**: 2, Winter, pp 67–79.
4. National Economic Development Office/Training Commission (1988) *Young People and the Labour Market: A Challenge for the 1990s*, London.
5. Alban-Metcalf, B and Nicholson, N (1984) *The Career Development of British Managers*, British Institute of Management, London.
6. Guerrier, Y and Philpot, N (1978) *The British Manager: Careers and Mobility*, British Institute of Management, London.
7. Robbins, Lord (1963) *Report of the Committee on Higher Education*, Cmnd 2154, HMSO, London; Franks, Lord (1983) *British Business Schools*, British Institute of Management, London.

8. Griffiths, B and Murray, H (1985) *Whose Business? – A Radical Proposal To Privatise British Business Schools*, Institute of Economic Affairs, London; *Financial Times*, 29 November 1991, p 16.
9. Constable, J and McCormick, R (1987) *The Making of British Managers*, BIM, London; Handy, C (1987) *The Making of Managers: A Report on Management Education, Training and Development in the United States, West Germany, France, Japan and the UK*, NEDO, London.
10. *The Economist* 6 April 1985, p 69.
11. National Economic Development Office/Royal Institute of Public Administration (1990) *Women Managers: The Untapped Resource*, Kogan Page, London.
12. Rothwell, S (1985) 'Women's management careers', *Business Graduate*, April, pp 34–9; McIntosh, A (1980) 'Women at work: a survey of employers', *Employment Gazette*, Department of Employment, November, pp 1142–9.
13. The Reward Group (1991) *Employee Benefits* quoted in IDS Top Pay Unit (1991) *Monthly Review of Salaries and Benefits*, 128, October, p 5.
14. Woodley, C (1990) 'The cafeteria route to compensation', *Personnel Management*, May, pp 42–5.
15. Pickard, J (1990) 'When pay gets personal', *Personnel Management*, July pp 41–5.
16. Bird, D, Stevens, M and Yates, A (1991) 'Membership of trade unions in 1989', *Employment Gazette* June, pp 337–343.
17. Bamber, G J (1986) *Militant Managers? Managerial Unionism and Industrial Relations*, Gower, Aldershot, p 50.
18. Claydon, T (1989) 'Union derecognition in Britain in the 1980s', *British Journal of Industrial Relations*, XXV 11, 2 July, pp 214–24.
19. Holbrook, D (1985) 'Can collective bargaining ever change? The ICI experience', *Personnel Management*, January.
20. Scase, R and Goffe, R (1989) *Reluctant Managers: Their Work and Lifestyles*, Unwin Hyman, London.
21. Dopson, S and Stewart, R (1990) 'What is happening to middle management?', *British Journal of Management*, 1, pp 3–16.

Chapter Thirteen

Employee Relations in Smaller Enterprises*

Ian Roberts, Derek Sawbridge and Greg Bamber

After defining a small firm, this chapter elaborates a systematic approach to managing key aspects of employee relations in such firms. We use the term *employee*, rather than *industrial* relations, as it is increasingly seen as more appropriate in the context of small and medium-sized enterprises, which are usually managed informally and rarely unionized. We consider the formulation of a human resources plan which includes the processes of recruitment, induction and training. We explore the issues of pay, communications, workplace regulations, dismissals and trade unionism.

Since the influential Bolton Report (1971), there has been an enormous growth of research on and publications about small firms in general. However, there has been a relative neglect of *employee relations* in small firms. Owner/ managers generally accord a lower priority to employee relations than to such other aspects of their business as their output (a product or a service), selling it and accounting for it. Hence, one writer describes those who work in the small business sector as 'the invisible labour force'.[1] This neglect reflects a belief that small firms have 'good' (ie harmonious) employee relations. The belief is fuelled by the indicator that strikes are rare in small firms.

None the less, in recent years, there has been a growing body of research on alternative indicators. When such issues as labour turnover, health and safety records, pay and the number of unfair dismissal cases are examined, the typical pattern of employee relations in small firms may appear to be worse than that in many of their larger counterparts.[2] Analysing such alternative indicators has given rise to another view of small firms, which has more to do with notions of the 'sweat shop' and exploitation than with notions of harmony.

Although there are examples which approximate to either one of these good or bad characterizations, most small firms fit somewhere between those two poles. In short, there are many different styles of employment relationship. The small-firm sector is diverse. There is a difference both in the external constraints

* The authors acknowledge that much of this chapter draws on a research project 'Management and industrial relations in small firms', which was funded at Durham University Business School by the Department of Employment. However, the views expressed here are personal ones, rather than those of the Department. The authors gratefully acknowledge the helpful comments of Jim Kitay and Mike Scott.

and typical management styles, for instance, in a software house on the one hand, and an owner-managed transport firm on the other.

Being 'small' in terms of numbers of employees is not the only determinant of the pattern of employee relations. The industrial subculture is also important. The traditions of specific industries may exert a greater influence on the expectations of owner/managers and workers than the number of employees in a firm. For example, in view of the strong traditions of trade unionism in the printing industry, there is a high level of union membership in many small printing firms; but unionism is invariably absent in small firms in most other industries (as discussed later). Moreover, the style of employee relations varies considerably, even within the same industry. Among other variables, the style reflects the personalities involved, especially those of the owner/managers.

WHAT IS A SMALL FIRM?

While an engineering firm employing 15 people could be described as small, a hairdressers employing the same number could be seen as rather large. There is no one accepted definition of a small firm. As shown in Table 13.1, the definition in terms of size also varies greatly from one country to another.

Table 13.1 *International definitions of small and medium-sized firms*

Country	Definition of small and medium firms
Australia	1 to 100 employees
Belgium	1 to 50 employees
Denmark	6 to 50 employees
Federal Republic of Germany	1 to 499 employees
France	6 to 500 employees
Eire	1 to 50 employees
Italy	1 to 500 employees
The Netherlands	1 to 100 employees
United Kingdom	1 to 200 employees

Source: Industrial Democracy and Employee Participation: A Policy Discussion Paper, Working Environment Branch, Department of Employment and Industrial Relations, Australian Government Publishing Service, Canberra, 1986: 70; *Report on the Future of Small and Medium-Sized Business in Europe*, Document No 4555 presented to the Parliamentary Assembly Committee on Economic Affairs and Development, Brussels, 1980.

The international range of definitions illustrates that any cut-off point in terms of numbers employed is arbitrary. The Bolton Committee, recognizing this problem, identified three qualitative criteria for defining small and medium-sized firms:

- a small market share and therefore only limited power to influence trading conditions;
- personalized management, with the owners themselves actively participating in all aspects of management;

■   financial independence, with the owners having effective control of the business.*

These qualitative criteria are important, because they set the context in which styles of employee relations are developed. Despite the diversity of the small-firm sector, when these three qualitative criteria are emphasized, there are many similarities between small firms across different industrial sectors. The most important feature is the personalized form of management, especially where the owner(s) actively participate in all aspects of management.

Most big firms have a personnel department, which includes specialists in the various aspects of employee relations, including recruitment, training, pay and so on. In most small firms, however, an all too often harassed owner/manager has to handle all such aspects in any 'spare time' left over from the other functions of business management. Hence, personnel and employee relations issues are often accorded a low priority.

The prime indicator of success for the owner/managers of most small firms is the market performance of their output. In addition, most of them are intensely committed to the success of 'their' firm. With some owners this commitment becomes an obsession. Success at any price may be an admirable quality in an individual, but can lead to problems if this principle is transferred to the management of people, particularly as owner/managers tend to view employee relations issues in a unitary framework.** Most owner/managers assume that their firm's goals are rational; therefore, as long as employees do what is good for the firm, they are also doing what is best for themselves. Managing employee relations is seen as a matter of 'common sense'. Hence, in the absence of a strike or other overt problem, such elements of management can be left to look after themselves.

Many writers on small firms have concluded that such informal management, based on the close relations between the owner and employees, is 'better' than the impersonal bureaucratic management which characterizes most larger firms. However, later research has questioned this conclusion:

> Small firms do offer more varied work roles and greater opportunities for close face-to-face relations in a flexible social setting with less of the bureaucracy of the larger enterprise. But, these conditions also offer greater opportunities for interpersonal conflict.[3]

---

* The financial independence and effective control criterion is problematic, given that many small and medium-sized firms are financially *dependent* on larger ones, for example, for contracts, franchise arrangements, bank loans and so on.
** Such a framework is defined by the emphasis placed upon the common objectives and values, which are seen to bind all members of the organization together; so the only employee behaviour seen as rational is that which supports the goals of the company, as defined by management. See Gunnigle, P and Brady, T (1985) 'The management of industrial relations in the small firm', paper presented to the Eighth National Small Firms Policy and Research Conference. On the distinction between unitary and pluralist frameworks, see Fox, A (1986), *Man Mismanagement*, 2nd edn Hutchinson, London.

This, then, is the key to understanding the reality of employee relations in small firms. Relations are not of the impersonal 'structured' type, characteristic of many larger firms. But neither are they merely a collection of individual interpersonal relationships, involving a loosely structured distribution of power, as in ties of friendship. Rather, the characteristic feature of small firms is the overlap between personal and employee relations.[4]

We advocate an approach which aims to maximize the potential benefits of the close personal relationships in most small firms, while recognizing that these relationships are also structured by an employment relationship. A systematic management approach is needed to settle the conflicts which may arise if and when the more personal ties 'turn sour'. The rest of this chapter is devoted to such a systematic approach to managing employee relations in small firms.

EMPLOYING PEOPLE

Given that most small-business owner/managers are output-oriented, they often see employing people as a nuisance or a 'necessary evil', that the labour law is too complicated and that one mistake can often mean the end of their business. This view is reinforced by some 'experts'. One book which purports to explain the law to small business, devotes 2 pages (out of 40) to employing people, and begins this advice with a warning, which typifies the whole section: 'One of the many minefields that any expanding small business has to negotiate is the hiring of employees. Hiring has deep perils.'[5]

Such a view has become the conventional wisdom among small-business owners. An ACAS analysis of inquiries from small businesses in the northern region during 1985 revealed that many owner/managers believed (mistakenly) that their business was governed by regulations on hours, pay, conditions etc. Of course employing people is not easy, but it is wrong to exaggerate the stringency of the law and the possible penalties for transgressing it.

To be a successful employer, a degree of planning and a systematic approach is generally necessary. There is an inevitable indeterminancy about the effort expended by employees in exchange for pay (the effort-reward bargain). Unless the pay system is completely based on performance, employees sell merely their *capacity* to labour. It is much harder for an owner/manager to plan precisely what the input from employees will be, than to estimate the rate at which a piece of machinery can work.

The managerial problem, then, is to maximize the potential input from employees. Should managers attempt to specify and closely control the rate at which employees work, as in the scientific-management style (sometimes called Theory X), or to harness the commitment and enthusiasm of the employees in order to maximize the 'variable' input of labour (Theory Y)?[6] Most styles involve some degree of both the X and Y approaches, but the latter is often more suitable in a small firm, which can usually exercise control less formally than a large firm. Most employees work closely with the owner/manager, so their performance is easily visible. Yet, in spite of this small-firm context, many owner/managers are inclined to start by being autocratic and unthinkingly to adopt a Theory X style of management.

A human resource plan

The first step in establishing a small firm should be to formulate a business plan. This should include plans for the output, selling, finance and so on. If the business is to employ people, it should also include a human resource plan. Such a plan should specify the dimensions of the workforce, both in terms of quantity and quality. Furthermore, the plan should have a time dimension: employment needs should be projected as far into the future as practicable. Such projections should be revised periodically, in the light of changing circumstances and new information. Attention must be paid to the structure of demand for the particular product or service. The owner/manager should consider whether demand is stable over a given period (a year, for example), or whether there are peaks and troughs to plan for. In the shorter term, does demand fluctuate? If so, is this best accommodated through the employment of casual or part-time workers, or by subcontracting?

Once developed, the plan will enable the owner/manager to integrate the costs of employment with the available capital resources. This should ensure the most efficient use of all factors of production and avoid the pitfalls of increasing labour costs, which may arise, for instance, from overstaffing and skill shortages. In the initial stages, the production of such a plan will probably be the sole responsibility of the owner/manager. However, as the firm develops, it will be necessary to review progress and update the projections. At these later stages owner/managers should remember that planning the size and quality of the workforce affects the interests of existing employees, so it is 'important that they and their representatives should be involved in each stage of the process'.[7]

Owner/managers who see the firm as their own creation and as private property may be reluctant to involve employees in planning 'their' firm. But such involvement can benefit the owner/manager by inducing the commitment and enthusiasm of the firm's employees. For an owner/manager, involving employees in such planning has at least two more advantages: assimilating the workers' knowledge of the production process; and informing them in a direct way of the external constraints within which the firm has to operate.

Recruiting

Having formulated a human resource plan and decided to recruit (given that no internal solution to a labour shortage can be found), an owner/manager should evaluate the precise requirements of each job vacancy. A task analysis of a job should specify its duties and responsibilities, and the ways in which the job is to be done. Such an analysis should also specify the desired relationships between the job holder and the superiors, any subordinates and colleagues. Then a job description should be drafted, listing the job's main elements and its general purpose. Next, a job specification should be produced. This defines the qualifications, experience and personal qualities needed to do the job.

Where do applicants come from? *Employing People: The ACAS Handbook for Small Firms* provides a guide to the main sources:

- *jobcentres* provide a free nationwide recruitment and advisory service;
- *employment agencies* can assist with the recruitment and selection process and provide other services;

- *local education authority careers services* can give employers information on suitable school leavers and other young people who are less than 18 years old, based on regular contacts with local schools;
- *advertisements* in local newspapers or specialist journals often attract good applicants at relatively low cost;
- *word of mouth* can be a useful method if the employer is able to judge the reliability of an employee's opinion.[8]

When recruiting, small firms tend to rely to a considerable extent on non-formal agencies of recruitment, entailing word-of-mouth recommendations from friends, relatives or existing employees. Owners often prefer to employ someone by personal recommendation, because such a relationship can provide a way of exerting pressure on the new recruit to perform satisfactorily. There is nothing intrinsically wrong with personal recommendations as a source of candidates; however, it may be unwise for a growing firm to rely entirely upon such sources, which:

> may lead to discrimination claims if it reduces the opportunity for all races and both sexes to apply. It is therefore recommended that this recruitment method should not be used where the workforce is wholly or predominantly white or black and the labour market is multi-racial.[9]

Perhaps of more importance than possible legal sanctions, is the limitation that overreliance upon this method of recruitment builds into the firm. Recent research at Durham revealed several examples of the collapse of such recruitment strategies. Well-established small firms encountered difficulties when the 'personal network' dried up. Not only were there no established systematic procedures for recruiting, but also, when 'outsiders' were recruited, they found it difficult to fit into workplaces mostly staffed by established friends and relatives. As a result, labour turnover increased and, where several 'outsiders' were recruited, they tended to form a clique, often leading to a degree of conflict between them and the more established workers.

Nevertheless, the advantages of recruiting personally-recommended candidates can be considerable and lead to a more integrated workforce than might otherwise be the case, as long as those candidates are suitable. It is absurd for owners to employ a friend or relative of either themselves or an existing employee if that person does not fit the job specification.

With the aim of employing the best person, employers should make a shortlist of candidates from more than one source from which they can choose their new employee. Because individuals have different strengths and weaknesses the criteria to be considered in the interview should be standardized as far as possible. To this end, the job specification should be divided into simplified headings to be used at the interview. Two of the most popular methods are the seven-point plan developed by Alec Rodger and the five-point grading system produced by Munro Fraser.[10] The former includes:

- physical make-up – health, physique, appearance, bearing and speech;
- attainments – education, qualifications, experience;
- general intelligence – intellectual capacity;
- special aptitude – mechanical ability, manual dexterity, facility in the use of words or numbers;

- interests – intellectual, practical, constructional, physically active, social, artistic;
- disposition – acceptability, influence over others, steadiness, dependability, self-reliance;
- circumstances – domestic circumstances, occupations of family.

The Munro Fraser system includes similar points, but listed under five headings:

- impact on others;
- acquired qualifications;
- innate abilities;
- motivation;
- adjustment.

The use of such systems should help to prevent engaging someone who is very good at performing at interviews, but less good at doing the job. Employers should be clear about the relative priority of individual attributes – whether they are essential or merely desirable. Furthermore, these systems should not be seen as exhaustive; extra items can be added. For example, if it is important to the owner that a candidate has some connection with a person already at the firm, this can be included.

In some circumstances, it may be possible to administer a selection test to measure individual ability. While this is relatively easy with potential typists, it is more difficult, say, for potential supervisors, whose job is less easily defined. Nevertheless, it can be useful to seek advice from a specialist recruitment consultant, who can administer a validated aptitude test. (Many owner/managers are too shy of using such external resources, which can provide valuable help.)

References can also provide an important stage in the recruitment process: first, to check the factual information given by candidates about previous jobs, pay, reasons for leaving etc; and secondly, to gain opinions about the character of candidates and their suitability for the specified post.

Choosing the correct candidate is inevitably a compromise; it is rare to find one who can achieve a maximum rating on all criteria. It is important, therefore, to standardize comparisons, not be swayed by outstanding ability in only one or a few areas.

Recruitment is influenced by the external labour market conditions. It is generally believed that when there is a slack rather than a tight labour market, employers have a larger available pool of labour to choose from and there is less upward pressure on pay levels. However, small firms can experience greater difficulty in finding the right employee under such conditions. First, because such an employer may be overwhelmed by the number of applicants, so that selection can be difficult and time-consuming. Secondly and more importantly, people may apply for work with which they will be less than happy. This factor rather than lack of technical skill, often underlies the complaint from small-business owners that they cannot get the right quality of staff. So, even in such favourable conditions, it is necessary to take a systematic approach to recruitment.

Induction

Once employees have been engaged, few small firms pay enough attention to induction. Typically, they are shown to their workstation, then expected to get on with the job immediately. Perhaps such expectation follows because the firm is small or because new employees were recommended personally or have already had experience in the industry. Sometimes new recruits are introduced to a worker doing the same type of work, who is expected to provide an example to follow. (This approach may be called 'sitting by Nellie'.) Such an approach can be a useful element of the induction process, but is insufficient. Much labour turnover occurs shortly after people join a firm; this is often known as the *induction crisis*. Furthermore, the level of such labour turnover is often under-reported in smaller firms as, when asked about labour turnover, owner/managers often do not include workers who left within a few days or even weeks.

A properly planned induction programme can speed up the process of integrating a new worker into the firm. This has benefits both for the individual concerned and for the firm. An induction programme should involve two aspects.

1. *A technical aspect*. How to do the job, including where tools and materials are located and, for a worker with experience of similar work, any methods specific to the individual firm.
2. *A personnel aspect*. Introductions to all members of the firm and a description of their function (supervisory staff are not always easily identified in the small firm). Factual information such as the location of eating, toilet, safety and health facilities etc. should also be detailed.

These two aspects should not be considered in isolation. The explanation of how the firm works is best undertaken on a tour of the establishment, where appropriate introductions can also be made. This gives new recruits an idea not only of where their job fits in, but also where they will fit in the social system of the workplace. Recruits should be encouraged to ask questions; the information flow should be in both directions and it is important for the manager to get to know recruits, as well as for them to know the work environment.

Explaining the functioning of one small print shop is simpler than explaining how a large multinational enterprise functions. However, the goal is the same: employers should aim to integrate new employees into their organizations as smoothly and quickly as possible.

Training

An induction programme is not the only form of training that a small firm needs to offer. The need for the subsequent training and development of staff is probably even greater than in larger establishments, for at least three reasons. First, in most small firms, there is less division of labour, so it is more important for small firms to develop a flexible and adaptable workforce. This is one function of a good training scheme. Secondly, in view of their small size, the potential for promotion is relatively limited. Therefore, unless there is scope for other forms of development, such as more variation in work or increased responsibility, workers may look elsewhere for career progress. (This has been the experience of many small firms employing professional workers in the high-tech sectors.) Thirdly, investment in the human resources of small firms is important because, compared with larger firms, they tend to be more dependent on the input from labour; most small firms are less capital-intensive than their larger counterparts.

Having established the need for training, what should it consist of? The requirements vary between types of business. However, the firm must initially specify the need and then ensure that the training suits both the employee and the firm. It makes no sense to train someone for non-existent jobs; the trained employee will be frustrated and may leave, so the firm gets no return on the investment.

Even in the smallest of firms it may be possible to initiate a self-development scheme for highly motivated employees and, as long as the training goals have been clearly identified, the practice can be relatively informal. Owner/managers often suspect external training; they criticize it as irrelevant to the specialized needs of their firm. This used to be a reasonable criticism, but recently many external providers of training have specifically aimed to satisfy the requirements of smaller firms. Information on training schemes is available from many sources including:

- the Training Agency;
- employers' and trade associations;
- local chambers of commerce and small business clubs;
- industry training boards and other specialist training organizations;
- the Department of Employment's Small Firms Service;
- business schools, small business centres and/or industrial liaison officers in educational institutions.

Any form of training must be seen in its social context. Training, to some degree, will be relevant to all members of the firm. It is shortsighted to concentrate solely on one or two high-flyers. Such training may become a source of jealousy and envy, leading towards interpersonal conflict, which is usually counter-productive to the firm's goals.

Pay

In general, pay levels are lower in small firms than in larger ones, for broadly equivalent grades of labour,[11] but there are considerable variations by sector and industry. For example, some of the small high-tech computer firms pay higher salaries than IBM and other multinationals in the same sector. None the less, most large firms offer more in the way of job security and opportunities for promotion.

The general pattern of lower pay in small firms may be linked with a specific orientation to work among small-firm employees. One researcher argued that such workers seem to be less motivated by money, but have more of an expressive orientation to work (ie they like working 'with people' and 'for companionship'). Small-firm workers may not always aim to maximize their economic rewards; instead they may be seeking other benefits, for example, a distinctive working environment which may be typical of small firms.[12] However, subsequent researchers challenged this finding; they concluded that the difference in attitudes between small and large-firm employees had been exaggerated.[13]

Owner/managers usually claim that their firm pays 'what it can afford'. Nevertheless, such claims should be treated warily; if they were true, pay levels would fluctuate much more than they do in practice. How, then, do small firms determine pay levels? There are at least four external influences over pay levels.

1. Statutory regulation is conducted by wages councils. These used to set minimum pay and conditions in the lowest-paying sectors, which tend to consist mainly of small businesses. At their peak, in the late 1940s, wages councils covered some 15 per cent of all workers.[14] Since then, however, successive governments have abolished some of them. In the 1980s, the government restricted the remaining wages councils to determining one minimum rate of pay and overtime, and has removed young people under the age of 21 from the scope of wages councils.
2. There are many national and/or local pay agreements with trade unions. For example, there are agreements between the printing unions, and firms which belong to the relevant employers' associations. Many small firms follow these agreements informally, irrespective of whether their workers are unionized or whether the firm formally belongs to an employers' association. These agreed rates often serve as an approximate guide, around which in-house discussions may take place about other elements of pay, including overtime and bonuses.
3. Most localities have small-business clubs, which may circulate details of the local 'going rate' for key jobs. There may be a tacit acceptance that such rates in small firms in the area are usually lower than those in the larger ones.
4. Wider market forces are also important. Pay in small firms appears to decline more in a slack labour market than in larger firms.[15]

While such external factors are real constraints, owner/managers do have considerable scope for determining precise levels of pay. It is important for owner/managers carefully to consider their own special requirements in terms of attracting, motivating and retaining particular individuals, and groups. Also, in some contexts, bargaining can be important.

Bargaining

Formal company-level collective bargaining is rare in small firms, except in some unionized firms in the traditional manufacturing sector. In the services sector, employers usually determine pay more or less unilaterally, subject to the external factors mentioned above. However, there may be some individual bargaining in the face of labour shortages, especially in relation to highly skilled workers, for instance, professionals in high-tech companies.

Many large employing organizations have been trying to link pay more closely to performance than hitherto. This can be very difficult for large employers, given the complex interrelationships between different parts of their organizations. Making such a link can be easier in a small firm. Rather than making much attempt to evaluate different levels of performance or contribution to the firm, however, in practice owner/managers often determine an individual's pay subjectively, according to their own prejudices. They tend to reward those individuals who appear to be 'good workers' and to penalize those assumed to be 'troublemakers'.

Owner/managers should attempt to overcome such prejudices. Job evaluation is one useful way of establishing a more rational pay structure which can cover all employees. An optional element of performance-related pay can then be added on to the basic pay structure. Such an element can be in the form of bonuses related to objective indicators of group (or individual) performance. Incidentally, the structure must accord with the legal requirement for equal pay for men and women doing work of equal value.

Fairness is a key factor to be observed when determining pay, as employees usually have an accurate view of who are the good workers. An appropriate pay structure will reinforce the collaborative working patterns which are particularly necessary in a smaller firm; an inappropriate structure may destroy them. Whether a firm chooses a time-rated pay system or an incentive system based upon performance will depend upon the type of work and style of management. However, in general, most small firms prefer time-rated systems, as they are simpler to operate and cheaper to administer.

COMMUNICATIONS

Many people assume that communications in small firms are automatically good. The frequency of contact is thought to guarantee ease of communication, rendering formalized channels of communication obsolete: 'In a small firm, the manager can know, and be known by, all the employees. Communication is easy because the workers can see the boss virtually every working day.'[16] This view can be challenged, however; the Commission on Industrial Relations Report:

> called into question both the ease of communications . . . and the effectiveness of such communications as did actually take place. Communications tend to be one-way, because, as the report said of small businessmen, 'it is not in their nature to consult'.[17]

Ordinary day-to-day personal contacts do not automatically lead to a satisfactory pattern of communication and consultation. Many owners put great faith in an 'open door' policy, but too often no news is seen as good news. Such an approach is too passive; to ensure effective two-way communications, a more active approach is required.

In most firms, it is a good practice to set up systematic channels of communication. For instance, regular consultative meetings can be arranged. The pattern and content of these meetings depends on the type of work, the location of employees and so on. For a group of employees in one location where the market is changing rapidly, it might be appropriate to have short daily or weekly briefly meetings. In a more stable market situation, where it is necessary to bring people together from several locations, it may be more practical to have monthly or even quarterly meetings. Meetings should not be so frequent that there is nothing new to say, nor so infrequent that there is no continuity between them.

Such meetings should not be too formal, but it will help to have an agenda. This is important as it helps to differentiate the content of the meeting from the less structured everyday interactions. Owner/managers could have much to gain from having a dialogue with employees, who usually have a great deal to contribute if encouraged to do so. Therefore, owner/managers should beware of turning these meetings into an opportunity to 'preach a sermon'. They should also ensure that such occasions do not turn into regular 'moaning sessions'. Besides confronting problems, meetings should also focus on more positive issues, such as the firm's progress and development. Indeed, as a firm grows it may be necessary to shift from meetings with all employees to ones in which section representatives can communicate the views of a wider constituency. The move from direct democracy towards representative democracy may be an anathema to most owner/managers, but if growth is positively sought such a forum will need to be developed. Particularly in non-union firms such a body will present the opportunity to voice any collective issues before they can become collective problems. An important issue in facilitating change, particularly in the area of productivity and working practices, has been seen to be the ability of the owner/manager to convince the workforce collectively of the need for development.[18]

To complement collective meetings, personal discussions are also important, particularly so that individuals can be informed about how their job is contributing to the enterprise and how their own performance is evaluated. In such discussions the emphasis should also be upon dialogue, rather than monologue. Where dialogue is not seen as important, other communication channels can be used. A company newsletter, handbook or folder can contain general information. For other types of information, the use of noticeboards or enclosures in pay packets can be effective. Such communication practices themselves should be subject to joint discussion. Above all, information must be exchanged and messages must get through, for in the absence of effective communication the unsettling power of rumour can be a potent force.

A good communication system need not be gauged merely against the potential problems that would occur in its absence; such a system is intrinsically valuable. One lesson to be learned from the best Japanese managers is that, although time-consuming, a consultative management style is likely to pay dividends. In order to build high-trust working relationships, and improve employee commitment to the firm's goals, communication channels and consultation both need to be given a high priority.

RULES AND REGULATIONS

With the informality which is a hallmark of most small firms, rules and regulations are often seen as anathema. Where there are written rules, they are often a mock bureaucracy, oriented to meeting external legal criteria, rather than to regulating the day-to-day functioning of the firm. This view is short-sighted. The purpose of rules is to provide standard procedures for all employees of the firm. This is especially important in the areas of discipline and grievances; the personalized relationships in a small firm can become a disadvantage when there is a breakdown of such relationships between employer and employee. In such a situation the availability of an impersonal, objective set of rules can be particularly useful.

Rules can also be useful in relation to other aspects of behaviour. Therefore, it is useful to make a concise company rule-book, so that the important information can be found in one place. Rules should be systematic and in writing, but this does not mean that they should be complicated. It is necessary to review the rules periodically, in the face of changing circumstances in the firm and outside it. Once formulated, the rules should be given to all employees (including part-time workers).

No set of rules is exhaustive and application should depend on the merits of each case. For example, where an employee has infringed a rule, were there any mitigating circumstances? It is helpful for the rules to illustrate the distinction between two types of unacceptable conduct: misconduct (which may lead to a warning) and gross misconduct (which could lead to summary dismissal). Examples of these two types of behaviour may vary between different types of business. One example of misconduct may be repeated lateness; however, working dangerously or stealing could be seen as gross misconduct. Other areas that company rules should cover include:

- absence procedures – who to notify and when;
- health and safety practices;
- standards of work performance;
- advice on special clothing requirements;
- the use of company facilities, eg telephones;
- timekeeping;
- holiday entitlements.

These rules should be framed in a way that suits the needs of each firm; the stress should be upon simplicity and fairness. Punishment for infringement of the rules should not be overstated, while the aim of improvement should be emphasized. While the rules should be applied with sensitivity, the element of impersonal regulation that such rules imply is necessary, particularly in the small-firm setting. This can be illustrated in relation to dismissal, an issue that is often problematic.

Dismissal

The Conservative Government has highlighted the issue of discipline and the small firm. Thus, the Government rejected the 1986 ACAS draft code of practice on disciplinary procedures. In January 1987, the minister of employment stated that the 1986 draft code seemed, 'to be aimed primarily at lawyers and personnel managers in large firms'. As well as its 'excessive legalism' he also criticized it as being too long and complex. When revising this draft, ACAS was obliged to ensure that it could be understood in small firms.

As noted earlier, owner/managers often have an exaggerated view of the extent to which their business is subject to legal regulation, especially by the labour law. The British law on unfair dismissal is relatively mild, compared with some other European countries, yet there is a myth among owner/managers 'that it is now impossible to sack people'. During the first 10 years of these laws (1972–81), we estimate that less than 1 per cent of all employment terminations led to a complaint to a tribunal. However, small firms accounted for a disproportionately large number of these complaints.

This over-representation does not reflect the speed with which small-firm owner/managers may sack an employee whom they suspect is damaging their business. On the contrary, our evidence is that when there is a problem with an employee breaking a rule, owner/managers often do nothing and let the situation drift. The problem is allowed to continue until the employer can ignore it no longer, a confrontation ensues, both parties lose their tempers and the employee is summarily dismissed. Problems, which initially would have responded to *corrective* discipline, end with the application of *punitive* discipline and dismissal. The intense relationships within small firms can have a negative effect. Thus, discipline and dismissal need to be handled impersonally and in a 'cool' manner.

There should be several stages to a disciplinary procedure, for example:

- *a formal oral warning* issued for minor offences;
- *a written warning* issued for a more serious offence or a repeat of a minor offence;
- *a final written warning* issued for further misconduct (making clear that dismissal will follow if there is no improvement);
- dismissal, where the appropriate length of notice should be given.

If an employer uses this code in all disciplinary cases, the chance of an employee being able to bring a successful claim for unfair dismissal will be minimal. Although, to reiterate, the probability of an employee making such a claim is less than imagined by most owner/managers.

There is a similar need for an impersonal set of rules in relation to handling grievances. If there are only one or two tiers of management, it may be hard to convince employees that grievances will receive a fair hearing. Thus, such procedures should be in writing and known by all employees. A minimum of two stages will be necessary in order to provide the right of appeal; a short delay between stages will be helpful for the parties to cool down, although this delay should not exceed a few days and most firms should be able to complete all stages within seven working days. In this way, the procedure should be seen as a fair process, through which redress of grievances can be sought. The alternative is a situation where no one complains (which should not be confused with harmony), but frustrations are bottled up.

TRADE UNIONS

In general, individual membership and recognition of trade unions are both much less usual in small firms than in larger ones. Most owner/managers and small-firm advisers see unions as irrelevant in small firms. A large majority of owner/managers think that union recognition in their companies is unlikely in the immediate future.[19] However, the manufacturing sector is more likely to be unionized than the service sector.

Small-firm employees may have a less sympathetic view of unions than their larger-firm counterparts. But the low level of union membership in small firms can also be explained in terms of the objective problems for unions of organizing many small establishments, the resistance of most owner/managers and the lack of union policies tailored specifically to the problems of workers in small firms.

Although most owner/managers dislike unions, few have much knowledge of how unions actually operate. Even in a small firm, unions can, if the right atmosphere is created, play a positive role. They can provide an effective channel of communication in the workplace. Moreover, full-time union officials have in some cases proved to be effective and almost 'independent' arbitrators in cases of discipline and grievance.

In industries where unionization is relatively high, it may be in the interest of the employer to anticipate any move towards unionization by the workforce, by inviting an appropriate union into the firm. In this way employers can choose a time that is suitable for themselves to arrange a good deal with the union. Thus, they may wish to seek a single-union agreement, to avoid the complications that can accompany multi-union representation.

When employees approach a firm asking for union recognition, the owner/manager has several options. There is no statutory obligation to recognize a trade union, although if a majority of the workforce support the union, the consequences of an outright refusal might precipitate some form of industrial action. If owner/managers think there is insufficient workforce support to justify full collective recognition, they may concede individual representation rights. In this case the union will have the right to represent individuals, for instance, in disciplinary cases or where an employee has a grievance. Alternatively, owner/managers may concede full negotiating rights and enter into a collective bargaining arrangement, whereby rules and procedures are jointly agreed with the union. This provides a method of jointly regulating employees' terms and conditions of employment.

In the foreseeable future, there is not likely to be much growth of unionization across the small-firm sector as a whole. There are fewer economies of scale for unions recruiting and representing people employed in small firms than in large organizations. However, the collapse of many heavy industries and other shifts in the industrial structure imply a continued decline in the traditional strongholds of union membership, while many small firms have a long-term future.

Therefore, several unions have begun to pay more attention to recruiting in small firms. For example, in early 1987 the two large general unions – the TGWU and GMB – launched initiatives aimed at recruiting new members among temporary and part-time workers, particularly within the small-firm sector. Certain groups were chosen for special attention, such as contract cleaning workers (in the case of the TGWU). More recently there has been emerging evidence that unions are taking the issue of membership within the realms of small firms and the self-employed more seriously. The GMB, for example, have initiated the development of regional self-employed units providing a 'one stop shop' of advice and services for the self-employed. In this way they hope to initiate a union presence in enterprises at the initial level, in the form of the membership of the owner himself. It is believed that as growth occurs in some of these enterprises it will be easier to extend union membership to employees than in firms where owner/managers have never had a contact with trade unions. While union officials report some success in these endeavours, this kind of approach inevitably makes heavy demands upon union resources. It remains to be seen whether, in the long term, such approaches will succeed, or whether recruiting and retaining small firm members will continue to present intractable difficulties for unions.

CONCLUSION

Many owner/managers do not seek to maximize the growth of their firm, but view it as a supplier of income for themselves and their families. Hence it has been argued that:

> Small firms in Britain run out of steam as generators of new jobs when their workforce reaches 20, even though firms employing up to 20 people are the only net creators of jobs among the different sizes of businesses.

Why is the cut-off figure about 20, rather than 5, 15 or 30? We can answer this question in terms of employee relations issues. When the number employed in a firm approaches 20, the limits of informality become apparent. At these staffing levels, problems arise in at least three areas.

1. Informal networks for recruitment are likely to be less satisfactory. Perhaps the limit of potential employees known to the owner/manager is exhausted, or a social gulf has emerged between the owner/manager and potential shop floor employees. In the absence of systematic recruitment policies, owner/managers can experience great difficulty in finding employees of the right quality.
2. When there are more than about 20 employees, informal styles of management are no longer appropriate. Communication becomes more difficult, as there are fewer occasions when the whole workforce is conveniently gathered together.
3. As enterprises grow, they tend to find that *ad hoc* responses to personnel issues are less satisfactory; conflict is more likely among workers and between employees and management. Thus, as the number of employees increases, a distinct personnel function begins to be viable and necessary.

An over-reliance upon the informal or non-formal regulation of employee relations in small firms may yield only a precarious harmony. Indeed, it has been argued that too much informality with respect to Human Resource Management may almost be a predictor of business failure.[21] Therefore a means of managing discord is necessary. Owner/managers should realize their potential for constructing high-trust employment relationships but they should avoid the pitfalls of the non-formal approach. They must avoid being duped by an illusion of harmony. The first step, then, is to realize that a personnel management function is necessary. This function cannot simply look after itself; if so, tensions are likely to grow which, if left undetected, can undermine the efficiency of the firm as much as the under-utilization of capital resources.

In developing a small-firm personnel management function, owner/managers should realize that relations with 'their' workers are primarily based upon an *employment* relationship. Hence a systematic approach is necessary. Such an approach does not imply the formalization of day-to-day relationships between the 'boss' and the workers. This personal element of small-firm employment should be fostered. However, it is possible to develop personnel practices which are not arbitrary, nor too bureaucratic. These practices should be applied creatively. We advocate a blend of informality and systematic procedures. The precise mixture will depend upon the context of each small firm and the choices made by the owner/manager and the workers.

Given a systematic approach to personnel management, most employment legislation and external regulations will have little effect upon the firm:

> independent research has consistently failed to find that employment legislation inhibited small employers from taking on employees or that the legislation played other than a marginal influence in day-to-day employer-employee relations.

In view of this finding, policy-makers should perhaps aim to improve the management of employee relations in small firms, rather than focusing so much effort on the issue of legal regulation. Nevertheless, it seems likely that the current Conservative government will continue with its policies of seeking to deregulate the small firm sector in particular.

References

1. Curran, J (1986) 'Bolton fifteen years on: a review and analysis of small business research in Britain 1971–1986', The Small Business Research Trust; also see Committee of Inquiry on Small Firms, chairman J E Bolton (1971) *Report* Cmnd 4811, HMSO, London.
2. See Daniel, W W (1984) 'Who didn't get a pay increase last year?', *Policy Studies,* **5** Part 1, July; Daniel, W W (1985) 'The first jobs taken by the unemployed compared with those they lost', *Policy Studies,* **6** Part 1, July, Craig, C, Garnsey, E and Rubery, J (1984) *Payment Structures and Smaller Firms: Women's Employment in Segmented Labour Markets,* Department of Employment, Research Paper No 48, London.
3. Curran, J (1986) 'The width and the depth: small enterprise research in Britain 1971–1986', paper presented to the Ninth National Small Firms Policy and Research Conference.
4. For an elaboration of this view, see Roberts, I P (1986) 'Industrial relations in small firms: in search of a framework', paper presented to the Ninth National Small Firms Policy and Research Conference.
5. Fazey, I H (1985) 'The How To Of . . . Small Business,' *Financial Times,* London.
6. On Theory X and Theory Y, see McGregor, D (1960) *The Human Side of Enterprise,* McGraw Hill, New York.
7. *Employment Policies* (1984) Advisory Booklet No 10, ACAS, London
8. *Employing People: The ACAS Handbook for Small Firms* (1985) ACAS, London.
9. ibid.
10. Rodger, A (1952) *The Seven Point Plan,* National Institute of Industrial Psychology, London and Fraser, J M (1966) *Employment Interviewing,* 4th edn, McDonald & Evans, London.
11. Daniel, W W (1984) op cit.
12. Ingham, G K (1970) *Size of Industrial Organisation and Worker Behaviour,* Cambridge University Press, London.
13. Curran, J and Stanworth, J (1981) 'A new look at job satisfaction in the small firm', *Human Relations,* **34**: 5, May.
14. Bamber, G J and Snape, E J (1987) 'British industrial relations', in Bamber, G J and Lansbury, R D (eds) *International and Comparative Industrial Relations: A Study of Developed Market Economies,* Allen and Unwin, London, Sydney and Boston.
15. Daniel, W W (1985) op cit.
16. Wood, G (1974) 'The owner manager and other small firm phenomena', *Personnel Management,* **6**: 11, November.
17. Rainnie, A and Scott, M G (1986) 'Industrial relations in the small firm', in Curran, J et al *The Survival of the Small firm,* Vol 2, Gower, Aldershot; also see Commission

on Industrial Relations, *Small Firms and the Code of Industrial Relations Practice*, Report No 69, HMSO, London.

18. Joyce, P, Woods, A, McNulty, T and Corrigan, P (1990) 'Barriers to change in small businesses: some cases from an inner city area', *International Small Business Journal*, 8: 4, July/Sept.

19. Beaumont, P and Rennie, I (1986) 'Organisational culture and non-union status of small business', *Industrial Relations Journal, 17: 3, Autumn.*

20. *Guardian*, 13 October 1986.

21. Hendry, C, Jones, A, Arthur, M and Pettigrew, C (1991) '*Human resource development in small to medium sized enterprises*', Employment Department Research Paper, No 88, HMSO, London.

22. Curran, J et al (1986) op cit.

Chapter Fourteen

Pay, Payment Systems and Job Evaluation

Colin Duncan

Developments during the 1980s created new pressures and opportunities to revise and improve pay determination processes. Major changes in the composition and structure of employment, and rapid diffusion of microelectronics technology, increasingly challenged the relevance of traditional approaches. There was also the need to respond locally to major processes of organizational and collective bargaining devolution. Declining trade union influence, together with fashionable HRM thinking, were associated with a significant shift from collective to individual-based approaches to labour accommodation that required new responses in the pay field. Also significant was direct political influence, including fiscal encouragement of profit-sharing and major pay restructuring in the public sector. All such changes were in the context of most volatile economic conditions, with many organizations confronting the recessionary conditions of the early 1990s with pay strategies developed during the Lawson boom years.

The problems facing organizations in formulating appropriate remuneration policies in such a context are compounded by the vast array of systems and methods of payment on offer. This chapter considers the process of selecting and implementing suitable systems of payment, discusses the main systems and methods available, and reviews some recent trends in remuneration policy.

CLASSIFICATION OF PAYMENT SYSTEMS

Payment systems are simply methods of relating pay to the work done by employees, although the term is sometimes also used when referring to an organization's wage or salary structure. They can broadly be classified into two categories: *payment by time* and *payment by results*. The former represents the simplest method of payment, where a fixed sum is received per hour, week or month. In its broadest sense, payment by results (PBR) refers to payments arising from a wide range of schemes that seek to relate some proportion of pay to aspects of performance other than time spent at work.

Table 14.1 shows that one-quarter of full-time men and nearly 15 per cent of women received such payments in 1991. The figures also show a progressive decline in the proportion of employees receiving PBR, especially evident in the case of manual employees from the mid-1980s. This may indicate some disenchantment with the concept of incentive pay, but recent establishment-level surveys have generally pointed to the opposite trend. For example, a survey

Table 14.1 *Coverage of PBR*

% of full-time employees receiving PBR payments	1981	1985	1988	1991
Men:				
Manual	44.5	43.2	39.0	35.5
Non-manual	17.8	16.7	16.3	16.0
Total	32.4	30.8	28.1	25.0
Women:				
Manual	32.0	33.3	29.8	26.2
Non-manual	12.3	11.7	12.0	12.0
Total	17.0	16.6	15.9	14.6

Source: New Earnings Surveys

carried out by ACAS in 1988 found that employers were showing increasing interest in all forms of incentive pay, with three-quarters of the managers interviewed reporting the existence of some kind of incentive scheme for at least some workers in their establishment.[1] The chief explanation may lie rather in changing employment composition and a relative fall in the shares of employment of those manual occupations and industries most associated with PBR. Moreover, New Earnings Survey data underestimate the incidence of PBR in failing to pick up merit or performance pay systems that integrate payments into basic pay, a class of incentive scheme that grew markedly in the latter 1980s.[2]

Time rate or incentive

Simple time rate systems nevertheless remain the most popular method of payment in Britain and there are few situations to which they are wholly unsuited. There are two chief forms of time rate: a simple flat rate for each hour, week or longer period worked by an employee; and the use of fixed scales with automatic increases based upon length of service. Incremental systems of this sort are most common within the public sector, but are also widespread in banking and financial services. While subsequent discussion focuses upon different forms of PBR, the relative popularity and merits of time rate systems should be borne in mind:

- they are simple and cheap to operate;
- forecasting of labour costs is easy;
- they produce stability and predictability of earnings for employees;
- pay anomalies are less likely to arise;
- they are generally associated with fewer industrial relations disputes.

The chief drawback of time rates, of course, is that little incentive exists to maintain or improve performance.

Terminology

In the literature on payment systems, and in common usage, terms are used so inconsistently that popular names have become almost meaningless. The term 'PBR' is a particular source of confusion. In government statistics, and in the sense used above, the term embraces nearly all payment systems with a variable pay element including, for example, profit-sharing schemes, but elsewhere it is commonly applied only to those systems which systematically relate wages to the measured output of individuals or groups. To avoid this confusion the latter systems are referred to in subsequent discussion as *output-related systems*.

INTRODUCING A PAYMENT SYSTEM

Objectives and expectations

There is often confusion about what are the objectives of payment systems. This reflects two factors. First, managers tend to rely on pay in pursuing *multiple* objectives which can include:

- ensuring that firms can recruit the appropriate quantity and quality of staff;
- reducing labour disputes;
- motivating high performance;
- achieving equitable pay differentials;
- reducing labour turnover;
- controlling costs;
- encouraging labour flexibility;
- inducing company loyalty;
- compensating for adverse working conditions.

Indeed, some commentators have argued that too many objectives are pursued via pay:

> In our view using money in all these different ways defeats its own purpose because the aim for achieving any one of the above objectives is to pay those employees to whom that particular objective applies more money relative to other employees. But by paying more money to groups of employees to whom each of the above objectives apply, the employer ends up cancelling out the impact of one differential by superimposing on it another which may go in a different direction.[3]

A second source of confusion is that there are invariably differences in what people expect from the payment system, not only as between managers and employees, but also within management hierarchies and among employees and their representatives.

The first point has implications for payment system choice; the second for the process of implementation.

Payment system choice

Three questions need to be considered:

1. What are the chief objectives to which the payment system is intended to contribute? This should be decided from an analysis of the most important aspects of performance from the company's point of view and will involve the setting of priorities as between conflicting objectives.
2. What payment systems are available? The main options are discussed shortly.
3. Which payment system(s) is most likely to contribute to the intended objectives in the particular circumstances of the firm? This involves more

than a simple matching process, as the system will require tailoring to particular characteristics of the firm and its environment.

Considerable progress has been made in developing systematic techniques to assist in choosing the 'best fit' system to satisfy given objectives.[4]

The above procedure, sometimes labelled the 'contingency approach', may seem self-evident, but is all too often ignored. There seems instead more than an element of fashion in pay system choice, and little evidence that the major trends wholly reflect convergence of pay objectives, or of the characteristics or circumstances of firms. Accordingly, enthusiasm for fashionable systems invariably wanes as disappointing results and difficulties become apparent, as occurred for example with productivity-based systems in the 1960s and 1970s, and profit sharing in the 1980s, with similar doubts now emerging concerning the performance of merit-based systems. The contingency method, on the other hand, warns against a panacea approach to pay system choice. Rather, payment system choice and design should be a process almost unique to the organization concerned, and there is evidence that schemes so designed and selected tend to perform better than those where such contingent factors have not been taken into account.[5]

The process of implementation

A further finding of the work of Bowey and her colleagues was that the extent of consultation and negotiation in designing and implementing a system can be more influential in determining its success than even the type of system chosen:

> Matching the payment system to the social and economic system of the organization, with its attitudes, motivations, inter-relationships, past history, expectations and interpretations, is more important than matching the type of payment system to non-social characteristics of the organization and its environment.[6]

In other words, good results can be obtained with several different types of payment system in any organization provided the chosen scheme is broadly suited and a number of ground rules are followed at the design and implementation stage.

1. *Consult early*. Early consultation with employees and their representatives has several advantages: local knowledge can be of much value in determining the operational requirements of a successful scheme; gauging employee opinion early on can avoid wasting time, money and effort on an unacceptable system; and the system will be better understood and accepted if employees have been fully involved in its design.
2. *Communicate the system*. The role and purpose of the scheme should be spelt out to all concerned. This will involve briefing employees and supervisors, including information on procedures to be followed in the event of disputes; training supervisors and employee representatives on the workings of the scheme; and ensuring that support functions (eg purchasing, sales, maintenance, stores) are made aware of the demands of the new system.
3. *Monitor and review*. A joint approach is best and machinery should be set

up to deal with problems occurring during the 'debugging' phase and for the regular review of the system in the light of changing circumstances.

4. *Allow adequate time.* Many systems fail because the programme is crashed through too quickly, say, over six months. Four or five years later companies can still be trying to debug the system and overcome employee or trade union hostility. Two years is considered to be a good guideline for the time required to design, implement and debug a payment system.

When contemplating changing a payment system it is important to bear in mind that the existing system may well serve purposes and reflect expectations other than those for which it is ostensibly designed. For example, the chief rationale underlying many productivity incentive schemes introduced in the latter part of the 1970s was simply to circumvent incomes policy and increase earnings for employees. The 'hidden agenda' of the existing system therefore requires careful investigation if meaningful negotiations are to take place and unanticipated consequences of change avoided.

OUTPUT-RELATED SYSTEMS

For manual workers in Britain output-related systems are still the most common class of incentive scheme. *Piecework* is the oldest and simplest form, where a money 'price' is paid for each physical unit of output, while under *standard time systems* (sometimes also referred to as *premium bonus systems*) earnings are made to depend on the difference between the time taken to complete a job and an allowed time. This may be preferred to piecework where a physical output is difficult to identify or measure. Most output-related systems, even simple piecework systems, now embody some element of time rates, for example in the form of fall-back rates where the bonus rides on top of the time rate, or waiting time.

Setting standards

The methods of fixing standard prices or times vary from casual judgement on the part of a rate-fixer to the more refined techniques of *work study*. The latter is now the more common approach and is more reliable. Work study combines a number of techniques, but the two most important elements are *method study* and *work measurement*. The former is concerned with establishing the most efficient method of working, including properly planned layouts and defined methods of operation, and ideally should precede work measurement. Work measurement, on the other hand, is a three-stage process: the time taken to perform a given task is first measured; then the effort of the worker or work group is *rated*, that is, an assessment is made of work performance relative to what is considered to be a standard pace; and a standard allowable time or price is then set on the basis of the first two stages, with due allowances for personal needs, relaxation and varying contingencies. The most subjective element of the process is effort rating and even experienced work study officers can recommend rates which are too loose (lucrative) or too tight.

Where jobs have been timed over a lengthy period data will have accumulated which can be used to calculate times for jobs which have not been studied

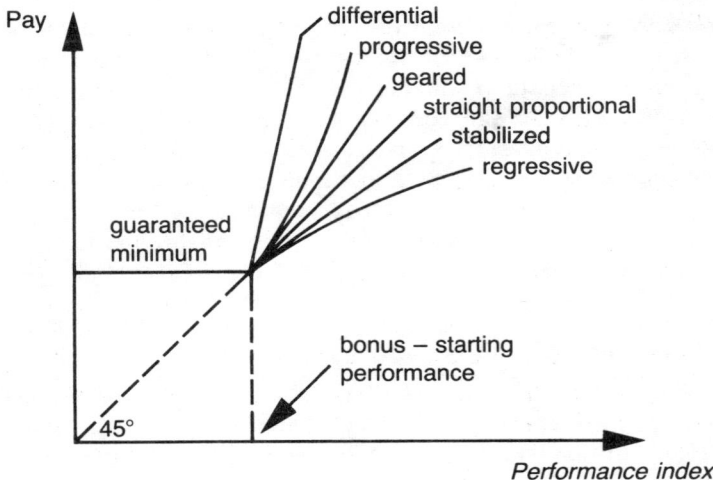

Figure 14.1   *Pay–performance relationships under various schemes*

individually or tasks which do not lend themselves easily to time study. Under predetermined motion time systems (PMTS), tasks can thus be allocated synthetic standard times, an approach which can avoid disputes about the accuracy of standards, and reduce the cost and time of work study.

Sources of variation

There are an enormous variety of output-related systems which differ with respect to a number of subsidiary features in order to meet varying requirements. For example, some link payment to individual output while others relate bonus to group performance. The period to which bonus is related can also vary, being daily, weekly, monthly or even longer. Perhaps the most fundamental distinction is the way in which earnings are made to vary with changes in performance. There are several variations, as illustrated in Figure 14.1, each with a distinctive objective – to encourage learners, to encourage workers to beat a certain standard, or to discourage excessive performance, for example.

If earnings and performance vary in the same proportion then the scheme is described as *straight proportional*. In *geared* schemes the rate of change of earnings, although constant, is greater than the rate of change in performance. If the change of earnings is less than the change of performance the scheme is known as *stabilized*. These relationships are linear in that the bonus *rate* does not vary with performance. In non-linear relationships, on the other hand, the bonus rate varies with performance levels. When the rate of change in earnings gradually increases with increases in performance, the scheme is termed *progressive* and, when it gradually falls, it is called *regressive*. *Differential* schemes are a combination of two or more schemes, changing from one to another at specified levels of performance.

Preconditions

The following have been suggested as the conditions ideally suited to output-related systems.

1. The work should be measurable and directly attributable to an individual or group. In practice, this generally means that the work should be almost entirely manual, repetitive and consist of fairly short-cycle operations.
2. The pace of work should be controlled to a significant degree by the worker, rather than by the machine or process being tended.
3. Management should be capable of maintaining a steady flow of work, and of absorbing at least short-term fluctuations in demand and output.
4. The tasks involved should remain fairly constant through time, that is they should not be subject to very frequent changes in methods, materials or equipment.[7]

The process of decay

Output-related systems have attracted harsh criticism over the years on account of their being prone to 'erosion' or 'decay'. This tendency is exacerbated by poor system choice, hasty implementation, and inadequate monitoring and control of the system. The more common manifestations are listed below.

Rate drift   Times allowed for jobs become slack over time when changes in product or method require frequent renegotiation of rates, especially in circumstances of strong workplace representation. Minor improvements in technology or methods which are too small to warrant retiming of jobs can, over time, produce the same phenomenon, as can the 'learning curve' effect.

Worker fiddles   A particularly common fiddle is that of 'cross-booking' of time between tasks. This can have several objectives for workers: to hide loose rates arising from poor work study (thereby encouraging restriction of output); ironing out fluctuations in pay arising from factors out of the workers' control; or simply to maximize bonus earnings. For the firm such practices can restrict output, inflate earnings relative to effort and can also distort the picture of labour costs for particular products, thereby inhibiting efficient production planning and control, and distorting pricing policies.

Shortcuts   Shortcuts towards achieving high bonus can reduce quality, damage machinery and endanger safety.

Labour inflexibility   Cumulative errors in work study manifesting in loose and tight rates can breed inflexibility. The perceived benefits of the scheme might also cause employees to resist change.

Pay anomalies   These can arise from a number of factors, including poor work study, or the varying bargaining capacities of individuals or groups. The situation can arise where semi-skilled workers on PBR earn more than skilled PBR workers or craft workers outside the scheme (eg maintenance), and this can create problems of morale, leapfrogging pay claims and spiralling wage costs.

Responding to decay

Careful preparation and control can do much to slow down the process of decay, but some erosion of the scheme is more or less inevitable over time, and five years is regarded in much of the literature as the standard life-cycle of such systems. Moreover, excessive adherence to formal rules and controls may prove counter-productive: evidence suggests that some degree of informality and flexibility is required in operating a successful scheme. For example, a study of the Coal Board's scheme following the reintroduction of incentives into coal-mining in 1977–8 found that the system's success owed much to the informal actions of colliery managers in relaxing incentive scheme rules and compromising costs for other benefits such as co-operative union relationships, sustained worker motivation and reduction of industrial disputes.[8]

One popular response during the 1960s and 1970s was to move to systems of *measured daywork*. Such schemes represented a 'halfway house' between an output-related system and payment by time by offering employees a fixed sum for maintaining performance at or above a predetermined level. Hence, workers were geared to an incentive level of performance but pay did not vary in the short term with actual performance. The system thereby aimed to avoid the problems associated with conventional output schemes by allowing more effective control, and predictability of output and costs. However, measured daywork seems to have fallen much from favour. In the 1988 ACAS survey just 6 per cent of respondents, chiefly from the public sector, reported its use. This reflects disappointing results with schemes in coal-mining, the docks and car manufacturing during the 1970s when they proved just as prone to erosion as conventional output systems. Effort drift simply replaced rate drift as the grounds for dispute changed from output prices and times to manning levels and the speed of the line.

Current trends

It is often assumed that output-related systems are falling from favour, not only because of their proneness to decay and other traditional problems, but also because they are becoming increasingly unsuited to modern conditions. New production techniques and forms of working have weakened direct links between effort and output, and there is a shifting emphasis from speed to quality and flexibility objectives. Moreover, such systems rarely generate high trust relations and may thus be unsuited to the unitary perspectives embraced in recent HRM strategies. Yet the systems remain widespread in both the public and private sectors, and there is no consistent evidence that they are in significant decline as means of rewarding manual workers. The 1988 ACAS survey, for instance, found that the incidence of individual piecework systems had remained stable or grown marginally during the 1980s, though a later joint NEDO/IPM survey suggested a significant decline in individual piecerate systems in the latter 1980s.[9] However, in traditional piecerate industries the change seems to be towards other forms of output-related incentive. For example, Courtaulds Textiles and Coats Viyella are moving from individual piecework towards group-based output incentive schemes, reflecting a trend in the industry towards small batch production requiring team-based work processes.[10]

PLANT OR ENTERPRISE-WIDE SYSTEMS

Under plant or enterprise-wide systems a collective bonus is paid on the basis of the overall labour performance of the plant or firm. The simplest systems link bonus to volume of output or to sales value over a set period, but many systems in the UK are derived from the *Scanlon Plan* or *Rucker Plan*.

Scanlon schemes are based on the ratio of total payroll costs to sales value of production. The ratio is estimated over a representative period and the figure derived gives a norm against which future performance is assessed. Bonus becomes payable when the ratio decreases over an agreed period.

The Rucker Plan is similar, except that the ratio is payroll costs to *added value*. Added value is essentially a measure of the income generated by the application of employees' skill and company investment to bought-in materials and, under the Rucker system, is calculated as the difference between sales revenue of production minus the costs of bought-in materials and services. This meets the objection that under Scanlon schemes, bonus is payable if prices increase to cover increased costs of raw materials and services.

Bonus calculations under each system are illustrated in Table 14.2 by means of an example. Assume that 25 per cent of savings go into reserve to provide a bonus in those months when no bonus would otherwise be payable; the remainder is divided equally between the company and employees. Thus, under Scanlon the employees' share is:

$$\frac{£(2,000 - 500)}{2} = £750 \text{ or } 7.5\% \text{ of the wage bill.}$$

Under Rucker the figures are:

$$\frac{£(1,667 - 417)}{2} = £625 \text{ or } 6.25\% \text{ of the wage bill.}$$

Advantages and limitations

Points in favour of these schemes and their variants are as follows.

1. They are economical to install and operate: it is not essential to have work measurement and excessive clerical costs are avoided.
2. A wider section of the workforce can be brought under the same scheme.
3. They reward co-operative effort, not only with respect to output, but in economy of materials, maintenance and general labour costs. Teamwork is thereby encouraged and further fostered through production or suggestion committees that are established for improvements in efficiency.
4. They may be conducive to union/management co-operation in that close consultation with union members is required and more information is disclosed to trade unions about the operation of the firm.

However, they have several limitations.

1. There is potential for inter-group/departmental rivalry if workers feel they are carrying others who are not pulling their weight.
2. They may have little incentive value because of the tenuous link between

Table 14.2 *Example of bonus calculations under the Scanlon and Rucker Plans*

Base period calculations

		£
Net sales over 3-year reference period	=	1,000,000
Less bought-in materials, supplies and services	=	400,000
Added value over 3 years	=	600,000
Payroll costs over 3 years	=	200,000

$$\text{Percentage ratio of payroll costs to net sales (Scanlon)} = \frac{200,000}{1,000,000} \times 100 \qquad = 20\%$$

$$\text{Percentage ratio of payroll cost to added value (Rucker)} = \frac{200,000}{600,000} \times 100 \qquad = 33.3\%$$

Bonus calculations

		£
Net sales over 1 month	=	60,000
Less bought-in materials etc	=	25,000
Added value	=	35,000
20% of net sales	=	12,000
Less actual wage bill	=	10,000
Savings available for distribution under Scanlon	=	2,000
33.3% of added value	=	11,667
Less actual wage bill	=	10,000
Savings available for distribution under Rucker	=	£ 1,667

effort and reward. Incentive is reduced the greater the number of workers covered and bonus may become regarded simply as part of basic pay.

3. Production or suggestion committees can be a poor substitute for work measurement in identifying inefficiencies.

4. The bonus can be influenced by external conditions such as reduced selling prices or loss of markets, and while adjustments to the norm are possible, frequent refinements can lead to undue system complexity, and reduced understanding and interest on the part of employees.

The schemes are much more than simple accounting ratios and require just as much preplanning, consultation and control as apparently more complex systems. They imply an open, participative management style which is not always favoured by trade union representatives, especially if suggestion committees and other facets of the scheme are perceived as designed to weaken trade union influence or bypass formal channels of representation. They are best suited where there is plant-wide acceptance of efficiency as a major objective, and where the market and technological environment are relatively stable. The existence of adequate records (output, sales, wages etc) over a representative period is a further precondition. It is sometimes suggested that the limit of effective coverage is about 1000 workers, although some firms have claimed success with company-wide schemes covering many thousands of employees.

PROFIT-SHARING AND EMPLOYEE SHARE OWNERSHIP

There was a sharp increase during the 1980s in profit-based methods of remuneration. Such schemes can be roughly grouped into cash-based systems where a bonus in cash is paid from profits, and share-based systems where employees receive a profit bonus in the form of shares or are provided with incentives to acquire shares in the enterprise. Each type has several forms. Under cash systems, for example, the bonus can be related to a fixed proportion of pre- or post-tax profits; to a proportion of profits above a stated threshold; to the dividends paid on share capital; or the amount may be determined on a purely discretionary or arbitrary basis. Sources of variation in share-based schemes include the rights attached to the shares issued, their marketability and various inducements offered to discourage early conversion to cash.

Nearly all the advantages and limitations of plant/enterprise-wide systems apply also to profit-sharing, though share-based systems have some additional features that can confer advantages. For example, payment of bonus does not affect cashflow, and they give employees a stake in the *ownership* of the enterprise that can reinforce commitment to company objectives.

Measured in terms of the proportion of companies operating such schemes, the spread of profit-sharing during the 1980s was most significant. One survey estimated that profit-based systems accounted for 66 per cent of all new systems introduced between 1979 and 1984.[11] A subsequent survey carried out in the mid-1980s found that as many as 65 per cent of companies operated at least one type of scheme, though this figure also included value-added and non-individual incentive bonus schemes, which were considered to be types of profit-sharing and accounted for around 10 per cent of the total.[12] Growth has been most spectacular in the case of share-based systems which, prior to the 1980s, were almost wholly restricted to executive employees.

The provision of fiscal incentives has been identified as by far the greatest stimulus to the spread of profit-sharing. By 1985 Inland Revenue-approved schemes accounted for 70 per cent of those systems that allowed all employees in a business unit to participate,[13] and the coverage of tax-assisted schemes has continued to grow. There are five main schemes which currently attract tax advantages.

1. Approved all-employee profit-sharing schemes (APS), sometimes also called approved deferred share trust (ADST) schemes, as first introduced in the Finance Act 1978. These are share incentive schemes where employees receive a bonus in shares which are held in trust for a minimum of two years. After this period the employee may dispose of the shares, but will be liable for income tax on their value, unless the shares remain in trust for a further

three years, when they can be disposed of without incurring income tax. Had the bonus been paid in cash rather than as shares it would have been subject both to income tax and national insurance contributions. The company can also offset the costs of the scheme against corporation tax.

2. Save as you earn (SAYE) schemes introduced in the Finance Act 1980. These are savings-related share option schemes where employees save a regular amount under a standard SAYE contract for either five or seven years, and then choose whether to take the money saved or buy shares at a pre-established price when the contract expires. Under approved schemes the employee is not liable to income tax on any gains made in exercising the option.

3. Discretionary share option schemes set up under the Finance Act 1984. As with SAYE schemes these involve the granting of options over shares, any gain realized when the option is exercised normally being free of income tax. Unlike APS and SAYE schemes, however, there is no obligation on the company to include all employees and the vast majority in operation are, in fact, executive share option schemes.

4. Profit-related pay schemes as introduced by the Finance Act 1987. In this system cash pay varies in relation to movement in the profits of the business. The aim of the Inland Revenue scheme was to encourage firms to convert an element of previously fixed pay to a profit-related form so that 'normal pay' would vary significantly with profits. This differs from conventional cash-based profit sharing where the profit bonus is clearly distinguished from, and is additional to, normal wage and salary payments. The profit-related pay element is exempt from income tax under approved schemes, up to certain limits. From April 1991 the limits were raised to the lower of £4000 or 20 per cent of salary. The schemes require to cover at least 80 per cent of full-time workers in the profit centre to which they apply in order to gain Inland Revenue approval.

5. Employee share ownership plan (ESOP) trusts, which purchase shares in a company and distribute them to employees. The ESOP is funded either by loans or grants from the company or by external borrowings which may need to be guaranteed by the company. Under the Inland Revenue terms for statutory ESOP trusts, which were created by the 1989 Finance Act, the company is entitled to relief from corporation tax for its payments to the trust and, from April 1991, for the costs of setting up schemes. Shareholders can also receive relief on capital gains tax when selling shares to the trust.

A number of objectives were pursued in promoting such schemes. The Conservative Government's twin aim of creating an enterprise culture and a share-owning democracy was chiefly pursued by the promotion of 'all-employee' share schemes (APS, SAYE, ESOPs), together with priority share allocations to employees in the context of privatizations. By contrast, the aim of executive share option schemes, according to former chancellor Nigel Lawson, was 'to attract top calibre company management and to increase the incentives and motivation of existing executives and key personnel by linking their rewards to performance'.[14] With regard to profit-related pay, the same chancellor in his 1987 Budget speech envisaged two main benefits:

First, the workforce would have a more direct personal interest in the profits earned by the firm or unit in which they work: and second, there would be a greater degree of pay flexibility in the face of changing market conditions. Such flexibility is vital if, as a nation, we are to defeat the scourge of unemployment.

Setting up a tax-approved scheme will typically involve wide consultation with interested parties, including the board of directors, shareholders, company solicitors and possibly registrars, consultants, stockbrokers, auditors and building societies. However, most companies have adopted the position that such schemes, and indeed profit-sharing in general, are non-negotiable with trade unions. The experience of companies operating APS or SAYE suggests a period of about ten months to prepare the scheme and obtain Inland Revenue approval.

Penetration of schemes

It is now apparent that the growth of profit-sharing and employee share ownership has been less significant than has commonly been supposed. While the numbers of registered APS and SAYE schemes were each approaching the 1000 mark by the end of the 1980s, participation rates were typically low (between 20–30 per cent), and about 2 million employees, roughly 8 per cent of the employed workforce, were estimated as participating.[15] Executive share option schemes grew fastest, and currently account for about twice the number of APS and SAYE schemes combined, but participation is generally confined to senior personnel and the scheme is widely considered simply as an executive perk. Concern over this led to changes in tax relief, so that from 1 January 1992 the share option strike price for executive schemes can be discounted at 15 per cent below the market value, but only in companies that also have an all-employee scheme. The growth of profit-related pay has been especially sluggish. Launched in a wave of publicity, with a target coverage of 1 million employees by 1989, the numbers participating by June 1991 had reached just 353,900.[16] Similarly, ESOPs have yet to take off to any appreciable extent, with only 16 non-statutory ESOPs and 1 statutory scheme recorded by the ESOP centre by the end of 1990.[17]

Moreover, the contribution of schemes to employees' remuneration has generally been modest, with cash-based schemes typically contributing just 2–4 per cent to total pay, while in the case of tax-approved share schemes the proportion of share capital owned by employees has been typically less than 1 per cent.[18] Such schemes have also operated in the context of a marked shift in company ownership from private to institutional investors that denotes little progress towards the broader political goal of a share-holding democracy. Though the numbers of individuals owning shares increased from 3 million to 11 million by the end of the 1980s, around three-quarters of shareowners owned less than three shareholdings each and the proportion of equity held by private relative to institutional investors steadily fell from about 30 per cent in 1979 to 18 per cent in 1989.[19] In the early 1990s the number of personal shareholders began to fall, with ProSHare, the wider share ownership group, estimating the figure as 9,800,000 by 1992. The proportion of adults owning shares in their companies had remained stable at just 4 per cent.[20]

Performance of schemes

Recent surveys of British employers show that the reason most frequently cited for introducing financial participation schemes is to promote worker identification and commitment to the organization. While managers operating schemes have generally rated them positively on this score, the evidence that they lead to positive attitudinal changes on the part of participating employees is not strong.

One comprehensive review of work in this field found evidence that financial participation and other components of the 'new industrial relations' were associated with positive employee attitudes towards the techniques themselves, especially if financial gains were expected to result. However, the most methodologically sound studies revealed also that schemes rarely had any impact on underlying attitudes of 'them and us'. The authors identified four main factors relating to the implementation and management of schemes that had impeded attitudinal restructuring.

1. *Lack of choice.* Workers are rarely consulted in decisions on whether to adopt or participate in schemes, thus reducing the prospect of more favourable attitudes emerging. Moreover, where little choice is perceived other than to co-operate, the schemes can act to bolster existing adversarial attitudes.
2. *Lack of trust.* In general, there is little evidence that employees trust either the motivation or ability of employers to operate schemes that will confer benefits to employees, especially where plants are unionized.
3. *Unequal status and outcomes.* The meagre attitudinal impact of schemes also reflects their actual and perceived failure to improve employee status in terms of earnings, job security or influence. Instead, the operation of schemes during the 1980s coincided with a marked widening in the dispersion of earnings and erosion of job security, together with apparently deep employer hostility towards any radical extension of worker influence that might lead to genuine equality of status.
4. *Lack of institutional support.* Top management support for schemes has tended to be instrumental, superficial and only forthcoming if profitable results are envisaged, and existing power and status relations maintained.[21]

If success with profit-sharing requires that such impediments are not present it seems doubtful that schemes can be beneficially adopted on a wide scale. While the first two constraints may be tackled by improved procedures of implementation, they reflect also the third and fourth factors. These imply that employer commitment to the managerial aims of schemes is rarely accompanied by endorsement of the egalitarian principles through which such aims may be realized.

This ambivalence is evident in the ambiguity of objectives revealed by managers operating schemes, where decisions to proceed seem chiefly guided by fashion, wishful thinking or fiscal gain, rather than systematic evaluation from contingency perspectives. Baddon et al, for instance, found little evidence of coherent management strategies pursued through financial participation. Rather, managerial objectives tended to be articulated in a *post hoc* rationalization of the purpose and achievements of a scheme. There was also evidence that employers often chose the wrong type of profit-sharing scheme relative to stated objectives.[22]

An additional difficulty in the case of profit-related pay has been the perceived incompatibility of the twin objectives the scheme is designed to achieve: positive attitudinal change is not easily pursued in a context of significant pay variability. The following were among the more specific reservations expressed by employers in the consultative period prior to the launch of the Government's scheme:

- it is hard to imagine why employees should feel 'involved' merely through the existence of a scheme which may or may not provide a bonus, especially as employees are not compensated for risk-taking by decision sharing;
- difficulties in determining profit centres, measuring profit, allocating overheads and allowing for transfer pricing within a company could lead to arbitrary decisions on the level of profit attributable to particular employees and therefore produce a demotivational effect;
- external factors adversely affecting profits and hence pay could again be demotivational, and indeed, under conditions of falling profitability, lower pay may be accompanied by increased workload;
- profit cannot be assessed nor audited quickly enough to secure early reductions in pay when market conditions deteriorate rapidly;
- to maximize the PRP element of pay, employees could be motivated to resist recruitment, reduce numbers employed and favour short-term profit maximizing at the expense of investment;
- managers could find themselves bargaining over two different parts of the pay packet at different times of the year and making one part of the pay packet insecure could make bargaining harder for that part which is secure.[23]

To date, participating firms have fallen into three chief categories: small private companies; companies which already had cash-based profit sharing and stood to gain by adapting these and claiming tax relief (eg the John Lewis Partnership); and partnerships, building societies etc which are not eligible for tax relief via the more popular APS scheme. The response to poor take-up has been to improve tax relief and, though this may do little to convince employers of the merits of the scheme, one commentator has suggested that 'non-PRP' could now be considered as a tax worth avoiding.[24]

Summarizing, the evidence suggests that despite the thinking behind tax concessions, profit-sharing and share ownership schemes are unlikely, in isolation, to affect significantly the industrial relations climate or change organizational culture. If carefully chosen and implemented, however, they may usefully serve to reinforce a participative culture which already exists.

MERIT AND PERFORMANCE PAY

During the latter 1980s systems of remuneration based upon performance appraisal techniques replaced profit-sharing as the fastest-growing method of payment. The systems grew in parallel with performance management concepts and initially were mostly confined to senior personnel, but their application is now filtering down organizational structures to non-managerial and manual grades.

There have been varying estimates of the penetration of appraisal-related pay that have differed according to the characteristics of survey samples and differences in definitions and classifications employed. Taken together, however, the evidence suggests that up to three-quarters of all employers may now be using some form of performance appraisal to determine pay. Though managerial grades are most affected, about half of employers apply such systems to other non-manual grades and around a quarter to manual employees. The growth of schemes has been especially marked in the public sector. One survey by Incomes Data Services (IDS) in 1990, covering local authorities, health authorities and higher education, found that 56 per cent of organizations had introduced performance pay in the space of just one year.[25] Little is known, however, of the degree of penetration as measured by proportions of employees covered or the contribution of schemes to total pay.

The concept of relating pay to individual merit is not new. By 1950, factor-based merit rating systems were well established in Britain. The trend from the mid-1980s, however, was from an emphasis upon personal qualities that characterized conventional merit rating towards assessments of performance against working objectives. One author refers to this shift as to rewarding output rather than input,[26] though in contrast to conventional bonus schemes, performance output is not measured solely by attainment of quantified targets. Rather, individual objectives are set by reference to company goals, and important qualititative aspects of performance are also subject to appraisal.

It is difficult to convey in a brief account the variety and complexity of current schemes, both with respect to appraisal methods, and mechanisms for linking appraisal results to pay, and managers contemplating such schemes should first seek detailed guidance.[27] Typically, however, elaborate performance management systems entail setting an individual broad objectives or 'accountabilities'. Several shorter-term goals may be attached to each objective. Scoring systems are then incorporated to assess performance against objectives and these typically distinguish at least three levels of attainment. Some systems also combine complex 'output' measures of this sort with behavioural analysis of 'imputs' needed to meet the requirements of a post. Such complex systems clearly require much effort and time to operate, and can entail around 30 checks on performance for each individual being appraised. Appraisal interviews usually occur annually, but sometimes more frequently, with continuous informal monitoring throughout the year. Schemes for manual workers are generally simpler, with the main focus upon skills assessment and acquisition, especially where schemes operate alongside changes in working methods.

The simplest method of relating performance assessment to pay is the provision of an unconsolidated lump-sum bonus, though this seems less common than other methods. A second approach, common in the public sector, is the linking of incremental progression to the appraisal results, or the provision of extra specific performance increments. Such performance payments are generally consolidated and staff would normally also receive an annual general increase. More common in the private sector are salary range schemes. Under such systems the 'rate for the job' or market rate is often represented by the mid-point of a salary range specifying a minimum and maximum. Typical ranges are 80 to 110 per cent, 85 to 115 per cent or 80 to 120 per cent of mid-points, with placing dependent on performance. Increases are generally consolidated, but under some schemes staff may not be guaranteed an annual general increase.

Some schemes have abandoned the separation of an annual pay award from individual merit payments. One model has been to determine only the overall cost of an annual increase by reference to market or other pay criteria, or through negotiations with trade unions, while employees receive amounts below or above costed increases depending upon individual performance. This and similar schemes are sometimes described as 'all merit', though most provide at least some annual increase to the majority of staff, including poor performers.

The growth of performance pay is easily linked to a range of business initiatives and preoccupations that surfaced in the latter 1980s: the perceived need to foster a 'performance culture' incorporating total quality and customer-care concepts; responses to new technology and competition that required a flexible but motivated workforce, a twin-goal not easily achieved through conventional bonus schemes; harmonization policies that ill-fitted the diversity and external 'ownership' of existing machinery determining pay; and more generally the individualization and localization of pay embraced in the new HRM philosophy. In the public sector especially, performance pay was also regarded as a cost-effective method of relieving recruitment and morale difficulties affecting key staff, by allowing selective pay enhancement in a context of uncompetitive national rates.

Though specific objectives have been pursued through performance pay, current orthodoxy is that pay should be a relatively minor feature of performance management systems, subsidiary to the broader aim of improving corporate and individual performance, and there are several successful performance management schemes that do not include performance pay.

Assessment

Performance pay is currently entering the downside of the familiar cycle characterizing panacea approaches to pay system choice, whereby initial promise and broad appeal is followed by growing doubts rooted in disappointing results. Such doubts intensified following the results of a major study of performance management systems conducted by the Institute of Manpower Studies (IMS) in 1991 which found no general link between improved company performance and either performance pay or other forms of performance management. The chief explanation offered was of misplaced emphasis upon pay in performance management systems relative to other human resource activities:[28]

> If performance management is to meet any of the expectations it has raised about improving the bottom-line, more emphasis needs to be placed on [employee development] rather than allowing performance management systems to become a narrow vehicle for the delivery of reward and remuneration policy.

This verdict was challenged in IDS commentary on the findings, which argued that performance management objectives revealed in the study were already too broad and vague for operational purposes. These included improvements in motivation, training and development, 'improving organizational effectiveness' and 'changing organizational culture'. Rather, the role of pay in performance systems needed to be clarified rather than downgraded: managers needed to specify more clearly and preferably in measurable terms what they hoped to achieve through performance systems, and judge the efficacy of performance pay in this light.[29]

More specific reservations have also emerged, chiefly concerning the motivational impact of performance pay, and problems of pay cost and pay system control.

Motivation Reliance upon subjective judgements in appraisal processes can give rise to suspicions by employees or their representatives of the 'blue-eyed boy' syndrome – that is of assessments influenced by personality rather than performance. In the civil service and elsewhere schemes have also allegedly discriminated against women.

Some schemes have become so complex that they are not easily understood by employees. Employee trust and motivational impact are thereby undermined.

It has proved difficult to differentiate merit from other pay increase criteria in schemes, and even 'all merit' systems generally incorporate market increases. Responses to the market may creep into schemes in subtle ways. For example, though long-serving employees are often more effective than new recruits, many schemes allow higher percentage awards at the bottom of a pay scale than at the top, to reflect the pattern of shortages and avoid employees breaking through grade ceilings. Cynicism and demotivation can therefore result when pay is poorly related to merit or employees are excluded from schemes on market grounds. Using performance pay as a recruitment device also decreases its motivational impact for those benefiting, as payments become viewed as an automatic perk rather than to be earned.

The systems tend to benefit 'high flyers' who may not stay long, but do little for the 'valuable plodder' without whom the organization could not function. Moreover, demographic trends imply greater reliance in the future on new sources of labour, including women with children, older workers and part-timers. Such employees tend to value job and pay stability, and predictability, rather than the 'get on or get out' philosophy often embraced in performance systems.

Focus upon the individual risks fracturing teamworking, and job flexibility may also be undermined where opportunities for demonstrating merit vary from job to job.

Schemes are often pushed through against trade union antipathy, if not outright resistance, an approach at variance with contingency thinking and likely to fuel suspicions that the real purpose of schemes is to downgrade union influence.

In successful schemes the proportion of employees in high performance categories should rise. Otherwise, the scheme will simply reward and perpetuate an existing, natural distribution of performance standards. Yet cost control considerations have led to the use of 'forced distributions' of performance and reward, especially in the case of manual and other schemes that cover large numbers of employees.

Pay costs/system control   Elaborate schemes are costly and extremely time-consuming to administer, especially where large numbers of employees are appraised.

When payments reflect market as well as performance criteria, differential or selective rewards can be difficult to justify. Pressures then build up to extend payments on a blanket basis, with further amounts required on top to reward genuine performance improvements.

Performance payments consolidated into basic pay can upset grading structures and lead to pressures to restore traditional relativities.

Consolidation of payments also represents a permanent addition to labour costs that may not be justified by future performance.

Characteristics of successful schemes

The contingency approach is as relevant to performance pay as to any other pay system. If the selection, design and implementation of the system is informed by this method, then it is more likely to perform well. This view is consistent with the findings of one recent study which identified three main features that distinguished successful performance pay schemes.

1. Managers were not seeking an immediate payback, but saw performance pay as part of an overall package of human resource initiatives designed to improve employee motivation and performance in the long run.
2. Senior managers were committed to developing an effective and valid performance appraisal procedure, supported by well-resourced training programmes and introduced through consultation rather than being imposed.
3. The objectives of the payment system were related to those of the organization, with the criteria for individual reward clearly linked to factors critical to the success of the business.[30]

The coexistence of the first and third conditions in some organizations implies that the IMS and IDS positions need not be mutually exclusive.

Performance pay is less likely to succeed where trade union representation and collectivist values are strong, where the organizational culture is collegiate or where team effort is of paramount importance. It has also been argued that systems conceived in the Thatcher era of competitive growth and individualism may not now be appropriate. Team effort and contribution to corporate success may now be more important than the previous focus upon the individual, and simpler forms of performance pay such as one-off, team-based bonuses may better fit the tougher conditions of the 1990s than the elaborate systems now in vogue.[31]

PAY STRUCTURES AND JOB EVALUATION

No less important than deciding the appropriate system of payment in an organization is achieving an appropriate internal structure of pay, and indeed the two processes should ideally be considered in tandem as each has implications for the other. Symptoms of a malfunctioning pay structure include: problems of recruitment and retention; an increasing frequency of claims and disputes relating to restoration of pay differentials; disputes about the matching of jobs to grades; lower grades becoming empty as many jobs drift to the top of the structure; and manipulation of the existing structure by both management and unions.

The most common method of dealing with distortions in the pay structure is job evaluation. Job evaluation is concerned with establishing the relative position of jobs in a hierarchy by looking at the content and demands of the work. Its purpose is to enable organizations to develop a rational and defensible basis for their pay structures. Job evaluation differs from a payment system in that it evaluates the demands of jobs rather than the performance of job-holders. Moreover, although it is concerned with establishing acceptable pay relationships, it does not in itself establish the pay of different jobs. This is a separate process normally determined through negotiation. Nor is job evalua-tion a science: the aim is to be systematic and the process involves a degree of subjectivity, not least in the choice and weighting of assessment criteria. Because it is not a scientific nor 'objective' procedure, a degree of employee participation in the design and implementation of the system is usually considered essential. Without this, the scheme will be built on management perceptions of what is fair and employees may remain unconvinced.

Methods of job evaluation

The four basic techniques of job evaluation are *ranking*, *grading* (or *classification*), *points rating* and *factor comparison*. The first two are usually described as non-analytical; the second two are described as analytical or quantitative. Non-analytical techniques assess jobs as a whole and produce simple rankings whereas analytical techniques break down jobs into a number of component factors or characteristics so that rankings and rank distances can be expressed numerically.

Job ranking This is the simplest form of job evaluation. A job description is prepared for each job to allow its duties, responsibilities and qualifications to be identified. Each job is considered as a whole and is given a ranking. A ranking table is then drawn up and the ranked jobs grouped into grades to which pay levels or ranges are allocated. As the evaluation team requires an all-round knowledge of every job the method is more appropriate for small organizations with no more than 30 to 40 jobs. More can be handled if 'benchmark' jobs are used as yardsticks against which other jobs can be assessed without having to complete a full evaluation of every job.

The chief advantage of ranking is its simplicity: it is easily understood, instal-lation costs are low and it does not make heavy demands on time or on administra-tion. However, the results of the exercise can be difficult to defend as they are based on impressionistic judgements rather than clearly defined ranking criteria. A further drawback is its failure to measure the difference between jobs; it can show job A to be more difficult than job B, but not how much more difficult.

Paired comparisons Paired comparisons is a refinement of job ranking which is sometimes considered less subjective and which introduces an element of scoring to indicate the degree of importance between two jobs. Again, each job is considered as a whole, but is then ranked against every other job in turn (this is unnecessary with basic job ranking) and points are awarded according to whether its overall importance is judged to be less than, equal to, or more than, the other job. The points allocated in each case are usually zero, one and two respectively. By totalling up the scores a rank order is produced, as illustrated in Table 14.3.

Table 14.3   *Paired comparisons*

Job	A	B	C	D	E	Total score	Rank order
A	–	0	2	0	2	4	2
B	2	–	2	2	2	8	1
C	0	0	–	2	0	2	5
D	2	0	0	–	1	3	3
E	0	0	2	1	–	3	3

One difficulty with this approach is that as the number of jobs increases the number of paired comparisons rises rapidly. If X jobs are to be ranked then the number of comparisons required is

$$\frac{X(X-1)}{2}$$

Hence if $X = 10$, 45 comparisons are needed, while if $X = 20$, the number of comparisons rises to 190. The number of calculations will therefore be impractical for a large number of jobs in the absence of computing facilities.

Job grading (or classification)   Job grading is similar to ranking but starts from the opposite end: grades and grade characteristics are established first, and the jobs are then fitted into them at the most appropriate level. The grade definitions are normally based on broad differences in skill, responsibility or qualifications. Jobs considered typical of each grade are selected as benchmarks, the other jobs are compared with these benchmarks and the grade description, and slotted in.

The method is easily understood, quick and inexpensive, as there is no need to compare individual jobs against each other. It is somewhat less subjective or arbitrary than ranking because, although whole jobs are still compared, the method does identify the qualities and experience necessary for different jobs. Moreover, the decisions reached can be justified by reference to the grade definitions and, as the grades are determined first, the problem of quantifying differences between jobs is avoided. The method is best applied to a fairly homogeneous family of jobs, differentiated in terms of the qualifications or skills needed to handle extra responsibility (eg as in clerical or administrative functions). On account of the inflexibility of grade definitions, job tasks should also be reasonably stable over time. The method has been widely used in the public sector and for clerical staff by many private sector companies.

The main weakness of job grading is that complex jobs are often difficult to fit into the system as they may straddle grade boundaries, and it can be difficult to decide whether to grade them up on the basis of some facets or down on the basis of others. Accordingly, there is a tendency over time for the original grades to become subdivided, rendering the scheme more complex and unwieldy. This difficulty may be eased if separate classification structures are used for different job classes. Nor is the technique as objective as it might first appear: evaluation may in reality be occurring prior to objective examination of job specifications, as arbitrary impressions of job worth might prejudice the definition of job grades. Indeed, without employee involvement in grade definitions or, ideally, their preparation by an independent body, there is scope for conscious or unconscious sex bias or for an employer to seek to depress pay by defining grades in such a way that most jobs fall into lower categories.

Points rating. Points rating is the most widely used technique in Britain. It is an analytical method which, instead of comparing whole jobs, breaks down jobs into a number of selected factors. Each factor or sub-factor is further broken down into degrees, to which points are attached. The number or range of points allocated determines the *weighting* or relative importance of different factors. Once the factors are defined and weightings established, benchmark jobs are again identified and evaluated as reference points, and the remaining jobs are examined against the factor definitions and benchmark job scores. The summation of the points for each factor, duly weighted, produces a total points score which determines the position of each job in the hierarchy.

Manual schemes normally include as factors skill, responsibility, effort and working conditions, but the factors chosen will vary with organizational requirements and the types of jobs covered. Table 14.4 illustrates the factors and weightings used by Imperial Tobacco Ltd in a scheme which covered the majority of its salaried employees in secretarial, clerical, technical, scientific and professional occupations. The scheme contained nine factors, each of which was rigorously defined in the job evaluation manual, as were the degrees or discrete levels of demand under each factor. Evaluating a job involved deciding which degree under each factor most closely corresponded with the level of demand in the job.

Table 14.4 *Staff job evaluation scheme, Imperial Tobacco Ltd, table of points values*

Factors	Degrees and points										Maximum % of highest possible score (331)
	A	B	C	D	E	F	G	H	J	K	
Job knowledge and skills	10	20	30	40	50	60	70	80	90	100	30.2
Problem solving	10	20	30	40	50	60	70	80	–	–	24.2
Scope (ie discretion)	8	16	24	32	40	48	–	–	–	–	14.5
Commercial significance	8	16	24	32	–	–	–	–	–	–	9.7
Supervision	5	10	15	20	25	–	–	–	–	–	7.6
Clerical operations	3	6	9	12	15	18	–	–	–	–	5.4
Manipulative tasks	2	4	6	8	–	–	–	–	–	–	2.4
Contacts:											
difficulty	2	4	6	8	10	12	–	–	–	–	3.6
relevance	2	4	6	8	–	–	–	–	–	–	2.4

Source: Imperial Tobacco Limited, *Staff Job Evaluation Scheme Manual*, p 42

Points rating has several advantages over other schemes.

1. It is more objective and consistent in that common standards provide a structured discipline for evaluators; by focusing attention towards specific factors or characteristics it helps break down traditional views of job worth and avoids the tendency under other schemes of assessing the individual rather than the job.
2. It allows differences between jobs to be quantified and the evaluated structure is easier to explain and justify.
3. It is the most adaptable of all methods and can be applied across a very wide range of diverse jobs.
4. New jobs or regrading appeals can be easily measured against existing factors or weightings, without upsetting the placings of other jobs. The method therefore tends to be stable and durable over time.
5. The method can help reduce traditional job demarcations.

The disadvantages of points rating are as follows.

1. It is costly and time-consuming to set up and maintain; the large variety of job characteristics to be covered by a limited number of factors or degrees requires a long and costly series of discussions.
2. The choice of factors and weightings relies on human judgement and can be hard to justify; quite small diferences in factor weightings can alter the positions of jobs.
3. The use of numerical measures can convey a spurious impression of precision which may breed rigidity.
4. The greater the number of factors, the higher the possibility of the same aspect of a job being assessed from different angles. This results in over-weighting of that factor.
5. The method is prone to grade drift, as minor changes in jobs can provide grounds for regrading appeals.

Factor comparison   Factor comparison is an extension of the points rating method which attempts to rank jobs and attach monetary values concurrently. Jobs are again examined in terms of selected factors of which they are thought to be composed. Benchmark jobs are then examined factor by factor to produce a rank order of the benchmark jobs for each factor. This shows the relative importance of each factor within each job. For example, if A, B and C represent the benchmark jobs, and X, Y and Z the factors, then the ranking produced under each factor could be shown as in Table 14.5.

Table 14.5   *Factor comparison – jobs*

		X	r		Y	r		Z	r
		A	1		A	1		C	1
Jobs		C	2		B	2		A	2
		B	3		C	3		B	3

r = rank order

An attempt is then made to establish how much of the current wage rate for each job is being paid for each of the factors. For example, suppose the weekly wage rates for jobs A, B and C are £200, £180 and £160 respectively, then the results of this stage might be as shown in Table 14.6. If the two rankings agree in their positioning of the jobs under each factor, as in the simplified example in Table 14.5 and 14.6, the benchmark jobs are accepted. If not, the money values of the anomalous jobs are adjusted or else they may be rejected from the calculations. The procedure results in a scale or range of money values for each factor, which is representative of the benchmark jobs in respect of that factor. The remaining jobs are then evaluated factor by factor against these scales, giving a total rate for each job.

Table 14.6   *Factor comparison – wage rates*

		Factors						
		X	r	Y	r	Z	r	Total
Jobs	A	£75	1	£75	1	£50	2	£200
	B	£65	3	£70	2	£45	3	£180
	C	£70	2	£35	3	£55	1	£160

In practice, however, this technique is highly complex, time-consuming and costly. It relies heavily upon choosing good benchmark jobs, which must display a sufficient range of variation under each factor, and rather more such jobs are typically required (about 15 to 20) than under points rating schemes. A further requirement which can be difficult to meet is that the pay rates for these jobs must not be in dispute. The method is not easily understood on account of the number of hierarchies involved and there is a clearly arbitrary element in the way existing wage rates are ascribed to different factors. It can also result in reduced pay flexibility in that, once differentials have been established, future pay increases need to be on a percentage basis if the integrity of the scheme is to be maintained.

Perhaps the major advantage of the factor comparison method is that in requiring custom-built installation, it can be more closely adapted to any special needs of an organization or unusual features of its jobs. For example, a modified form of the technique was successfully applied by the BBC to professional, technical and administrative posts, as other methods were felt to be unsuited to the unusual content of these jobs and particular organizational needs.

Other methods   The methods described are those most commonly in use, but their limitations have encouraged attempts to find other ways of evaluating jobs. One approach which departs from traditional methods is to rank jobs on the basis of the types of decisions made by the job occupants. The best-known examples are Jaques's time-span of discretion method and Paterson's decision-band method. The former ranks jobs on the basis of the longest period which may elapse before the use of marginally substandard discretion in a job would be detected. Paterson's method, on the other hand, uses a scale of six different kinds of decisions (or bands), whereby a job is ascribed to the highest band in which any of its tasks fall. Such schemes are still relatively uncommon and are not easily applied to manual occupations. Moreover, they come close to evaluating the individual rather than the job.[32]

There has also been a proliferation of consultants' proprietary schemes in recent years, which are either refinements of the basic schemes described or are 'hybrid' or composite schemes which combine the principles of two or more techniques. For example, the 'Direct Consensus Method', developed by Imbucon, is an off-the-peg form of paired comparisons. The Price Waterhouse Urwick 'Profile Method' is a streamlined version of points rating, while the consultants, Arthur Young, offer a refinement of Paterson's decision-band method. A composite scheme has been devised by PA consultants which is a form of points rating with factor weightings determined by paired comparisons. Perhaps the most widely adopted proprietary scheme is the 'Hay Guide Chart Profile Method' of Hay–MSL Ltd, which is a variation of the points rating method, except that the factors used are aspects of the decisions taken in jobs.

Equal value implications

The Equal Value (Amendment) Regulations 1983 that came into force in January 1984 have several implications for job evaluation. Prior to the Amendment a woman could claim equal pay under the Equal Pay Act 1970, only if she was paid less than her chosen comparator for 'like work' or work rated as equivalent under a job evaluation exercise. Under the Amendment, however, she (or he) may claim equal pay, even though her work has not been rated as equivalent by job evaluation, on the ground that the work done, although different, is of *equal value* in terms of the demands that it makes. Moreover, there is scope in the legislation for challenging a firm's existing job evaluation scheme as discriminatory.

The legislation is widely perceived as necessitating some reconsideration of current methods of determining relative pay, including job evaluation, if firms are to reduce their vulnerability to claims. For example, in *Bromley & ors* v *H & J Quick Ltd* (1988) ICR 623, the Court of Appeal held that a valid job evaluation scheme under the Regulations must be 'analytical' and evaluate jobs under various demand headings, criteria which the company's paired comparisons method on a 'whole jobs' basis did not meet. An integrated, analytical job evaluation scheme (eg points rating covering both blue-collar and white-collar workers) is conventionally considered the best method of reducing employer vulnerability to claims. If such a system is negotiated with the union(s), and accepted by both parties, it will be difficult to convince a tribunal of sex bias in the scheme and the claim could be blocked at the pre-hearing stage. However, such a system can be difficult to apply in a consistent fashion as factors appropriate to blue-collar jobs (eg difficult working conditions) might be irrelevant to white-collar jobs, and vice versa. Nor do such systems constitute an insurmountable barrier to a claim under the Amendment. For instance, the scheme may be considered sex-biased if factors such as effort, physical strength and working conditions are over-represented or over-weighted, relative to factors such as manual dexterity or mental concentration. Several guides exist as to how employers might avoid bias creeping into schemes and reduce their vulnerability to claims.[33]

Trends and developments

The ACAS survey in 1988 found that some 40 per cent of manufacturing and 35 per cent of service-sector establishments then used job evaluation. However, nearly two-thirds of larger establishments (those employing more than 500 people) operated schemes. About three-fifths of schemes were based upon analytical points rating methods, while simpler job ranking, paired comparisons or job classification systems accounted for the remainder. The survey results also suggested an upward trend in the use of schemes, albeit at a slow pace.

Equal value It is unclear to what extent employers are responding to equal value legislation through integrated schemes. One survey conducted in 1989 uncovered evidence of such a trend. Thirty-eight per cent of new schemes being introduced covered all occupations, and almost no new systems were being introduced for blue-collar or manual grades alone.[34] However, the ACAS survey found that just one in eight respondents with job evaluation reported using schemes that covered all or most occupational categories.

Unless such schemes further other company objectives such as harmonization or job flexibility, and in the absence of definitive case law, many employers may be justifiably reluctant to pursue major pay structure reform solely on equal value considerations. Some rulings have raised doubts about the value of integrated schemes as a defence. For example, in *Reed Packaging Ltd* v *Boozer* (1988) IRLR 333, the Employment Appeals Tribunal accepted the employer's argument that two separate pay structures based on different schemes had arisen from the necessity of negotiating with two separate trade unions, and that this constituted a genuine material factor defence justifying the difference in pay between applicants and comparator.

Pay flexibility Job evaluation is often criticized as imposing a strait-jacket upon organizations which are attempting to cope with changing markets, technologies or other pressures that have implications for relative wages. It may represent no more than a temporary solution to such pressures, which will continue to exist and eventually will undermine the new structure. In such circumstances, maintaining the scheme can come to assume higher priority than organizational needs. An alternative approach would be to identify the chief causes of pay distortions and then design a pay structure that is as resistant as possible to these causes. How this approach might be tackled systematically, while avoiding some of the inflexibilities of job evaluation, is described by Lupton and Bowey.[35]

The present emphasis, however, is not upon accommodating but responding to market and other pressures through flexible pay strategies and individual performance criteria. Such approaches are fundamentally incompatible with job evaluation only insofar as they challenge the whole concept of an established pay and grading structure, and indeed there are examples of firms such as Cable and Wireless that have abandoned grading structures altogether. Generally, however, even the most innovative firms have recognized the value of a grading structure as a tool for managing internal pay relativities and ensuring that market or merit-driven systems are tempered in line with organizational objectives and values.

The chief approach has been to pursue flexibility through flatter structures with fewer grades, but wider pay bands attached to grades and greater management discretion in deciding placings on pay ranges. The view that job evaluation is inconsistent with this approach rests on a misunderstanding of the technique. The evaluation process may provide an agreed hierarchy of jobs from which a grading structure can be built, but need not determine the actual structure, and the setting of pay differentials and ranges is also normally quite separate from the evaluation process. Indeed, job evaluation has featured extensively in major processes of pay structure reform that occurred in both the private and public sector in the latter half of the 1980s, as an aid to devising, and assimilating jobs into, the new grading structures that formed the basis of more flexible remuneration strategies.

There are, however, some circumstances unsuited to traditional job evaluation. It may be difficult to operate schemes alongside multi-skilling policies or job rotation. It is also unsuited to organizations whose business is project-based, subject to change, and reliant on the flexible use of people's knowledge and skills such as software houses, consulting engineers and other professional groups with a project-orientation. In such cases there may be no fixed 'job' that can be evaluated, and it may be more relevant to link pay chiefly to individual competencies and skills. The difficulty here is in devising defensible pay approaches that also meet organizational requirements, rather than rewarding competencies or skills the organization cannot use. Systematic approaches to devising grading structures are thus emerging that are built upon job evaluation principles, but where factors assessed are those skills and competencies of individuals that are relevant to organizational needs, rather than the demands of specific jobs.

Such systems work best when applied to specific job families. They can provide a career map for employees to encourage the acquisition of relevant skills and can also be linked into performance management systems. It is an approach that is still in its infancy in the UK, and requires sophisticated management and generous resources to work well. Moreover, some schemes implicitly endorse such principles as equality of opportunity or even lifetime employment which may impede longer-term flexibility. Skill and competency-based pay can also provide unions with bargaining levers, including demands for training and job openings which employers may find irksome or impossible to concede.[36]

Computer-assisted schemes   The use of computers to facilitate evaluation processes is an important development that is likely to gain wide application. Such systems normally entail the use of job analysis questionnaires in place of traditional job descriptions, and as data are gathered in a common format, statistical analysis using mathematical models can lead to more rigorous assessment processes. Thus, job evaluation can be carried out more quickly and efficiently with less demands on management and employee resources. Some commentators also envisage such systems as providing exciting possibilities beyond the remit of job evaluation. Data generated could form the basis for conceptual modelling and expert systems covering such areas as job analysis and design, career planning, training policy and performance management.[37]

HARMONIZATION

Harmonization refers to the trend towards introducing the same conditions of employment among all employees. 'Single status' and 'staff status' are terms which are sometimes used synonymously with harmonization when describing this process, although each term implies a slightly different approach. The IPM distinguished the three terms as follows.

1. *Single status* is the removal of differences in basic conditions of employment to give all employees equal status. Some organizations take this further by putting all employees into the same pay and grading structure.
2. *Staff status* is a process whereby manual and craft employees gradually receive staff terms and conditions of employment, usually upon reaching some qualifying standard, for example length of service.
3. *Harmonization* means the reduction of differences in the pay structure and other employment conditions between categories of employees, usually manual and staff employees. The essence of harmonization is the adoption of a common approach and criteria to pay and conditions for all employees. It differs from staff status in that, in the process of harmonization, some staff employees may have to accept some of the conditions of employment of manual employees.[38]

Pressures towards harmonization

Harmonization has proceeded at a slow but steady pace since at least the Second World War. Some quickening in the pace of change was noticed in the early 1970s and again in the 1980s. The process is often justified by management on the view that traditional distinctions in employment conditions are irrelevant, anachronistic and unjust. However, there have been several recent pressures towards harmonization of which, in the view of the IPM, questions of morality are probably of least importance.

New technology Status differentials can obstruct efficient labour utilization and the ability of firms to react quickly and flexibly to new technology. Indeed, concessions on harmonized conditions are invariably exchanged as part of an explicit agreement for more efficient work practices, such as reducing overtime or eliminating demarcation lines.

Moreover, technology, by deskilling many white-collar jobs, has made differential treatment more difficult to defend. It has also contributed to a declining manual worker base so that the costs of harmonization for many firms is also declining.

Legislation Legislation concerning equal pay, sex and racial discrimination, and employment protection, has narrowed differences and extended rights to manual workers in areas previously the preserve of staff (eg maternity pay, time off for public duties). The directives and recommendations of the European Commission have also encouraged harmonized conditions. Moreover, pay restraint imposed by incomes policies led to bargaining by manual workers over non-pay issues, setting precedents for widening the scope of collective bargaining. A number of legislative initiatives have also provided opportunities for administrative savings through harmonization. Statutory sick pay and the removal of restrictions on cashless pay are examples.

Recession   Recession and intensification of competitive pressures have enhanced the perceived importance of co-operative attitudes, flexibility and commitment from employees, qualities which tend to be undermined by traditional divisions.

Benefits and costs

More specifically, where companies have pursued harmonized conditions, it has usually been to achieve one or more of three objectives: improving labour productivity; simplifying personnel administration and thus reducing costs; and changing employee attitudes to improve co-operation, motivation and morale.

Harmonization will, of course, incur costs, the extent of which will be determined by the scope of the exercise and the nature of existing differences. Even where the aim is directly to reduce costs through rationalization of administrative procedures, there can be unanticipated problems. For instance, manual workers might not view cashless pay as a benefit and some cash inducement may be required to effect the change. Moreover, staff employees or unions might demand compensation, monetary or otherwise, for erosion of status differentials resulting from improved manual conditions. In general, there is likely to be a net increase in costs in the short term, as many of the perceived benefits of harmonization, such as improved attitudes, are unlikely to produce immediate financial gains. For this reason most companies adopt a gradualist, cautious approach towards the exercise.

Occasionally, however, companies may opt for the 'complete package' or 'grand design' approach towards harmonizing a whole range of conditions including integration of pay structures and systems, the working week, sick pay arrangements, pensions, canteen facilities and many other items. This is really in the nature of an elaborate productivity deal and has all the same resource implications – a long consultative process and heavy demands upon management time and skills in negotiating, costing, administering and monitoring the change. A deal of this sort was negotiated by the Rover Group in 1992, in which Japanese-style working practices were conceded not only in return for harmonized conditions but a 'jobs-for-life' guarantee. Normally, however, such elaborate programmes are more commonly associated with companies setting up on greenfield sites, especially Japanese or US multinationals, where costs may be reduced by avoiding entrenched attitudes and working practices. Costs are nevertheless incurred in the careful recruitment and induction programmes required, and in the generous pay and benefits packages invariably offered in exchange for restrictions on normal trade union activity, such as single union agreements, pendular arbitration and no strike clauses.

Harmonization and pay

Harmonization has proceeded furthest in respect of conditions of service such as holidays, sick pay or pensions, but more recently there has been progress in the more sensitive area of pay and payment systems. For example, some firms have moved in the direction of reducing the variability of manual pay relative to non-manual by consolidating bonus schemes into fixed salaries in exchange for concessions on working practices. There have also been moves towards aligning overtime base rates and calculators as between manual and white-collar staff. The repeal of the Truck Acts by the Wages Act 1986 removed the right of manual workers to insist on being paid in cash (unless there is a contractual obligation to this effect) and has hastened the trend towards integrated non-cash methods of wage payment.

Some companies have also made more elaborate moves towards integrated, single-grading payment structures, often based upon a common job evaluation scheme. Equal value considerations have pushed in this direction, as have new bargaining patterns. For example, trade unions in engineering and elsewhere have recently supported moves to single-table bargaining, to counter single-union deals, but match the competitive advantage that such deals have secured for companies on greenfield sites.[39] Moreover, current union amalgamation trends make it increasingly likely that manual and non-manual workers will find themselves organized in the same union. The newly privatized water companies represent recent examples of moves towards integrated pay, where single-table bargaining, integrated salary structures and revised working practices have accompanied moves to shorten the working week. The new deal at Rover also provides that Rover's 11 unions will now negotiate through one bargaining unit.

Questions for organizations

Harmonization should aim towards removing illogical and indefensible differences, but where their removal is not clearly to the mutual benefit of employer and employees, the process should be viewed as akin to productivity bargaining. In deciding whether to embark upon a programme of harmonization ACAS advises that organizations should first seek answers to the following questions:

- What differences in the treatment of groups of employees are a rational result of differences in the work or the job requirements?
- Is it possible to estimate the direct costs of removing these differences?
- What differences in status are explicitly recognized as part of the 'reward package' for different groups in the labour force? What would be the possible repercussive effects of harmonization?
- How do the existing differences affect industrial relations in the organization?[40]

'CAFETERIA BENEFITS'

Flexible compensation systems, often referred to as 'cafeteria benefits', allow employees some choice in the make-up of the benefits they receive. Sometimes the choice is limited to four or five fixed packages, incorporating different levels or mixes of such benefits as pensions, company cars, holidays or medical insurance, with no facility for cross-trading benefits or substituting benefits for cash. Usually, however, the term refers to choice from a full 'menu' of different benefits at different levels, and employees can also alter the balance of benefits and cash pay as desired. The concept is consistent with the trend towards the 'total remuneration package', whereby companies treat basic salary and benefits as a total costed package, but cafeteria benefits offer choice and flexibility in the make-up of the package. Schemes operate by setting an 'option price' for different levels of benefits, and allocating a 'credit' amount to spend, often based on the existing salary, grade or service of employees.

Such systems are now well established in the US, where a favourable tax regime and escalating costs of medical insurance acted as catalysts during the 1980s. Though still rare in Britain, the schemes are expected to grow during the 1990s.[41] They have attracted much interest among leading-edge firms in the private sector and semi-autonomous public sector organizations that are now using new-found freedoms to embark upon fashionable core/periphery labour strategies. The following are among the chief benefits envisaged.

1. *Recruitment and retention.* Many existing benefits packages are rigid and unsuited to present or projected employee profiles. The rise of the dual income family, for instance, has meant over-provision of some aspects of joint incomes, such as company cars or family medical insurance. Moreover, demographic trends have led employers to target new sources of labour to supplement the dwindling supply of school leavers and graduates, including women with children, older people and part-timers. Flexible compensation can cater for the diverse needs of such groups more effectively than blanket provision of benefits or pay-only inducements, thus sharpening recruitment and retention strategies.
2. *Labour costs.* A selective rather than universal benefits package is potentially less costly. It avoids spending money on benefits that are little appreciated and there is greater potential for controlling future cost increases. If a particular budget escalates in cost, the employer need not automatically pick up the bill when setting individual benefit budget levels. New benefits can also be introduced at minimal cost.
3. *Employee commitment.* The system fits well the trend towards individualization of employment relations. It may foster a climate of trust and openness, and reinforce corporate messages about personal responsibility. The higher value placed by employees on an individually-tailored benfits plan may also lead to improvements in commitment and morale.

However, there are a number of problems associated with flexible benefits systems that have acted to impede take-up:

1. *Administration.* The system may create an administrative burden that outweighs the benefits. Setting up a scheme and communicating it to employees itself constitutes a major exercise. Ongoing commitments include: valuing benefits and establishing new benefits; routinely recording employee preferences; and keeping abreast of tax, actuarial and legal issues affecting schemes. The complexities are such that designing and running a scheme is likely to require significant imput from external consultants, though the recent computerization of personnel functions has made in-house administration of schemes more practicable.[42]
2. *Tax implications.* One worry is that offering individuals a cash alternative in lieu of a benefit can render the benefit option taxable at its cash value, even if the individual opts to take the benefit. Recent Inland Revenue and VAT rulings dealing with company cars are illustrative.

3. *Cost control*. There are several reasons why labour costs may increase, at least in the short term: employees may trade under-utilized benefits (eg holiday entitlement) for benefits they take up fully; there could be increases in the costs of benefits through loss of discounts arising from lower take-up; and premiums for risk benefits such as medical insurance may rise because of the effects of 'adverse selection'. Administering the system can also build in longer-term recurring costs.

4. *Union reaction*. There may be union resistance to flexible benefits plans where they are perceived as threatening standard terms and conditions, or undermining collective values.

CONCLUDING COMMENTS

Pay determination processes were greatly affected during the 1980s by major transformation of the economic and political landscape, including the dismantling of the corporate state, deregulation of finance and industry, and downgrading of union influence and collectivist values. Pay responses were towards flexibility and market sensitivity, greater individualization and differentiation of reward according to criteria of merit and skill, and reward strategies that sought to bridge traditional divisions between capital and labour.

One difficulty that has always confronted centrally-promoted reforms in the pay sphere is that of reconciling simple ideological premises or macro-economic aims with the complex functions typically performed by organizational pay systems, and the need to gear system choice and design to specific company objectives and circumstances. Using pay as a direct vehicle of social or economic reform, as was apparent in the promotion of profit-sharing and in pay reforms imposed on the public sector, is especially problematic in fostering a uniformity of approach that cannot be suited to all circumstances.

While recent trends clearly reflect legitimate and independent management responses to changed circumstances, there are also indications that patterns of change have been guided by fashion and experimentation rather than systematic assessment of options in line with longer-term strategic goals. This is despite the growing body of material now available to managers to guide pay reform processes, and is apparent in evidence of ambiguity of objectives and superficial management commitment to the principles of such schemes as profit-sharing and performance pay. The result has been a general failure of the schemes to deliver desired outcomes.

There are also indications that the well-documented limitations of market and merit-led pay were poorly appreciated by many organizations. One frequent criticism of current approaches by pay monitoring bodies such as IDS has been of 'short-termism'. This is an inevitable feature of market-based approaches in economic conditions as volatile as those of the last decade – a credit-led boom sandwiched between two deep and protracted recessions. Other problems now emerging include corruption of pay structures, loss of labour cost control and associated motivational difficulties, problems that threaten to outweigh the benefits of greater pay flexibility.

Moreover, the material and social legacy of Thatcherism has, in many respects, acted against the professed aims and sentiments of current pay approaches.

Table 14.7   *Dispersion of earnings of full-time adults – lowest and highest deciles expressed as a percentage of the corresponding medians*

	Men		Women	
	Lowest 10%	*Highest 10%*	*Lowest 10%*	*Highest 10%*
1981	65.6	167.7	68.0	172.6
1986	60.8	171.5	65.8	164.5
1991	57.9	183.0	61.7	180.6

Source: New Earnings Survey

Most obviously, schemes that seek to bridge traditional divisions and reduce antipathetic attitudes have operated alongside a marked and unprecedented widening in the dispersion of pay over the last decade, as is shown in Table 14.7.

Other countervailing influences have included the shifting balance of share ownership from individuals to institutional investors, and the enormous inflation of executive pay in recent years. Excessive increases for public figures leading newly-privatized monopolies were especially controversial and generated considerable public cynicism in being clearly unrelated to business performance. More generally, developments such as financial deregulation, the merger and takeover booms, and the need to fend off corporate raiders, have contributed to a meaner and leaner business environment. Excessively male-dominated, and obsessed by short-term financial return, the prevalent corporate ethos that has emerged is not altogether conducive to 'enlightened' personnel approaches based upon trust and partnership.

Pay approaches will need to respond to a fresh set of pressures in the significantly altered political and economic environment of the 1990s. The challenge for organizations is to tailor pay responses sensitively and variably to change as it affects their specific circumstances, in order to achieve greater continuity and effectiveness of strategy than was apparent in the 1980s.

References

1. ACAS (1988) *Developments in Payment Systems: The 1988 ACAS Survey*, Occasional Paper 45.
2. Casey, B et al (1991) 'Payment systems: a look at current practice', *Employment Gazette*, August.
3. Bowey, A M and Thorpe, R (1986) *Payment Systems and Productivity*, Macmillan, London, p 33.
4. Lupton, T and Gowler, D (1969) *Selecting a Wage Payment System*, Engineering Employers' Federation Research Paper No 111, London; for a useful summary of the techniques, see Lupton, T and Bowey, A M (1983) *Wages and Salaries*, 2nd edn, Gower, Aldershot, Chapter 3. Systematic approaches to reforming bargaining levels and structures are described in Palmer, S (ed) (1990) *Determining Pay: A guide to the issues*, Institute of Personnel Management, London.
5. Bowey, A M et al (1982) *Effects of Incentive Payment Systems: United Kingdom: 1977–80*, Department of Employment Research Paper No 36, HMSO, London.
6. Bowey, A M and Thorpe, R, op cit, p 150.
7. National Board for Prices and Incomes (1968) *Payment by Results Systems*, Report No 65, Cmnd 3627, HMSO, London.
8. Edwards, C and Heery, E (1985) 'Formality and informality in the working of the National Coal Board's incentive scheme', *British Journal of Industrial Relations*, 23: 1, March.

9. Cannell, M and Long, P (1991) 'What's changed about incentive pay?', *Personnel Management*, October.
10. Incomes Data Services (IDS) (1991) *Report*, 591, April.
11. Confederation of British Industry (1985) *Incentive Payments*, London.
12. Baddon, L et al (1989) *People's Capitalism: A Critical Analysis of Profit-sharing and Employee Share Ownership*, Routledge, London, p 62.
13. Poole, M (1989) *The Origins of Economic Democracy: Profit sharing and employee-shareholding schemes*, Routledge, London, p 46.
14. IDS *Study* (1986) 357, 'Profit sharing & share options', March.
15. IDS *Study* (1990) 468, 'Profit sharing and share options', October.
16. IDS *Report* (1991) 600, September.
17. IDS Top Pay Unit (1990) *Research File*, 16, 'Personnel tax guide 1990/1991', November, p 37.
18. Baddon, et al, op cit, pp 71, 289.
19. Oldham, G (1990) 'TAURUS and the private shareholder', *Economic Affairs*, 11: 1, October/November.
20. *Financial Times*, 11 March 1992, p 23.
21. Kelly, J and Kelly, C (1991) '"Them and US": social psychology and "The new industrial relations"', *British Journal of Industrial Relations*, 29: 1, March.
22. Baddon, et al, op cit, Chapter 5.
23. Duncan, C (1988) 'Why profit related pay will fail', *Industrial Relations Journal* 19: 3, Autumn.
24. Luther, R (1991) 'The Government's profit-related pay initiative: three years on', *Fiscal Studies*, 12: 3, August.
25. IDS (1990) *Public Service Employment*, 24, October, p 2.
26. Fowler, A (1988) 'New directions in performance pay', *Personnel Management*, November.
27. Helpful guidance material from IDS includes: (1989) *A Guide to Performance Related Pay*, IDS Public Sector Unit, August; IDS *Study* (1989) 442 'Appraising manual workers' performance', September.
28. Bevan, S and Thompson, M (1991) 'Performance management at the crossroads', *Personnel Management*, November, p 39.
29. IDS (1991) *Focus* 61, 'Performance pay', December.
30. Kinnie, N and Lowe, D (1990) 'Performance-related pay on the shopfloor', *Personnel Management*, November.
31. IDS, *Focus* 61, op cit.
32. For a critique of the Jaques and Paterson techniques, see Lupton, T and Bowey, A M, op cit, pp 20–8.
33. See Equal Opportunities Commission *Job Evaluation Free of Sex Bias* (1991), Manchester; Ghobadian, A and White, M (1987) 'Factors contributing to the implementation of unbiased job evaluation schemes', *Personnel Review*, 16: 5.
34. Spencer, S (1990) 'Devolving job evaluation', *Personnel Management* January.
35. Lupton, T and Bowey, A M, op cit, ch 7.
36. For further discussion of such systems, see IDS, *Focus* 60, 'The pay/jobs match', pp 9–12; Murlis, H and Fitt, D (1991) 'Job evaluation in a changing world', *Personnel Management*, May.
37. For further discussion of computer-assisted schemes, see Murlis, H and Pritchard, D (1991) 'The computerised way to evaluate jobs', *Personnel Management*, April; Spencer, S (1990) 'Job evaluation: a modern day "genie" for management information?', *Employment Gazette*, June.
38. Roberts, C (ed) (1985) *Harmonisation – Whys and Wherefores*, Institute of Personnel Management, London.
39. Marginson, P and Sisson, K (1990) 'Single table talk', *Personnel Management*, May.
40. ACAS (1982) *Developments in Harmonisation*, Discussion Paper No 1, March.
41. As argued, for example, by Woodley, C (1990) 'The cafeteria route to compensation', *Personnel Management*, May.
42. Advice on setting up and administering schemes is contained in IDS *Study* (1991) 481, 'Flexible Benefits', May.

Part Three
The Law in Industrial Relations

Chapter Fifteen

The Legal Background: An Overview

Karl J Mackie

LAW AS STRATEGY: REFORMING THE UK INDUSTRIAL RELATIONS CULTURE

Much of the thrust of government policy throughout the 1980s was aimed at undermining the industrial relations culture which had dominated union, business, public and government thinking, arguably for most of this century, and certainly from 1945 onwards. Within this change effort, trade union and employment laws played a central part as targets, and instruments, of change. The question of the rights and wrongs of these changes, and their permanence, are matters for political judgement and evaluation, and are touched on in the conclusion of this chapter on likely futures for employment law in Britain. However, the primary aim of this chapter is to set out the legal objectives and mechanisms of the changes made in this period.

What were the elements of the British industrial relations culture which came under attack? Its most favoured concept as far as lawyers of British industrial relations were concerned was that of *voluntarism* or abstentionism; the notion that it was, in Kahn-Freund's words: 'the policy of the law to allow the two sides by agreement and practice to develop their own norms and their own sanctions, and [to abstain] from legal compulsion in their collective relationship.' The clearest expression of this policy was in the area of the statutory 'immunities' for industrial action, the provisions which protected British trade unions from legal actions for which the common law (judges) would have otherwise made them liable. It was a system which was effectively in place by 1906 and gave formal political approval to the legality of trade unions and their methods, but in the simple form of a shield rather than an arsenal of legal rights. The voluntarist system has always had both its exceptions (for example, in emergency powers or wages councils' authority) and its tensions – it was subject to amendment during both world wars and after the 1926 General Strike, but otherwise became the 'norm' of practice in British industrial relations.[1]

However, the strains arising from unchecked industrial action became pronounced again the the 1960s, with concern over the impact of industrial action on the economy and a lengthy debate about how to reform the 'British disease'. A variety of ideas for legal measures were canvassed in the period (most especially in the Donovan Royal Commission Report and the Labour Government's proposals in *In Place of Strife*), culminating in an attempt by a Conservative Government to restructure industrial relations law completely in the Industrial Relations Act 1971. The attempt was widely recognized as having failed[2] and the Labour Government which came to office in 1974 restored, in an amended form, the traditional approach, while maintaining and extending some of the new legal provisions affecting employers, such as unfair dismissal. The period since 1979, following the re-election of a Conservative Government, has seen a remarkable transformation in industrial relations culture, spearheaded by legal reforms.

THE ELEMENTS OF CHANGE

Although one can set the legal changes descriptively within sophisticated academic debates around issues of voluntarism or interventionism in British industrial relations,[3] the central strategic objective behind government legislative policies since 1979 has been a simple one: *to shift the balance of power from trade unions to employers*.

The government campaign on this issue in the 1979 election repeatedly referred to the need to restore a proper balance of power between employers and trade unions. The trade unions were said to have abused their privileged position, exercising industrial pressure regardless of the country's social or economic interests. In the re-election campaigns of 1983, 1987 and 1992, the same theme was prominent, although by then the message to the electorate was a warning not to endanger the achievements of the government in restructuring the industrial relations culture of the country. Also, talk of 'balance' had given way to statements merely stressing the need to prevent a return to the abuses of union power.

The immediate concerns expressed in the 1979 campaign were consequent on the 'winter of discontent' of 1978–9 with its examples of extensive secondary picketing and secondary industrial action, and of trade unions which were ready to confront both employers and government to achieve their industrial objectives.

An important element of the changes since 1979, therefore, has been the reform of law affecting *industrial action*. This has entailed re-regulation, first, to create a legal structure which constrains industrial action to within more narrowly defined boundaries of disputes between workers and their own employer. A second, related set of regulations has been devised to support this framework by means of legal controls on *union organization and activities* – union membership agreements, elections, political funds and other aspects of union internal affairs.

Although industrial action and forms of union organization are distinct issues, the government's view was that they were linked facets of the 'union problem'. If one were to represent the Conservative view at its most basic, it ran something along the following lines: industrial action was initiated by unrepresentative and politically-motivated activists or militants inside the unions, leaders who were often unanswerable to the members at large; this leadership then used their power to invoke industrial action for wider industrial or political ends, relying in particular on the institution of the closed shop to control dissident members with threats of expulsion and therefore loss of job.

This line of reasoning helps to explain why a government party which claimed to be committed to 'deregulation' could be so ready to turn to *increased* regulation of the unions beyond merely outlawing certain forms of action. The regulations were regarded as a necessary component of freeing employers and government from what was viewed as illicit exercise of union power.

Underpinning the desire to set union conduct within a more constrictive legal framework, lies a government drive to ensure business competitiveness and 'free market' conditions. For the same reasons, the government has therefore altered legal constraints on *employer power* – industrial relations legislative policies moving in a contrasting direction of freeing employers from some of the earlier regulations which determined or set minimum standards on *employer–employee* relations, with the aim of giving employers more flexibility in their management of labour (at a time, as other chapters document, when economic conditions and employer policies have, in any case, induced a significant shift to more 'flexible' work patterns of, and in, employment).

One must also, however, acknowledge the existence of contradictory or countervailing forces to this simple analysis of the legal reforms since 1979 as representing merely a power-realignment strategy. That is, there is evidence also of *increased* regulation of employers. The sources of this can be traced to at least three factors.

1. The desire of the government to limit public spending has, in certain circumstances, led to a shift of responsibility for social security payments from administration by government to administration by employers, as in the case of sickness and maternity benefits.
2. The influence of membership of the EC has continued to make itself felt in, for example, the imposition on employers of new duties to employees on the transfer of undertakings, or the extended coverage of sex discrimination and equal pay claims. This 'new wave' of regulation reached a crisis point in 1991 at the Maastricht Summit on European Union, when the UK government refused to sign the Social Chapter of the new Treaty.
3. There are occasions where the government has continued to accept an 'encouragement' role for regulation of employer–employee relations in areas that generally match their policies, requiring employers to provide facilities for trade union workplace ballots in certain circumstances, requiring statements in company annual reports of measures adopted to encourage employee involvement, providing improved taxation treatment for share-owning or profit-sharing schemes.

LAW AS TACTICS: EFFECTING CHANGE

The above is an outline of the regulatory policies which have reshaped British industrial relations law since 1979. In understanding these changes, one must also take account of the fact that the nature of the law-in-action is not merely a matter of the substantive principles of law, the rights and obligations created. The law's effectiveness is also determined by questions of procedure, legal remedies, ease of access to adjudication, and by the alternative means of control available to the parties in dispute. These remain vital factors in understanding the impact of law and changes in the law.

One of the principal features of an earlier Conservative Government's attempt (in the Industrial Relations Act 1971) to achieve the same objective of increased restraint on union/worker conduct, was the failure of the legal measures to make a sufficient impact on the practices of employers and unions. There are aspects of this evident in the post-1979 legislation. However, it is also widely acknowledged that these measures have been far more successful in achieving their aims. While this success must be in part attributed to the presence of a more chastening economic climate, it is also a measure of a more sophisticated approach to legislative control.

The 1979 government was at pains to emphasize the need for a 'step-by-step' approach to removing union 'abuses'. Thus, the legislation whose content is described below, is the outcome of a series of measures, in particular a major Act passed every two years of the Conservatives' period of office – the Employment Acts 1980, 1982, the Trade Union Act 1984, the Wages Act 1986 and the Employment Acts 1988 and 1990.

Alongside this important 'gradualist' approach, building on changing attitudes and experience (of public, government and legal drafting), the nature of the procedures and remedies made available by the Acts helped to sidestep some of the tactics the unions used to resist the Industrial Relations Act. First, the legislation was drafted to help to avoid the direct clashes between the trade unions and government (or special institutions created for the purposes of the legislation) which were typical of the earlier Act, such as over-registration of unions or 'cooling-off' periods to be called by the secretary of state for employment. Secondly, the legislation built on existing rights rather than created new ones – for example, merely narrowing down the traditional 'immunities' rather than creating direct statutory prohibitions, thus returning industrial action to scrutiny by traditional common law principles; attacking the closed shop through the medium of unfair dismissal claims and compensation rather than declarations of unlawfulness for the practice. In a similar fashion the legislation has relied on established institutions – industrial tribunals, Certification Officer, High Court – rather than creating new ones.

This step-by-step approach has also been evident in the case law around the legislation, although here there is more of an element of chance. While employers generally were hesitant to test the new rights in relation to their 'domestic' unions, other significant and well-publicized cases emerged from outside the mainstream, cases where an employer was in a less close relation with a union (as in the *Stockport Messenger* case). The success and publicity attaching to such cases provided other employers with the confidence and example to apply to the law where they might have hesitated before (and the unions with examples which diminished confidence among officials and members). In this way, change in conduct (for example in relation to use of ballots before industrial action) has been a clear outcome of the legislative programme.

Finally, the re-emergence in law of the liability of trade unions *as organizations* allowed the courts when seeking to enforce judgments to cause severe economic damage to unions concerned, rather than imposing martyrdom on individual officials. (The same process was apparent through the miners' strike of 1984–5, but in that dispute the main cases involved were member complaints against their union, actions derived under traditional common law rules rather than the new statutory rules.) This helped erode the initial union refusal to recognize the validity of the laws, thereby gradually establishing the legitimacy of legal intervention in a way which had never been wholly successful under the 1971 Act. The fact that this legitimacy also had an opportunity to establish itself over three terms of Conservative Government office is, of course, a final factor in consolidating the legitimacy of the new laws as a new 'Queensberry Rules' in industrial relations.

Space does not permit an adequate analysis of case law developments (judicial interpretation of legislation) over the period since 1979, but this aspect of the tactics of legal intervention is a crucial one, quite separate from the issue of the nature of the new legal rules. It is also worth commenting on the fact that not only has judicial attention continued to play a significant part in the interpretation of the survived remnants of the pre-1979 legislation, but also that the miners' strike of 1984–5 has created a body of case law within the common law which is likely to be highly significant for some time in the future.

In line with the earlier analysis of the regulatory objectives of the governments of the period, a more detailed discussion of the main changes in the law is set out in the rest of this chapter under three headings: employer–employee relations; industrial action; trade union organization and activities. A final section provides an evaluation of the significance of this decade of reform, and speculates briefly on possible future directions.

Before discussing the legal changes in more detail, it is useful to demonstrate the extent of legislation enacted by the Conservative Government since 1979 by a summary of the changes made in these substantive areas. (Discussion of pensions law, health and safety and taxation law developments has had to be limited. The other items listed in the following chart are intended as an *aide-mémoire* rather than as a precise description of legal provisions.)

LABOUR LAW: MAIN CHANGES SINCE 1979

Employer–employee relations

Industrial tribunal procedures
Pre-hearing assessments introduced with warning on costs and possibility of awarding costs on grounds of unreasonable as well as frivolous or vexatious claims. Secretary of state given power to require applicants to pay a deposit before they can bring a case.

*Summary judgments** possible.

Equal pay procedures with 'independent expert' to conduct job evaluation where 'equal value' claim.

Non-union members given *right to join union* and other workers before tribunal where individual dismissed or victimized for non-union membership; right to claim *interim relief;*** *compensation* made significantly higher than ordinary dismissal claims for dismissals on relevant union or non-union grounds.

---

* ie reasons for decision may be written in summary form in most cases (although parties may request full reasons).
** ie a special procedure for obtaining rapid relief by way of re-employment or continuation of contract until a full hearing is held.

Unfair dismissal
Length of service requirement increased to two years.

Reasonableness. Equal burden of proof rather than employer to prove; 'size and administrative resources' factor to be taken into account.

Fixed-term contracts. One-year period sufficient for employee to agree to waive rights to claim unfair dismissal or redundancy.

Compensation amendments (loss of minimum basic award; conduct other than that contributing to dismissal can be taken into account; higher minimum basic award and 'special award' system for dismissals for non-union/union reasons).

Dismissals for *industrial action.* Employer immunity extended.

Dismissals or victimization of *non-union member* unfair. Legal support for the closed shop ended.

Protection where *transfer of undertakings*, unless reasonable dismissal for 'an economic, technical or organizational reason entailing changes in the workforce'.

Redundancy
Employer rebates withdrawn unless fewer than ten employees.

Terms and conditions
Wages Councils' powers. Abolished powers of setting wage levels for workers under 21 years, non-wage conditions and above-minimum differentials. Powers restricted to setting minimum adult hourly rate and overtime rate/live-in accommodation payment maximum.

Wages Councils' structures. Simpler abolition or variation powers for Secretary of State; more independent members, small employer representatives; three-year term of office; statutory requirement to have regard to effect of order on employment levels in the industry, in particular regional areas of low employment.

Cashless pay. Truck Act restrictions abolished for new contracts.

Truck Acts repealed. New right for all workers to go to tribunal for unlawful deductions from pay (where non-statutory, no prior written notification in contract or written agreement); one-tenth limit on deductions in any one pay day for retail workers (where cash shortages/stock deficiencies).

Fair Wages Resolution rescinded.

Repeal of 'comparable terms and conditions' arbitration procedure ('recognized' terms in collective agreements or 'general level' claims).

Statutory sick pay introduced to replace direct state benefit for up to 28 weeks.

Statutory maternity pay to replace maternity allowance.

Transfer of undertakings require transfer of contracts and collective agreements in appropriate cases.

Duty on employers to respond promptly to *employee request to terminate union subscription check-off from pay or to vary check-off deduction amount where employee contracts out of union political levy.*

Repeal of legislation on women's hours of work.

Pension transfers across employments improved.

Maternity rights
Right to reasonable *time off for ante-natal care* with pay.

Right to return to work. Introduction of extended written notice requirements to retain right to return to work. If not reasonably practicable for employer to offer old job back, can offer suitable alternative or, in the case of employer with five or fewer employees, can refuse to take back.

Sex discrimination
Equal pay for work of equal value introduced where not in the same or similar job as the comparator man in the same employment.

Sex discrimination in relation to *retirement* provisions. Unlawful in relation to dismissal, demotion, promotion, transfers, and training.

Eligible employment extended. Right to claim sex discrimination in relation to employment in private households or for small employers.

Employee or trade union involvement or consultation
Employers required to state in *annual reports* what consultation and employee involvement measures have been introduced.

Share ownership and profit-related pay tax incentives.

Right for union to claim *recognition* from employer abolished.

Union (or non-union) labour only or union recognition/consultation clauses in commercial contracts void; unlawful to discriminate against or victimize contractors on these grounds.

Reduced minimum period of trade union *consultation on redundancies.* Thirty days where 10–99 employees/new right to *consultation on transfer of undertakings.*

Pension scheme consultation requirements with employees and trade unions.

Data protection safeguards for personal information held about individuals on computer. Rights of access to, and amendment of, data.

Industrial action

Trade union liability for damages. Can be sued for unlawful industrial action.

Trade dispute definition narrowed to disputes between workers and their employer, for action 'wholly or mainly' related to industrial relations issues.

Selective dismissals and re-engagement simplified.

Social security benefits for strikers' dependents subject to a 'deemed' union strike payment.

Secondary and sympathetic action or picketing made unlawful.

Ballots required for any union-supported action.

Industrial action to enforce union membership made unlawful.

Union membership and subcontractors. Industrial action to compel union membership (or non-membership) or union recognition/consultation by other employers made unlawful.

Trade union organization and activities

Ballots required: before *industrial action* made official; every five years or less for union *principal executive committee* members and presidents and general secretaries; every ten years or less to maintain a *political fund*.

Candidates in elections must be given the opportunity to have *election addresses* sent out.

Qualified *independent scrutineers* must be appointed to supervise election and political fund ballots.

Public funds available to pay certain postal ballot expenses.

Right to use employers' premises for certain ballots.

Register of members' names and addresses must be maintained.

Broader and updated definition of 'political objects' when political fund necessary.

Rights for union members:
— *to prevent industrial action without a ballot*;
— *not to be 'unjustifiably disciplined'* (for not supporting industrial action or for making assertions that the union is acting unlawfully);
— *to inspect union accounts*;
— *to prevent misuse of union funds* to indemnify unlawful conduct or use of union property by trustees for unlawful purposes;
— *to pursue grievances against the union in the courts* after six months of internal procedures.

Commissioner for the Rights of Trade Union Members appointed to assist members to enforce certain statutory rights.

Right for individuals to claim *unreasonable expulsion/exclusion from union membership* where UMA (union membership agreement) exists.

EMPLOYER–EMPLOYEE RELATIONS

The main policy emphasis in this area has been the stress on 'deregulation' in order to allow the labour market to work more freely and to allow employers to concentrate on the question of the production of goods and services rather than on external systems of rules and legal diversions. Many of the legal changes reflect this philosophy. However, in other respects this has been an area of reform and modification rather than deregulation. In addition, other burdens have fallen on employers where other elements of government policy –

European legal requirements, transfer of aspects of public spending on to employers' shoulders – have overridden the search for deregulation. Finally, it is worth making the point that 'deregulation' merely replaces rule by statutory provision with the older 'common law regulation' of the contract of employment (or, more frequently than before 1979, contracts for 'self-employment' arrangements).

It was, of course, the inadequacy of the earlier protection which led to the addition of modern statutory controls. However, a return to the older regulation also takes place in a different socio-economic context. Thus, the formalization of contracts, encouraged by the statutory requirement of written statements of terms and conditions, and a more legalistic (and more white-collar) environment, may perhaps mean a greater number of disputes will take place around the contract of employment than was once the case for personnel managers. The effect, however, is probably relatively insignificant compared with the impact of the statutory rights. Even within these rights, the question of individual contract remains important, for instance, in terms of the factors which go into assessments of 'reasonableness' in unfair dismissal or of constructive dismissal claims, in terms of questions of suitable alternative employment in redundancy and maternity rights cases, and in calculation of compensation by industrial tribunals.

The interlinking of contract and collective agreements has always been one of the curious features of British industrial relations law, the courts managing to recognize the collective bargain without giving it any legal status or intent in its own right, by finding it incorporated (in appropriate cases) into individual contracts of employment. This was one area which the 1971 Act completely misjudged, seeking to establish a system of legally binding agreements but allowing a disclaimer clause which was universally used. Despite this issue rumbling on in government circles from 1979, it has remained one the government has thought better to avoid (perhaps because the 'balance' of advantage in a legally binding agreement is not entirely clear?). However, collective aspects of employer–employee relations inevitably find their way into a number of elements of law in employer–employee relations and the amendments to these since 1979 are also discussed below.

Industrial tribunals and unfair dismissal*

The sphere of individual employee rights has been the most consistent sector of government policy since the 1960s when statements of contract and redundancy payments were first introduced. These established the industrial tribunals as the primary 'labour court' in the country, their presence already familiar to employers as an appeal body from industrial training levy decisions. Their work expanded with the explosion of regulation in the 1970s into unfair dismissals, maternity rights, sex and racial discrimination cases, and equal pay, alongside issues of victimization and dismissal of union members and activists, claims for time off and other rights. Their jurisdiction is now extensive.

However, the tribunals have still not been given any powers to deal with general employment disputes, even those arising over contracts of employment

---

* See Chapter 17 for a more detailed treatment of the law on unfair dismissal.

(the power to extend their jurisdiction into this area remains: s 131 of the Employment Protection (Consolidation) Act 1978); they are limited to the specific provisions of the statutes. Further, the vast majority of claims they deal with concern unfair dismissal, suggesting a reticence by employees to tackle their employers in such a forum until their relationship has been severed. The 'severed relationship' factor is also an important element in the fact that only a minuscule number of cases lead to re-employment, although the orders for reinstatement and re-engagement were once intended to be the primary remedy of the tribunals.[4] This fact and the associated aspect that tribunals cannot enforce such orders but merely increase the compensation element if the employer refuses re-employment has remained a sore point with trade union critics of the system.

For their part, employers prior to 1979 were apt to stress the 'unrealistic' nature of tribunal decisions and (especially small employers) the interference and expense involved in spending time away from their business. It was these claims which the Conservatives stressed in emphasizing the need to induce a sense of realism and proportion in the regulation of employee rights. However, the period since 1979 has been less one of deregulation of the elements of tribunal jurisdiction (although there are important elements of that) than one of technical amendments and procedural points. Employers have, for the most part, learned to live with tribunals and many acknowledge, at least in private, that the dismissals legislation has helped employers to become more professional about matters of discipline and dismissal.

The desire to reduce the burden of employment legislation on employers led primarily to amendments directed at unmeritorious applicants. The rule on costs in tribunals, that they would not normally be awarded except against cases brought or conducted 'frivolously or vexatiously', was extended to include those who acted 'otherwise unreasonably'. To reinforce this, a new interim procedure was introduced at the same time, the pre-hearing assessment, where a party who had a *prima facie* weak case could be warned that a costs award might be made against them at the full hearing should they lose their case, although they were entitled to continue to a full hearing by a separate tribunal. This procedure has deterred many applicants, although of those who did continue despite the warning, it appears that a sizeable minority (of around 13 per cent) still win their case. A suggestion by the government in 1986 that in addition a deposit for all tribunal claims (refunded if successful) could be charged to deter unfounded applications was dropped after widespread opposition to the proposal, but returned in 1988 with a power to introduce such a scheme given to the secretary of state. Finally, the tribunals can now, if they wish, issue their decisions in summary form in most cases, rather than full, reasoned judgments, although parties may request the fuller statement.

Other reforms were directed at the main category of complaint before the tribunals (ie unfair dismissals), but again were for the most part relatively limited in effect. The test of unfair dismissal remains that of 'reasonableness' in all the circumstances, but now includes an additional phrase that the circumstances include the 'size and administrative resources' of the employer's undertaking. Again intended to assist small employers, this amendment appears merely to have confirmed existing practice in the tribunals rather than to have altered their approach. Similarly, there is little evidence of any effect from the change in the onus of proof which now requires the tribunal to find that the dismissal was reasonable (or not) rather than requiring the employer to show that it was reasonable. (The employer is still required to show he has a relevant reason for dismissal.) These amendments were accompanied by a number of adjustments to the system of compensation in ordinary cases, for example the ending of a system of a minimum entitlement to two weeks' pay as a basic award (the part of compensation based on length of service with a company calculated in a similar manner to statutory redundancy payments), and the widening of the circumstances tribunals could take into account in reducing compensation because of an employee's conduct. There was, however, a more drastic review of the compensation system in relation to dismissal of non-union (and union) members. The reforms in this area are outlined in the section below on collective relations in employment.

The most significant deregulation element of the changes since 1979 has been the gradual raising of the qualification period for claiming unfair dismissal, from six months (to which the Labour Government had gradually reduced it by 1979) to two years. The rationale for this is to allow employers time to assess their need for an employee (and his or her acceptability). (For a short period, this rationale led to a difference in qualification periods for large and small employers, the latter allegedly needing more freedom from such legal restraint in order to establish themselves or to grow. On similar grounds, the government proposed at one stage that they would raise the weekly hours of service required over the two years from 16 to 20.) The research evidence in this field has consistently indicated that employment legislation is a long way from most employers' minds as a business problem, and the limited deregulation introduced by the government suggests an acknowledgement of this. Employers in this area, as in the field of industrial action, tend to look for stability in their environment so that they can get on with their main interests. However, on the union side, there is concern about the growing army of temporary and part-time workers not protected by any effective employment legislation.

As regards the case law of tribunals, there has also not been much for employers to become indignant about. The general test behind most tribunals' assessments – 'Is this decision within the range of responses of a reasonable employer?' – has provided limited scope for tribunals to be idiosyncratic or to set advanced standards, while experience in personnel departments and the assistance of a growing army of experts on employment law, briefing documents, legal insurance schemes etc has provided employers with more than a measure of guidance on how to avoid liability. The number of successful applicants before tribunals has therefore tended to decline (to below 30 per cent of those who reached a hearing, by 1984) alongside union enthusiasm for the system. Related to this, the value of being represented, especially being represented by a lawyer, also seems borne out by the statistics. Many employers still settle, however, rather than face the costs, time and doubts of going to a full hearing, or because by this stage they have been informed that they have a weak case.

Terms and conditions of employment

The impact of other aspects of government policy has in most cases been more significant than the hue and cry over the tribunal system in the 1970s. Thus, one may contrast the limited degree of deregulation or tribunal rights (which, after all, still affects only limited numbers of employers at any one time) with the government's readiness to 'privatize' the cumbersome administration of statutory sick pay on to the shoulders of all employers in the interests of seeking saving on public sector manpower costs. An element of reimbursement of employer administrative costs, as well as of the basic sickness payment, was introduced after protests from employers over the original scheme, but the scheme is likely to remain something of a headache for small employers (and an uncertainty for employees).

A repeat run of this took place over statutory maternity pay, introduced in April 1987. This latter reform combines with earlier reforms (more complex written requirements for women to claim maternity leave; rights to time off for maternity care) to make 'maternity management' a sophisticated element of personnel practice.

More central to the government's ideology have been the reforms affecting payment systems. One of the earliest measures to be repealed as inappropriate to free market conditions was Schedule 11 of the Employment Protection Act 1975 (itself an extension of an earlier Act), which had provided trade unions with a form of access to unilateral arbitration for claims based on 'recognized' or 'general level' terms and conditions for comparable workers. A similar rationale led to the Fair Wages Resolution (covering employment terms and conditions of contractors on government department contracts) being rescinded. Also repealed some time later were the Truck Acts which had required manual workers to be paid in the current coin of the realm. The Wages Act 1986 removes this right, unless it is part of the employee's contract (an element giving some cause for confusion in relation to existing employees' rights), freeing employers from the costs and constraints of payment in cash. The provisions in the Truck Acts providing safeguards for employees against fines and deductions from their pay, have been replaced with new legal rights against unauthorized deductions, and maximum limits on deductions from the pay of retail workers for cash shortages or stock deficiencies.

Similarly, the government has been unhappy with the effects on the labour market of Wages Councils (which set legally binding minimum terms and conditions in sectors of employment which have traditionally had limited degrees of union organization), particularly their impact on the 'rigidity' in young workers' earnings. Although the option of abolishing the Councils was considered, and their numbers reduced, the government opted for surgery rather than abolition in the 1986 Act, although it was fairly severe surgery. The power of Wages Councils to set any rates for workers under the age of 21 was abolished. For adult workers, the Wages Councils were restricted to setting one minimum hourly rate (compared to a range of rates in recognition of differentials) and one overtime rate. Their powers to set other conditions (eg holidays) were repealed (apart from setting a maximum level of payments made by workers for living accommodation). Also, the constitution of Wages Councils was revised to add more independent members (for shorter terms of office), more small employer representatives, and a requirement imposed on Councils to have regard to the effect of their orders on employment levels in an industry, in particular regions with low levels of employment. (This latter aspect relates to a wider initiative of the government to increase flexibility in payment systems, and especially to loosen the hold of 'national bargaining' processes.)

An added regulation in the field of payment systems in 1983 provided unwelcome news for employers, with the finding of the European Court that the UK government was in breach of European law (not for the first or last time) over the Equal Pay Act 1970. The result was a complex set of regulations (the Equal Pay (Amendment) Regulations 1983) providing women (or men) effectively with the right to claim a job evaluation exercise if they claimed that their work was of equal value to a man (woman) in the same employment doing a different job. Although the case law has proved this area is also a minefield for applicants, it still represents something of a slowly-ticking time bomb under many payment systems if one assumes that pay differentials in many parts of industry represent long-held but now unlawful assumptions about 'women's work' (for example, canteen assistants, clerical workers, paramedical professions). (One must also make the assumption that the tribunals and 'independent experts' appointed to report on these cases will be able to detect this through job evaluation techniques.) Recognition of the difficulties of protracted hearings over individual cases has led some employers and trade unions to opt for collective bargaining to seek to arrive at more stable pay structures.

Similarly, employers have had to rethink their treatment of men and women approaching retirement, following from the Sex Discrimination Act 1986, which incorporated the results of the *Marshall* case in the European Court, declaring it unlawful to discriminate between the sexes in age of compulsory retirement (or in a range of other aspects of employment, such as opportunities for promotions, transfers, access to training, etc). In the same Act the government was, for once, usefully able to combine sex equality with deregulation, by provisions phasing out the existing restrictions on women's hours of working. (A similar approach was taken to restrictions on young persons' working hours.) Regulation of sex discrimination matters has continued to expand with the increasing activism of the European Court.

Collective relations in employment

Many aspects of employment relations are linked to collective issues and these, too, were subject to scrutiny in an attempt to root out what were regarded as undesirable statutory requirements, but with other requirements again added, however, in pursuit of other policy aims. The provisions (ss 11–16 of the Employment Protection Act 1975) allowing trade unions to claim recognition from an employer by means of ACAS conciliation, investigation and recommendation, were repealed. A similar distaste for the unnecessary extension of trade unionism other than by the voluntary wish of the workers directly involved, or their employer, led to the Employment Act 1982 (ss 12, 13) depriving employers of any legal right to require other employers (or those seeking to tender for contracts) to recognize, consult or negotiate with trade unions, or to employ union labour only. In the interest of strict equality, the latter rule applies also to attempts to extend non-unionization.

The concern for protecting individual freedom against union and/or employer coercion into membership led in the 1980 and 1982 Acts to an extension of the protection for non-union members against dismissal or victimization, and the extension of the circumstances where non-members could claim unfair dismissal or victimization in the closed shop.

By 1988 the government felt confident enough, despite evidence of some employer support for such agreements (and despite the fact that a majority of ballots held did meet the high level of support required for legal recognition of the closed shop), to dispense with the remaining legal support for the closed shop. The Employment Act 1988 (s 10) made unlawful industrial action to enforce union membership practices and repealed (s 11) the remaining legal support for dismissal or victimization for non-union membership in the limited circumstances where closed shop agreements had applied. (The joinder provisions remain applicable to all dismissals or victimization for non-union membership reasons.) The 1990 Act made it unlawful to refuse employment to persons because they are not members of a union (or because they are).

The 1982 Act recognized the ineffectiveness of current compensation levels in achieving re-employment offers from employers, by dramatically increasing the compensation available for unfair dismissals for reasons of non-union membership (and by extending the interim relief procedure to claims of dismissal for non-union membership). A new minimum basic award was to apply, currently £2700 (compare the earlier repeal of the two-week minimum payment for claimants generally.) Further, where the unfairly dismissed employee asked for re-employment, a payment of 104 weeks' pay was to apply (£13,400 minimum) if the tribunal did not order it, and 156 weeks' pay (minimum £20,100) if it did, but the employer refused to take the employee back (unless the employer proved it was not practicable to do so). Again in the interests of equality these provisions applied to protect union members where they were dismissed by reason of becoming or remaining union members or because of their union activities (at an appropriate time).

European requirements led to extended consultation rights for workers and trade unions in the limited cases (outside share purchase takeovers) where the new Transfer of Undertakings (Protection of Employment) Regulations 1981 applied. Further encouragement of consultation was approved by the government in imposing a requirement in the 1982 Act for annual reports of companies with more than 250 employees to state what action had been taken with regard to informing, consulting with or involving employees in company issues. A similar desire to encourage employee identification with the company led in the Finance Acts to new tax benefits for share purchase and profit-related pay schemes. On the other hand, the lower time limit required for consulting with trade unions about intended redundancies (60 days where 10–99 workers) had been halved to 30 days in 1979. In 1986, when most of the 'labour shake-out' in traditional manufacturing industry had taken place, the government ended the entitlement of employers to a rebate (then 35 per cent) on their statutory redundancy payments, with the exception of employers with less than ten employees.

INDUSTRIAL ACTION

The restoration after 1974 of the traditional immunities for trade unions and for industrial action did not create any stable political consensus on the issue. In particular, the major national disputes in the 'winter of discontent' around Labour government incomes restraint gave the Conservatives a popular electoral platform on which to condemn a system which offered such opportunities for disruption of business and public life, although the public were perhaps less concerned with the subtle nuances of the immunities system than with the fact of social disruption as such.

Conservative and employer complaints about the legal framework focused especially on two aspects of this disruption. The first was the extent to which trade unions were involving other employers and workers (through picketing and sympathy or secondary action) to add to pressure on the employer in dispute. This was seen to be harming other businesses and members of the public who were not immediately concerned with the issues in the dispute nor necessarily in a position to influence their outcome. Second, there was concern that trade unions were exercising the power they held over members, through closed shop agreements in particular, to rally support for action from unwilling members who would not have wished to be involved.

The post-1979 reforms have therefore attempted to single out these practices for reform, by making secondary action and picketing unlawful and by providing a requirement that trade unions adopt secret ballots in order to show they have the backing to authorize or endorse (lawful) industrial action. The effectiveness of these measures in terms of their impact on practice is discussed elsewhere in this book, but their significance in terms of an attack on the traditional legal framework, alongside the other measures outlined below, is profound.

Trade dispute

The 'golden formula' underlying immunity from tort actions in industrial disputes covered acts taken 'in contemplation or furtherance of a trade dispute'. This formula still applies to protect those actions by individuals or trade unions which are not otherwise declared outside its scope by the reforms of secondary action, action without ballots etc. In line with the government's intent to narrow the extent of the immunities system, the scope of this formula has also been narrowed by s 18 of the 1982 Act. It now covers only a dispute 'between workers and their employer' over industrial matters (rather than disputes between workers and workers or workers and employers generally, or a trade union and an employer independent of employee support). Also, the dispute must be 'wholly or mainly related to' one or more of the industrial relations issues listed in the Trade Union and Labour Relations Act (TULRA) 1974, s 29, rather than, as in the older formula, be merely 'connected with' them. The significance of this change was demonstrated in the *Mercury* case, where the refusal of telecommunications workers to link up a new telecommunications competitor to the telephone network, as part of a campaign against privatization and fear of loss of jobs, was suggested not to be wholly or mainly related to the loss of jobs, but primarily political in intent and therefore outside the protection. The new rules also limit the occasions when a trade dispute can exist in relation to matters outside the UK. This will only apply if the persons involved in this country are 'likely to be affected' with respect to their terms and conditions or other industrial relations matters listed in the 1974 Act, s 29.

Secondary action

This was first declared (s 17 of the 1980 Act) outside the bounds of immunity protection except in certain detailed circumstances. By 1990, the government felt able to remove legal protection from all secondary action. 'Sympathy' action, ie action taken to express support for fellow workers or union members (eg to show solidarity with a pay claim by the nurses), is of course secondary and therefore unlawful.

Secondary picketing

Section 16 of the 1980 Act redefined s 15 of the 1974 Act to restrict lawful picketing to a person attending at or near his own place of work. 'Place of work' is generally seen as implying a restriction to one's normal working premises, ie it would not extend to other plants or sites of one's employer even where there is a common dispute across sites, let alone to another employer's premises (whether or not any of the tests of lawful secondary action would apply to action taken by workers on that site). There are exceptions: for mobile workers or workers who find it impracticable to picket their place of work (who can picket any premises from which they work or from which their work is administered); for union officials who are accompanying members whom they represent; and for employees dismissed in connection with a trade dispute (who may picket their former place of work).

Although the section does not deal directly with the problem of 'mass picketing', guidelines in a Code of Practice issued by the Secretary of State for Employment suggest that six pickets at any one entrance is a reasonable number, a figure stressed in some of the cases arising from the miners' dispute and in subsequent disputes.

Ballots

The introduction of a requirement to hold secret ballots in connection with official industrial action, in s 10 of the Trade Union Act 1984 (as amended by the Employment Act 1988), marked a significant stage in the government's growing confidence in the effectiveness of its legal reforms. The provision was intended to moderate calls for strikes or other industrial action by the requirements to show majority support among those to be involved (an intention also evident in the requirement that the ballot paper mention without qualification that the action may be in breach of the contract of employment). Failure to hold a properly conducted ballot leads to a loss of immunity where the union authorizes or endorses the action, or fails effectively to 'repudiate' action by its members. The detailed requirements of the Act ensure that this is a likely source of much litigation on technical grounds, although most employers are likely to be more concerned with the substantive question and result.

In addition to the possibility of employers or their suppliers or customers pursuing actions in tort, the 1988 Act (s 1) provided a statutory right for individual members (who are likely to be induced to take part) to go to court for an order preventing union support of industrial action where a valid ballot was not held. The Act also added to the legal technicalities surrounding industrial action ballots by imposing a requirement of separate workplace ballots, except where the workers across the sites have a distinct occupational factor or factors in common. (This provision is intended, according to government claims, to prevent manipulation of ballot results by use of artificial constituencies, but may also be a 'step' towards a more general requirement in future legislation.) The 1990 Act added further detailed requirements.

There is growing evidence that ballots are becoming an accepted part of union practice in industrial disputes, although their moderating influence is less evident than their use as part of the standard negotiating tactics in a dispute.[5] The majority of ballots on industrial action result in support for the action, although in many cases this is merely a signal to employers to re-open negotiations on their last offer.

Trade union liability

One of the most important reforms in the law for the success of legislative efforts to restructure the balance of power in industrial disputes, was to restore trade union liability for tortious acts (ie civil wrongs such as inducing a breach of contract etc). Section 14 of TULRA, going back to the reforms of the 1906 Act, had given trade unions as organizations blanket immunity from actions in tort (with some exceptions outside the field of industrial relations). The immunity given by the traditional 'in contemplation or furtherance' formula mainly applied, therefore, on behalf of individual union officials who were alleged to be acting unlawfully. Trade unions, as such, were protected from most tort actions. Section 15 of the Employment Act 1982 removed this general immunity to make trade unions open to legal actions where they acted outside the new restricted range of immunities. By this means, litigants and the courts were able to avoid 'martyring' individual officials (although this route is still the only option in the event of unofficial action, which is repudiated by the union). Orders of the court (injunctions) and actions in damages could be awarded against the union and its funds, although the Act specified limits on the amount of damages claimed, according to the membership size of the union. This change in the law was particularly important in undermining the unions' campaign of opposition to the new laws, as unions which disobeyed court orders found themselves liable to penalties for contempt of court which exceeded the limits on damages laid down in the Act. In the case of repeated disobedience, not only could the fines multiply but sequestration of union assets (receivership in the case of the miners' union) followed in a number of cases, facing unions with a choice of compliance or of eventual major losses of members' funds, if not bankruptcy.

Experience of such clashes led the government, in the Employment Act 1988, to introduce new statutory rights for union members to go to the courts where union funds are being used to indemnify individuals for criminal offences or contempt of court (s 8), or where trustees are permitting or carrying out unlawful application of union funds.

Industrial action and trade union recognition

Another area where immunity was lost relates to attempts to influence the union practices of subcontractors or other employers. In keeping with its other measures to prevent the practice of 'secondary unionization', by employers requiring other employers to employ union labour only (or non-union labour), or to recognize, negotiate or consult with unions, immunity was withdrawn from industrial action with these purposes. Section 10 of the Employment Act 1988 went even further, withdrawing immunity from industrial action intended to enforce a closed shop with one's own employer.

Dismissals/strike benefit

Finally, two other reforms confirmed the government's readiness to add to the pressure on workers to avoid industrial action. First, s 9 of the 1982 Act amended the rules relating to dismissals taking place during industrial action. The previous rules in the 1978 Act (s 62) had given the tribunals jurisdiction to hear claims of unfair dismissal only in cases where there were selective dismissals or selective re-engagement offers among any employees taking part in the action. A leading case on this section had decided that the measure of selection applied in respect of all workers who had taken part in the action, even where a number had returned to work (*Stock* v *Frank Jones (Tipton) Ltd*). The amendments ensured that:

- the criterion of selection only applied at the date of the dismissal and did not include those who might have participated earlier but had since returned to work;
- the test was only applicable at one establishment and did not require an 'all or none' approach across all sites affected;
- there was a limited time period (three months from the dismissals) during which the 're-engagement offer' discrimination test applied.

The 1990 Act removed protection for dismissal from those taking part in 'unofficial' action. A second change in the law sought to reduce the state 'support' for industrial action, by reducing social security benefits to strikers' dependents by an amount representing a 'deemed' union payment to the striker. (The individual taking part in industrial action was already ineligible for such benefit.)

TRADE UNION ORGANIZATION AND ACTIVITIES

Much of the legislation on trade unions since 1979 has reflected a government belief (supported by opinion polls of union members) that union actions did not reflect a true level of support by members for many of the activities in which trade unions and trade union leaders engage. This accompanied concern at the pressure individual members may face to participate in industrial action, or the pressures exerted on non-unionists to join the union.

The legislation in this area has therefore broadly sought to emphasize the 'voluntary' aspect of trade unions as organizations, to give individuals rights to opt out of membership and other activities, or to express without interference or pressure their views on key affairs of the union. This programme was phrased both in terms of the rights of the individual over the organization and in terms of the need to support the workings of democracy in union affairs – the need to 'hand the unions back to their members'.

A somewhat different approach was taken to union recognition by employers, repealing an earlier measure which gave trade unions a right (normally following an inquiry and ballot of workers by ACAS) to require an employer to recognize their authority to negotiate on behalf of employees. (And in the celebrated case of GCHQ, the government as employer withdrew established union membership and recognition rights on the grounds of threat to national security.)

Trade union recognition

The attempt to establish a legal procedure (ss 11–16 of the Employment Protection Act 1975), whereby trade unions could seek recognition from an employer on the basis of a degree of employee support was repealed by the Employment Act 1980. The repeal was justified on the grounds that none of the parties, including ACAS which was responsible for the first stage of investigation and recommendation, had found the previous procedure satisfactory. A number of employers had disliked the outside intervention and challenged details of the procedure in the courts, initially with considerable success; trade unions had found it slow and often ineffective, and raising awkward issues of inter-union rivalries; ACAS had been unhappy at the effect on its conciliation work of its involvement in a quasi-compulsory capacity. Whatever the merits of such arguments they were in tune with the inclinations of the incoming government to repeal rather than seek to amend or improve the statutory provision.

In retrospect, with the cutbacks in traditional areas of union membership to follow, and the trends to non-unionism and withdrawal of union recognition in some sectors, it seems likely that many in the trade unions must now doubt the wisdom of their stance. More broadly, future policy-makers are left with the question of the inequity of legislative policies advancing the argument of 'extending democracy' in union affairs, while effectively abolishing one of its significant manifestations (the right for employees to decide who should speak for them) as between employees and their employer.

Secondary recognition and unionization

The traditional practice of trade unions exerting pressure on their own employer to ensure that other employers with whom he contracts use union labour or recognize, negotiate or consult with trade unions has been another object of the government's attention. Section 14 of the 1982 Act removed any immunity from industrial action taken against employers with these purposes. Immunity is, therefore, not saved in this particular instance merely because a worker is in dispute with his or her own employer, nor is it relevant that the other workers may be working on the same site, or haulage contractors may be entering or leaving the site. Thus, it is more appropriate to dub this restriction as one of 'secondary unionization' rather than one of secondary action. (The section also prohibits secondary 'non-unionization', although this was inserted more on the grounds of equality of treatment rather than on any widespread campaign by employees or employers to compel others to be non-unionists.)

The restrictions on secondary unionization (and non-unionization) were also extended to common employer practices with the same purposes. Sections 12–13 of the Act made it a breach of statutory duty for one employer to terminate a contract or discriminate against others in seeking or awarding tenders etc, where these practices are one of the reasons for so doing. Finally, this same philosophy is applied to contractual provisions. The Act makes void any term in a contract with the same effects.

Union membership and union membership agreements

A final element in the government's restrictions on means to extend union membership were its various amendments to the legislation on dismissal or victimization of non-union members. From its entry into office in 1979, the Conservative Government never concealed its dislike for the closed shop or 'union membership agreement' (UMA) as the law terms it. Nevertheless, it sufficiently recognized its extent, its support among many employers (on the grounds of orderly collective bargaining), and the fact that it could be continued informally even when formally repealed, not to seek its outright abolition initially. It used other legal tactics in the 1980 and 1982 Acts to restrict its scope to a point where its effective legal validity was more tenuous. In addition, other factors such as the decline of employment in traditional strongholds of unionism and the difficulties raised by the law for employers contemplating new UMAs have contributed to a decline in its extent.[6] Thus, the possibility of ending legal support for the closed shop was realized in the Employment Act 1988, in the sense of making industrial action to enforce a closed shop unlawful and repealing the earlier provisions which made it fair to dismiss (or take action short of dismissal against) a non-union member where there was a valid UMA. The 1990 Act created similar protection for job applicants.

Further measures to discourage trade unions and employers from enforcing union membership are found in other remedies made available to the tribunals. First, applicants and/or employers may 'join' trade unions (ie sue them as well as the employer in the tribunal action) and others as respondents where they claim the employer was induced to dismiss (or take action short of dismissal) by reason of industrial action or threats to that effect. If the tribunal finds the dismissal unfair they may make any compensation, or any part of it, payable by the joined party. Secondly, a special system of remedies has been created for dismissals for non-union membership. This system of relief has been in part inspired by, and extended to dismissals on union grounds also (membership or union activities at an appropriate time), although the compensation elements were largely in response to non-unionist dismissals. The dismissed employee may claim interim relief (formerly only available to trade union members who produced a certificate from a union official saying he had reason to believe the dismissal was because of union grounds). This allows an early award of re-employment or continuation of contract with the employer. Also, compensation levels have been increased considerably to add to the pressure on respondents to re-employ, or not to dismiss in the first place.

Individual rights against the union

A series of measures other than those already outlined were introduced to protect union members (and in some instances non-members) from union actions, and to allow individual members to control or monitor union affairs. Most of these were introduced by the Employment Act 1988. One of the most significant innovations in the Act was the creation of a Commissioner for the

Rights of Trade Union Members, who may provide assistance (by way of legal advice or representation or paying legal costs) to union members who are considering legal action against their union in relation to a number of the statutory rights.

Section 1 of the Acts gives to union members, who are likely to be induced to take part in industrial action, a right to take their union to court where action has been authorized or endorsed without a valid secret ballot (see below). Section 3 of the Act, at the same time, prevents unions from disciplining individuals who fail to take part or support industrial action or who indicate opposition to it, whether or not a ballot has been held. The section also protects individuals from being so 'unjustifiably disciplined' where the discipline is taken because of a member making assertions that the union or its officers are acting unlawfully or in breach of union rules, or because of a member consulting the Certification Officer or the new Commissioner for the Rights of Trade Union Members. Complaints of unjustifiable discipline can be taken to the industrial tribunals, with a separate later claim necessary (to a tribunal or the Employment Appeal Tribunal, depending on whether or not the union has responded to a tribunal declaration) where compensation is sought.

Other rights provided by the 1988 Act include: a right to pursue a grievance against a union through the courts after six months of internal procedures have elapsed (whatever union rules or court practices there may be to the contrary) (s 2); a right to inspect a union's accounting records and be accompanied by an accountant for this purpose (s 6); a right to prevent deduction of union subscriptions by the employer as soon as the employee notifies the employer of his resignation (s 7); a right to prevent union funds being used to indemnify individuals in respect of criminal offences or for contempt of court, and to prevent union trustees applying union property for unlawful purposes (ss 8, 9).

Secret ballots

State funding The government made a cautious attempt to encourage wider use of secret ballots in trade unions in 1980 (s 1 of the Act and the regulations made thereunder) by offering a refund from public funds for a range of important ballots, if those ballots were postal ballots and the trade unions applied for reimbursement for basic postal costs from the Certification Officer. (Section 2 of the Act also provided a legal right to request the use of an employer's premises for similar ballots.) The scheme was boycotted initially by the TUC and its affiliates, but this eventually broke down after pressure from some of its members who used postal ballots extensively and because of the increasing range of areas of union activity in which a legal requirement to ballot was becoming necessary. The scheme covers ballots on industrial action, employer offers, union amalgamations or rule changes, national officer or national executive elections, political fund ballots.

Industrial action This requirement, introduced in Part II of the 1984 Act (as amended by the 1988 Act), has also been described above. Like the other ballot requirements of the 1984 Act, this was a more direct intervention in union affairs and one which has had a lasting impact. The Act specified in detail the conditions which had to be satisfied for the ballot to attract immunity (assuming the intended action was otherwise lawful):

- allowing voters to vote in secret and without interference;
- balloting only those whom it was reasonable to believe would be called on to take action and no others;
- holding a ballot no more than four weeks before the industrial action and giving support only after the ballot and within four weeks of it;
- asking separate questions for a strike or other industrial action (and specifying that these may be in breach of the contract of employment);
- informing constituents as soon as reasonably practicable of the detailed results.

Trade unions could use either a postal ballot or a workplace or semi-postal ballot, not aggregating the votes from separate workplaces, unless there was a genuine occupation factor (or factors) common to those voting.

Principal executive committee elections   Part I of the 1984 Act required that voting members of union principal executive committees be elected at least every five years by secret ballot (postal, workplace or semi-postal) of members or defined constituencies of members. Detailed conditions were again laid down (including maintaining a register of members' names and addresses) and members could complain of non-compliance to the Certification Officer or the High Court. The latter could issue an enforcement order against the union, specifying steps to be taken to remedy the non-compliance.

A number of reforms to these provisions were enacted in the Employment Act 1988, reflecting government concern at the slow pace of reform in union rules, the lack of cases being taken by members to the High Court, continuing controversies over the reliability of some election results, and the fact that major union influence could be exerted by certain national officials who nevertheless had no vote on their union's executive committee. The 1988 Act therefore extended the balloting requirement (with effect from mid-1989) to all members of a principal executive committee (including those attending other than in a purely informatory or advisory capacity) and to the positions of union president and general secretary (s 12). Election candidates were given the right to prepare an election address and have it distributed with ballot papers (s 13). Ballots were to be postal ballots only and to be supervised by a qualified independent scrutineer (ss 14, 15). The Act also gives the secretary of state power to issue Codes of Practice on election procedures (and on political and industrial action ballots) (s 18), and of course the new Commissioner for the Rights of Trade Union Members will be able to support any individual claims to the High Court over the conduct of election ballots.

Political fund ballots   Secret ballots to establish a fund to be used for political purposes (support for political parties and political candidates) had been established by the Trade Union Act 1913. In Part III of the 1984 Act, the government extended this legislation. In future, authorization for the use of political funds was required to be subject to ballots at least every ten years. The trade unions who had established such funds many years earlier were given one year from the Act's commencement date to hold such a review ballot. Members could complain to the High Court if a union continued to collect contributions after a resolution to have a political fund ceased to have effect. Also, stricter rules were laid down with regard to the management of the funds and the occasions when proposed expenditure required the establishment of a political fund. The round of ballots which followed the Act delivered something of a rebuff to the government, every union (including some without such a fund previously) receiving a majority vote in favour of holding such a fund (see Chapter 16).

CONCLUSION

Working to legal rules: a revolution in industrial relations?

It is difficult to evaluate the labour law of the 1970s or 1980s without acknowledging the importance of politics and political beliefs. Both decades have demonstrated in different ways the remarkable extent to which political beliefs, underpinned (more or less systematically) by theories of economics and industrial relations, can inform the legal rules which adjust power balances in industrial relations.[7] More open to question in the earlier period of the 1970s was the extent to which laws can act as a primary force to change social attitudes or to move resistant social forces such as employers or trade unions. Yet both the 1970s and 1980s show that legal rules can foster significant changes in the exercise of power in industrial relations.

The 1970s first established the legal notion that an employer ought to have a reason, and be able to demonstrate the reasonableness of its application in dismissing a worker; that he should have equal rates of pay for men and women doing similar work; that he should offer women workers the right to return to their work after maternity leave. One can argue about the exact impact of such developments, in particular whether they achieved all that was hoped for them (and in most cases they did not). However, they still constituted a revolution of a kind in past employer practice which recent Conservative Governments have both eroded and in some instances extended, certainly not reversed. However, they did reverse much of the 1974-9 (and earlier) gains of trade unions in extending legal support for collective bargaining – recognition claims, fair wages arbitrations, extended wages council powers.

The changes in the law during the 1980s also constituted their own kind of revolution, this time setting new boundaries on the flexibility of conduct by trade unions. The latter revolution, however, is perhaps of more significance not only in having a longer period to consolidate the legal rules as the new 'Queensberry Rules' of industrial relations, but also because there had been greater doubts as to whether the trade unions, by their nature as collective organizations or by tradition, could as easily be made to conform as employers to legislative norms in the areas of industrial action or internal affairs. That they have to a great extent done so, testifies as much to the changing nature of trade unions and their members as to the skilled crafting of the law.

Of course there are other social factors, such as unemployment, which assisted the legislation in making the impact it did, particularly the failure of the unions to mount the campaign of opposition to the post-1979 legislation which they mounted against the Industrial Relations Act 1971. Until there is a revival of conditions of full employment (and there are some who would argue that this is beyond the capacity of the modern economy), it is difficult to assess the long-term hold of the new legal framework without knowing the exact weight of the different contributory factors.

Nevertheless, the later period suggests one should not underestimate the power of the forces of law, nor the changing attitudes of union members to law and to union practices. Law can be a primary as well as a secondary force in altering human conduct. In the changed climate of the late 1980s, it is easy to forget the difficulties the government faced after the experiences of 1978–9 and the campaign of resistance to the 1971 Act, in wondering whether it had the capacity to overcome union resistance in well-rooted areas such as the closed shop, secondary action and picketing, union internal procedures.

Nor should one underestimate what can be done *tactically* in the way legal change is approached and legal rules framed – one of the main lessons the Conservatives had gleaned from the Industrial Relations Act experience. The legislation since 1979 has been remarkable in the care given to its phasing (step-by-step) and to the drafting of the rules and procedures necessary to achieve its objects, down to the detail of specifying that a ballot paper on industrial action should inform the worker that industrial action may be in breach of contract. Even those parts of the legislation which were condemned by the courts as so obscure as to leave the players baffled as to the rules of the game (such as the initial provisions dealing with secondary action), were rationalized by government spokespersons – why worry about the rules of the game appearing complex when one would prefer the sport (of industrial action) to stop? (It is a moot point whether the same philosophy lies behind the complexities of the regulations dealing with workers' rights on transfer of undertakings, or equal pay for work of equal value.)

The return of industrial action and picketing into the arms of the common law, combined with trade union liability for official industrial action, was a particularly significant move in the step-by-step approach to reform, relying on those employers who were more able and/or more willing to take on the power of the unions to establish the effectiveness of the reforms, supported by the financial penalties exacted by the courts for contempt of court where injunctions were resisted. The legal actions by some union members in the miners' strike on the basis of common law principles (the contract between the union member and his union/fellow members) were also significant in contributing to a more legalistic culture and to the political objectives underlying the legal rules, and in turn provided experience for some of the detailed statutory regulation of union internal affairs provided by the Employment Act 1988.

Similarly, the government tackled the statutory reform of internal union affairs on the basis largely of areas of union activity – leadership elections, strike ballots, the political fund, the closed shop – where the political groundwork had already been laid to make it difficult for trade unions to make a popular political case even among their own members.

The assumption in the voluntarist tradition that a major social group was best left to set its own rules proved too simplistic in the face of wider political undercurrents of 'public interest' in debates on 'democracy', 'individual freedom' and 'industrial disruption'. The traditions (sceptics called them 'privileges') of trade unionism proved no more popular in this wider domain than those of the legal profession (although the latter's version of self-government mechanisms has perhaps been more delicately handled by the government). Hence the attack on the closed shop on the basis of individual freedom, despite evidence of support among many employers for its operation; hence the use of the term 'democracy', a concept itself so much part of union tradition, to win support for a formalized, uniform system of balloting procedures among trade unions which had had a variety of traditional methods of interpreting accountability to members.

The political impact of the legislative goals and reforms revealed the complacency of tradition in the unions rather than its values. The fact that the extent of change in union practices in these areas is still more patchy in reality than the legal rules might lead one to expect, should not detract from a recognition of the extent and direction of the changes towards a legal rule-bound industrial relations culture which were set in process.

INDUSTRIAL RELATIONS LAW: AGENDA FOR THE 1990s?

By the early 1990s many commentators observed that the strategy to redistribute power from trade unions to employers, in terms of legal reforms, had run out of steam. In 1991, the year before another general election, it was true that the Conservative Government was issuing yet another consultation paper in line with its 'step-by-step' or 'abuse-by-abuse' approach seeking further controls on union activity. However, there was a sense that this was a case of scratching around for new initiatives rather than an urgent priority for parliamentary or employer action, a sense that was itself a testimony of the success of the 1980s in establishing a climate and legal framework for control of the so-called 'abuses' of the 1970s.

Trade union regulation was sufficiently advanced and legislation on employee rights sufficiently restrained and stable, to free the way for employers to concentrate single-mindedly on pursuing economic success – albeit that by 1991 this economic goal was proving very elusive.

There were only two clear threats on the horizon to the continuation or even extension of the industrial relations law strategy of the 1980s. The first was a change in the political complexion of the government (or of a devolved Scottish government), which might restore a sense of a new social agenda for legal action in the workplace/market place. Secondly, there was the 'incoming tide' of European law which had, throughout the 1980s, provided one of the key countervailing forces to the UK government's emphasis on deregulation of labour/social conditions – 'the only card game in town' as one union leader observed at a TUC conference in the 1980s. The contradictory trend of Europeanization of UK law reached a highpoint in a showdown at the 1991 Maastricht Summit of EC leaders meeting to agree the terms of a new Treaty of European Union. UK government resistance to the relatively minimal social regulations envisaged in the proposed Social Chapter of the Treaty, ensured that the Chapter was eventually dropped. However, it was retained in the form of a separate Protocol which 11 of the 12 members of the EC signed, thus establishing a perhaps irresistible magnet for reform of employment law in the UK at some point during the 1990s.

The European dimension alone thus ensures that there will be a continuing pressure to establish minimum social standards from which employment relations can negotiate upwards.

The European dimension to UK practice also leaves open the scope for comparative claims on issues of employee consultation and industrial democracy structures, whether expressed in terms of legal rights to union recognition, works councils or supervisory boards of directors including employee representatives. A complementary pressure towards such practices may also arise from shareholder interest groups with exposure of management 'abuses' in the financial euphoria of the late 1980s – illicit share dealings, pension fund manipulation, 'excessive' pay increases or share option deals and other practices of the 'corporate barons' of the 1980s who substituted for the 'union barons' of the 1970s.

The Conservative Government which took over UK industrial relations reform for the decade of the 1980s had hit an appropriate public interest chord in recognizing the need for 'balance' and appropriate mechanisms to regulate such balance in the exercise of social power within a democratic industrial society. However, the meaning of 'balance' and its expression in the rules and procedures of law will undoubtedly continue to fuel a keen debate in the field of employment law during the 1990s.

Leaving aside questions of European pressures to achieve minimum employment standards (and thus a 'level playing field' for employers across the European Union), there will be a number of arenas for continuing debate – recognition of union or employee claims to influence the management of enterprises; the legal protection (or lack of it) afforded to temporary and part-time workers; the claims to equity in resources provided for pay in major areas of the public sector (and thus the role of pay review bodies and other third-party mechanisms to redress imbalances in the market place); means of access to job security, retraining and further education in a society subject to rapid transformations of technology, business ownership and business strategies; protection for pension fund ownership and rights; continuing attempts to outlaw sex and racial discrimination practices; question marks around the effectiveness of the current industrial tribunal system to deal with employment grievances outside of its primary work on assessing compensation for unfair dismissals. A listing of such areas of concern indicates that while industrial relations law debates may have run out of steam for the time being, debates on employment law practices are likely to be highly vulnerable to a shifting balance of political legal power in the 1990s.

References

1. Mackie, K J (1979–80) 'The changing role of law in British industrial relations', *Industrial Relations Journal*, **10**: 4, Winter, pp 57–65.
2. Weekes, B, Mellish, M, Dickens, L and Lloyd, J (1975) *Industrial Relations and the Limits of the Law: the Industrial Effects of the Industrial Relations Act 1971*, Blackwell, Oxford.
3. For a sense of the different emphases, see Lewis, R (ed) (1986) *Labour Law in Britain*, Blackwell, Oxford, Chapter 1; and Wedderburn, Lord (1986) *The Worker and the Law*, 3rd edn, Penguin, London, Chapter 1.

4. For a recent survey of the operation of industrial tribunals, see Dickens, L, Jones, M, Weekes, B and Hart, M (1985) *Dismissed: A Study of Unfair Dismissal and the Industrial Tribunal System*, Blackwell, Oxford.
5. See *Annual Report 1986*, March 1987, ACAS.
6. Millward, N and Stevens, M (1986) *British Workplace Industrial Relations 1980–1984*, Gower, Aldershot.
7. See Wedderburn, op cit.
8. Undy, R and Martin, R (1984) *Ballots and Trade Union Democracy*, Blackwell, Oxford.

Chapter Sixteen
Ballots, Picketing and Strikes

Derek Fatchett MP

For most students of industrial relations, conflict is seen as a central motivating characteristic of the system. Mostly that conflict will be latent rather than manifest, subject to control through joint procedures and regulation. The ability to influence the outcome of these regulatory processes will depend upon the power of the parties, and the extent to which they can mobilize that power. The pursuit of outcomes, however, through the exercise of power, has itself been subject to further regulation by the State: an intervention which can be interpreted in contrasting ways, either as the State as the benign, impartial umpire on the one hand, or as the supporter of one side in the conflict, on the other.

This chapter will be mainly concerned with aspects of open, often dramatic, conflict; but it will, in relation to the question of ballots and picketing, analyse a context in which, especially under the Conservative Government first elected in 1979, the State has sought to influence the means by which, and the extent to which, trade unions are able to mobilize support. In particular, the last decade has seen continuing government intervention designed to restrict the freedom of action of trade unions.

BALLOTS

Ballots have always formed an important aspect of trade unionism. Their use has been widespread and varied: at branch level, for the election of branch officers; at the workplace, to offer support or guidance to wage negotiators, or to demand or sanction industrial action; at all levels, to elect members of a union's national executive committee, or, in certain cases, to elect the union's full-time officials.

As the subject of balloting can be extensive, so can the means by which the ballots have been conducted; from a show of hands at a branch meeting, or at a packed factory gates meeting, to the more formal provision of a postal ballot.

Despite the trade unions' considerable formal commitment to the use of ballots, there can be little doubt, from the mid-1960s onwards, with a gathering pace in the 1970s, that questions of internal union democracy assumed a greater salience in the broader political context. The reasons for this were mainly twofold: first, there was often articulated a feeling that trade union leaders, be they elected or appointed, were out of touch with their members, thereby forcing the rank and file members into a more militant stance than they would otherwise have adopted; and, secondly, there was detailed criticism of particular approaches to balloting, either because it was felt that the expression of choice was circumscribed by pressure or intimidation, or because it was asserted that particular approaches would enhance turnout rates, with a consequent greater degree of democracy and reliability in the result. The factory gate meeting was seen by many critics as the least representative of views, and the one most likely to be influenced by intimidation.

It is certainly open to a good deal of debate as to whether these particular arguments could be supported by strong factual material. That, however, became almost irrelevant, as facts often do: perceptions and political pressures moved inexorably in the direction which demanded a greater scope for a more formalized balloting system.

Changes in the requirements for balloting

The most significant changes were introduced by the Trade Union Act 1984 and the Employment Act 1988, which set out the requirements for balloting in relation to the election of members of a union's principal executive committee, to the conduct of industrial disputes and to the endorsement of a union's political role through the continuation of its political fund.

It was the political fund change which initially attracted so much controversy, as, with the available evidence showing the sharp loss of support by the Labour Party in the 1983 election, it appeared more than possible that the vast majority of unions would vote to discontinue their political funds and, hence, to sever their links with the Labour Party. The conditions imposed by the Trade Union Act made it difficult, if not impossible, for a union to bypass the balloting requirements: any member would be able to take action to declare the collection of political funds ultra vires, if an affirmative ballot had not taken place within the previous ten years. As the 37 political fund-holding unions had not held a ballot within the specified time-scale, all were caught within the net imposed by the 1984 Act.

Although the 1984 Act did not set out a specific form for the ballots to follow, along with the provisions of the Trade Union Act 1913, it did provide the certification officer with sufficiently firm guidance to ensure that a definable pattern emerged; in broad terms, voting at geographical branch meetings was excluded, while workplace and individual postal balloting were regarded with considerably greater favour. The Employment Act 1988 now excludes the possibility of a workplace ballot: s 14 states that ballots held for deciding on political funds must be postal. Perhaps this development can best be construed as largely ideological, as evidence, referred to later in this chapter, seems to support a greater potential for participation in workplace, rather than postal, ballots.

In many respects, the change involving internal union elections introduced by the 1984 Act was more significant in terms of relationships between unions and the State than the provision concerning the political funds. Since the *Osborne* case,[1] and the consequent 1913 Act, the State had set down ground rules against which unions must conduct their political role. No such ground rules had previously existed as far as internal union elections were concerned; a union could organize itself to satisfy its own formal requirements and those of its members. Indeed, the process of election to union executive committees varied substantially: some unions operated systems of indirect election whereby,

324 A Handbook of Industrial Relations Practice

following election to a subordinate committee, members of that committee elected their representative on to the union's executive body: others, very much a minority, conducted their election on the basis of individual postal ballots. The differences reflected a variety of factors: the skilled–unskilled origin of the union, its current spread of membership, and the way in which the union's current structure had emerged as a result of merger and takeover.

The historical splendour of that diversity was immediately put at risk by the 1984 Act: balloting would now have to conform to a pattern which allowed direct elections, and equality of access for each individual member. Unions would be forced into change, or face the risk of every election being declared invalid. The Employment Act 1988 takes the process of State prescription a stage further, by, in s 14, insisting that the election for members of a trade union governing body, including non-voting members, should be held on a postal ballot.

Balloting and industrial action

The 1984 Act also confronted a third area of balloting, relating to industrial action. The rationale for change in this context could not have been made more explicit: no longer, it was argued, was it acceptable for a union to call out its members for industrial action without a ballot, which was secret, and conducted without intimidation. The workplace mass meeting was no longer acceptable, and the penalty for not conforming to the Act's requirements was substantial. Although the Employment Acts 1980 and 1982 had severely curtailed the scope of the immunities previously enjoyed by the unions, the 1984 Act made these immunities conditional upon holding a ballot on the question of industrial action.

The unions defended their existing practices, especially against those accusations which suggested that union leaders or rank-and-file activists simply forced their members into industrial action. It was pointed out, for instance, as we shall see later in this chapter, that many strikes assume the character of spontaneous reactions to managerial decisions, thereby making more formal processes of balloting less appropriate. In addition, the argument was made that it is extremely difficult, if not impossible, to maintain or to spread a dispute without the consent of those involved. Three separate provisions included in the Employment Act 1988 will further restrict the ability to strengthen or to spread a strike. Section 1, for instance, gives a right to a union member to obtain a court order to require his union to withdraw authorization of a strike given without the backing of a properly conducted ballot, while s 3 gives a right to continue working during a strike without fear of union discipline. Furthermore, in the context of a closed shop, even one approved by the requisite ballot, dismissal on the grounds of non-union membership is deemed unfair.

In this context, as in others, the 1988 Act is typical of the approach adopted by the Conservative Government. The emphasis was on a step-by-step approach, with every new piece of legislation built upon the secure foundations of the previous legislation and extending the legal controls upon trade union action. Although experience under the 1984 and 1988 Acts is inevitably somewhat limited, certain conclusions can be drawn. First, there can be little doubt that the legislation has changed trade union practice and thinking. Unions have been forced, often with a great deal of disquiet, to change the way in which they conduct ballots. In addition, and maybe more importantly, unions have started to accept that ballots will continue to form a part of this behaviour. This was first clearly seen during the debate at the 1986 TUC Congress when the joint Labour party/TUC document, *People at Work: New Rights, New Responsibilities*,[2] was discussed.

The TUC general secretary, Norman Willis, explained the provision in the document which granted to individual union members a right to have a secret ballot on decisions relating to strikes. 'Balloting is here to stay', he said, 'because our members favour it. We are committed to making the trade union movement even more representative and more democratic because that way we will be stronger and more effective.'[3] It is difficult to imagine quite the same form of words from a TUC general secretary a few years earlier.

Secondly, and somewhat ironically given the character of previous debates, the trade union's initial experience of ballots under the 1984 Act had been rather encouraging. On strike ballots, the 1985 Annual Report of the Advisory, Conciliation and Arbitration Service (ACAS) offered the following information:[4]

> At the end of the year the service had become aware of 94 cases in which ballots had been organized, involving no fewer than 37 trade unions. Of these 68 resulted in a majority vote for industrial action and 25 against, with one tie. In 38 of the cases where voting was in favour of action, stoppages or other industrial action took place and 23 resulted in no action. It is not clear whether all ballots had complied with the strict terms of the Act. In 15 cases we were aware that injunctions had been sought by employers in the courts, either because no ballot had taken place before industrial action began, or because they considered that ballots which had been held did not meet all the requirements of the Act.

From the ACAS figures, it is not unreasonable to conclude that industrial action ballots have not, in themselves, been particularly damaging to trade unions. In over 70 per cent of the cases, members had supported industrial action. Furthermore, it is worth noting that ballots had taken place in no more than 12 per cent of reported disputes: in 1985, there were 813 officially recorded stoppages, but only 94 ballots.

As McIllroy has argued, on the question of ballots about industrial action, unions were showing that they could not only live with the law, but they also had the capacity to turn it to their advantage. He points out that:[5]

> of the total of 246 ballots on industrial action held by the end of 1986, 189 went in favour of the union position, 54 against and 3 were tied. It was clear that ballots on industrial action, while still small-scale in relation to the overall picture, were becoming as ACAS put it, a permanent part of the negotiating scene. In 1987 a further 280 ballots were held. In 251, or 90 per cent, the ballot went in favour of the union's position.

The political fund ballots

If the experience of industrial action ballots has been far less damaging than feared by the trade unions, the results of political fund ballots exceeded the unions' wildest dreams. During the 12 months from April 1985 to March 1986, 37[6] balloted, and with, by the standard of union elections, a reasonably high turnout of 51 per cent, only 2 unions failed to achieve an affirmative level of support of less than 70 per cent of those voting. Indeed, in 21 out of the 37 unions, the vote in favour of maintaining a political fund exceeded 80 per cent.[7] These were quite remarkable results, especially against a background of early opinion poll evidence which suggested that the number of unions likely to record a 'yes' vote could be counted on one hand.

The experience of ballots on both industrial action and on the continuation of political funds suggests that the fear of ballots, so deep in the rhetoric of union debate, if not in practice, may have been misplaced. The notion that a silent moderate majority would automatically surface, thereby preventing the more radical and militant options, proved illusory and chimerical: when the union leadership, at whatever level, campaigned for their case, without taking the members' support for granted, the members, on the whole, seemed to respond.

Another aspect of interest emerged in relation to the political fund ballots. It had often been asserted that individual postal ballots would invariably guarantee a turnout higher than other methods of voting. The case for this has more often rested upon optimism and prejudice rather than hard facts. While an analysis of postal, as against geographical branch ballots, will mostly, but not always, come out in favour of the former, when compared against workplace ballots the evidence is considerably more mixed. This was certainly the case with the political fund ballots, where, as we have already seen, the requirements of the 1913 and 1984 Acts virtually ensured that union executives had little alternative but to opt for a postal or a workplace ballot, or a mixture of both. For comparison purposes, it is unfortunate that only four unions adopted a full postal ballot. This, however, did not prevent Leopold feeling able to conclude that 'those unions which conducted their ballot in the workplace had turnouts on average 30 per cent higher than those using postal ballots'.[8]

The evidence of the political fund ballots scarcely seemed to influence government thinking. The 1988 Act, and the Code of Practice on ballots published in the following year, loaded the dice in favour of postal ballots, on a compulsory basis for internal union elections, and on a strongly persuasive basis for industrial action ballots.

In many ways, the debate about ballots has often taken place on false ground, with the impression being given that the trade unions are, by nature, hostile to ballots. Several sustainable conclusions show that such assertions, while valuable debating points, may bear little relevance to the facts: unions have always extensively employed ballots; the main argument has been about the method of balloting, and not the principle itself. That argument has now moved on: the unions have found both in relation to industrial action and the political funds that they have been able to secure support. The demand now is, given that ballots have come to be regarded as an integral part of union decision-making, they must be so organized as to maximize participation. For the TUC, workplace ballots offer the most effective means of encouraging involvement. Willis reflected this viewpoint in his speech to the 1986 TUC congress: 'We want ballots with proper facilities, polling stations at the workplace, meetings in working time.'[9]

The government soon rejected the TUC proposals for greater facilities for workplace balloting; for the government the need was to extend the subject matter of balloting, and to introduce, in certain contexts, mandatory postal balloting.

As for subject matter, the government, both in its consultative document of February 1987,[10] and in its subsequent Employment Act 1988, have established two further areas in which balloting should take place. First, the Trade Union Act 1984 restricted the benefit of immunities to those strikes which had been endorsed by a ballot. As we have seen from the earlier quoted ACAS figures, unions have not felt that it was invariably necessary to conduct a strike ballot. Through s 1 of the Employment Act, the government sought to enforce ballots by imposing upon the union a duty to its members not to authorize industrial action without obtaining majority approval from those likely to take part. Through this method, it is anticipated that a ballot would become the inevitable practice. However, with the existence of many short strikes, it is unlikely that the hope will ever become the invariable rule.

Secondly, while the 1984 Act, as we have seen, provided for direct balloting for the election of the union's principal executive committee, the provision did not extend to non-voting members of the executive. The government came to see this as a loophole, perhaps largely because of the decision of the National Union of Mineworkers to deprive their president and general secretary of a vote on the union's executive. For this reason, it was argued that:[11]

> the sensible course seems now to be to extend the requirements to include all general secretaries, presidents and executive members whether elected or appointed. In this way the members themselves would be given a direct say in the appointment of all members of the union's governing body. Only then could there be any strong certainty that officials who speak for the union (and may be seen in some sense by the public as being the union itself) fully represent those for whom they speak.

The government's suggested course was given statutory backing in the Employment Act 1988.

Postal ballots

In addition to the wider scope for ballots, the government also gave a further push to postal balloting. The justification offered for this approach mainly rested upon the assertion that pressure could be applied upon individual members in the context of a workplace ballot.[12]

> Because of the scope for subtler forms of pressure in a workplace ballot, however, there is a real question whether such ballots can ever be totally free from suspicion. Having ensured that individuals have a right to participate in ballots the government is determined to ensure that they are able to do so without constraint and that all the votes cast are properly reflected in the result. If necessary, therefore, because of their greater degree of security the government is prepared to take the further step of insisting on postal ballots for executive elections and for political fund ballots.

While the subsequent Code of Practice was not wholly prescriptive about postal ballots, the government's thinking and preference were clear.

These proposals will help to ensure that balloting will remain on the broader political agenda, with the trade unions, on the one hand, emphasizing their commitment to, and practice of, democracy, and arguing for the statutory provision of the necessary facilities to secure workplace ballots, and with the government, on the other hand, stressing the rights of the individual union member and placing their faith in postal ballots.

PICKETING

In relation to industrial action, ballots have always offered one means of mobilizing support. Another method, not necessarily mutually incompatible, involves picketing fellow workers, in order to persuade them to take steps which might be sympathetic to the objectives of those initiating the industrial action. The persuasion, implicit in the picketing, could vary from encouraging others to take industrial action, to asking workers not to handle the goods of the employer involved in the dispute or not to service that employer in other ways. These attempts, through picketing, to broaden the base and the scope of industrial action have inevitably always formed part of trade union activity. Equally, they have always been activities fraught with difficulty as far as the relationship between the individual picket and the law is concerned.

Before commenting on detailed aspects of the law on picketing, it is worth while challenging a particular image of picketing. For very many of the general public, with no personal direct experience, picketing easily becomes synonomous with the events captured on television screens in disputes such as those at the Messenger Group, Wapping, or in the miners' strike. Picketing is then seen as involving large numbers of both strikers and their supporters, on one hand, and the police, on the other, with a strong attendant risk of violence and illegality.

In contrast to these perceptions, the fact is that in any one year, there will be hundreds, if not thousands, of strikes with the vast majority involving some form of picketing, and usually taking place without the presence of any police officers. Overwhelmingly, picketing is peaceful: a conclusion supported by Khan and her colleagues,[13] and by Evans.[14] And even in the 1984/5 miners' strike, which has been held up as characteristic of all that is wrong with unions, in general, and picketing, in particular, the National Council for Civil Liberties was confident enough, on the basis of its analysis of the strike, to conclude:[15]

> contrary to the impression inevitably created by media concentration on incidents of mass picketing and violent confrontation, most of the picketing during the strike has been orderly and on a modest scale.

Liability for picketing

Liability for the individual picket can arise through both the civil and criminal law. Consistent with the attitude of the common law towards trade unionism and industrial action, picketing was regarded as both a criminal offence and a civil wrong. This liability was first restricted by the Conspiracy and Protection of Property Act 1875; and after further judicial intervention opened up the loopholes which Parliament considered that it had closed by the 1875 Act, s 2 of the Trade Disputes Act 1906 provided a framework which, with alteration, has carried forward into the Employment Act 1980.

Section 16(1) of the Employment Act 1980 now sets out the current legal parameters for picketing:

> (1) It shall be lawful for a person in contemplation or furtherance of a trade dispute to attend (a) at or near his own place of work, or (b) if he is an official of a trade union, at or near the place of work of a member of that union whom he is accompanying and whom he represents, for the purposes only of peacefully obtaining or communicating information, or peacefully persuading any person to work or abstain from working.
>
> (2) If a person works or normally works (a) otherwise than at any one place, or (b) at a place the location of which is such that attendance there for a purpose mentioned in subsection (1) is impracticable, his place of work for the purposes of that subsection shall be any premises of his employer from which he works or from which his work is administered.

Further, subs (3) permits the definition of his own place of work to extend to a worker whose contract of employment has been terminated in relation to a trade dispute, or whose dismissal was a cause of the trade dispute; and subs (4) defines the scope of trade union officials.

A number of significant points emerge. First, while the Act talks of certain action being lawful, characteristically of English labour law the Act does not provide a legal right to picket. As with other aspects, immunities are provided in relation only to those actions which are in contemplation or furtherance of a trade dispute. This means that, given the action would have to fall within the definition of a trade dispute, picketing, for instance, in the context, say, of a boycott of South African goods, or similar activities which may be regarded as political, and, therefore, being outside the scope of the definition, would not be covered; nor would the immunity be extended to picketing in the non-employment context, such as, for instance, by tenants outside the offices of their landlord.

Second, the immunity provides only for picketing at or near one's place of work. While this might appear a somewhat specific point, it is worth noting that the provision does not allow employees to occupy, to sit in or to work in at a place of work. These forms of industrial action, usually associated with attempts to resist closures and redundancies, cannot be regarded as picketing. Liability, for instance, in relation to the civil law of trespass, would almost invariably be present in the circumstances of an occupation of a workplace.

Third, the definition of place of work assumes relevance in a number of respects. For some workers, such as the classic example of lorry drivers, the place of work is not easy to define or to locate: in this context the 1980 Act referred specifically to premises from which an employee may work, or from which his work may be administered. For others, while the immediate place of work may be self-evident, the employer may operate from a number of interrelated locations, increasingly in practice, in separate companies forming part of an overall, interdependent organization. Often, for such employees, the need to spread the dispute to other sections of the organization is quite pressing, indeed vital to the successful prosecution of the dispute. However, given the interpretation of a place of work adopted by the courts, there appears to be little room for doubt that lawful picketing can take place only at the immediate workplace, and not at other workplaces in the group: a conclusion which was reinforced in the Stockport Messenger newspaper group dispute[16] in which work was transferred between companies in the same group, and in which picketing by displaced employees at other workplaces in the group was deemed to be unlawful.

Section 16 of the Employment Act, then, can be considered as severely restricting the ability to picket, especially in relation to secondary or sympathetic action. Attempts to extend disputes in order to gain the support of other workers through sympathetic action has always formed part of the trade union response. Even though the practice of secondary action attracted widespread publicity in the 1970s, its historical respectability can scarcely be questioned. The 1980 Act, however, ensures that, for the present, sympathetic action enjoys immunities only in the following contexts: when pickets at their own place of work persuade other workers, employed by another company, not to cross the picket line; and when workers, at their own place of work, organize picketing in support of other workers who are involved in a trade dispute. The practice, therefore, of workers from the primary dispute sending pickets to other workplaces, on the pattern, say, of the miners picketing the power stations, would not enjoy immunity under s 16.

In addition to the statutory immunities, the law of picketing becomes more complex because of the powers of the police, in relation to what are normally described as public order offences. A picket may be behaving in such a way as to fall within the scope of s 16, yet still be committing a criminal offence. Some of these offences may, in fact, be clear-cut: an assault would most often fall into that category. There are, however, grey areas, such as aspects of threatening behaviour, obstructing the police in the course of their duty or obstructing the highway, which can give rise to argument, and, in the context of a dispute such as the 1984–5 miners' strike, a great deal of controversy.

According to McIllroy,[17] figures on the miners' strike of 1984–5 showed:

> 9808 people were arrested during the strike in England and Wales and 1483 arrested in Scotland. In England and Wales only 80 per cent of those arrested were charged, and in Scotland the figure was 57 per cent. The charges brought were minor ones. In England and Wales 98 per cent of charges were for breach of the peace, obstructing the police, breach of bail conditions or vandalism, and in Scotland the figure was 75 per cent.

These offences illustrate the widespread powers of the police in relation to any picket or indeed, any demonstration. It is not too great an exercise of licence to suggest that pickets are always at the mercy of the police, though, as we know, picketing is mostly tedious, and without a police presence. Certain cases emphasize the width of the police powers.

In order to illustrate that judicial restrictiveness dates back for a number of years, and that it is not just a characteristic of recent years, it might be worth while to look at the case of *Piddington* v *Bates* [1961] WLR 162. In that case, a police officer felt that two pickets only were necessary at the back entrance of an employer's premises. A third person attempted to join the picket, refusing to accept the police officer's determination that two were sufficient. A conviction for obstructing the police officer was upheld, because it was concluded that the police officer had reasonable grounds for believing that there might have been a breach of the peace, unless he restricted the number of pickets to two.

It was the miners' strike which brought into sharp public focus the extent of police powers; in no way more so than in the willingness of the police to prevent miners travelling to those pits which were still working. At its most dramatic, this power was used to prevent Kent miners travelling through the Dartford tunnel on their way to the Nottinghamshire coalfield. It would appear from *Moss and others* v *Mclachlin* (1985) IRLR 76, that the police can rely upon roadblocks and arrests to prevent pickets gathering, as long as they have reasonable grounds for believing that a breach of the peace is likely to occur. The reasonable grounds can arise out of what has already happened at picket lines, or what, from other information, including newspaper reports, can be reasonably anticipated to happen.

Mass picketing

At this stage, a word about mass picketing may be appropriate. In many ways, mass picketing is a modern phenomenon, made possible by extensive access to private travel, and popularized by its alleged success during the 1972 miners' strike at the Saltley power station. In relation to that dispute, it is always necessary to assess coolly the contribution made by mass picketing to the outcome of the strike: other factors, particularly the dramatic shift in relative fuel prices, can be considered as of greater significance. Effective or not, the tactic of the mass picket has been pursued in other contexts, although never on numerous occasions.

The nature of mass picketing is such that it might be seen more as a demonstration. The dividing line may not always be easy to establish, but there is one defining characteristic of a mass picket: the action is designed to persuade or to prevent others from carrying out their contract of employment. Such an intention, it is suggested, would not be present in relation to a demonstration.

Judicial comment on mass picketing *per se* is somewhat limited, but, from *Thames and others* v *NUM South Wales* (1985) IRLR 136, it is safe to conclude that a mass picket will be regarded as unlawful because it will be associated with unreasonable harassment. And, from *obiter dicta* by Lord Reid in *Broome* v *DPP*, it would appear that mass picketing is likely to constitute the criminal offence of wilful obstruction of the highway. According to Lord Reid:[18]

> it would not be difficult to infer as a matter of fact that pickets who assemble in unreasonably large numbers do have the purpose of preventing free passage. If that were the proper inference then their presence on the highway would become unlawful.

DoE code on picketing

Given the controversy and the complexity surrounding the existing law on picketing, it is scarcely surprising that there have been both attempts to clarify acceptable practice, and to argue for reform. In relation to practice, the most important document is the Department of Employment Code on Picketing.[19] Three aspects of that code are worthy of further comment: the number of pickets: the organization of picketing; and the provision of essential goods and services. Before looking at these detailed areas, it is necessary to point out that the code in itself has no legal basis, although it is persuasive in evidential terms.

In relation to numbers, *Piddington* v *Bates* had already indicated the extent of police powers in determining the acceptable number of pickets. As for the Code, 'the main cause of violence and disorder on the picket line is excessive numbers.'[20] Without denying that excessive numbers can be a cause of disorder, it would be presumptuous to read too much into that general statement, given that large numbers are not normally associated with picketing. However, having defined the problem in these terms, the Code goes on to offer the following advice:[21]

> pickets and their organizers should ensure that in general the number of pickets does not exceed six at any entrance to a workplace; frequently a smaller number will be appropriate.

The conditions in which that smaller number would be appropriate are not stated: nor is the reasoning which leads to the conclusion that six pickets should be the maximum number. The Code would have offered greater practical assistance if these issues had been adequately addressed.

A key role is, therefore, accorded to the picket organizer, who is seen by the authors of the Code as an experienced person, preferably a full-time trade union official. That person should be authorized by his union, and be mainly responsible for liaison and negotiation with the police. In addition to that pivotal task, the Code sets out five other areas of responsibility for the picket organizer:

- to ensure that pickets understand the law and the provision of the Code and that picketing is conducted peacefully and lawfully;
- to be responsible for distributing badges or armbands, which authorized pickets should wear so that they are clearly identified;
- to ensure that employees from other places of work do not join the picket line and that any offers of support on the picket line from outsiders are refused;
- to remain in close contact with his own union office, and with the offices of other unions if they are involved in the picketing;
- to ensure that such special arrangements as may be necessary for essential supplies or maintenance are understood and observed by the pickets.[22]

This is an exhaustive and onerous set of responsibilities, with the duties in relation to essential supplies and services being strongly emphasized, partly as a result of the public sector strikes during the so-called Winter of Discontent in 1978/9. The Code is clear as to responsibility:[23]

> pickets should take very great care to ensure that their activities do not cause distress, hardship or inconvenience to members of the public who are not involved in the dispute.

The list of essential supplies and services is itself lengthy, covering all those activities which provide, in a public context, for the young and the elderly, and which, also, can be seen as intrinsically related to public health and safety. While that list may not give rise to controversy, even though the pay and conditions for those providing the services may be a source of serious dispute, the overall phrase, used in the Code, about not causing distress, hardship or inconvenience to members of the public, may be of little value. In certain disputes, for instance in public transport, it is an inevitable consequence of an industrial dispute that public services are adversely affected. Similarly, referring once more to disputes in the coal industry, the ability to disrupt the supply of electricity has always offered the miners a potent weapon. The inability to threaten electricity supplies was central to the weakness of the miners during the 1984/5 strike.

Defining a list of essential services may be none too difficult or controversial: giving such a provision legal substance may be much more hazardous.

In addition to these three aspects to which attention has been drawn in some detail, the Code also comments on the role of the police: 'It is not the function of the police to take a view of the merits of a particular trade dispute'.[24] This statement of police neutrality would earn widespread approval. Yet, in practice, the law seems to work in such a way as to lessen the chances of the police being regarded as impartial. While, on the one hand, there is clearly a duty to make it possible for people to go to work if they so wish, there is no corresponding duty to allow individuals to picket. This flows from the legislation itself, which gives no legal right to picket, and from the fact that the law was drafted more than 100 years ago. At that stage, it was impossible to envisage coaches full of strike-breakers, or lorries loaded with basic materials for a factory, speeding through a picket line. When that happens the opportunity to persuade and to inform peacefully does not exist.

Clause 99 of the Employment Protection Bill

The problem posed by the practical restriction on the exercise of the right to picket was addressed by the then government in 1975 with cl 99 of the Employment Protection Bill. The clause sought to allow pickets the ability:[25]

> to persuade any other person (whether in a vehicle or not) to stop for the purpose of peacefully obtaining or communicating information from or to that other person or peacefully persuading him to work or abstain from working.

Quite what cl 99 would have achieved is unclear. The government held it to be a 'declaratory' provision, not changing the law but making explicit what they felt to be implicit in s 15 of the Trade Union and Labour Relations Act 1974, that pickets had a right to seek to persuade others not to enter their place of work. The clause was, however, defeated, with the Conservative opposition members of the Standing Committee objecting on the grounds that the proposed clause would, in effect, confer a right to stop vehicles; and with the government's own supporters feeling that the declaration contained in cl 99 was of no value. As a further illustration of that viewpoint, a government backbencher, Jeff Rooker, proposed an amendment to the clause which would have allowed pickets to stop any lorry, and which would have made any lorry driver driving through the picket line, guilty of breaches of the peace. For Rooker:[26]

> the ideal of picketing, . . . is not so much to prevent people or vehicles entering a factory as to put the strikers' case, so that people may be persuaded not to enter a particular factory.

The amendment would aim not just to make it possible to stop vehicles, but it would, in Rooker's view, overcome some of the causes of mass picketing:[27]

> the reason we have mass picketing . . ., is that it is realized that the only chance strikers have of even stopping a vehicle is to have mass picketing.

While the Rooker amendment was defeated, it can be argued that it sought to tackle the main difficulty inherent in the current law of picketing. Buses and lorries can be driven through picket lines, thereby effectively eliminating the possibility of peaceful persuasion, while in practice, both casting the police in such a role as to be seen as sympathetic to the employer and the strike breakers, and, at the same time, inflaming passions, and the feeling of impotence on the part of the pickets. That scenario can only be changed by achieving a more effective legal balance between those picketing and those wishing to cross the picket line.

Current proposals

For the current government, however, the desired balance must always lean towards those trying to exercise the right to work. This much is clear from the arguments used by government ministers during the course of industrial disputes. It is further reinforced by a proposal contained in *Trade Unions and Their Members*, published in February 1987:[28]

> The government believes that a decision to take industrial action should be a matter for the individual. Every union member should be free to decide for himself whether or not he wishes to break his contract of employment and run the risk of dismissal without compensation. No union member should be penalized by his trade union for exercising his right to cross a picket line and go to work.

From this assertion, it is argued that the powers exercised by unions to discipline members who refuse to join in strike action should be severely curtailed. By granting, through s 3 of the 1988 Act, a union member the right to continue working through a strike, the government aims to achieve its objectives of further reducing union power. All of which scarcely suggests that both the necessary balance between the right of strikers and non-strikers, and the impartiality of the role of the police, are about to be achieved. But, without that balance, and given the complexity of the existing law, it is not unreasonable to conclude that picketing will continue to be a hazardous pursuit.

STRIKES

Picketing and ballots often, but not invariably, form part of industrial action: strikes constitute but one form of industrial action. Works-to-rule, go-slows and overtime bans are all collective actions, usually in breach of the individual contract of employment, which seek to impose pressure upon an employer with the objective of seeking benefit or securing redress for employees. Strikes will virtually always be prosecuted as a last-resort measure, as it will be in the interest of workers, who will lose financially as a result of the strike, to adopt approaches through collective bargaining and the threatened imposition of sanctions, which might provide beneficial results at little or no cost.

Different types of strike action

Before turning to the extent and causes of strikes, it would be useful to differentiate between different types of strike action. The usual categories in this respect are official and unofficial; and constitutional and unconstitutional. The distinction between official and unofficial reflects not upon the merits of a particular dispute, but upon the attitude of the union towards the stoppage. An official strike will simply be a dispute which has been officially sanctioned by the appropriate body in the union, usually the National Executive Committee. By definition, it follows that an unofficial dispute will not have received that sanction. However, it would be naïve and misleading to conclude from this that the union officially looks askance at such disputes. Mostly, strikes are short in duration, and arise more or less spontaneously from issues which have occurred at the place of work: in these circumstances they are usually resolved before a national union committee has an opportunity to meet, and either to approve or disapprove. Furthermore, the fact that the strike remains unofficial can provide a full-time union official with a useful bargaining lever: while distancing the union from the action which has been taken, the official may be able to argue that his influence with his striking members will only be enhanced if management were to make an improved offer. Then, of course, he might feel in a strong enough position to advocate a return to work.

While the official/unofficial category relates to decisions which are internal to the union, the constitutional nature of strike action refers to the established industrial relations procedures for a particular firm or industry. In all collective bargaining contexts, two sets of agreements will emerge: those relating to substantive issues, such as pay and conditions, and which are subject to periodic renegotiation; and those relating to procedural matters, which are rarely changed, and which provide a framework in which industrial conflict can be controlled and managed. It is against these procedural arrangements that the constitutionality of a strike is judged. Those procedural agreements usually offer a series of steps, typically initially from the workplace to an eventual final step outside the immediate firm. Going through all these procedures can take some time, often months, and there is a great temptation or need on occasions to speed up the resolution of the dispute by taking industrial action, which would then be regarded as unconstitutional. Indeed, characteristic of strikes in the 1950s and 1960s was the so-called wildcat strike: often likely to last for no more than two shifts, not sanctioned by the union, and in breach of the procedural agreements. It was this type of strike which gave rise to so much political debate in the 1960s and which was one of the main reasons for the creation of the Donovan Commission between 1965–8.

By the mid-1960s unofficial and unconstitutional strikes accounted for about 87 per cent of all workers involved in strikes and 69 per cent of the working days lost through strike action. As Table 16.1 indicates, during the period of the 1960s the recorded level of stoppages was regularly between 2000 and 3000 per year. The economic boom of that period, with low levels of unemployment, gave workers the ability to mount effective short strikes. From the mid-1970s, however, the pace of economic decline quickened, especially during the early years of the Thatcher Government.

Table 16.1   *Recorded number of industrial stoppages 1960–69*

1960	2832		1965	2354
1961	2686		1966	1937
1962	2449		1967	2166
1963	2068		1968	2350
1964	2524		1969	3116

Source: Department of Employment Gazette (Various issues)

Whether unemployment was deliberately used as a means of reducing trade union power is open to political debate: the impact of unemployment on trade union power, however, is clear. As one would anticipate, the willingness to take industrial action, given the knowledge that high unemployment often enables the employer to resist effectively, has been reduced. The pattern of a falling number of strikes emerged slowly at first, but gained strength in the 1980s with 1985 recording no more than one-third of the stoppages experienced in 1975 (see Table 16.2). The pattern continued at the end of the 1980s, with a further downfall in 1990, as the economic recession started to bite.

Table 16.2   *Recorded number of industrial stoppages in progress 1975–85*

1975	2332	1980	1348	1986	1074
1976	2304	1981	1344	1987	1016
1977	2737	1982	1538	1988	781
1978	2498	1983	1364	1989	701
1979	2125	1984	1221	1990	630
		1985	903		

Source: Department of Employment Gazette

It is, of course, not just unemployment alone which has transformed the pattern of strikes in this country. Also taking place has been a significant restructuring of the economy, characterized by the decline of traditional industries in which unionization was high and in which there was a markedly above-average propensity to strike; and by a growth in the service sector, which exhibits the constraining features of low unionization and a deep reluctance or ability to take strike action. These changes, combined with the effects of high unemployment, may ensure that the experience of the 1960s, with its preponderance of short, unofficial strikes may not be repeated, at least not in the near future.

Emphasis for this change has been placed upon economic factors. For some, this may be surprising, given the legal constraints imposed by the Employment Acts of 1980, 1982 and 1988, and by the Trade Union Act 1984. Perhaps the legal risks are in the minds of those taking and organizing industrial action. Nevertheless, it is reasonable to suggest that in relation to the law two other factors are of more relevance; first, most people organizing and participating in industrial action expect any strike to be over in days rather than weeks; and secondly, there is a feeling that, even though there are well-publicized cases of legal intervention in disputes, it will not happen in your case with your employer. After all, it is only a small minority of cases in which the courts are asked to intervene.

The re-emergence of the official strike

Alongside the declining number of strikes, the last 20 years have experienced a partial re-emergence of the official strike. While unofficial action will tend to be localized, involving relatively small groups of workers, the official strike will, in contrast, involve more workers, often a whole industry or firm. In other words, official strikes, while remaining few in numbers, will influence the calculation of days lost through strike action simply because of their likely duration and numbers involved, and they will most likely attract public attention. For instance, in 1984, 27,130,000 working days were lost, about seven times the annual average for the 1960s, mostly caused by the dispute in the coal industry. Even in 1989, when the recorded number of strikes was 701, the days lost equalled 4,100,000, higher than the average for the 1960s.

Again, the most powerful explanation for this partial re-emergence of official strikes can be found in economic factors. First, because of the falling ability of the economy to afford wage increases, governments have intervened directly in the wage bargaining process, either as an employer itself in the public sector or through some form of incomes policy. The consequence of these interventions has been to restrict the scope for compromise, thereby ensuring that, if a dispute takes place, it will be an official confrontation between union and government. In this way, governments of all political persuasions have politicized industrial relations and the traditional role of the State as umpire has been overtaken by the State as active participant. Secondly, again because of incomes policies, employers have found themselves unable to make a wage offer which may be regarded as appropriate for the particular firm's circumstances. This again is likely to produce a context in which official strike action becomes a response. And, thirdly, given the squeeze upon profits resulting from the economic recession and the often perceived requirement to shed labour, employers have found it necessary, both in the public and the private sector, to define disputes much more in principled terms rather than subject to the normal possibilities of compromise. These factors have combined to reactivate the official strike, often with an impact upon days lost, if not on the number of strikes.

The 1980s then, can be seen as a decade in which the number of strikes was falling; but, in which, because of a few lengthy official strikes, the number of days lost through industrial action would vary considerably.

A LEGAL REVOLUTION

From the viewpoint of trade unionists, the most often expressed wish in relation to the law and the courts is that they should simply keep out of industrial relations practices. Sometimes that view is put forward because it is felt that lawyers possess little understanding of what happens in a factory, shop or office: on other occasions, the argument is couched in stronger terms, asserting that the courts are intrinsically anti-trade union. Regardless of whether judges reflect only the views of the narrow social class background from which they overwhelmingly originate, English law will almost inevitably appear to be against the trade unions, as the fundamental doctrine of the legal system is based upon the individual, and the primacy of contract, and not upon collective interest and collective action. For this reason, the common law was never able to develop concepts out of which could have been built a set of collective rights, such as the rights to organize, to picket and to strike.

Parliament also has never intervened to shift the balance from the individual to the collective. Parliament has only felt persuaded to provide immunities from the legal consequences of certain collective action. Nevertheless, that approach provided, for more than half a century, an acceptable and tolerable framework, and assisted the development of voluntarism which was so much the cornerstone of the industrial relations system. But, now, it is possible to argue that the previous consensus has been destroyed. The government has enthusiastically assisted in the destruction of the old consensus: by legislation which restricts immunities; by the extension of individual rights as against collective rights; and by action as employer often showing a determination not to bargain with employees. Private sector employers have been encouraged to join in: so, too, it could be argued, have the courts, which have noted not just the detail of change, but the climate of change, as well. All of this reflects a new philosophy of individualism, designed to marginalize the traditional voluntarism of industrial relations.

McIllroy has entitled a recent analysis of the trade union legislation introduced by Conservative Governments as a possible permanent revolution. The permanence of the revolution will depend upon political factors external to the industrial relations system. The Labour Party is committed to redefining the immunities enjoyed by trade unions and, in so doing, opening the possibilities for a limited extent of legal secondary action. There is also a commitment to extend individual employment rights, drawing upon European practice, and upon the EC Social Charter.

It is in this mixture of precise changes to the law relating to collective action, and in the enthusiastic support for individual employment rights, that it is possible to sketch out the nature of the permanence of the legislative changes introduced by the Conservatives.

Some of the legal changes are, if not considered desirable, nevertheless accepted in practice. The use of ballots offers the most potent illustration of this point. But, alongside this acceptance of certain changes, there is on the part of trade unionists a feeling that the balance of power has been shifted strongly to their disadvantage.

The April 1992 General Election result will, however, put the trade unions under pressure to come to terms with even more of the Conservative legislation. The cavalry, in the form of a Labour government, is not now just over the horizon.

The emphasis on individual rights is, however, more interesting. It may simply reflect a reaction to the legal constraints introduced in the 1980s. The chances are, however, that the reasons are deeper. Two recessions in a decade, coupled with the restructuring of traditional, heavily unionized industries, have done much to weaken the trade unions' source of power and membership. The new areas of employment in the services and in information technology have so far proved difficult recruiting ground for the trade unions. An effective strategy for the unions, when faced with the loss of membership in traditional areas, and the difficulties in recruitment in new employment fields, would be to look to a possible Labour government to deliver individual rights to employees. In this way, the unions could claim some influence, thereby making membership a more attractive proposition.

Whether all of this amounts to a permanent revolution is questionable: it is difficult to imagine a period of years without further legislative intervention in industrial relations and the Conservative Government has already announced its intention of introducing further legislation, this time aimed at check-off arrangements for the collection of union subscriptions. We might, however, be entering the 1990s facing an interesting paradox, with the Conservatives essentially concerned about weakening collective rights, often by extending the ability of the individual to challenge the wishes of the collective, and the trade unions becoming increasingly anxious to extend individual rights, both as a reflection of their own weakness, and as a means of securing collective bargaining opportunities. In either case, the law is still going to influence practice in relation to ballots, picketing and strikes. All the electorate and the politicians have to do is to decide what sort of law they want, and where they want to define the balance of power.

References

1. The case of the *Amalgamated Society of Railway Servants* v *Osborne* [1910] AC 87 prevented unions from financing political activity out of general funds. For this reason, the Trade Union Act 1913 developed the concept of a separate political fund, out of which political activities could be financed.
2. TUC/Labour Party (1986) *People at Work: New Rights, New Responsibilities*, London.
3. As reported in *The Times*, 2 September 1986.
4. Advisory, Conciliation and Arbitration Services (1985) *Annual Report*, p 15.
5. McIllroy, J (1991) *The Permanent Revolution*, Spokesman Books, Nottingham.
6. See Fatchett, D (1987) *Trade Unions and Politics in the 1980s*, Croom Helm, London, and Fatchett, D (1984) 'Trade union political funds' *Industrial Relations Journal*, Vol 15, No 3.
7. Reference is made to 37 unions with membership in the UK. In addition, the Scottish Carpet Workers Union also held a successful ballot.
8. Leopold, J (1986) 'Trade unions political funds: a retrospective analysis,' *Industrial Relations Journal*, Vol 17, No 4, Winter.
9. As reported in *The Times*, 2 September 1986.
10. 'Trade unions and their members', HMSO, Cmnd. 95, February 1987.
11. ibid, para 5.29.
12. ibid, para 5.14.
13. Khan, P, Lewis, N, Livock, R and Wiles, P (1983) *Picketing – Industrial Disputes, Tactics and the Law*, Routledge and Kegan Paul, London.
14. Evans, S (1985) 'Picketing under the Employment Acts,' in Fosh, P and Littler, C (eds) *Industrial Relations and the Law in the 1980s. Issues and Future Trends*, Gower, Aldershot.
15. National Council for Civil Liberties (1984) *Civil Liberties and the Miners Dispute; First report of the Independent Inquiry*, London.
16. *Messenger Newspapers Group Ltd* v *NGA* [1984] IRLR 397.
17. ibid, p 89.
18. [1974] ICR 84, 90.

19. Department of Employment (1980) *Picketing*, Code of Practice.
20. ibid, para 29.
21. ibid, para 31.
22. ibid, para 34.
23. ibid, para 37.
24. ibid, para 26.
25. Minutes of Standing Committee F, 17 July 1975, col 1488.
26. ibid, col 1488.
27. ibid, col 1488.
28. ibid, para 2.22.

Chapter Seventeen
Unfair Dismissal and Tribunals*

Paul Lewis

THE ESSENCE OF THE LAW OF UNFAIR DISMISSAL

The essence of the law of unfair dismissal is the right of the employee not to be unfairly dismissed by his employer. In deciding cases, industrial tribunals go through a two-stage process. They ask the following questions. Has the employer established a fair reason for the dismissal? Did the employer act reasonably or unreasonably?

The statute defines fairness rather than unfairness. The fair reasons for dismissal – the first stage of the process – are:

- the capability or qualifications of the employee;
- the conduct of the employee;
- the employee was redundant;
- the employee could not continue in his work without contravention of a statutory duty or restriction; and
- some other substantial reason (SOSR).

A dismissal will also be fair if it can be shown that its purpose was to safeguard national security.[1] If an employer cannot establish a fair reason his case will fall. On the other hand, if a tribunal is satisfied that one of these reasons has been shown, it must then decide whether the employer acted reasonably or unreasonably in treating it as a sufficient reason for dismissal. The second stage of the process, therefore, is a test of reasonableness. The statute says little about reasonableness except that tribunals must take into account 'the size and administrative resources of the employer's undertaking', and decide the issue, 'in accordance with equity and the substantial merits of the case'.[2] In practice, reasonableness comes down to proper procedure, consistency and the appropriateness of dismissal as the form of disciplinary action to be taken. The last of these involves consideration of the severity of the employee's offence, as well as any mitigating factors such as length of employment, good record, provocation and domestic or personal difficulties.

The onus of proof for establishing a fair reason lies with the employer. The employee, may, however, wish to bring evidence and put arguments in order to challenge the reason put forward. On reasonableness, the onus of proof is neutral. Both parties will need to present arguments and evidence on this point. If the act of dismissal itself is denied the employee will be responsible for

---

* This chapter relates to the law as at 1 February 1992.

establishing dismissal within the statutory meaning. The employee will also be responsible for proof of loss for compensation purposes. If the dismissal is alleged to be on grounds of sex or race discrimination, an employee with two years' continuous employment will be able to use unfair dismissal law, where the onus of proof of the reason for the dismissal is upon the employer. Those without the qualifying employment will be restricted to use of the discrimination legislation, where the onus of proof is on the complainant. If the dismissal is alleged to be on union or non-union grounds the unfair dismissal legislation can be used, irrespective of whether or not there is qualifying employment. However, where the applicant has less than two years' continuous employment, the onus of proof of reason will lie with him rather than with the employer.

MEANING OF DISMISSAL AND EFFECTIVE DATE OF TERMINATION

Where the words used are unambiguously those of dismissal or resignation, they alone may be sufficient to determine the issue. However, the context may also need to be taken into account. Even words which are unambiguous may not represent real intentions when spoken (or shouted) during a heated exchange (*Sovereign House Security Services Ltd* v *Savage*). Thus, some short period of cooling-off might be reasonable before the decision becomes final. This gives the parties an opportunity to communicate with each other.

Agreements to exclude unfair dismissal rights are void (but see the ACAS Conciliation Officer exception opposite). A mutual termination by consent, to avoid the act of dismissal, was such an agreement and was therefore void according to the Court of Appeal in *Igbo* v *Johnson Matthey (Chemicals) Ltd*. However, if an agreement to terminate is made with proper advice and no duress it is a valid mutual termination, and no question of dismissal arises (*Logan Salton* v *Durham County Council*).

Dismissal is defined as:

- termination of the contract by the employer with or without notice;
- the expiry of a fixed-term contract without renewal;
- constructive dismissal (see below, pp 354–5); and
- failure to permit a woman to return to work after confinement.

The effective date of termination (EDT) is when any notice expires or, if there is no notice, the actual date of termination. For the woman who is refused her right to return to work the dismissal is taken as having effect on the notified day of return. Where notice given by the employer is less than the statutory minimum, the EDT (for the purposes of qualifying employment for unfair dismissal and written reasons claims, and the calculation of the basic award) becomes the date on which the statutory minimum notice would have expired. In constructive dismissal the EDT is at the end of whatever period of notice the employer would have had to give if he had dismissed on the date of the employee giving notice or terminating (whichever applied).

Sometimes the contract of employment can end because one party is no longer capable of performing it in the way the parties envisaged. This is called 'frustration'. The circumstances are likely to be external, unforeseen and not the fault of either party (*Paal Wilson & Co* v *Partenreederei*). Long-term illness is an example. A borstal sentence was frustration in *F C Shepherd & Co Ltd* v *Jerrom*. The contract may be said to be frustrated after the passage of time. The significance of frustration is that it is not a dismissal, therefore no question of unfair dismissal or redundancy would arise.

The expiry of a fixed-term contract is itself a dismissal. Such a contract must have definite starting and finishing dates, although there may be provision for termination by notice within its period (*BBC* v *Dixon*). This contrasts with a 'task' contract which is discharged by performance. Its expiry does not constitute a dismissal (*Wiltshire County Council* v *NATFHE and Guy*).

EXCLUSIONS

The following are excluded.

- Anyone who is not an employee (see Chapter 18, pp 360–1).
- Anyone who is employed for fewer than 16 hours a week (but see below).
- Anyone who has reached normal retiring age. Where there is a normal retiring age and it is the same for men and women, that age applies even if it is different from 65. In any other case 65 will apply.[3]
- Anyone with less than two years' employment with their present employer.
- Anyone who, at the time of dismissal, was taking part in unofficial industrial action.
- Anyone who is the subject of a certificate excepting them from the legislation in the interests of national security or confirming that they have been dismissed for that same reason.
- Anyone in a number of specified occupations, namely share fishermen, the police and the armed forces.
- Those who ordinarily work outside Great Britain.
- Those with contracts for a fixed term of one year or more who have agreed in writing to waive their rights.
- Those covered by a dismissal procedure which is exempted from the legislation by ministerial order.
- Anyone who has made an agreement to refrain from proceeding further with or making a complaint to a tribunal 'where a conciliation officer has taken action'.[4]
- Anyone whose employment contract has an illegal purpose (eg to defraud the Inland Revenue). An unknowingly illegal contract may not restrict statutory rights.[5]

The legislation does apply to Crown Servants and to House of Commons staff.

The hours qualification arises out of the legal definition of continuous employment.[6] An employee must either be employed for 16 hours or more per week, or work under a contract which normally involves employment for 16 hours or more. Those with five years' continuous employment enjoy continuity if the contract is for eight or more hours per week. Continuity is also preserved where there are gaps in the employment contract because of incapacity, a temporary cessation of work (*Ford* v *Warwickshire County Council*), custom or arrangement, and pregnancy or confinement. However, separate contracts with the same employer cannot be aggregated to obtain sufficient hours and therefore sufficient continuous qualifying employment (*Surrey County Council* v *Lewis*), although there could be a 'global' contract. There is no continuous employment qualification if the dismissal is for reason of race, sex, trades unionism or non-unionism, although race and sex discrimination cases would have to be taken under the Race Relations Act 1976 and Sex Discrimination Act 1975, rather than the unfair dismissal provisions of the Employment Protection (Consolidation) Act (EP(C)A) 1978 in the absence of two years' continuous employment. The qualification is one month where the dismissal is on medical grounds specified in Schedule 1 of the EP(C)A.

Continuous employment begins on the date specified in the contract of employment, even if this is not a working day, rather than when the employee actually starts to do the work (*General of the Salvation Army* v *Dewsbury*).

Normal retiring age (NRA) means contractual retiring age where there is one which is strictly applied. A contractual retiring age which is not strictly applied creates a presumption that the NRA is the same. In such circumstances, and also where there is no contractual retiring age at all, the overall test is the reasonable expectation of employees (*Waite* v *GCHQ*). The reference group for establishing NRA will be determined by the 'position' held by the employee.[7] Position means the following taken as a whole: status as an employee, nature of the work, and terms and conditions (*Hughes* v *DHSS*). A NRA in excess of 65 will allow unfair dismissal claims up to that NRA. This contrasts with redundancy where eligibility for redundancy payments (RPs) is restricted to those who have not reached 65 years, even if the NRA is in excess of 65.

FAIR REASONS

Capability

It is fair to dismiss an employee on the grounds of capability or qualifications, but subject to the test of reasonableness. Capability refers to 'skill, aptitude, health or any other physical or mental quality'. Qualifications means any 'degree, diploma or other academic, technical or professional qualification'.[8] In practice, dismissals on the grounds of capability fall into two categories: those involving incompetence; and those involving ill-health. Where incompetence reflects the fact that the employee is working below capacity, rather than a lack of ability, the issue is to be treated as one of misconduct, rather than one of capability (*Sutton and Gates (Luton) Ltd* v *Boxall*). Loss of confidence in an employee, more likely in a management position, can amount to incapability. The overall test for capability as a reason is that the employer must have an honestly and reasonably held belief that the employee is not competent, and have reasonable grounds for that belief (*Taylor* v *Alidair Ltd*).

Conduct

This ranges from the mundane (clocking offences, theft, drunkenness, fighting) to the more unusual (having long hair, not wearing a tie properly and even losing the company cat). The Employment Appeal Tribunal (EAT) has set out what it considers is the correct approach for tribunals to take. Known as the *British Homes Stores* v *Burchell* test and endorsed by the Court of Appeal in *W Weddell and Co Ltd* v *Tepper*, it requires the tribunal to ask:

- Did the employer have 'a reasonable suspicion amounting to a belief' that the employee had committed the misconduct, at the time the dismissal decision was taken?
- Did the employer have reasonable grounds for this belief?
- Did the employer carry out a reasonable investigation?

These three requirements – belief, reasonable grounds and reasonable investigation – are widely applied by tribunals. As a result there is a duty imposed upon employers to handle misconduct cases with some care, although they will not be expected to establish an employee's guilt beyond all reasonable doubt as would be necessary in the Crown Court.

Certain offences normally attract the label 'gross misconduct':

- theft, fraud, deliberate falsification of records;
- fighting, assault on another person;
- deliberate damage to company property;
- serious incapability through alcohol or being under the influence of illegal drugs;
- serious negligence which causes unacceptable loss, damage or injury;
- serious acts of insubordination; and
- working for a competitor or otherwise damaging the company's commercial interests.

What constitutes gross misconduct is a matter of fact for tribunals to decide (*Dalton* v *Burton's Gold Medal Biscuits Ltd*): there is no definition in law. Gross negligence, in the absence of any element of intention, does not amount to gross misconduct (*Dietmann* v *London Borough of Brent*).

Redundancy*

Redundancy is defined in the EP(C)A as a dismissal which is 'attributable wholly or mainly to': an actual or intended cessation of business, either generally, or in the place in which the employee is employed; or an actual or expected diminution in the requirements of the business for employees to carry out 'work of a particular kind', either generally, or in the place in which the employee is employed.[9]

The expiry of a fixed-term contract could be dismissal for redundancy if redundancy was the reason for non-renewal.

Redundancy is essentially a management prerogative and, in the absence of bad faith, there will normally be no challenge to it (*Moon* v *Homeworthy Furniture (Northern) Ltd*). The fact of needing fewer employees is what matters; once this has been established few tribunals will put the reasons under a microscope. The statutory rights of unions in this field are limited to advance warning and consultation; there is no legal right to a share in decision-making.

---

* The Industrial Relations Code of Practice 1972, which included provisions on redundancy, was revoked during 1991.

A properly carried out dismissal by reason of redundancy will be a fair dismissal, although the employee, if qualified, may be entitled to a statutory redundancy payment (see Chapter 18). Properly carried out in this context means that the dismissal passes the general test of reasonableness and, in addition, satisfies the selection requirements laid down in the statute. These are that selection must not be: because of the employee's proposed or actual union membership or activities; because of union non-membership; in contravention of a customary arrangement; in contravention of an agreed procedure.

If the selection fails on any of these points the dismissal is automatically unfair, and the Stage 2 test of reasonableness is not applied. Otherwise, reasonableness must be judged, and this can include selection criteria (*Bessenden Properties Ltd* v *Corness*). In examining whether there has been a breach of customary arrangement or agreed procedure it should be noted that such a breach is permissible if there are 'special reasons' justifying it. In practice, employers will have to substantiate any arguments they put forward for special reasons by, for example, reference to the needs of the business. Employees, on the other hand, will need to provide evidence to establish a customary arrangement. Agreed procedures will normally apply only in unionized workplaces. If there is no customary arrangement and no agreed procedure, the employer has a free hand in selection, subject to the general test of reasonableness and providing that selection is not on grounds of unionism, non-unionism, race or sex. Selection on grounds of pregnancy is automatically unfair following the House of Lords ruling in *Brown* v *Stockton-on-Tees Borough Council*.

There should be consultation with employees or their representatives (*Graham* v *ABF Ltd*). In non-union workplaces, it may be deemed unreasonable if the employee is not consulted and given some advance warning. Reasonableness will also include an investigation of the possibility of alternative work. The larger the organization, the more demanding will be the tribunal's requirements on this point, but ultimately there is no obligation to provide alternative employment (*MANWEB* v *Taylor*). Selection will have to pass the general test of reasonableness, as well as meeting the specific statutory requirements described earlier. Tribunals will want to identify the candidates for redundancy and to know the criteria used for selecting between them. They will also want to know how the selection was operated, and by whom. In general, they will look for an objective approach, which includes taking into account length of employment. It may be, however, that a tribunal will apply the 'any difference' test to deficiencies, such as lack of consultation and failure to investigate alternative employment prospects (*British United Shoe Machinery Co Ltd* v *Clarke*). The difference may be perceived as simply a postponement of the redundancy. This would give rise to a finding of unfair dismissal with compensation limited to the period during which the redundancy would have been delayed. The 'any difference' test should not be applied to the question of whether or not the dismissal is unfair, but may legitimately affect the compensation (*Polkey* v *A E Dayton Services Ltd*) (see p 351).

In 1982 the EAT laid down some guidelines in *Williams and others* v *Comp Air Maxam Ltd*. These comprised the need for advance warning, consultation, objective selection criteria, fair selection process and examination of possible alternative work. Subsequent decisions make it clear that the absence of one or more of these will not necessarily lead to a finding of unfair dismissal.

Contravention of statutory duty or restriction

This reason is likely to apply, for example, to people who drive on the public road as part or the whole of their job. Loss of licence means that they cannot do this job without a breach of law. More generally the employer should check that there would, in fact, be a breach of statute if the employee continued to do his normal job and seek expert advice if there is any doubt. Secondly, can the job be done by that person in any other way, for example, by using public transport? If driving is only a small part of the job, this may be feasible. Moreover, the general Stage 2 test of reasonableness applies. Has the employee been warned of the risks of losing his job if he loses his licence? Has the employer looked at the possibility of alternative work? Has proper procedure been invoked? Are there mitigating factors such as a good record and long service?

Some other substantial reason (SOSR)

The dismissal of a temporary replacement for someone on maternity leave or someone suspended on medical grounds specified in Schedule 1 of the EP(C)A would be a dismissal for SOSR if the replacement was informed in writing at the outset that they would be dismissed on the return of the absent employee. A dismissal for economic, technical or organizational reasons arising out of the transfer of an undertaking is also a dismissal for SOSR.

The main application of SOSR, however, is where the employer seeks to change employees' terms and conditions of employment unilaterally as a result of some form of reorganization. The justification for doing this, which is usually accepted by tribunals, is the need for business efficiency or financial saving (*Hollister* v *National Farmers' Union*). The financial problems facing firms in recent years have greatly influenced tribunals in this respect, but management will need to show a sound business reason for introducing the change, and evidence of some advance consultation with employees. Moreover, anyone dismissed for not agreeing to the change will need to be given due procedural rights – investigation of their circumstances, warnings, right to put their case, right of appeal etc. In other words, the test of reasonableness will have to be satisfied. It is possible that an employee may justifiably resign as a result of the employer's actions and claim constructive dismissal. A finding of constructive dismissal may result, but it will not necessarily give rise to an unfair dismissal (see p 354–5). Where the reorganization leads to a requirement for fewer employees this will be a redundancy. The employee who is confronted by an imposed change in terms and conditions of employment (eg a wage reduction) may, of course, invoke common law procedures in order to obtain remedy. In the light of the employer's repudiation of contract the employee may continue working and sue for damages for the breach (*Ferodo Ltd* v *Rigby*). Changing terms by terminating existing contracts and offering re-engagement on new terms removes the threat of common law actions, but may open the door to unfair dismissal claims as in *Gilham and others* v *Kent County Council*.

The expiry of a fixed-term contract can be SOSR. The employer will need to show: that he had a genuine need for a fixed-term contract in the first place; and why that reason has ceased to operate. The dismissal would then have to stand the test of reasonableness. As noted earlier, a dismissal as a result of the expiry of a fixed-term contract could be for reason of redundancy rather than SOSR.

SOSR could include the dismissal of people with personal characteristics that are unconventional or socially unacceptable. Such people have little protection unless the characteristics have no bearing at all on the work situation. In fact, employers can nearly always argue that such factors do have a bearing because, for example, of the effect on relationships with other employees and/or customers. Because of this it remains to be seen whether the dismissal of AIDS virus carriers will be unfair. The dilemma for people with something to hide is that hiding it will help them obtain a job, but after discovery by the employer the deceit will count against them in any unfair dismissal claim. The Rehabilitation of Offenders Act 1974 offers protection in certain employments to some of those who have criminal records.

REASONABLENESS

Meaning

Reasonableness is not defined but the ACAS Code on Disciplinary Practice and Procedures in Employment, and a wealth, if not a surfeit of case law, provide a clear indication of what is meant.[10] In short it means:

- following proper disciplinary procedure, including carrying out a reasonable investigation;
- being consistent in the application of discipline;
- that the disciplinary action taken needs to be appropriate for the particular case or, to borrow a phrase from criminal law, the punishment must fit the crime; and
- taking into account any mitigating circumstances (eg long service, good record, provocation, domestic or personal problems).

The standard of proof required is that facts need to be established on the balance of probabilities.

A breach creates no liability, but the Code is admissible in evidence in a case under the Act and must be taken into account by a tribunal where relevant. This means, for example, that a hiccup in a disciplinary procedure (eg a failure to investigate properly) does not in itself render the employer liable. However, if the employee is dismissed and applies to a tribunal claiming that he was unfairly dismissed, the breach of code is admissible and must be considered by the tribunal if relevant. The Code deals with both rules and procedures. The former set standards of conduct at work, the latter provide means of dealing with a failure to meet those standards.

The general test

The approach to be adopted, as laid down by the appellate courts, is as follows:

- the tribunal should not put itself in place of the respondent and say what it would have done if it, the tribunal, had been the employer;
- rather, it should note that for any disciplinary offence there will be, among

employers, a range of reasonable responses (*British Leyland (UK) Ltd* v *Swift*); and

■ the tribunal should ask itself if the response of the employer before it falls within that range.

If it does, the employer has behaved reasonably. If, on the other hand, no reasonable employer would have behaved in that way, the employer before it has behaved unreasonably.

In *W Devis and Sons Ltd* v *Atkins* it was decided that post-dismissal evidence, not connected with the reason which the employer gave for the dismissal, could not be admitted except in the determination of compensation. Similarly, the test of reasonableness is to be applied to the employer's behaviour at the time of the dismissal, on the basis of the facts that he had at his disposal, or should have had if a reasonable investigation had been carried out. However, post-dismissal facts which emerge during any internal appeal can be taken into account in deciding reasonableness (*West Midlands Co-operative Society Ltd* v *Tipton*). Ultimately, reasonableness is a question of fact for the tribunal to determine (*Union of Construction, Allied Trades and Technicians* v *Brain*).

Disciplinary rules

The Code states that rules should be reasonable; they should be readily available; management should do all it can to ensure that employees know and understand them; and management should make employees aware of the likely consequence of breaking any particular rule. Faced with an industrial tribunal, management will want to be able to give positive answers on these points. From the employee's point of view, however, each of the above provides a potential mitigating factor to be offset against the breach of discipline.

Management should be in a position to provide a tribunal with a copy of the disciplinary rules, as well as with evidence that the dismissed employee had the rules drawn to his attention. If rules are not communicated properly, the employee will have the defence that he did not know of a particular rule. That argument will be difficult to sustain if the employer has evidence (eg signature for receipt) that a rulebook was given to the employee. The assumption in law is that the employee will have read the rules. Possibly, if the rules are unclear, he can argue that he knew of the rule, but had not been told that he could be dismissed for breaking it. An employer should be ready to demonstrate that the rules are fully applied in practice, and are applied in a consistent and non-discriminatory manner. Establishing this should form part of the disciplinary investigation (*West Midlands Travel Ltd* v *Milke and Poole*). If it can be shown that management often turned a 'blind eye' to breaches of rule there may be doubts about the reasonableness of dismissing. Good disciplinary rules will clearly distinguish, by examples, between gross misconduct (usually subject to dismissal) and other misconduct, and will provide sufficient flexibility to allow mitigating circumstances to be considered (*Hadjioannou* v *Coral Casinos Ltd*).

Disciplinary procedures

The Code states that procedures should be speedy and in writing. They should indicate the range of disciplinary action and specify which levels of management have authority to take particular action. Immediate superiors should not have power to dismiss without reference to senior management. The Code envisages a system of warnings which is typically in four stages:

- a formal oral warning for minor offences;
- a written warning for subsequent minor offences or a more serious offence;
- a final written warning (or a disciplinary suspension) for further misconduct, making clear that dismissal may follow if there is not adequate improvement; and
- dismissal if there is not adequate improvement.

Sometimes the procedure may be entered at the second or third stage if there is serious misconduct, and of course the right exists to dismiss summarily for gross misconduct. Previous warnings may be relevant to dismissal, even if they were for different reasons. An employer can take into account:

- the substance of previous warnings;
- how many previous warnings there have been;
- the date(s) of previous warning(s); and
- the period of time between warnings (*Auguste Noel Ltd* v *Curtis*).

The Code goes on to lay down a number of requirements which have become quite prominent in the deliberations of industrial tribunals.

- The employee has a right to know the charges against him, and to have an opportunity to state his case – principles derived from the concept of 'natural justice'. (See *Pritchett and Dyjasek* v *J McIntyre Ltd*, however, in which these requirements were not met but the dismissal was nevertheless judged to be fair.)
- He has a right to be accompanied by a union representative or some other person.
- Except for gross misconduct there should be no dismissal for a first offence. Instead, a system of oral and written warnings should be used. A warning, however, is not just a general exhortation to improve. It spells out the offence and indicates what will or may happen if it recurs, or if there is no improvement.
- There should be a careful investigation before any disciplinary action is taken.
- The reasons for the choice of disciplinary penalty should be explained to the employee.
- The employee should be given a right of appeal, and told of his right and how to exercise it.

The Code distinguishes between suspension with pay while an alleged breach is being investigated, and the use of suspension without pay as a disciplinary penalty. Criminal offences outside employment should not be taken as automatic reasons for dismissal. The main consideration is whether it makes the employee unsuitable or unacceptable in his employment. Records of disciplinary breaches should be kept, as should details of warnings (including oral ones) and disciplinary penalties. Although records may be kept, the 'slate' ought to be wiped clean after a period of satisfactory conduct. The length of the period is not specified in the Code.

Tribunals have added the chance to 'make good' or improve to the questions they are likely to ask of an employer. They have also been influenced by the principles of natural justice (see p 350). These include the requirement that nobody should be a judge in their own interest. This is significant particularly in relation to appeals. It prevents those taking the original decision from being involved in any subsequent appeal against that decision. An appeals body should act in good faith (*Khanum* v *Mid-Glamorgan Area Health Authority*). Refusal to grant a right of appeal, which is part of the contract of employment, may lead to a finding of unfair dismissal (*West Midlands Co-operative Society Ltd* v *Tipton*; but see *Batchelor* v *British Railways Board*).

Where there is gross misconduct an employer may dismiss summarily. However, this does not mean that proper procedure can be dispensed with; an opportunity to explain will be necessary in most cases (*W & J Wass Ltd* v *Binns*). There should always be a full investigation and a chance for the employee to put his case. Typically, the employee will have been sent home following his misconduct. A period of suspension, therefore, can be used to gather the facts, hear the employee's side of the story and arrive at a decision. That decision would not be at risk, if the employee's misconduct is criminal, simply by virtue of an acquittal in the Crown Court. The Court and the tribunal are deciding different issues, and different degrees of proof are necessary. An employee may be not guilty, but the employer may still have dismissed fairly.

Taking into account the 'size and administrative resources of the . . . undertaking' may affect such factors as the offering of alternative work, but is not an excuse for the absence of a proper investigation.

Until recently, tribunals applied the 'any difference' test to breaches of procedure in order to determine whether or not a dismissal was fair (*British Labour Pump Co Ltd* v *Byrne; W & J Wass Ltd* v *Binns*). This test asks whether the proper application of procedure would have made any difference to the outcome. For example, would dismissal have been averted if the applicant had had an opportunity to state his case, or if a warning had been given? Often the answer has been that it would have made no difference, or at best that it would have delayed the dismissal (eg pending fuller investigation). As a result of the House of Lords ruling in *Polkey* v *A E Dayton (Services) Ltd*, however, the application of the 'any difference' test is normally likely to be restricted to questions of compensation. A reduction can be made to reflect the chance that a dismissal would still have occurred even if the correct procedure had been followed. This '*Polkey* reduction' is separate and distinct from any reduction for contributory fault. The substantive matter of the fairness or otherwise of the dismissal will be decided according to what the employer did, rather than what he might have done. The correct statutory tests are fair reason and reasonableness. The *Polkey* decision is a reminder, therefore, that lack of a proper procedure does not mean that a dismissal is automatically unfair (*West Midlands Co-operative Society Ltd* v *Tipton*). Exceptionally, perhaps, an employer may be able to dispense with the procedural niceties on 'no difference' grounds and still be reasonable. A procedural deficiency can be remedied on internal appeal by a rehearing of the case, but not merely by a review (*Whitbread and Co plc* v *Mills*).

Consistency

The reference in the statute to 'equity' has been taken as the basis for the need for consistency of treatment as part of reasonableness. Where comparisons are drawn with how other people have been treated in the past, including elsewhere in the organization, consistency is to be applied to the organization and not to individual managers (*Post Office* v *Fennell*). If more than one person is being dismissed as a result of an incident:

- are they being dismissed for the same offence?
- are there any differences between the cases, eg past records, mitigating factors? (*Eagle Star Insurance Co Ltd* v *Hayward*).

In practice, some degree of inconsistency may be reasonable if the facts of different individual cases can be distinguished, as in *British Steel Corporation* v *Griffin*.

SPECIAL CASES

The two-stage process of unfair dismissal law involves the establishing of a fair reason and the satisfying of the test of reasonableness. It now has to be added that some dismissals are not subject to this process because the statute provides specially for them.

Automatically unfair dismissals

In certain cases the statute instructs that dismissals are to be regarded as automatically unfair once the reason for dismissal is established. This applies to the following.

- Dismissals on grounds of proposed or actual trades union membership or activity, or proposed or actual non-membership. (Prior to the operation of the Employment Act 1988, the dismissal of a non-unionist in a 'closed shop' could sometimes be fair.[11]).
- Unfair selection for redundancy (see above, pp 345–6).
- Dismissals on grounds of pregnancy.

Dismissals on grounds of union activity or membership, or non-union membership, are not subject to the requirement for qualifying employment, nor to the usual age limits. If the applicant has the normal qualifying employment the onus of proof lies with the respondent (*Shannon* v *Michelin (Belfast) Ltd*). Otherwise it lies with the applicant (*Smith* v *The Chairman and other councillors of Hayle Town Council*). Even in the former circumstances, however, the applicant will have to adduce evidence that the reason for dismissal was trades unionism, as well as rebutting the employer's reason. The statute says that union activities must be at the 'appropriate time' if they are to be protected – namely, outside working hours, or in working hours with the employer's agreement or consent – but does not say what constitutes such activities. The courts have interpreted the term narrowly, for example, by ruling that these activities do not include the actions of the union itself (*Therm-A-Stor Ltd* v *Atkins and others*), or the acts of a union member not done formally within the union's responsibility

(*Drew* v *St Edmundsbury Borough Council*). However, in a recent case, dismissal for past union activities elsewhere was interpreted by the Court of Appeal as being dismissal because of a fear that such activities might be repeated in the present employment. Thus, the dismissal was on grounds of trades union activity and was automatically unfair (*Fitzpatrick* v *British Railways Board*).[12] A non-unionist has the right not to be dismissed for refusing to make a payment (eg to a charity) in lieu of a union subscription.

In pregnancy dismissals the employer has the following defences:

- at the date of termination of employment the employee could no longer do her work adequately;
- that she could not have continued working after termination of employment without contravening a statute (eg the Health and Safety at Work etc. Act 1974).

Even if one of the above applies, the employer or successor must still offer suitable alternative employment, if there is any, on terms which 'are not substantially less favourable to her'.[13] The onus of proof will be upon the employer to show that he made a suitable offer or that there was no suitable available vacancy. Selection for redundancy on grounds of pregnancy will automatically be unfair dismissal following the House of Lords ruling in *Brown* v *Stockton on Tees Borough Council*, and in any case opens up the prospect of a claim on grounds of sex discrimination (*Hayes* v *Malleable Working Men's Club*). It should be noted, however, that dismissal because of pregnancy is not automatically sex discrimination. Much depends upon how a man would have been treated if he had had a similar absence record (*Webb* v *Emo Cargo (UK) Ltd*). However, recent decisions of the ECJ suggests that in European law, pregnancy dismissals may automatically be sex discrimination (*Dekker* v *Stichting Vormingscentrum voor Jong Volwassenen (VJV Centrum) Plus; Handels-og Kontorfunktionaerernes Forbund i Danmark (acting for Hertz)* v *Dansk Arbejdsgiverforening (acting for Aldi Marked K/S)*). A failure to recruit because of pregnancy would also be direct sex discrimination. As regards illness arising from pregnancy, an employer must not dismiss during statutory maternity leave. Thereafter, the relevant test (for sex discrimination rather than unfair dismissal purposes) is how a man with a similar absence record would be treated. The right not to be unfairly dismissed because of pregnancy is subject to the normal qualifying employment and hours requirement for unfair dismissal claims.* Where these qualifications and requirements are not met, the claim may be pursued as sex discrimination under the Sex Discrimination Act.

In addition to the automatically unfair dismissals mentioned above there are some further special cases. These are dismissal of strikers; constructive dismissals; failure to permit a woman to return to work after confinement; dismissals associated with transfers of undertakings.

---

* The requirement for a period of qualifying employment is likely to be removed to allow the UK to conform with the EC's proposed Directive on the Protection of Pregnant Women at Work.

Dismissal in connection with industrial action

Dismissal in connection with a lock-out, strike or other industrial action is largely excluded from unfair dismissal law. Where there are union members and the strike is unofficial, tribunals have no jurisdiction whatsoever. This is because an employee has no right to claim that he was unfairly dismissed if, at the time of his dismissal, he was taking part in unofficial industrial action.[14] Where the strike is official, or all the strikers are non-unionists, tribunals have a limited jurisdiction. If everyone is treated the same, no complaint of unfair dismissal can be heard. If, however, some are dismissed and others are not, there is a possible unfair dismissal claim. The selectivity must apply, however, at the time of the complainant's dismissal, rather than from the beginning of the strike. Thus, if 100 people go on strike and all are still on strike a month later, the dismissal of the 6 strike leaders may give rise to unfair dismissal claims. The dismissal of all 100 will not. Moreover, if 40 people had returned to work after a month, the dismissal of the remaining 60 would not give rise to claims, since there was no selectivity among those on strike at the time of the dismissal.

Where all strikers are dismissed, but only some are re-engaged, the critical factor will be the time interval between the dismissal of those re-engaged and their re-engagement. If this period is three months or more, none of the people who have not been re-engaged will have a claim. Whether a person is taking part in industrial action is a matter of fact for the tribunal to decide (*Coates and Venables* v *Modern Methods and Materials Ltd*). The law regards a strike as breach of contract (*Simmons* v *Hoover*).

Constructive dismissals

A constructive dismissal is termination by the employee, with or without notice, in circumstances where the employee is entitled to terminate the contract without notice because of the employer's conduct. These are circumstances where the employer is guilty of gross misconduct as a result of which the employee has a right to resign and claim that he has been unfairly dismissed. It is important to note not only that the onus of proof will be upon the applicant, but also that the two-stage process does not apply. Instead, the test is whether there has been a fundamental breach of contract (*Western Excavating (ECC) Ltd* v *Sharp*). This, however, establishes only the fact of dismissal, and not its fairness or otherwise.

It has to be stated that, perhaps surprisingly, constructive dismissals are not automatically unfair (*Savoia* v *Chiltern Herb Farms Ltd*; see also *Vose* v *South Sefton Health Authority*). The employer may argue that it was necessary to change the contract of employment unilaterally in the interests of the business. This would have special weight if the business was in trouble or had to make specified savings. Other breaches would be less easy to defend, for example, breach of trust (an implied contractual term; *Wood* v *W M Car Services (Peterborough) Ltd*), abusive language, failure to provide proper safety arrangements, or reducing an employee's pay and/or status.

The employee does not have to resign and claim constructive dismissal (ie accept the employer's repudiation of contract). He can affirm the contract, either accepting the change, or rejecting it but carrying on working and suing for damages (*Ferodo Ltd* v *Rigby*).

Refusal of right to return to work after confinement

Next, there is the position of the woman who is refused her right to return to work after confinement. It was noted earlier that this was part of the statutory definition of dismissal. It will not be treated as dismissal, however, if the employer has five or fewer employees and it was not reasonably practicable to allow her to return to work or offer her alternative employment on 'terms not substantially less favourable to her'.[15] Nor will it be a dismissal, irrespective of the size of the firm, if it is not reasonably practicable to take her back, but she is offered alternative employment which she unreasonably refuses. The onus is upon the employer to show that there was no dismissal.

Dismissals in connection with transfers of undertakings*

Finally, there is the question of dismissals in connection with the transfer of undertakings. Regulations issued under the European Communities Act 1972 apply where there is a transfer, but not where there is simply a change in the ownership of share capital. Undertaking includes 'any trade or business . . . in the nature of a commercial venture'.[16] Contracts of employment automatically transfer with the business, as do rights and duties under the contract, including continuity of employment. Dismissals arising out of the transfer are automatically unfair, unless there is some economic, technical or organizational reason for them 'entailing changes in the workforce'.[17] Such a reason, including redundancy, would constitute SOSR. Thus, the mere change of identity of the employer does not give an employee the right to resign and claim unfair dismissal or redundancy. However, a detrimental and substantial change to the employee's working conditions will give a right to claim unfair dismissal.

INDUSTRIAL TRIBUNALS

Industrial tribunals are statutory judicial bodies. They were first established under the Industrial Training Act 1964 to hear employers' appeals against levies made by the training boards that were set up under the Act. Since then the tribunals have been given the task of deciding many other types of disputes, typically those between individual employees and their employers. In addition to handling unfair dismissal cases, tribunals deal with:

- whether an employee is receiving the amount of redundancy pay to which he is entitled;
- claims for equal pay between men and women;
- claims that there have been unlawful deductions from wages;
- claims in respect of time off for union representatives;
- claims in respect of race and sex discrimination in the employment field; and
- other issues put within their jurisdiction by various statutes.

---

* This subject is explored more fully below, see Chapter 18, pp 368–70.

Unfair dismissal complaints account for over half of the tribunals' caseload.

Tribunals currently operate as a result of the Employment Protection (Consolidation) Act 1978,[18] with most of the procedural details set out in regulations issued under that Act.[19] Except in rare cases tribunals comprise three people: one from a panel nominated by the unions; one from a panel nominated by the employers; and a legally-qualified chairman. The chairman is appointed by the Lord Chancellor (Lord President in Scotland), while the two other members are appointed by the Secretary of State for Employment. The purpose of having a combination of lay members and a lawyer is to get a blend of legal knowledge and industrial experience. A majority decision suffices, but in all except a handful of cases, the decision is unanimous.

The tribunal process is triggered off by an individual who thinks he has been unfairly dismissed completing an originating application form, known as an IT.1, and sending it to the Central Office of the Industrial Tribunals (COIT) within three months of the effective date of termination. An application may arrive later than this if it was not reasonably practicable to apply within three months, but in practice tribunals enforce the three-month rule quite strictly. The individual may or may not have already exercised his separate legal right to request and obtain from his former employer a written statement of the reasons for the dismissal. This right is given to those who had two years' or more continuous employment with their employer prior to termination.[20] The claim for compensation for failure to give written reasons is usually put on the same IT.1 as the unfair dismissal claim itself, and must be at COIT within three months. The respondent employer has 14 days in which to reply to the request for written reasons. An unreasonable refusal to comply will result in a tribunal making a penalty award of two weeks' pay. The two weeks' pay is gross and, since the right to have written reasons is separate from the right not to be unfairly dismissed, there is no percentage deduction for any contributory fault. The award will usually be made at the end of the hearing of the substantive unfair dismissal claim.

Regardless of whether a request for a written statement of reasons has been made, the respondent employer will need to reply to the originating application. A copy of the IT.1 will be sent to him, together with a form IT.3 on which the reply can be made. The IT.3, known as the 'Notice of Appearance', should be returned to the specified regional office within 14 days. This act secures for the respondent the right to take part in any hearing which might ensue. A copy of the IT.3 is sent to the applicant. The regional office of the industrial tribunals then sets in train the arrangements for a hearing. A brief questionnaire is sent to the parties asking about representation at the hearing, and about the number of witnesses they will be bringing. Finally, the regional office will fix a date for a hearing and notify the parties.

The above description constitutes the minimum of what might happen. There may be more. First, COIT will notify an applicant if it looks as though the case is not within the tribunals' jurisdiction, and will indicate that the case may be struck out unless the applicant confirms in writing that he is determined to go ahead. Secondly, the regional chairman may decide that a full hearing of the case should not go ahead until there has been a pre-hearing assessment (PHA). This device was introduced in order to prevent meritless cases being pursued.

It can be requested by either party, or ordered by the chairman of his own volition. A PHA involves the full tribunal in a brief, perhaps 30–minute hearing, at which the arguments are put, but little or no evidence is given. The regulations say that the tribunal may consider the IT.1, the IT.3, any representations in writing and any oral argument. If the tribunal considers that a party's case has 'no reasonable prospect of success', it may warn that party of the possibility of costs being awarded against it if it continues. The outcome of a PHA therefore is either a 'costs warning' or no such warning. In any particular case, the tribunal dealing with the PHA will have a different membership from that dealing with any subsequent hearing. The Employment Act 1989 provides for regulations to replace PHAs with a system of pre-hearing reviews and cash deposits, but no such regulations have yet been made.[21]

Irrespective of whether or not the case involves a PHA there may be a preliminary matter to settle before a full hearing of the case is considered. Such matters usually concern eligibility.

- Is the applicant an employee?
- Was the IT.1 received in time?
- Has the employee the requisite length of qualifying employment?
- Is the applicant under normal retiring age?

If there is no PHA, and there is no preliminary matter to decide, the parties will not meet the tribunal until the full hearing. They might, however, meet the chairman if there are any procedural difficulties. Such difficulties might arise if the parties choose to implement the interlocutory procedure. This procedure allows the parties to deal with each other, requesting and providing information, and exchanging documents. Ultimately there may be an agreed bundle of documents. In the event of a refusal to co-operate by one of the parties, a tribunal order may be sought by the other.

The tribunal regulations allow orders for discovery and inspection of documents, and for further particulars of the grounds of the case. Discovery means finding out what documents the other side is relying upon, while inspection is the right to see one or more of those documents. If the other party refuses, it will be necessary to make out a case to the regional chairman, and a hearing in chambers (ie in the chairman's room) will be held at which his decision will be given. The other members of the tribunal are not present. The same process will be necessary if the other party refuses to provide further particulars of their case.

The tribunal may also compel witnesses to attend. Application for witness orders is made to the chairman. If the orders are granted they will be sent to the party requesting them and that party serves them on the witnesses. Failure to abide by tribunal orders is a criminal offence punishable by fine.

There is an important role for ACAS. Copies of the papers – the IT.1 and the IT.3 – are sent to the regional office of ACAS. The purpose of this is to allow ACAS to perform its statutory duty, which is to conciliate. The duty is 'to endeavour to promote a settlement of the complaint without its being determined by an industrial tribunal'.[22] The duty to conciliate applies if ACAS is requested to do it by the parties, or in the absence of such a request, if the conciliation officer considers that there is 'a reasonable prospect of success'.

Where it is sought by the applicant, and where it is 'practicable', the conciliation officer must try to promote re-employment rather than a cash settlement.

ACAS defines conciliation in the way that the process is commonly understood. The essential features are that the outcome (ie the agreement) is a joint decision of the two parties, the employee and the employer, and that the conciliator does not impose, nor even recommend what the particular outcome should be. The vast majority of agreed settlements are in the forms of cash compensation rather than re-employment. The tribunal may promulgate the agreed decision.

Any information conveyed to a conciliation officer is privileged – it cannot be admitted in evidence at the hearing without the permission of the person who communicated it. Moreover, it should be noted that once ACAS has conciliated and an agreed settlement has been reached, the right to pursue the case through to a tribunal hearing is lost. The same is not true if the settlement is agreed without ACAS. The ACAS role can continue until all questions of liability and remedy have been decided (*Courage Take Home Trade Ltd* v *Keys*). This means that ACAS could be used to conciliate over compensation if the tribunal decides on unfair dismissal but leaves it to the parties to settle compensation.

Since settlements tend to be in the form of a sum of money, it is useful to have some idea of what a tribunal might award. In most cases tribunal awards comprise two elements, as follows.

1. A basic award calculated in the same way as a statutory redundancy payment, ie according to age, length of employment and earnings, with the $\frac{1}{12}$ reduction operating from the age of 64 in the case of both men and women. The maximum basic award from 1 April 1992 is £6150.*
2. A compensatory award arrived at by establishing the applicant's net loss as a result of the dismissal. The maximum possible under this head from 1 April 1991 is £10,000 and there was no increase from 1 April 1992.

It may be more difficult for the respondent to do this calculation, since only the applicant will know the detail of his own losses, and in any case future loss is something of an imponderable. Nevertheless, a rough estimate will inform the bargaining process. Interest is now payable on industrial tribunal awards when they remain unpaid 42 or more days after the tribunal decision is promulgated.[23]

The parties may represent themselves or be represented by a person of their own choosing. Because legal representation is not compulsory, legal fees can be avoided. Legal advice is available under the Legal Aid and Advice Scheme, but legal aid (including representation) is not. The normal legal rule under which the loser pays the victor's costs does not apply. Costs will be awarded only if a party acts frivolously (ie pursues a hopeless case), vexatiously (ie pursues a case in order to inconvenience the other party) or behaves unreasonably in some other way.

Legal procedure is used. This means that the representative will proceed by examining witnesses (ie asking them questions). Each witness is examined first

---

* In dismissals on grounds of union membership or non-membership there is also a minimum basic award. From 1 April 1992 this is £2700.

by the representative of the party for whom the witness is appearing. Then the witness will be examined by the representative of the other 'side' (ie cross-examined). At this stage the tribunal may well ask some questions. Finally, the witness may be re-examined by the representative of his own 'side'. Representatives will need to be familiar with the substance of the law and with the procedure of industrial tribunals.

References

1. Employment Protection (Consolidation) Act (EP(C)A) 1978, c 44, Schedule 9, para 2(1).
2. EP(C)A, s 57(3).
3. Sex Discrimination Act 1986, c 59, s 3.
4. EP(C)A, s 140(2)(*e*).
5. Wedderburn, Lord (1986) *The Worker and the Law*, 3rd edn, Penguin Books, Harmondsworth, p 235.
6. EP(C)A, Schedule 13.
7. EP(C)A, s 153.
8. EP(C)A, s 57 (4).
9. EP(C)A, s 81.
10. ACAS (1977) Code of Practice, *Disciplinary Practice and Procedures in Employment*, HMSO, London. See also: ACAS (1987) *Discipline at Work*, Advisory, Conciliation and Arbitration Service, London.
11. Employment Act 1988, c 19, s 11.
12. Under EP(C)A, s 58(1)(*b*).
13. EP(C)A, s 60(3)(*c*).
14. Employment Act 1990, c 38, s 9.
15. EP(C)A, s 56A.
16. The Transfer of Undertakings (Protection of Employment) Regulations, SI 1981/1794, r 2(1).
17. Transfer of Undertakings Regulations, r 8(2).
18. EP(C)A, s 128.
19. Industrial Tribunals (Rules of Procedure) Regulations, SI 1985/16.
20. Increased from six months by Employment Act 1989, c 38, s 15. The two years' qualification applies to any employment commencing on or after 26 February 1990. (Employment Act 1988 (Commencement and Transitional Provisions) Order, SI 1990/189).
21. Employment Act 1989, s 20.
22. EP(C)A, s 134.
23. Employment Act 1982, c 46, Schedule 3, para 7 and the Industrial Tribunals (Interest) Order, SI 1990/479.

Chapter Eighteen
Other Individual Rights*

Paul Lewis

INTRODUCTION

In the main, this chapter is concerned with the rights of the individual employee or worker. From time to time, however, a departure is made in order to deal with the rights of trades union members (in relation to employers and to their own unions) and the rights of unions as conferred upon their officials. The common law contract of employment is still the essence of the employment relationship; therefore, contractual as well as statutory rights are examined.

A broad summary is provided at the expense of much detail. In particular, little space is devoted to areas of law where the essentials are unchanged or which have had little usage. Instead the focus is upon those areas which have been the subject of substantial change or have caused difficulty of interpretation. Social security law (including pensions, sick pay and maternity pay) is excluded, and the chapter does not extend to data protection and access.

STATUTORY EMPLOYMENT PROTECTION RIGHTS

Meaning of 'employee'

An employee is defined as 'an individual who has entered into or works under (or where the employment has ceased, worked under) a contract of employment'. A contract of employment means 'a contract of service or apprenticeship'.[1] Unfortunately this does not get us very far, since the critical question – 'How is it to be decided if the worker is employed under a contract of service?' – is left unanswered. In fact, the common law of contract and case law provide some tests to be applied, although no single test is generally conclusive. The issue is whether the worker is an employee, working for an employer under a contract of employment (or service), or a person in business on his own account providing services for a customer under a contract for services.

Tribunals should consider the following.

- Who has the right to control the manner of work? (The 'control' test.)
- Is the worker integrated into the structure of the organization? (The 'organizational' test.)
- Whose business is it – who takes the risks, who takes the profits? (The 'entrepreneurial' test.)

---

* This chapter relates to the law as at 1 February 1992.

- Who provides the tools, instruments and equipment? (However, some employees by custom provide their own tools.)
- Is the employer entitled to exclusive service?
- Are there wages, sick pay and holiday pay? If yes, who pays them? A fixed payment for a specified period suggests a contract of employment. Payment by task argues for a contract for services, but not conclusively.
- Who has the power to select and appoint; dismiss; fix the place and time of work; fix the time of holidays?
- Is there a mutual obligation – the employee to work, the employer to provide it? (See *Nethermere (St Neots) Ltd* v *Gardiner and Taverna*.)
- What contractual provisions are there?
- Is there a duty of personal service?
- What arrangements are there for tax and national insurance, eg is tax deducted via PAYE?
- Is the relationship genuinely one of self-employment or is there an attempt to avoid protective legislation?

Redundancy

An employee dismissed by reason of redundancy* may be entitled to a statutory redundancy payment (RP).[2] To qualify, the employee must have been continuously employed by the employer (or an associated employer) for two years or more, and be under 65 years or under normal retiring age if lower than 65 (see p 344).

Employment before the age of 18 does not count towards continuous employment. Those working under a contract for less than 16 hours per week are excluded, unless there have been 5 or more years of continuous employment at 8 or more hours. Share fishermen, Crown Servants, most merchant seamen and certain other miscellaneous categories are also excluded.

A redundancy payment is calculated by taking the number of years' employment in each of the age ranges in Table 18.1 (see p 362) and multiplying by the appropriate number of weeks' pay. No employment beyond 20 years is counted, so the maximum payment is $20 \times 1\frac{1}{2} = 30$ weeks' pay. There is a maximum level of weekly pay which is counted. Since 1 April 1992 this has been £205. Where a week's pay varies with the amount of work done, an average hourly rate is to be calculated over the last 12 weeks of employment. In such circumstances overtime hours are to be included, but must be treated as if paid at the non-premium rate. This can give rise to the anomaly of those working overtime having a lower hourly rate for RP (and unfair dismissal basic award) purposes than those who do not work overtime (*British Coal Corporation* v *Cheesbrough*). The RP is reduced by $\frac{1}{12}$ for each month beyond the age of 64.[3]

An employee has six months in which to claim RP by applying to an industrial tribunal or writing to the employer. The employee will lose any right to an RP, however, if the employer offers 'suitable' alternative

---

* Redundancy is defined on p 345. The 'relevant date' for determining the length of continuous employment is the end of the notice period, or where there is no notice, the date of termination.

Table 18.1   *Formula for computation of RPs*

Age	No of weeks' pay
under 22	$\frac{1}{2}$
22–40	1
41 and over	$1\frac{1}{2}$

employment and the employee 'unreasonably' refuses it.[4] Where the terms of the new employment differ from those of the old there is a requirement for a 'trial period' of at least four weeks to establish whether the employment is suitable, without loss of entitlement to claim the RP.

An employee may claim a payment, or any unpaid part of it, direct from the National Insurance Fund, after taking all reasonable steps (other than legal proceedings) to recover the payment from the employer, or when the employer is insolvent. An employee given notice of dismissal by reason of redundancy may be entitled to a reasonable amount of time off before the expiry of that notice in order to look for new employment or make arrangements for training for future employment.[5]

Maternity

There is no minimum qualifying employment for the right to antenatal time off.[6] The woman must have an appointment. For any second or subsequent appointment she must provide a medical certificate as proof of pregnancy and evidence of the appointment (eg an appointment card).

The right to return to work applies until the end of the period of 29 weeks beginning with the week in which the child is born, although it may be extended in certain circumstances.[7] The qualifying period of employment is 2 years at 16 or more hours, or 5 years at 8 or more, up to the 11th week before the expected week of confinement, as medically certified.* The woman must continue to be employed, but does not necessarily have to be at work, up to the 11th week before confinement. She must inform the employer of her intention to return, and her expected (or actual) week of confinement. This must be done in writing at least 21 days before maternity absence, or as soon as it is reasonably practicable. If requested by the employer she must produce for inspection the medical certificate showing the expected week of confinement. The employer has the right to send a written request within 49 days from the notified date of the beginning of confinement asking for confirmation of intention to return. He must explain that a failure to give written confirmation within 14 days (or as soon after as is reasonably practicable) will lose her the right to return. She must, in any case, notify the employer in writing of her proposed date of return at least 21 days beforehand.

The right to return will not apply if there has been a redundancy and there is no suitable alternative work, or an offer of such work is unreasonably refused. Similarly, if the employer can argue that it is not reasonably practicable to take

---

* The proposed EC Directive on the Protection of Pregnant Women at Work would (if adopted in the form currently proposed) require the abolition of the qualifying period.

the woman back in her original job, but that he has offered suitable alternative work which she has unreasonably rejected, the right to return will be lost. An employer with five or fewer employees can argue that it was not reasonably practicable to take her back, nor to offer her suitable alternative work. Suitable means that the terms, conditions and location are not substantially less favourable than those of her employment prior to maternity absence.

Time off for public duties[8]

An employee is entitled to time off for duties arising out of holding one of the following public positions:

- justice of the peace;
- member of a local authority;
- member of a statutory tribunal;
- member of an NHS trust or authority (including a family health services authority);
- member of the National Rivers Authority;
- member of the governing body of an educational establishment maintained by a local authority, a grant-maintained school or a higher education corporation; and
- member of a board of visitors for prisons, remand centres etc.

The amount of time off is what is 'reasonable in all the circumstances'. There is no obligation upon an employer to pay for the time off. Any employee refused time off may apply to a tribunal within three months. The tribunal may make an award which is 'just and equitable', taking into account any loss sustained and the infringement of rights.

Payment of wages

This area was radically altered by the Wages Act 1986.[9] There is now a general restriction on deductions from wages which applies to both manual and non-manual workers. There is no qualifying period of employment or minimum number of hours of work, and the rights extend to Crown employees. A deduction from wages may not be made unless it is authorized by statute, or by a relevant provision of the worker's contract, or by the worker himself in advance, in writing.

A copy of the appropriate contractual term, or notification of it in writing, must be given to the worker in advance of any deduction. Neither contractual changes nor the worker's agreement can be used to authorize deductions retrospectively.

The term 'wages' includes weekly and monthly pay, and includes salaries. It includes any holiday pay, commission, bonuses and other pay, whether contractual or non-contractual, as well as statutory sick and maternity pay, and various statutory payments such as guarantee pay and pay for time off. It does not include advances of wages, payments of expenses, pensions, *ex gratia* payments, redundancy payments or payment to the worker otherwise than in his capacity as a worker. Payments or benefits in kind are excluded from wages, except for vouchers with a fixed monetary value (eg luncheon vouchers), which are capable of being exchanged for money, goods or services. Wages in lieu of notice are not wages and therefore are not claimable under the Wages Act: they are damages for breach of contract (*Delaney* v *Staples*).

Certain deductions from wages are not subject to the above rules, including agreed deductions payable to third parties (eg a trades union), deductions arising from industrial action and deductions to obtain recovery of overpayment of wages. However, according to the Employment Appeal Tribunal (EAT) in *Home Office* v *Ayres*, the recovery of overpayments can be dealt with under the Wages Act if it is not lawful at common law. The recovery of overpayments will not automatically be lawful.

In addition to the general restrictions on deductions, there are special restrictions applicable to retail employment. This includes not just shop assistants but also many others handling money, for example bus conductors, drivers who collect fares, cashiers, ticket clerks. These apply to deductions for cash shortages or stock deficiencies, including those arising from the dishonesty or negligence of the worker. The deduction is limited to 10 per cent of gross wages on any pay day, although there is no limit at the termination of employment. Deductions, or the first of a series of deductions, must be made within 12 months of the employer's discovery of the shortage or deficiency, or from any earlier date when the employer ought reasonably to have made the discovery.

Both the general and the special retail rules governing deductions apply equally to employers' demands for payments. The employer may take the usual steps for recovery, providing that within the 12-month period he made a written demand, on a pay day, showing the employee's total liability. The right of application to an industrial tribunal replaces the worker's right to go to the county court over the matters contained in the Wages Act.

The repeal of the Truck Acts means that manual workers no longer have a statutory right to be paid in cash. The issue will be subject entirely to matters of employment contract and union–employer negotiation. It may well be that those employees paid in cash have an implied term in their contracts that cash will be the method of payment. The imposition of cashless pay, therefore, could result in claims for damages for breach of contract. For employees starting on or after 1 January 1987, employers are likely to insist on cashless pay as part of the contract, unless unions can persuade them otherwise. The repeal of the Truck Acts has no bearing on the frequency of pay (ie weekly or monthly), which remains a matter of contract and collective bargaining.

The Wages Act does not affect the employee's right under the Employment Protection (Consolidation) Act (EP(C)A) 1978 to have an itemized pay statement.[10]

Minimum wages

There is no general minimum laid down by law. There are, however, minimum levels laid down for certain industries through the medium of wages councils.* Originally trade boards, under the Trade Boards Act of 1909, they were to

---

* The government is considering the abolition of wages councils and in a recent White Paper, 'People, Jobs and Opportunity' (p 39) states that wages councils 'can have no permanent place in our system of wage setting': Cm. 1810, HMSO, London.

afford protection to employees in industries which were low paid, and where trades union organization was weak. They now operate under the Wages Act 1986.[11] A wages council consists of equal numbers of employers' and workers' representatives appointed by their respective organizations, and up to five independent members, one of whom takes the chair. Small business interests are specifically required to be represented on the employer's side. Wages orders are enforceable as implied terms of the contract of employment and implementation is monitored by a wages inspectorate. In fixing minimum rates wages councils must consider the possible effect on levels of employment. The orders cannot be retrospective. A period of 28 days exists for objections to the proposed rate.

A worker may sue for arrears for up to six years, but the wages inspector can, in fact, institute civil proceedings on behalf of a worker. If the wages inspector instigates criminal proceedings the worker may obtain up to two years' arrears, and the employer may face fines of up to £400, or £2000 if false records are kept or false statements made.[12] Just over 2 million workers are covered by the wages council system in industries such as clothing manufacture, catering, hairdressing, toy manufacture, retail distribution and laundries. A notice of the current wages order must be displayed and home workers notified. The employer must keep records. Orders may fix a single minimum rate of remuneration for basic hours and a minimum overtime rate, and set a limit on deductions in respect of living accommodation. The orders do not apply to anyone under the age of 21. Underpayment may allow an employee to resign and claim unfair constructive dismissal. Any redundancy payment must be based on a figure no less than the statutory minimum, otherwise an application may be made to a tribunal to establish the proper amount of the payment.

Guarantee pay

The EP(C)A provides for a daily guarantee payment where the employer is unable to provide any work at all during a day when the employee would normally be required to work.[13] Crown employment is included. One month's qualifying employment is needed and any employee on a fixed-term contract of 3 months or less, or on a specific task contract expected to last for 3 months or less is excluded, unless there is already 3 months' continuous employment, ie under a contract for, or working 16 hours or more per week (8 hours or more if there is already 5 years' continuous employment).

If the failure to provide work stems from industrial action in the employer's firm or any associated employer's firm, no payment will be due. Nor will it be due if suitable alternative employment (even if not permitted by the contract) is unreasonably refused, or if the employee does not conform to the employer's requirements relating to availability for work. The amount of the daily payment is the number of normal hours multiplied by the hourly rate, subject to a statutory maximum of £14.10 per day from 1 April 1992. No payment is due where there are 'no normal working hours on the day in question'. The maximum number of days' guarantee pay is five in any three-month period. An employee may complain to an industrial tribunal that his employer has not paid part or all of the guarantee payment. This complaint must be made within three months of the day to which the application relates. Any remuneration for the day may be offset against the liability to pay statutory guarantee pay. Where there is a collective agreement on guarantee pay, and at the request of the parties, the minister may issue an order exempting from the statutory provisions the employees covered by that agreement. Guarantee pay has no bearing on the issue of whether the employer has a right under the contract to dispense with some or all of the employee's pay during a lay-off or short-time working when there is insufficient work. This will depend on the terms of the contract.

Medical suspension

Under the EP(C)A an employee, or someone in Crown employment, who is suspended on medical grounds under one of a limited number of sets of regulations specified in Schedule 1 to the Act, has a right to be paid for up to 26 weeks.[14]

Notice periods

The EP(C)A lays down minimum notice periods.[15] The right is given to those employees with 1 month or more of continuous employment, and is as follows: if the continuous employment is less than 2 years, 1 week's notice; 1 week's notice per year of continuous employment from 2 years to 12. The minimum legal notice to be given where length of employment exceeds 12 years is still 12 weeks. The minimum notice which has to be given by the employee to the employer is one week. This does not increase with length of employment. None of the above removes the employer's right to dismiss summarily (ie without notice or wages in lieu of notice) for gross misconduct.

Written particulars

Not later than 13 weeks after the commencement of employment the employer must give the employee a written statement of the main terms of his employment.[16] Crown Servants and employees who normally work outside Great Britain are excluded, as is anyone working under 16 hours a week (or under 8 if they have 5 years or more continuous employment).

The statement must identify the employer and employee, the date when the employment began, and whether any employment with a previous employer counts as continuous employment and, if so, when the continuous employment began. The following particulars have to be given:

- scale or rate of pay or method of calculating it;
- interval of payment;
- any terms and conditions relating to hours of work, holiday pay, sufficient for holiday pay entitlement to be calculated, sick pay, pensions;
- length of notice on both sides; and
- the title of the job the employee is employed to perform.

If there are no terms under any of these headings the statement should say so. An additional note should specify disciplinary rules and grievance procedures, and whether a pensions contracting-out certificate is in force.

The above details do not actually have to be provided in the statement. The statement can simply refer the employee to other documents containing the details (eg works rules, collective agreements).

Employers with fewer than 20 employees are not required to provide details of disciplinary rules and procedures, but in arriving at the total number of employees those employed by any associated employer must be included.[17]

The Proof of Employment Relationship Directive, adopted by the EC in 1991, requires domestic legislation to be in operation by 30 June 1993.[18] No draft of proposed legislation is yet available, but it appears that employers will have to provide the main details of employment within two months of the employee commencing work. Of considerable importance is the likelihood of the legislation applying to employees (and perhaps some other workers) working for more than 8 but less than 16 hours per week without the current 5-year continuous employment qualification. The information to be provided is largely the same as that already required under s 1 of the EP(C)A. It will need to be provided, on request, to those already in employment, within two months of the request.

Rights of employees on insolvency[19]

Insolvency rights fall into two categories:

- some debts are given priority (up to a statutory maximum which may be changed from time to time by the Secretary of State); and
- some debts (including any unmet priority debts) can be paid out of the NI Fund.

Priority debts   These include:

- statutory guarantee payments;
- remuneration payable on suspension on medical grounds;
- payment for time off for union duties, or to look for work, or arrange training on being made redundant;
- remuneration payable under a protective award;
- payment for time off for antenatal care;
- statutory sick pay;
- up to four months' wages or salary;
- accrued holiday pay; and
- contractual sick pay and holiday pay.

Debts which may be claimed from the NI Fund   These are:

- arrears of pay for up to and including eight weeks – pay includes wages, salaries, bonuses, commission, overtime pay and the statutory items which make up the priority debts above; the maximum earnings limit of £205 per week (from 1 April 1992) applies;
- holiday pay for up to and including 6 weeks – again the maximum earnings limit applies: the entitlement must have occurred within the previous 12 months;
- pay for the statutory notice period or compensation for the employer's failure to give proper statutory notice (again the earnings limit applies);
- unpaid basic award of unfair dismissal compensation;
- reasonable reimbursement of apprentices' or articled clerks' fees;
- statutory maternity pay; and
- statutory redundancy pay.

Change of ownership of a business

The EP(C)A states that where a trade, business or undertaking is transferred from one person to another, the period of employment of someone employed at the time of transfer will count as employment with the transferee.[20] The transfer does not break the continuity. However, the transfer must involve the business and not just the physical assets (*Woodhouse and Staton* v *Peter Brotherhood Ltd*). The EP(C)A does not define trade or undertaking but defines business to include 'a trade or profession . . . and any activity carried on by a body of persons, whether corporate or incorporate'.[21]

In addition to the EP(C)A provisions are the Transfer of Undertakings Regulations.[22] These apply where there is a transfer 'effected by sale or as a result of a sale, by some other disposition, or by operation of law', but this does not include changes in control which arise simply from changes in share ownership. They apply to undertakings. An undertaking is 'any trade or business . . . in the nature of a commercial venture'. Deciding what is a commercial venture is a matter of first impression for the industrial tribunal (*Woodcock and ors* v *(1) The Committee for the time being of the Friends School, Wigton (2) Genwise Limited*).

Where there is 'hiving down' of a business by a receiver – ie the separation of the employees from the business in order to make the latter more attractive to potential buyers – the initial transfer to a subsidiary is not covered by the regulations, so that contracts of employment do not transfer. The transfer of leases, involving a double transfer (back to the lessor and then from lessor to new lessee) can count as a transfer under the regulations (*Foreningen af Arbejdsledere i Danmark* v *Daddy's Dance Hall A/S*). So, too, can the transfer of a lease back to the lessor, followed by the sale of the business to a new owner, and the rescission of a lease, followed by the owner taking over the running of the business (*P Bork International A/S (in liquidation)* v *Foreningen af Arbejdsledere i Danmark; Landsorganisationen i Danmark* v *Ny Molle Kro*).

The general principle appears to be that the application of the EC directive (to which the regulations purport to give effect) is not precluded provided that the undertaking retains its identity as an economic unit. The EAT later upheld this principle in relation to franchises in *(1) LMC Drains Ltd (2) Metro Rod Services Ltd* v *Waugh*.

The regulations are complex and a certain amount of difficulty has been encountered in operating them. For example, in *Banking, Insurance and Finance Union* v *Barclay's Bank plc*, a union complaint that the company failed to consult them about a transfer was dismissed because transfer of the staff and the business separately meant that no transfer had occurred for the purposes of the regulations. Also, the various rights conferred by the regulations depend on the employee being employed at the time of the transfer. Dismissals prior to transfer have sometimes resulted in these rights being lost.

This problem has now been settled by the decision of the House of Lords in *Litster* v *Forth Dry Dock and Engineering Co Ltd*. Where dismissal arises out of a transfer and there is an economic, technical or organizational (ETO) reason to justify it, any liability is determined according to the principle in *Secretary of State for Employment* v *Spence and others*. The *Spence* principle makes it clear that responsibility would lie with the transferor if the effective date of termination (EDT) or 'relevant date' preceded transfer and with the transferee if it came after it.* There might still be difficulty in establishing the timing of the transfer. The *Spence* principle would also apply to dismissals not arising out of the transfer. By contrast, where the dismissal arises out of a transfer, but there is no ETO, the rule in *Litster* applies. This holds that where an employee has been dismissed prior to the transfer, he is to be treated as if he had not been dismissed. Any liability thus passes to the transferee.

The regulations reverse the normal common law position that a change in ownership automatically terminates the contract of employment. Instead, the regulations state expressly that the contract of employment will continue, as will rights and duties under it, including continuity of employment. Thus, the mere change of identity of the employer does not give an employee the right to claim a redundancy payment. As already noted, the employee's statutory rights are transferred by virtue of the EP(C)A. Maternity rights are also transferred. Liability for tortious acts (eg negligence) committed in relation to an employee also appear to transfer (see *Secretary of State for Employment* v *Spence and others* on this general question). Criminal liabilities do not transfer, and occupational pension schemes are expressly excluded from automatic transfer. Protective awards do not transfer according to the EAT in *Angus Jowett and Co* v *The National Union of Tailors and Garment Workers*, although the failure to pay, being a matter of contract, perhaps might.

A dismissal before or after the transfer will be automatically unfair if the reason is the transfer itself or something connected with it. Automatic means that the second stage test of reasonableness does not apply. There is, however, an exception. The dismissal can be justified as fair if it is for an economic, technical or organizational reason entailing changes in the workforce. The Court of Appeal has ruled, in *Berriman* v *Delabole Slate Ltd*, that changes in the workforce mean a deliberate change in the numbers and functions of employees. Straightforward changes in terms and conditions will, it seems, not constitute ETO. In *Wheeler* v *(1) Patel (2) Golding Group of Companies*, the EAT held that an ETO must relate to the conduct of the business.

An ETO constitutes SOSR under dismissal law, and requires the normal second stage (ie the test of reasonableness) to be entered. The onus of proof for ETO lies with the employer (*Litster*). *Gorictree Ltd* v *Jenkinson* showed that dismissal for an ETO prior to a transfer can simultaneously be dismissal for redundancy, giving rise to entitlement to a redundancy payment. This would be true even if the applicant was re-engaged subsequently, including immediately after the transfer, by the transferee. Where the dismissal is post-transfer because the transferee requires fewer employees, this can also be due to an ETO (*Meikle* v *McPhail (Charleston Arms)*). Where redundancy is the reason for dismissal, the statutory provision relating to unfair selection will apply.

Nothing in the regulations removes the individual's right to resign and claim a fundamental breach of contract, either for unfair dismissal or common law damages purposes. However, this right is circumscribed to a degree by the

---

* 'Relevant date' is defined on p 361 above; EDT in Chapter 17, p 342.

wording of the regulations which says that either: 'a substantial change is made in his working conditions to his detriment'; or the change in identity of the employer itself is 'significant' and 'to his detriment'.

Collective agreements also transfer automatically, but unless specifically provided otherwise in the agreement, these will not be legally enforceable. However, the collective agreement terms may be incorporated into individual contracts, which can be enforced (*Marley* v *Forward Trust Group Ltd*). Occupational pension schemes are again excluded from automatic transfer. Trades union recognition transfers automatically if the union is independent. Any redundancy agreement will have been transferred automatically, so in the event of a redundancy this will be relevant to the question of unfair selection.

The employer has a duty to inform and consult union representatives. These are the representatives of independent trades unions recognized by the employer. Consultation concerns employees who may be affected by a projected transfer. The information to be divulged, in writing, comprises:

- the fact of the transfer, the date and reasons;
- the legal, economic and social implications; and
- measures the transferor and the transferee propose to take *vis-à-vis* the employees. If there are no measures this must be stated.

Consultation involves considering union representations and replying to them, giving reasons for the rejection of any of them. As with redundancy consultation the employer may argue 'special circumstances'. Unions may complain to an industrial tribunal within three months. Compensation of up to two weeks' pay may be awarded to each affected employee on the basis of what is 'just and equitable', taking into account the seriousness of the employer's breach of duty.

CONTRACTUAL RIGHTS

Although statute limits to some extent what can be agreed between the parties, much of the substance of the employment relationship stems from express and implied contractual terms, works rules, custom and practice, and, where applicable, collective agreements between unions and employers. Like the statute-imposed terms, the implied terms are of particular importance because they lay down some ground rules for all employment contracts. The following obligations are prominent.

Employer	*Employee*
To pay wages for work done	To obey the employer's lawful commands
To take reasonable care for the employee's safety	To take reasonable care and skill in going about the work
To act in good faith	To give faithful and honest service and not to act manifestly against the employer's interest

The main employee duties can be seen to be co-operation, care and fidelity. It is submitted that co-operation includes a duty to adapt to reasonable change

(*Cresswell* v *Board of Inland Revenue*; *MacPherson* v *London Borough of Lambeth*). The employer has no general duty to provide work, but in the absence of a term to the contrary the common law holds that payment will nevertheless be due. The employer's duty to treat the employee fairly and reasonably, on the one hand, and the employee's duty to give faithful and honest service, on the other, import into the contract a term of mutual trust and confidence (*Woods* v *W M Car Services (Peterborough) Ltd*).

In general, a breach of a major term will amount to a repudiation of contract which the other party may accept and treat as grounds for ending the contract. Alternatively, that party may affirm the contract and insist on its further performance (*W E Cox Toner (International) Ltd* v *Crook*). The remedies for the breach would be a claim for compensation for constructive dismissal or suing for damages. It may also be possible to affirm the contract while standing on the original terms and sue for the breach. Thus, in *Ferodo Ltd* v *Rigby*, a worker continued the employment contract but sued for the damages arising out of a wage reduction imposed by the employer. The employer's biggest advantage in contract is the legitimacy given to his commands and the fact that many terms become part of the contract by imposition because employees fail to challenge rules or changes – 'silence is consent'.

In any dispute about the terms of a contract the courts may imply a term. The approach taken is that such a term should be so obvious that the parties did not feel a need to state it expressly. In practice, of course, it is difficult in the absence of express provisions, to decide what was intended by the parties. Sometimes evidence can be found in the terms of collective agreements, or in custom and practice. The former may be incorporated into the contract either expressly or by implied means. Thus, although a collective agreement is not itself legally enforceable, its terms nevertheless may be enforceable because of the process of incorporation into individual contracts of employment.

Courts will generally enforce contract terms without reference to their fairness to the respective parties, providing that the contract itself is not illegal or contrary to public policy, the terms are not made void by statute and the contract was entered into willingly.

Exceptionally, the courts will grant an injunction restraining a party from breaching a contract of employment. Such cases are rare because it is not thought desirable to order specific performance of a contract against the wishes of one of the parties. Special circumstances need to apply, as they did in *Hill* v *C A Parsons and Co*. In *Irani* v *Southampton and South-West Hampshire Area Health Authority* there were again special grounds: there was still confidence between employer and employee, a disputes procedure was available, and damages would not have been adequate as a remedy. An injunction was also granted in *Powell* v *London Borough of Brent*. The injunctions in *Hill*, *Irani* and *Powell* were all temporary. All of the above cases involved employees seeking injunctions to prevent dismissal, but there have been occasions when employees have sought injunctions for other purposes. For example, in *Hughes and others* v *London Borough of Southwark*, social workers obtained an injunction to stop their employer transferring them to a different type of work. On the other hand, the High Court would not grant an injunction in *MacPherson* v *London Borough of Lambeth* to stop the employer withholding pay because the employees would not operate a new computer. The employees were not able and willing to perform their contractual duties.

The development of industrial action based on partial performance of duties has given prominence to another aspect of the employment contract. Can an employer deduct some, or perhaps all, of the employee's pay if there is a partial withdrawal of labour, as there was, for example, in the long-running teachers' dispute? In *Miles* v *Wakefield Metropolitian District Council* the House of Lords held that an employer may refuse to accept partial performance and may withhold all of the pay. However, if partial performance is accepted by the employer, only part of the pay may be withheld (*Wiluszynski* v *London Borough of Tower Hamlets*). A different view (but with the same effect) is that where partial performance is accepted full wages are payable, but with an amount set off to cover the breach (*Sim* v *Rotherham Metropolitan Borough Council*).

A further contractual issue is whether dismissal is wrongful, ie not in accordance with the terms of the contract. In *Dietmann* v *London Borough of Brent* dismissal was wrongful because the disciplinary procedure had not been invoked, but its use was a term of the contract of employment.

Many employees faced with a repudiatory breach of contract by an employer will prefer the simpler, quicker and cheaper route of claiming unfair constructive dismissal to processing a claim for damages. This may, perhaps, be less true where a claim for damages is compatible with continued employment, and where the legal services of a trades union are available (both of these applied in *Ferodo*). In practice, many employees will probably reluctantly accept the employer's imposed change because of the need to keep their job. Many employers will prefer a dismissal, which can be defended as fair by using a mix of contract and statute arguments, to a claim for damages against the employee. Obtaining injunctions may have important advantages for both employers and employees.

JUDICIAL REVIEW

A person might have a remedy under public law. Where a person's rights are affected by a decision made by someone empowered by public law, judges may enforce duties or quash decisions if they are, for example, illegal, irrational or procedurally deficient (*Associated Provincial Picture Houses Ltd* v *Wednesbury Corporation*; *Council of Civil Service Unions and others* v *The Minister for the Civil Service*). In cases of dismissal, judicial review has an advantage over unfair dismissal law for the dismissed person, in that it allows the dismissal to be reversed. The general rule is that this remedy is available only where there is no other means of challenging the decision in question. Exceptionally, however, courts will depart from this rule, as in *Calveley and others* v *Merseyside Police*, where decisions to dismiss were quashed by the Court of Appeal. To obtain a judicial review, the person applying must be affected by the decision about which he is complaining.

EQUAL OPPORTUNITIES

Equal pay

The Equal Pay Act 1970 operates by inserting an equality clause into the contract of employment.[23] This means that there should be equality where a man and a woman are employed:

- on 'like work' – work of the same or a broadly similar nature; or
- on 'work rated as equivalent' – work of equal value under a non-discriminatory job evaluation scheme; or
- on work which is of equal value.

'Like work' does not mean that the work has to be the same (*Capper Pass Ltd v Lawton*). It can be 'broadly similar', but the differences must not be of any 'practical importance'. The time at which the work is done does not affect whether it is 'like work' (*Dugdale* v *Kraft Foods Ltd*). What has to be examined is the work actually done, rather than what could be done under the contract (*Electrolux Ltd* v *Hutchinson*). Job evaluation schemes allow a comparison of different jobs for the purposes of equal pay claims. The scheme must be non-discriminatory, impartial and must constitute a proper analysis (*Eaton Ltd* v *Nuttall*; *Bromley and others* v *H & J Quick Ltd*). Equal pay can be claimed irrespective of the jobs being completely different, provided that the demands made (under such headings as effort, skill and decision) are of 'equal value'.[24]

The British legislation states that equal value claims are permitted only if neither 'like work' nor 'work rated as equivalent' claims are possible. In *Pickstone and others* v *Freemans Plc*, however, the House of Lords held that this was a restriction of the wider European right to pursue an equal value claim. Thus, the present domestic law is deficient and complainants can rely on the wider European interpretation. This means, for example, that the existence of a man doing work that is the same as the complainant's and being paid the same, does not preclude an equal value claim using some other man as the comparator.

The Act does not apply solely to pay. It also extends to other terms. However, the House of Lords has rejected the argument that the whole remuneration package has to be considered, rather than just pay. The basic rate must be the same regardless of other contractual benefits (*Hayward* v *Cammell Laird Shipbuilders Ltd*). The Act applies to both men and women. The comparator has to be in the 'same employment' as the claimant. This means employed by the same (or an associated) employer at the same establishment, or at a different establishment if there are common terms (see *Leverton* v *Clwyd County Council*). A woman may compare herself with a male predecessor (*MacCarthys v Smith*). It is not provided under the Act, however, for comparison with a 'notional' man, ie to argue that a man doing the same job *would* have been paid more. It will be for the applicant to establish like work, equally-rated work and the same employment. Conversely, these issues will provide a basis for the employer's defence.

If the applicant succeeds in establishing the comparison, the employer may then argue that the variation in male/female terms is nothing to do with sex. The equality clause does not operate if the variation is 'genuinely due to a material factor'. This can include economic and other factors, as well as individual differences such as skills, qualifications, age and experience (*Rainey v Greater Glasgow Health Board*). Different pay structures may be a material factor, as in *Leverton*, and in *Reed Packaging Ltd v Boozer and Everhurst*. The onus of proof is on the employer to show a material factor. Such factors must be justifiable, ie caused by a real need on the part of the undertaking, appropriate to meet that need and necessary (*Bilka-Kaufhaus GmbH v Weber Von Hartz*).

The decision in *British Railways Board v Paul* makes it appear that there is no time limit for complaints made by individuals to industrial tribunals, nor, by inference, for applications by employers. However, the interpretation of the statute in this case is perhaps doubtful. It may be wiser to regard the time limit as being six months from the date of termination. Applications can also be made where employment is continuing. The Secretary of State may take cases to tribunals, either while the complainant is still employed or within six months of leaving.

Where the claim is successful the remedies are damages and up to two years' arrears of pay. A special procedure operates for equal value claims. First, the tribunal must dismiss the claim if it is satisfied that there are no reasonable grounds for determining that the jobs are of equal value. Secondly, if the case progresses, an expert (from a panel drawn up by ACAS) will be called in to do an assessment of the value of the respective jobs, and to present a report to the tribunal.

The Act is comprehensive in its application. Few occupations are excluded, and there are no hours or length of employment qualifications for making a claim. It applies to those who are 'employed', which is a category wider than employees (see *Quinnen v Howells*).

Although the British equal pay legislation includes items other than pay (ie other contractual terms), it does not go as far as the concept which has been developed by the European Court of Justice (ECJ). Recent ECJ cases show that contractual and statutory sick and redundancy pay, and occupational pensions, are pay within the meaning of Article 119 of the Treaty of Rome.* Therefore, they are subject to the principle of equal pay and Article 119 can be directly relied upon in preference to the narrower domestic legislation. As a result, differences in pensionable age and in benefits payable under an occupational pension scheme are a direct breach of the principle of equal pay as laid down in European law (*Barber v Guardian Royal Exchange Assurance Group*).

Moreover, there is, in another recent decision, the basis of an approach to the equal pay comparison which is entirely different from that used in the UK (*Handels-og Kontorfunktionaerernes Forbund i Danmark v Dansk Arbejdsgiverforening (acting for Danfoss)*. Domestic legislation requires a women to use one or more individual comparators as the basis for her case. By comparison, the

---

* Article 119 of the Treaty of Rome, which established the European Economic Community, holds that there should be 'equal pay for equal work'. An equal pay directive requires member countries to give effect to this principle through their own legislation (75/117/EEC; OJ L45).

ECJ in *Danfoss* stated that it was sufficient for the complainant to show a statistical imbalance between men's and women's pay to throw the burden of proof on to the employer to justify the imbalance. The context was one in which discretionary elements of pay were being distributed between individuals on a basis which was not clear.

Race and sex discrimination

It is unlawful in relation to employment to discriminate against a person because of their sex, because they are married, or on grounds of colour, race, nationality, or ethnic or national origins. Discrimination takes the following forms.[25]

1. *Direct*. Treating a person 'less favourably' than another person is or would be treated, on one of the prohibited grounds (eg colour). This includes segregation on racial grounds and sexual harassment (*Strathclyde Regional Council* v *Porcelli*).
2. *Indirect*. Applying a 'requirement or condition' which is or would be applied equally (eg to women and men), but which is such that the proportion of one group (eg women) who can comply with it is 'considerably smaller' than the proportion outside that group who can comply. Exclusion of groups of people from particular terms (eg part-timers from redundancy pay), where those groups are predominantly of one sex, may constitute indirect sex discrimination if it cannot be objectively justified by factors unrelated to sex. Thus, since statutory sickness payments made by an employer are defined as pay under Article 119, denial of such pay to part-timers, affecting women more than men, constitutes indirect sex discrimination (*Rinner-Kühn* v *FWW Spezial-Gebäundereinigung GmbH & Co KG*). Similarly, since severence payments under a collective agreement were also pay, the exclusion of part-timers, most of whom were women, constituted indirect sex discrimination and there was an entitlement to proportionate benefits (*Kowalska* v *Freie und Hansestadt Hamburg*). However, in *R* v *Secretary of State for Employment ex parte Equal Opportunities Commission*, the exclusion of part-timers from certain UK employment legislation was found to be objectively justified by the need to preserve jobs.
3. *Victimization*. Treating a person less favourably because they have, or are suspected of having, used the legislation, or because they intend to use the legislation, or have properly alleged breaches of the legislation. The legislation referred to is the Sex Discrimination Act 1975, the Equal Pay Act 1970 and the Race Relations Act 1976.

In addition to discrimination there is a series of other unlawful acts, including discriminatory advertising, instructing or putting pressure on others to discriminate, and aiding or assisting in the committing of an unlawful act.

Both the Race Relations Act and the Sex Discrimination Act allow discrimination where it is a 'genuine occupational qualification'. This means that a person of a particular sex, race, nationality etc can be chosen for a job because of their sex, race, nationality etc. The circumstances are limited and there are differences between the two Acts.

The Equal Opportunities Commission and the Commission for Racial Equality are charged with overseeing the working of the legislation, and have issued

Codes of Practice for their respective areas.[26] The Race Relations Code of Practice encourages ethnic monitoring. The Court of Appeal has given support to this practice, and to the use of the results of monitoring for evidential purposes when claims are brought (*West Midlands Passenger Transport Executive* v *Singh*).

While the Equal Pay Act applies to terms of employment, the two other discrimination Acts apply to:

- recruitment and selection arrangements (eg a discriminatory interview as in *Brennan* v *J H Dewhurst Ltd*);
- the terms on which jobs are offered;
- refusal to offer employment;
- opportunities for promotion, transfer or training, or access to any other benefits, facilities or services; and
- dismissal or any other detriment.

The Race Relations Act additionally contains terms of employment, conferring a right equivalent to that contained in the Equal Pay Act for women.

Remedies are obtained by applying to an industrial tribunal within three months of the act which is the subject of complaint. The tribunal may make a declaration of rights, an order for compensation and a recommendation that the respondent take a particular course of action. The maximum compensation is the same as the compensatory award for unfair dismissal. This was increased to £10,000 on 1 April 1991, but was not increased from 1 April 1992. The question of whether compensation can exceed this limit in a case pursued directly under EC law is currently being considered by the European Court of Justice (*Marshall* v *Southampton and South West Hampshire Health Authority (No 2)*).

Compensation may be awarded for injury to feelings and may include aggravated damages which compensate for the manner of, or motive for, the discrimination. Exemplary damages can also be awarded in order to punish the offender and deter others from similar unlawful conduct (*Alexander* v *The Home Office*; *Noone* v *North West Thames Regional Health Authority*; *City of Bradford Metropolitan Council* v *Arora*).

Discriminatory provisions in collective agreements and works rules are void, but discrimination in relation to death and retirement is permitted, except for retirement provisions which affect promotion, demotion, dismissal, training and transfer.

RIGHT OF TRADES UNIONISTS AND NON-UNIONISTS*

Access to employment

It is unlawful to refuse someone a job on the grounds that they are, or are not, a trades union member.[27] An advertisement containing such a requirement will

---

* Legislation relating to trades unions has just been consolidated (Trade Union and Labour Relations (Consolidation) Act 1992).

not in itself be unlawful, but it will be taken as conclusive evidence that an unlawful act was committed if a non-unionist or union member is subsequently refused employment, does not have the required status as specified in the advertisement and makes a claim to an industrial tribunal. Any requirement that a person must agree to join or leave a union if appointed is also unlawful. Union discrimination is unlawful whether practised by an employer directly, or indirectly through an employment agency.

Claims are made to an industrial tribunal within three months against employers, employment agencies or both. Provision exists for joining parties to the proceedings (eg a trades union insisting on union members only being recruited, or an employer if the original action is against an employment agency). Remedies are a declaration, and such compensation as is just and equitable, including for injury to feelings. The tribunal can make a recommendation of action to ease the complainant's position, and increase the compensation if it is not complied with. Maximum compensation is £10,000 and this figure was not increased on 1 April 1992. It should be noted that advertisement is defined widely to include any notice even if it is not made public.

Action short of dismissal[28]

Employees are given a right not to have action short of dismissal taken against them by their employer: because of their actual or proposed membership of an independent trades union; because of their actual or proposed union activities; or to compel them to join a union. In addition, the non-unionist must not have action short of dismissal taken against him if he refuses to make some other payment (eg to a charity) instead of a union subscription. It appears that paying a wage increase to members of one union, but withholding it from members of another can constitute action short of dismissal for union reasons (*National Coal Board* v *Ridgway and Fairbrother*).

Time off for union officials and members[29]

These rights arise not simply out of being an employee, but out of being an employee *and* a union member or official. The term 'official' means an officer of the union or a person who is not an officer but is elected or appointed in accordance with the union's rules to represent some or all of the members. The rights give a 'reasonable' amount of time off during working hours, and are of two types.

Paid time off for union officials   This is for:

- duties concerned with negotiations with the employer over matters for which the union is recognized;
- duties concerned with any other functions on behalf of employees of the employer which the employer has agreed the union may perform; and
- training for the duties mentioned above.

The duties must relate to or be connected with any of the following matters:[30]

(*a*) terms and conditions of employment, or the physical conditions in which any workers are required to work;

(*b*) engagement or non-engagement, or termination or suspension of employment or the duties of employment, of one or more workers;

(*c*) allocation of work or the duties of employment as between workers or groups of workers;

(*d*) matters of discipline;

(*e*) the membership or non-membership of a trade union on the part of a worker;

(*f*) facilities for officials of trade unions; and

(*g*) machinery for negotiation or consultation, and other procedures, relating to any of the foregoing matters, including the recognition by employers or employers' associations of the right of a trade union to represent workers in any such negotiation or consultation or in the carrying out of such procedures.

Time off, with no obligation to pay, for union members   This is for union activity regardless of whether or not it is related to the employer.

The provisions relating to paid time off for union officials (but not unpaid time off for members) were altered by the Employment Act 1989.[31] The effect of this is to limit rights to paid time off, so that they no longer cover duties:

- which neither concern negotiations with the employer nor have been agreed by the employer;
- which do not relate to or are not connected with any of the matters listed in (*a*) to (*g*) above;
- which relate to any associated employer(s) but not to the employer himself;
- which concern negotiations with the employer over matters for which the union is not recognized, where the employer has not agreed to the duties being performed.

The term working hours is defined to mean contractual hours, so excluding any non-contractual overtime. To attract paid time off training must be relevant to the official's duties, and approved either by the TUC or the official's own union. The rights of both officials and members in relation to time off are subject to the union being independent and recognized by the employer. The right to unpaid time off will be relevant to union officials who hold positions in geographically-based branches, or hold higher positions in unions where their duties may not (in the main) relate to their own employer. An ACAS Code of Practice, revised in 1991 following the changes made by the Employment Act 1989, provides detailed guidance.[32] A complaint may be made to an industrial tribunal within three months, alleging refusal to give time off or refusal to pay for time off.

Redundancy consultation*

These are rights given to union officials under the Employment Protection Act 1975.[33] The union must be recognized by the particular employer, and be independent. In fact, the right is given to the 'trade union representative', which means 'an official or other person authorized to carry out collective bargaining with the employer in question by that trade union'. An employer must actually

---

* The EC is currently considering ways of strengthening these rights.

be proposing redundancy rather than just considering it if the Act is to apply. Consultation rights extend to non-unionists of the same description as the members represented by the union.

Consultation must begin 'at the earliest opportunity'. More specifically:

- where the employer proposes to make redundant 100 or more employees at one establishment within 90 days or less, the consultation must start at least 90 days before the first dismissal;
- where the number is 10 employees or more in one establishment within 30 days or less, it must start at least 30 days before the first dismissal.

An employer must also notify the Secretary of State for Employment within the above time periods. Failure to do so could result in a fine.

The consultation process itself comprises an employer disclosing in writing to trades union representatives the whole of the following:

- the reason for his proposals;
- the numbers and descriptions of employees whom he proposes to dismiss;
- the total numbers of such description(s) employed at that establishment;
- the proposed method of selection; and
- the proposed method of carrying out the dismissals, having regard to any agreed procedure, and the period over which they are to take effect.

An employer must consider any representations made by union representatives, and reply to them, stating reasons if any of them are rejected. An employer may argue that there were 'special circumstances' for failing to comply with one or more of the statutory provisions. If a tribunal finds an infringement of the statute, it must make a declaration to that effect, and may also make a 'protective award'. This is an award that the employer shall pay the employee remuneration for a protected period. An employee whose employer fails to pay him during the protected period may apply to a tribunal within three months of the last day of non-payment, and the tribunal may order the employer to pay.

Disclosure of information[34]

This is another right given to the 'trade union representative', defined in the same way as in the redundancy consultation rights. Again, the union must be independent and recognized. Union representatives have a right to information about the company which is both information without which they would 'be to a material extent impeded' in their bargaining; and is information which it is good industrial relations practice to disclose.

An ACAS Code of Practice[35] sets out good practice as including disclosure of information on pay and benefits, conditions of service, manpower, company performance and company finance. An employer does not have to disclose information in certain circumstances, including when disclosure would cause 'substantial injury' to the company (apart from through any effect on collective bargaining).

If a union considers that an employer has failed to disclose the required information, it may make a complaint to the Central Arbitration Committee. The Committee may ask ACAS to conciliate, but if that fails it will hear the complaint. If the complaint is upheld, the Committee will specify the information to be disclosed, and a period of time in which disclosure must take effect. A failure to disclose then gives the union a right to apply again to the Committee, this time for an award of improved terms and conditions. If the Committee makes such an award it has effect as part of the individual employees' contracts of employment, and is enforceable.

Individuals' rights in relation to trade unions

These rights are a mixture of common law and statute. On joining a union, the individual (regardless of whether they are an employee or, for example, an unemployed person) enters into a contract of membership with the union. The essence of the contract is a subscription in exchange for the provision of benefits and services. The terms of the contract are to be found in the rulebook. Thus, a member may use the ordinary courts to prevent a union breaching its own rules. A claim that the union was in breach of contract by not representing a member properly may fail because of the absence of a term in the contract on which the action could be based (*Iwanuszezak* v *General Municipal Boilermakers and Allied Trades Union*). However, a claim in tort for negligence might be possible in these sorts of circumstances.

Union rules will not reign supreme if they involve a breach of the principles of 'natural justice'. In particular, a person must be told the charge against him, and be given an opportunity to put his case. Nobody hearing the appeal should have a vested interest in the decision. Nor will rules reign supreme if they conflict with a statutory provision. There is now a substantial amount of statute law governing the internal functioning of trades unions. Here, the focus is upon rights given to individuals in connection with exclusion or expulsion from unions, under the Employment Act 1980, and upon rights conferred by the Employment Act 1988.[36]

A person unreasonably refused admission to or unreasonably expelled from a trades union in a closed shop may make a complaint to an industrial tribunal within six months of the refusal or expulsion. A tribunal will decide the matter 'in accordance with equity and the substantial merits of the case'.[37] The matter to be decided is whether the trades union acted reasonably or unreasonably. Acting in accordance with its rules is not conclusive evidence of reasonableness, nor is acting in breach of them conclusive evidence of unreasonableness. If the tribunal upholds the complaint it will make a declaration to that effect. The individual may then make a claim for compensation after four weeks have elapsed, but within six months of the date of declaration.

As a result of the operation of the Employment Act 1988, there is now a statutory right given to union members and ex-members not to be unjustifiably disciplined. This includes the right not to be disciplined for failing to participate in industrial action and applies even if the majority of members have voted in favour of the action in a ballot. The member may complain to an industrial tribunal. The Act also provides that union members seeking to exercise their legal rights shall not be denied access to the courts. Moreover, the Act establishes a Commissioner for the Rights of Trade Union Members to help members take cases against their own unions. Members are also given rights of access to their union's detailed accounts and have the right to be accompanied by a professional adviser. Members may seek court orders if union funds are used to indemnify individuals against penalties arising from criminal offences or contempt of court, and if trustees make unlawful use of union property. There is also a right to stop employers deducting union subscriptions once union membership has been terminated.*

Right to hold a ballot on the employer's premises[38]

In firms with over 20 employees an independent, recognized union has a right to hold one of the various ballots which attract public funding (eg on industrial action, principal executive committee elections, amending rules, amalgamations) on the employer's premises. The employer must comply if it is 'reasonably practicable' to do so.

References

1. Employment Protection (Consolidation) Act (EP(C)A) 1978, c 44, s 153.
2. EP(C)A, s 81.
3. EP(C)A, Schedule 4, para 4.
4. EP(C)A, s 82(5).
5. EP(C)A, s 31.
6. Employment Act 1980, c 42, s 13.
7. EP(C)A, ss 45 and 56.
8. EP(C)A, s 29.
9. Wages Act 1986, c 48, ss 1–11.
10. EP(C)A, s 8.
11. Wages Act 1986, ss 12–16.
12. Maximum amounts on the standard scale of fines are to be increased under the provisions of the Criminal Justice Act 1991, c 53, s 17.
13. EP(C)A, s 12.
14. EP(C)A, s 19.
15. EP(C)A, s 49.
16. EP(C)A, s 1.
17. EP(C)A, s 2A (inserted by Employment Act 1989, c 38, s 13).
18. EC Directive on Proof of Employment Relationship, 91/553/EEC; OJ L288.
19. EP(C)A, ss 122–7; Insolvency Act 1985, c 65; Insolvency Act 1986, c 45.
20. EP(C)A, Schedule 13, para 17.
21. EP(C)A, s 153.
22. The Transfer of Undertakings (Protection of Employment) Regulations, SI 1981/1794. These were issued under the European Communities Act 1972, c 68 to give effect to the EC 'Acquired Rights' Directive (77/187/EEC; OJ L61).
23. Equal Pay Act 1970, c 41.
24. Equal Pay (Amendment) Regulations, SI 1983/1794. These were issued under the European Communities Act 1972, following *Commission of the European Communities v UK* in which the UK was found to have not fully implemented EC Equal Pay Directive 75/117/EEC under Article 119 of the Treaty of Rome.
25. Sex Discrimination Act 1975, c 65, ss 1, 3 and 4; Race Relations Act 1976, c 74, ss 1–2.
26. Commission for Racial Equality (1983) Race Relations Code of Practice, London; Equal Opportunities Commission (1985) Sex Discrimination Code of Practice, Manchester.

---

* The Green Paper (1991) *Industrial Relations in the 1990s*, Cm 1602, July, HMSO, London, proposed that written, annual employee consent should be needed for check-off (p 26). After consultation, the government announced that it would be proceeding with legislation in this area, but with consent needed every three years (Secretary of State for Employment's Statement to the House of Commons, 28 January 1992).

27. Employment Act 1990, c 38, s 1.
28. EP(C)A, s 23.
29. EP(C)A, ss 27–8.
30. Trade Union and Labour Relations Act 1974, c 52, s 29(1).
31. Employment Act 1989, s 14. This amended EP(C)A, s 27(1).
32. ACAS (1991) Time off for Trade Union Duties and Activities, ACAS Code of Practice 3, revised edn, HMSO, London.
33. Employment Protection Act (EPA) 1975, c 71, s 99.
34. EPA, s 17.
35. ACAS (1977) Disclosure of Information to Trade Unions for Collective Bargaining Purposes, ACAS Code of Practice 2, HMSO, London.
36. Employment Act 1980, ss 4–5; Employment Act 1988, c 19, Part I (as amended by the Employment Act 1990). Further rights are proposed in the Green Paper 'Industrial Relations in the 1990s' (1991) HMSO, London. The government announced on 28 January 1992 that it would be proceeding with much of what it had proposed in the Green Paper.
37. Employment Act 1980, s 4(5). The DE's Code of Practice on Closed Shop Agreements and Arrangements was revoked during 1991.
38. Employment Act 1980, s 2.

Chapter Nineteen

Health and Safety at Work*

Paul Lewis

HEALTH AND SAFETY AT WORK ETC ACT 1974

General duty of employers to their employees

The philosophy behind this legislation is that the duties of employers should be set out in broad terms covering all sorts of employment situations, ie shops, offices, factories etc. The Act covers all persons at work except domestic servants in private households. Sets of regulations issued under the Act then deal with different types of work situations or different health and safety issues.

All those receiving training or work experience from an employer in the workplace, and who are not employees, are deemed to be employees for the purposes of health and safety legislation.[1]

The essence of the Health and Safety at Work Act (HSWA) is a general duty imposed upon employers which requires them 'to ensure, so far as is reasonably practicable, the health, safety and welfare at work' of all their employees.[2] This general duty includes health and safety in relation to the:

- provision and maintenance of plant and systems of work;
- arrangements for use, handling, storage and transport of articles and substances;
- maintenance of the place of work, and access to and egress from it;
- working environment;

and includes the duty to provide:

- adequate welfare facilities;
- necessary information, instruction, training and supervision;

and to consult with union safety representatives if there are any. A notice containing the main provisions of the Act must be posted.[3]

An employer must prepare a written statement of his policy with respect to the health and safety at work of his employees, and show it to an inspector if requested to do so. The statement must indicate the organization and arrangements in force to give effect to the policy and must be revised as often as is appropriate. The statement, and any revision of it, must be brought to the notice of all the employees.[4] There is a provision for exceptions, but the only exemption granted to date is for employers who employ fewer than five employees.[5]

---

* This chapter relates to the law as at 1 February 1992.

Where, under HSWA, a safe system of work for the employer's own employees involves giving information and instruction to persons other than his own employees (eg the employees of a contractor) it must be given (*R* v *Swan Hunter Shipbuilders Ltd and Telemeter Installations Ltd*). Thus, employers have a duty to provide relevant safety information to the employees of other employers working on their premises.[6]

Meaning of 'practicable' and 'reasonably practicable'

'Practicable' means something less than physically possible. It means feasible – possible in the light of current knowledge and invention. Where the requirement is that something should be as safe as is practicable, this means that the duty must be performed unless it is unreasonable to do so (*Marshall* v *Gotham and Co Ltd*). The word 'reasonably' requires that a comparison be made between the risk of injury (including the severity of any injury which might occur) and the time, trouble and expense of preventive action. If there is gross disproportion between them (ie risk is insignificant compared with the preventive measures needed), the defence that an employer has done what was reasonably practicable will succeed (*Edwards* v *National Coal Board*). The onus of proof lies upon the accused to show that it was not practicable or reasonably practicable to do more than was done.[7]

Duties owed to non-employees

The HSWA operates where people are at work rather than by specifying particular types of workplace. With the exception of where there is Crown immunity, it therefore covers all premises including vehicles, movable structures and offshore installations. Under the Act an employer has a responsibility to show the same standard of care towards non-employees (eg visitors, contractors etc) as he is required to show to his employees, and this duty includes provision of information and instruction.[8] The duty owed to non-employees is not restricted to the employer's premises and a self-employed person has similar duties.

Persons who have 'to any extent, control of premises' (but not domestic premises), or control access to or egress from such premises, have duties to persons other than employees and must take such measures as are reasonable for a person in that position to take, as far as is reasonably practicable. This does not extend to taking measures to guard against unexpected events (*Austin Rover Group Ltd* v *HM Inspectorate of Factories*).

The Act also covers control of the emission into the atmosphere of noxious or offensive substances from prescribed premises. These are premises and substances laid down in the Health and Safety (Emissions into the Atmosphere) Regulations 1983, as amended.[10] The duty imposed is to use the 'best practicable means' for preventing the emission and to render harmless or inoffensive any substances emitted. (Part I of the Environmental Protection Act 1990 and regulations thereunder introduce new controls over air pollution.)

Duties of designers, manufacturers etc

Duties are also placed upon designers, manufacturers, importers and suppliers to require the safe design and construction of articles, testing and examination, and the provision of information indicating the designed use and precautions needed to avoid risks. Designers and manufacturers must carry out necessary research. Those erecting or installing articles are also responsible for safety. Parallel requirements exist in relation to manufacturers, importers and suppliers of substances. The standard of care is what is reasonably practicable to achieve safety and absence of risks to health. This section of the Act has been strengthened by the Consumer Protection Act 1987.[11] Manufacturers etc must now consider reasonably foreseeable risks. Moreover, these risks are to be considered in relation to handling, maintenance and storage, as well as use. The requirement to provide health and safety information is also widened so that it covers revision (eg in the light of new knowledge), applies not just to use and covers situations such as foreseeable errors by users. Manufacturers etc must also take account of non-domestic premises other than workplaces to which they supply substances.

Duties of employees

The employee has a common law duty to go about his work with reasonable care. This is supplemented by the 1974 Act which lays upon the employee a statutory duty of reasonable care towards himself and those who may be affected by his acts or omissions. There is also a statutory duty to cooperate with the employer or any other person in meeting the statutory requirements. Reasonable care includes the use of equipment provided for his safety. The employer must make sure that the employee knows of the equipment and must take steps, as far as is reasonably practicable, to get the employee to use it. Following a EC directive, the Health and Safety Commission (HSC) has recently issued draft regulations governing the use of personal protective equipment, and technical standards are laid down as a result of a separate EC directive (see p 400–1).

The duties of employees include not intentionally or recklessly interfering with or misusing anything provided for health, safety and welfare purposes in pursuance of the statutory provisions. (This is a duty placed upon all persons and not just employees.)

Individual employees can be, and occasionally are, prosecuted by the inspectors under these provisions. Moreover, as noted below (see p 392) senior managers (as well as the organization) may be liable under s 37 of the HSWA where they consented to or connived at the commission of an offence or neglected their duties.

No charge must be made for anything done or provided in respect of any *specific* requirement of health and safety legislation. Thus, if a regulation states that eye protectors must be worn in a particular situation, there can be no charge. If an employer provided them simply in an attempt to fulfil his *general* duties under s 2 of HSWA, he could charge. The duties of employees apply to all employees including those who hold managerial positions.

Safety representatives

Regulations under the Act allow a recognized trades union to appoint safety representatives, with specified functions:

- to investigate potential hazards, dangerous occurrences and the cause of accidents;
- to investigate and process members' complaints about health and safety at work;

- to deal with management over general questions of health and safety;
- to carry out workplace inspections;
- to represent members in discussions with inspectors;
- to receive information from the inspectors;
- to attend meetings of health and safety committees.[12]

A code of practice and guidance notes give further detail.

The HSC's draft general regulations (see pp 398–9) include modifications to the Safety Representatives and Safety Committees Regulations 1977. An employer would be required to provide reasonable facilities and assistance for safety representatives, and to consult them in respect of:

- any measure which might substantially affect the health and safety of the employees represented by those safety representatives;
- arrangements for appointing or nominating 'competent' persons to implement safety measures;
- information to be provided to employees;
- the planning and organization of health and safety training; and
- the health and safety consequences of the introduction of new technology.

As far as is reasonably practicable a safety representative (SR) should have been employed by his employer for the previous two years, or have had at least two years' experience of similar employment. Employers must provide facilities for SRs for inspections, including for independent investigation and discussion. However, employers are entitled to be present during inspections. SRs can have access to any documents kept by their employer for statutory health and safety purposes, except those relating to the health and safety of individuals, and in general are entitled to information which it is necessary for them to have to perform their duties. SRs are not entitled to information where disclosure (apart from health and safety effects) would cause 'substantial injury to the employer's undertaking'. There are other (limited) restrictions on disclosure.

Safety representatives are the appropriate people to receive information from the inspectors about particular occurrences in the workplace, and any action that inspectors take or propose to take. The safety representatives are given a right to time off in order to perform their functions, and also for training.[13] A safety representative may complain to an industrial tribunal if refused reasonable time off or refused pay for such time off. Where at least two SRs request it in writing, an employer is required to establish a safety committee. The overall function of such a committee is to keep health and safety measures under review.[14]

OTHER LEGISLATION*

Factories Act (FA) 1961[15]

Until repealed and replaced by regulations under the HSWA, the FA remains important. In general, the person or company in immediate control of the

---

* Parts of this legislation are likely to be replaced in the near future by regulations under the HSWA (eg Workplace (Health, Safety and Welfare) Regulations; Provision and Use of Work Equipment Regulations).

premises is responsible for ensuring compliance with the Act and the many sets of regulations issued under it[16] (see *Dexter* v *Tenby Electrical Accessories Ltd*).

A factory is a place where people are employed in manual labour in any process for, or incidental to, the making, repairing, altering, cleaning, adapting for sale or demolition of any article. With a number of exceptions (eg government, local authorities), this must be done for gain or for trading purposes. An employer will have rights of access and control. Manual labour means that the work is done primarily or substantially with the hands. A number of specific processes are also defined as factory processes so that they are covered by the Act, eg shipbuilding or repairing or breaking up.

The Act lays down conditions for cleanliness, overcrowding, ventilation, temperature, lighting and drainage, and provides for the secure fencing of dangerous machinery. Various rules are laid down for lifting equipment (eg hoists, lifts, cranes) and lifting tackle (eg chains and ropes). Workplace floors, stairs and gangways must be soundly constructed, properly maintained and, as far as is reasonably practicable, kept free of obstructions and slippery surfaces. There may need to be a handrail on staircases. Openings in floors must be fenced whenever practicable. There are provisions to protect people from being overcome by fumes in confined spaces, and to protect against fire and explosion in such circumstances. Other sections deal with steam boilers and air receivers. Specific requirements in relation to all pressure plant, including pipework and fittings, have recently come into force (see pp 390–1).

The welfare provisions of the Factories Act require an adequate supply of drinking water, adequate and suitable washing facilities, and accommodation for non-work clothing. Seats must be provided for workers who have the opportunity to sit without detriment to their work. There are detailed rules where the work can properly be done sitting. Provision of protective clothing is required by various sets of regulations under the Act. Eye protection is subject to the Protection of Eyes Regulations 1974, as amended.

The Act contains a number of other provisions. A list of any homeworkers must be provided to the local authority. A person intending to use premises as a factory must notify the inspector at least four weeks in advance. Where premises are occupied by separate factories, the owner is responsible for the common parts. Otherwise, the occupier is liable. Where a particular individual fails to fulfil a statutory duty imposed upon him, and the employer has taken all reasonable steps, the employer will not be liable. An employee causing an accident by interfering, eg with a guard, would be in breach of his statutory duty not to wilfully interfere with or misuse anything provided in pursuance of the Act's objectives. There is also a duty upon employees to use anything provided under the Act for their health and safety. A breach of the Act by an employee may mean that both he and the employer are criminally liable. Women must not be employed in a factory within four weeks of childbirth.

As far as is reasonably practicable, there must be a safe means of access to any place where a person has to work. Moreover, that place must be kept safe while the person is working there.[17]

Offices, Shops and Railway Premises Act 1963

Most of the Act's provisions are similar to those of the Factories Act 1961, including the requirement to notify the business to the inspectorate. The Act applies where people are employed. It applies generally to all offices and shops, and to most railway buildings near the permanent way. It covers offices and shops which are part of buildings used for other purposes, as well as associated areas, eg stairs, passages, toilets etc. There are specific requirements for the cleaning of premises and furnishings. Floors and steps must be swept or washed at least once a week. In a room where people work, there shoud be at least 3.7 metres^3 of floor space in respect of each person and 11.0^3 metres if the ceiling is lower than 3.0 metres. An exception is made where the room is open to the public. Temperature should be reasonable, and generally not below 16°C after the first hour, and a thermometer must be prominently displayed. There must be adequate supplies of fresh or artificially purified air. The Act lays down requirements for toilets and washing facilities, and for drinking water, storage of clothing and seats. Provisions similar to those in the Factories Act apply to stairs, passages etc. There are provisions for the fencing of dangerous machinery and restrictions on the lifting of excess weights.

Generally, the occupier is responsible for complying with the Act, although some responsibilities are given specifically to employers (eg the duty to notify the inspectorate of the commencement of business). If the premises are used by more than one employer the owner becomes responsible for health and safety in the common parts. The defence against alleged breach of duty under the Act is that all due diligence was used.[18]

Reporting of Injuries, Diseases and Dangerous Occurrences Regulations 1985 (RIDDOR)[19]

Injuries resulting from accidents at work which cause incapacity for more than three days must be reported to the enforcing authority in writing within seven days of the accident. Any of the major injuries (including fatalities) which are specified in the regulations must be notified immediately by the quickest practicable means, eg telephone, as well as reported in writing within seven days. The same applies to dangerous occurrences. A record of all reportable injuries and dangerous occurrences must be kept.

Diseases must be reported if they are listed in RIDDOR, if there is written diagnosis from a doctor showing that the employee suffers from the disease and if the employee is in one or more of the work activities specified in the regulations.

Control of Substances Hazardous to Health (COSHH) Regulations 1988[20]

The starting point of the provisions is the requirement for an employer to carry out an assessment of work tasks which are likely to create risks for the health and safety of his employees from exposure to hazardous substances. From the assessment should flow decisions about the measures necessary to prevent or control such exposure. The central requirement is the duty to prevent or control exposure to substances hazardous to health. The regulations then go on to require maintenance of control measures and, in certain cases, the monitoring of exposure and health surveillance. Workers exposed to hazardous substances have rights to information, instruction and training.

The regulations apply regardless of the type of workplace and cover virtually all substances hazardous to health. Substance means 'any natural or artificial substance whether in solid or liquid form or in the form of a gas or vapour (including micro-organisms)'[21] It is a defence for any person 'to prove that he took all reasonable precautions and exercised all due diligence' to avoid committing an offence by contravening the regulations.[22]

The Noise at Work Regulations 1989[23]

These regulations specify three action levels for noise – a first level of 85dB(A) and a second level of 90dB(A). The measure dB(A) indicates loudness in decibels in a way that is adjusted to the character of the human ear. These action levels relate to daily noise exposure – the total exposure over the whole working day – without taking into account the use of ear protectors. In addition, there is a peak action level – a peak sound pressure of 200 pascals – to protect people against explosive noise. An employer has a general duty to reduce risk of hearing damage to employees to the lowest level practicable.

If an employee's exposure is likely to reach any of the action levels the employer must arrange for a noise assessment to be carried out by a competent person. Records of assessments must be kept. Where the noise level is likely to reach 90dB(A) or the peak level, exposure must be reduced, as far as is reasonably practicable, by means other than ear protectors.

Where the noise level reaches 85dB(A), but not 90dB(A), an employer must provide suitable ear protectors if requested to do so by an employee. Where the noise level reaches 90dB(A) or sound pressure 200 pascals, an employer must provide suitable ear protectors, has a duty to ensure so far as is reasonably practicable that they are worn, and must designate the area as an 'ear protection zone'.

The Electricity at Work Regulations 1989[24]

In the main, these regulations are concerned with prevention of danger from electric burn, electric shock, electrical explosion or arcing or from fire or explosion stemming from electrical energy. They cover all workplaces to which the Health and Safety at Work Act 1974 applies, and relate to any electrical equipment even if manufactured and installed prior to April 1990 (when the regulations became operational) and any work activity. Some of the regulations impose absolute duties, ie ones which must be fulfilled irrespective of costs and other factors.

The onus is upon the employer to assess the work activities which use electricity or which may be affected by it. Employers must have regard to all foreseeable risks. Duties are also placed on the self-employed and employees. Where matters are within their control, persons in each category become duty-holders. In criminal proceedings a duty-holder has the defence that all reasonable steps were taken and all due diligence exercised in an attempt to avoid committing the offence. However, this may not provide an adequate defence where the regulations lay down absolute standards.

The Health and Safety (First-Aid) Regulations 1981[25]

These regulations place a general duty upon employers to make adequate first-aid provision for their employees if they are injured or become ill at work. Employers must provide, or ensure that there are provided, adequate and appropriate equipment and facilities 'for enabling first-aid to be rendered'.[26]

An employer is under a duty to inform his employees of the arrangements made in connection with first-aid. A self-employed person has a duty to make adequate first-aid provision for himself. The regulations have widespread application, and are accompanied by an Approved Code of Practice, which was revised in 1990.

The Fire Precautions Act 1971

The provisions here are enforced by local fire authorities, while fire risks arising out of the production process itself are dealt with by the HSE and other enforcement agencies. The 1971 Act places duties on occupiers or controllers of premises in respect of:

- measures for providing warning of fire;
- means of escape in case of fire.

A fire certificate is required for any building where:

- more than 20 people are employed; or
- more than 10 are employed on any floor other than the ground floor; or
- flammable materials are stored in or under the building.

The certificate will lay down conditions which must be complied with, including the provision and maintenance of:

- the means of escape in case of fire;
- fire doors;
- fire alarms and fire fighting equipment;
- emergency lighting and exit signs.

Moreover, the certificate will require that employees be instructed in the:

- fire drill (which is to be held at least once a year);
- locations and use of fire fighting equipment and fire alarm points;
- use of fire doors;
- stopping and isolation of machinery;
- arrangements for evacuation.

The Pressure Systems and Transportable Gas Containers Regulations 1989[27]

In relation to transportable gas containers, the regulations lay down that they must be verified as conforming to certain approved design standards or specifications. Checks must be made when containers are filled, and non-refillable containers must not be refilled. There are requirements in relation to modification and repairs. Various records must be kept.

As regards pressure systems, duties to provide information are placed upon designers, suppliers, importers, repairers and those who modify systems. The installer is under a duty to ensure that nothing in the manner of the installation gives rise to danger and the user is required to establish the system's safe operating limits. Various records must be kept.

Major provisions relating to pressure systems, contained in regulations 8–12, do not become operative until 1 July 1994. These include the requirement for a pressure system user to have a written scheme for the periodic examination of specified parts of the system by a competent person. The defence for a person accused of being in breach of the regulations is that:[28]

> the commission of the offence was due to the act or default of another person not being one of his employees . . . and that he took all reasonable precautions and exercised all due diligence to avoid the commission of the offence.

Construction regulations

These apply where there are 'building operations' and 'works of engineering construction'.* The term building operations includes the following in relation to buildings: construction, structural alteration, repair, maintenance, repointing, redecorating, external cleaning, demolition, preparatory work (including the laying of foundations). The term works of engineering construction includes construction of a railway line or siding (except on an existing railway) and the construction, structural alteration or repair of docks, harbours, tunnels, canals, bridges, reservoirs, roads, sewers, pipe-lines etc. Demolition is also included.

The main regulations   There are four main sets of regulations, namely: the Construction (General Provisions) Regulations 1961; The Construction (Lifting Operations) Regulations 1961; the Construction (Health and Welfare) Regulations 1966; the Construction (Working Places) Regulations 1966. Taken together, these regulations include provisions in respect of the following:

- the handling of materials;
- vehicles on sites;
- ladders;
- gangways and runs;
- stairs;
- excavations, shafts and tunnels;
- scaffolding;
- dangerous locations (eg roofs);
- hoists;
- lifting appliances;
- demolition.

They cover the whole range of construction activities from ground works to working at heights and specify precautions to be taken at each stage. In addition, they require statutory inspections of workplaces, plant and equipment, and specify the time intervals between such inspections.

The Construction (Head Protection) Regulations 1989[29]   The person in control of a site can make rules governing when and where head protection should be worn. Employees must wear such protection when instructed to do so by their employer or to comply with rules made by the person in control of the site. Self-employed workers must similarly wear head protection when instructed by a person in control, or when required by rules drawn up by that person.

---

* These terms are to be found in the Factories Act 1961, s 176, as extended.

Employers must provide suitable head protection for their employees and the self-employed must provide it for themselves. The protection must be maintained and replaced whenever necessary. Employers and others must ensure that workers wear suitable head protection whenever there is any foreseeable risk of head injury.

ENFORCEMENT OF HEALTH AND SAFETY LEGISLATION

Enforcement is principally by the HSE, although local authorities are responsible for enforcement in certain premises and for enforcing the implementation of general fire precautions. The allocation of enforcement responsibilities is determined by the Health and Safety (Enforcing Authority) Regulations 1989, issued under s 18 of HSWA. Broadly speaking, local authorities have responsibility under the 1989 regulations for: premises where the main activity is the sale or storage of goods for retail or wholesale distribution; office activities; hotels and catering; places of entertainment.

If there is a breach of duty an inspector may serve an improvement notice, or a prohibition notice, or may prosecute. An improvement notice will apply where the inspector alleges a breach of statutory duty. It will specify a time period within which the improvement(s) must be made. An employer may appeal to an industrial tribunal within 21 days against either the allegation of a breach or the shortness of the time period if, eg this would cause undue difficulty for the production process. The appeal has the effect of suspending the notice. Where an inspector believes that there is a risk of serious personal injury he may serve a prohibition notice, which can have immediate effect. There is again a right of appeal, but this does not suspend the notice unless an industrial tribunal so directs.

Because the Crown cannot prosecute itself, the HSC issues Crown notices where improvement or prohibition notices would be used (eg in the civil service), although these have no legal force.

Any breach of the general duties in the 1974 Act, or of specific duties under other health and safety legislation, is a criminal offence, as is obstructing an inspector or giving him false information. An employer will be liable for the acts of his employees during or arising out of the course of their employment. Where an offence is committed with the consent or connivance of, or due to the neglect of, any 'director, manager, secretary or other similar officer' the individual as well as the organization is to be held guilty (see, eg *Armour* v *Sheen*).

Where there is a breach of an approved code of practice issued under s 16 of HSWA, this will be taken (in criminal proceedings) as conclusive proof of a contravention of a requirement or prohibition, unless the court can be satisfied that there was compliance by some other method. Prosecution for breaches of the HSWA is limited to inspectors save for permission otherwise by the Director of Public Prosecutions; nor can the Act be used for the purposes of civil claims, ie for breach of statutory duty. Regulations under HSWA and legislation enacted prior to HSWA can be used for civil purposes unless they state otherwise.

The powers of inspectors are considerable, including the right to enter premises, to obtain information and to take possession of articles and substances. A successful prosecution requires proof beyond all reasonable doubt. The maximum fine in the magistrates' courts is £2000, although this will become £5000 when the standard scale of fines is increased in October 1992.[30] Moreover, there is a maximum of £20,000 for certain offences.[31] In the Crown Courts, on indictment, the fines are unlimited and in the case of a number of offences there can also be up to two years' imprisonment.

NEGLIGENCE AT COMMON LAW

The basis of a worker's claim for damages arising out of an employer's negligence is as follows:

- the employer owes the worker a duty of care;
- the employer has not fulfilled that duty;
- as a result, the worker has suffered injury or damage to health.

The duty of care

The employer has a duty of reasonable care for the safety of his employees and the responsibility extends to the premises of third parties to which he sends his employees. He also has a duty to care towards the independent contractor, although the degree of care is less in such cases. In general, reasonable care means avoiding acts and omissions which a person can reasonably foresee would be likely to injure his neighbour (*Donoghue* v *Stevenson*). A neighbour is anyone who is so affected by my acts or omissions that I ought reasonably to have these effects in mind. Liability arises, therefore, where there is not reasonable care to prevent reasonably foreseeable risk. Foresight has to be assessed on the basis of what is known (or should reasonably be known) at the time.

It follows that the degree of care required is determined by balancing risk against the actions necessary to prevent or reduce it. Risk is judged in terms of how likely it is that an injury will occur and how serious it would be. The cost of preventive action will figure highly in the equation. The degree of care may vary according to the worker, eg whether he has a lot or a little experience.

The duty of care may be divided into a number of specific parts:

- safe premises;
- a safe system of work;
- safe plant, equipment and tools;
- safe fellow workers.

The duty to take reasonable care in relation to plant, equipment and tools has implications for testing and maintenance, and may ultimately require the item to be replaced. Fellow workers will be safe if they have adequate training, instruction and supervision. Part of a safe system of work is the provision of safety equipment. In *Crouch* v *British Rail Engineering Ltd*, the duty of care was not fulfilled by making safety goggles available for collection from a point about five minutes away. The lack of immediate availability encouraged risks to be taken. In *Pape* v *Cumbria County Council*, the employers provided gloves for cleaners handling chemical cleaning materials, but the duty of care went beyond this; it extended to warning the cleaners about handling such materials with unprotected hands and instructing them as to the need to wear gloves at all times.

Negligence

Negligence occurs where there is a breach of the duty of care. In terms of the above definition of the duty of care, this means that the actions taken by an employer to prevent or reduce risk were inadequate for the level of risk which was reasonably foreseeable. An employer cannot use a contract term or a notice to exclude or restrict liability for death or personal injury resulting from negligence.[32] The onus of proof of negligence lies within the plaintiff, who must also show causation, ie that the negligence caused the injury, and that the employer had a reasonable and safer alternative to what he did. However, in the absence of an explanation of the cause of the injury, there is what almost amounts to a presumption of negligence.

If the action is against the defendant in his capacity as employer it will need to be established that the plaintiff was acting in the course of his employment when he received his injury. Where the injury was sustained in working hours on the employer's premises this is likely to prove difficult to challenge, especially if the employee was performing tasks in the employer's interest. Acting in the course of employment means carrying out acts which have been authorized by the employer, as well as some that have not been authorized, in order to fulfil contractual obligations. The latter, however, must be connected with authorized acts, in that they can be regarded as ways of performing such acts. Anything normally and reasonably incidental to a day's work (eg going to the toilet, to the canteen, or to collect tools or materials) will also be included.

Where the action lies against the defendant in his capacity as occupier of premises the test is again whether there has been a breach of the duty of care. As a result of the Occupiers' Liability Act 1957, a statutory duty of care is owed to persons authorized to be on the premises.[33] The occupier's actual degree of control over the premises will be an important factor in determining liability. The Occupiers' Liability Act 1984 defines the duty owed to trespassers.

Actions for damages

The general rule is that employers (principals) will be liable for the acts and omissions of their employees (agents); that is, they will be vicariously liable. The limiting factor is that the employee's act or omission must be in the course of employment or linked with it in the ways described earlier. Moreover, the courts have held that the person entitled to tell the employee how to do work would generally be liable for that employee's negligence, even if the employee is an employee of another company (see, eg *Sime* v *Sutcliffe Catering (Scotland) Limited*).

The time limit for commencement of claims is three years from the time of knowledge of cause of action.[34] Where the person is fatally injured, the three years can be applied from the time of death or from the date of the personal representative's knowledge, whichever is later. Other exceptions are possible on grounds of equity. Employers must be insured against such actions as a result of the Employers' Liability (Compulsory Insurance) Act 1969.

Damages are divided into two categories: special and general. The former covers provable loss to the date of the trial, eg loss of earnings, damage to clothing. The loss of earnings is net loss. The general damages cover the remaining forms of loss, eg pain and suffering before and after the trial, and future loss of earnings. The broad aim is restitution – putting the injured person back where he was before the accident happened, in as much as money can do this. Where appropriate, a money value will be put on disfigurement, loss of enjoyment of life, nursing expenses and the inability to pursue personal or social interests.

Defences

Contributory negligence   An employer may argue that the injured person was careless or reckless and was solely or partly to blame for his own injuries, eg by ignoring clear safety rules. Contributory negligence might include contribution to the seriousness of the injury, eg by the failure to wear available safety equipment.

Injuries not reasonably foreseeable   An employer may argue that the type and/ or the extent of injuries sustained by the plaintiff were not reasonably foreseeable as a result of the employer's breach of duty of care. The plaintiff has the burden of proof in demonstrating that such injuries could be foreseen as arising out of that particular negligence.

Voluntary assumption of risk   In extreme cases an employer may succeed in escaping liability on the grounds that the employee had consented to taking risks as part of the job, ie risks other than those inherent in performing the job as safely as is reasonably practicable.

Injury not sustained in the course of employment   It may be argued that the injury was not sustained in the course of employment. This could be because:

- the injury was not sustained at work at all; or
- it was sustained at work and during working hours, but the employee was performing unauthorized acts, which could not be regarded simply as unauthorized ways of performing authorized functions. A defence to liability here will be an express prohibition. Such a prohibition will not, however, remove liability as regards unauthorized methods of performing authorized tasks.

Absence of vicarious liability   An employer may try to avoid liability by arguing that he is not vicariously liable. In cases of alleged vicarious liability it has to be established: first, that the employee is liable; and secondly, that his employer is vicariously liable for his act(s) or omission(s). There may not be liability for the actions of an employee where:

- the employee is 'lent' to another employer and is working for, and under the control of, that other employer.

Vicarious liability may be transferred in such cases, the question of control being paramount.

- The employee knows (or should know) that what he has done is expressly outside the limits of his authority;
- The actions of the employee are excessive, eg a security guard who uses excessive violence against an intruder.

SAFETY DISCIPLINE

Disregard of safety rules or procedures

Employees who disregard safety rules and procedures may be subject to discipline, including dismissal, in the same way as if there was a breach of some other type of rule. All the usual requirements laid upon employers need to be met, eg rules must be reasonable and applied consistently and fairly, rules must be communicated to employees and the procedure for handling disciplinary breaches must be reasonable. A dismissal for a safety breach would need to be defended in the light of the normal requirements of unfair dismissal law.

An employer may seek to change existing safety rules or introduce new ones. If the change is a direct result of new legislation, the requirements automatically become an implied term of contracts of employment. Where the change stems from a policy change rather than a change in legislation, an employer will need to consider the existing terms of employment and whether the change can represent a breach of contract. The procedure for implementation (eg advance warning, consultation etc) may be important. For example, employers introducing no-smoking policies might justify their actions on the basis of their general duties under the HSWA, provide employees with evidence to support this, give advance warning, perhaps survey employee opinion, or consult in other ways and provide some facilities for smokers after the rule becomes operative.

Refusal to work on grounds of lack of safety

What is the legal position if an employee refuses to work because what he is being asked to do seems to him to be unsafe? On the one hand, the employee has a contractual duty to take reasonable care, so that he may feel that he will be in breach of such a duty. Moreover, he may feel he is in breach of statutory duties also. On the other hand, he is required by the terms of his contract of employment to obey the lawful commands of his employer. The critical question here is whether the employer's command is lawful. This means it must not only be within the terms of the contract, but also must not involve the employee engaging in a criminal act, or indeed being unable to act with due care. The problem is that opinions may well differ and neither party is likely to be able to wait for a legal ruling. The advice of specialists (safety managers, union safety representatives and perhaps even a factory inspector) is about as far as one can go. If there is a refusal to work the matter may then become a disciplinary one.

As part of their contractual duty to provide their employees with a safe system of work and take reasonable care of their safety, employers must investigate all bona fide complaints about safety brought to their attention by employees (*BAC Ltd* v *Austin*). Failure to do so could give grounds for an employee to resign and claim constructive dismissal. If the employee chooses to stay but refuses to do the work, the question of whether or not the employer is in breach of a contractual term or a statutory duty will not be conclusive in determining the fairness or otherwise of any consequent dismissal. The test will be reasonableness

(*Lindsay* v *Dunlop Ltd*). Relevant factors may include the attitude of other employees in the same position and what steps the employer is taking to deal with the safety problem. Employers might fare better if they did not treat refusal to work on safety grounds as straightforward disobedience. Dismissing for refusal to work before there has been a proper investigation of the employee's complaint, and before the results of that investigation have been communicated to the employee, may well be unfair. If an employee has a special condition, he ought to be treated as sympathetically as possible and any alternative duties considered, especially if the condition is likely to be temporary. Pregnant women anxious about the effects of working at VDUs might fall into this category.

In *Piggott Brothers and Co Ltd* v *Jackson and ors*, an employer's failure to get a definitive explanation of the cause of the employees' symptoms (experienced as a result of exposure to fumes) was held to amount to unreasonableness. This was so even though ventilation had been improved and the problem had been investigated by HSE inspectors who thought it was a one-off that had ceased to exist. Dismissals for refusal to work were held to be unfair. The Court of Appeal would not disturb these findings – the decision was a permissible option on the facts.

THE EUROPEAN DIMENSION

EC emphasis on health and safety at work

Because of changes introduced by the Single European Act (SEA) 1986, which became operative in July 1987, health and safety has become an important area of European legislation. Two aspects of the SEA are of particular significance.

First, the introduction of Article 118A into the Treaty of Rome gives health and safety a particular prominence in the objectives of the EC. Article 118A states that particular attention shall be paid to encouraging improvements in the working environment as regards the health and safety of workers in order to harmonize conditions within the community. To help achieve this, the qualified majority voting procedure introduced by SEA can be used to adopt directives. This means that health and safety matters are less likely to get held up in the EC legislative machine, since unanimity is no longer required. The vehicle of a 'framework' directive (see below) has been used to give effect to the objectives of Article 118A.

The second aspect of the SEA that is particularly relevant to health and safety is the new Article 100A. This allows the Council to adopt by a qualified majority, in cooperation with the European Parliament, measures to further the establishment and functioning of the internal market. While Article 100A excludes matters of taxation, free movement of people, and provisions relating to the rights and interests of employed people, it has been held to *include* technical standards and safety requirements for specific products.

The EC is agreeing a single set of rules on technical standards to replace the legislation in individual member states. The main means of achieving this will be a set of directives ('new approach' directives). A new approach directive sets out the range of products covered by the directive and the essential requirements, eg in relation to safety, which must be met before the product can be sold in the EC. There has to be attestation – a demonstration that the essential requirements have been met. This can be done by:

- a manufacturer's declaration (backed up by test results);
- a certificate from an independent body;
- the provision of test results by an independent body.

The CE mark may then be displayed. Conforming with a European standard shows that the EC's requirements have been met. Such standards are prepared by two EC committees.

A number of new approach directives have been adopted and some new UK legislation has already been introduced. The directives cover:

- toy safety;
- simple pressure vessels;
- construction products;
- electromagnetic compatibility;
- gas appliances;
- personal protective equipment;
- machinery safety including
  mobile machinery and lifting equipment;
- active implantable medical devices;
- non-automatic weighing instruments;
- telecommunication terminal equipment.

The health and safety aspects of the 'new approach' directives may be far-reaching. For example, the machinery directive – relating to the design and construction of machinery – has extensive health and safety requirements relating to (among other things):

- materials;
- lighting;
- handling;
- control systems and devices;
- starting and stopping including emergency stops;
- maintenance;
- protection against mechanical hazards;
- guards and protection devices;
- other hazards (noise, fire, radiation etc);
- indicators (eg warning devices).

Most machinery made or sold in the UK, including imports, will have to meet these requirements from and including 1 January 1995.

In addition to developments arising out of the introduction of Articles 100A and 118A, which use the qualified majority voting procedure, there are health and safety provisions in the Charter of Fundamental Social Rights (the 'Social Charter') and in the EC's environmental protection programme.

Major directives already adopted under Article 118A

Directive on the introduction of measures to encourage improvement in the safety and health of workers at work (the 'framework directive')[35] The 'framework' directive, adopted in 1989, can be seen as a EC equivalent of the HSWA. It lays down broad duties akin to those contained in s 2 of HSWA and embodies the principle (found in British law, in, for example, the COSHH and Noise

Regulations) that the risks inherent in work activities should be assessed and appropriate control (including preventive) measures introduced.

The HSC has recently published draft regulations to give effect to this directive. Employers with five or more employees would have to make their assessment in writing and identify any group of workers who were at high risk. Arrangements would have to be made to give effect to the preventive and protective measures identified as necessary as a result of conducting the assessment. These arrangements are concerned with the management of health and safety – planning, organization, control, monitoring and review. Employers with five or more employees would have to record these arrangements in writing.

Employers, with exceptions for the self-employed and bodies which are not corporate, but subject in these cases to the nature of the activities, size and competence, must appoint 'one or more competent persons' to assist them in undertaking the preventive and protective measures flowing from the risk assessment.

Procedures for dealing with serious and imminent danger would have to be established, including the circumstances in which employees could stop work or take other remedial action. Information would need to be provided to employees, eg on risks, preventive and protective measures, emergency procedures etc.

Where employees of different employers work together, there would have to be co-operation and co-ordination, perhaps involving a safety co-ordinator. Every employer would have to provide 'adequate' health and safety training. Employees' duties would include notifying employers of safety shortcomings and using machinery, equipment etc only in the manner in which they were instructed or trained.

Temporary and agency workers would have to have information from employers and/or agencies in respect of any special skills or qualifications needed for safe working, and details of any health surveillance which was required. The Safety Representatives and Safety Committees Regulations would be amended to provide more detail of safety representatives' rights to consultation, and to provide a right to reasonable facilities and assistance.

Other health and safety at work directives   The framework directive has so far given rise to nine 'daughter' directives. Two of them have implementation dates in 1993: Asbestos (1 January 1993) and Biological Agents (26 November 1993). The remainder, described below, have to be implemented by 31 December 1992. It must be stressed that:

■ these directives have to be given effect through domestic legislation;
■ existing domestic legislation may or may not be adequate to meet the requirements of the directives.

Workplace health and safety[36]   This directive lays down minimum standards in respect of a number of areas including:

■ the keeping clear of escape routes and emergency exits;
■ workplace cleanliness;

- maintenance of machinery and equipment, and the rectification of faults;
- structural stability;
- electrical installations;
- fire detection and fighting equipment;
- room ventilation, temperature and lighting;
- rest room and sanitary facilities

Use of work equipment[37]   Some new legislation is needed to give effect to this directive, even though much of what it requires is already contained in the present UK provision. The HSC has decided to take the opportunity to introduce a set of regulations which consolidates the existing legislation, as well as meeting the needs of the directive. Thus, there will be a comprehensive set of new regulations governing work equipment and this will replace various existing regulations, as well as sections of the Factories Act, Offices, Shops and Railway Premises Act, and Mines and Quarries Act. The new regulations will contain the following.

General provisions

- selection, suitability and maintenance of work equipment;
- restrictions on the use of work equipment where there are specific risks;
- the provision of adequate information and, where appropriate, written instructions;
- training must be adequate;
- work equipment must be to EC technical standards.

Specific requirements

- guards and protection devices for dangerous parts and machinery;
- protection against failure;
- high or very low temperatures;
- controls for starting or making a significant change in operating conditions;
- stop and emergency stop controls;
- controls and control systems;
- isolation from sources of energy;
- stability;
- lighting;
- maintenance operations;
- markings;
- warnings.

It is intended that the general provisions would apply from 1 January 1993. The specific requirements would apply:

- from 1 January 1993 for work equipment first provided after 31 December 1992;
- from 1 January 1997 for work equipment first provided before 1 January 1993. (This would still be subject to the present legislation until 1 January 1997.)

Use of personal, protective equipment (PPE)[38]   This directive lays down that PPE should be used when risks cannot be avoided or sufficiently limited by collective protection or by reorganization of the work (Article 3). The HSC has produced draft regulations which would place a duty upon employers to provide suitable PPE for their employees. The regulations would not apply to the extent that other regulations, eg COSHH and Control of Lead at Work apply. PPE would need to conform to EC requirements as laid down in a separate PPE products directive.

Employers would need to carry out an assessment of risks and of the characteristics required of the PPE. The characteristics of available PPE would then need to be compared with the characteristics sought. PPE would need to be maintained and, where necessary, replaced, and put in appropriate accommodation when not being used.

An employer would need to provide adequate information, instruction and training for users of PPE, and would have to take all reasonable steps to ensure that PPE was properly used. There would be a duty placed upon employees and the self-employed to make full and proper use of PPE, and to take all reasonable steps to return it to the accommodation provided. Loss of or defects in PPE would need to be reported. No charge should be made to employees for PPE used at work.

Manual handling of loads[39]   This directive requires that employers avoid the need for manual handling which involves a risk of injury to workers. Where such manual handling cannot be avoided, an employer must make an assessment, in advance if possible, and take appropriate measures to eliminate or reduce the risk of injury in the light of the assessment.

The HSC's draft regulations would require manual handling which involves a risk to be avoided 'so far as is reasonably practicable'. Otherwise, a 'suitable and sufficient' assessment would have to be conducted and appropriate steps taken to reduce the risk of injury to 'the lowest level reasonably practicable'. In making the assessment regard would need to be had to:

- the task, eg body posture, frequency, duration;
- the load, eg weight, size, stability;
- the working environment, eg lighting, floor condition, amount of space;
- individual capability, eg need for unusual strength, height etc or special knowledge.

Employees undertaking manual handling which involves a risk would have to be provided with general, and where reasonably practicable, precise information about the weight of each load and the heaviest side of any load whose centre of gravity is not positioned centrally.

An employee would have to make full and proper use of any equipment of system of work provided to avoid or reduce risks from manual handling, and to inform his employer about any physical condition suffered by him which might reasonably be considered to affect his ability to undertake manual handling safely.

Display screen equipment (VDUs)[40]   This directive must be the subject of domestic legislation to be in force by 31 December 1992. Employers will be responsible for ensuring that all equipment installed from that date onwards meets the legal requirements. Existing equipment must be brought up to standard by the end of 1996. The legislation is likely to apply to most VDUs in commercial use.

The directive provides for:

- mandatory inspections of computer equipment and associated furniture;
- training in health and safety;
- the restructuring of job functions to allow periodic breaks from screen work;
- regular free eye tests and special glasses where necessary;
- minimum standards in relation to computer screens, keyboards, desks, chairs, lighting, noise, humidity and software.

Employers will need to carry out an assessment of work stations.

Carcinogens[41]   This directive lays down that employers must carry out an assessment of the risks related to exposure to carcinogens at work and use substitute substances or processes where possible. Where substitution is not possible, work should be conducted in a controlled environment. Otherwise, exposure should be reduced to as low a level as possible. Emergency procedures must be established. Workers' health will have to be monitored and the results of surveillance made available to them.

Temporary workers[42]   This directive applies to those working under fixed-term contracts and those workers supplied by agencies. An employer will be responsible for the health, safety and welfare of staff supplied by agencies, and must provide information, training and medical surveillance for temporary workers on the same basis as for those who are 'permanent'.

The draft regulations intended to give effect to the framework directive are also intended to provide for the implementation of this directive.

Proposals

A number of directives are proposed which have their origins in the Social Charter. These directives will lay down minimum standards:

- for medical assistance on board vessels;
- for work at temporary or mobile construction sites (eg health care provision);
- for the drilling industries, quarrying and open-cast mining (the extractive industries);
- on fishing vessels (especially in relation to working procedures);
- on information about certain dangerous industrial agents (provision of 'data sheets' etc);
- on exposure to risks from certain physical agents (eg vibration, electro-magnetic radiation);
- on activities in transport, including the handling of loads;
- for safety signs at the workplace.

In addition, a directive has been put forward under Article 118A on the protection of pregnant women at work. A common position was reached on this in December 1991, along the following lines:

- 14 weeks' paid maternity leave irrespective of length of employment and at a rate no lower than the rate of SSP prevailing in the particular member state;
- there to be no qualifying period of employment for the right not to be unfairly dismissed on grounds of pregnancy;
- a duty to be placed upon employers to assess the risks to the health and safety at work of pregnant women, and to take health and safety measures in the light of the assessment.

It seems fairly clear that if this directive is adopted there will be increased eligibility in respect of both statutory maternity pay and maternity leave, since the respective qualifying periods of six months and two years are likely to disappear. The proposed directive on working time is also put forward as a health and safety measure but a common position has not yet been reached.

References

1. The Health and Safety (Training for Employment) Regulations, SI 1990/1380.
2. Health and Safety at Work Act (HSWA) 1974, c 37, s 2(1).
3. The poster is entitled 'Health and Safety Law: What you should know'. The requirement to display it arises out of The Health and Safety (Information for Employees) Regulations, SI 1989/682 (operational from 18 October 1989).
4. HSWA, s 2(3).
5. Health and Safety Policy Statements (Exception) Regulations, 1975.
6. s 2(1) – general duty, s 2(2)(*a*) – safe system of work, and s 2(2)(*c*) – information and instruction.
7. HSWA, s 40.
8. s 3(1).
9. s 4(2).
10. SI 1983/943, as amended by SI 1989/319. The Alkali etc Works Regulation Act 1906 and other provisions require that certain works must be registered with the Secretary of State for the Environment. The registration system was modified recently by SI 1989/318.
11. HSWA, s 6; Consumer Protection Act 1987, s 36 and Schedule 3.
12. Safety Representatives and Safety Committees Regulations, SI 1977/500 (SRSC Regulations).
13. There is a separate Code of Practice concerning time off for training: Code of Practice on Time Off for the Training of Safety Representatives. This was issued under regulation 4 (2)(*b*) of the SRSC Regulations (1978) HSC, London.
14. HSWA, s 2(7).
15. 1961, c 34. The present account is not exhaustive.
16. s 155.
17. s 29(1).
18. OSRPA 1963, s 67.
19. RIDDOR, SI 1985/2023. See Reporting an Injury or a Dangerous Occurrence (1990) Health and Safety Executive, London; and Reporting a Case of Disease (1990) HSE, London.
20. SI 1988/1657.
21. COSHH, reg 2, para 1.
22. COSHH, reg 16.
23. SI 1989/1790.
24. SI 1989/635.
25. SI 1981/917. See also First-Aid at Work (1990) Code of Practice No 42, HMSO, London.
26. SI 1981/917, reg 3.
27. SI 1989/2169.
28. SI 1989/2169, reg 23.

29. SI 1989/2209.
30. Criminal Justice Act 1991.
31. Offshore Safety Act 1992. The provision is not limited to offshore activities.
32. Unfair Contract Terms Act 1977, s 2.
33. Occupiers' Liability Act 1957; Occupiers' Liability (Scotland) Act 1960.
34. Limitation Act 1980.
35. 89/391/EEC.
36. 89/654/EEC.
37. 89/655/EEC.
38. 89/656/EEC. Technical standards are determined by 89/686/EEC which has to be operative in member states by 1 July 1992.
39. 90/269/EEC.
40. 90/270/EEC.
41. 90/394/EEC.
42. 91/383/EEC.

LIST OF CASES CITED

Alexander v *The Home Office*, CA (1988) IRLR 190

Angus Jowett and Company v *The National Union of Tailors and Garment Workers*, EAT (1985) ICR 646

Armour v *Sheen*, CS (1977) IRLR 310

Associated Provincial Picture Houses Limited v *Wednesbury Corporation* (1947) 1 KB 223

Auguste Noel Limited v *Curtis*, EAT (1990) IRLR 326

Austin Rover Group Limited v *H M Inspectorate of Factories*, HL (1989) IRLR 404

Banking, Insurance and Finance Union v *Barclay's Bank plc*, EAT (1987) ICR 495

Barber v *Guardian Royal Exchange Assurance Group*, ECJ (1990) IRLR 240

Batchelor v *British Railways Board*, CA (1987) IRLR 136

Berriman v *Delabole Slate Limited*, CA (1985) ICR 546

Bessenden Properties Limited v *Corness*, NIRC (1974) IRLR 338

Bilka-Kaufhaus GmbH v *Weber von Hartz*, ECJ (1986) IRLR 317

Brennan v *J H Dewhurst Limited*, EAT (1983) IRLR 357

British Aircraft Corporation Limited v *Austin*, EAT (1978) IRLR 332

British Broadcasting Corporation v *Dixon*, CA (1979) IRLR 114

British Coal Corporation v *Cheesbrough*, HL (1990) IRLR 148

British Home Stores Limited v *Burchell*, EAT (1978) IRLR 379

British Labour Pump Company Limited v *Byrne*, EAT (1979) IRLR 94

British Leyland (UK) Limited v *Swift* CA (1981) IRLR 91

British Railways Board v *Paul*, EAT (1988) IRLR 20

British Steel Corporation v *Griffin*, EAT (1986) 316 IRLIB 10–11

British United Shoe Machinery Company Limited v *Clarke*, EAT (1977) IRLR 297

Bromley and ors v *H and J Quick Limited*, CA (1988) IRLR 249

Brown v *Stockton-on-Tees Borough Council*, HL (1988) IRLR 263

Calveley and ors v *Merseyside Police*, CA (1986) IRLR 177

Capper Pass Limited v *Lawton*, EAT (1976) IRLR 366

City of Bradford Metropolitan Council v *Arora*, CA (1991) IRLR 165

Coates and anor v *Modern Methods and Materials Limited*, CA (1982) IRLR 318

Council of Civil Service Unions and ors v *The Minister for the Civil Service*, HL (1985) ICR 14

Courage Take Home Trade Limited v *Keys*, EAT (1986) IRLR 427

Cresswell and ors v *Board of Inland Revenue*, High Court (1984) IRLR 190

Crouch v *British Rail Engineering Limited*, CA (1988) IRLR 404

Dalton v *Burton's Gold Medal Biscuits Limited*, NIRC (1974) IRLR 45

Dekker v *Stichting Vormingscentrum voor Jong Volwassenen (VJV Centrum) Plus*, ECJ (1991) IRLR 27

Delaney v *Staples (T/A De Montfort Recruitment)*, HL (1992) IRLR 191

Dexter v *Tenby Electrical Accessories Limited*, High Court (1991) GLR 22.2.91

(1) LMC Drains Limited (2) Metro Rod Services Limited v *Waugh*, EAT (1991) 443 IRLIB 10–11

Logan Salton v *Durham County Council*, EAT (1989) IRLR 99

Macarthys v *Smith*, ECJ (1980) IRLR 210

Macpherson v *London Borough of Lambeth*, High Court (1988) IRLR 470

Marley v *Forward Trust Group Limited*, CA (1986) IRLR 369

Marshall v *Gotham and Company Limited*, HL (1954) AC 360

Marshall v *Southampton and South-west Hampshire Area Health Authority (No 2)*, HL (1991) 437 IRLIB 12

Meikle v *McPhail (Charleston Arms)*, EAT (1983) IRLR 531

Merseyside and North Wales Electricity Board v *Taylor* High Court (1975) IRLR 60

Miles v *Wakefield Metropolitan District Council*, HL (1987) IRLR 193

Moon v *Homeworthy Furniture (Northern) Limited*, EAT (1976) IRLR 298

National Coal Board v *Ridgway and Fairbrother*, CA (1987) ICR 641

Nethermere (St Neots) Limited v *Gardiner and Taverna*, CA (1984) IRLR 240

Noone v *North-west Thames Regional Health Authority*, CA (1988) IRLR 195

Paal Wilson and Company A/S v *Partenreederei Hannah Blumenthal*, HL (1983) AC 854

Pape v *Cumbria County Council*, High Court (1991) IRLR 463

P Bork International A/S (in Liquidation) v *Foreningen Af Arbejdsledere I Danmark*, ECJ (1989) IRLR 41

Pickstone and ors v *Freemans plc*, HL (1988) IRLR 357

Piggott and Company Limited v *Jackson and ors*, CA (1991) IRLR 309

Polkey v *AE Dayton (Services) Limited*, HL (1987) IRLR 503

Post Office v *Fennell*, CA (1981) IRLR 221

Powell v *London Borough of Brent*, CA (1987) IRLR 466

Pritchett and Dyjasek v *J McIntyre Limited*, CA (1987) IRLR 18

Quinnen v *Howells*, EAT (1984) IRLR 227

R v *Secretary of State for Employment ex parte Equal Opportunities Commission*, High Court (1991) IRLR 493

R v *Swan Hunter Shipbuilders Limited and Telemeter Installations Limited*, CA (1981) IRLR 403

Rainey v *Greater Glasgow Health Board*, HL (1987) IRLR 26

Reed Packaging v *Boozer and Everhurst*, EAT (1988) IRLR 333

Rinner-Kühn v *FWW Spezial–Gebäudereinigung GmbH and Co KG*, ECJ (1989) IRLR 493

Savoia v *Chiltern Herb Farms Limited*, CA (1982) IRLR 166

Secretary of State for Employment v *Spence and ors*, CA (1986) IRLR 248

Shannon v *Michelin (Belfast) Limited*, CA (1981) IRLR 505

Sim and ors v *Rotherham Metropolitan Borough Council and ors*, High Court (1986) ICR 897

Sime v *Sutcliffe Catering (Scotland) Limited*, CS (1990) IRLR 228

Simmons v *Hoover Limited*, EAT (1976) IRLR 266

Smith v *The Chairman and other Councillors of Hayle Town Council*, CA (1978) IRLR 413

Sovereign House Security Services Limited v *Savage*, CA (1989) IRLR 115

Strathclyde Regional Council v *Porcelli*, Court of Session (1986) IRLR 134

Surrey County Council v *Lewis*, HL (1987) IRLR 509

Sutton and Gates (Luton) Limited v *Boxall*, EAT (1978) IRLR 486

Taylor v *Alidair Limited*, CA (1978) IRLR 82

Therm-a-stor Limited v *Atkins and ors*, CA (1983) IRLR 78

Union of Construction, Allied Trades and Technicians v *Brain*, CA (1981) IRLR 224

Vose v *South Sefton Health Authority*, EAT (1985) 314 IRLIB 12

Waite v *Government Communications Headquarters*, HL (1983) ICR 653

W and J Wass Limited v *Binns*, CA (1982) IRLR 283

W Devis and Sons Limited v *Atkins*, HL (1977) IRLR 314

Webb v *Emo Air Cargo (UK) Limited*, CA (1992) IRLR 116

W E Cox Toner (International) Limited v *Crook*, EAT (1981) IRLR 443

Western Excavating (ECC) Limited v *Sharp*, CA (1978) IRLR 27

West Midlands Co-operative Society Limited v *Tipton*, HL (1986) IRLR 112

West Midlands Passenger Transport Executive v *Singh*, CA (1988) IRLR 186

West Midlands Travel Limited v *Milke and Poole*, EAT (1989) 388 IRLIB 10

Wheeler v *(1) Patel (2) J Golding Group of Companies*, EAT (1987) IRLR 211

Whitbread and Company plc v *Mills*, EAT (1988) IRLR 501

Williams and ors v *Comp Air Maxam Limited*, EAT (1982) IRLR 83

Wiltshire County Council v *NATFHE and Guy*, CA (1980) IRLR 198

Wiluszynski v *London Borough of Tower Hamlets*, CA (1989) IRLR 259

Woodcock and ors v *(1) The Committee for the Time Being of the Friends School, Wigton (2) Genwise Limited*, CA (1987) IRLR 98

Woodhouse and Staton v *Peter Brotherhood Limited*, CA (1972) 3 All ER 91

Woods v *W M Car Services (Peterborough) Limited*, CA (1982) IRLR 413

W Weddell and Company Limited v *Tepper*, CA (1980) IRLR 96

Useful Addresses

Advisory, Conciliation and Arbitration Service (ACAS)
Head office 27 Wilton Street, London SW1X 7AZ Tel 071–210 3000

Scotland
Franborough House, 123–57 Bothwell Street, Glasgow G2 7JR
Tel 041–248 1400

Wales
Phase 1, Ty Glas Road, Llanishen, Cardiff CF4 5PH Tel 0222 762636

London Region
Clifton House, 83–117 Euston Road, London NW1 2RB Tel 071–338 5100

Midlands Region
Alpha Tower, Suffolk Street, Queensway, Birmingham B1 1TZ Tel 021–622 5050

Nottingham Office, 66–72 Houndsgate, Nottingham NG1 6BA Tel 0602 693355

Northern Region
Westgate House, Westgate Road, Newcastle upon Tyne NE1 1TJ Tel 091–261 2191

North-west Region
Boulton House, 17–21 Chorlton Street, Manchester M1 3HY Tel 061 228 3222

South-east Region (as London)

South-west Region
Regent House, 27a Regent Street, Clifton, Bristol BS8 4HR Tel 0272 744066

Yorkshire and Humberside Region
Commerce House, St Albans Place, Leeds LS2 8HH Tel 0532 431371

British Institute of Management (BIM)
2 Savoy Court, Strand, London WC2R 0EZ Tel 071–497 0580

Central Arbitration Committee (CAC)
39 Grosvenor Place, London SW1X 7BD Tel 071–210 3738/3737

Certification Office for Trade Unions and Employers' Associations
27 Wilton Street, London SW1X 7AZ Tel 071–210 3734

Commission for Racial Equality (CRE)
Elliot House, Allington Street, London SW1E 5EH Tel 071–828 7022

Birmingham Alpha Tower (11th Floor), Suffolk Street, Queensway, Birmingham B1 1TT
Tel 021–632 4544

Leeds Yorkshire Bank Chambers (1st Floor), Infirmary Street, Leeds LS1 2JT
Tel 0532 434413/4

Leicester Haymarket House (4th Floor), Haymarket Shopping Centre, Leicester
LE1 3YG Tel 0533 517852

Manchester Maybrook House (5th Floor), 40 Blackfriars Street, Manchester M3 2EG
Tel 061–831 7782/8

Commonwealth Trade Union Council (CTUC)
Congress House, Great Russell Street, London WC1B 3LS Tel 071–631 0728 *or* 636 4030
ex 290

Confederation of British Industry (CBI)
London Centre Point, 103 New Oxford Street, London WC1A 1DU Tel 071–379 7400

Eastern 14 Union Road, Cambridge CB2 1HE Tel 0223 65636

East Midlands 17 St Wilfred Square, Calverton, Nottingham NG14 6PP Tel 0602 653311

Northern 15 Grey Street, Newcastle upon Tyne NE1 6EE Tel 091–232 1644

Northern Ireland Fanum House, 108 Great Victoria Street, Belfast BT2 7PD Tel 0232 226658

North-western Emerson House, Albert Street, Eccles, Manchester MS0 0LT Tel 061-707 2190

Scotland Beresford House, 5 Claremont Terrace, Glasgow G3 7XT Tel 041–332 8661

South-eastern Tubs Hill House, London Road, Sevenoaks, Kent TN13 1BX Tel 0732 454040

Southern Bank Chambers, 10a Hart Street, Henley on Thames, Oxon RH9 2AU Tel 0491 576810

South-western 8–10 Whiteladies Road, Bristol BS8 1NZ Tel 0272 737065

Wales Pearl Assurance House, Greyfriars Road, Cardiff CF1 3JR Tel 0222 232536

West Midlands Metropolitan House, 1 Hagley Road, Edgbaston, Birmingham B16 8PS Tel 021–454 7911

Yorkshire and Humberside Arndale House, Station Road, Crossgates, Leeds LS15 8E4 Tel 0532 644242

Employment Department
Caxton House, Tothill Street, London SW1H 9NF Tel 071–273 6969
Moorfoot, Sheffield S1 4PQ Tel 0742 753275

Engineering Employers' Federation (EEF)
Broadway House, Tothill Street, London SW1H 9NQ Tel 071–222 7777

Employment Appeal Tribunal (EAT)
Audit House, Victoria Embankment, London EC4Y 0DS Tel 071–273 1041

Equal Opportunities Commission (EOC)
Overseas House, Quay Street, Manchester M3 3HN Tel 061–833 9244

European Trade Union Confederation (ETUC)
Rue Montagne Aux Herbes Potagères 37, 1000 Brussels, Belgium Tel 010–322 218 3100

European Trade Union Institute (ETUI)
Boulevard de L'Imperatrice 66, Brussels, Belgium Tel 010–322 512 3070

General Federation of Trade Unions (GFTU)
Central House, Upper Woburn Place, London WC1H 0HY Tel 071–387 2578

Health and Safety Commission
Baynards House, 1 Chepstow Place, Westbourne Grove, London W2 4TF Tel 071–229 3456

Incomes Data Services (IDS)
193 St John Street, London EC1V 4LS Tel 071–250 3434

Industrial Injuries Advisory Committee
157–66 Blackfriars Road, London SE1 8EU Tel 071–962 8065

Industrial Participation Association
42 Colebrooke Row, London N1 8AF Tel 071–354 8040

Industrial Relations Services (IRS)
18–20 Highbury Place, London N5 1QP Tel 071–354 5858

Industrial Society
Robert Hyde House, 48 Bryanston Square, London W1H 7LN Tel 071–262 2401

Industrial Tribunals
London and North 19/29 Woburn Place, London WC1H 0LU Tel 071-273 3000

Institute of Directors (IOD)
116 Pall Mall, London SW1Y 5ED Tel 071-839 1233

Institute of Personnel Management (IPM)
IPM House, Camp Road, Wimbledon, London SW19 4UW Tel 071-946 9100

International Confederation of Free Trade Unions (ICFTU)
Rue Montagne aux Herbes Potagères 37/441, 1000 Brussels, Belgium Tel 010-322 217 8085

International Labour Organization (ILO)
CH-1211, Geneva, Switzerland Tel 010-4122 799 6111
London office, Vincent House, Vincent Square, London SW1 2NB Tel 071-828 6401

Labour Research Department
78 Blackfriars Road, London SE1 8HF Tel 071-928 3649

Local Government Information Unit (LGIU)
1-5 Bath Street, London EC1V 9QQ Tel 071-608 1051

Low Pay Unit
27/29 Amwell Street, London EC1R 1UN Tel 071-713 7616

National Institute of Economic and Social Research (NIESR)
2 Dean Trench Street, Smith Square, London SW1P 3HE Tel 071-222 7665

Office of the Commissioner for the Rights of Trade Union Members
Bank Chambers (First Floor), 2a Rylands Street, Warrington, Cheshire WA1 1EN Tel 0925 415771

Trades Union Congress (TUC)
Congress House, Great Russell Street, London WC1B 3LC Tel 071-636 4030
Scotland 16 Woodlands Terrace, Glasgow G3 6ED Tel 041-322 4946
Wales Transport House, 1 Cathedral Road, Cardiff CF1 0SD Tel 0222 372345
Northern Ireland Committee (ICTU) 3 Wellington Park, Belfast BT9 6DJ Tel 0232 681726
Northern Swinburn House, Swinburn Street, Gateshead NE8 1AX Tel 091-490 0033
Yorkshire and Humberside York Place, Leeds LS1 2ED Tel 0532 429096
North-west Baird House, Merton Road, Bootle, Merseyside L20 7AP Tel 051-933 6067
West Midlands 10 Pershore Street, Birmingham B5 4HU Tel 021-622 2050
East Midlands 61 Derby Road, Nottingham NG1 5BA Tel 0602 472444
East Anglia 119 Newmarket Road, Cambridge CB5 8HA Tel 0223 66795
South-east Congress House, Great Russell Street, London WC1B 3LS Tel 071-636 4030
South-west 1 Henbury Road, Westbury on Trym, Bristol BS9 3HH Tel 0272 506425

TUC Affiliated Unions
Amalgamated Association of Beamers, Twisters and Drawers (Hand and Machine) 27 Every Street, Nelson, Lancashire BB9 7NE Tel 0282 64181
Amalgamated Engineering and Electrical Union 110 Peckham Road, London SE15 5EL Tel 071-703 4231
Amalgamated Society of Textile Workers and Kindred Trades Foxlowe, Market Place, Leek, Staffordshire ST13 6AD Tel 0538 382068
Amalgamated Union of Asphalt Workers Jenkin House, 173a Queens Road, Peckham, London SE15 2NF Tel 071-639 1669
Associated Metalworkers' Union 92 Deansgate, Manchester M3 2QG Tel 061-834 6891

Associated Society of Locomotive Engineers and Firemen 9 Arkwright Road, Hampstead, London NW3 6AB Tel 071–431 0275

Association of First Division Civil Servants 2 Caxton Street, London SW1H 0QH Tel 071–222 6242

Association of University Teachers United House, 1 Pembridge Road, London W11 3HJ Tel 071–221 4370

Bakers, Food and Allied Workers' Union Stanborough House, Great North Road, Stanborough, Welwyn Garden City, Herts AL8 7TA Tel 0707 260150

Banking, Insurance and Finance Union Sheffield House, 17 Hillside, Wimbledon, London SW19 4NL Tel 081–946 9151

British Actors' Equity Association 81 New Road, Harlington, Hayes, Middlesex UB3 5BG Tel 081–759 9331

British Association of Colliery Management BACM House, 317 Nottingham Road, Basford, Nottingham NG7 7DP Tel 0602 785819

Broadcasting Entertainment and Cinematograph Technicians Union 111 Wardour Street, London W1V 4AY Tel 071–437 8506

Card Setting Machine Tenters' Society 36 Greenton Avenue, Scholes, Cleckheaton, West Yorkshire BD19 7DT Tel 0274 670022

Ceramic and Allied Trades Union Hillcrest House, Garth Street, Hanley, Stoke-on-Trent ST1 2AB Tel 0782 272755

Civil and Public Services Association 160 Falcon Road, London SW1P 2LN Tel 071–924 2727

Communication Managers' Association Hughes House, Ruscombe Road, Twyford, Reading, Berkshire RG10 9JD Tel 0734 342300

Confederation of Health Service Employees Glen House, High Street, Banstead, Surrey SM7 2LH Tel 0733 53322

Council of Civil Service Unions 58 Rochester Row, London SW1P 1JU Tel 071–834 8393

Educational Institute of Scotland 46 Moray Place, Edinburgh EH3 6BH Tel 031–225 6244

Electrical and Plumbing Industries Union Park House, Wandsworth Common, North Side, London SW18 2SH Tel 081–874 0458

Engineering and Fastener Trade Union 42 Gaiton Road, Warley, West Midlands B67 5JU Tel 021–429 2594

Engineers' and Managers' Association Station House, Fox Lane North, Chertsey, Surrey KT16 9HW Tel 0932 564131

Film Artistes' Association 61 Marloes Road, London W8 6LF Tel 071–937 4567

Fire Brigades Union Bradley House, 68 Coombe Road, Kingston upon Thames KT2 7AE Tel 081–541 1765

Furniture, Timber and Allied Trades Union Fairfields, Roe Green, Kingsbury, London NW9 0PT Tel 081–204 0273

General Union of Associations of Loom Overlookers Overlookers Institute, Jude Street, Nelson, Lancashire BB9 7NP Tel 0282 64066

GMB (including Clothing & Textile Section) 22 Worple Road, London SW19 4DD Tel 081–947 3131

Graphical Paper and Media Union Graphic House, 633–67 Bromham Road, Bedford, Bedfordshire MK40 2AG Tel 0234 351521

Greater London Senior Staff Guild Room 158 North Block, County Hall, London SE1 7PB Tel 071–633 6727

Health Visitors Association 50 Southwark Street, London SE1 1UN Tel 071–378 7255

Hospital Consultants and Specialists Association Number One Kingsclere Road, Overton, Basingstoke, Hants RG25 3JP Tel 0256 771777

Inland Revenue Staff Federation Douglas Houghton House, 231 Vauxhall Bridge Road, London SW1V 1EH Tel 071–834 8254

Institution of Professional Managers and Specialists 75–9 York Road, London SE1 7AQ Tel 071–928 9951

Iron and Steel Trades Confederation Swinton House, 324 Grays Inn Road, London WC1X 8DD Tel 071–278 8378

Manufacturing Science and Finance 64–6 Wandsworth Common, London SW18 2SH Tel 081–871 2100

Military and Orchestral Musical Instrument Makers Trade Society 2 Whitehouse Avenue, Borehamwood, Hertfordshire WD6 1HD (no telephone number)

Musicians Union 60–2 Clapham Road, London SW9 0JJ Tel 071–582 5566

National League of the Blind and Disabled 2 Tenterden Road, Tottenham, London N17 8BE Tel 081–808 6030

National and Local Government Officers' Association 1 Mabledon Place, London WC1H 9AJ Tel 071–388 2366

National Association of Colliery Overmen, Deputies and Shotfirers Simpson House, 48 Netherhall Road, Doncaster, South Yorkshire DN1 1PZ Tel 0302 84813

National Association of Co-operative Officials Saxone House, 56 Market Street, Manchester M1 1PW Tel 061–834 6029

National Association of Licensed House Managers 9 Coombe Lane, Raynes Park, London SW20 8NE Tel 071–947 3080

National Association of Probation Officers 3–4 Chivalry Road, London SW11 1HT Tel 071–223 4887

National Association of Schoolmasters/Union of Women Teachers Hills Court Education Centre, Rose Hill, Rednal, Birmingham B45 8RS Tel 021–453 6150

National Association of Teachers in Further and Higher Education 27 Britannia Street, London WC1X 9JP Tel 071–387 3636

National Communications Union Greystoke House, 150 Brunswick Road, London W5 1AW Tel 081–998 2981

National Union of Domestic Appliances and General Operatives Imperial Buildings, Corporation Street, Rotherham, Yorkshire S69 1PB Tel 0709 382820

National Union of Hosiery and Knitwear Workers 55 New Walk, Leicester LE1 7EB Tel 0533 556703

National Union of Insurance Workers 27 Old Gloucester Street, London WC1N 3AF Tel 071–405 1083/6798

National Union of Journalists Acorn House, 314–20 Grays Inn Road, London WC1X 9DP Tel 071–278 7916

National Union of Knitwear, Footwear and Apparel Trades The Grange, 108 Northampton Road, Earls Barton, Northampton NN6 0JH Tel 0604 810326

National Union of Lock and Metal Workers Bellamy House, Wilkes Street, Willenhall, West Midlands WV13 2BS Tel 0902 66651

National Union of Marine, Aviation and Shipping Transport Officers Oceanair House, 750–60 High Road, Leystonstone, London E11 3BB Tel 081–989 6677

National Union of Mineworkers Holly Street, Sheffield, S1 2GT Tel 0742 766900

National Union of Public Employees Civic House, 20 Grand Depot Road, Woolwich, London SE18 6SF Tel 081–854 2244

National Union of Scalemakers 1st Floor, Queensway House, 57 Livery Street, Birmingham B3 1HA Tel 021–236 8998

National Union of Footwear, Leather and Allied Trades The Grange, Earls Barton, Northampton NN6 0JH Tel 0604 810326

National Union of Teachers Hamilton House, Mabledon Place, London WC1H 9BD Tel 071–388 6191

Northern Carpet Trades' Union 22 Clare Road, Halifax HX1 2HX Tel 0422 60492

Pattern Weavers' Society 38 St Pauls Road, Kirkheaton, Huddersfield Tel 0484 24988

Power Loom Carpet Weavers' and Textile Workers' Union Callows Lane, Kidderminster Worcestershire CY10 2JG Tel 0562 823192

Prison Officers' Association Cronin House, 245 Church Street, Edmonton, London N9 9HW Tel 081–803 0255

Rossendale Union of Boot, Shoe and Slipper Operatives 7 Tenterfield Street, Waterfoot, Rossendale, Lancashire BB4 7BA Tel 0706 215657

Scottish Prison Officers' Association 21 Calder Road, Saughton, Edinburgh EH1 3PF Tel 031–443 8105

Scottish Union of Power-Loom Overlookers 3 Napier Terrace, Dundee, Tayside DD2 2SL Tel 0382 612196

Sheffield Wool Shear Workers' Union 50 Bankfield Road, Malin Bridge, Sheffield, Yorkshire S6 4RD Tel 0742 333668

Society of Shuttlemakers 21 Burnley Road, Colne, Lancashire BB8 2JD Tel 0282 866716

Society of Telecom Executives 1 Park Road, Teddington, Middlesex TW11 0AR Tel 081–943 5181

Transport and General Workers' Union Transport House, Smith Square, Westminster, London SW1P 3JB Tel 071–828 7788

Transport Salaries Staffs' Association Walkden House, 10 Melton Street, London NW1 2EJ Tel 071–387 2101

Union of Communication Workers UCW House, Crescent Lane, London SW4 9RN Tel 071–622 9977

Union of Construction, Allied Trades and Technicians UCATT House, 177 Abbeville Road, Clapham, London SW4 9RL Tel 071–622 2442

Union of Shop, Distributive and Allied Workers Oakley, 199 Wilmslow Road, Fallowfield, Manchester M14 6LJ Tel 061–224 2804

United Road Transport Union 76 High Lane, Manchester M21 1FD Tel 061–881 6245

Wire Workers Union Prospect House, Lama Lane, Sheffield S3 8SA Tel 0742 721674

Writers' Guild of Great Britain 430 Edgware Road, London W2 1EH Tel 071–723 8074

Yorkshire Association of Power-Loom Overlookers Inveresk House, 31 Houghton Place, Bradford BD1 3RG Tel 0274 727966

Some unions not affiliated to the TUC
Electrical, Electronic, Telecommunications and Plumbing Union Hayes Court, West Common Road, Bromley BR2 7AU Tel 081–462 7755

Royal College of Nursing of the United Kingdom 20 Cavendish Square, London W1M OAB Tel 071–409 3333

Union of Democratic Mineworkers The Sycamores, Moor Road, Bestwood, Nottingham NG6 8UE Tel 0602 736468

Training Enterprise and Education Directorates
London 236 Grays Inn Road, London WC1X 8HL Tel 071–278 0363

South-east Telford House, Hamilton, Basingstoke, Hants RG21 2UZ Tel 0256 29266

South-western 4th Floor, The Pithay, Bristol BS1 2NQ Tel 0272 273710

East Midlands 21/23 Castlegate, Nottingham NF1 7AQ Tel 0602 410360

West Midlands Alpha Tower, Suffolk Street, Birmingham B1 1UR Tel 021–631 3555

Northern Wellbar House, Gallowgate, Newcastle upon Tyne NE1 4TP Tel 091–232 7575

Yorkshire and Humberside City House, New Station Street, Leeds LS1 4JH Tel 0532 341044

North-west Washington House, New Bailey Street, Piccadilly Plaza, Manchester M3 5ER Tel 061–833 0251

Index